Phil Edmonston

LEMON-AID

2007-2017

NEW AND USED CARS AND TRUCKS

DUNDURN
TORONTO

Editor: Catherine Leek of Green Onion Publishing
Design: Kim Monteforte of WeMakeBooks.ca
Printer: Webcom

ISBN: 978-1-45973-697-9 (pb)
ISBN: 978-1-45973-698-6 (pdf)
ISBN: 978-1-45973-699-3 (epub)

1 2 3 4 5   21 20 19 18 17

We acknowledge the support of the **Canada Council for the Arts** and the **Ontario Arts Council** for our publishing program. We also acknowledge the financial support of the **Government of Ontario**, through the **Ontario Book Publishing Tax Credit** and the **Ontario Media Development Corporation**, and the **Government of Canada**.

Care has been taken to trace the ownership of copyright material used in this book. The author and the publisher welcome any information enabling them to rectify any references or credits in subsequent editions.

J. Kirk Howard, President

The publisher is not responsible for websites or their content unless they are owned by the publisher.

Printed and bound in Canada.

VISIT US AT

 dundurn.com | @dundurnpress | dundurnpress | dundurnpress

Dundurn
3 Church Street, Suite 500
Toronto, Ontario, Canada
M5E 1M2

Preface
A TIME TO HECKLE, A TIME TO HAIL

It came out of the blue, last November, Conservative Senator Bob Runciman Ontario's former Minister of Consumer and Commercial Relations, complimented APA Director George Iny for his smooth presentation during Senate Bill S-2 hearings on a new law for car recalls. "Not like Phil Edmonston." He added, "I was presenting new consumer laws over three decades ago and he heckled me from the back of the room."

Heckle time is over, Bob; it's time for applause. Amendments currently working their way through the Senate and Parliament will finally see reforms to correct defects that date back to the inception of Canada's Motor Vehicle Safety legislation in 1971. Senate Bill S-2 will finally give Transport Canada the authority to order a recall. Under our current Act, the government has to ask the Federal Court to order an automaker to send its customers a *letter* stating that their vehicle is defective; our legislation does not require the carmaker to actually pay for repairs to fix safety defects. Canadians benefit from a free repair largely by riding on the coattails of more robust American protection or at the pleasure of the automakers.

Currently about one in five recalled vehicles is never repaired. With the proposed amendments, Canadians will get real-time recall look-up capability and Transport Canada will be able to fine carmakers (Fiat Chrysler are you listening?) that routinely fail to comply with timeliness and reporting requirements. An important additional measure needed is to have some of the fines paid by automakers dedicated to independent research to improve vehicle and road safety, and not just paid into general government revenues.

When enacted, the changes have the potential to morph Transport Canada from "zombie" to "zealot." And that's not all. The Auditor General has provided a road map for Transport Canada in a recent report prepared by his office. After waiting 45 years for many of these changes, and witnessing all the missed opportunities along the way, you may well imagine that nobody is happier than I to see the proposed amendments on the way to becoming law.

Phil Edmonston
December 2016

AUTOMOBILE PROTECTION ASSOCIATION TEAMS UP WITH *LEMON-AID*

Phil Edmonston invited us to collaborate with him on this year's *Lemon-Aid* guide, and the Automobile Protection Association's (APA) team went to work. The APA expanded the information on Leasing and Vehicles for Seniors in Part One and enhanced the used car information in Part Two. In Part Four the APA added its road test and reliability information to the reviews. We also provided new information on recommended preventive maintenance to address known weaknesses with several vehicles.

The guide contains more detailed technical information and actual consumer comments than you could ever keep in your head. With the benefit of the information in these pages you'll have a heads-up for problems that could present themselves down the road with the vehicle you currently own and the vehicles you are thinking of buying. That's because *Lemon-Aid* has always been about more than just the cars; it's about empowering consumers.

George Iny
APA Executive Director
December 2016

APA's PRINCIPAL CONTRIBUTORS TO THE 2017 *LEMON-AID* GUIDE

George Iny, *Executive Director*

A leading consumer advocate for more than 30 years. Dozens of investigations and reports on auto retailing, repair practices, leasing, and financing. Thousands of interviews for local and national radio, television and print media. George last contributed to the *Lemon-Aid* guide in 1985 and is pleased to be back for the current edition.

Ron Corbett, *Staff Writer*

APA's principal vehicle reviewer for new and used vehicles, Ron has driven more than 500 cars, trucks and SUVs during his career. Ron is also a contributor to *Protégez-Vous*, the French language consumer magazine distributed in Quebec, and a regular guest on the *Lemon-Aid Car Show*, broadcast on the Rogers Community Television network. This is Ron's third book-length collaboration.

Mark Toljagic

A professional freelance journalist, Mark was the *Toronto Star* Wheels used-car columnist and a news feature writer for 18 years. He received the AJAC Journalist of the Year award in 2007. Mark currently contributes to a number of websites, including MSN.

CONTENTS

Introduction
What You Don't Know *Can* Hurt You 2

Part One
NEW CARS AND OLD TRICKS 5
More Choice, Better Deals 6
Buying Tips 7
Which New Car, Truck, SUV, or Van? 11
When and Where to Buy 17
Buying the Right Car or Truck 20
Safety 21
Highway High-Tech 25
Safety Features that Kill 31
Comfort 33
"Senior" Cars 34
Other Buying Considerations 47
Saving on Servicing Costs 56
"Hidden" Costs 59
Surviving the Options Jungle 61
Lemon-Aid's Review of Standard and Optional Features 62
Unnecessary Options 73
Dealer Options 76
Aftermarket Accessories 80
Paying a Fair Price 80
Leasing Fleecing: Why Leasing Costs More 87
The Contract 95
Trade-In Tips 98
Summary 101

Part Two
OLD WHEELS AND GOOD DEALS 103
Secret Warranties and Special Programs 103
Auto Insurance 111
Three Decades of Hits and Misses 115
Safety First 118
Used Better Than New 119
Used Is the Smart Choice 120
When and Where to Buy 125
Buying with Confidence 125
Don't Pay Too Little 129
Financing Choices 135
Dealer Scams 137
Private Scams 141
Helpfule Websites 142
Summary 146

Part Three
"ROBBERS" AND RECOURSES 149
It Pays to Complain 149
Two Warranties 152
Supplementary Warranty Scams 154
Supreme Court Tackles "Fine Print" 156
Broken Promises 158
Negligence 159
Reasonable Durability 161
The Art of Complaining 163
Seek Outside Help 168
Contact the Right People 170
Twenty-One Legal "Tips" You Should Know 171
Using Government Agencies 186

v

Part Four

2007-2017 RATINGS "GOOD CARS, BAD CARS" 187

2016-2017: An Opportunity for Buyers 188
Five Ways to Get a "Good" Car 189
Best Model Choices 191
South Korea: Boasting; Japan: Coasting; Volkswagen: Roasting 191
Don't Believe in the "Fuel Fairy" 194
Take Advantage of Depreciation 196
How *Lemon-Aid* Picks the "Best" and "Worst" 198
Definition of Terms Used in Part Four 200
Real-Time Recall Lookups in Canada 206

American Models 209

American Car Quality 210
Fiat Chrysler and Jeep 210
FIAT CHRYSLER AUTOMOBILES 214
JEEP 242
FORD 259
GENERAL MOTORS 304
General Motors SUVs and Pickups 342

Japanese and Korean Automakers 360

ACURA 360
HONDA 369
HYUNDAI 395
INFINITI 415
KIA 424
LEXUS 442
MAZDA 451
MITSUBISHI 468
NISSAN 474
SUBARU 510
SUZUKI 522
TOYOTA 527

European Vehicles 563

AUDI 564
BMW 585
MERCEDES-BENZ 603
MINI 620
VOLKSWAGEN 625
VOLVO 642

MODEL INDEX 643

ACKNOWLEDGMENTS

A book like this one involves the contributions of many people. The APA cannot name them all here, but we are taking this opportunity to acknowledge the following people:

Kevin Bavelaar, Auto Showplace, Toronto
Andrew Bleakley, Car Inspector, Montreal
Denis Charron, Patrick Darche and Isabelle Dubé, Garantie Nationale, Montreal
Lisa Christensen, Auto Mechanic and Host of The Car Show, CJAD 800 Montreal
Joe de Paola, Alain Paquette and Pierre Phaneuf, Montréal Auto Prix
Dennis Desrosiers, Desrosiers Automotive Consultants, Richmond Hill, Ontario
Sam Kassam, Sam's Diesel Service Centre, Saint-Laurent, Quebec
Anton Koschany, Brett Mitchell, CTV *W5*

John Lespoir and Jay Zinnegar, Talon Tire, Montreal
Eli Melnick, Start Auto Electric, Toronto
Chris Muir, Auto Mechanics Instructor, Centennial College, Toronto
Dick Noble, retired auto dealer, Ladysmith, British Columbia
John Raymond, Community Producer, *Lemon-Aid Car Show*, RogersTV, Toronto
John Wallischeck, Autolinks
Chris Woods, Excellence Auto, Scarborough, Ontario

CONTENTS

KEY DOCUMENTS

Introduction
2006-07 GM Special Coverage
   Adjustment – catalytic converter
   warranty extension *3*
2006-08 Honda engine block warranty
   extension *4*

Part One
NEW CARS AND OLD TRICKS *5*
2017 Models: New, Dropped *7*
2007-2010 – Nissan CVT customer
   satisfaction program *10*
Top 20 Safety Defects *33*
Deadliest Vehicles *33*
Good "Senior" Car Choices *45*
Fuel Economy Fantasies *50*
Vehicles with Class-Leading Fuel
   Consumption *61*
The Top 10 Most Frequently Stolen
   Vehicles Across Ontario *63*
Winter Tire Recommendations *68*
Additional Contract Clauses *97*

Part Two
OLD WHEELS AND GOOD DEALS *103*
Secret Warranty Roundup *104*
GTA Insurance Rates vs. Ontario
   Average *112*
Bill of Sale *126*

Part Three
"ROBBERS" AND RECOURSES *149*
Reasonable Part Durability chart *161*
2006-13 Honda Civic paint chalking,
   cracking, or clouding *163*
2011-15 Chevrolet Caprice and 2012-15
   Chevrolet Impala – special coverage
   adjustment – engine cooling fan
   motor *163*
Complaint Letters – samples *166*
Claim Limits for Small Claims
   Courts *178*
2011-2012 Chevrolet Cruze – special
   coverage adjustment – coolant leak/
   drip on automatic tranny shifter
   grommet *186*

Part Four
2007-2017 RATINGS "GOOD CARS, BAD CARS" *187*
5-Year ACSI Trend – Domestic and
   International Automobiles *193*
Black Book Highest Retained Value by
   Vehicle Segment *197*
American Models
TIPM Units Faulty on Various
   Chrysler Products *229*
Chrysler fuel spit back *235*
Ram 1500 catastrophic engine failure
   fix *240*
Doors that Won't Latch *260*
2011-14 Ford excessive transmission
   clutch shudder and/or automatic
   transmission fluid leak *266*

2008-11 Ford paint degradation/road abrasion *270*

2011-14 Ford rear axle vent – oil leak *280*

2009-11 Ford transmission – slip/neutral out – 5th gear start from stop – backup camera on in drive *292*

2011-2015 Ford A/C – exhaust odor in cabin *294*

2010-2014 Ford – excessive oil consumption, smoke from the exhaust *296*

Aluminum Panels *299*

2011-14 Ford delayed engagement park to forward or reverse *303*

2015-2016 GM – engine cylinder head gasket leak *305*

2012-13 Cadillac crankshaft rear oil seal – oil leaks *306*

2008-15 GM "sag or hesitation" on acceleration – normal *316*

2012-14 GM excessive oil consumption – oil leaks – blue exhaust smoke – MIL – or fuel trim codes *317*

2013 GM steering clunk no power assist *318*

2014 GM wet carpet on driver's side *318*

2010-14 GM power steering stick-slip *324*

2013-14 GM bearing damaged or engine will not rotate *325*

2014 GM 2-3 upshift or 3-2 downshift clunk noise *329*

2014 GM tail lamp gasket seal *330*

2007-13 Cadillac clunk noise after shifting from reverse to drive or drive to reverse and then accelerating *333*

2010-15 GM steering shudder (vibration) during slow speed maneuvers *345*

2007-14 GM engine oil consumption on aluminum block/iron block engines with active fuel management *352*

2014 GM shift lever contacts ignition key *359*

Japanese and Korean Automakers

2008-12 Honda high oil consumption – faulty engine rings *386*

Kia steering/suspension – pull or drift concern *441*

2007-14 Lexus HVAC evaporator drain hose clogged due to insect intrusion *450*

Nissan Doube CVT Warranty *475*

2007-12 Nissan engine – oil leak from upper end of oil cooler *482*

2007-12 Nissan brake master cylinder *489*

Nissan rear suspension member, bushing replacement *492*

2009 Nissan L/H rear suspension knuckle *495*

2014 Nissan campaign #PC311 to replace engine on/off push button *499*

2003-12 Nissan grinding/knocking noise from rear on turns *500*

2010-12 Nissan navigation system – screen goes blank *502*

A Reliable Supplier for Rebuilt 2.5L Subaru Engines *510*

"Boxed" by Subaru *513*

European Vehicles

2007-15 Audi electrical – harness damage from animal bites *574*

Mercedes-Benz – Defective Gears Cost Big Money *605*

Volkswagen – Diesel *625*

2011-12 Volkswagen intake manifold & fuel injectors *633*

Introduction

Volkswagen Executives Have Started Hiring Criminal Defense Lawyers

There are little things that can tell you that the proverbial *scheisse* is about to hit the fan. One of those is when you cheat on emissions and executives start resigning. A much bigger one is when everyone starts hiring criminal defense lawyers, as *Bloomberg* reports:

> Dozens of Volkswagen Group executives in Germany have hired U.S. criminal defense lawyers as the Justice Department ramps up meetings with managers to gather evidence that may lead to charges, people familiar with the matter said.

> ... As dire as that may seem for the VW executives, they do have one annoying ace up their sleeves – as *Bloomberg* notes, Germany's constitution doesn't allow the extradition of its citizens outside the European Union. (Michael Ballaban, December 5, 2016, *Jalopnik.com*)

Slippery Slope

In August of 2009, after ruptured airbag inflators in Honda vehicles were linked to at least four injuries and a death, the automaker quietly requested a design change and did not notify U.S. regulators.... The previously undisclosed redesign could make Honda and Takata more vulnerable in more than 100 pending federal lawsuits and dozens more state suits. The request shows that Honda understood the safety risks posed by the inflators long before it started expanding recalls by the millions in 2014, the attorneys and law professors said. (Paul Lienert and Jessica Dye, *Automotive News*, March 24, 2016)

No wonder car owners in Canada are suffering from "recall fatigue:" From 2000 to 2016 exploding Takata airbags used by 18 automakers that can rupture and spray metal shards at passengers have resulted in eleven deaths in the U.S. (fortunately none reported in Canada). Over 28 million inflators have been recalled in the U.S. and Canada; replacing another 60 million air bags won't be completed before 2019. Over 30 million GM cars were recalled to replace ignition switches that can shut off the vehicle on the road. Jeeps from 2007 to 2015 can suddenly stall out, lose power steering and brakes, and disable their airbags. All these formerly hidden dangers made 2014 to 2016 a record period for safety-related recalls, not due so much to assembly line mistakes, but as a consequence of factory cost-cutting run wild and widespread remediation to correct corporate cover-ups. Furthermore, 20% of the affected vehicles may never get fixed because owners can't be found, or they have lost interest.

GM's recall could have happened a lot sooner if the company had replaced its ignition switches about ten years ago when first alerted to the defect. The payout would have been $37.7 million, according to confidential General Motors documents released by the U.S. Congress. The cheaper $14.2 million repair that GM authorized saved the company $23.5 million – a savings that has ballooned into a cost of almost $5 billion.

Automakers will sometimes continue manufacturing a vehicle that is potentially defective because it costs less to stonewall complaints and pay off victims than to make a safer vehicle. Consumer advocates learned this lesson many years ago after reading the court transcripts in *Grimshaw v. Ford* (fire-prone Pintos) from 1981. Reporter Anthony Prince wrote the following assessment of Ford's indifference in an article titled "Lessons of the Ford/Firestone Scandal: Profit Motive Turns Consumers into Road Kill," *People's Tribune* (Online Edition), Vol. 26, No. 11, November 2000:

> Rejecting safety designs costing between only $1.80 and $15.30 per Pinto, Ford had calculated the damages it would likely pay in wrongful death and injury cases and pocketed the difference. In a cold and calculating "costs/benefits" analysis, Ford projected that the Pinto would probably cause 180 burn deaths, 180 serious burn injuries, [and] 2,100 burned vehicles each year. Also, Ford estimated civil suits of $200,000 per death, $67,000 per injury, [and] $700 per vehicle for a grand total of $49.5 million. The costs for installing safety features would cost approximately $137 million per year. As a result, the Pinto became a moving target, its unguarded fuel tank subject to rupture by exposed differential bolts shoved into it by rear-end collisions at speeds of as little as 21 miles per hour [34 km/h]. Spewing gasoline into the passenger compartment, the car and its passengers became engulfed in a raging inferno.

Carmakers lobby for "zombie" consumer protection laws (neither dead nor alive), set up "secret" warranties, hide behind bankruptcy filings, and slap gag orders on settlements. Often, progress on vehicle emissions and safety is the result of successful lawsuits and government initiative, with Washington and California leading the way, while Transport Canada (vehicle safety), Canada's Competition Tribunal (misleading advertising), Environment Canada (emissions recalls), and Energy and Natural Resources Canada (fictional fuel economy ratings) exhibit a determined passivity. When it comes to auto regulations, Ottawa often seems more comfortable singing "Kumbaya" with the carmakers than being perceived as a cop on the beat.

SHHHH...More Secret Car Warranties

Automobile manufacturers use secret warranties or "special policies" to compensate car owners for performance-related defects long after the original warranty has expired, sometimes up to ten years. These extensions of the standard warranty are often found in confidential Technical Service Bulletins (TSB) sent to dealers, but seldom seen by car owners.

Part Four has dozens of special policies, warranty extensions and secret warranties that will pay for the repair or replacement of defective parts, including engines, transmissions, catalytic converters, brakes, and computer modules, even if you bought your vehicle used. Look at the following little-known warranty extensions that will pay for large repair bills up to 13 years out.

General Motors

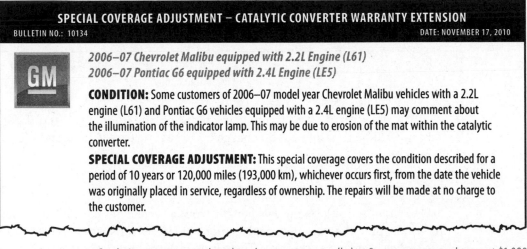

SPECIAL COVERAGE ADJUSTMENT – CATALYTIC CONVERTER WARRANTY EXTENSION

BULLETIN NO.: 10134   DATE: NOVEMBER 17, 2010

2006–07 Chevrolet Malibu equipped with 2.2L Engine (L61)
2006–07 Pontiac G6 equipped with 2.4L Engine (LE5)

CONDITION: Some customers of 2006–07 model year Chevrolet Malibu vehicles with a 2.2L engine (L61) and Pontiac G6 vehicles equipped with a 2.4L engine (LE5) may comment about the illumination of the indicator lamp. This may be due to erosion of the mat within the catalytic converter.

SPECIAL COVERAGE ADJUSTMENT: This special coverage covers the condition described for a period of 10 years or 120,000 miles (193,000 km), whichever occurs first, from the date the vehicle was originally placed in service, regardless of ownership. The repairs will be made at no charge to the customer.

Catalytic converters attach to the exhaust system, usually last 8 years or more, and can cost $1,000 each to replace. GM's 10-year extended warranty may mean $2,000 savings for two converters. Remember, warranty extensions should apply whether the vehicle was bought new or used.

2005-07 SUVs with defective fuel level sensors will have the part replaced for free up to 10 years or 120,000 miles. Previous repair costs will be refunded. Affected models are 2005-06 Chevrolet SSR, Trailblazer EXT, GMC Envoy XL; and the 2005-07 Buick Rainier, Chevrolet Trailblazer, and GMC Envoy. Cite GM Campaign #10054E.

Honda

2006-09 Civic engines may have a cracked engine block. This warranty extension will pay for a new engine block. If the engine is "cooked" from overheating, the entire engine will be replaced, gratis.

ENGINE BLOCK WARRANTY EXTENSION

CAMPAIGN NO.: 10-048   DATE: DECEMBER 18, 2013

APPLIES TO: 2006-08 Civic - VINs beginning with 1HG or 2HG: 2009 Civic - VINs beginning with 1HG, 19X and 2HG

BACKGROUND: On some 2006-08 and early production 2009 Civics, the engine (cylinder) block may leak engine coolant, resulting in engine overheating. To increase customer confidence, American Honda is extending the warranty of the engine block to 10 years from the original date of purchase, with no mileage limit. The warranty extension does not apply to any vehicle that has ever been declared a total loss or sold for salvage by a financial institution or insurer, or has a branded, or similar title under any states law. To check for vehicle eligibility, you must do a VIN status inquiry.

CUSTOMER NOTIFICATION: Customers were originally sent a notification of this warranty extension that indicated the warranty on the engine block was being extended to eight years. They will receive another notification that the warranty on the block is being extended to 10 years.

CORRECTIVE ACTION: If confirmed by your diagnosis, install a new engine block.

To save "he said, she said" disputes with the dealership's service manager, present a copy of one of the service bulletins in this book.

2006-11 Civics with cracked or chalking paint on the hood, roof, trunk, or front fenders will be repainted at no charge up to seven years. Cite Honda Campaign #12-049.

Nissan

2002-05 Altima and Maxima models benefit from a recall that pays for new bushings and seals, plus the complete replacement of the lower suspension assembly, all affected by premature corrosion. There is no mileage limit under Campaign #P5216.

Let's take a closer look at the car industry and give you the low-down on the many new and used vehicles on the market.

1 *Part One*

NEW CARS AND OLD TRICKS

Merge Fiat with Chrysler

"A 2012 Trillium study of vehicle advertising in Ontario found that approximately 73 percent of automobile advertisements placed by automobile manufacturers were not in the spirit of the Motor Vehicle Dealers Association – where a consumer could understand the final cost of a vehicle in a clear, comprehensive and prominent manner. In other words, if a dealer would have placed similar ads, we are confident the dealer would be in violation of the MVDA's advertising regulations."

Trillium Automobile Dealers Association (TADA) 2016, as submitted to the Ontario Committee on Finance and Economic Affairs

Lemon-Aid supports TADA's conclusion that carmakers' ads are deceptive. And, coming from Canada's largest provincial new car dealer association with a membership of over 1,000 dealers – that's almost a third of all new car dealers in Canada – governments mustn't ignore this accusation.

MORE CHOICE, BETTER DEALS

Fueled by low crude-oil prices, rock-bottom interest rates and extended-term loans, consumers binged on new vehicles, making for record sales in 2015 in North America – and 2016 looks like another banner year, too. At the same time, passenger-car sales have slumped as consumers embraced crossovers, SUVs and pickup trucks, encouraged by cheaper gas, improved fuel economy and the perceived utility of driving a multipurpose vehicle. Changing consumer tastes enabled Fiat Chrysler, Ford and General Motors to make windfall profits by pushing fully-loaded, technology-laden trucks and sport utilities.

During the past two years, oil prices have fallen precipitously from over $110 USD per barrel to $45 for some grades of crude. Although motorists welcome the savings at the pump, lower gas prices aren't entirely good for the auto industry or the environment. Shoppers have been turning away from "greener" mini-compacts, diesels, hybrid and electric vehicles – with the exception of the $100,000 Tesla Model S.

The trend has prompted Fiat Chrysler Automobiles to drop the slow selling (and unreliable) Dodge Dart and the Chrysler 200, while General Motors will retire the Buick Verano (a Chevrolet Cruze clone) for 2017. Slow sedan sales are particularly troublesome for GM. Sales of the redesigned Chevy Impala grew, but the model is expected to move from Oshawa to a Michigan plant.

Despite the sudden drop in the Canadian dollar against the U.S. currency, carmakers have managed to mostly hold the line on price increases of new vehicles. To "move the iron" dealers are sweetening rebates, adding standard equipment and offering new car loans for up to 96 months to shrink monthly payments, often at zero percent interest. Leasing is immensely popular again, especially when it comes to luxury brands. There have been some price increases, of course, that the industry has camouflaged by increasing "Transport and Preparation" fees, reducing dealer margins, and promoting bargain-priced models in their advertising – which you will have trouble finding stocked at dealerships.

On the used-car side, Canada's weakening loonie has resulted in a robust export market to the United States for used luxury vehicles, pickups and SUVs, and driven up prices for used vehicles. Agents acting on behalf of U.S. dealers are buying up late-model used vehicle inventories from Canadian dealers, leaving consumers to sift through the remainders. According to auto industry analyst Dennis DesRosiers, some 200,000 used cars and trucks were plucked from the Canadian market in 2015 and shipped to waiting customers in the U.S. The trend continues in earnest in 2016.

Here Today, Gone Tomorrow

For 2017 it will take a sharp eye to spot which of the new and upgraded models are worth more money than last year's offerings.

2017 Models: New, Dropped

NEW OR SIGNIFICANTLY CHANGED MODELS FOR 2017

Audi A4
Audi A5
Audi Q7
Buick LaCrosse
Buick Encore
Buick Envision
Cadillac CT6
Cadillac XT5
Chevrolet Bolt
Chevrolet Cruze
    Hatchback
Chevrolet Malibu
    Hybrid
Chevrolet Sonic
Chevrolet Trax
Chrysler Pacifica
Fiat 124 Spider
Ford Escape
Ford Fusion
Genesis G90
GMC Acadia
Honda Civic Hatchback
Honda Ridgeline
Hyundai Elantra
Hyundai Genesis G90
Hyundai Ioniq
Infiniti Q60
Infiniti QX30
Jaguar F-Pace
Jaguar XE
Jeep Wrangler
Kia Niro Hybrid
Kia Cadenza
Kia Optima HEV
Kia Sportage
Lincoln Continental
Mazda CX-9
Mazda MX-5 RF
Mercedes-Benz GLC
    Coupe
Mercedes-Benz E-Class
Mini Clubman
Mitsubishi Mirage
    Sedan
Nissan Armada
Porsche Boxster
Subaru Forester
Subaru Impreza
Toyota C-HR
Toyota Corolla
Volkswagen Golf
    Alltrack
Volvo S90

DROPPED

Buick Verano
Chrysler 200
Chrysler Town &
    Country
Dodge Dart
Honda CR-Z
Toyota Venza

Buying Tips

It's good to be a patient shopper.

Time works to your advantage as better products make their debut and low oil prices continue to impact prices of fuel-sipping economy cars, compacts, hybrids and electrics. Shoppers may look forward to discounts of 5-10 percent, beginning with the holiday promotions at the end of the calendar year. That's because many more Canadians are rushing to dealers to acquire expensive, less efficient, all-dressed large trucks, SUVs and European luxury vehicles during the autumn new model season. After being nagged for years about oil shortages and gas that would reach $7 a gallon, we have found ourselves awash in cheap oil and greater competition in the oil patch. Our collective consciousness says, "It's time for a treat. I want mine. Bigger is better."

In addition to fuel savings from low oil prices, there are a number of other ways car buyers can save from $5,000 to $15,000 on a vehicle purchase.

1. Buy a vehicle that is relatively uncomplicated, easy to service and has been sold in large numbers over many years. This will ensure that cheaper, independent repair shops can provide service and there is a good supply of less expensive aftermarket parts.

2. Begin your vehicle research anytime, but wait until the depth of winter, if you can, to negotiate a more reasonable price. Car shopping between December and February can yield savings; the new-model-introduction hoopla has died down, holiday incentives are on and dealers are hungrier when frigid weather keeps buyers at home. Seasonal prices vary even more for used vehicles, with winter offering the best deals.

3. For maxium savings on a new vehicle, look for a model that's finishing its model run during the summer, or the previous generation of a used vehicle before the most recent redesign.

4. Don't buy European offerings, unless you know local servicing that is competent and reasonably priced. Dealership networks are notoriously weak for these cars after the warranty is over, parts can be inordinately expensive and hard to find, and few independent garages will invest in the expensive equipment needed to service complicated emissions and fuel-delivery systems. CBC aired a story of an Ontario woman who bought a used 2010 Mini (made by BMW) and after seven months was given an estimate for a $10,000 engine rebuild. The old axiom that there is a right way, a wrong way and an expensive European way to fix a car still holds true for most models from the European luxury carmakers.

5. Think twice before you buy a hybrid or electric vehicle. Most give a poor return on expenditure, are complicated to service and dealer-dependent. Many hybrids don't provide the fuel economy or savings they hype. The exceptions are Toyota models like the Prius and hybrid Camry with the Hybrid Synergy Drive system. These are durable hybrids (400,000 km and more in taxi service) that deliver fuel savings of 30 percent compared to similar conventional vehicles. Contrary to perceptions, recent VW diesels are much less reliable than most gasoline vehicles and they're expensive to repair.

6. Be wary of Chrysler, Dodge or Jeep models if you're buying a new vehicle to own for the long haul. Chrysler is the weakest of the Detroit Three and its lineup has a history of serious safety- and performance-related defects, with the TIPM module being a case in point. A defective Totally Integrated Power Module, or TIPM, can introduce a tsunami of electrical faults, including no-start conditions, dead instruments, no cooling fan (leading to engine overheating) and random stalling at speed. Automatic transmissions, brakes, the electrical system and air conditioners on Fiat Chrysler group vehicles are also troublesome.

On the other hand, the full-size Dodge Charger and Chrysler 300 break the mould and are recommended buys. The Dodge Ram is a good used truck buy when equipped with the Cummins inline-six diesel; that engine beats the competition for power and reliability. However, the new V6 Fiat diesel in the Ram 1500 light-duty pickup has been very troublesome. This year, the Chrysler group will launch a plug-in hybrid version of the next-generation Chrysler minivan, called the Pacifica. The hybrid version will be powered by a gasoline engine and a battery pack. Buyers should keep their fingers crossed.

7. Don't be blinded by luxury brands. Higher-priced vehicles don't ensure you will get a higher level of quality or reliability. Think Cadillac ATS, XLR, and XTS, Lincoln MKS, MKT (with EcoBoost), MKX, and the VW Touareg. Many of the premium European brands, including Audi, BMW and Mercedes-Benz, are touted as the pinnacle of luxury and perfection, yet seasoned owners will tell you that these complex machines can break down regularly, especially after the factory warranty and maintenance plan (a common sales incentive) expire. Post-warranty, owners have to contend with expensive component costs, waits for parts delivery, and pay a premium for service. If you want a luxury badge, the Asian brands offer better reliability, with Lexus and Acura offering the best dependability.

8. Avoid turbocharged engines. Auto manufacturers are turning to turbocharged small engines to hit ever more ambitious fuel-economy targets set by the government. Unfortunately, in real-world driving they are often little more fuel efficient than larger six-cylinder and V8 engines, and not as smooth. For instance, the Automobile Protection Association (APA) found that 2013-2015 Fords with EcoBoost four-cylinder engines burn more fuel than similar models with conventional four-cylinder

engines. Turbo-equipped vehicles can generate rosy numbers in laboratory fuel economy tests, where the acceleration cycle is so gentle that the turbo is hardly working, but the APA's real-world evaluations revealed that the actual fuel consumption of some models is disappointing and the likelihood of expensive repairs down the road is higher.

9. Don't buy a 2011-14 Ford vehicle equipped with a dual-clutch (DSG) automatic transmission. Developed by Ford and Getrag, the automated six-speed is essentially two manual transmissions, each with its own clutch alternating shift duty. Electric solenoid actuation provides quick and efficient shifts, avoiding the hydraulic losses associated with torque converters. While it enhances economy, the complex transmission is jerky in operation and, ultimately, unreliable. Found in Focus and Fiesta models, the automatic transmission is extremely expensive to replace after the end of the warranty. Dual-clutch automatic transmissions in VW and Audi products are also troublesome, with expensive failures after the warranty expires.

10. Choose a used vehicle with a conventional hydraulic automatic transmission, or a manual gearbox if you are comfortable with a gearshift. Be wary of continuously variable (CVT) automatics in used vehicles. With the exception of Synergy Drive transmissions used in the Prius and other Toyota hybrids, all the automakers selling vehicles in North America with CVT automatics have been bedeviled by poor durability. Nissan CVT-equipped vehicles have been so failure prone that the company extended its warranty for up to ten years on vehicles produced until 2010. Nissan's transmission subsidiary, Jatco, has supplied the same CVT transmission to other makes, such as Jeep. Fortunately, new vehicles with CVTs have become less risky, as materials, lubricants and computer programming have evolved to address durability concerns.

NISSAN CVT – CUSTOMER SATISFACTION PROGRAM

The following is a list of vehicles included in the Nissan CVT Warranty Extension program:

NISSAN	2007	2008	2009	2010
	Murano	–	Murano	Murano
	–	Rogue	Rogue cube®	Rogue cube®
	Sentra	Sentra	Sentra	Sentra
	Versa 1.8SL	Versa 1.8SL	Versa 1.8SL	Versa 1.8SL
	Maxima	Maxima	Maxima	Maxima
	Altima	Altima	Altima	Altima
	Altima Coupe	Altima Coupe	Altima Coupe	Altima Coupe
	Altima Hybrid	Altima Hybrid	Altima Hybrid	Altima Hybrid

Nissan's ten-year "goodwill" warranty covers almost any ... eventuality.

11. Check to see if the vehicle comes with a spare tire and jack, not a spray can of sealant and air compressor. Include this stipulation in the contract. If you wait until after the vehicle is delivered, the dealer will likely charge you $350+ for a space-saver spare, jack and tie-down assembly. Some models, like the Mini and certain BMWs, have no provision for a spare tire in their cargo areas. In that case, you will likely be stuck with hard-riding and more expensive runflat tires, or required to call roadside assistance when a conventional tire goes flat.

12. Don't buy a new vehicle with below-average reliability. Yes, an extended warranty can help address the risk due to a reputation for past failures, but choosing a better vehicle is the better solution. New vehicles with poor reliability eventually suffer from plunging depreciation, which impacts your pocketbook at trade-in time.

13. Use your credit card for the down payment and put down as little money as possible. If you want to cancel a sales contract or work order *because a promised service wasn't delivered*, it's easier to do with a credit card than with cash.

Which New Car, Truck, SUV, or Van?

I remember in the '70s, American Motors gave away free TVs with each new car purchase, just before shutting its doors. In the past decade, General Motors gave away free Dell computers and VW hawked free guitars with its cars. The Detroit Three automakers continue to build some poor-quality cars and trucks, although there appears to be some improvement in recent years. The gap between Asian and American automobile quality has narrowed; however, this may reflect only a lowered benchmark following recent Honda, Nissan, and Toyota powertrain, and electrical system glitches, and a substantial increase in recalls.

Nevertheless, Asian makes continue to dominate dependability surveys, while American and European models are mostly ranked below the industry average, but some are trending upward. Ford, long the darling for improved quality scores, has crashed in the past five years due to chronic infotainment electronic failures, faulty EcoBoost (turbocharged) powertrains, and false fuel-economy ratings with its C-Max and Fusion hybrids. Ford was sued by owners of the 2013 Fusion Hybrid and C-Max Hybrid, who complained the company's official fuel economy figures were science fiction. The company settled out of court.

So, what to buy? Here are some helpful steps to follow as you contemplate buying new or used.

Step 1: Be Patient and Practical

First, keep in mind that you are going to spend much more money than you may have anticipated – almost $32,000 for the average car and $40,000 for most minivans, according to Dennis DesRosiers, a Toronto-based industry consultant. Then there are extra fees, like freight charges and so-called administration costs that are added to the bottom line. But, with cutthroat discounts from the manufacturers, and armed with tips from this guide that will help you avoid costly extras, you can bring that amount down by a few hundred to a couple of thousand dollars.

According to the Canadian Automobile Association (CAA), the average household owns two vehicles, which are each driven about 20,000 km annually and cost an average of $800 a year for maintenance; DesRosiers Automotive Consultants calculates maintenance at $1,100 annually.

It's practically impossible to buy a bare-bones car or truck because automakers know most buyers will move up from the low prices for basic models in their ads, so they tend to cram new vehicles with costly, non-essential performance and convenience features in order to increase profits. Nevertheless, money-wasting features like factory-installed electronic navigation, self-parking systems, giant glass moonroofs, and voice-command capability can easily be passed up with little impact on safety or convenience. In fact, features like voice command and in-dash controls accessed via touch screens can be very distracting while driving – with a negative safety effect. On the other hand, park sensors, backup cameras, full-torso side curtain airbags, automatic braking with collision avoidance (AEB), now standard or being phased into vehicles, are all important safety equipment that are well worth the extra expense.

Our driving needs are influenced by where we live, our lifestyles and our ages (see "Senior" Cars, below, for a discussion of vehicles best suited to mature drivers). The sweet spot for buying is a less expensive three-or-four-year-old model (it can easily save you $10,000 or more on the purchase price compared to a new vehicle) that is crashworthy, with minimal high-tech, in-dash features to distract and annoy, and does not cost much to maintain.

Keep it simple

In the city, a small wagon, hatchback, or crossover is more practical and less expensive than a mid-sized car like the Honda Accord or Toyota Camry. Also, keep in mind that most compacts, cars like the newer Civic and Elantra, have grown in size and are excellent substitutes for a larger sedan. What once were small cars are now quite large, relatively fuel-efficient, and equipped with more horsepower than you'll need. Nevertheless, if you're going to be doing a lot of highway driving, regularly transporting groups of adults, or loading up on accessories, a medium-sized sedan, wagon, or small sport-utility could be a better choice for comfort. Of course, nothing beats a minivan for multiple passenger seating, comfort and cargo space.

Don't let low fuel prices stampede you into buying a vehicle unsuitable to your driving needs. If you travel less than 20,000 km per year, mostly in the city, choose a small car or SUV equipped with a 4-cylinder engine that produces about 140 hp to get the best fuel economy without sacrificing performance. Anything more powerful is likely a waste. Extensive towing demands the cruising performance, extra power for additional accessories, and durability of a larger, 6-cylinder or V8 engine. Believe me, fuel savings will be the last thing on your mind if you buy an underpowered truck.

Carmakers give false figures in five areas: Fuel economy, emissions, rear legroom, payload, and towing capacity. Confirm these claims with a test drive, and get the recommendation of a dealer for the trailer or boat you intend to haul.

Step 2: Seek Out Alternatives

Sometimes a cheaper "twin" will fit the bill. Twins are nameplates made by different auto manufacturers, or by different divisions of the same company, that are virtually identical in body design and mechanical components, like the Chevrolet Silverado and GMC Sierra pickups.

Compact South Korean SUVs like this recommended Hyundai Tucson AWD ($28,999 nicely equipped) are ideal for small families and light commuting. Remember, Hyundai owns Kia and their vehicles are quite similar under the skin. In this segment, the redesigned Kia Sportage LX AWD is similarly equipped at $27,529. So, if a Hyundai dealer doesn't have the model or offer the price you want, go to a Kia outlet. Take fuel economy and horsepower claims with a grain of salt – both automakers have fudged these figures in the past.

Step 3: Enlist a Friend

Car shopping can be bewildering. Visiting the showroom with your spouse, a level-headed relative or a sensible friend will help you steer a truer course through all the non-essential options you'll be offered.

Getting a female perspective can be really helpful. Women make the salesmen (yes, less than 10 percent of the sales staff working on the showroom floor

O-100 KM TIME?
HOW MANY SPEAKERS?
WOWIE! THAT'S REAL
LEATHER?

GROAN

HOW FAST WILL IT GO FROM
100 KM/H TO 0? CAN YOU
INSTALL THE BABY SEAT?
LEMON-AID SAYS THE CAR
STALLS...

Women ask the important questions and listen. Men get "gadget-giddy." Take your mother, wife, or sister along.

are women) work harder to make a sale. Most salespeople agree that female shoppers are more level-headed about what they want and less impulsive during negotiations than men, who tend to be mesmerized by the available techno-toys available.

In increasing numbers, buyers are choosing compact SUVs, and pickups believing they are more versatile than conventional passenger cars. Many drivers, especially women, have discovered they feel safer sitting higher in these vehicles. Having spotted a profitable trend, automakers are offering increased versatility combined with unconventional styling in so-called "crossover" vehicles. These are commonly "wagons on stilts" that use a lighter, unibody car platform, but incorporate key features of a truck, such as all-wheel-drive and somewhat higher ground clearance. You'll pay more for this versatility, compared to a compact car, both to buy the vehicle and in fuel expenses.

Step 4: Stick to Your Budget

Determine how much money you can spend, and then decide which vehicles in that price range interest you. Have more than one model in mind so that the overpriced one won't tempt you as much. As your benchmarks, use the ratings, alternative models, and estimated purchase price. Logic and budgeting are the first casualties of showroom hype, so carefully consider what you actually need and how these things will fit into your budget before comparing models and prices at a dealership.

Write down your first, second, and third choices relative to each model and the equipment offered. Browse the automaker websites both in Canada and in the States, and consult manufacturer websites and the APA's pricing database for the Canadian manufacturer's suggested retail price (MSRP), promotions, and package discounts. Some dealers quote lower opening prices that may apply only to Internet-generated referrals. Once you get a good idea of the price variations, query some dealers by e-mail and make them bid against each other (see E-mail Bids, below). Call the lowest-bidding dealership, ask for an appointment to be assured of getting a sales agent's complete attention, and take along the downloaded price info from the Canadian automaker website and the manufacturer's advertising, as many salespeople are not familiar the latest promotions, or will open their pricing at a higher amount, in the hope that you may not know better.

Don't get taken in by the "Buy Canadian!" chanting from Chrysler, Ford, General Motors, and the Canadian Auto Workers. While Detroit-based automakers are beating their chests over the need to buy American, they buy Asian auto parts and have been moving production to Mexico. Imported Chinese auto parts have had a poor reliability record over the past decade, running the gamut of leaking tire valve stems affecting all automakers who bought cheap imported stems to "grenading" Chinese-made Getrag MT-82 manual transmissions in 2011-13 Mustang GTs that also shift poorly in cold weather.

This brings up the question as to whether Chinese automakers can be trusted to make safe, reliable parts and vehicles that aren't misrepresented. *Lemon-Aid* thinks not. Chinese manufacturers sold millions of failure-prone tire stem valves to American car companies, and entered the North American market with low-quality, counterfeit brand tires. In China, they copied GM's Daewoo subcompact and renamed it the "Chery." GM sued when the Chinese manufacturer used a disguised GM Daewoo in a crash test in place of the Chery (China Motor Vehicle Documentation Centre. Retrieved 2011-03-12). And now they are ripping off Land Rover by selling a copy of the Evoque SUV and marketing it as the 2016 "Landwind X7."

The China-made Landwind X7 knockoff is expected to sell for the equivalent of $22,000, or about $30,000 cheaper than the Evoque. The birds are real.

Vehicles that are produced through co-ventures between Detroit automakers and Asian manufacturers have better quality control, and the knowhow acquired during these joint ventures has helped the American auto industry. For example, Toyota and Pontiac churned out identical Matrix and Vibe compacts in Ontario and the U.S.; however, the Ontario-built Matrix has the better reputation so you'll usually save money by buying a used Vibe. On the other hand, Volvo's quality declined when Ford bought the automaker, and Volvo is just getting on its feet again under Chinese ownership.

Sometimes choosing a higher trim line that packages many options as standard features will cost you less than ordering all the features separately. And when it's time to sell your vehicle, a basic version of the higher trim line may command a higher price than a lower trim line loaded with options ordered individually. This is especially true of pickup trucks.

In North America, auto buyers are buying larger vehicles. In Canada, there is a major shift from small cars to compact sport utility vehicles (which are actually fairly large and heavy vehicles), and mid-size sedans into crossovers; pickup sales are going through the roof. *TrueCar.com*, an American auto analyst, says transaction costs reflects this trend: Mid-size SUVs average $6,465 more than mid-size sedans and compact utilities sell for $5,379 more than compact cars. Since an SUV costs automakers only about $1,500 more to make than a sedan on the same platform, manufacturers are making record profits selling these vehicles in record numbers. Not only are women joining the upscale crowd, seniors as well have embraced "bigger is better." Edmunds, a publisher of car reviews, says nearly half of compact SUV and crossover buyers are older than 55. The taller roofline, which improves ease of entry and visibility in traffic, has a lot to do with the trend.

Consider a low-mileage (less than 5,000 km) demonstrator, or a model near the end of its last year before being redesigned. You may get a generous end-of-model-year rebate, a lower price for the extra mileage on the demonstrator, or a more generous discount from the dealer. Remember, if the vehicle has been pre-registered to another company or individual by the dealer so they could qualify for an end-of-the-month bonus, it is no longer legally a demo and should be considered used. With a demo, the CarProof (*www.carproof.com*) VIN search for possible collision damage is likely pointless, as dealers do not report incidents affecting vehicles in their fleets.

The APA has found that the savings most dealers offer with a demonstrator are small – in the range of $500 to $1,500 for a current model year vehicle, and that they often carry dealer-installed features like anti-theft etching and accessories that are built into their prices and reduce your savings. Many dealers jack up their demo prices with transportation and preparation charges for a vehicle that may already have been in service. You should not be paying a separate charge for Freight and Vehicle Preparation on a demonstrator. Finally, if you're considering a real demonstrator, or a "pre-registered" car with no mileage, be sure to ask about the start date for the warranty; sellers sometimes neglect to inform you that several months of coverage have elapsed.

When to Buy

Start doing your new-car research anytime, but wait until the depth of winter, if you can, to negotiate a more reasonable price. And shoppers who wait until summer or early fall can double-dip from additional automakers' dealer incentive and buyer rebate programs that may be in place to clear out the outgoing models. Vehicles made between March and August offer the most assembly-line fixes, and, hence, fewer factory-related glitches.

Visit the showroom near the end of the month, when the salesperson will want to make that one last sale to meet the month's quota. If sales have been terrible, the sales manager may be willing to do some extra negotiating in order to boost sales staff's morale. This is especially true for the Fiat Chrysler Dodge and Jeep brands and Hyundai, whose dealers are under constant pressure from their manufacturers to meet their sales quotas or walk the plank.

Where to Buy

Large cities have more selection and more competition. Dealers rely on sales volume and apply pressure in the business office to make up for lost margins due to vehicle discounting. Least expensive is likely a suburban dealer about 30-45 minutes outside a large metropolitan market; they're usually more likely to drop their prices to attract a customer from the city, and have the lower overhead costs typical of dealers in smaller communities.

But, price isn't everything and good dealers aren't always the ones with the lowest prices. Buying from someone you know is relatively honest and gives reliable service is just as important as getting a low price. Check a dealer's honesty and reliability by talking with motorists in your community who drive vehicles purchased from the local dealer (identified by the nameplate on the vehicle's trunk). If these customers have been treated fairly, they'll be glad to recommend their dealer. You can also check the dealer's repair standards by getting your current vehicle serviced, if it is the same make.

How can you tell which dealers are the most honest and competent? Well, judging from the hundreds of reports I receive each year, dealerships in small suburban and rural communities are often fairer than big-city dealers because they're more vulnerable to negative word-of-mouth testimonials and to poor sales – when their vehicles aren't selling, good service picks up the slack. Their prices may also be competitive, but don't count on it.

Be skeptical of testimonials on some third-party ratings sites. The APA has obtained variable results in secret shopper visits to dealers who were recommended by third parties on dealer websites.

The quality of new-vehicle service is directly linked to the number and competence of dealerships within the network. If the network is weak, parts are likely to be unavailable, repair costs can go through the roof, and the skill level of the mechanics may be subpar, since better mechanics command higher salaries. Among foreign manufacturers, Hyundai and Kia have a much improved overall dealer representation across Canada, primarily due to record-breaking sales during the last few years. However the customer service at Kia and Hyundai can be weak or nonexistent, as their after-sales support has not kept pace with their rapid expansion. Servicing has always been problematic with European makes. Prices tend to be costly and servicing is particularly dealer-dependent.

You will get better treatment by going to dealerships that are accredited by consumer groups like the APA or Car Help Canada, or auto clubs like the CAA. Auto club accreditation is no ironclad guarantee that a dealership will be honest or competent; however, if you're cheated, or given bad service by a recommended dealer or repair shop (look for the accreditation symbol in a dealer's ads, on the Internet, or on their shop windows), the consumer association or auto club is one more place to take your complaint to apply additional mediation pressure.

Automobile Brokers

Car brokers are independent agents who act as intermediaries to find the new or used vehicle you want at a price below what you'd normally pay. They have their smartphone contact lists, speak the sales lingo, know all of the angles and scams, and can generally cut through the bull to find a fair price – usually within days. Their services cost from $300 and up, usually paid for by the dealer out of the markup. You can save a couple of hundred dollars on your purchase of a basic vehicle, or more than a thousand dollars if you're in the market for a luxury vehicle. Just as important, you'll save the stress and hassle associated with the dealership experience, which some people find unpleasant.

Brokers get new vehicles through dealers. The broker's job is to find a vehicle that meets a client's expressed needs and then to negotiate its purchase (or lease) on behalf of that client. The majority of brokers tend to deal exclusively in new vehicles, with a small percentage dealing in both new and used vehicles. Used vehicles are usually picked up at auctions open only to auto dealers, or were taken in trade by the broker. Ancillary services vary among brokers; most are no frills, and will prefer that you have already picked the model and features you want, and have taken a test drive and done some price shopping to set a benchmark. Brokers can usually arrange financing through the dealer so you benefit from below-market interest rates available on new vehicles.

The cost of hiring a broker can be charged either as a flat fee or as a percentage of the value of the vehicle (usually 1-2 percent). Reputable brokers are not beholden to any particular dealership or make, and they'll disclose their flat fee up front or tell you the percentage amount they'll charge on a specific vehicle.

Good brokers are hard to find, particularly in western Canada. Buyers who are looking for a broker should first ask friends and acquaintances if they can recommend one. Word-of-mouth referrals are often the best because people won't refer others to a service with which they were dissatisfied. Your local credit union and the APA or Car Help Canada may be able to help.

Consumer Association Buying Services

The best-known buying services offered by not-for-profits in Canada are those offered by the APA and Car Help Canada. These two consumer associations offer unique counselling and referral service that will help you purchase a new vehicle at the right price in a non-adversarial environment from a knowledgeable seller.

The APA (*APA.ca*) provides its members with detailed price reports on requested new vehicles, specifying the cost savings members receive on individual trim levels and even option packages. The APA works through approved dealers, often the fleet sales manager or association specialist, to deliver a low, competitive price without haggling. Depending on the model and market conditions, savings run from a couple of hundred dollars to well over a thousand dollars. The membership fee is $77 for the first year and $44 to renew annually. The service is available in the Toronto, Montreal, and Vancouver/Victoria markets. Group auto insurance is offered to Ontario residents.

CarHelpCanada.com provides consumers with the best possible pricing information when researching a new or used vehicle purchase. Members can take their pre-negotiated price to a dealer of their choice, or preferably choose one of the recommended dealerships. They also offer group auto insurance discounts. Members pay $65 plus tax annually. The service is available in the Greater Toronto market and parts of Southern Ontario.

Frivolous Freight Charges

Lemon-Aid has always cautioned new-car buyers about inflated transportation and PDI (pre-delivery inspection) fees or suggested they should be reduced by half to match the equivalent charges for the same vehicles sold in the U.S. This advice is even truer today in light of recent price increases for these charges in Canada that have seen them climb to almost $2,000. Transport and prep should be included in the price of the vehicle, like other consumer products, or limited to the average cost of delivering the vehicle to the dealer. Currently, the high charges amount to a cash grab by the manufacturer or dealer, and are priced well above their actual cost of delivery. Consider that Hyundai charges $1,895 for delivery of the Made-in-USA Santa Fe compared to Toyota's $1,760 charge for the similarly sized 4Runner, which comes all the way from Japan.

Front-Wheel Drive

Most cars are front-wheel drives, and, for most users, front-drive is the system that offers the best value for money. Front-wheel drive directs engine power to the front wheels, which pull the vehicle forward, while the back wheels simply support the rear and assist with braking. The biggest benefit of front-drive is foul-weather traction. With the engine and transmission up front, there's lots of weight pressing down on the front-drive wheels, increasing tire grip in snow and on wet pavement. When towing a heavy trailer, however, the weight shifts and you lose the traction advantage.

Front-drive vehicles provide a bit more interior room (no transmission hump), more car-like handling, and better fuel economy, but damage from potholes and fender-benders is usually more extensive, and maintenance costs (especially premature suspension, tire, and brake wear) may be a bit higher than with rear-drives.

Rear-Wheel Drive

Rear-wheel drive is on the way out, even for pickups, because the majority of buyers prefer the all-weather convenience of four-wheel drive. Rear-drive directs engine power to the rear wheels, which push the vehicle forward. The front wheels steer, brake, and support the front of the vehicle. With the engine up front, the transmission in the middle, and the drive axle in the rear, there's plenty of room for larger and more durable drivetrain components. This makes for less crash damage, lower maintenance costs, and higher towing capacities than with front-drives.

Ford's rear-drive 2013 Mustang ($15,000) comes with a V6 that's almost as powerful as its earlier V8 and it's $10,000 cheaper. Mustangs are Above Average performers that hold their value and are easily repaired at independent shops.

On the downside, rear-drives don't have as much weight over the driving wheels, so they can't provide as much traction on wet or icy roads. You'll need to carry a shovel and traction aids for winter in most of Canada.

Four-Wheel Drive (4x4)

Four-wheel drive (4x4) directs engine power through a transfer case to all four wheels, giving you much better traction on snow-covered roads. On most models, the driver can select rear-drive when four-wheel drive isn't required. The large transfer-case housing makes the vehicle sit higher, giving you additional ground clearance. Traditional 4x4 systems also provide a low-range gear for off-road conditions.

Keep in mind that extended driving over dry pavement with part-time 4x4 engaged may cause the driveline to bind and result in serious damage. Some buyers prefer rear-drive pickups equipped with a winch and four dedicated winter tires.

Negatives with older SUVs built on truck platforms are a rough and noisy driveline, vague handling, high repair costs, and poor fuel economy.

All-Wheel Drive (AWD)

AWD is four-wheel drive that's on all the time. Almost universal in new luxury vehicles and popular in today's crossover models, AWD never needs to be deactivated when running over dry pavement and doesn't require the heavy transfer case that cuts fuel economy and raises the centre of gravity, which makes the vehicle less stable. AWD-equipped vehicles aren't recommended for off-roading because of their lower ground clearance and fragile driveline parts, which aren't as rugged as 4x4 components. But very few vehicles are ever driven off road, even among those with off-road capability.

SAFETY

Which Safety Features Are Best?

Automakers have loaded 2016-17 models with features that wouldn't have been imagined several decades ago. Some of the more effective safety features are head-protecting side airbags, electronic stability control, antilock brakes, automatic emergency braking (AEB), rearview cameras, adjustable brake and accelerator pedals, integrated child safety seats, seat belt pretensioners, adjustable head restraints, and sophisticated navigation systems.

Seat belts provide the best means of reducing the severity of injury arising from both low- and high-speed frontal collisions. In order to be effective, seat belts must be adjusted properly and feel comfortably tight without undue slack. Seat belts have improved significantly over the years, but some owners still complain that seat belts don't retract enough for a snug fit, are too tight, chafe the neck, or don't fit children properly. Automakers have addressed these problems with adjustable shoulder-belt anchors that allow both tall and short drivers to raise or lower the belt for a snug, more comfortable fit. Another important seat belt innovation is the pretensioner (now found on most front seat belts), a device that automatically tightens the safety belt in the event of a crash. If you're buying a used vehicle, check out the recall status of any vehicle equipped with Takata-made seat belts, especially Hondas.

Crashworthiness

A vehicle with a high crash protection rating is a lifesaver. In fact, improvements in crashworthiness over the past 50 years have paid off handsomely, with benefits similar to large public health initiatives when it comes to lives and injuries saved. By surrounding occupants with a protective cocoon and deflecting crash forces away from the interior, auto engineers have successfully created safer vehicles without increasing vehicle size or cost unduly. And purchasing a vehicle with the idea that you'll be involved in an collision someday is not unreasonable. According to the Insurance Institute for Highway Safety (see below), the average car will likely have two accidents before being scrapped, and it's twice as likely to be in a severe frontal collision as a side-impact.

Since some vehicles are more crashworthy than others, and since size doesn't always guarantee crash safety, it's important to buy a vehicle that gives you the best protection from frontal, side, and rear collisions while keeping its rollover and roof-collapse potential to a minimum.

Two Washington-based organizations monitor how vehicle design affects crash safety: The National Highway Traffic Safety Administration (NHTSA) and the Insurance Institute for Highway Safety (IIHS). Crash information from these two groups doesn't always correspond because tests and testing methods vary.

NHTSA crash-test results for vehicles and tires are available at *www.safercar.gov/Safety+Ratings*. Information relating to safety complaints, recalls, defect investigations, and service bulletins can be found at *www.safercar.gov /Vehicle+Owners*. IIHS results may be found at *www.iihs.org/ratings*. NHTSA has archived millions of owner complaints from the last four decades and lists them by model and year.

Don't get taken in by the five-star crash rating hoopla touted by automakers. Vehicles that do well in the easier NHTSA side and front crash tests may not do very well in IIHS offset crash tests, or may have poorly designed head restraints that can increase the severity of neck injuries. Before making a final decision on the vehicle you want, look up its crashworthiness and overall safety profile in Part Four.

Cars versus trucks

Occupants of large vehicles have fewer severe injury claims than do occupants of small vehicles. This was demonstrated in a 1996 NHTSA study showing that collisions between light trucks or vans and small cars resulted in the car occupants having an 81 percent higher fatality rate than the occupants of the light trucks or vans.

Vehicle weight improves protection in two-vehicle crashes. In a head-on crash, for example, the heavier vehicle drives the lighter one backward, which decreases forces inside the heavy vehicle and increases forces in the lighter one. All heavy vehicles, even poorly designed ones, offer this advantage in two-vehicle collisions. However, their advantage is lessened in single-vehicle crashes; that is, when the car or truck leaves the roadway and collides with a guardrail, tree, or other fixture.

Crash test figures show that SUVs, vans, and trucks also offer more protection to adult occupants than do passenger cars in most crashes because their higher set-up allows them to ride over other vehicles (Ford and Volvo were leaders in lowering the fronts of their SUVs to reduce the effect of override). Conversely, because of their high centre of gravity, easily overloaded tires, and unforgiving suspensions, these vehicles used to have a disproportionate number of single-vehicle rollovers, which are far deadlier than frontal or side collisions; the introduction of electronic stability control (ESC) across the board (required by law in Canada on all 2012 and newer models) has significantly reduced the occurrence of pickup truck and SUV rollovers.

Interestingly, a vehicle's past crashworthiness rating doesn't always guarantee that subsequent model years will be just as safe or safer, although carmakers are taking much more care not to degrade occupant protection when redesigning models than they used to.

Rollovers

According to *Safercar.gov*, although vehicle rollovers represent only two to three percent of crashes, they cause *one-third* of all traffic deaths in what are usually single-vehicle accidents, resulting from a loss of control that causes the vehicle to leave the roadway. Rollovers occur less frequently with passenger cars and minivans than with SUVs, trucks, and full-sized vans (especially the 15-passenger variety). That's why ESC systems are so important in top-heavy vans, pickups, and SUVs.

More Safety Considerations

According to Transport Canada, 91 per cent of front-seat occupants use their seatbelts, while only 85 per cent of rear-seat passengers do – a troubling statistic when you consider that the rear seat is often where children and young adults are riding.

In light of the dramatic reduction in automobile accident fatalities and injuries over the past four decades, safety experts believe that additional crash protection features will likely pay smaller dividends in the future. One school believes it's time to target the driver more aggressively, but programs need to be science-based and have broad public support to be effective. The NHTSA believes that we could cut automobile accident fatalities by half through 100 percent seat belt use and the elimination of drunk driving.

Another school believes that effective measures that target the driver should be augmented with technology to help *avoid* a collision. This includes new features like automatic braking, backup cameras, more sophisticated "black box" data recorders, more-stringent licensing requirements, including graduated licensing and de-licensing programs directed at teens and seniors, and stricter law enforcement.

Incidentally, police studies have shown that there's an important side benefit to arresting traffic-safety scofflaws. They often net career criminals or seriously impaired drivers before they have the chance to harm others.

Active safety

Advocates of active safety stress that accidents are caused by the proverbial "nut behind the wheel," and believe that safe driving can be best taught through schools or private driving courses. Active safety components are generally systems, such as ABS brakes, high-performance tires, and traction control, which may help a driver avoid accidents if they're skilful and mature.

The theory of active safety has several drawbacks. A study of seriously injured drivers at the Shock Trauma Center in Maryland showed that 51 percent of the sample tested positive for illegal drugs while 34 percent tested positive for alcohol (*www.druggeddriving.org/ddp.html*). Drivers who are under the influence of alcohol or drugs cause about 40 percent of all fatal accidents. All the high-performance options and specialized driving courses in the world will not provide much protection from impaired drivers who draw a bead on your vehicle. And, because active safety components get a lot of use – you're likely to need ABS brakes 99 times more often than you'll need an airbag – they have to be well designed and well maintained to remain effective. Finally, consider that several independent studies have shown that safe driving taught to young drivers doesn't necessarily reduce the number of driving-related deaths and injuries (*Lancet*, July 2001; 1978 DeKalb County, Georgia, Study):

> The DeKalb Study compared the accident records of 9,000 teens that had taken driver education in the county's high schools with 9,000 teens that had no formal driver training. The final results showed no significant difference between the two groups. In other words, DeKalb County, Georgia, paid a large amount of money for absolutely no value.

With young drivers, controlling their behaviour appears to make a greater contribution to their risk profile than focusing on their skill levels. Impulse control is lower in adolescence compared to full adulthood, and peer pressure and thrill-seeking contribute to their higher collision involvement.

Passive safety

Passive safety assumes that you will be involved in life-threatening situations and should be either warned in time to avoid a collision or automatically protected from rolling over, losing traction, or bearing the brunt of collision forces. Head-protecting side airbags, ESC, brake override systems, daytime running lights, and a centre-mounted third brake light are five passive safety features that have paid off handsomely in reduced injuries and lives saved.

Passive safety features also assume that some accidents aren't avoidable and that, when those accidents occur, vehicles should provide as much protection as possible to drivers, passengers, and other vehicles that may be struck – without depending on the driver's reactions. Passive safety components that have consistently been proven to reduce vehicular deaths and injuries are seat belts, laminated windshields, and vehicle structures that enhance crashworthiness by absorbing or deflecting crash forces away from the occupants.

Collision avoidance

Avoiding a collision is the next frontier in vehicle safety. New features, such as automatic braking that uses sensors mounted in front of the rearview mirror or at the front of the vehicle, can actually intervene to prevent a collision, whether the driver responds or not. This suite of technologies includes blind-spot detection, lane-keeping assist, and cross-traffic alert (for reversing out of parking spaces). Some are still not completely proven, and not all are equally effective, but early results are promising. A U.S. IIHS study of automatic braking systems determined there was a 39 percent reduction in the number of frontal collisions, when combined with forward collision warning systems. David Zuby, IIHS chief research officer, said

> As this technology becomes more widespread, we can expect to see noticeably fewer rear-end crashes. The same goes for the whiplash injuries that often result from these crashes.

HIGHWAY HIGH-TECH

Faster wireless systems, dash-mounted video cameras, LED front lights, radar, and lithium ion batteries are five technologies that should post the most growth within the next five years.

High-speed 4G wireless connections, seven times as fast as previous 3G cellular services, have come to the car. If automaker marketing is to be believed, they are expected to make driving safer and highway travel more predictable. General

Motors is the current leader for in-car 4G communications, offering it even on their cheapest vehicle, the $11,595 Chevrolet Spark.

With 4G, drivers can download directions, turning their cars into roving Wi-Fi hot spots for up to seven devices. In effect, the car will have access to the same information that one could get from home or off a smartphone, including the hundreds of car-friendly "apps" that can make driving safer, cheaper, and more pleasant, but also more distracting.

Most drivers are well aware of the potential all this technology has for distraction. We can expect things to get worse going forward, as new communication technology migrates into vehicles without being field-tested with large groups of users over time to measure their impact on driving safety. The likely result will be Band-Aid solutions that are not supported by science, like the hand-held cellphone ban. Whether hand-held or hands-free, talking on the phone impairs your driving due to "cognitive blindness." This is a major reason the automakers are in a hurry to put active collision-avoidance into their vehicles; they're attempting to compensate for the new tech they are loading onto dashboards.

Widely used in commercial vehicles such as delivery trucks and police patrol cars, dash-mounted event data video recorders are gaining popularity among auto owners as a safety feature that can record accidents, breakdowns, and crimes. Although dash cameras have not been offered as a dealer option yet, they are widely available on the Internet from Amazon and Garmin, among others, starting at less than $200. Some of the higher-end aftermarket navigation systems are now bundled with a dash cam mounted on their reverse side.

The G1W (top) and G1W-C (bottom) are recommended by a number of independent testers. They cost between $75-$100 USD (*thewirecutter.com/reviews/best-dash-cam/*).

Helpful Automobile Apps

Mobile apps, or software applications, are self-contained programs that take advantage of today's powerful web browsers to increase the functionality of smartphones. Apps allow users to do with the phone's browser in a few clicks what used to be done on a desktop computer. The accessed information doesn't need a bookmark or URL to be found, and the image can be enlarged to be easily read on the phone's display.

In the "connect-me-now" world of communication, smartphones have replaced cellphones, MP3 players, global positioning systems (GPS), personal data assistants (PDA), and, in some cases, even computers. That's because these phones are much cheaper, multi-functional, and more mobile than most computers. Here is a selection of apps that you may find useful.

- **SaferCar:** A free app downloaded from the NHTSA, the SaferCar mobile app is available for iPhones (*itunes.apple.com/us/app/safercar/id593086230?ls=1&mt=8*) and Androids (*play.google.com/store/apps/details?id=gov*). The SaferCar app allows you to receive immediate information on your phone when you register to receive safety updates. Other aspects of the app include:
  - *Real time news:* The app forwards NHTSA safety headlines and information, including recalls on vehicles you own. You receive timely news that may bear on the safety of you and your family.
  - *Complaints:* With the SaferCar app, you can notify NHTSA of a complaint, concern, or safety issue you discovered with your car. Other owner complaints are also listed.
  - *Safety ratings:* Using the app, you can review and compare safety data for cars you own or are considering for purchase.
  - *Safety seats:* Information on safely installing child safety and booster seats is provided, along with help finding local support to have your seat checked or properly installed.
  - *Recall campaigns:* Find out if your car is under investigation, has been recalled, *and* if it has been fixed according to automaker data.

- **Waze (*www.waze.com*):** Waze is a community-based traffic and navigation app that allows drivers to report police or road hazards, and see what other motorists have reported. This powerful navigation app is not only free, but it works on both the iPhone and Android platform and is applicable to drivers on both sides of our border. Accident and construction delays are indicated in real time in both official languages. This is a full-fledged navigation application that threatens most automakers' navigation devices that sell for thousands of dollars.

Breaking the "Black Box"

Since 1996, cars sold in the U.S. have been required to provide a connection for mechanics and inspectors to measure what's going on electronically under the hood. The system, called On-Board Diagnostics generation two (OBD-II), uses a 16-pin connector mounted somewhere near the instrument panel to gather maintenance, component failure, and safety information and stores it in a vehicle's "black box," much like airplane electronic data recorders (EDRs).

Aftermarket manufacturers have developed gadgets that transmit uncoded stats in real time, such as fuel economy, engine speed, temperature, vehicle speed, and pertinent safety information relative to airbag deployment and braking application prior to a crash. You get a comprehensive view of your car's performance, efficiency, safety-related defects, and emissions control malfunctions. Here are just a few of these gadgets and apps.

1. **GoPoint** (*www.gopointtech.com/products/*): The free GoPoint app works with iPhones and Android devices and uses a wireless Bluetooth-enabled connector (which costs $120) that plugs into your car's OBD-II port to give you real-time information from your vehicle's built-in diagnostic system, much like a technician's scan tool. The app and required BT1 connector can uncover what set off the dreaded Check Engine light. It also monitors the efficiency of your vehicle and tells you how your driving habits impact fuel economy in real time. Bosch offers a similar free app called "fun2drive," which uses a non-proprietary Bluetooth OBD-II connector that is sold widely online.

2. **GasBuddy:** An awesome free app for drivers who simply want the cheapest gas available, thereby, avoiding the annoyance of fueling up and then spotting cheaper gas a mile down the road. GasBuddy quickly locates stations in Canada and the U.S. with the most competitive price. It searches by city, postal code, or your own GPS-mapped location. Plus, GasBuddy will map the route to the cheapest station and show what other amenities the station provides, such as a car wash, compressed air, ATM, convenience store, etc. *GasBuddy.com* recently acquired Canada's popular Tomorrow's Gas Prices Today website.

3. **RepairPal:** This free iPhone application works quickly to get you a repair estimate and locate a mechanic nearest your GPS location to do the work. The user simply registers the make and model of the vehicle, then suggests the repair required. An estimated price range from dealerships and independent shops in the area will display on the phone's screen. This will be followed by a list of other things that could go wrong and a local mechanic's recommendation as to what should be tackled first. RepairPal will also connect the user to roadside assistance or the manufacturer's customer assistance centre. The bad news: The service only works in the U.S. for now, though the company has pledged to expand into Canada soon, given the extraordinary interest in the app.

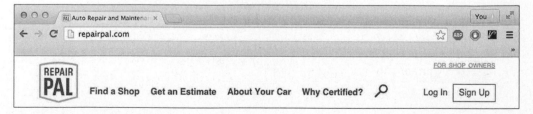

4. **iLeaseMyCar Pro:** This is very useful tool for iPhone and iPad users who aren't sure whether they want to buy or lease a new car. The $1.99 USD application infuriates dealer salespeople because it quickly determines the monthly payment for an auto loan or lease down to the penny by using the same information found in dealership programs. If you are new-car shopping, this app can save your calculations for different vehicles so you don't get confused by all the figures. There is also a useful reverse lease/loan calculator that shows the selling price that will meet your desired payment.

5. **My Max Speed 2.0:** Using the accelerometer in an Android phone, this $4.99 USD app logs speed and location every five seconds and can export the data to a spreadsheet. It's a great way to monitor a teen's driving habits or provide evidence to beat a traffic ticket. The app also shows where the vehicle has traveled and sends a message if the phone carrying the app travels outside a preset boundary (geo-fencing).

6. **AccuFuel:** A $0.99 USD iPhone app is primarily a fuel efficiency tracker, but also keeps a real time record of what you spend on fuel. Fuel use data is given in Society of Automotive Engineers (SAE), imperial, and metric units that can be stored for multiple vehicles.

7. **Car Minder Plus:** We're all guilty of ignoring the scheduled maintenance outlined in our owner's manual. Car Minder Plus manages your car maintenance needs from logging repairs to tracking fuel economy. It detects potential problems early by tracking fuel consumption. The $2.99 USD app lets you save data for multiple cars and tracks them individually. When you store service history, the app will cross-verify it with the service warnings so that anything that looks like a potential problem is brought to your attention immediately.

Driven to Distraction

Driving while distracted is a major cause of automobile accidents that can be prevented by driver's using common sense (active safety), which isn't very likely with the popularity of smartphones and the advent of cars that rove the Internet. Distracted driving can take many forms: Cognitive disengagement, or being lost in thought, is the most common, followed by adjusting the radio, gawking at visual distractions such as a disabled vehicle or a billboard, eating behind the wheel, talking on a phone, and texting.

Interestingly, a 2006 University of Utah study compared cellphone use to drunk driving (*www.distraction.gov/research/PDF-Files/Comparison-of-CellPhone-Driver-Drunk-Driver.pdf*). Researchers found impairments associated with using a cellphone while driving can be as profound as those associated with driving with a blood alcohol level at 0.08 percent, a "driving under the influence" level widely used in Canada and the United States.

In another experiment, people using a driving simulator were more likely to hit a pedestrian when their cellphone rang, even if they had planned in advance not to answer it (*www.ncbi.nlm.nih.gov/pubmed/22871271*).

Phones don't have to be used to be a distraction; studies show that our antennas are always up. People's performance on basic laboratory tests of attention gets worse if a cellphone is merely visible nearby. (See abstract: *psycnet.apa.org/index.cfm?fa=buy.optionToBuy&id=2014-52302-001.*)

What about stricter law enforcement? Don't get your hopes up. A 2010 study carried out by the Highway Loss Data Institute reviewed insurance claims in New York, Connecticut, and California and compared the data to other areas without cellphone bans. The conclusion? Laws banning the use of hand-held devices while driving did not reduce the rate of accidents in the three states and the District of Columbia (*www.cnn.com/2010/US/01/29/cellphone.study/index.html*).

Voice Controls – A Mixed Bag

In order to make use of the features reviewed above less distracting, carmakers and infotainment suppliers have enthusiastically embraced "voice recognition." Even government agencies like NHTSA are backing voice controls since their own research has shown that the crash risk rises threefold when drivers take their hands off the steering wheel and eyes off the road. They predict these new features will lead to fewer accidents as drivers keep their hands on the wheel and stay mentally "connected" to the road ahead.

Wrong.

Many of the new systems have simply changed one distraction for another. And, this is in addition to drivers balking at having to remember robotic phrases and practice Professor Higgins diction.

Actually, features like Apple's Siri electronic assistant (first used in 2013 models) may be as mentally taxing as the buttons and knobs they replace, says the American Automobile Association's Foundation for Traffic Safety. Test subjects scored 4 points on a 5-point scale used to measure mental strain while using Siri – it's more of a distraction than talking on a cellphone or fooling with radio knobs. More worrisome? Siri was being used when three simulated crashes were registered during the experiments. Researchers also tested similar Toyota Entune, Ford SYNC, and Chevrolet MyLink systems.

The takeaway? Research confirms that voice-controlled systems don't make driving safer. Instead, they allow drivers to drift into a "zombie" state – the eyes look ahead, but don't see (known as cognitive blindness); hands are on the steering wheel, but don't react. Then, when the system doesn't work as expected, drivers will look at the screen to figure out what's wrong. And we're back to square one.

SAFETY FEATURES THAT KILL

In the late '60s, Washington forced automakers to include essential safety features like collapsing steering columns and safety windshields in their cars. Mandatory safety and crashworthiness standards were passed in 1966 U.S. legislation (Ottawa passed its own watered-down version in 1971's *Canadian Motor Vehicle Safety Act*). Since the American law came into force U.S. highway fatalities dropped from 55,704 in 1972 to 33,561 in 2012 while miles driven increased almost fourfold. As the years have passed, the number of mandatory safety features increased to include rear shoulder belts, airbags, and crashworthy construction. These improvements met with public approval until reports of deaths and injuries caused by ABS and airbag failures showed that defective components and poor engineering could compromise the potential life-saving benefits associated with having these devices.

For example, one out of every five ongoing NHTSA defect investigations concerns inadvertent airbag deployment, deactivation of the front passenger airbag, failure of the airbag to deploy, or injuries suffered when the bag did go off. In fact, airbags are the agency's single largest cause of current investigations, exceeding even the full range of brake problems, which runs second.

Side Airbags – Good and Bad

Side and side curtain airbags are designed to protect drivers and passengers in rollovers and side-impact crashes, which are estimated to account for almost one-third of vehicular deaths. They have also been shown to help keep unbelted occupants from being ejected in rollovers. Head-protecting side airbags can reduce serious crash injuries by 45 percent. Side airbags without head protection reduce injuries by only 10 percent. Ideally, you want a side airbag system that protects both the torso and head.

There's a downside to increased side airbag protection. Sit properly in your seat, or risk serious injury from the deploying side airbag. Airbags may be deadly to children or to any occupant sitting too close to the airbag, resting his or her head on the side pillar, or holding onto the roof-mounted assist handle. Research carried out in 1998 by safety researchers (Anil Khadikar of Biodynamics Engineering Inc. and Lonney Pauls of Springwater Micro Data Systems, *Assessment of Injury Protection Performance of Side Impact Airbags*) shows there are four hazards that pertain to most airbag systems:

1. Inadvertent airbag firing (short circuits, faulty hardware or software);
2. Unnecessary airbag firing (sometimes the opposite-side airbag will fire; the airbag may deploy when a low-speed side-swipe wouldn't have endangered occupant safety);
3. A small child, say, a three-year-old, restrained in a booster seat could be seriously injured; and
4. Out-of-position restrained occupants could be seriously injured.

At the time, nearly all of the side airbags located in the rear seat were chest (torso) or head/chest combination side airbags. The NHTSA did issue a consumer advisory warning against seating children near side airbags in 1999. By contrast, the newer-generation side and curtain airbags have proven to be much safer for children, provided they are securely seated using a three-point seatbelt. The NHTSA now states on its *SaferCar.gov* website that it has not seen any indication of risks to children from current roof-mounted head side airbags.

Protecting yourself

Vehicle owners have reported instances when airbags have not deployed during a serious collision, or have set off inadvertently without cause. You should take the steps below to reduce the danger from airbag deployment:

- Buy a vehicle with head-protecting side curtain airbags for front and rear passengers.

- Make sure that seat belts are buckled and all head restraints are properly adjusted (to about ear level).

- Choose vehicles with head restraints that are rated "Good" by IIHS (see Part Four).

- Request that passengers who are frail or short or who have recently had surgery sit in the back. If they prefer, they should sit in front, with the seat positioned as far back as possible.

- Ensure that the driver's seat can be adjusted for height and has tracks with sufficient travel to allow short drivers to remain at a safe distance (over 25 cm or 10 in.) away from the airbag and still be able to reach the accelerator and brake. Adjusting the steering wheel toward the instrument panel (if it telescopes) is an alternative.

- Consider buying pedal extensions to keep you at a safe distance away from a deploying airbag if you are very short. Suppliers such as Creative Controls can be found online.

Top 20 Safety Defects

The U.S. government's online safety complaints database contains almost half a million vehicle owner questionnaires (VOQs), going back to the year 2000. Although the database was originally intended to record only incidents of component failures that relate to safety, you will find every problem imaginable dutifully recorded. This information is posted at NHTSA *safercar.gov* (see Helpful Automobile Apps, above).

A perusal of the listed complaints shows that some safety-related failures occur more frequently than others and often affect one manufacturer more than another. Here is a summary of the most commonly reported failures.

1. Sudden unintended acceleration
2. ABS brake failure; wheel lock-up
3. Airbag malfunctions
4. Tire-tread separation
5. Electrical/fuel-system fires
6. Stalling
7. Sudden electrical failures
8. Erratic transmission engagement
9. Unintended transmission shifts
10. Steering and suspension failures
11. Seat belt malfunctions
12. Collapsing seatbacks
13. Defective sliding doors and locks
14. Poor headlight illumination; glare
15. Dash reflecting onto windshield
16. Hood flying up
17. Wheel falling away
18. Steering wheel lifting off
19. Transmission lever pulling out
20. Exploding windshields

Although the chances of dying in a collision have been reduced in recent years, some vehicles have significantly higher rates of death than others. In general, the smallest and lightest vehicles resulted in the highest death rates, with most of them being entry-level models without advanced safety features at the time of the study (model years 2008-2011). Here is a ranking of the deadliest vehicles from the recent study of U.S. crash statistics conducted by the IIHS. The numeral indicates the number of driver deaths recorded per 1 million registered vehicles. The average for all vehicles sold in the U.S. was 28 deaths per million registered vehicle years.

Deadliest Vehicles		
1	Kia Rio four-door	149 deaths
2	Nissan Versa sedan	130 deaths
3	Hyundai Accent four-door	120 deaths
4	Chevrolet Aveo	99 deaths
5	Hyundai Accent two-door	86 deaths
6	Chevrolet Camaro	80 deaths
7	Chevrolet Silverado 1500 crew 4WD	79 deaths
8	Honda Civic two-door	76 deaths
9	Nissan Versa hatchback	71 deaths
10	Ford Focus	70 deaths

COMFORT

Do You Feel Comfortable in the Vehicle?

The advantages of many sports cars pale in direct proportion to your tolerance for a harsh ride, noise, a claustrophobic interior, and limited visibility. SUVs and four-wheel-drive pickups may have awkwardly high step-ups, wind noise, and be too large for urban driving. With these drawbacks, some buyers find that after falling in love in the showroom, they end up regretting their purchase – all the more reason to rent your intended choice for a day or two if you're moving into a new vehicle segment. A short showroom test drive on unfamiliar roads next to the dealership with the salesperson talking is not sufficient to evaluate a vehicle. Try to schedule a longer test drive. Luxury-segment buyers, especially repeat customers, may be able to schedule the loan of a demonstrator vehicle for a couple of hours or a day.

Check to see if the vehicle's interior is user-friendly. For example, can you reach the sound system and AC controls without straining or taking your eyes off the road? Are the controls just as easy to operate by feel as by sight? What about dash glare onto the front windshield, and headlight aim and brightness? Can you drive with the window or sunroof open and not be subjected to an ear-splitting roar? Do rear-seat passengers have to be contortionists to enter or exit, as is the case with many two-door vehicles?

To answer these questions, you need to drive the vehicle over a period of time to test how well it responds to the diversity of your driving needs, without having some impatient sales agent yapping in your ear. If this isn't possible, you may find out too late that the handling is less responsive than you'd wanted and that the infotainment electronics create an Orwellian environment.

You can conduct a few showroom tests. Adjust the seat to a comfortable setting, buckle up, and settle in. Can you sit 25 cm (10 in.) away from the steering wheel and still reach the accelerator and brake pedals? Do the head restraints force your chin into your chest? When you look out the windshield and use the rear- and side-view mirrors, do you detect any serious blind spots? Will optional mirrors give you an unobstructed view? Does the seat feel comfortable enough for long trips? Can you reach important controls without moving your back from the seatback, or taking your eyes off the road? If not, shop for something that better suits your needs.

"Senior" Cars

A group of pensioners were discussing their medical problems over coffee at Tim Hortons one morning.

"Can you believe it?" said one. "My arm is so weak I can hardly hold this coffee cup."

"Yes, I know." replied the second. "My cataracts are so bad I can't see the breakfast prices."

"I can't turn my head," rejoined the third, "because of the arthritis in my neck."

"My blood pressure pills make me dizzy," commented the fourth, adding, "I guess that's the price we pay for getting old."

"Well, it's not all bad," shouted out the first. "At least we can still drive, eh!"

Anonymous

Seniors are the fastest growing segment of the driving population and driving is vital to their health and independence. Nevertheless, the Canadian Association of Occupational Therapists warns that older driver mortality and morbidity is on the rise for seniors:

> In fact, the leading cause of accidental deaths for persons 65 to 75 years old in Canada today is driving-related accidents. More specifically, individuals over 75 have a 3.5 times higher crash rate compared to 35 to 44 year olds (Canada Safety Council, 2005). With the senior population on the rise, it is projected that by 2040 there will be almost double the number of older drivers in Canada.

Those living in households that are car-dependent spend 25 percent of their income on transportation. By living closer to work, shopping, restaurants and other amenities, households can reduce transportation costs substantially.

Husbands do the bulk of family driving, which usually involves short trips (11-17 km (6-10 mi) per day, on average) for medical appointments and visits to family, friends, and shopping malls. This puts older women, who tend to outlive their husbands, in a serious bind because of their lack of driving experience – particularly in rural areas, where driving is a necessity rather than a choice.

Seniors, like most other drivers, want cars that are reliable, relatively inexpensive and fuel efficient. Additionally, older drivers need vehicles that compensate for some of the physical challenges associated with aging and provide protection for accidents more common with mature drivers (side impacts, for example). Furthermore, as drivers get older, they find that the very act of getting into a car (sitting down while moving sideways, without bumping their heads or twisting their necks) demands considerable acrobatic skill. And don't even ask about shoulder pain when reaching up and over for the shoulder belt!

Here's an overview of issues concerning senior's and driving:

Some head restraints are pure torture, especially for seniors. Some of the worst designs that push your head forward and into the chest to comply with new whiplash regulations appeared five years ago.

Traffic safety researchers were expecting a spike in collision rates among older drivers in the last decade, largely as a consequence of the growing cohort of the population over 60. The increase has yet to happen – in fact the collision rate among American drivers 60 and over *declined* according to data from the American Insurance Institute for Highway Safety. Everything suggests that boomers will continue driving as they get older, possibly more safely due to increases in longevity, and certainly in greater numbers because there are more of us and more of us hold a driver's license than previous generations.

The Profile of Senior Drivers

Let's look at some of the compensating factors that reduce the risks associate with driving as we get older. Older drivers self-regulated even before the science of traffic research identified what those risk reducing behaviours were:

- They are much less likely to drink and drive. Alcohol involvement in fatal collisions among those over 60 is lower than the rest of the driving population.
- Impulse control at the wheel seems better. We are less likely to speed or to drive aggressively as we get older.
- Seniors drive less at night and on unfamiliar roads. They may avoid high-speed roads due to concerns about merging and speeds.
- The car stays at home during the worst driving conditions.
- Seniors are more likely to drive during off-peak hours.

One opportunity that some couples fail to realize is the importance of sharing the driving while this is still possible. In many couples, the husband may be doing all the driving, especially after the household's second car has been sold. The spouse continues to hold a license but it may have been a few years since she drove with any regularity – until the day her husband is incapacitated. A better solution is for both members of a couple to share the driving while they are still able to.

When it comes to driving, as in many other facets of human activity, experts have begun to segment the senior population. The younger group – roughly comprised of retired or semi-retired individuals no longer working a regular full-time schedule – is engaged in a broad range of physical activities. They may be taking regular medication but are able to undertake most activities they did earlier. Eyesight, mobility and rapid decision-making likely peaked a decade ago, but they've pretty fully compensated for them. Good impulse control, avoidance of unnecessary risk taking, off-peak driving, and less driving for commuting and at night all reduce their collision involvement.

After 80, the collision risk increases. Drivers in this group are already doing plenty to reduce their collision involvement on their own, including:

- Driving restricted to daytime, after rush hour.
- Short trips in their community along well-known routes for regular errands for food, medical appointments and social activities.
- No drinking, no speeding.

Cognitive abilities are declining, including the ability to process lots of information quickly, as is their eyesight. Medications may be interfering with "sharpness" and multiple medications, or dosage changes may require adjustment, which frequently occurs "behind the wheel."

At this age, many couples have gotten rid of a second vehicle, if they had one, and the healthier of the two spouses may be performing all of the driving duties.

Physical infirmity may impair driving, affecting actions as simple as turning a key or pulling a door handle. Navigating intersections crowded with cyclists in new bicycle lanes is stressful. Backing up is often done using the rearview mirror and an "audible warning," from tapping the vehicle behind you when parking.

Risk Factors

Here are some of the risk factors involving older drivers:

- We're more fragile after 60; seniors are three times more likely to be injured in a collision and take longer to heal than the younger-age drivers.

- Left turns across oncoming traffic become more dangerous. Older drivers are 40% more likely to cut across someone else's right of way during a left turn. Eyesight and cognitive abilities are the likely causes. Behaviour is not, as older drivers are probably more patient behind the wheel than other groups.

- Failing to yield or colliding with a vehicle in the next lane, particularly when changing lanes, becomes more likely than for other age groups .

Car dealers will tell you that vehicles owned by older drivers are more likely to have incurred minor dings and scrapes on the sides, and at all four corners. Wheel covers are frequently all scratched up from "kissing" the curb. "Parking by feel" in industry parlance often means an older person's car will need $500 to $1,500 in cosmetic repairs before it can be resold. It's also indicative of declining physical skills which manifest themselves slowly over time by an increase in minor incidents.

The Carmakers

The carmakers have split personalities when it comes to the older driving population. To begin with, vehicle marketing, even to older people, is tied up with youth or the preservation of youthful values like escaping into nature, and the lifestyle and socializing of an under-30 Never-Never Land. Styling has "bulked up" since 2000, influenced by macho SUVs like the Hummer and large Chevrolet Suburban and Yukon; this occurred as part of the Survival and Back-to-Nature movements that has the public wearing hiking boots to the mall and water bottles on belts for strolling in city parks. Side window lines on cars are higher, and windshields more raked; the rear visibility is so poor on new vehicles that a back-up camera has become a necessity. The sum total of all these changes is bigger vehicles that are harder to see out of, harder to maneuver in close quarters, and sometimes harder to get in and out of.

Vehicle controls also exhibit contradictory design objectives. Carmakers like Ford occasionally undertake to make gauges larger and easier to read, but then cram the speedo with tiny numerals up to 260 km/h; that's far faster than anybody needs. Heating and ventilation controls were simplified — the type with three large rotary knobs and few buttons is generally considered the simplest — but were then relocated on some vehicles to multiple use touch screens with scroll-through menus. In the most egregious examples, you probably should pull over to the side of the road to adjust the radio or climate controls.

The owner's manual for the complex dashboard interface that controls the sound system, heating and ventilation, phone and sometimes navigation on new vehicles is often bigger than the manual the explains operation of the rest of the vehicle! Clearly this explosion of in-dash technology competes for the attention of all drivers.

There is a positive side to advances in vehicle technology. Collision protection has improved significantly, with side impact airbags nearly universal. Side impact protection is particularly important to older drivers, because being hit from the side is more likely in this group. In the event of a side impact with an SUV or pickup truck, side curtain air bags are the only protection between your head and the window glass or bluff front end of the striking vehicle.

Electronic stability control has reduced single-vehicle-off-the-road fatalities and injuries by 30%. For SUVs, it has reduced rollovers by an astounding 50%.

"Active" electronic features hold much promise for the future. After being pioneered by Volvo, automakers are progressively introducing automatic emergency braking and/or pre-collision warning systems. Automatic braking has the potential to reduce rear-ender type collisions by over 30 percent.

Many new models now come with blind spot detection that will flash a light in the rearview mirror and eventually an audible alert if it detects the driver either drifting or merging into a lane where a another vehicle is in the blind spot. Although not all systems are equal, and the field data is still not in, the potential benefit to older drivers is greater than other groups.

Park Assist pioneered by Ford and Volvo, and now copied by others, allows the vehicle to parallel park miraculously at the touch of a button, without gauging distances, or steering. While this is not likely to reduce injuries, it will relieve an older driver with restricted mobility from having to parallel park conventionally; it may reduce the incidence of unintended acceleration during parking (sometimes caused by having part of the foot on the accelerator after the body has rotated to back up). Park assist should also reduce the inevitable dings and scraped bumper corners that cars owned by older drivers seem to accumulate.

When to Give Up Driving

You should give up driving at the point when the risk of injury or property damage to yourself and others becomes too high. Determining when that is can be a thorny question, and involves trade-offs. Here are a couple of indicators:

- Your friends no longer want to get in the car with you at the wheel.
- Family members insist on taking their vehicles when you go out together.

Older drivers are not the riskiest group of license holders. That distinction belongs to young males whose fatality involvement per license holder is four times higher than the average. However, older drivers are not a single homogenous group. Before

80, their record is good, one of the many dividends of increased longevity in the era we live in. After 80, the risk increases but it can be tricky to pin down. Per license holder, older drivers are still doing pretty well, showing less involvement than 16-18 year old males. But per kilometre driven, they're doing worse. That's because older drivers avoid becoming a statistic, by avoiding driving. They drive so much less that it can conceal the increasing hazard associated with their driving.

There are competing issues that make seniors want to drive for as long as possible. For many seniors, driving represents autonomy. Public transportation in many communities is underdeveloped, may involve standing-room-only even during so-called off-peak daytime trips. Subway and overhead rail systems require negotiating obstacles like stairs. These inconveniences are magnified when carrying home groceries and other necessities that are purchased on a regular basis. The loss of autonomy that results from giving up driving, especially for a person living alone, can contribute to isolation, and a reduction of community, social and recreational activities, elements that contribute to longevity and health. In a more perfect world, the places people live would more closely mimic urban development before the Second World War, when towns were relatively compact, with a defined and walkable Main Street for shopping, and neighbours you knew who could check up on you and help with errands, but that's not the reality in most North American communities.

The person who can recognize the right moment to give up driving voluntarily appears to be a rare breed. In surveys, 80% of drivers of all ages believe they are a "better than average" driver – a statistical impossibility that demonstrates our emotional attachment to and perceptual bias in favour of our mobility.

Sean McAlister was the former head of driver licensing in the Province of British Columbia, with more than three decades of experience In vehicle safety issues. According to Sean, age alone is a poor criteria for determining competence behind the wheel. "There are 45 year olds who shouldn't be driving," he told the APA, "but they do, and we accept it."

The provinces have addressed the issue of older drivers in a variety of ways. After age 80 a medical report from a physician confirming you are able to drive may be required along with an eye examination.

In some cases a medical exam alone is insufficient, so a driving exam is ordered under the auspices of the provincial driving authority. The assessment lasts about half an hour using your own vehicle on unfamiliar roads, located near the test center. The examiner uses a series of subjective and objective measures to determine fitness to drive. Inevitably, it's easy-to-quantify measures like turning left into the wrong lane, rolling through or missing a stop sign, or not braking before entering a street from a driveway that may result in a failing grade and revocation of the driving privilege. The driver is likely to have been making some of these errors many years before they became a senior.

In the eyes of the test subject, revocation of their license is sometimes perceived as arbitrary, and the consequence is draconian. In some cases you may not even be able to drive the car home, let alone plan an orderly retreat from driving and arrange alternate transportation over the next few weeks. The theory, of course, is that by failing you have instantly become a menace. The reality is the test, over a short period, under semi-controlled conditions, may reflect the impact of stress, a certain amount of disorientation and variability due to traffic conditions and the presence of an examiner.

A driving test failure is experienced as traumatic by the test subject, and sometimes as long overdue by their relatives and friends. Ideally, driving evaluations would be performed at regular intervals beginning at age 65, allowing the subject to establish a relationship with the examination process, and performed as a diagnostic tool to maintain driving skills and adaptations before becoming an all-or-nothing evaluation. This is unlikely to happen – driver's education has a poor record for collision reduction in North America, and is generally confined to those in "driver rehab" among the population of those already driving. Because ongoing testing and evaluation programs are so limited, they are believed to be ineffective for older drivers; this contributes to the prevailing belief that one becomes "untrainable" after 60. In fact for all age groups, driver's education as it is currently taught in North America has a limited or zero influence on collision reduction. Coincidentally, the latest advances in neuroscience are teaching us that the brain can be exercised to stay in shape longer and repair cognitive decline well into our senior years.

What the APA Can Do for Seniors

The APA's counsellors can walk you through the purchase of a vehicle. This includes buying the right used or new vehicle for your needs. You don't want too much vehicle.

Paying the right price: Seniors, especially women, who may have left the car-buying decision to their spouse for most of their lives, are perceived as easy marks by some auto retailers. Here are some common dealership ploys used to snare seniors:

- Leasing is not for older seniors who rarely accumulate the mileage included with the lease payment, do not need to replace a vehicle every 3-4 years, and do not want to be stuck with ongoing payments on a vehicle if serious health issues intervene.

- Life and health insurance on a car loan sold by dealers is usually overpriced and may have exclusions for pre-existing conditions common to seniors that are glossed over in pre-purchase materials.

- Expensive extended warranties are likely a poor value for a vehicle that will be driven less than 10,000 km a year, and rarely in the harshest weather.

Selling Your Last Car

With the help of local car dealers, the APA has developed a service to help seniors sell their last vehicle. The typical situation involves a vehicle that has been owned for many years, but has been parked for several months or even years, because the driver has stopped using it. Sometimes the driver has passed away or is in a long-term-care facility, and the job of disposing of a vehicle has fallen upon their spouse or relatives, who have plenty of other demands pressing upon them. Here is what APA will do for members in the Greater Toronto and Montreal areas:

- Send roadside assistance to get the vehicle started or tow it to a facility that will get it running again. This is an owner-paid service, usually at a commercial rate. Alternatively, a participating dealer will go to the location to inspect the vehicle.

- Perform a vehicle appraisal to determine what cosmetic repairs (repainting bumpers, attending to minor dings and dents, buffing out faded paint) and what mechanical repairs like a new battery or correcting a lit Check Engine light, should be performed before the vehicle is offered for sale. The dealer will also indicate which repairs not to perform as they are unlikely to recover their cost when the vehicle is resold (this typically includes large-scale repainting or rust repairs).

- The dealer will quarterback performance of the repairs performed at a commercial rate where possible, through approved service providers. This will save the vehicle owner 30-50% on reconditioning costs prior to sale, compared to contracting repairs personally.

- Provide a vehicle appraisal with a binding offer to buy the vehicle good for 30 days. The dealer will also provide a valuation for retail sale of the vehicle via classified advertising, in the event the owner or their family wants to try this route.

- The APA will provide information to the member or their family regarding cancellation of loan insurance, and mechanical protection in the event refund money may be available. For leased vehicles, a lease takeover is likely the best solution.

Driving Through the Ages

Accident death rates are higher for older occupants than for younger age groups. This is because our fragility increases as we age, and our ability to withstand the forces involved in crashes become much lower. Of course, our driving skills also deteriorate as we age, although most of us are reluctant to admit it.

- In our 40s: Thought processing starts slowing down, multi-tasking becomes more difficult, night and peripheral vision worsens, and glare blinds you for a longer period of time.

- In our 50s: Nine in ten people use bifocals, reaction time slows, and distractions increase.

- In our 60s: Muscle strength and range of motion decrease by as much as 25 percent. Hearing acuity is reduced.

- **By age 70:** Arthritic joints may make movement painful and restrict mobility, and conditions such as stroke, Parkinson's disease, hypertension, and diabetes may impair cognitive ability or affect behaviour.

Access and Comfort

Drivers with arthritic hands sometimes have to insert a pencil into their key ring to twist the key in the ignition.

Since hand and grip strength can be a problem for seniors, make sure your ignition lock doesn't require that much effort. A thicker steering wheel also requires less hand and wrist strength to grip and handle to make turns. Power locks, trunk and tailgate closers, mirrors, and windows are a must, especially if the vehicle will be operated with hand controls. A remote keyless fob will allow entry without fumbling with the door lock. Cruise control can be helpful for those with lower-body mobility challenges. Also, consider vehicles with adjustable pedals, a tilt steering column, and a height-adjustable, power-assisted driver's seat with memory.

Ideally, you want adequate lumbar support and the ability to reach the pedals and see over the dashboard, without putting stress on muscles that are losing some flexibility.

Some vehicle types are more senior-friendly:

- **Four-door vehicles:** Doors are lighter and easier to open than two-door coupes. Sports cars have seats with more heavily padded side and thigh bolsters, which force occupants to "climb out" of their seats.

- **SUVs and pickups:** Easier to get in and out of than a sedan, since the higher seats require less bending. The step up to floor level can be a challenge, especially with higher four-wheel-drive models. Cargo area of an SUV can provide useful loading ability for a wheelchair.

- **Minivans and small people movers:** A higher seat, superior forward visibility, and a lower floor is the best compromise for many people. Easiest for loading equipment like a wheelchair.

 Look for vehicles that are easy to enter and exit, with door openings that are wide enough for easy access. Ensure that the door catches when opened on a slight incline so that it doesn't close as you are exiting. Vans, SUVs, and trucks should also have a low step-up and an easily reached inside-grip handle, as well as other handles located throughout the interior. Other vehicles need low thresholds beneath the doors because many older drivers have a great deal of difficulty lifting their legs to get out. The trunk or rear cargo area should also have a low lift over and room to stow a wheelchair or scooter.

Drivers with limited mobility need a seated position that is close to standard chair height: Not too low so that you fall into it, and not too tall that you have to climb up and then back down. Many small crossovers, like the Subaru Forester, provide seating at the correct "H-Point" to allow the hips to slide into place. Concave bucket seats may complicate exiting the vehicle. Heated seats with adjustable lumbar support are great for occupants with back pain. Bench seats are preferable because they're roomier and easier to access, but they have pretty much gone the way of the dodo (a few used domestic sedans and some pickups offer this configuration).

General Motors Mobility (*www.gm.ca/gm/english/corporate/mobility/home*) offers an extensive array of adaptive devices that can be fitted in their vehicles through authorized installers in Canada. Other manufacturers and aftermarket suppliers also offer a variety of devices designed for the rapidly growing segment of aging drivers.

Most people prefer the versatility of a van like the Dodge Grand Caravan or the full-sized GM Express/ Savana, but well-equipped smaller versions can accommodate the physically-challenged, just as well.

Safety Features for Older Drivers

Generally you want controls with larger buttons, more readable labeling, rear-backup cameras, active emergency braking, convex mirrors added to the side mirrors, and cross-traffic alert that detects passing vehicles when you're backing up. Lane keeping assist, which will warn you by tugging at the steering wheel when you drift or actually steer the vehicle back into its lane looks promising, as is blind-spot detection, though both are too new to predict their potential collision reduction.

- A low beltline (the lower edge of the glass area) improves the driver's downward sightlines, making parking easier. As drivers age, reduced flexibility in the shoulders and neck can restrict head movement, so having more glass area is a big help.

- Large, wide-angle side mirrors and rear-view mirrors help compensate for reduced vision caused by minor strokes and glaucoma, limited range of motion, or difficulties twisting to check for blind spots while merging or backing up. A rear-mounted camera helps when backing up; however, the rear image may be distorted, making it impossible to judge where the vehicle's corners are accurately.

- The driver's seat should be mounted high enough for a commanding view of the road (with slower reaction times, seniors need earlier warning). The driver's seat must offer enough rearward travel to attenuate the force of an exploding airbag, which can be particularly hazardous to older or short occupants, and anyone recovering from surgery. Adjustable gas and brake pedals are a big plus for short-legged drivers.
- Head restraints shouldn't force your chin into your chest and should be easily adjustable.
- Cars that are brighter and lighter in colour are easier for other drivers to see at night and when it rains.
- Drivers with a high sensitivity to glare will find extendable sun visors helpful.
- Remote-controlled mirrors are a must, along with adjustable, unobtrusive head restraints and a non-reflective front windshield (some drivers put a cloth on the dash-top to cut the distraction).
- Check to confirm that the brake and accelerator pedals aren't mounted too close together.
- A superior crashworthiness rating is important, as well as dual-stage torso- and head-protecting side airbags, since many intersection collisions involving mature drivers occur when drivers are making a turn into oncoming traffic. The extra head protection can make a critical difference in side impacts. Dual-stage and dual-threshold airbags are recommended to attenuate the force of airbag deployments. Deployment force depends on crash severity, distance between the air bag and the driver or passenger, and the weight of the occupant.
- Look for headlights that give you a comfortable view at night, as well as turn signal indicators that are easily seen and heard. Ensure that the vehicle's knobs and switches are large and easy to identify and that any backlit gauges are sufficiently bright so they don't wash out in daylight or produce too much glare at night.
- Features that are especially important to drivers wearing bifocals: A blue-green light colour that measures 505 nanometres is the ideal gauge colour in terms of being easiest to see. The belief that instruments illuminated or marked in red are easiest to see is a myth. Check the dash for windshield glare (more common with light-coloured dash panels).
- An antilock braking system, or ABS, prevents wheels from locking during emergency braking, and has been standard on all but the most basic cars for a decade. Drivers using ABS can stop the car and retain control without "pumping" the brakes, which can be challenging for older drivers.
- Electronic stability control (ESC) is a feature that helps prevent loss of control in turns, or during a sudden stop, especially on slippery roads. ESC may compensate for slower reaction times and make quick corrections. By law, all 2012 and newer vehicles come equipped with ESC standard, and many models prior

to 2012 provided the technology. Look for the ESC indicator light or a push button on the instrument panel of older models if you are buying used.

- Having an easily accessed spare tire and a user-friendly lug wrench and jack is also important, or to be even safer, a valid roadside assistance plan.

Ford's Confusing Electronics

Some safety, performance, and convenience features may not work as well as advertised and issue false, distracting alerts, or be costly to service. Chief offenders are Ford's MyTouch and SYNC options found on many of its cars since 2011. Owners find these features very buggy, slow, and not-at-all intuitive.

Says one Ford owner:

> Ford's MyTouch infotainment system integrates multiple controls and info readouts via what used to be the entertainment system in what is a way busier approach than reaching over towards the center stack to make adjustments via rotary knobs or push buttons. I don't need to be cursoring up and down through menu options – while I am driving in heavy traffic, period. It isn't as bad as texting while driving, but it is close.

Good "Senior" Car Choices

These new and used vehicles are recommended by *Lemon-Aid* and the APA for ease of entry and exit, visibility, driving position, and logical easy-to-use controls. Most have a better-than-average reliability rating, and all but the Yaris prior to 2011, and older Vibe and Matrix provide standard ESC.

SMALL CARS
Nissan Versa hatchback
  (2011-2013)
Nissan Versa Note hatchback
  (2014-2017)
Pontiac Vibe (2005-2010)
Scion Xd and iQ (all years)
Toyota Matrix (all years)
Toyota Yaris hatchback (all years)

MID-SIZE/LARGE CARS
Chevrolet Impala (2014-2017)
Honda Accord (2008-16)
Hyundai Genesis AWD (2015-16)
Toyota Avalon (all years)
Toyota Camry (all years)

SMALL CROSSOVER/SUV
Buick Encore (all years)
Chevrolet Trax (better visibility
  and cheaper than Encore)
Honda CR-V (all years)
Kia Rondo (2013-2017)
Kia Soul (all years)
Mazda 5 (2012-2016)
Mazda CX-5 (2012-2017)
Mercedes B250 (2017, lease only)
Subaru Forester (2009-13, 2014-17)

MID-SIZE/LARGE CROSSOVER/SUV
Lexus RX (2010-17)
Subaru Outback (2010-14, 2015-17)
Toyota Highlander (all years)
Toyota Sienna minivan (all years)
Toyota Venza (2009-2016)

Adaptive Aids

For most people, driving a motor vehicle has become essential to the tasks of everyday living – commuting, running errands, or taking children to school, for example – and synonymous with freedom, independence, and self-sufficiency. Driving in vehicle-congested areas is challenging enough for drivers without disabilities; for a person with a physical disability driving to the local grocery store can be daunting. But it can be done. After rehabilitative assessment and evaluation, the driving needs of people with temporary or permanent disabilities can be accommodated through the use of adaptive vehicle equipment, safe driver training, or both.

Many persons with physical disabilities can safely drive using some of the considerable variety of adaptive devices available today. Some of these devices are found in almost all vehicles and are used by people with and without physical disabilities.

For example, some of the commonly found adaptive aids are:

- Left foot accelerator – eliminates left leg cross-over;
- Right hand turn signals – eliminate right hand cross-over;
- Foot pedal extensions – raise height of brake and accelerator pedals;
- Hand controls – operate horn, wipers, turn signals, dimmer switch; can also operate brake and accelerator;
- Steering devices – allow steering by spinner knobs, amputee ring, quad fork, or tri-pin;
- Custom seating – creates balance, positioning, and stability; and
- Lifts and ramps – permit access into and out of the vehicle.

Adaptive aids compensate for the disability or inability to perform the needed function. For example, if a driver is missing a right leg, a left foot gas pedal allows them to drive with their left foot.

Simple assistive devices are available to make driving safer and easier. Items such as seat belt adjusters, handibars, or expanded mirrors are available either in home catalogues or at medical supply or auto parts stores. Other items that are available from the factory or aftermarket are easy-locking seat belts, visor extenders, steering wheel covers to improve grip, seat and back support cushions to relieve back pain or improve the ability to see over the steering wheel, and doors that automatically lock and open.

To begin adaptive-on-the-road driving, a person should first become familiar with the current state-of-the-art adaptive vehicle equipment and rehabilitative driver training available in their province. One Ottawa-based national group that works with many regional associations is Independent Living Canada, *www.ilcanada. org*; phone: 613-563-2581; TTY/TDD: 613-563-4215; e-mail: *info@ilc-vac.ca*.

For specific equipment, a good place to start is by searching your auto manufacturer's online information. For example, Toyota Canada has a mobility program that features the Sienna minivan, and General Motors Mobility offers an extensive array of options for its vehicles. Some aftermarket conversion companies offer important services too, like *GoldLineMobility.com* in London, Ontario.

Where to Go for More Information

Here are some other websites that may be helpful.

- The National Mobility Equipment Dealers Association (NMEDA) supports the use of safe, reliable vehicles and modifications to enhance accessibility for people with special needs (see: *www.nmeda.org.*).
- The National Highway Traffic Safety Administration (NHTSA) addresses automotive safety issues for persons with disabilities (see: *www.nhtsa.dot.gov/ cars/rules/adaptive*).
- See AAA's "Safe Features for Mature Drivers" (*www.aaaexchange.com/Main/ Default.asp?CategoryID=18&SubCategoryID=86&ContentID=388*).
- AAA's list of vehicles and their options suitable for seniors can be accessed at: *www.aaapublicaffairs.com/Assets/Files/20083211031180,SFMD-VehicleListv6.2.pdf*.

OTHER BUYING CONSIDERATIONS

When "New" Isn't New

Nothing will cause you to lose money more quickly than buying a new car that's older than advertised, has previously been sold and then taken back, has accident damage, or has had the odometer disconnected or turned back.

Even if the vehicle hasn't been used, it may have been left outdoors for a considerable length of time, causing premature body and chassis rusting, or severe rusting of internal mechanical parts, which leads to brake malfunction, fuel line contamination, hard starting, and stalling.

You can check a vehicle's age by looking at the date-of-manufacture plate usually found on the driver-side door pillar. If the date of manufacture is 7/15, your vehicle was probably one of the last 2015 models made before the August-September changeover to the 2016s. Redesigned vehicles or those new to the market are exceptions to this rule. They may arrive at dealerships in early spring or mid-summer and are usually designated as the next year's models. They'll depreciate more slowly in the first couple of years because they're one model year "newer," but this difference narrows over time.

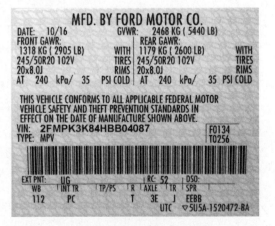

Sometimes a vehicle can be too new and cost you more in maintenance because its redesign glitches haven't yet been worked out. As Honda's North American manufacturing chief, Koki Hirashima, so ably put it, carryover models generally have fewer problems than vehicles that have been significantly reworked or just introduced to the market. Newly redesigned vehicles get quality scores that are, on average, 2 percent worse than vehicles that have been around for a while, says J.D. Power. Some surprising poor performers were the redesigned 2006 Honda Civic (its incorrectly cast aluminum engine block could crack, the suspension was unsettled), and 2009 Toyota Corolla (electric steering system can cut out, various minor issues).

Because they were the first off the assembly line for that model year, most vehicles assembled between September and February are called "first-series" cars. "Second-series" vehicles, made between March and August, incorporate more assembly-line fixes and are better built than the earlier models, which may depend on less effective "field fixes" to mask problems. Even a conscientious manufacturer can take a couple of years to correct all the quality and design glitches after a new model is launched.

There's also the very real possibility that the new vehicle you've just purchased was damaged while being shipped to the dealer, and was fixed in transit or at the dealership. It's estimated that this happens to about 5 percent of all new vehicles. Although there's no specific Canadian legislation allowing buyers of vehicles damaged in transit to cancel their contracts, B.C. legislation says that dealers must disclose damage of $2,000 or more, and Ontario requires disclosure of a "material fact." In a more general sense, Canadian common-law jurisprudence does allow for cancellation or compensation whenever the delivered product differs markedly from what the buyer expected to receive.

Fuel Consumption

In 2009, the Obama administration raised U.S. fuel economy standards to 35.5 miles per gallon by 2016, then again in 2012 to a lofty 54.5 mpg by 2025. The U.S. Environmental Protection Agency's (EPA) objectives were threefold: To combat climate change, reduce oil imports, and reverse the gradual slide in fuel economy that had occurred in the previous 20 years. In a move to harmonize the standards, the Canadian government under Stephen Harper somewhat reluctantly adopted the same plan in 2014. Under the Regulations Amending the Passenger Automobile and Light Truck Greenhouse Gas Emission, average fuel consumption of new 2025 cars and light trucks must increase, on an average industry fleet-wide basis, to 163 g/mile of carbon dioxide, which is equivalent to 54.5 mpg U.S. or 4.3 litres/100km, using a government test procedure. Because the lab-based procedures yield considerably different fuel economy numbers than real-life on-road outcomes, what the average consumers should expect to see will be closer to 36 mpg or 6.5 litres/100km.

The automakers have responded by reducing the weight of redesigned vehicles, while maintaining the same or even increasing vehicle dimensions and structural protection. More efficient fuel delivery to the engine, more turbochargers married to smaller engines, and tweaks to valve timing, the charging system, engine cooling, and computer controls have been introduced. Some vehicles now turn off the engine automatically at red lights, and then restart it when the driver's foot lifts off the brake pedal. Automatic transmissions have gone from four forward gears up to as many as nine speeds; the continuously variable (CVT) transmission, which theoretically has an infinite number of speeds, has made a comeback.

As a consequence of all these changes, today's new vehicles typically use 25 percent to 30 percent less fuel than the equivalent 2008 model, with no compromise in performance and utility. Improvements have been most impressive with the largest vehicles, but all classes use less fuel. Prices of conventional gas vehicles have not increased anywhere near the projected lifetime savings in fuel costs. However, new vehicles use more complex technology that could prove failure prone down the road, and is already more expensive to repair. The appearance of oil-sensitive turbochargers on economy cars (Volkswagens and even some models of the Honda Civic), compact SUVs, and even full-size pickup trucks (think Ford) is surprising, given the sometimes casual maintenance provided by second and third owners of vehicles in these segments. Expensive synthetic oil is a necessity for most turbocharged engines.

Unfortunately for long-range energy planning, gasoline prices plummeted and consumers are using the fuel savings to "upsize" their purchases by moving out of small cars into compact SUVs with all-wheel-drive; an SUV consumes 25 percent or more fuel than a compact car. Sales of new mid-size SUVs (notwithstanding their indicated size, these are *large* vehicles), pickups, and luxury vehicles are also breaking records in Canada.

Some provinces have taken a different strategy. Instead of focusing on lowering fossil fuel consumption, they are promoting zero emissions. Quebec and Ontario both offer very large subsidies (up to $8,000) to purchasers of fully electric vehicles, and are backing charging infrastructures in the hope of kick-starting electric vehicle sales. So far the public hasn't been buying, and with the possible exception of the Tesla Model S, electric vehicle sales have been a footnote. Almost all EV buyers come from multi-vehicle households in which the electric vehicle supplements conventional gasoline models; it's not unusual to see a Range Rover or Porsche SUV sharing the driveway with a Tesla. Had the Harper government been sincere about collaborating with the provinces to reduce our reliance on oil or impacting climate change, they would have aligned their fossil fuel reduction strategy with the provinces' conversion to electrification. Gasoline taxation would have increased to maintain prices at the pump at historic levels, to discourage the current migration to larger vehicles. Right now, we have a two-track federal-provincial energy conservation dance, with the public rejecting both partners and going to the bar for another drink.

Fuel Economy Fantasies

For two decades, Canada's Energuide fuel consumption ratings had a large element of whimsy in them. Tests were conducted in automaker laboratories on rollers using the government's two-cycle test procedure. The car was cooled by a breeze and accelerated gently without taxing the engine, the turbocharger spinning lazily and automatic transmissions shifting into higher gears earlier than on real roads. Tire and wheel packages could be chosen for optimal fuel consumption on rollers, rather than the size most commonly sold on the vehicle.

Beginning with the 2015 model year, Natural Resources Canada belatedly introduced a five-cycle test procedure that better approximates typical driving conditions, resulting in fuel consumption ratings that are more representative of a vehicle's on-road fuel use. The new procedures account for air conditioner use, cold temperature operation, and driving at higher speeds with more rapid acceleration and braking. The APA compared the new ratings with real-life driving (see box).

The Automobile Protection Association discovered that Canada's new fuel consumption ratings still correlate imperfectly with the real-world fuel consumption of some vehicles. In a recent test of 2016 luxury SUVs, the APA obtained the following consumption figures during a group test drive conducted over 250 kilometres on a mix of highway and secondary roads, without air conditioning, and using the recommended premium fuel:

	Actual L/100 km	Energuide Highway L/100 km	Variance %
Acura RDX	8.6	8.6	0
Audi Q3	9.0	8.2	9
2015 BMW X1	9.6	7.2	33
Infiniti QX50	10.7	9.7	10
Mercedes GLA	8.0	7.4	8

The Acura RDX exactly matched its highway rating, which is both unusual in APA testing, and commendable. On the identical trip, the BMW X1 exceeded its highway rating by a substantial one-third. The three other vehicles were somewhere in between.

Fuel consumption ratings for hybrids tend to be inflated, sometimes by as much as 25-30 percent. *Consumer Reports* (*CR*) found the vast majority of hybrid models fell short of their EPA estimates in real-world driving tests conducted a few years ago. As a group, hybrids missed their estimates by 10 percent. The most disappointing were the latest hybrids from Ford and Volkswagen. The Lincoln MKZ Hybrid model, for example, was rated 45 mpg overall in EPA tests, yet returned only 35 mpg in *CR* tests, a discrepancy of nearly 25 percent.

But Chrysler, Ford, GM, Honda, Lexus, Toyota, and VW don't tell potential buyers which of their fuel-frugal hybrids, ethanol-friendly, diesel-powered, and turbocharged models are high-tech, feel-good PR machines that won't deliver their promised fuel-efficiency. More than three-quarters of cars with small, turbocharged engines also missed their EPA numbers in *CR* tests. Currently it costs more to run vehicles equipped with special power trains or able to accept alternate fuels. Then there's Ford's EcoBoost turbo noisemaker, as this owner discovered:

> I own a car with a 3.5-liter EcoBoost, and it sounds like a whale with indigestion, all groans and clicks from the intake and injectors. Sometimes I don't know whether to take it to the dealer or a gastroenterologist.

Yet most public environmental protection groups and government agencies, seconded by the major automobile clubs, genuflect whenever the hybrid, ethanol, or diesel alternative is proposed. We have to be aware of the lies. *Automotive News, Car and Driver,* and *Edmunds* have also found that diesel and hybrid fuel consumption figures can be 30-40 percent more than advertised.

Fuel economy misrepresentation

Fuel economy misrepresentation is actionable, and there is Canadian jurisprudence that allows for a contract's cancellation if the gas-mileage figures are false. Most people, however, simply keep the car they bought and live with the fact that they were fooled. One strategy for checking if the salesperson is lying about the fuel economy of a vehicle you are considering is to pay a visit to the service department of the same dealership on your way out of the showroom; present yourself as a current owner of the model you are thinking of buying and ask the people at the counter what fuel mileage you should be getting. The APA learned that the service departments of Ford dealers regularly told customers to expect fuel consumption of their new turbocharged Ford Escape that was three to four L/100 km *higher* than represented in the showrooms at the same dealerships!

There are a few choices you can make that will lower fuel consumption. First off, choose a compact car; that's the best compromise in terms of economy, comfort, cabin space, and collision protection. Second, select conventional induction rather than a turbocharged engine; even if the non-turbo engine has larger displacement the fuel consumption penalty is likely to be small or non-existent. Third, a V6 or V8 engine with a cylinder-deactivation feature or variable valve timing will increase fuel economy by 8 and 3 percent, respectively, over an engine without these features.

Ethanol

Why are we so hard on ethanol? After all, in its 2007 budget the federal Conservative government committed $2 billion in incentives for ethanol, made from wheat and corn, and for biodiesel. The Canadian Renewable Fuels Association trumpeted ethanol as "good for the environment," a position echoed by the Manitoba and Saskatchewan governments, which emphasized that ethanol "burns cleaner" than gasoline.

Hogwash! Environment Canada's own unpublished research says ethanol "burns no cleaner than gasoline."

Scientists at Environment Canada studied four late-model vehicles, testing their emissions in a range of driving conditions and temperatures. "Looking at tailpipe emissions, from a greenhouse gas perspective, there really isn't much difference between ethanol and gasoline," said Greg Rideout, head of Environment Canada's toxic emissions research. The study was broadcast by CBC on March 30, 2007, and can be found at *www.cbc.ca.*

Environment Canada found no statistical difference between the greenhouse gas emissions of regular unleaded fuel and 10 percent ethanol blended fuel. Although it did note a reduction in carbon monoxide, emissions of some other gases, such as hydrocarbons, actually increased under certain conditions.

Other drawbacks of ethanol: It's hard to find, it eats fuel line and gas tank components, it performs poorly in cold climates, it gives you 25-30 percent less fuel economy than gasoline, and it contributes to world hunger (the crop used to produce one SUV fill-up of ethanol could feed a person for a year).

Smart drivers should continue to ignore automaker gas-saving hype, hunker down, and keep their paid-for, reliable, gas-guzzling used vehicles, because the depreciation savings will more than offset the increased cost of fuel.

Hybrids

As practical as the promise of ethanol fuel for everybody seemed to be at first, hybrids use an alternative fuel system that requires expensive and complex electronic and mechanical components to achieve the same fuel economy that a basic Honda Civic or other compact car can achieve for about two-thirds the cost – and without polluting the environment with exotic toxic metals leached from battery packs and powertrain components.

Among the available hybrid systems, Toyota's has the best track record. Early Prius taxicabs used in Vancouver, many of which were rebuilt American wrecks, regularly accumulated over 400,000 km (nearly 250,000 miles) before being retired with their original battery packs still in service. The CVT transmission used in the Prius and other Toyota hybrids is the only CVT to have established a track record for durability. Replacement battery packs are available at reasonable prices in the aftermarket and from Toyota. When used in other Toyota models like the Camry, RAV4, Highlander, and Lexus RX, the Synergy Drive hybrid system delivers a 30 percent reduction in fuel consumption compared to the available conventional gas engine, with the greatest benefit occuring in city driving.

Consumer Reports tested six pairs of vehicles, with each pair including a conventional vehicle and the equivalent hybrid model, and published the astonishing results in its April 2006 edition. *CR* found that in each category of car, truck, and

SUV, the overall cost after accounting for fuel savings for the hybrid version was *higher* than the cost of the same vehicle equipped with a conventional propulsion system.

Other disadvantages of hybrids are their mechanical and electronic complexities, dependence on specialized dealers for basic servicing, overblown fuel-efficiency numbers (owners of the Honda Civic hybrid reported getting 40 percent less mileage than promised), and the eventual cost to replace their battery packs.

Finally, consider that hybrid vehicles use rare-earth minerals such as lanthanum, scandium, and yttrium mixed oxides and aluminas (which are used in almost all automotive emissions control systems). Neodymium is another rare element needed for the lightweight permanent magnets that power hybrid motors. It's a radioactive substance mined almost exclusively in China, which has threatened to restrict its sale and slapped on heavy export duties. And there's a good reason why mining has been mostly restricted to China – the government there doesn't care if the mining and refining of these toxic minerals poisons the environment and sickens villagers – something North American "green" advocates overlook.

Western nations cannot afford to mine and refine neodymium within their borders due to the enormous environmental toxicity that mining it produces. In a sense, China is not cornering the neodymium market using their mineral reserves, but rather their willingness to sacrifice their environment and expose their populace to a higher cancer rate. In the end, North American motorists may trade a dependence on Middle Eastern oil for a troubling dependence on Chinese-sourced neodymium that's poisoning the Chinese people in the process.

Diesels

Only one percent of personal vehicles sold in North America are diesels. Thanks to favourable fuel tax treatment, around 50 percent of Europeans choose a diesel. Yes, diesels run much cleaner than they used to, but they're still dirtier than a gas engine on the road. On the plus side, among the alternative fuels tested by independent researchers, diesel comes closest to its estimated fuel economy figures. This increased fuel economy allows diesels to go up to 1000 km (650 miles) between fill-ups. Modern diesels have gobs of low-end torque for fast acceleration from a standing position. The torque advantage also attracts SUV and truck owners who want good towing capability with quick pick up.

Independent service for a diesel is harder to find and repairs require a steep learning curve for non-specialists because of the complex fuel delivery system, exhaust aftertreatment, and advanced electronics. Unlike hybrids, diesels are reasonably priced (about $2,000 more than gasoline-powered vehicles) and most models hold their value quite well, which compensates for the higher new purchase price.

Despite a limited market that's likely to decline in the long term, a wide array of diesel-powered cars, sport utilities, and trucks are available from an increasing number of automakers, including BMW, Chrysler, Ford, General Motors, Jeep,

Land Rover, Mercedes, and Porsche. Mazda's diesel debut in North America has been delayed, likely indefinitely, and Volkswagen/Audi/Porsche diesels (2009-16) can't yet be sold without an emissions recall fix.

Diesel reliability varies

European imports offer the most reliable, durable diesel engines. Asian manufacturers have not embraced the diesel for North America. Except for Chrysler's Cummins diesel, most Detroit-made vehicles equipped with diesel engines are a letdown. Owners report horrendously expensive maintenance costs, considerable repair downtime, and worsening reliability resulting from attempts to clean up diesel emissions over the past decade, with Ford's Powerstroke, GM's Duramax and more recently the EcoDiesel V6 supplied by Fiat's VM Motori for Ram pickups. Additionally, new diesel engines require that owners regularly fill up with urea to meet emissions standards – an unexpected extra expense and inconvenience.

A yearly urea refill can be expected since the urea tank contains roughly 8 gallons (U.S.), which is good for about 19,300 km (12,000 miles) of standard operation. Generally, automakers will add the urea solution at every scheduled maintenance visit. Mercedes-Benz BlueTEC diesels will not run if the urea tank doesn't contain a certain amount. If the tank reaches one gallon, the car notifies the driver. It does so again with only 20 starts remaining. To reset the system, at least two gallons of AdBlue – or four half-gallon bottles at $7.75 each – must be added. Not a lot to clean the environment, you say? Read on.

Consumer Reports was charged an outrageous $317 USD to put 7.5 gallons of AdBlue in its Mercedes GL320 test car at $32/gallon for the fluid. That was in 2010 when AdBlue (generically called DEF) was relatively hard to find. Today, auto supply stores and most gas stations stock the stuff at a far more reasonable cost – and owners can refill the tank themselves. Incidentally, the urea systems require an in-tank heater for cold Canadian weather that can regularly fail. A broken AdBlue heating element reportedly costs $1,000 to replace on a Volkswagen Passat TDI after the warranty is over. The emissions system on the BMW diesel used in the 3 series sedan and X3 SUV for the 2011-2013 model years can go into limp mode below -10C, triggering a Service Engine warning and allowing high emissions.

More dirt on diesels

The only reasons to buy a diesel-equipped vehicle are for their potential to deliver better-than average fuel economy and for their perceived lower maintenance and repair costs when compared with similar-sized vehicles powered by gasoline engines.

Let's examine the fuel-savings issue first. In theory, when compared with gasoline powerplants, diesel engines are up to 30 percent more efficient in a light vehicle and up to 70 percent cheaper to run in a heavy-duty towing and hauling truck or SUV. They become more efficient as the engine load increases, whereas gasoline engines become less so. This is the main reason diesels are best used where the driving cycle includes a lot of city driving – slow speeds, heavy loads, frequent stops, and long idling times. At full throttle, both engines are essentially equal from a fuel-efficiency standpoint. The gasoline engine, however, leaves the diesel in the dust when it comes to high-speed performance.

Diesel fuel should cost about $0.05 a litre less than regular gasoline. However, in some regions, the cost of diesel fuel is more than regular gasoline, in fact the price can be as much as a dime over regular fuel. The diesel engine's reputation for superior reliability may have been true in the past, but no longer. This fact is easily confirmed if you cross-reference owner complaints with confidential auto-maker service bulletins and independent industry polling results put out by J.D. Power and others, a task done for you in Part Four's ratings section. In a nutshell, Chrysler had the best diesel in its Dodge pickups (engine supplied by Cummins, not the new Fiat-derived diesel), while GM and Ford come in second and third among Detroit pickups. Some owners of diesel-equipped trucks have been frustrated by chronic breakdowns, excessive repair costs, and poor road performance. It's practically axiomatic that bad injectors have plagued Ford Power Stroke and GM Duramax engines, and (to a lesser extent) Dodge Cummins diesels.

In the past, defective injectors were often replaced at the owner's expense and at a cost of thousands of dollars. Now, General Motors and Ford use "secret warranty" programs to cover replacement costs long after the base warranty has expired. Chrysler has been more recalcitrant in making payouts, apparently because fewer vehicles may be involved and costs can be quite high (expensive lift pumps and injectors may be faulty).

Current Volkswagen diesels have serious repair and maintenance issues that should give buyers pause before acquiring a second-hand TDI model. Most disconcertingly, owners report that the motor's high-pressure fuel pump is prone to failure, grinding itself to smithereens and contaminating the fuel system. Other reported issues include: Failed fuel injectors, bad fuel pressure sensors, broken turbochargers, frozen intercoolers, and clogged particulate filters. Component costs are very high. In addition, the TDI uses a timing belt that needs changing religiously, along with the water pump.

Leasing a European luxury SUV with a diesel engine can make sense. The monthly payment is frequently the same or not much more than for the gasoline version, and you stand to save $15-$25 a week in fuel costs; over the life of the lease that will add up to several thousand dollars. And if your engine or turbo self-destructs, the vehicle will still be covered by the manufacturer's warranty.

Excessive Maintenance Schedules

Alan Gelman, a well-known Toronto garage owner and co-host of Toronto AM740's "Dave's Corner Garage," warns drivers:

> There are actually two maintenance schedules handed out by car companies and dealers. The dealer inspection sheets often call for far more extensive and expensive routine

maintenance checks than what's listed in the owner's manual. Most of those checks are padding; smart owners will stick with the essential checks listed in the manual and have them done by cheaper, independent garages.

Getting routine work done at independent facilities will cost about one-third to one-half less than usually charged by dealers and major tire and repair chains. Just be sure to follow the automaker's suggested maintenance schedule so no warranty claim can be rejected for neglected servicing, and keep your records (these will also help you get more for your vehicle when you resell it). An ALLDATA service bulletin subscription ($26.95 USD per year) will keep you current as to your vehicle's factory defects, required check-ups and recalls, tell you what's covered by little-known "goodwill" warranties, and save you valuable time and money when troubleshooting common problems.

SAVING ON SERVICING COSTS

Warranty Coverage

There's a big difference between warranty promise and warranty performance. All automakers offer "bumper-to-bumper" warranties that are good for at least the first 3 years/60,000 km, and most models get powertrain coverage up to 5 years/100,000 km. Hyundai, Kia, and Mitsubishi offer an industry-leading 5-year/100,000 km base warranty, with Mitsubishi kicking in a 10-year/160,000 km powertrain warranty. Virtually all the luxury brands provide a comprehensive warranty for 4 years/80,000 km. Some, like Buick and Cadillac, offer 6 years/110,000 km of powertrain coverage. Mazda is breaking the mould by offering unlimited mileage as part of its 3-year basic warranty and 5-year powertrain coverage.

It's also becoming an industry standard for car companies to pay for roadside assistance, a loaner car, or hotel accommodations if your vehicle breaks down while you're away from home and it's still under warranty. This assistance may be for as long as 5 years, without any kilometre restriction. *Lemon-Aid* readers report few problems with these ancillary warranty benefits.

Don't be warranty-dependent

If you pick a vehicle rated Recommended by *Lemon-Aid*, breakdowns should be rare and you won't need to spend money on additional warranty protection. On those vehicles that have a history of engine and transmission breakdowns, an extended warranty backed by the manufacturer is good insurance, especially if you're looking at keeping some Fiat Chrysler Jeep models, or a Cadillac, Lincoln or European luxury vehicle past the end of the standard warranty. If the vehicle has a poor overall repair history, you will likely need to budget $1,800 to $3,500 for a comprehensive extended warranty that covers major components, including fragile and expensive electronic parts. But first ask yourself this question, "Why am I buying a vehicle that's so poorly made that I need to spend several thousand dollars to protect myself until the warranty company grows tired of seeing my face?"

When is comes to used car warranties sold by independent dealers, just like the weight-loss product ads you see on TV, what you see isn't always what you get. For example, powertrain coverage for a year from the dealer may have a low claim limit of just $1,500 or $2,000; that's too small for even one large engine or transmission repair. Coverage may not include oil leaks (called "seals and gaskets" protection), and you may be required to adhere to a warranty company maintenance schedule, rather than the one that came with the vehicle. There may be a mandatory warranty "activation" step required after you have taken delivery of your new vehicle – fail to do it and guess what? No warranty coverage.

Bumper-to-bumper coverage usually excludes stereo components, brake pads, clutch plates, and other expensive "wear items," but you should not be asked to pick up the tab if one of these components was already well on the way to a failure when you picked up your used vehicle.

Some automakers will pull every trick in the book to make you pay for their factory screw-ups. These tricks include blaming your driving or your vehicle's poor maintenance, penalizing you for using an independent garage or the wrong fuel, or simply stating that the problem is "normal" and it's really you who is out of whack.

Part Three has all the answers to the above lame excuses. There, you will find plenty of information that will make automakers and their dealers think twice about rejecting your claim.

Don't pay for repairs covered by "secret" warranties

Automobile manufacturers are reluctant to publicize their secret warranty programs because they believe that such publicity would weaken consumer confidence in their products and increase their legal liability. The closest they come to an admission is to send out a "goodwill policy," "special policy," or "product update" service bulletin intended for dealers' eyes only. These bulletins sometimes propose free repairs for defects that can include faulty paint, air conditioning malfunctions, or engine and transmission failures.

If you're refused compensation, keep in mind that secret service bulletins can be considered an admission of manufacturing defects. You can usually find them in technical service bulletins (TSBs) that are sent daily to dealers by automakers. If polite negotiations fail, you could challenge the denial of coverag in court on the grounds that you should not be penalized for errors by the manufacturer that are described in a bulletin to its dealers.

Service bulletins are written by automakers in "mechanic speak." They're good guides for warranty inspections (especially the final service before the warranty expires), and they're useful in helping you decide when it's best to trade in your vehicle. Manufacturers try to weasel out of their obligations by claiming that they never wrote such a bulletin.

If your vehicle is out of warranty, show these bulletins to less-expensive, independent garage mechanics so they can quickly find the trouble and order the most recent upgraded part or software, ensuring that you don't replace one defective component with another. A sampling of the latest secret warranties now applicable can be found throughout Part Four.

Make sure you copy these secret warranties as they are shown here in *Lemon-Aid* because service managers and automakers often deny that these bulletins exist, or they may shrug their shoulders and say that they apply only in the U.S. However, when they're shown a copy, they usually find the corresponding Canadian bulletin in their files. The problems and solutions don't change from one side of the border to another. Mechanical fixes do differ in cases where, for example, a bulletin is for California only, or it relates to a safety or emissions component used only in the U.S. but these instances are rare. It is quite gratifying to see some automakers like Honda candidly admit in their bulletins that no-charge "goodwill" repairs are available. What a shame other automakers aren't as forthcoming!

The best way to get bulletin-related repairs carried out is to visit the dealer's service department and to attach the specific ALLDATA-supplied service bulletin covering your vehicle's problems to a repair order.

Getting your vehicle's service bulletins

Free summaries of automotive recalls and technical service bulletins listed by year, make, model, and engine can be found at the ALLDATA (*www.alldata.com/TSB*) and NHTSA (*www.safercar.gov*) websites. But, like the NHTSA summaries, ALLDATA's summaries are so short and cryptic that they're of limited use. You can download the complete contents of all the bulletins applicable to your vehicle from ALLDATA at *www.orders.alldatadiy.com* if you pay the $26.95 USD annual subscription fee, which covers vehicles since 1982. Check the enthusiast websites for your model vehicle (every car and truck has at least one) for discussions about TSBs; community members will often post a link to the full TSB you need.

Trim Insurance Costs

Insurance premiums can average between $900 and $2,000 per year, depending on the type of vehicle you own, your personal statistics and driving habits, and whether you can obtain coverage under your family policy.

There are some general rules to follow when looking for insurance savings. For example, vehicles older than ten years do not necessarily need collision coverage, and you may not need loss-of-use coverage or a rental car. Other factors that should be considered are noted below.

- When you phone for quotes, make sure you have your vehicle identification number, or VIN, in hand. Many factors, such as the make of the car, the number of doors, if there's a sports package, and the insurer's experience with the car, can affect the quote – most of this information is encoded in the VIN. And be honest, or you'll find your claim denied or reduced, the policy canceled, or your premium cost boosted.

- Where you live and work also determine how much you pay. In the past, auto insurance rates have been 25-40 percent higher in Greater Toronto than other areas of Ontario because people drive more kilometres and claims are higher. Similar disparities are found in British Columbia and Alberta.

- Taking a driver-training course can save a new driver hundreds of premium dollars.

- You may be able to bundle your home or apartment insurance with your vehicle(s) as part of a premium package that's eligible for additional discounts.

InsuranceHotline.com, based in Ontario but with quotes for other provinces, says that it pays to shop around for cheap auto insurance rates. The group has found that the same insurance coverage can vary in cost by a whopping 400 percent. *CarHelpCanada.com* and the APA offer competitive group insurance rates to their members in Ontario.

"Hidden" Costs

A Lower Resale Value

Depreciation is the biggest – and most often ignored – expense related to new vehicle ownership. You'll encounter it when you trade in your vehicle or when a collision or theft forces you to buy another vehicle earlier than you intended. Vehicles with high depreciation can lose almost 50 percent of their value in their first three years.

The best way to limit depreciation losses on a new vehicle is to choose a model that is reliable and economical to operate, and then keep it for ten years or more. If you plan to change vehicles more frequently, choose a lower-depreciating vehicle – like one that keeps at least half its value over four years. You'll retain more equity that will give you a bigger down payment and fewer loan costs with your next purchase.

If buying new, you want a vehicle that depreciates slowly, like a Subaru Impreza, Toyota RAV4, or Honda Civic, Accord, or CR-V. As a rule, Japanese vehicles are the slowest to depreciate, with Honda, Subaru and Toyota leading the way. American cars lose their value the quickest, but domestic pickup trucks retain their value, even when they are older. European models vary. South Korean automaker vehicles depreciate almost as quickly as domestic models, but can offer savings due to their lower original purchase price for well-equipped models.

However, if you're in the market for a *used* vehicle, you should be on the look-out for fast-depreciating vehicles that are also reliable and overall good performers, like a recent Chevrolet Impala, Kia Soul, or a Hyundai Accent, Elantra, or Santa Fe. Anything from Ford, or Fiat Chrysler? Yes, intermediate sedans like the Fusion, and Chrysler 300 and Dodge Charger. Among full-size pickups, the F150 offers the best combination of price and availability in the used vehicle market.

Hybrid cars

The Toyota Prius is the best of the hybrid lineup from a reliability and performance standpoint. In a polling of taxi drivers across Canada, the Prius is considered a definite money-saver when used as a high-mileage urban transporter. With cheap gas prices, used Prius values have cratered.

Automakers have sold several hybrids like the Prius, Honda Civic and Accord Hybrids, the Ford C-Max, and some Hyundai/Kia variants. They use a gas engine/electric motor combo for maximum fuel economy and low emissions while providing the driving range of a comparable conventional car and avoiding the long charge times and range anxiety of plug-in vehicles. Yet the hybrid still has some drawbacks.

- Real-world fuel consumption can be 20-30 percent higher than advertised. This has resulted in out-of-court settlements by Honda, Kia, and Ford for misleading advertising. These settlements compensate owners with a pre-paid fuel charge card that is renewed annually.
- Cold weather and hilly terrain can cut fuel economy by 10-30 percent, seemingly more than a conventional gas engine.
- Air conditioning will increase fuel consumption, as with a conventional engine.
- Interior cabin heat may be insufficient.
- Electrical systems can deliver a life-threatening 275-500 volts if tampered with through incompetent servicing or during an emergency rescue.

- If you're buying a used hybrid not covered by a warranty, battery packs cost $4,000 and up.
- Depending on the model and your usage, it will take five to eight years or more for the fuel savings to equal the hybrid's extra costs.
- Hybrids cost more to insure, and some depreciate just as quickly as non-hybrid vehicles that don't have expensive battery packs to replace.
- Hybrids make you a captive customer of the dealer, as few independent shops have taken even the basic coursework required to provide routine maintenance.

Here are hybrid models that offer the best value:

- Chevrolet Volt (plug-in)
- Toyota Camry Hybrid, RAV4 Hybrid
- Toyota Prius (non-plug-in conventional hybrid version)

If you find the limitations of a gas-electric hybrid too daunting, why not simply buy a more fuel-efficient compact car? Or, get a comfortable higher line of used car? Here are some vehicles with class-leading fuel consumption recommended by the APA and *Lemon-Aid*.

Vehicles with Class-Leading Fuel Consumption

SMALL CARS
Honda Fit and Civic
Mazda 3 with SkyActiv 2L engine
Nissan Versa Note hatchback
Subaru Impreza hatchback (with
    standard AWD, as an alternative
    to a compact SUV)
Toyota Yaris and Corolla
Toyota Matrix and Pontiac Vibe
    hatchbacks

MID-SIZE SEDANS
Honda Accord
Hyundai Sonata
Kia Optima
Nissan Altima
Toyota Camry

COMPACT SUVS
Buick Encore
Honda CR-V
Hyundai Tucson
Kia Sportage
Mazda CX-5
Nissan Rogue
Toyota RAV4 (conventional or
    hybrid)

PEOPLE MOVERS
Mazda 5
Honda Odyssey
Kia Rondo (2014 or newer)
Toyota Sienna

SURVIVING THE OPTIONS JUNGLE

The best options for your buck are an automatic transmission, air conditioning, a rearview camera, and a sound system with good phone connectivity. These features may bring back one-third to half their value come trade-in time. Although

Lemon-Aid doesn't recommend them, a sunroof, or better still a see-through moonroof, will improve the resale value and appeal of a used luxury vehicle. Extravagantly equipped vehicles hurt your pocketbook in three ways: They cost more to begin with but return only a fraction of what they cost when the vehicle is resold; some options increase maintenance costs; and features like roof racks and bigger alloy wheels and tires increase fuel consumption slightly.

Dealers make vastly higher margins with dealer-installed add-ons like rust-proofing, and insurance-type products than on new vehicles. No wonder the knives come out when you go into the business office! Before agreeing to dealer-installed options, take a look at aftermarket alternatives, which typically cost less. Similarly, check with your car or life insurer, or credit union before purchasing expensive dealer loan insurance or replacement cost insurance.

Lemon-Aid's Review of Standard and Optional Features

One problem with options is that you sometimes can't refuse them. Dealers sell very few bare-bones models, and dealers in some markets pack vehicles with dealer-installed features that they may not be willing to remove. You'll be forced to dicker over the total cost of what you are offered, whether you want extras like a "green tire package" or anti-theft etching or not. In these circumstances, it isn't a case of "yes" or "no," but more a decision of "at what cost?"

Adjustable Pedals and Extensions

This device moves the brake and accelerator pedals forward or backward about 10 cm (4 in.) to accommodate short-statured drivers and protect them from airbag-induced injuries.

If the manufacturer of your vehicle doesn't offer optional power-adjustable pedals, there are several companies selling inexpensive pedal extensions through the Internet; for example, go to *www.creativemobilitygroup.com/shop/pedal-mates/*. If you live in southwestern Ontario, check out *www.mobilityinmotion.net*.

Adjustable Steering Column

This option allows easier access to the driver's seat and permits a more-comfortable driving position. It's particularly useful if more than one person will drive the vehicle. Best is a steering column that both tilts and telescopes.

Air Conditioning

Nowadays, a vehicle without air conditioning is harder to resell and worth significantly less in most markets in Canada. AC systems are far more reliable than they were decades ago, when they had a lifespan of five to seven years. Repair costs can exceed $1,000, but they're less common than they once were.

AC will increase fuel consumption by 10-20 percent in city driving; the difference is more noticeable with small vehicles. Does AC waste or conserve fuel compared to driving with open windows at highway speeds? *Edmunds.com*, a popular automotive information website, conducted fuel-efficiency tests and concluded that there wasn't that much difference between open or closed windows, a finding confirmed by *Consumer Reports*. Here's the conclusion from Edmunds:

> While the A/C compressor does pull power from the engine wasting some gas, the effect appears to be fairly minimal in modern cars. And putting the windows down tends to increase drag on most cars, cancelling out any measurable gain from turning the A/C off. But this depends on the model you're driving. When we opened the sunroof in our SUV, the mileage did decrease even with the A/C off. Still, in our experience, it's not worth the argument because you won't save a lot of gas either way. So just do what's comfortable.

AC provides extra comfort, reduces fatigue and wind noise by not having to roll down the windows, and improves window defogging. Tip: The air conditioning compressor is usually engaged automatically by the ventilation system when you select the windshield defogging function. If you don't need to dry the air, many systems allow you to select "ECON" (economy) or "AC off" to disengage the compressor when demisting the windshield.

Pickups and SUVs: A Hot Target

The Insurance Bureau of Canada (IBC) reports 73,964 vehicles were stolen in 2014. The 10 most stolen models across Canada were various model years of the Ford F350 and F250 heavy-duty pickup trucks, along with Cadillac Escalades. Nothing else made the top 10. "This should come as no surprise," says IBC's Dubin. "Many of these higher-end vehicles are stolen in Atlantic Canada and Quebec and they end up being 'title-washed' and sold in other parts of the country. It's a lucrative market for big, rugged vehicles."

Perhaps more telling is the list of top-10 stolen vehicles in Ontario:

The Top 10 Most Frequently Stolen Vehicles Across Ontario

Rank	Model	Rank	Model
#1	2003 Cadillac Escalade	#6	2013 Toyota Highlander
#2	2010 Acura ZDX	#7	2005 Hummer H2
#3	2009 BMW X6	#8	2014 Toyota Venza
#4	2013 Acura MDX	#9	2011 BMW X6
#5	2003 Chevrolet Avalanche	#10	2004 Chevrolet Avalanche

Note: Every time this list comes out, I yearn for a list of those cars that are so unwanted that no self-respecting thief would steal them. Until an official alert is sent out by the IBC, here's my own list of "Cars Thieves Hate:" Chrysler Sebring/ Avenger, Chevrolet Cobalt/Pontiac Pursuit, Dodge Caliber, GM minivans, Kia, Nissan Quest, Saturn Ion and L-Series, and VW New Beetle. All of the above cars can be safely parked on the street, unlocked, with the key in the ignition – except on trash pickup day.

Heavy-Duty Battery

A good option for northern climates is the optional heavy-duty type offered on many trucks for about $100. It's a worthwhile purchase, especially for vehicles equipped with lots of electric options. Heavy-duty batteries give you an extra year or two for about 20 percent more than the price of a standard battery.

Child Safety Seat (Integrated)

Integrated safety seats are designed to accommodate any child more than one year old or weighing over 9 kg (20 lb.). Since the safety seat is permanently integrated into the seatback, the fuss of installing and removing the safety seat and finding someplace to store it vanishes. When not in use, it quickly folds out of sight, becoming part of the seatback. Two other safety benefits: You know that the seat has been properly installed, and your child gets used to having his or her "special" seat in back, where it's usually safest to sit.

Cruise Control

Automakers bundle this convenience feature with other convenience features; it's nearly universal on all but basic vehicles. The constant rate of speed saves some fuel and lessens driver fatigue and leg discomfort during long trips. Cruise control should not be used on wet or icy roads as it can make the vehicle hard to control. Malfunctioning cruise-control units were also suspected of contributing to sudden acceleration incidents. Cruise control can be disconcerting to inexperienced drivers who are unaccustomed to the system.

Adaptive cruise control is the latest evolution of this feature. When it senses a vehicle ahead of you is too close, adaptive cruise control automatically reduces your speed, even applying the brakes if necessary. Although large-scale field data is still lacking, adaptive cruise control has the potential to reduce highway rear-enders resulting from driver inattention.

Electronic Stability Control (ESC)

IIHS studies found that stability control is second only to seat belts in saving lives because it reduces the risk of fatal single-vehicle collisions and rollovers. ESC was first used by Mercedes-Benz and BMW on the S-Class and 7 Series models in 1995 and then was featured on GM's 1997 Cadillacs and Corvettes.

It helps prevent the loss of control in turns, on slippery roads, or when you must make a sudden steering correction. The system applies the brakes to individual wheels or cuts back the engine power when sensors find the vehicle is beginning to spin or skid. It's particularly useful in maintaining stability with SUVs.

Nevertheless, NHTSA safety complaint postings are full of incidents where the electronic stability control either kicked in at the wrong time, worked partially, or didn't work at all. It has been required on new vehicles in Canada since 2012, and already equipped most vehicles before that. ESC is highly recommended if you are purchasing a used pickup truck or SUV made before 2012.

Engines (Cylinder Deactivation and Turbocharging)

In most cases it's preferable to choose the available non-turbo 6- or 8-cylinder engine over a turbocharged 4 if one is available. Generally, full-size pickups with V8 engines are easier to resell. The industry is currently promoting turbocharging based on the mistaken premise that it will deliver greater power and increased fuel economy, with no loss of reliability. You can't have it all. There have been many owner complaints relative to turbocharged engines with stop-start systems that work poorly, as well as failure-prone Ford EcoBoost turbocharged engines that malfunction, burn excess fuel, or stall out.

Cylinder deactivation is unobtrusive and delivers consistent fuel savings in steady-state driving. Honda employs cylinder deactivation to cut fuel consumption by 10-15 percent in its Odyssey minivan. The V6 runs on all 6 cylinders when accelerating, and on 3 cylinders when cruising. GM uses a similar system on the V8s used in its pickup trucks and other automakers offer it too.

Engine and Transmission Cooling System (Heavy-Duty)

This relatively inexpensive option provides extra cooling for the transmission and engine and is often part of a package. It can extend the life of these components by preventing overheating when heavy towing is required. It's a recommended feature for pickups, especially Ford and Chrysler models with a history of unreliable transmissions.

Keyless Entry (Remote)

This convenience option saves you from fiddling with your key in a dark parking lot, or taking off a glove in cold weather to unlock or lock the vehicle. Keyless entry systems are combined with factory anti-theft measures, like an ignition kill switch or some other disabler. Incidentally, some automakers no longer make vehicles with an outside key lock and key fobs can fail. *Lemon-Aid* has found that some locking systems also malfunction, trapping occupants inside or barring them from entering. Make sure the vehicle has a manual override.

Paint Colour

Choosing a popular colour can make your vehicle easier to sell for a better price.

- Black, silver, grey, white: These colours have been very popular over the years.
- Bright red: This colour shows sun damage, so keep your car in a garage or shady spot if possible, and have it waxed occasionally.
- Pearl finishes: These paints are the most difficult to work with. If the paint needs to be retouched, it must be matched to look right from both the front- and side-angle views.
- Champagne, gold, green: Popular in the 1990s, these colours were overused and never came back. Vehicles in these colours are harder to sell.

Power-Assisted Features

Power seats with memory are useful if more than one person regularly drives the vehicle. Automatic window and seat controls currently have few reliability problems, and they're fairly easy to troubleshoot and repair. As a safety precaution, look for a window control that has to be lifted. This will ensure no child is strangled from pressing against the switch on older vehicles. A power-window lockout switch on the driver's door is important. Power-sliding doors on minivans are more dangerous. They continue to be failure-prone on all makes and probably shouldn't be purchased by families with young children.

Wheels and Tires

We are in the Fantasy Era of vehicle tire and wheel sizes. The steel rims with plastic wheel covers on basic models are the most resistant to damage, but lack the curb appeal of alloys. Hard-riding "sport" suspensions with ultra-low profile tires on large wheels may look sharp, but they're not suited to the road conditions in most of Canada. The extra-large, wide wheels on new vehicles mated to low profile tires are ideal for dry days at the racetrack, but a pain for everyday use. Fragile low-profile tires and rims sustain expensive damage when going over potholes. They're heavier, which uses more gas and is harder on the backs of repair personnel who will have to service the vehicle. Wide tires are also more likely to hydroplane when they wear, and are a packaging nightmare for the engineers who have to fit them around crowded engine compartments. As a general rule, *Lemon-Aid* recommends you stick with the standard wheel and tire size.

Larger wheels and tires may improve handling, but there's a limit. For example, many cars come with 17-inch original equipment (OE) tires supplied by the carmaker. Moving up to a slightly larger size, say a 18-inch wheel, could improve your dry weather grip and handling a bit. Getting any larger wheels can have serious downsides, though, like making the vehicle harder to control, more likely to hydroplane ("float" over wet surfaces), and cause SUVs and pickups to roll over more easily. Large tires also cost more.

Keep tires inflated

Keep tires correctly inflated. Moderate underinflation reduces tire life by about 25 percent. Significant underinflation can affect vehicle cornering and increases the risk of tire failure at speed from a blowout. Check the air pressure in the spare tire, which may not have been verified since the vehicle left the assembly plant. A compact or space saver spare requires about twice the air pressure of a conventional tire.

Which tires are best?

Tire applications and sizes have exploded in the last two decades, in large part due to pressure from the automakers who are driving this proliferation. Passenger vehicles and light trucks are usually delivered with one of the following tire types:

- **All-Season:** The most common, and more accurately a three-season tire for Canada.
- **Touring All-Season:** Sharper handling than a standard tire, it may cost a little more. Tire life is comparable. A worthwhile upgrade if you're replacing four original all-season tires on your vehicle.
- **Performance All-Season:** This tire carries a high-speed rating, usually V for sustained driving up to 240 km/h. It's common on European sedans and performance vehicles, and is frequently the upgrade tire included with the sport suspension package offered for some standard vehicles. Tread life is 30-50 percent less than standard and touring tires and it will cost more to replace. If you're a lease customer, this type of tire will likely require replacement before the lease is over. Be careful before you put your money down for the cheapest replacement tires; many leases now require replacement tires of "like kind and quality." Although these tires are called "All-Season," most are unsuitable for winter.
- **Performance summer tire:** Exclusive to high-performance vehicles, the speed rating is likely V (240 km/h), W (270 km/h) or Z (300+ km/h). Expensive, rapid wearing and not suitable for winter.
- **M&S Tires:** Mud and Snow tires are a type of all-season tire featured on pickups and SUVs. They feature stylish deep tread lugs, which contribute to superior traction on loose surfaces. Those big treads usually result in higher road noise and less precise handling. The hard tread compound used on M&S tires is intended for year-round use but not optimized for cold weather; a dedicated winter tire will perform better on snow and ice.

Replacement all-season car, truck, and SUV tires cost between $100 to $250 per tire. Unknown-make tires imported from China are the cheapest but may not be a bargain.

Which tires are best for winter?

All-season tires are a compromise since they won't get you through winter with the same margin of safety as snow tires. Dedicated winter tires provide the best traction on snowy surfaces, thanks to aggressive treads and soft rubber compounds. Four winter tires are highly recommended for Canada; they're mandatory in the Province of Quebec. In Ontario, your insurance provider likely offers a discount if you put winter tires on your vehicle. When possible, drop by one or two inches of wheel diameter for winter (for example, from the standard 17-inch alloys to smaller 16-inch steel wheels). Steel wheels for winter will stand up better to pothole damage, and the higher profile winter tires to match the smaller wheel will provide a larger cushion of air.

The softer rubber and spongier tire tread wears more quickly in hot weather, so it's important to remove winter tires in spring. Use a slightly narrower tire size for winter driving if possible, as wide tires tend to float more in snow.

Car dealers now compete with the large tire chains when it comes to offering winter wheel and tire packages for new vehicles. Their prices are much more competitive than before, often due to bulk buying by their manufacturer or dealer network, and there is the opportunity of rolling the tire purchase into below market interest rates for new car financing.

Below you will find the winter tire recommendations based on test results published by the APA (*www.apa.ca/tire_wintertireratings.asp* for the complete report):

Winter Tire Recommendations

BEST
Bridgestone WS 80
Nokian Hakkapelitta
  R2 and R8

VERY GOOD
Continental
  WinterContact SI
Gislaved Nord*Frost
  100
Michelin X-ice Xi3
Pirelli Ice Zero FR
Toyo Observe GSi5

GOOD
Dunlop Winter Maxx
General Altimax
  Arctic
Hercules Avalanche
  R-G2

Nokian Nordman 5
Pirelli Carving Edge
Vredestein SnowTrac 5
Yokohama IceGuard
  IG51c

ACCEPTABLE
BF Goodrich Winter
  Slalom KSI
Firestone Winterforce
Goodyear Ultra Grip
  Winter
Hankook Winter
  i*Pike RS
Toyo Observe G3 ICE

DECENT BUDGET TIRES
Eskay Winter X
GT Radial Champiro
  IcePro

MEDIOCRE BUDGET TIRES
Max Trek Trek M7
Sailun Ice Blazer
  WST1
Saxon Snowblazer
  Passenger
Uniroyal Tiger Paw Ice
  & Snow II

BELOW AVERAGE
Hercules HSI S
Nexen Winguard 231
Westlake 606

AVOID
Jinyu YW51 S
Weathermate HW 501

Spare tires

Some vehicles come without a standard spare tire. A can of tire sealant and pump may provide a temporary fix if the hole is small, but you'll be stranded in the event of a blowout. Manufacturers like Kia and Hyundai charge upwards of $300 if you want to add a spare, with a tie down and jack assembly on their basic models sold without one. It may be possible to obtain the components for much less from a recycler (junkyard).

The location of the spare can also have safety implications. With spares stowed under the chassis or mounted on the rear hatch, the attaching cables and bolts can rust out or freeze, so the spare falls off, or becomes next to impossible to use when you need it.

Self-sealing and run-flat tires

Today, there are two technologies available to help maintain vehicle mobility when a tire is punctured: Self-sealing and self-supporting/run-flat tires.

- Self-sealing: Punctures from nails, bolts, or screws up to 3/16 of an inch (0.48 cm) in diameter are fixed instantly and permanently with a sealant. A low air-pressure warning system should be included. Expert testers say a punctured self-sealing tire can maintain air pressure for up to 200 km (124.5 mi) – even in freezing conditions.

- Self-supporting or run-flat: Priced from $175-$350 per tire, about 30 percent more than the price of comparable premium tires. Goodyear's Extended Mobility Tire (EMT) run-flat tires were first offered as an option on the 1994 Chevrolet Corvette and then became standard on the 1997 model. Many BMWs sold since 2006, Minis since 2002, and other vehicles feature run-flat tires with stiff sidewalls that are drivable even after losing air. However, a run-flat can run "flat" only once; it's rarely repairable, and the rigid sidewall contributes to a hard ride when it's correctly inflated.

Run-flat tires are engineered to carry the weight of the car at a speed up to 80 km/h (50 mpg) for a distance of 150 km (90 mi) even after all air pressure has been lost, according to BMW. You won't feel the tire go flat; your vehicle's tire-pressure monitor must warn you before the side wall collapses and you begin riding on your rim. Even when fully inflated, run-flats give your vehicle a harsher ride, and you'll likely notice more road noise. The all-wheel-drive Toyota Sienna's Dunlop run-flat tires have a well-earned reputation for premature wear, with owners reporting the need to replace all four tires at 25,000-30,000 km (15,000-20,000 mi). Owners of other models and tire brands have reported similar issues with tire longevity and uneven wear.

Trailer-Towing Equipment

Just because you need a vehicle with towing capability doesn't mean that you have to spend big bucks. First determine the maximum load weight you'll be towing, what kind of vehicle you want to do the job, and whether your tires will handle the extra burden. For most towing needs (up to 900 kg/2,000 lb.), a passenger car, small pickup, or minivan equipped with a 6-cylinder engine will work just as well as a full-sized pickup or van (and will cost less to operate). If you're pulling a trailer that weighs more than 900 kg, most passenger cars won't handle the load unless they've been specially outfitted according to the automaker's specifications. Pulling a heavier trailer (up to 1,800 kg/4,000 lb.) will likely require a larger vehicle equipped with V6 or V8 power.

Automakers reserve the right to change limits whenever they feel like it, so write any sales promise about towing into your contract. A good rule of thumb is to reduce the promised tow rating by 20 percent and then check that figure with an independent expert. Don't rely only on a verbal assurance from the seller. In assessing towing weight, factor in the cargo, passengers, and equipment of both the trailer and the towing vehicle. Keep in mind that five people and luggage add 450 kg (almost 1,000 lb.) to the load, and that a full 227L (60 gal.) water tank adds another 225 kg (almost 500 lb.). The manufacturer's gross vehicle weight rating (GVWR) takes into account the anticipated cargo and supplies that your vehicle is likely to carry.

Automatic transmissions are fine for trailering. Manual transmissions tend to experience greater clutch wear caused by towing. The best compromise is to shift an automatic transmission manually, both for maximum control and performance going uphill, and downhill so as not to overheat the brakes.

Unibody vehicles (those without a separate frame) can handle most towing chores as long as their limits aren't exceeded. Front-drives aren't the best choice for pulling heavy loads in excess of 900 kg (2,000 lb.), since they lose some steering control and traction with all the weight concentrated in the rear.

Whatever vehicle you choose, keep in mind that the trailer hitch is crucial. It must have a tongue capacity of at least 10 percent of the trailer's weight; otherwise, it may be unsafe to use. Hitches are chosen according to the type of tow vehicle and, to a lesser extent, the weight of the load.

Most hitches are factory-installed, even though independents can install them more cheaply. Expect to pay at least $200 for a simple boat hitch and a minimum of $600 (plus installation) for a fifth-wheel version for your truck.

Equalizer bars and extra cooling systems for the radiator, transmission, engine oil, and steering may be necessary for towing a heavier load than 900 kg (2,000 lb.). Heavy-duty springs and brakes are a big help, too. Separate brakes for the trailer may be necessary to increase your vehicle's maximum towing capacity.

Be wary of the towing capabilities bandied about by automakers and dealers. The domestic automakers routinely exaggerate the towing capability of their pickups. Another towing caveat: Dealers seldom mention the need for expensive optional equipment, or that the top safe towing speed may be only 72 km/h (45 mph). In the showroom, poorly trained sales reps will assure you the vehicle's load limit matches your needs, without actually confirming that your trailer and their vehicle are compatible. Best to doublecheck yourself, using information from the automaker and trailer manufacturer, and to write your requirements or any verbal assurances made by the seller into the sales agreement.

Generally, 3L to 4L V6 engines will safely accommodate light to medium towing needs. Smaller 4-cylinder engines can handle small utility and tent trailers, but pulling a heavy trailer will likely offer a white-knuckle experience when merging with highway traffic or traveling over hilly or winding terrain.

You may have to change your driving habits to accommodate the type of vehicle you purchase when towing. Braking efficiency on ABS-equipped vehicles is compromised if you pump the brakes. With large vans and pickups, and you may scrub the right-rear tire during sharp right-hand turns until you get the hang of making wider turns. Limited rear visibility is another challenge, requiring drivers to carefully survey side and rear traffic before changing lanes or merging.

Transmissions

Despite its many advantages, the manual transmission is an endangered species in North America. In fact, manuals have gone from 20 percent of sales to less than 5 percent in the last 20 years. Today they are mostly featured in high-performance sports cars, basic versions of small pickups, and small, inexpensive econocars. The most recent casualty is the 2015 and later Subaru Legacy sedan (a stick is still available on the Outback crossover). A manual gearbox is simpler to service and repair than an automatic, and until recently manual transmissions usually added a mile or two per gallon over automatics.

One theory explaining why the manual transmission is falling out of favour? North American drivers are too busy juggling smartphones, text messaging, and cappuccinos to shift gears. Interestingly, buyers in Europe continue to opt for a manual transmission, despite high traffic congestion there.

Of the three types of automatic gearboxes available, the most reliable and cheapest to repair are conventional hydraulic automatics, with five or six dedicated speeds. The all-new ZF 9-speed automatic gearbox used in 2014-15 Acura, Chrysler, and Jeep models may be a "lemon." It has generated a large number of safety-related complaints and a recall of Chrysler Dodge and Jeep vehicles (in one rollaway, the Cherokee dragged its owner into 10 feet of water at a local lake). *Car and Driver* reported that at one time Jeep dealers were replacing 12-15 Cherokee transmissions a week (*blog.caranddriver.com/holy-shift-zf-9-speed-automatic-problems-mount-chrysler-releases-third-software-update-for-jeep-cherokee/*):

[T]hese allegations are far worse than the sluggish and delayed gear changes we've experienced testing the Cherokee and Evoque (and yet absent in the 200 and TLX). Cherokee, 200, and TLX owners have each reported conditions such as sudden lunges from unexpected downshifts, a lack of kickdown upon entering highways, front-axle vibration in low gears, and complete failures in which the transmission shifts into Neutral while driving and lights up the dash with warning lights. Other owners have reported rollaways in which the vehicle indicated it had engaged Park when it was actually in Neutral.

Incidentally, this problem may continue to grow in size. The new Land Rover Discovery Sport, Jeep Renegade, and Fiat 500X also carry the 9HP automatic.

A "Macho Cherokee" that will make you cry as it shifts from 9 to 0 gears.

From NHTSA postings:

Two times the Cherokee's transmission warning came on to "service transmission" with no response from depressing the accelerator. At these two times the vehicle was at a full stop and the dash was full of warning lights for different things. When the transmission was shifted from Drive to Park, there was a loud and violent jerking by the transmission. This transmission has had its software updated many times, which has not helped. Dealer tech was able to observe this condition and replaced the transmission valve body. After replacing the valve body and after driving about 50 miles on an interstate highway, the service transmission warning came on, again. The car would lunge and jerk violently trying to go. Shut the engine off and let the car reset itself. I will not drive the vehicle again and will ask Chrysler to supply a rental vehicle at their expense until they have replaced my vehicle. This makes three times the vehicle has been in the shop for transmission problems. This transmission issue as far I am concerned is a major safety issue.

Fiat Chrysler CEO Sergio Marchionne had these words of sympathy for owners of Cherokees equipped with the failure-prone 9HP tranny. "We have had to do an inordinate amount of intervention on that transmission, surely beyond what any of us had forecast."

The second automatic transmission design is the complex, expensive, and failure-prone dual-clutch gearbox (DSG), a favourite with Ford and European automakers like Audi, BMW, and VW. The design uses two automated clutches, one for gears 1, 3, and 5, while the other operates gears 2, 4, and 6, allowing the transmission to shift rapidly. However, judging from service bulletins and owner feedback, it also delivers early breakdowns, rough shifting, excessive noise, and very expensive dealer-dependent repairs that can take weeks. The Ford Focus and Fiesta both use a Getrag dual-clutch automatic that has proven to be a disaster for some owners.

The third design, and growing in popularity, is the continuously variable automatic transmission (CVT), used by some American and Japanese automakers. CVT transmissions don't have gears; they use a less durable chain instead, moving between two cones to provide an "infinite" number of gear ratios. When the drive system fails, the whole transmission is overhauled at great expense. CVTs have also been criticized for their unfamiliar response and "feel" when you press on the gas pedal. However, they do deliver efficiency gains and manufacturers need them to hit rising fuel-economy targets. Nissan subsidiary, Jatco, is a major supplier of CVTs to several automakers and it has been toiling to improve the transmission's durability.

Unnecessary Options

All-Wheel Drive (AWD)

Mark Bilek, editorial director of *Consumer Guide's* automotive website (*consumerguideauto.howstuffworks.com*), is a critic of AWD. He says AWD systems generally encourage drivers to go faster than they should in adverse conditions, which creates trouble stopping in emergencies. Automakers like AWD as "a marketing ploy to make more money," Bilek contends. My personal mechanic adds, "Four-wheel drive will only get you stuck deeper, farther from home." Four dedicated snow tires, and a vehicle with decent ground clearance and front-wheel drive will get you through the winter, with slightly lower running costs.

Electronic Instrument Readout

If you've ever had trouble resetting a digital clock display, you'll feel right at home with this electronic gizmo. Gauges are presented in a series of moving digital patterns that may be confusing, distracting, and unreadable in direct sunlight. This system is often accompanied by a trip computer and vehicle monitor that indicate average speed, signal component failures, and determine fuel use and how many kilometres you can drive until the tank is empty.

Fog Lights

A pain in the eyes for some, a pain in the wallet for others who have to pay the high bulb replacement costs. Fog lights aren't necessary for most vehicles with well-aimed original-equipment headlights.

Factory GPS Navigation Systems

This navigation aid links Global Positioning System (GPS) satellites to the vehicle. The factory navigation system is usually bundled with other features into a high-end in-dash "infotainment" system. Functionality of factory navigation system varies by manufacturer and generation of their system. Updates are an expensive owner-pay proposition, even during the new-vehicle warranty period, and the system is certain to be obsolete long before the vehicle is retired.

In reality, many system functions can be performed by a smartphone, and the factory navigation screen is sometimes washed out in sunlight, and harder to manipulate than the better aftermarket devices. A portable GPS unit made by Garmin or others is more user-friendly and cheaper, in the range of $200-$300, and can be updated for less or replaced periodically.

A better long-term strategy for in-dash vehicle electronics is a large clear screen and superior connectivity for your cellular phone, via a platform like Apple CarPlay or Android Auto. That way your phone, which gets replaced every 2-3 years, will provide the technology and features to maintain vehicle connectivity that's up to date.

High-Intensity Headlights

These headlights are much brighter than standard headlights, and they cast a blue hue. Granted, they provide additional illumination, but they are also annoying to other drivers, who may think your high beams are on. Systems used in Europe have a device to maintain the light beam closer to the road so that other drivers aren't blinded.

Keyless Ignition or Pushbutton Start

This convenient option is a silent killer responsible for at least 19 carbon monoxide deaths to date. It uses an electronic pushbutton on the dash to turn the vehicle on or off – no key needed, just a fob in your pocket. Only problem is that one may not know for sure if the engine has stopped running. A driver may accidently fail or forget to turn off their vehicle when parking indoors overnight. Fatalities can occur after the home fills with deadly carbon monoxide, if the garage is attached, or a garage fire spreads to the rest of the house.

The newest vehicles with Pushbutton Start buttons incorporate features that can help prevent deaths from carbon monoxide poisoning. Some cars beep if left running for too long and others have an automatic shutoff.

START: Maybe. STOP: Maybe not.

Power-Assisted Minivan Sliding Doors

Not a good idea if you have children. These doors have a high failure rate, sometimes opening or closing for no apparent reason with the potential to injure children caught between the door and post. They're popular with adults who have mobility restrictions, as an alternative to the conventional heavy manual sliding doors on minivans.

Rollover-Detection System

This feature makes use of sensors to determine if the vehicle is leaning over beyond a safe angle while driving. If so, the vehicle's electronic stability system is engaged, and if that doesn't work the side airbags are automatically deployed and remain inflated to make sure occupants aren't injured or ejected in a rollover accident.

Rooftop Carrier

This largely decorative feature on SUVs and some minivans provides additional baggage space and may allow you to meet all your driving needs with a smaller vehicle. However, even an empty rack can increase your highway fuel bill by 5-10 percent.

Seat and Steering Wheel Warmers

A feature on luxury vehicles that has migrated to all vehicle segments thanks to Hyundai and Kia. Over the years, the NHTSA has logged over 1,260 complaints on seat heaters, mostly concerning overheating, resulting in 287 injuries and over 500 fires. Seat and steering wheel warmers are popular with new vehicle buyers. Using seat warmers is a bad idea when carrying babies, kids, or people with sensory impairments who may not notice when the seat overheats.

Sunroof

Although a sunroof is rarely opened after the first weeks of good weather in spring and summer, owners love the design that features a tinted glass or plastic panel, for the additional light it allows into the interior when it's closed. Unless you live in a temperate region year-round, which excludes most of Canada, the advantages of having a sunroof are far outweighed by the disadvantages.

NHTSA's *safercar.gov* website is replete with owner complaints of the glass sunroof suddenly shattering when the car door is shut, the ambient temperature drops, or for no discernable reason when the vehicle is underway. Moreover, you aren't going to get better ventilation than a good AC system would provide, and a sunroof may plague the interior with wind noises, rattles, water leaks, and road dust accumulation. A large glass roof also increases fuel consumption slightly (extra weight), reduces night vision because overhead highway lights shine through the roof opening, and can reduce headroom by several centimetres. However, a luxury car without a sunroof is harder to sell and commands a lower price.

Tinted Glass

Tinting jeopardizes safety by reducing your night vision. On the other hand, it does keep the interior cooler in hot weather, reduces glare, and hides vehicle contents from prying eyes. Dark tinted side glass is standard on vans and SUVs, except for base models, and worth the extra cost, since cheaper aftermarket products (costing about $200) can peel away after a few years. Some aftermarket tinting can run afoul of provincial highway codes that require a certain level of transparency for windshields and front side windows.

DEALER OPTIONS

Aftermarket Anti-Theft Systems

Insurance Bureau of Canada (IBC) statistics show that automobile theft costs Canadians close to $1 billion a year, including $542 million for insurers to fix or replace stolen cars, $250 million in police, health-care, and court-system costs, and millions more for correctional services.

The IBC collects auto theft reports from its member insurance companies and government agencies throughout Canada and publishes its "most stolen vehicles" list each year. The insurance group says that despite declines in recent years, auto theft is still big business in Canada.

Rick Dubin, Vice-President of Investigative Services, reports that thieves have changed their strategy to avoid getting caught. "Organized criminals are now dismantling higher-end vehicles and exporting them in pieces instead of as whole vehicles because they are less likely to be detected." These vehicles get reassembled as far away as West Africa and then resold, he says.

All new vehicles come with electronic anti-theft protection that is supposed to ensure a thief cannot start the vehicle unless they have a key with the correct programming. In provinces where amateurs are responsible for stealing most vehicles for joyrides, an effective theft deterrent is a visible device that complicates the job like a steering-wheel lock. Aftermarket anti-theft devices usually require interfering with delicate factory wiring and if there are problems, it can cause random hard-to-diagnose issues with the vehicle. Some manufacturers are quick to void their warranty even if the anti-theft system is not the cause of the electronic malfunctions. That's one reason for paying a bit more for the dealership to install extra-cost electronic theft protection on a new vehicle; the work quite likely won't be any better, but it will afford the dealer and automaker one less opportunity to pass the buck if there is a problem down the road.

GPS tracking systems sold by independent retailers are effective for theft recovery, but won't protect a vehicle from being stolen.

Anti-Theft Marking

Dealer-applied anti-theft marking is a scam. The government doesn't require it, and thieves and joyriders aren't deterred by it. It costs about $60 per vehicle and dealers in some markets occasionally apply it to all vehicles in inventory whether you want it or not. That's called a "tied sale" and it's prohibited under Canada's competition laws. The retail charge for dealer ID etching ranges from $199 to $399, and it is sometimes bundled with a top-up of your insurance settlement in the event of a vehicle theft, usually only on condition that you repurchase a vehicle from the same dealer.

If you want to etch just the window glass for your own peace of mind, several private companies will sell you a $30 kit that does an acceptable job (try *www.vinetcher.com*). Properly applied vehicle anti-theft marking may make the vehicle less attractive if it's being stolen for parts. The recognised leader in eastern Canada is Sherlock (*www.sherlock.ca*), which provides a very complete application and maintains a database for use by police in the event the vehicle or its parts are discovered after a theft. Their application retails for $300 at the dealer, and $269 at the Lebeau network of aftermarket shops. Many insurers offer a small premium discount on the theft component of your coverage with vehicle etching.

Extended Warranties

Not necessary for most of the vehicles recommended in *Lemon-Aid*. However, an extended warranty from the manufacturer is recommended for new European luxury models, as well as new vehicles with below average predicted reliability if you foresee holding onto them after the end of the standard warranty. Manufacturer extended warranties may cost more, but they have the advantage of more generous coverage and of being accepted at every dealership selling the brand. Look for the following warranty features:

- **Full coverage.** Powertrain coverage alone is not enough nowadays, because expensive failures of electronic components and air conditioning are more likely.

- **Zero or a low deductible of no more than $50 per visit.** With a high deductible, some dealers will "throttle" the number of repairs they do on each visit, so you return more than once and pay another deductible.

- **No maximum limit on the value of repairs covered,** or a repair limit equal to the value of the vehicle. Used vehicle warranties sold by independent companies have claim limits that can be as low as $1,500. That won't pay for the cost of even one major repair.

Car manufacturers limit the markup on their extended warranty to 25-30 percent, and many of them publish retail price lists that customers can consult. Independent companies do not publish price lists and permit higher markups, which is why some franchised dealers prefer them. The APA reports that car dealers routinely mark up aftermarket warranties to $750-$1000, that they purchased from the warranty company for just $300 or $400.

Nitrogen Tire Inflation

Calgary new car dealers visited by secret shoppers acting for the APA were quoted a mandatory charge of $149 to $299 for replacing the air normally used to inflate tires with nitrogen. Nitrogen is supposed to maintain more consistent inflation pressure than air under racing conditions and during extreme temperature fluctuations. Tire manufacturers design tires to perform well with regular air, which incidentally is already 78 percent nitrogen. Filling with nitrogen shouldn't exceed about $8 per tire (Costco provides it free). If you need to top up a tire, you'll be doing it with air, which will negate the benefit of the nitrogen you paid for.

Paint and Fabric Protectors

Selling for $495-$698, paint "sealants" add nothing to a vehicle's resale value. Although paint lustre may be temporarily heightened, this treatment is not more effective than regular waxing, but costs a lot more. Auto fabric protection products are nothing more than variations of Scotchgard, which can be bought in aerosol cans for a few dollars – a much better deal than the $149 to $495 charged by dealers.

Remote Starters (Aftermarket)

Remote starters are a risky option. If they aren't original equipment there's a greater chance of having been installed improperly. Apart from being unreliable, aftermarket remote starters may cause a fire or damage electronic circuits and computers, and *Lemon-Aid* takes a dim view generally of leaving an unattended vehicle with the engine running. An engine block heater with a timer is a better idea, although it is going out of fashion. It's an inexpensive investment that will provide cabin heat sooner and reduces fuel consumption by allowing you to start out with a semi-warm engine.

Rustproofing

Dealer-applied rustproofing is not recommended. Even if the dealer's rustproofing company is still in business when you have a claim, you're likely to get a song and dance about why the warranty won't cover so-called internal rusting, or why repairs will be delayed until the sheet metal is actually rusted through.

Most vehicles built today are much less rustprone than they were several decades ago, thanks to more-durable body panels and better designs. When rusting occurs, it's usually caused by excessive environmental stress (road salt, etc.), poor paint application, poor design that traps salt and humidity in enclosed areas (GM and Chrysler's foam insulation around fuel filler doors and inside fenders for example) – many of these causes are excluded from rustproofing warranties.

Instead of dealer rustproofing, invest in periodic aftermarket rustproofing and park your vehicle in a dry, unheated garage or under an outside carport and then wash it every few weeks. Clean your vehicle regularly and keep it as dry as possible during the spring thaw when humidity and salt are the most active. If you live in an area where roads are heavily salted in winter, or in a coastal region, have your vehicle sprayed annually; check the APA website for a recommendation (Krown Rust Control Tel. 1-800-267-5744, nationally, for annual rustproofing and Barry's Rustproofing Tel: 514-344-1168 in Montreal for a grease treatment). Effective rustproofing protects vital suspension and chassis components, can make the vehicle ride more quietly, and may allow you to command a higher price at trade-in time. The downside is that the application may give off an unpleasant odour for a few days, and it may drip, soiling your driveway.

Make sure the rustproofing application includes the rocker panels, the bottom edge of the rear hatch or tailgate where applicable, and the wheel wells. It's a smart idea to stay at the shop while the work is being done to see that all areas have been covered and the overspray has been cleaned.

Be wary of electronic "black box" rustproofing. Selling for $495-$1,195 these devices claim to inhibit vehicle corrosion by sending out a pulsed current to the grounded body panels, protecting areas that conventional rust-inhibiting products can't reach. There is debate as to whether these devices are worth their high prices and if they work at all.

Gas-Saving Gadgets and Fuel Additives

Ah, the search for the Holy Grail! Magic software and miracle hardware that will turn your gas-hungry Hummer into a fuel-frugal Prius when the right additive is poured into your fuel tank.

The accessory market has been flooded with hundreds of atomizers, magnets, and additives that purport to make vehicles less fuel-thirsty. However, tests on over 100 gadgets and fuel or crankcase additives carried out by the EPA have found that only a handful produce an increase in fuel economy, and the increase is tiny. These gadgets include warning devices that tell the driver to ease up on the throttle or shift to a more fuel-frugal gear, hardware that reduces the engine power needed for belt-driven accessories, and spoilers that channel airflow under the car. The use of many of these products is a quick way to lose warranty coverage and could conceivably result in a failure on provincial emissions tests.

PAYING A FAIR PRICE

The most effective way to improve your odds is to use a consumer group or credit union buying service, like the ones offered by the APA and *CarHelpCanada.com*. You will have access to independent unbiased advice from association staff and a referral to a dealer or auto broker in Southern Ontario, Montreal, or Vancouver for fair treatment and a good price on a new vehicle. If you prefer to fly solo, here are a some strategies.

Price Guidelines

Two of the more common prices quoted are the MSRP (what the automaker advertises as the maximum fair price) and the dealer's invoice cost (which is supposed to indicate how much the dealer paid for the vehicle, but isn't exactly the same because of holdbacks and incentive money). The MSRP can be verified by viewing the manufacturer's website. If you want an invoice price from an independent source, visit *www.apa.ca* or *www.carhelpcanada.com* or one of the commercial invoice pricing services.

Buyers who live in small markets or in western Canada sometimes face inflated auto prices compared to those charged in major metropolitan areas. A good way to get a more competitive price without buying out of province is to check online to see if any dealers in nearby urban markets are offering promotions. Bring a printout of a dealer ad with the selling prices, preparation charges, and transportation fees, and use it locally for your negotiations.

Another tactic is to take a copy of a local competitor's car ad to a competing dealer selling the same brand and ask for a better price. Chances are they've already lost a few sales due to the ad and will work a little harder to match the deal; if not, they're almost certain to reveal the tricks in the competitor's promotion to make the sale.

Dealer Incentives and Customer Rebates

The timing of sales incentives hasn't changed much in the past 20 years. When vehicles are first introduced in the fall, they're generally priced high; by Christmas time, they'll sell for less. During the summer, they may sell for less through a combination of dealer sales incentives (manufacturer-to-dealer), cash rebates (manufacturer-to-customer), zero percent interest financing (manufacturer's-finance-company-to-customer), and discounted prices (dealer-to-customer).

In most cases, the manufacturer's rebate is applied to the selling price. There are other rebate programs that require financial participation on the dealer's part – it's unfair to the dealer who is essentially strong-armed by their manufacturer into giving away margin they may not want to part with. These shared incentive programs tempt dealers to offset losses by inflating the selling price or pocketing the manufacturer's rebate.

Some rebate ads will include the phrase "from dealer inventory only." So if your dealer doesn't have the vehicle in stock, you won't get the rebate.

Sometimes automakers will suddenly decide that a rebate no longer applies to a specific model, even though their ads continue to include it. When this happens, threaten to take all brochures and advertisements showing your eligibility for the rebate plan to provincial consumer protection officials or the federal Competition Bureau. They can use false advertising statutes to force automakers to give rebates to every purchaser who was unjustly denied one.

If you are buying a heavily discounted vehicle, be wary of mandatory dealer option "packages" for unwanted protection (rustproofing, paint sealants, and upholstery finishes) or excessive "Administration" or "Documentation" charges for preparation, filing fees, loan guarantee insurance, and credit life insurance.

Holdback

Ever wonder how dealers who advertise vehicles at the invoice price can make a profit? They may be counting on the manufacturer's holdback.

In addition to the MSRP, the invoice price, dealer incentives, and customer rebates (available to Canadians at *www.apa.ca*), another element in every dealer's profit margin is the manufacturer's holdback – the quarterly payouts dealers depend on when calculating gross margin.

The holdback was set up almost 50 years ago by General Motors as a guaranteed profit for dealers tempted to bargain away their entire markup to make a sale. It usually represents 1-3 percent of the sticker price (MSRP). There are free Internet sources for holdback information, but they're geared to the U.S. market. The most comprehensive are *www.edmunds.com* and *www.kbb.com* for American buyers. Although there may be a difference in the holdback between American automakers and their Canadian subsidiaries, their operation is similar.

"We Sell Below Invoice"

It happens rarely, but is possible. Manufacturers sometimes offer incentives to dealers who beat monthly sales quotas or exceed service standards that can drop the dealer's cost of acquisition to an amount below what appears on the invoice when the vehicle arrives from the factory. This has been especially true at Fiat Chrysler Jeep and Hyundai dealerships where monthly "stair step" all-or-nothing incentive programs require the dealer to meet sales targets or lose their entire bonus for the month, including bonuses on vehicles already sold and delivered.

When you take financing from a bank at market rates, the dealer receives a commission of $300 to $600 for writing up the loan. Some dealers drop their price on the vehicle below invoice, but earn the money back with excessive administration fees and mandatory extras like nitrogen in tires and vehicle ID etching that are not part of the invoice and amount to over $500 in some markets.

Beware of Financing and Insurance Traps

After you and the dealer have settled on a price for the vehicle, you aren't out of the woods yet. You'll be handed over to an F&I (financing and insurance) specialist, whose main goal is to convince you to buy additional financing, loan insurance, paint and seat cover protection, rustproofing, and extended warranties. These items will be presented on a computer screen as adding "only a couple of dollars" to your payments.

Compare the dealer's insurance and financing charges with those from an independent provider that likely offers better rates and better service. The dealer gets a generous kickback for selling insurance and financing products that would make a conventional insurance broker or agent green with envy – markups of 40-75 percent are normal when not prohibited by provincial rules. And guess who pays for it? The F&I closer's hard-sell will take all your willpower to resist, because most shoppers believe the selling has ended after they've agreed on a price for the vehicle; for the F&I specialist, the selling has just begun.

Add-on charges are the dealer's last chance to stick it to you. Dealer preparation charges, "Documentation" fees, "Administration" fees, and extra handling costs are ways the dealer gets extra money for just doing their job. Dealer preparation is often a once-over-lightly affair, with a car seldom getting more than a wash job and some gas in the tank.

GPS-based vehicle immobilizing

Some loan companies operating in Canada require borrowers to allow the installation of a starter-interrupter device that prevents the vehicle from starting if the loan is in arrears. Triggered by a remote signal from the loaner, the car can't be started until the device has been reset. Though it has yet to receive a formal complaint, the Office of the Privacy Commissioner of Canada is "actively following the issue, specifically the data collection made possible by the growing deployment of automotive sensors." In public hearings, some witnesses have complained the starter-interrupter shut off their cars while they were driving.

The borrower's vehicle is continuously tracked through these devices and drivers have to give up any right of privacy until their loan is paid.

after the time for me to cure this nonpayment has run out. I agree that I have no right to privacy regarding the use of the GPS device to track the location of the vehicle, but in the event that a court, arbitrator, dispute resolution organization or state or federal authority should determine that such a right exists, I hereby waive such right to the fullest extent possible. I understand the GPS unit is not being used to make monies beyond those due and owing under this Agreement and my Contract, but is being used to secure collection of monies I hereby acknowledge I owe and, where allowed, to repossess the Vehicle as allowed.

Buyer: _____ Co-Buyer: _____

A contract template posted on the Passtime USA website. The driver gives up "the right to privacy."

Except for Quebec, neither Transport Canada nor the other provinces have adopted a clear position banning or regulating the use of these devices. In Quebec, the government requires lenders to provide consumers with 30 days' notice before they repossess a car through a bailiff. Activating a starter-interrupter is considered a form of repossession.

E-mail Bids

Send an invitation for bids to area dealerships, asking for their bottom-line price for a specific model, trim level, and options. Spell out your specifications carefully, because you want to compare apples to apples, and let the dealer know if you will be a cash buyer, finance, or lease customer. Be clear that all final bids must be sent by a certain day. When all the bids are received, the lowest bid is sent to the other dealers to give them a chance to beat that price. After that, the lowest all-in price, including extra dealer charges, gets your business. This technique will not work for your trade-in, as any offer you receive will be no more than an estimate subject to reduction after an on-site appraisal.

Dozens of *Lemon-Aid* readers have told us how this bidding approach has cut thousands of dollars from the advertised price and saved them from the degrading song-and-dance routine between the buyer, sales agent, and sales manager ("he said, she said, the sales manager refused").

A *Lemon-Aid* reader sent in the following suggestions for buying by fax or e-mail.

First, I'd like to thank you for writing the *Lemon-Aid* series of books, which I have used extensively. I have written evidence from dealers that I saved a bare minimum of $700 on the Accord (but probably more) and a whopping $900 on the Elantra through the use of tendering, over and above any deals possible through Internet-tendering and/or showroom bargaining.

Based on my experience, I would suggest that in reference to the tendering process, future *Lemon-Aid* editions emphasize the issues below.

Casting a wide geographical net, which helped tremendously in increasing the number of serious bidders as long as you're willing to pick the car up there. One car was bought locally in Ottawa, the other in Mississauga.

Unless you don't care much about what car you end up with, be very specific about what you want. If you are looking at just one or two cars, which I recommend, specify trim level and all extended warranties and dealer-installed options. Otherwise, you'll end up with quotes comparing apples and oranges, and you won't get the best deal on options negotiated later. Also, specify that quotes should be signed. This helps out with errors in quoting.

Dealerships are sloppy. There is a 25-30 percent error rate in quotes. Search for errors and get corrections, and confirm any of the quotes in serious contention over the phone.

Phone to personally thank anyone who submits a quote for their time. Salespeople can't help themselves, they'll ask how they ranked, and often want to then beat the best quote you've got.

Another reader, in British Columbia, was successful with this approach.

Thanks for all the information that helped me decide to purchase a new Honda Odyssey EX-L for a super price from a good dealer.

After completing my research (and vacillating for a few weeks) I ended up issuing a faxed "request for quotation" (RFQ) from several dealerships. I can tell you that some of them were not happy and tried to tell me that Honda Canada was clamping down on this activity. In the end, one dealership did not respond and one "closer" salesperson called to attempt to get me in their dealership so he could "assess my needs." I told him that my needs were spelled out very specifically in my request but he refused to give me a price.

In the end, I received five quotations by phone, fax, and e-mail. I purchased my van in Chilliwack for about $2,200 off list. It turned out that the salesperson just started selling cars two months ago and was very appreciative of my business. The whole deal was completed in half an hour. I was in full control but treated every respondent fairly. I did not play dealers off one another and went with the lowest first offer.

Leftovers

Previous model-year leftovers are being picked clean as the 2017s arrive this fall. Older models can be good buys, if you can amortize the first year's depreciation by keeping the vehicle for eight years or more. But if you're the kind of driver who trades every two or three years, you're likely to come out a loser by buying an end-of-the-year vehicle. The reason is that, as far as trade-ins are concerned, a leftover is a "used" vehicle that has depreciated an additional model year. The savings the dealer gives you probably won't equal that first additional depreciation.

Shopping for a demonstrator? Ask the dealer for all work orders relating to the vehicle, including the PDI checklist, and make sure that the odometer readings follow in sequential order. Remember as well that most demonstrators should have less than 5,000 km (3,000 mi) on the ticker and that the original warranty has been running since the day the vehicle was first put on the road. Also, ask for written confirmation that there was no collision damage. If the vehicle's provincial ownership record shows that it was registered to a daily rental company or any other third party, you're probably buying a used vehicle disguised as a demo. You should walk away from the sale – you're dealing with a crook.

Rebate versus Low or Zero Percent Financing

If you aren't offered much of a discount for cash, financial planners say it can be smarter to finance a new vehicle at a subsidised automaker rate or zero percent. The cashflow that you free up should be used to repay debt running at high interest rates (like credit cards) or to invest in a retirement savings account and earn a tax deduction.

If you have a choice between a price rebate and low-interest-rate financing, choose the one that provides the lowest total overall cost, including the vehicle, taxes, and interest. Most salespeople can perform the calculations necessary for this comparison, but few will do it unless you ask them to. Ask for printouts with the numbers.

If the total cost for both is similar, the rebate is usually the better deal, because it is earned right away. With low interest rate financing, you'll have to stick with the vehicle until the end of payments to earn the full benefit. If the vehicle is written off early, you'll lose the remaining interest benefit, whereas the rebate was earned at the beginning.

Getting a Loan

Borrowers must be at least 18 years old (the age of majority), have a steady income, prove that they have discretionary income sufficient to make the loan payments; if not, you should be able to guarantee the loan with additional collateral or the help of a co-signer.

Before applying for a loan, you should have established a good credit rating via a paid-off credit card and have a small savings account with your local bank, credit union, or trust company. Prepare a budget listing your assets and obligations. This will quickly show whether or not you can afford a car. Next, prearrange your loan with a phone call. This will provide an alternative to the smoke-and-mirrors at the dealership.

Incidentally, if you do get in over your head and require credit counselling, contact Credit Counselling Service (CCS), a not-for-profit organization located in many of Canada's major cities (*www.creditcanada.com*).

Hidden Loan Costs

The APA's undercover shoppers have found that most deceptive financing deals involve major banking institutions rather than automaker financing.

In your quest for an auto loan, remember that the Internet offers help for people who need an auto loan and want quick approval, but don't want to face a banker. The BMO (Bank of Montreal: *www.bmo.com*), RBC (Royal Bank of Canada: *www.rbc.com*), and other banks allow vehicle buyers to complete loan applications on their websites. Loans are available to any web surfer, including those who aren't current BMO or RBC customers.

Contact the financial institutions to find out the following:

- The annual percentage rate on the amount you want to borrow, and the duration of your repayment period;
- The total cost of the loan, including sales taxes and interest;
- The minimum down payment that the institution requires;
- Whether taxes and licence fees can be included in the overall loan;
- Whether lower rates are available for different loan periods, or for a down payment;
- Whether discounts are available to depositors, and, if so, how long you must be a depositor before qualifying; and
- How much more it will cost for a fixed rate loan compared to a variable rate loan.

When comparing loans, consider the annual rate and then calculate the total cost of the loan offer – that is, how much you'll pay above and beyond the total price of the vehicle.

Dealers may be able to finance your purchase at interest rates that are competitive with the banks' because of the rebates they get from the manufacturers and some lending institutions; the major banks often prefer to pay the dealer a commission to write up an auto loan at a higher rate than what they could offer you directly. When dealing with banks, keep in mind that the traditional 60-month new vehicle loan has now been stretched to 84 or 96 months. Longer payment terms make each month's payment more affordable, but over the long run, they increase the cost of the loan considerably. A shorter term is preferable, or look for a below-market interest rate through automaker financing.

Be wary of dealers that charge a "processing" or "document" fee for writing up a loan application. This double dipping is more common with independent dealers selling used cars; dealers working with financial institutions already receive a generous commission from the lender for writing the loan. Most bank lenders pay a bounty to the dealer if they bump up the lending rate by an extra 1-2 percent for good credit risks. This is similar to lending institutions adding "points" to mortgages, except that with auto loans, it's unjustified and not disclosed. In fact, dealers in the United States are the object of state lawsuits and class actions for inflating loan charges. Credit unions usually offer auto loans that are not nearly as punitive because customers are members of the institution. By the way, automakers do not pay dealers commissions for writing up loans.

Loan Protection

Credit insurance guarantees that the vehicle loan will be paid if the borrower becomes disabled or dies. There are three basic types of insurance that can be written into an instalment contract: Credit life, accident and health, and comprehensive. Some plans will make some of your loan payments if you become unemployed. Most bank and credit union loans are already covered by some kind of loan insurance, but dealers sell the protection separately at an extra cost to the borrower. For this service, the dealer gets a hefty 20-60 percent commission. The additional cost to the purchaser can be significant.

Collecting on these types of policies isn't easy. There's no payment if your unemployment was due to your own conduct or if an illness is caused by some condition that existed prior to your taking out the insurance. Generally, credit insurance is unnecessary if you're in good health, you have no dependants, and your job is secure. Nevertheless, if you need to cancel your financial obligations, the same company that started LeaseBusters now offers FinanceBusters (*www.financebusters.com*). They provide a similar service to a lease takeover, but for customers who have vehicle loans.

Personal loans from financial institutions (particularly credit unions) now offer lots of flexibility, like fixed or variable interest rates, a choice of loan terms, and no penalties for prepayment. Precise conditions depend on your personal credit rating. Leasing is less flexible.

LEASING FLEECING: WHY LEASING COSTS MORE

Approximately 25 percent of cars are leased today (about halfway between the low of 7 percent in 2009 and the 45 percent peak in 2005). Because leases are so profitable for dealers and automakers alike, the industry is offering a truckload of incentives to support leasing. All this effort is paying off with a proliferation of leasing deals mostly on high-end sports and luxury cars and fully-loaded trucks and SUVs. Insiders say that almost all new vehicles costing $60,000 or more are leased. Car dealers love leasing because it guarantees they will be seeing you back in three or four years, with an opportunity to put you into another new vehicle.

Yet, there are reasons why leasing is a bad idea for many people. It's often touted as an alternative that can make high-priced vehicles more affordable, but it's really more expensive than buying outright. A useful website that takes the mystery out of leasing is *www.federalreserve.gov/pubs/leasing* run by the U.S. Federal Reserve Board. It goes into incredible detail comparing leasing versus buying, and has a handy dictionary of the terms you're most likely to encounter.

Is Leasing Cheaper?

The short answer is No!

Over the long run, leasing is more expensive because you'll be trading vehicles every three to four years. Changing vehicles often costs more because *depreciation is highest earlier in a vehicle's life.* Even though payments may *appear* lower when you lease, they become a permanent fixture in your household budget. When you finance your car, it's easier to extend your ownership cycle past the end of car payments, and you'll have some equity in the vehicle to put into your next purchase.

Leasing Advantages

Leasing does offer advantages.

First, it saves some of your cash flow, which you could theoretically use to pay down other consumer debt running at much higher interest rates, like credit card balances – but few consumers actually do that. Alternatively, your monthly payment savings could be put into a retirement savings plan and generate a tax benefit at the end of the year.

If you like the idea of changing vehicles frequently, on a three- or four-year schedule, and understand that there is a price to pay for it, leasing makes sense because the automaker is assuming the risk on the loss of value at the end of the lease term. It's easier to turn in a leased vehicle than dealing with a trade-in, especially a trade where the value of the vehicle is lower than the remaining balance of the loan. (That's called being "upside down" in the business.)

If you want to indulge yourself by trying something different, say a sports car or a convertible, but foresee that your needs will be changing (a move, growing family), the three-to-four-year term of most leases could suit your needs.

If you are taking a chance on a new model that hasn't been proven, or an expensive domestic or European luxury brand with high servicing costs and so-so reliability, you'll know that your vehicle can be dropped off at the dealership when the lease expires, which will likely coincide with the end of the warranty.

But taking a chance on an unproven model raises several questions. What are you doing choosing such a risky venture in the first place? Admittedly, by always driving a newer vehicle covered by the manufacturer's warranty, you have use of a free loaner vehicle while your luxury lemon waits for parts to arrive from Europe, or while a mechanic is learning to repair the latest technology on your car. Suppose you want to keep the car after the lease expires? Your guaranteed buy-out price will likely be 10-15 percent higher than what the vehicle is worth on the open market.

Who Should Avoid Leasing

Seniors, students, and used-car buyers are sometimes encouraged to lease a vehicle because they will be able to drive a new vehicle every few years, for the same or a lower monthly payment than financing. Most of the time, the salespeople who make this pitch are misleading you. They gloss over the fact that the lease customer will always have payments, has to pay the dealer "upfront" fees on top of the lease payment when they replace their vehicle every few years, and loses the equity available with a paid-up used car.

Leasing is a particularly bad idea for older seniors (70+). They stopped working years ago, and consequently will likely never accumulate the annual mileage included in the price of the lease. Dealers love to lease vehicles to seniors because many turn them in with just 40,000 or 50,000 km after four years instead of the allowable 80,000 km or 96,000 km. That low-mileage lease return becomes a gift to the dealer and the subsequent buyer of the vehicle.

In the event of an illness, which causes a temporary or permanent inability to drive, a lease is harder to get out of than a loan. You will be more exposed to penalties and early termination costs, or end up having to continue making payments while your vehicle sits in a parking spot. Finally, older drivers tend to scrape the corners of their vehicles; this minor but very visible cosmetic damage can result in hefty reconditioning charges when it's time to turn in a leased vehicle.

Students are attracted to the low monthly payments leasing promises for brand-new wheels, but sometimes overlook the hangover from the high insurance premium charged to a young driver of a new vehicle. A small used car will usually cost less to run and offers the opportunity to unload it more easily in the event the car becomes a financial burden or plans change; for example, the opportunity to spend a year studying abroad.

Finally, if you are in the market for a used vehicle, leasing is almost certainly not for you. A used vehicle lease runs at a higher interest rate, and the monthly payment savings compared to leasing a new vehicle are usually wiped out when you add the cost of an additional warranty to bring coverage up to the level of a new vehicle and the additional maintenance that will be required on an older vehicle.

Decoding "Lease-Talk"

Take a close look at the small print found in most leasing ads and ask the seller about the following items before you sign a lease. Pay particular attention to these key words and phrases.

- **Total price of the new vehicle:** This is called the "capital cost" in the lease agreement. Over the life of the lease, you will pay down about half or two thirds of that value.

- **Down payment and other money due at signing:** This is part of the "upfront money." When you're leasing your goal is to keep the down payment as close to zero as possible. If you put down a large down payment, and the vehicle is stolen or written off after a collision, the lessor keeps all the money you prepaid. It is never reimbursed on a pro-rated basis.

- **Security deposit:** The security deposit has largely disappeared from automaker leases. This amount is equivalent to a monthly payment rounded up to the nearest $50, and should be refunded to you at the end of the lease if there is no excess wear and tear. Make a note to yourself to remember the refund and save the message somewhere you will find it when the least terminates.

- **Administration fee:** Most dealers charge an additional "administration" fee on top of the advertised or negotiated price of a new vehicle. The exception is the Province of Quebec, where consumer protection laws are better and the industry culture around new vehicle pricing is more disciplined. This extra charge, which ranges from $394 to $695 depending on the local market and dealership, is essentially a money grab by the dealer to cover general overhead – it doesn't correspond to the cost of any service provided by the salesperson or business office to "administer" the products and services they sold you, which all carry their own markups. Ask about these upfront charges and make sure they have been included in the all-in price for your vehicle during negotiations.

  In Quebec, Ontario, Manitoba, and Alberta the administration fee must be included in the advertised price for the vehicle. In British Columbia it is permitted to advertise a price without bundling the fee into the price, but the amount must appear in the ad or the charge is prohibited. If you believe the dealer is in violation of requirements related to extra fees, report it to the provincial dealer regulator; try to get a dealer print-out or pricing information on the back of a salesperson's business card to support your complaint.

- **Government charges:** Small charges to cover tire recycling (about $15) and registration of the lease in a provincial database (about $50) are part of the upfront money.

- **Number of included kilometres, and excess-kilometre penalty:** A competent salesperson will inquire about your projected annual mileage if you are leasing. Get it wrong, and you could be paying 10 to 20 cents a kilometre at the end of the lease for being over-mileage. Use the annual mileage of your current vehicle as an estimate. The standard mileage allowance in auto lease advertising and in most leases is 24,000 km a year for imports and 20,000 km for domestics. The mileage can alternate between the two allowances depending on the vehicle and promotion. It's almost always indicated in the fine print of lease advertising. Automakers also offer low-mileage leases, with a smaller 16,000 km annual allowance for a small savings on the monthly payment. If you think

24,000 km is insufficient, you can pre-buy additional mileage at a very good rate, in the range of 5-6 cents per kilometre added to your monthly payment; most automakers cap the maximum allowance to 30,000 km annually. If you drive more than this, a new-vehicle lease is not for you. Instead, a good alternative would be a lease takeover, from someone who did not use all their annual allowance. That underused mileage is essentially provided free to you as part of the takeover.

- **Monthly payment:** More often these days, this will be advertised as a biweekly or weekly payment. General Motors even tried a *daily* payment for the Cruze! The best strategy during negotiations is to keep the conversation focused on the monthly payment; hidden charges are very difficult to spot when you are looking at a small weekly payment. There are so many payments (260 weekly payments in a 5-year lease, for example) that even a small "error" of $3 a week, which is hard to spot, results in a payment bump of $750 over the life of the lease.

If you prefer to time your payments bi-weekly to coincide with your paycheque cycle, remember that the biweekly payment is *smaller* than half the monthly payment, because all months except February are longer than four weeks. Dividing the monthly payment in two to arrive at the biweekly payment results in a disguised price *increase*. A couple of automakers, notably Toyota, sometimes advertise semi-monthly payments; these are truly equivalent to half of a monthly payment.

FULLY EQUIPPED.
THE LOWEST PRICE ON THE MARKET.

- **Term:** Most automaker leases run for 36 or 48 months. Automakers occasionally promote 60-month leases, notably Toyota and Honda because of the strong resale value of their vehicles. On rare occasions, an automaker will feature short 24- or 30- month leases; these are normally expensive, unless the automaker is running a special promotion to bring down the monthly payment. The best is usually to stay within the sweet spot of the automaker's offer. With a 36-month lease there is a good chance that you will pay only for minor service like oil changes and tire rotation, and simple inspections. The 48-month lease will likely require tire replacement in the last year of the lease and a front brake job, both of which will reduce some of the payment savings possible with the longer term. Lease terms shorter than three years mean you will be back sooner, and paying arbitrary "administration" fees and other charges more frequently; that's one reason why dealers like them.

- **"Residual" or end value:** This estimated value of the vehicle at the end of the lease is of no concern if you don't intend to purchase the vehicle at the end of an automaker lease, which is the "closed end" or "walkaway" variety. As a rule, the end values of mainstream Toyota and Honda models are conservative, and you may know someone who wants to take the lease over in its final months to buy it out; this saves the double taxation that would occur if you waited to the end of the lease, bought the vehicle, and resold it immediately. With most luxury and high-end vehicles, the residual value is usually higher than what a private seller could obtain on the market. The manufacturer absorbs any shortfall on the end value when they resell the vehicle at auction; that's a big advantage of the closed end lease. Some dealers and finance companies still offer the old "open end" or operating lease. Originally developed for commercial businesses, an open-end lease makes the lessee responsible for any shortfall on resale, and is to be avoided.

Almost all leases include a purchase option that allows the lessee to buy the vehicle for the amount of the residual value. This option is valuable if you are facing high penalties for excess mileage or cosmetic damage on the vehicle; you'll avoid paying them if you buy out the vehicle and keep it for a couple more years. Bear in mind though, that a vehicle purchased at the end of a lease will no longer qualify for the manufacturer's subsidized low interest rate – you'll be paying interest at the higher market rates applicable to a three- or four-year-old used vehicle, currently 4-6 percent for low-risk borrowers.

- **Insurance requirements and other restrictions:** The lease sets minimum requirements for collision insurance and liability coverage. These are usually comparable to what a new vehicle buyer would purchase for a financed vehicle. The leases carry some restrictions on mobility – you can't move to the United States with the vehicle, for example. Some leases limit the amount of time a vehicle can be out of the country or outside Canada, a possible concern to snowbirds, but those clauses are rarely enforced unless payments are in arrears.

End-of-Lease Charges

The leasing agency or dealer may claim "reconditioning charges" when you return the vehicle, because it shows unreasonable wear and tear. Body dents and dings, scratched bumper paint, windshield damage and worn or mismatched tires are common reasons for extra charges. Come prepared by having the cosmetic repairs appraised independently if damage appears significant, and take photos of the vehicle prior to returning it. Most lease contracts now specify that you must return the vehicle with its original keys and fobs; if you've lost an electronic key, you may be facing a claim of up to $500 for a replacement. To save a couple of hundred dollars on a replacement key, it may be possible to get a used key fob for your model from a recycler and have it programmed for your vehicle. The APA's website has extensive advice on how to cope with lease damage; you can find it here: *www. apa.ca/readarticle.asp?id=374*. It's amazing how often these excess wear and tear charges disappear if you arrange to lease your next vehicle from the same dealer.

New car dealers offer a type of lease insurance, costing from $750 to $1,250, which will cover cosmetic damage up to $3,000 or $4,000. It's a high-margin sale for the business office, but can save you some headaches if you are casual about looking after your vehicle, or you park it in an area where bumper damage is inevitable. Make sure the coverage includes window glass, alloy wheels, and, ideally, worn tires. This coverage does not replace conventional auto insurance, but is supposed to pay for damage that is too minor to claim under your regular policy. Some manufacturer subsidiaries, like Toyota Financial Services, have entered the market and offer their own branded products that carry a lower markup and better assurance of avoiding surprises at lease-end.

Another nasty surprise in some leasing contracts is an extra charge added to the buyback if you decide to exercise your purchase option. The charge, which can range from $200 and up (it's $1,000 on some BMW and Mini leases), is buried in the fine print at the end of the leasing agreement and rarely mentioned by the salesperson when you are negotiating the lease. Most consumers only learn about the charge at the end of the lease when they are considering holding onto the leased vehicle.

Excess mileage will be charged to you at the end of the lease at about double the rate of pre-purchased mileage. If you drove significantly less than the mileage allowance, there is unfortunately no provision for refunding you any of the unused mileage.

Strategies for Negotiating a Good Deal on a Lease

The first thing a salesperson is likely to ask you when you say you are thinking of leasing is, "How much can you afford to pay?" After you respond, the seller will calculate a payment at the top end of your range, or a bit higher than the top end to see if you're good for a bit more money. Unless you already know the correct biweekly or monthly payment, you're almost certain to pay more than necessary working this way. There are so many variables in a lease that a seller can move them around to lower your payments without *ever reducing the price of the vehicle.* For example, the seller can increase the down payment, reduce the allowed mileage, convert the monthly payment to weekly or biweekly, or add an extra year to the lease, all of which will reduce your payments, while not discounting the vehicle.

Keep it simple

Focus on obtaining the lowest monthly payment and a mileage allowance suited to your needs. Always ask or a $0 down payment during the negotiations, and don't worry about the interest rate or residual value. You want the lowest total expense, including fees and taxes, over the term of the lease – one big number. Stick to a monthly payment period during discussions.

How to answer "How much can you afford?"

Start low. Come in with an advertised lease promotion for the vehicle from the automaker with a ridiculously low price, like $49 a week. That's likely to be a vehicle with a manual transmission and no air conditioning. Anchor your negotiations with this vehicle, which few dealers carry in inventory and stick with a zero down payment. The salesperson knows they'll have to bump you up, but they won't know how high you're prepared to go.

Or start low by coming in with an advertised lease promotion for a vehicle from a competing manufacturer for a similar ridiculously low price. The salesperson has a good idea of the deal you'll obtain at competing dealers selling their own brand, but no insider information about a competing brand. Plus there's the added risk that you'll like the other vehicle better.

Another strategy is not to reveal that you are planning to lease the vehicle, and negotiate the lowest purchase price possible before showing all your cards. That price then becomes the basis for lease calculations when you finally inquire about leasing. But it's not always that easy, since vehicle prices for a cash buyer, finance buyer, and lease customer may all be different, depending on the available promotions. If this sounds like a hassle, an alternative is to consider leasing with the help of a consumer association like the APA, Car Help Canada, or a buying group or auto broker. Their recommended deals usually carry a standard markup that is relatively consistent whether you are buying or leasing, and won't vary depending on what you answered when asked how much you can afford to pay.

An Alternative

Instead of leasing, consider purchasing a used model. Look for a three- to five-year-old lease-return vehicle with 60,000-100,000 km on the clock and some of the original warranty left. A used car or truck can be just as reliable for half the cost of one bought new or leased. Parts will be easier to find, independent servicing should be easier to find, insurance premiums will come down from the stratosphere, and your financial commitment will lessen considerably.

With an automaker "certified" used vehicle purchased from a new-car dealer, you may be eligible for below-market financing and one or two years of full warranty coverage equivalent to the new vehicle warranty.

THE CONTRACT

How likely are you to be cheated when buying a new car or truck? APA staffers posing as buyers visited 60 dealerships in three Canadian cities. About half the dealers they visited flunked their test, and (hold onto your cowboy hats) auto buyers in western Canada were especially vulnerable to dishonest dealers. Dealer ads left out important information, or vehicles in the ads weren't available, or were selling at higher prices. Fees for paperwork and vehicle preparation were frequently excessive.

The Devil's in the Details

Watch what you sign, since any document that requires your signature is a contract. Don't sign anything unless all the details are clear to you and all the blanks have been filled in. Be careful with anything you're asked to sign after receiving verbal assurances that the salesperson is merely putting the vehicle on hold. And when you are presented with a contract, remember it doesn't have to include all the clauses found in the dealer's pre-printed form. You and the sales representative can agree to strike some clauses and add others.

When the salesperson asks for a deposit, make sure that it's listed on the contract, and try to keep it as small as possible ($500 at most), and pay for it by credit card – in case the dealer goes belly up. If you decide to back out of the deal on a vehicle taken from stock, let the seller have the deposit as an incentive to cancel the contract (believe me, it's cheaper than hiring a lawyer). Few dealers will use the deposit to compensate the salesperson for their lost commission, which explains part of the salesperson's reluctance to cancel a sale, even when it results from an error on their part.

If you're ordering a vehicle not on the lot, scrutinize all references to the exact model (base, LX, or Limited), features, exterior and interior colours, charges, and delivery date. Make sure you specify a delivery date and protect the price from increases after you sign.

Key Contract Clauses

You can put things on a more equal footing by negotiating the inclusion of some of the sample additional contract clauses found on page 97. To do this, write in a "Remarks" section on your contract and then add, "See attached clauses, which form part of this agreement." Then attach a photocopy of the "Additional Contract Clauses" and ask the salesperson, or more likely their manager, to initial them. Although some clauses may be rejected, the inclusion of just a couple of them can have important ramifications later.

"We Can't Do That"

"We're not allowed to do that" is heard most often in reference to reducing the administration fee and extra dealer charges. Some dealers have been telling *Lemon-Aid* readers that they are "obligated" by a provincial authority, insurance companies, or law enforcement to add high charges. This is pure hogwash. Furthermore, the automakers clearly state that they don't set a bottom price, since doing so would violate Canada's *Competition Act* – that's why they put disclaimers in their ads saying the dealer may sell for less.

The Pre-Delivery Inspection

The best way to ensure that the PDI (written as "PDE" in some regions) will be completed is to write in the sales contract that you'll be given a copy of the completed PDI sheet when the vehicle is delivered to you. Then, with the PDI sheet in hand, verify some of the items that were to be checked. If any items appear to have been missed, have them noted for correction on a subsequent visit.

ADDITIONAL CONTRACT CLAUSES

1. **Financing:** This agreement is subject to the purchaser obtaining financing at _____% or less within _____ days of the date below.

2. **"In-service" date and mileage:** To be based on the closing day, not the day the contract was executed, and will be submitted to the automaker for warranty purposes. If a different "In service" date applies, and/or the vehicle has more than 50 km on the odometer, dealer is to write in the information here and both parties to initial: _____

   Dealer's representative: _____ Buyer/Lessee: _____

3. **Delivery:** The vehicle is to be delivered by _____, failing which the contract may be cancelled, and the deposit refunded if requested by the buyer/lessee.

4. **Protected price:** The vendor agrees not to increase the price of the new vehicle, the cost of preparation, or the cost of shipping. If an additional promotion, rebate, or other reduction from the manufacturer is forthcoming while waiting for vehicle delivery, the dealer undertakes to apply it to the selling price when eligible.

5. **Trade-in:** The vendor agrees that the value attributed to the vehicle offered in trade shall not be reduced, unless it has been significantly modified or has suffered from excessive or accelerated deterioration since the signing of the agreement.

6. **Courtesy car:**

   a) In the event the new vehicle is not delivered on the agreed-upon date, the vendor agrees to supply the purchaser with a courtesy car at no cost in the event the purchaser has given up the use of their current vehicle, sold it, or traded it in. If no courtesy vehicle is available, the vendor agrees to reimburse the purchaser the cost of renting a vehicle. This clause will not apply in cases where the buyer is driving a vehicle they have agreed to trade in to the dealer. Clause 5 concerning the trade-in value is applicable.

   b) If the vehicle is off the road for more than two days for warranty repairs, the purchaser is entitled to a free courtesy vehicle for the duration of the repair period. If no courtesy vehicle is available, the dealer agrees to reimburse the purchaser the cost of renting a vehicle.

7. **Work orders:** The purchaser will receive duly completed copies of all work orders pertaining to the vehicle, including warranty repairs and the pre-delivery inspection (PDI).

   Clause 8 is optional.

8. **Dealer stickers:** The vendor will not affix any dealer advertising, in any form, on the vehicle. Dealer's representative to initial if the buyer has requested this undertaking.

   Dealer's representative: _____

   Clause 9 is optional.

9. **Fuel:** Vehicle will be delivered with a free full tank of gas. Dealer's representative to initial if the buyer has requested this undertaking.

   Dealer's representative: _____

10. **Excess mileage:** New vehicle will not be acceptable and the contract will be void if the odometer has more than 200 km at delivery/closing. If a higher mileage has been agreed upon, write it in here _____ km.

_____	_____	_____
Date	Vendor's Signature	Buyer's Signature

Can You Get a Fair Price for Your Current Vehicle?

Many consumers negotiate hard for a low price on their new vehicle, but give up their gains by not paying attention to their trade. Generally, a franchised dealer is able to offer more if your vehicle belongs to the same brand they carry. Dealers sometimes offer ridiculously low trade-in values after agreeing on the new vehicle price, secure in the knowledge that you are committed to the purchase. The car industry expends a lot of energy warning consumers about the "dangers" of selling privately, but it can still work despite the hassle. If you have a desirable vehicle, you can easily earn one or two thousand dollars by selling their old vehicle privately, or asking an independent dealer to make you an offer for it. A private seller can post ads on *Autotrader.ca* and *Kijiji.ca* for free.

The APA and Car Help Canada offer a unique appraisal service via a Toronto-area used car dealer. Members are entitled to a no-charge on-site inspection of their vehicle, followed by a written offer to purchase the vehicle at a firm price. The customer is then free to shop their trade in the conventional manner at a dealership recommended by one of the two associations. If the new car dealer offers a higher amount, they get to keep the vehicle. If they offer less, the trade is sold to the original appraising dealer. The appraisal service is especially useful if you are driving an oddball that a franchised new car dealer will only be able to send to a wholesaler, for example a ten-year-old sedan with only 50,000 km. Used car dealers are lighter on their feet when it comes to unusual vehicles, and more likely to find a spot for them on their lot if the vehicle has some merit.

When to Sell

In general, the longer one keeps a vehicle, the less it costs to own. Desrosiers Automotive Consultants estimates that the annual cost of repairs and preventive maintenance for the average vehicle is about $900; it's under $500 in the first two or three years, increasing up to an average of $1,500 in years seven through ten. After the 12th year, maintenance costs taper off, partly because older vehicles accumulate less annual mileage. If you're happy with your vehicle's performance and features, and it's safe and dependable, it would pay to invest in maintaining it and continue using it.

But when the cost of repairs becomes equal to or greater than the depreciation on a new car, or a repair approximates the value of your current vehicle, it's time to consider disposing of it. Shortly before your vehicle's eighth birthday (or whenever you start to think about selling it), ask a mechanic to look at it to give you some idea of what repairs, replacement parts, or maintenance work it will need in the coming year. Check the review in this book and dealer service bulletin summaries to determine if it will need extensive repairs in the near future. Consider whether your vehicle can still be serviced easily. If it's no longer on the market, such as a Saab or a Suzuki, it probably has very little market value left; you may prefer to keep it until a large repair estimate means it's time to take it off the road.

Don't trade for fuel economy alone. The cost of acquiring a new fuel-efficient model is almost always much higher than the difference in gas receipts between it and your present ride – unless you're racking up 40,000 km a year, or driving a Hummer.

Reassess your needs. Has your family grown to the point that you need a new vehicle? Are you driving less? Are you taking fewer long trips? Let your car or minivan show its age, and pocket the savings if its deteriorating condition doesn't pose a safety hazard and isn't too embarrassing. If you're self-employed and are constantly on the road, it makes sense to trade every few years. In that case, the vehicle's appearance and reliability are prime considerations, particularly since the higher cost of depreciation may be tax deductible.

Selling to Dealers

Selling to a franchised dealer means that you're likely to get less than if you sold your vehicle privately. One Toronto woman we know was offered $14,000 for her mint, low-mileage Nissan 4x4 from two different dealers. Indignant, she sold it privately for $22,000.

Most owners are prepared to give up some of their equity to the dealer for the peace of mind that comes with knowing that their eventual buyer won't lay a claim against them and that they can time the sale of the vehicle with the delivery of their new one. A dealership that sells the same make as your current vehicle will likely give you a higher trade-in allowance because it's easier for them to resell their brand of vehicle – unless it's too old or has too much mileage for them to retail it.

Getting More for Your Trade-In

Customers who are on guard against paying too much for a new vehicle often give up their trade-in for too little.

To minimize the stress, don't sign a new vehicle sales contract unless your current vehicle has been sold or you've agreed on a price for your trade-in – you could end up with two vehicles. If you haven't seen any interest in your vehicle after two weekends, you might be attempting to sell it at the wrong time of year or have priced it too high.

Make Money – Sell Privately

If you want to make the most out of the deal, consider selling it yourself. You'll come out hundreds or even a couple of thousand dollars ahead – private buyers will pay more for your vehicle than dealers, unless it's an oddball or the local market for used vehicles is moribund (Christmastime). There's a large market for used vehicles in good condition in the $5,000-$8,000 range. Although many people prefer buying from a private individual over a dealer, they may still be afraid that the vehicle is a lemon. By using the suggestions below, you should be able to sell your vehicle more easily.

1. Know its value. Study dealer ads, and remember that their advertised "asking" prices will likely be negotiated down a bit to conclude the sale. Undercut the dealer's price by $1000 or more, and be ready to bargain down another 10 percent for a serious buyer. Prices fluctuate depending on which models are trendy, so watch the want ads carefully.

2. Afraid to sell it yourself? Visit some local independent dealers to see if they will offer more for your vehicle than the new car dealer. If you obtain a firm offer, make sure the new car dealer writes it into the sales agreement. That way you will pay sales tax only on the difference between the two vehicle prices, like a conventional trade-in.

3. Be especially careful to agree on who is responsible for repairs when selling to friends or family members. Anything short of perfection and you'll be eating alone.

4. Don't touch the odometer. If you do, you may get a few hundred dollars more – and a criminal record.

5. Make minor repairs. This includes an oil change, cosmetic touch ups, replacing missing or cracked wheel covers. If any warranty is transferable, use it as a selling point.

6. First impressions are important. Clean up the vehicle. Give the task to a professional detailer or spend a day scrubbing the interior and exterior. Polish the paint if you know how to do it. Clean the chrome, and peel off old bumper stickers. Make sure tools and spare parts have been taken out of the trunk to reduce rattles – buyers are more comfortable when looking at a clean orderly vehicle. If your driveway or parking area is cluttered, you may want to tidy it up too.

7. Consider replacing tires if they are completely worn out; used tires can do the trick. Tires on the same axle should match.

8. Write an effective ad. Look at other ads for an idea of how to do this. Buyers want to know about the vehicle. If you're the original owner, say so in your ad. If you have complete service records available, that is also a selling point. Always include the price and one or more easy ways to reach you.

9. Post notices on bulletin boards at your office or local supermarkets, and place a "For Sale" sign in the window of the vehicle itself. Online ads on *Autotrader.ca* and *Kijiji.ca* are free.

10. Keep important documents handy. Show prospective buyers the sales contract, repair records, owner's manual, and all other documents that show

how the vehicle has been maintained. Mention the fuel consumption if it's an advantage.

11. Be quick and available when you receive electronic inquiries.

12. Don't mislead the buyer. If the vehicle was in an accident or some financing is still to be paid, disclose it. Misleading statements could be used later against you in court. It's also advisable to have someone witness the actual transaction in case of a future dispute.

13. Both parties should sign a receipt if any money changes hands, be it a deposit or the payment.

14. Let the buyer have the vehicle inspected, and then accompany the prospective buyer to the garage. This gives you protection if the buyer claims you misrepresented the vehicle.

15. Finally, be wary of using your home address in advertising; in most cases an e-mail address or phone number will do. Consider arranging to meet in a public place if you live alone, or at a time when other people will be around.

Drawing Up the Contract

The province of Alberta has prepared a useful bill of sale applicable throughout Canada that can be accessed at *www.servicealberta.gov.ab.ca/pdf/mv/BillOfSaleReg 3126.pdf*. Your bill of sale should identify the vehicle (including the vehicle identification number) and include its price, whether a warranty applies, and the nature of the examination made by the buyer.

Summary

Now that you know how to get the cheapest, safest, and most reliable new car, let's take a look at the many used car buys that can save you up to $15,000 over a new vehicle, and provide a decade's worth of cheap, reliable transportation.

2 OLD WHEELS AND GOOD DEALS

SECRET WARRANTIES AND SPECIAL PROGRAMS

Almost all automakers use little-known "special policy" or "goodwill" extensions of their standard warranty to cover components with a high failure rate long after a vehicle's original warranty has expired. This creates a pool of vehicles that may be eligible for free repairs to correct common problems after their original warranties have expired.

We're not talking about merely a few months' extension on small items. In fact, some free repairs – like those related to General Motors, Nissan, and Honda – are authorized up to 10 years under a variety of "goodwill" or "special policy" programs (see Introduction). Most warranty extensions hover around the 5- to 7-year mark and seldom cover vehicles exceeding 160,000 km. Yet there are exceptions, like the catalytic converter special policy that will pay for the converter's replacement up to 10 years, or 193,000 km, on many Chevrolet models.

Incidentally, automakers and dealers claim that there are no "secret" warranties, since they are all published in service bulletins. Although this is partially correct, have you ever tried to get a copy of a service bulletin? Or, if you did manage to get a copy, did the dealer or automaker say the benefits are applicable only in the States? Pure weasel speak!

Secret Warranty Roundup

As a public service – and particularly because I enjoy getting the carmakers all riled up and giving auto owners more tools to get free repairs – here is a summary of the more important warranty extensions currently in effect that could save you thousands of dollars.

ALL YEARS, ALL MODELS

Problem: Premature wearout of brake pads, calipers, and rotors. Produces excessive vibration, noise, and pulling to one side when braking. **Warranty coverage:** *Rotors and pads:* "Goodwill" settlements confirm that brake rotors and pads that fail to last 2 years/40,000 km will be replaced for half the repair cost; components not lasting 1 year/20,000 km will be replaced for free.

Problem: Faulty automatic transmissions that self-destruct, shift erratically, gear down to "limp mode," are slow to shift in or out of Reverse, or are noisy. **Warranty coverage:** If you have the assistance of your dealer's service manager, or some internal service bulletin that confirms the automatic transmission may be defective, expect an offer of 50-75% in the first year or two after the end of the powertrain warranty. Coverage from Acura, General Motors, Honda, Hyundai, and Nissan varies between 7 and 10 years, depending on the model.

ACURA

2007-09 MDX; 2009-10 RL; and 2009-11 TL

Problem: Fix for a transmission judder or failure. **Warranty coverage:** 8 years/ 160,000 km radiator assembly and automatic transmission warranty extension, which covers "damage, repairs, replacement, and related towing resulting from this issue." Original and subsequent owner coverage.

BMW

2007-10 models

Problem: Premature failure of the high pressure fuel pump. **Warranty coverage:** BMW has extended the emissions warranty to 10 years/193,000 km, according to bulletin #SI B13 03 09, announced in BMW's November 2010 dealer letter.

CHRYSLER

2007-16 Jeep, Durango, minivans, and trucks

Problem: Stalling, no starts, and various electrical malfunctions. A defective Totally Integrated Power Module (TIPM) will cause the car to play out a scene from *The*

Exorcist: No starts, self-starts, stallouts, and headlights suddenly shutting off. Parked vehicles may produce other bizarre happenings, like the anti-theft alarm going off for no apparent reason, the radio and blower motor coming on or electric windows that roll down by themselves. All this can happen while the vehicle is on the road or parked, without a key in the ignition or a key fob nearby. **Warranty coverage:** Dealers may charge up to $1,300 for out-of-warranty TIPM repairs. However, owners who complain to Chrysler can get "goodwill" compensation on a case-by-case basis. This is a known "hidden" defect that affects a vehicle's "merchantability" as expressed in provincial consumer protection laws and business practices legislation.

Check out what some drivers reported in a California class-action lawsuit filed May 5, 2014, in California: *www.autosafety.org/sites/default/files/imce_staff_uploads/Chrysler%20TIPM%20-%20Gibbs%202nd%20Amended%20Complaint%205-14.pdf*:

> **2008 Dodge Grand Caravan:** While stopped at a red light, the van suddenly entered into an electrical chaos. The horn started blaring, the wipers started going full blast, and wiper fluid starting spraying. This kind of electrical problem has happened before but this time was the worst. The vehicle continued to drive while everything electrical flickered and continued to malfunction. Finally had to stop and remove fuses for horn and wiper fluid in order to get the malfunctions to stop. Van transmission also stopped shifting during this episode. Even after vehicle was stopped, there were multiple electrical popping noises throughout the engine as if it was trying to power up things that were no longer operational. I took vehicle into dealership and they identified problem as a failure of the TIPM. Looking online there are multiple complaints of similar problems and failures. The TIPM is actually backordered because of the demand.

JEEP

2007 Dodge Caliber and Jeep Compass and Patriot

Problem: Jeeps have serious corrosion issues that are addressed by a little-known extended warranty. We all know that the first Canadian Fiats were rustbuckets, but ironically, it now seems that Jeeps and Chrysler Calibers have contracted the same contagion. **Warranty coverage:** The premature corrosion of the front and rear suspension cross-members is now covered for 10 years with no mileage limitation. Cite TSB #23-012-14 issued on May 19, 2014, to get the free repairs. The first sign of this problem could be a vibration in the steering wheel.

FORD

2009-2011 Escape, Mariner; 2010-2011 Fusion and Milan vehicles equipped with a 2.5L or 3.0L engine built on or before 03/04/2011

Problem: A leaking/stuck canister purge valve. This condition may cause various intermittent driveability symptoms. **Warranty coverage:** 8 years under the Emissions Warranty.

Ford/Lincoln; 2009-11 Edge, Flex; 2011 Explorer; 2010–11 MXS; 2009-2011 MKX; 2010-11 MKT

Problem: Sluggish transmission. **Warranty coverage:** Change the valve body calibration under the 8-year Emissions Warranty.

2011-14 models equipped with the MyFord Touch touch screen entertainment and navigation system

Problem: Poor cell phone and Bluetooth compatibility; doesn't recognize voice commands; slow to respond; and not user-friendly. **Warranty coverage:** Ford is extending the warranty on the system to 5 years with unlimited miles, up from 3 years and 60,000 km. Lincolns will be covered for 6 years with unlimited miles, up from 4 years and 80,000 km.

GENERAL MOTORS

2006-07 Cobalt, G4/G5, and Ion

Problem: A faulty fuel pump module may produce a fuel odour or spotting on the ground. **Warranty coverage:** GM has extended the fuel pump warranty to 10 years/ 193,000 km, says TSB #09275A, issued March 3, 2010.

2006-07 Malibu and G6

Problem: Catalytic Converter failure. **Warranty coverage:** Under Special Coverage Adjustment #10134, dated November 17, 2010, GM will replace the converter free of charge up to 10 years/193,000 km.

2006-07 Buick Terraza; 2010 Buick Lucerne; 2006-07 Chevrolet Monte Carlo; 2006-08 Chevrolet Uplander; 2006-10 Chevrolet Impala; 2008-09 Chevrolet Malibu; 2006-08 Pontiac Montana SV6; 2006-09 Pontiac G6; 2006-08 Saturn Relay; 2007-09 Saturn AURA; all equipped with a 3.5L or 3.9L Engine

Problem: Some customers may comment on a coolant leak. The comments may range from spots on the driveway to having to add more coolant. If the coolant leak is coming from the front (accessory drive end) of the engine, the coolant crossover gaskets should be replaced. If the leak is found to be coming from a cylinder head gasket, the gasket must be replaced. **Warranty coverage:** GM's 8-year Emissions Warranty.

2006-09 Cadillac STS-V, XLR, XLR-V; 2007-08 Cadillac Escalade, Escalade ESV, Escalade EXT, XLR; 2006-09 Chevrolet Corvette; 2007-08 Chevrolet Silverado; 2008 Chevrolet Suburban; 2007-08 GMC Sierra, Sierra Denali, Yukon Denali, Yukon XL Denali; 2008 GMC Yukon XL; 2008-09 HUMMER H2; and 2008-09 Pontiac G8

Problem: Slips in Reverse or Third, Delayed Reverse or Drive Engagement, DTC P0776, P2715, P2723, Harsh 2-3 Shifts (Inspect 1-2-3-4/3-5-R housing and pump seal rings). **Warranty coverage:** GM's base warranty. Eligible for an undefined "goodwill" consideration since the housing and pump seal rings weren't reasonably durable.

2006-11 models

Problem: Engine Oil Consumption on Aluminum Block/Iron Block Engines with Active Fuel Management. Install AFM Oil Deflector and Clean Carbon from Cylinder and/or Install Updated Valve Cover. **Warranty coverage:** The 8-year Emissions Warranty.

2007-12 Chevrolet Silverado and GMC Sierra

Problem: Excessive rear interior wind noise, which GM attributes to "a void in the body filler within the C-pillar" or "a result of the design of the body rear panel acoustic insulator that is mounted behind the rear seat. The insulator is one of several early designs which demonstrated a lesser success of minimizing wind noise (Bulletin No.: 10-08-58-001F). **Warranty coverage:** GM will add padding in the cab area on a case-by-case basis at no charge under a "goodwill" policy.

HONDA

2006-09 Civic

Problem: The sun visor may come apart or split with use. **Warranty coverage:** 10 years/ 160,000 km.

2006-09 Civic

Problem: Engine overheats or leaks coolant because the engine block is cracking at the coolant passages. **Warranty coverage:** Honda will install a new engine block assembly free of charge under an 8 year "goodwill policy," as stated in its letter to Canadian owners.

2007-09 Civic

Problem: An engine oil leak from the front of the timing chain case cover on the oil pump assembly. **Warranty coverage:** Post-warranty free repairs may be eligible for goodwill consideration by the District Parts and Service Manager or your Zone Office.

2007-11 CR-V

Problem: AC failure. **Warranty coverage:** A warranty extension pays for a replacement of the compressor clutch up to 7 years/100,000 miles (miles because this extended warranty was approved in the United States).

2008-09 Accord

Problem: The leather seat covers may crack or the paint may rub off, delaminate, or peel. Honda attributes the problem to "an insufficient buffing process and material problem." **Warranty coverage:** Honda will replace the seat-back or seat cushion cover for an undefined period.

LEXUS

2007-13 Lexus ES; 2006-12 Lexus IS; and 2013 Lexus GS models

Problem: Emergency trunk release can break, trapping an occupant inside. **Warranty coverage:** Trunk release will be replaced for free; no time or ownership limitation.

MAZDA

2007 CX-7 and CX-9

Problem: These Mazdas may leak oil from the rear differential seal. In TSB 0300411, Mazda says the differential breather was placed too low and could easily become clogged by snow or water. **Warranty coverage:** A new differential with a raised breather covered by the breather boot will be installed for free on a case-by-case basis for an undefined period.

MERCEDES

Model Year 2005-06 ML (164), SLK (171), C (203), CLK (209), E (211), CLS (219), R (251), and Model Year 2005-08 G (463)

Problem: Faulty airbag wiring may cause the airbag warning light to remain lit. **Warranty coverage:** 10 years/160,000 km.

NISSAN

2005-10 Frontier, Pathfinder, and Xterra

Problem: Coolant may leak into the 5-speed transmission. **Warranty coverage:** 8 years/ 130,000 km torque converter coverage for the original owner and any subsequent owners. Owners who already had the radiator or transmission repaired were eligible for reimbursement.

2007 Altima and Sentra and 2008-12 Rogue with 4-cylinder engines

Problem: A leak from the upper end of the oil cooler (TSB NTB11015A). **Warranty coverage:** Removing the cooler and replacing the gaskets are covered under an undefined extended warranty.

TOYOTA

2006-08 RAV4, 2007-08 Solara, 2007-2009 Camry, 2007-2011 Camry Hybrid, 2009 Corolla, and 2009 Matrix

Problem: The 2.4L 4-cylinder engine may be an "oil-burner." In TSBs #SB002411 and #SB009411, the company said the problem was traced to the piston assembly. **Warranty coverage:** Toyota will replace the pistons and rings up to 10 years or 240,000 km.

VOLKSWAGEN

2009-11 Jetta and 2010-11 Golf, all with the 2.0L TDI engine

Problem: The company says it may have a remedy for diesels that won't start in cold weather. In TSB #2111-06 Volkswagen confirms that some vehicles might not start if left in temperatures below freezing. Moisture from the air intake may condense in the intercooler. **Warranty coverage:** VW recommends adding a cold weather intercooler kit that will be provided free of charge on a case-by-case basis for an undefined period.

Parts

Used parts can have a surprisingly long lifespan. Generally, a new gasoline-powered car or minivan can be expected to run with few problems for at least 200,000-300,000 km in its lifetime. Some repairs will crop up at regular intervals along with preventive maintenance, and your yearly repair costs should average about $1,000 after the warranty is over. Buttressing the argument that vehicles get cheaper to operate the longer you keep them, the U.S. Department of Transportation points out that the average vehicle requires one or more major repairs after every 5 years of use. Once these repairs are done, however, the vehicle can then be run relatively trouble-free for another 5 years or more, as long as the environment isn't too hostile. In fact, residents in outlying regions keep their vehicles the longest – an average of 11 years, or longer in some provinces.

Time is on your side in other ways, too. Three years after a model's launch, the replacement parts market usually catches up to consumer demand, although low-volume European makes may take longer.

Parts are unquestionably easier to come by after the 3-year mark through local garages, careful searching at auto wreckers, or looking on the Internet. And a used part usually costs one-third to half the price of a new part. Reconditioned components are another alternative, and they're often guaranteed for as long as, or longer than, new ones. In fact, some savvy shoppers use the ratings in Part Four of this guide to see which parts have a short life and then buy those parts from retailers who give lifetime warranties on brake parts, exhaust systems, tires, batteries, and so on.

Buying from discount outlets or independent garages, or ordering over the Internet can save you big bucks (30%, even more on the Internet but there are risks) comparted to the cost of new parts when compared with dealer charges. Mass merchandisers like Costco are another good source of savings; they cut prices and add free services and lifetime warranties on common replacement items like tires and batteries.

Body parts are a different story. Although car company repair parts can cost 50-100% more than generic aftermarket parts, buyers would be wise to buy original equipment manufacturer (OEM) parts supplied by automakers in order to get body panels that fit well, protect better in a collision, and have maximum rust resistance. Insurance appraisers often substitute cheaper, lower quality aftermarket body parts in collision repairs; however, policyholders who prefer OEM can get an endorsement on their insurance policy that provides OEM body parts for a small charge.

With some European models, you can count on aggravation and expense caused by the slow distribution of parts and high markups. Because these companies have a quasi-monopoly on replacement parts, there are few independent suppliers you can turn to for help. And junkyards, the last-chance repository for inexpensive car parts, are unlikely to carry foreign parts for vehicles that are more than 10 years old or were sold in small numbers.

It's a myth that Japanese and South Korean car parts are hard to find, or aren't very durable. Although this was true in the early 70s when the Japanese automakers just arrived in North America, there is now an abundance of foreign-made parts available. This is due in large part to the popularity of Japanese and Korean vehicles, an influx of independent suppliers, platform sharing where the same parts are used among many different models, and the large reservoir of used foreign parts stocked by junkyards. Among the Korean brands, Kia sometimes has trouble supplying parts for its new models, but after a few years, the supply of recycled and aftermarket parts fills the gap.

The aftermarket parts arena has been flooded by cheap Chinese components, some counterfeit, that don't have the same durability as replacement parts made by auto manufacturers or well-known parts makers. Exhaust systems, brakes, tires, tire valve stems, and a host of other maintenance items are commonly brought in from China. Ironically, these parts of dubious value are sometimes snapped up by carmakers and the big autoparts chains that are mainly interested in getting more for less and end up with poor-quality, failure-prone parts that cost their customers more when they wear out prematurely.

This Chinese-built car tested out as uncrashworthy.

This is one of the reasons that cars made in China have done so poorly in crash tests. An

American auto engineer asked his Chinese colleagues during one of these crash-worthiness trials, "Where is the crush space where crash forces are deflected away from the occupants?" Answer: "What crush space?"

Auto Insurance

The price you pay for insurance can vary significantly, not only between insurance companies but also within the same company over time. But one thing does remain constant in provinces with private auto insurance: Through careful comparison shopping, insurance premiums can be reduced substantially. Insurance premiums for used vehicles are usually cheaper than new-car coverage.

Beware of "Captive" Brokers

Using the Internet to find a lower auto insurance quote and accepting a large deductible are critical to keeping premiums low. Another option if you are in Ontario is to check with the Automobile Protection Association (APA) or the Automobile Consumer Coalition; both groups offer competitive group rates to members with relatively clean driving records.

Use InsuranceHotline.com

InsuranceHotline.com is the largest online quoting service for car insurance in Canada. The agency will run applicants' profiles through its extensive database of insurance companies to find the insurer with the lowest rate.

Here are some *InsuranceHotline.com* findings.

- A family car under $35,000 can cost more to insure than one over $35,000.
- SUVs under $35,000 don't always cost more to insure than a family car or a small luxury model.
- Luxury cars mean luxury premiums, costing on average about $500 more annually to insure than family cars and SUVs.
- Hybrid fuel savings can be wiped out by higher-cost insurance premiums that rival what you would pay to insure a muscle car.
- It does pay to shop around – sometimes, more than $900.

In Ontario, the more expensive markets for auto insurance are located in the Greater Toronto Area.

GTA Insurance Rates vs. Ontario Average

Rank	City	Avg. Annual Insurance Cost	Difference from ON Avg.
#1	Brampton	$2,393	+ 44%
#2	Woodbridge	$2,342	+ 41%
#3	Vaughan	$2,342	+ 41%
#4	Toronto	$2,017	+ 27%
#5	Mississauga	$1,998	+ 26%
#6	Hamilton	$1,987	+ 26%
#7	Thornhill	$1,884	+ 20%
#8	Markham	$1,829	+ 17%
#9	Richmond Hill	$1,755	+ 13%
#10	Ajax	$1,718	+ 11%

Ontario cities with the cheapest car insurance policies were: Belleville, Kingston, Cobourg, and Napanee. (The annual auto insurance premium average for Ontario of $1,538, was calculated by *Insurancehotline.com* based on a single, 35-year-old driver with a clean driving record).

ARC Insurance (*arcinsurance.ca/blog/average-car-insurance-rates-across-canadian-provinces/*) compared the cost of car insurance for 2015 throughout Canada and found the following rates among the provinces:

10. Quebec	$642	5. Alberta $1,004
9. Prince Edward Island	$695	4. Manitoba $1,027
8. New Brunswick	$728	3. Saskatchewan $1,049
7. Nova Scotia	$735	2. British Columbia $1,112
6. Newfoundland & Labrador	$749	1. Ontario $1,281

*indicates a province with public auto insurance. Quebec is a hybrid, with public insurance for injury and private insurance for collision repairs and property damage.

Of course the type of vehicle that's insured affects the cost of insurance as well, sometimes in surprising ways. *Insurancehotline.com* compared insurance premium quotes on 2015 cars, SUVs, trucks, and minivans in six Ontario cities – Ajax, Cambridge, London, Ottawa, Peterborough, and Toronto, and ranked them based on which ones cost less to insure than the rest:

1. Chevrolet Corvette Stingray
2. Volkswagen Golf
3. Porsche Boxster
4. Tesla Model S*
5. Mazda6
6. Honda Accord
7. Mazda3
8. Volkswagen GTI
9. Cadillac CTS
10. Ford Mustang GT
11. BMW M235i
12. Porsche Cayman

Incredible that a Corvette could cost less to insure than a Mazda3, but that's the figure Hotline agents came up with based on their fictional 40-year-old driver with a clean driving and insurance history. From the number one position to the twelfth, the difference in quoted premiums was $408.

There were similar surprises with insurance costs for trucks, SUVs, and minivans.

Trucks
1. Nissan Frontier
2. Honda Ridgeline
3. Nissan Titan
4. Toyota Tacoma
5. GMC Canyon
6. Dodge Ram
7. GMC Sierra
8. Chevrolet Silverado
9. Ford F-Series
10. Toyota Tundra

SUVs
1. Hyundai Santa Fe Sport
2. Dodge Journey
3. Jeep Wrangler
4. Ford Escape
5. Mazda CX-5
6. Jeep Cherokee
7. Nissan Rogue
8. Chevrolet Equinox
9. Honda CR-V
10. Toyota RAV4

Minivans
1. Kia Sedona
2. Chevrolet Orlando
3. Kia Rondo
4. Dodge Grand Caravan
5. Chrysler Town & Country
6. Honda Odyssey
7. Toyota Sienna
8. Mazda Mazda5

From the number one position to the tenth, the difference in quoted truck premiums was a low $165; SUV premium prices varied by $342; and the difference among minivans was $300.

Insurance-Paid Collision Repairs

The Automobile Repair Regulatory Council says the owner of a motor vehicle damaged in an accident has the right to choose the shop that will do the repairs. Be aware that anyone at the scene of an accident who is aggressively promoting a particular repair shop is likely receiving a kickback under the table. Collision repair shops that are eager to pay your insurance deductible, provide a free loaner vehicle or offer other inducements for your business may have paid out too much to perform a quality collision repair.

Do not waste your time or that of several shops getting several estimates. Select a repair facility you feel comfortable with, then notify your agent or insurance company, or ask the shop to call on your behalf. Before you sign any work orders, notify your insurance company or agent, and tell them where the damaged vehicle can be inspected. Your insurance adjuster will require that the damage to the vehicle be inspected. This can be done at an insurance drive-in claim centre or at the shop you have chosen using a video link to the insurance company.

The APA recommends you confirm that a dealer has their own collision repair facility before giving them your repair work. Dealers without their own body shops, or a related body shop in the dealer network, are mainly interested in the markup they'll make on parts sales for the repair and the undisclosed commission they're charging an independent shop for referring your business. When problems arise with the repair, they'll pass the buck. The exception would be an independent collision repair facility approved by the manufacturer for your brand of vehicle.

Most collision and repair centres guarantee their work to some degree, but may not include the paint job. Ask to see a copy of the shop's guarantee and have any information you do not understand clarified. As for the paint warranty, try to get at least a 1-year guarantee.

Choosing a Qualified Repair Shop

Look for signs that indicate repair technician certification and training. Membership in professional trade associations indicates that the shop is keeping up with the latest repair procedures. Also, affiliation with automobile associations like the Canadian Automobile Association (CAA), Alberta Motor Association (AMA), or British Columbia Automobile Association (BCAA) or APA is a plus, because you can use the association to exert pressure when the repair takes too long, or the work isn't done properly.

Before Driving Away with Your Repaired Car

- Check the appearance of the repaired area close up and at a distance.
- Examine the paint for colour match, texture, and overspray.
- Take a test drive to check mechanical repairs if any were required; check lights, the horn, and collision warning/avoidance systems if repairs were made to the front of the vehicle.
- Check that the vehicle is clean.
- Get copies of the paperwork, including the original estimate with parts listed.

If you are not satisfied, mention your concerns immediately and follow up with a written communication (copy your insurer) and ask for a scheduled time to complete the work.

Hits

Acura – CL Series, Integra, and Legend; Audi – A3, A4, A6, S4, S6, TT, TTs; BMW – 135i, 3 Series, and 5 Series; Chrysler – Colt, 2000, Stealth, and Tradesman vans; Ford – Crown Victoria, Econoline vans, Freestyle/Taurus X, Grand Marquis, Mustang, and Ranger; GM – Acadia, Cruze, 2014 Impala, Enclave, Equinox, Express, Firebird, Savana, Tahoe, Terrain, Traverse, Vandura, and Yukon; Honda – Accord, Civic, CR-V, Fit, Prelude, Pilot, and Ridgeline; Hyundai – Accent, Elantra, Genesis, Santa Fe, Tiburon, and Tucson; Kia – Forte, Rio, Rondo, and Soul; Lexus – All models; Lincoln – Town Car; Mazda – 323, CX-5, Mazda3, Mazda5, Miata, and Protegé; Mitsubishi – Outlander and Spyder; Nissan – Frontier, GT-R, Leaf, Rogue, Xterra, and X-Trail; Subaru – Impreza, Legacy, Outback, and Forester; Suzuki – Aerio, Grand Vitara and SX4; Toyota – Avalon, Camry, Corolla, Cressida, Echo, Highlander, Matrix, Sienna, Sequoia, and Tercel, VW – Golf.

Misses

Audi – Early A3, A4, A6, and A8; BMW – 7 Series, MINI Cooper, and X5; Chrysler – 200, Avenger, Dakota, Dart, Neon, Pacifica (the original), Sebring, Sprinter; Daewoo – All models; Fiat – All early North American models (except the 2000 Spider) and the new 500; Ford – Aerostar, C-Max, early Focus, Tempo, and Topaz; GM – Avalanche, Aveo, Catera, Cobalt, Fiero, G6, Grand Prix, HHR, Impala (through 2013), the Lumina/Montana/Relay/Silhouette/Terraza/Trans Sport/Venture/Uplander group of minivans, SRX, and STS; Hyundai – Excel, Pony, pre-2006 Sonata, and Stellar; Jaguar – All models; Jeep – Commander, Compass and Patriot; Kia – Sedona, Sephia, Sorento, Spectra, and 2006 and earlier Sportage; Lada – All models; Land Rover – All models; Lincoln – Continental front-drive; Mercedes-Benz – B-Class, ML, and R-Class; Nissan – Armada, Titan; Saab – All models; Saturn – L-Series, ION, and Relay; Suzuki – Samurai, Verona, and X-90; Toyota – Previa; VW – EuroVan and first-generation Touareg.

Note in the list above how many so-called premium luxury models fell out of favour. And after being abandoned by the automakers themselves, their hapless owners were left with practically worthless, unreliable cars that can't be serviced properly.

Chrysler Automatic Transmissions

Hard to believe, but true. Since the early '90s, practically all models in Chrysler's front-drive lineup have had failure-prone automatic transmissions. Chrysler regularly stiffs its customers with transmission repair bills that average more than $3,000 – about half the average vehicle's worth after 5 years – when the warranty expires. Since this is far less than what a new car or minivan would cost, most owners pay the bill and then hop onto the transmission merry-go-round, replacing the same transmission at regular intervals. Just ask any transmission shop.

And from *www.dodgeforum.com*:

According to *Consumers Reports*, the transmission is "clunky" in their tests. Well, it is, especially when cold. It wants to get into 2nd and 3rd so quickly, that the shift is a bit jerky . . . I bought my 2011 Dodge Grand Caravan in May and as soon as it hit 5000 miles, I noticed a bang between 1st and 2nd gear. It took 4 days to get an appointment at the local dealer. I told them I shouldn't be driving the car with this shifting problem, they didn't seem to be worried. I brought the van in and they had to wait 5 days for a part to come in for it. I got the van back to find out I had no reverse and the check engine light came on. Brought the van back the next morning and they told me they had done a complete rebuild on the transmission and that a pump had gone. Got the van back a week later and noticed the same banging from 1st to 2nd gear and a shudder when in reverse. Brought it back again, and just picked the van up today to find out it was low on transmission fluid. There is no dipstick, and the service manager said the only way to know the fluid is low is by going on the computer.

Beginning in 2014, Chrysler started changing over to a new powertrain with a re-engineered transmission that includes 9-speeds and the Pentastar V6 engine. Early reports show the powertrain is as unreliable as ever and potentially hazardous.

The 2014 Jeep Cherokee was the first light vehicle in the world with a 9-speed transmission. Chrysler says increasing the number of gears from six to nine helps to reduce emissions, improve fuel efficiency, and adds to the vehicle's off-road capability. These claims are disputed by owner postings to *safercar.gov* where the 2014-2015 Cherokee has racked up an inordinate number of safety-related complaints:

My transmission shifts hard from 1st to 2nd, and from 2nd to 3rd. It also has a pronounced "wobble" after it shifts from 1st into 2nd gear, and continues until it shifts hard into 3rd gear at about 20 mph. After a stop will not go into 1st gear for a second or two, then abruptly surges forward with more speed than the amount of accelerator you are giving it. When decelerating, the transmission will actually go into 4th gear and add fuel causing the tachometer to go up between 500 and 1000 rpm. The transmission, although touted as a "9-speed", is useless, as it will not go into 9th either automatically or manually at any speed below 75 or 76 mph even though it easily could at 67 or 68 mph with sufficient rpm to still maintain speed. When I reported these problems to the dealer, I was told that this is normal operation for this transmission.

. . .

Transmission failure three times in the first 3000 miles. First failure was while stationary. Second was at 30 mph and 3rd at 65 mph. Failure is unpredictable and causes immediate drop in speed which could result in an accident. Car was "fixed" by Jeep dealer each time; car failed in same manner all three times.

Diesel Defects

Chrysler

Although Chrysler's Cummins engine has been the most reliable diesel sold by American automakers, it also has had some serious manufacturing flaws, involving lift-pump failures that compromise injector-pump performance. Here's how independent mechanic Chuck Arnold (*chuck@thepowershop.com*) describes the problem.

> Low fuel pressure is very dangerous because it is possible for the engine to run very well right up to the moment of failure. There may be no symptom of a problem at all before you are walking. If you notice extended cranking before startup of your Cummins 24-Valve engine you should get your lift pump checked out fast. Addition of fuel lubricant enhancing additives to every tank of fuel may minimize pump damage and extend pump life.

Ford

F-Series equipped with the 6.0L Power Stroke diesel engine were so badly flawed that they couldn't be fixed, forcing Ford to buy back over 500 units. In late October 2013, the company settled a class-action lawsuit related to the 6.0L engine found in 2003-2007 SuperDuty trucks, vans, Excursions, and ambulances. Owners complained of a myriad of problems with the Navistar design. Components affected ranged from injectors, the fuel injection control module, EGR system, and turbocharger. Power Strokes also have a history of fuel injectors that leak into the crankcase, and, on the 7.3L diesel, water can leak into the fuel tank, causing the engine to seize. Other glitches affect the turbocharger, the fuel injection control pressure sensor, and the engine control software.

Both Ford and General Motors have had problems with snow accumulation in the air filter element, restricting air passage to the engine and possibly causing severe engine damage. Both companies are liable for the repair of any damage caused by this poor design. Or did they imagine Canada was a snow-free zone?

General Motors

GM's diesel engine failures primarily affect the 6.5L and 6.6L Duramax engine. The 6.5L powerplants are noted for cracked blocks, broken crankshafts, cracks in the main bearing webbing, cracked cylinder heads, coolant in the oil, loss of power, hard starting, low oil pressure, and oil contamination. Duramax 6.6L engines have been plagued by persistent oil leaks and excessive oil burning, and by defective turbochargers, fuel-injection pumps, and injectors, causing seized engines, chronic stalling, loss of power, hard starts, and excessive fuel consumption.

The APA has identified an independent truck service specialist in the Montreal area that can fix your defective Ford or GM pickup diesel engine and keep it running:

Sam's Diesel Service
9800 Henri Bourassa West
Saint Laurent, Quebec
Tel: 514-336-2045
(ask for shop owner Sam Kassam)

Safety First

Looking through Part Four can help you make a list of safe and reliable used car buys to consider before you even leave the house.

The best indicator of a car's overall safety is National Highway Traffic Safety Administration (NHTSA) and Insurance Institute for Highway Safey (IIHS) crash-worthiness ratings, applicable to most vehicles made and sold over the past several decades in North America. IIHS uses more severe standards and rates head restraint effectiveness, roof crush resistance, and offset frontal collision protection as well. Results from these two agencies are posted for each model rated in Part Four. For readers who wish to go directly to the respective website of either safety group, see *safercar.gov* or *www.iihs.org/ratings*.

Frontal-offset crash test of a Hyundai Tucson by the Insurance Institute for Highway Safety (IIHS).

Other national and international testing agencies can be found at *www.crashtest.com/netindex.htm*. This site shows the results of early crash tests of cars that were sold in Australia, Europe, and Japan and that are just now coming to the North American market.

Of course, no one expects to be in a collision, but NHTSA estimates that every vehicle will be in two accidents of varying severity during its lifetime. So why not put the average on your side by checking out the crashworthiness ratings in Part Four or at NHTSA's *safercar.gov*?

The Tata Nano is a primitive, no frills mini-compact. A radio and fire extinguisher are optional.

Used Better Than New

Almost two-thirds of the cars sold in Canada are second-hand, up from about 56% just over a decade ago. Of the 4.4 million automobiles that were sold in Canada in 2010, most were second-hand (2.9 million). Although a sizeable number of used Canadian SUVs and luxury cars are being shipped to the U.S. thanks to our weakened loonie, plenty of good quality used vehicles are still left on this side of the border. In fact the supply of used vehicles is once again becoming plentiful in Canada as more vehicles are beginning to come off 3- and 4-year leases.

Blame it on increased longevity – of the driver – and of the car (or more so, the truck). We discussed the phenomenon of senior drivers populating our highways in the previous chapter, but we also should mention that many older drivers are perfectly happy owning "senior" cars, as well. More than 6 million of the 31.7 million cars on the road (2013) are 11.4 years old or older and R. L. Polk Data says, half of all the cars manufactured in the last 25 years are still on the road today. Auto consultant DesRosiers notes that in Canada new car buyers keep their vehicle for 8-9 years. In the U.S., they usually sell around the 5th year of ownership.

Not surprisingly, pickups last longer than cars. Over 20% of all the Chevrolet pickups sold 25 years ago are still chugging along our highways and Chrysler and Ford pickups aren't far behind.

Buy Used and Save Thousands

Buying a used vehicle is easier and less annoying than buying new and with a little bit of homework and patience you can find reliable wheels for less than half what the car originally cost. Plus, there is less of a showroom shakedown – confusing figures, payment plans, and costly "extras" – awaiting you. You get a car that has already been pre-scratched, dented, and corroded, but this saves you from that sickening feeling when someone dents your car door while parked at the supermarket. The transformation from new to used occurs as soon as the sales title passes from dealer to a new owner, thus theoretically making every car sold a used vehicle that immediately loses 10-20% of its original value; that loss to the original owner benefits used car buyers.

Most dealers expect price haggling because they know competition from private sales gives buyers a large incentive to bring down inflated asking prices. Dealers also make more money selling used vehicles than they make selling new cars and trucks, and they aren't burdened by things like the manufacturer's suggested retail price, freight charges, options loading, new car "co-op" advertising charges imposed by the manufacturer, reduced margins, and warranty chargebacks. The savings generated by these simpler transactions often go straight into the dealer's and buyer's pockets.

Car dealers get their vehicles from fleets, lessees, wholesalers, trade-ins, and auctions. Some of the less reputable dealers buy damaged vehicles at auction that other dealers unloaded because they weren't good enough to sell to their own customers. Other dealers supply "curbsiders" dodgy used vehicles to sell from private homes posing as their original owners.

The majority of private sales are comprised of vehicles 6 years or older. Franchised dealers tend to limit themselves to vehicles that are 5 years old or newer. Independent used-car dealers run the gamut from 1-year-old daily rentals, 3- to 4-year-old lease returns, to anything that can be driven away.

USED IS THE SMART CHOICE

It costs a lot to purchase a new car or SUV. In fact, many of our readers tell us that the cost of their new car exceeded the downpayment on their first house! Read on for more reasons why Canadians increasingly prefer to buy used vehicles rather than new ones.

Less Initial Cash Outlay, Slower Vehicle Depreciation, and Better and Cheaper Parts Availability

New-vehicle prices average around $32,000 and insurance can cost almost $2,200 a year for young drivers. The CAA calculates that once you add financing costs, maintenance, taxes, and a host of other expenses over an average of 18,000 kilometers, the yearly outlay for a Honda Civic LX would be about $9,100 (or 51 cents per km). A Camry LE would cost over $1,400 more at $10,500 (58 cents per km) and the Chevrolet Equinox LT would require $11,900 (66 cents per km).

The annual new-car expenditure above can be reduced by up to 50% if a vehicle is purchased used, figuring in a substantially lower purchase price, lower taxes, and no freight or admininstration fees. (*www.caa.ca/wp-content/uploads/2012/06/CAA_Driving_Cost_English_2013_web.pdf*).

For a comprehensive comparative analysis of all the costs involved in owning a vehicle over 1- to 10-year periods, access Alberta's consumer information website at *www.agric.gov.ab.ca/app24/costcalculators/vehicle/getvechimpls.jsp.*

Depreciation works for you

If someone were to ask you to invest in stocks or bonds guaranteed to be worth less than half their initial purchase value after 3-4 years, you'd probably head for the door. But this is exactly the trap you're falling into when you buy a new vehicle that will likely lose 40-50% of its value after 4 years.

When you buy used, the situation is altogether different. That same vehicle can be purchased off-leases, 3 or 4 years old in good condition with some the manufacturer's warranty remaining for a bit more than half its original cost.

Defects Can't Hide

Avoid nasty surprises by having your chosen used vehicle checked out by an independent mechanic (for $80-$150) before you purchase. This examination protects you against the vehicle's defects and gives you a powerful negotiating tool, where the cost of any estimated repairs can be used to bargain down the purchase price.

Having the vehicle inspected prior to the sale is the most effective way of making sure you won't get stuck with a lemon or pay too much for a vehicle that needs a lot of maintenance. A complete vehicle inspection includes a visual examination of the body and chassis to spot obvious collision damage. A thorough inspection takes from about 45 minutes to 2 hours depending on the vehicle. A more complicated vehicle with lots of accessories, or a vehicle in uneven or poor condition, requires more time. Vans can also take longer because the engine bay is crowded. The inspection should include a road test and a written report should be provided.

Not all inspections are created equal. The facilities that follow have been chosen from the list of shops provided to APA members, and have performed well in the past.

MONTREAL AREA

Andrew Bleakley
Mobile Vehicle Inspection Service
(514) 890-5000

The APA's recommended mobile used car inspection service includes a meticulous examination of body and mechanical components and an inspection of the odometer for signs of tampering. The service costs $120 ($10 off for APA members) including taxes, plus an extra $10 or $20 if you're farther away from the city centre. A visit can usually be arranged within 1 or 2 days of your phone call. The inspection includes a detailed written report. This service is available on the Island of Montreal and some areas of Laval. There is a modest surcharge for off-island locations, including the South Shore, north to Saint-Jerome, and east to the Terrebonne and Mascouche areas.

GREATER TORONTO AREA

Start Auto Electric
401 Dundas St. E.
Toronto, Ontario
416-868-1727

Vertex Auto Repair
336 Birchmount Rd.
Toronto, Ontario
416-690-7196

Gary's Automotive
1435 Wallace Rd.
Oakville, Ontario
905-827-3771

Mark-Caesar Auto Service Ltd
986 Roselawn Ave.
Toronto, Ontario
416-783-6975

Wrenchspinner
901 Kipling Ave.
Etobicoke, Ontario
416-233-4671

Graf Auto Centre
151 Bentworth Ave.
North York, Ontario
416-789-3423

A basic inspection starts at $150 ($130 with the APA membership). Additional charges apply for VIN information.

ALBERTA

Kirkham Auto
9298 Horton Road S.W., Calgary, AB
(403) 253-2033

GREATER VANCOUVER

Obtaining a pre-purchase vehicle inspection in Vancouver can be difficult. Some repair shops perform only cursory inspections that will identify tune-up and light maintenance opportunities for the shop. Others will refuse an inspection outright because they don't want to get into a conflict with a dealer. The mobile inspection service recommended by some used car dealers mystery shopped by the APA performed an incomplete inspection and checked off items that had not been verified.

Eye on Collision Repairs
Dennis Pieschel
Located in Delta B.C.
604-323-3770
eyeoncollision@dccnet.com

If you're considering a rebuilt vehicle or have reason to believe the vehicle may have been involved in a significant collision, this is the must-see expert for consumers in the Lower Mainland. A pre-purchase inspection costs $150 and up at a facility in Delta, or for a small additional charge a mobile inspection at a location closer to the seller. If you bought a badly hit car, Dennis Pieschel is the expert you'll want in your corner to support your claim. A report with supporting photos that you can use in Court costs from $200 to $250. Mr. Pieschel also acts as an expert in accelerated depreciation cases for luxury vehicles that have lost value after extensive collision repairs. Mr. Pieschel is a former Insurance Corporation of British Columbia (ICBC) collision estimator. He offers an inspection-only service of the chassis and body for prior collision repairs; he does not offer a general mechanical inspection nor perform repairs.

Hemrich Brothers Garage
8506 Ash Street, (Marpole) Vancouver, B.C.
(604) 325-8511

A competent mechanical repair facility with good alignment equipment and the knowledge required to use it, derived from setting up vehicles for competition.

If you can't get permission to have the vehicle inspected elsewhere, you should probably walk away from the deal, no matter how tempting the selling price if it's a private sale. A private seller who forbids an inspection is likely trying to put one over on you. The standard excuses are that the vehicle isn't insured, that the registration or plate has expired, or that the vehicle has a dead battery. These are good indicators that you are likely dealing with a curbsider who is peddling junk that they may not even have registered in their name.

Quebec is the only province that requires dealers to permit both a road test and an offsite inspection at a location within a reasonable distance. APA secret shoppers discovered that in Toronto, about a third of franchised dealers prohibit a pre-purchase inspection, even of their newest pre-owned vehicles. Used car dealers were much more flexible. In some cases new and used vehicle dealers made getting the inspection so inconvenient that most consumers would pass. If you're faced with this situation, here are some partial workarounds.

- More than likely you will be told no independent inspection is needed, because the vehicle was checked by the dealer and is 100% OK. Ask for a copy of the dealer's inspection report and have the copy included with your paperwork.

- Before you sign, make the seller write into the sales agreement any representations made about the condition of the vehicle or its prior history: "Accident free, 100% original, no claims, full warranty" etc.

- Try to get the dealer to write a full warranty into the sales agreement, even if it's short (5 or 7 days). That will give you enough time to have the vehicle checked by a third party – it's not ideal, but the handwritten warranty might be just enough leverage to get the dealer regulator involved on your side. A powertrain warranty from a third party is not the same; you'll want a full warranty from the dealer, given that no inspection is permitted.

No Surprises

Smart customers shopping for a reliable used car can run an Internet history check on a vehicle and its previous owners through CarProof at *www.carproof.com/order*. A comprehensive search costs $51.45, or $71.45 if you want an ICBC full report as well. Try to get answers to the questions listed below from the seller or dealer before paying for a history search.

What is its ownership history?

The best is a one-owner vehicle. Original owners spend more to acquire their vehicle and are generally perceived as more motivated to maintain them. The original owner likely enjoyed the benefit of warranty coverage that provided free repairs.

A lease customer may not have considered themselves to be the "owner," and consequently skimped on maintenance. But a lease carries the benefit of a forced disposal after 3 or 4 years; unlike an owner, a lessee doesn't get to choose when to turn the vehicle in to avoid an expensive repair. Furthermore most lease returns are still covered by the balance of the factory new vehicle warranty.

Daily rental companies never report collision repairs to vehicle history services. A dealer who uses a history report to "prove" a former daily rental is collision free is usually lying.

The rental companies collude in the deception; if you call them with the vehicle's VIN you will be told the collision records have been destroyed or are otherwise unavailable.

How did you acquire the vehicle?

Best would be from the original owner who turned it in, or the retailer who sold the vehicle originally. This is usually the case only with franchised dealers. If the dealer sold the vehicle originally, they likely can provide at least partial service records and other information about its history.

What is the collision history?

Most dealers will disclose only what's in the vehicle history report. The APA discovered that reporting reliability varies by province. CarProof, generally recognized as the most complete report, was very reliable in British Columbia, picking up over 90% of damage identified by a professional vehicle appraiser, including vandalism, plus some other minor claims missed by the appraiser. CarProof was less reliable for Ontario market vehicles, but still very helpful. In Quebec more than 40% of accident repaired vehicles for sale on dealer lots in the APA study showed up clean in CarProof's reports; some of them had been rather severely damaged.

Not all collision damage is equal. In the absence of structural damage, replacing the front bumper, hood and a fender shouldn't preclude a sale. Cosmetic damage to the side or rear of the vehicle resulting in one or two panels repaired and repainted also should not put you off. The problem with extensive collision repairs is that a non-expert has no good way of determining if they were done properly or not, and mechanical repair shops that are likely to offer a pre-purchase inspection aren't qualified to examine bodywork. The worst place to buy a used car with a claim on it? Vancouver. The APA discovered many independent dealers there specialize in reselling poorly rebuilt, potentially dangerous, wrecks.

Is it a local vehicle or from out of province?

Theoretically it shouldn't matter, but it does. Dealers take advantage of loopholes in consumer protection and provincial vehicle inspection programs to export vehicles with a checkered history to another province. An unscrupulous seller may know that the history search is missing some important information about a vehicle from another province. Is there a sticker from the original dealer on the vehicle, or is their name on the license plate frame? It may be worth calling the dealer in the vehicle's home province for information on its service history.

Do you have the service records?

If the dealer sold the vehicle originally, they should have some information. The previous owner may have left paperwork in the glove box. Look inside; you may be surprised.

When to Buy

Used vehicles are best bought in the summer or fall when trade-ins swell dealer inventories and private sellers don't mind showing their vehicles outdoors. Prices are higher at this time of the year, but you'll have a good choice of vehicles and shopping is easy. In winter, prices decline substantially, and dealers and private sellers are generally easier to bargain with because buyers are scarce and weather conditions don't allow sellers to present their wares in the best light. In spring and early summer, prices go up significantly, as private sellers become more active and buyers who put off shopping over the winter come into the market.

Private Sellers

Private sellers are your best source for a cheap and reliable used vehicle because you're on an equal bargaining level with a vendor who isn't trying to profit from your inexperience. A good private sale price would be approximately 20% less than the asking price advertised by local dealers.

Remember, very few sellers, be they dealers or private parties, expect to get his or her asking price. As with price reductions on home listings, a reduction on the advertised price is common with private sellers. Dealers usually won't cut more than $500-$1,500 off their advertised prices for mainstream used vehicles, but there are exceptions.

It is also a good idea to draw up a bill of sale that gives all the pertinent details of your used-car transaction. (See the following pages for one that you may use as your guide.)

BUYING WITH CONFIDENCE

No matter from whom you're buying a used vehicle, there are a few rules you should follow to obtain a good price.

First, have a good idea of what you want and the price you're willing to pay. If you have a preapproved line of credit, that will keep the number crunching and extra fees to a minimum. Finally, be resolute and polite, but make it clear that you are a serious buyer and want to keep the transaction as simple as possible.

Here's a successful real-world technique used by Kurt Binnie, a frequent *Lemon-Aid* tipster.

> Imagine the surprise of the used-car salesman when I pulled out my BlackBerry and did a VIN search right in front of him using Carfax [*Lemon-Aid* recommends the Canadian firm CarProof]. Threw him right off balance. Carfax results for Ontario vehicles give a good indication, but not the complete MTO [Ministry of Transportation, Ontario] history. I bought the UVIP [Used Vehicle Information Package] . . . before closing the deal. For the car I ended

Bill of Sale

- **Sections 1 and 2 must be completed** in order to make this Bill of Sale acceptable for vehicle registration. Completion of section 3, on the back of this form, is optional.
- Two copies of this Bill of Sale should be completed. The buyer keeps the original and the seller keeps the copy.
- Alterations or corrections made while completing the vehicle information section should be initialled by the buyer and seller.

SECTION 1

SELLER(S) INFORMATION

Name(s) *(Last, First, Second)*   Telephone Number

Address   Street   City / Town   Province / State   Postal Code / Zip Code

Personal Identification:

VEHICLE INFORMATION

Year	Make	Model or Series	Style

Vehicle Identification Number (VIN) / Serial Number	Body Color	Roof Color	Odometer Reading

BUYER(S) INFORMATION

Name(s) *(Last, First, Second)*   Telephone Number

Address   Street   City / Town   Province / State   Postal Code / Zip Code

Personal Identification:

This vehicle was sold for the sum of:

_____ Dollars $_____

(Sum written in full)

(Subject to the terms and special conditions which appear in Section 3 on the back of this form)

SECTION 2

GENERAL INFORMATION

Dated at: _____

City / Town   Province / State   Country

on _____ .

I certify that all information shown above is true to the best of my knowledge.

_____   _____
Signature of Buyer   Signature of Seller

_____   _____
Signature of Buyer   Signature of Seller

_____   _____
Signature of Witness   Signature of Witness

REG3126 (2011/01)

SECTION 3 (OPTIONAL)

SPECIAL CONDITIONS OF SALE

1. The vehicle described on the front of this form is:
   Check the appropriate box(es)

   a) Free of all liens and encumbrances: ☐ Yes ☐ No   If No, please give names of lien holders:

   _____

   b) Being paid for in full: ☐ Yes ☐ No

   Being paid by: ☐ Cash ☐ Cheque ☐ Money Order ☐ Other *(please specify)*: _____

2. Payment Terms: _____

3. Vehicle was last registered in: _____

   Province / State   Country

4. Special conditions of sale *(if any)*: _____

   _____

   _____

   _____

General Information:

- The law in the Province of Alberta requires a vehicle to be insured prior to registration. Documentary proof of vehicle insurance is required. Legislation allows a person to whom a valid licence plate is issued to transfer the licence plate to a newly purchased vehicle to be registered within 14 days of the date on their Bill of Sale.

  The above does not apply to commercial vehicles used for the transportation of goods or passengers for compensation.

- A vehicle entering Alberta from another jurisdiction requires a safety inspection. Information can be obtained from a Registry Agent. A listing of local Registry Agents can be found in the telephone directory under Licence and Registry Services; or visit Service Alberta's website at www.servicealberta.gov.ab.ca for comprehensive registries and consumer information and services.

- In addition to the Bill of Sale, other identification is required to obtain Alberta registration. Where possible, obtain Section 2 of the previous Alberta vehicle registration certificate.

- The prospective purchaser can determine whether a vehicle is free of liens and encumbrances in Alberta by contacting a Registry Agent.

  In order to perform a search, a Registry Agent will require the vehicle identification number (VIN) / serial number of the vehicle. A request for a search can be made in person or in writing. There is a fee for this service.

- Vehicle Information Reports are available from a Registry Agent. There is a fee for each service.

- The buyer must produce a copy of a properly completed Bill of Sale, that includes the same information as shown on this standardized form, in order to register and licence a vehicle in Alberta.

This form is provided as a courtesy by Service Alberta to ensure that sufficient information is contained within the Bill of Sale to permit licensing and registration of the described vehicle by the new owner.

No liability attaches to the Crown through the use of this document in respect of the sale of this vehicle. Any dispute arising from the sale becomes a civil matter among the parties named in this document.

REG3126 (2011/01)

Source: Alberta government site: *www.registryedmonton.com/uploads/BillOfSaleReg3126.pdf.*

Kurt's letter goes on to describe how he avoids negotiations with sales staff and managers. He figures out the price he's willing to pay beforehand, using a combination of book values and the prices listed at *www.autotrader.ca* (*www.vmrcanada. com/canada_makes.htm* is also a good Canadian source for used car prices). He then test drives the vehicle, runs the VIN through his smartphone, and then makes a point-blank, one-time offer to the dealer. He has also found that used-car sales personnel often have no knowledge about the vehicles on their lots beyond their asking price.

Primary Precautions When Buying Privately

If you're buying privately write up a sales agreement, even if it's just handwritten, that includes a clause stating that there are no outstanding traffic violations or liens against the vehicle. If a lien does exist, you should contact the creditor(s) listed to find out whether any debts have been paid. If a debt is outstanding, you should arrange with the vendor to pay the creditor the outstanding balance. If the debt is larger than the purchase price of the car, it's up to you to decide whether you wish to complete the deal. If the seller agrees to clear the title personally, make sure that you receive a written relinquishment of title from the creditor before transferring any money to the other party. Make sure the title doesn't show an "R" for "rebuilt," since this indicates that the vehicle was written off as a total loss and may not have been properly repaired. A rebuilt title reduces the value of the vehicle by 30-50%, and is a good indication that your seller is really a curbsider passing him- or herself off as a private party.

Ask the seller to show you the vehicle's original sales contract and a few repair bills in order to ascertain how well it was maintained and if it has any unexpired repair warranties. The bills should show the odometer readings increasing progressively and will also indicate what repairs were performed. If none of these can be produced, that's a negative. The original contract of sale likely was accompanied by a financing contract. Verify that the loan was paid. If you're still not sure that the vehicle is free of liens, ask your bank or credit union advisor to check for you. If no clear answer is forthcoming, look for something else.

A vehicle sold as safety certified can still turn into a lemon or be dangerous to drive. The certification process can be sabotaged if a minimal number of components are checked, the mechanic is incompetent, or colluded with the seller. "Certified" is not the same as having a warranty to protect you from engine seizure or transmission failure. It means only that safety equipment like the lights, suspension, steering and brakes met the minimum safety standards on the day the vehicle was tested.

Flood damage can be hard to see, but it impairs ABS, power steering, and airbag functioning (potentionally making deployment slower). Parts of Canada have become havens for rebuilt American wrecks. Write-offs are also shipped from provinces where there are stringent disclosure regulations to provinces where there are lax rules or no rules at all. If you suspect your vehicle is flood-damaged, is a rebuilt wreck from the States, or was once a taxi, CarFax can help with its history.

Don't Pay Too Little

Don't be surprised to find that many national price guides have prices that appear unrealistic in your market. It's important not to focus too strongly on buying the cheapest vehicle. A better strategy is to shop for condition not price. It may be worth visiting a few high-priced sellers early in your search so you have a good idea of what the market can offer. Bring an ad from one of the cheaper sellers with you; you can always produce it as a negotiating tool.

If you'd like to buy smart when buying used, consider the tips below.

- Choose a vehicle that's 3 to 5 years old, has a good reliability record, and is easy to repair. The money you save from the extra years' depreciation and lower insurance premiums will more than make up for some additional maintenance costs compared to a new vehicle.

- Look for off-lease models with low mileage (50,000 to 80,000 km) and a good reputation.

- Buy a vehicle that's depreciated more than average simply because of its bland styling, unpopular colour (dark blue, beige, green and champagne are out; white, black and grey are in), lack of high-performance features, or discontinuation.

- Buy a cheaper twin or rebadged model like a fully loaded Camry instead of a Lexus ES, a Pontiac Vibe in lieu of a Toyota Matrix, or a Chevrolet Silverado instead of a GMC Sierra.

- Buy a well-equipped mid-size or large sedan, or a minivan. Your $20,000 savings will pay the gas bill many times over, and the vehicle can be resold a few years down the road, with moderate depreciation compared to a new version of the same model.

Figuring Out How Much to Pay

The best way to determine the price range of the vehicle you are looking for is to check local advertising on the Internet. The *Auto Trader* website at *www.auto trader.ca* will let you see what prices other Canadians are trying to sell your chosen vehicle for. From there, you may wish to get a second opinion by accessing Vehicle Market Research International's Canadian used-car prices at *www.vmrcanada.com*. It is one of the few free sources that list wholesale and retail values for used cars in Canada. The site even includes a handy calculator that adjusts a vehicle's value according to model, mileage, and a variety of options.

Black Book and *Red Book* price guides, found in most libraries, banks, and credit unions, are useful to anyone buying or selling a used vehicle. Both guides are accessible on the Internet. To read the *Canadian Black Book* values, simply copy the following URL into your web browser: *www.canadianblackbook.com/used-cars.html*. This site lists the vehicle's trade-in and future value, as well as the asking price based upon your Canadian postal code. No other identification is required.

Now, if you want to use the *Canadian Red Book Vehicle Valuation Guide*, which seems more attuned to Quebec and Ontario sales, you can order single copies of their used car and light truck wholesale and retail price guide for $19.95 at *www. canadianredbook.com* (an annual subscription costs $105). There are no restrictions as to who may subscribe. Price guides cannot realistically account for vehicle condition and local markets.

Cross-Border Sales

Now that the Canadian dollar is worth about $0.77 U.S., there's not much to gain buying a vehicle in the United States. However, shopping in the States for upscale exotic sports cars, luxury vehicles, or a convertible may be worthwhile if you have a particular vehicle in mind that has limited availability in Canada.

Here's what to do.

1. Check with Ottawa to see if the used vehicle you covet can be imported into Canada (call the Registrar of Imported Vehicles at 1-888-848-8240, or visit their website at *www.riv.ca*).

2. Take a trip across the border to scout out what is available from all dealers. Compare your findings with what's offered by Canadian cross-border dealers.

3. Verify if the price is appealing once taxes and transport charges are considered.

Hire a broker or deal directly with the dealer. Be wary of private sellers, because your legal recourses will be limited in cross-border transactions.

Rental and Leased Vehicles

Budget, Hertz, Avis, National, and other rental companies sell vehicles that have 1-2 years of service and 30,000-60,000 km on the odometer. These rental companies allow an independent inspection by a mechanic chosen by the buyer, as well as arrange for competitive financing. They may provide an in-house vehicle history as well.

Rental vehicles are recent models with popular equipment; they sell for significantly less than dealer demonstrators, and come with strong guarantees, like Budget's 30-day money-back guarantee at some of its retail outlets (including three in B.C.). Rental-car companies also usually settle customer complaints without much hassle. Rental agencies tend to keep their stock of cars on the outskirts of town near the airport (particularly in Alberta and B.C.) and advertise locally. Sales are held year-round as inventory is replenished. Late summer and early fall are usually the best times to see a wide selection because the new rentals arrive during this time period. Most rental vehicles received only basic maintenance and were used hard, but barring real neglect (no oil changes) or a major collision repair, vehicles are generally in decent condition and have a generous measure of their original warranty. If you're financing your purchase entirely, it can make more sense to buy a new car, as you will qualify for near-zero-rate financing that will erase some of the savings possible with a daily rental financed at market rates.

Vehicles that have just come off a 3- or 5-year lease are priced lower than former daily rentals, generally have low mileage, and are usually reasonably well maintained. You'll find these vehicles at new car dealers (often taken in trade) and independent dealers (bought at auction).

Repossessed Vehicles

Repossessed vehicles frequently come from bankrupt small businesses or subprime borrowers who failed to make their finance payments. They are usually found at auctions, but finance companies and banks sometimes sell them as well. The biggest problem with repossessed sport-utilities and pickups is that they may have been damaged or neglected by their financially troubled owners. Although you rarely get to test drive or closely examine these vehicles, a local dealer may be able to produce a vehicle maintenance history by running the VIN through their manufacturer's database and confirm that the warranty hasn't been cancelled.

New-Car Dealers

New-car dealerships aren't bad places to pick up good used cars or trucks. Sure, prices are about 20% higher than for vehicles sold privately, but discounting and 0% financing can trim used-car costs dramatically. Plus, dealers are insured against selling stolen vehicles or vehicles with finance or other liens owing. Most will allow prospective buyers to have the vehicle inspected by an independent garage or at their own facility (convenient and the inspection report can become part of the agreement), offer a much wider choice of models, and have their own repair facilities to do warranty work. In addition, if there's a possibility of getting post-warranty "goodwill" compensation from the manufacturer, your dealer can provide additional leverage, particularly if the dealership is a franchisee for the model you have purchased. Finally, if things do go terribly wrong, dealers have deeper pockets than private sellers, so there's a better chance of winning a court judgment.

Provinces are beginning to crack down on dealers who sell defective used cars. Under the revised regulations, a mechanical assessment will be completed by a licensed journeyman technician with a trade certificate as an Automotive Service

Technician or Heavy Equipment Technician under the *Apprenticeship and Industry Training Act*. (See: *www.transportation.alberta.ca*. under the "Drivers and Vehicles" tab.)

Manufacturer "Certified" used vehicles

The word "Certified" doesn't mean much. Ideally, it tells you the vehicle has been inspected and reconditioned under the manufacturer's supervision. You may be surprised to learn that there is no direct supervision by the automakers – nobody sent by the automaker to inspect the car, nobody double checking paperwork. Some dealers simply slap a "certified" sticker on the car, even before inspecting it, figuring they can take care of "certification" after they have a signed offer with some deposit money on the table.

The primary benefit of automaker certified used car programs is the complete and well-priced warranties offered with them. You can purchase coverage comparable to the original warranty for 2 or 3 years. Claims handling is available with no deductible or repair limit, and the warranty is accepted at all dealerships selling the brand; that's a greater degree of security and convenience than independent company warranties can offer.

Used-car leasing

Leasing a used car is a lousy idea. Sure, leasing has been touted as a method of making the high cost of vehicle ownership more affordable, but don't you believe it. It's generally costlier than an outright purchase, and, for used vehicles, the pitfalls far outweigh any advantages.

Lenders who lease used vehicles frequently want to benefit from the looser rules applicable to leasing disclosure and repossessions, compared to conventional installment sale financing. Used car lease payments are frequently only a little cheaper than new car leases after you add the price of an extended warranty. The used car lease has the disadvantages of both leasing (always making payments) and owning (repair bills, unpredictability). If you want to trade used vehicles often, the better solution is to go for a lease takeover on a site like *LeaseBusters.com*. You'll have the added benefit of no upfront fees when you take over someone else's lease.

Used-Car Dealers

The retailing environment is more relaxed at used car dealerships, and the personnel usually know more about their vehicles than the sales staff at new car dealerships. There is less pressure to close the deal; only rarely is a manager brought in to strong-arm a buyer.

Used-car dealers usually sell their vehicles for less than what new-car dealers charge. However, their vehicles may be worth less because they don't get the first pick of top-quality trade-ins. Some independent urban dealerships are marginal operations that can't invest much money in reconditioning their vehicles, which often come from auctions and new-car dealers reluctant to sell the vehicles to their own customers. And most used-car dealers don't always have repair facilities to honour the warranties they provide (but they are a valuable resource if you want to know where to get your vehicle repaired fast and inexpensively in their area). Often, their credit is easier to access (but more expensive) than financing offered by franchised dealers.

Used-car dealers operating in small towns are an entirely different breed. They're often family-run businesses that recondition and resell cars and trucks from within their communities. Routine servicing is usually done in-house, and more complicated repairs are subcontracted out to specialized garages nearby. These small outlets survive by word-of-mouth advertising and wouldn't last long if they didn't deal fairly with local customers. Their prices are sometimes higher than elsewhere due to the better quality of their used vehicles and the cost of reconditioning and repairing what they sell under warranty.

Auctions

First of all, make sure it's a legitimate auction. Many auctions open to private buyers are fronts for used-car dealers, pretending to hold auctions that are no more than weekend selling sprees.

Furthermore, you'll need patience, smarts, and luck to pick up anything worthwhile. Government auctions – places where the mythical $50 Jeeps are sold – are fun to attend but somewhat overrated as places to find bargains. The odds are against you: It's hard to determine the condition of the vehicles put up for bid; prices can go way out of control; and auction employees, professional sellers, their relatives, and their friends usually pick over the good stuff long before you ever see it.

To attend commercial auctions is to swim with the piranhas. They are frequented by "ringers" who bid up the prices, and by professional dealers who pick up cheap, worn-out vehicles unloaded by new-car dealers and independents. There are no guarantees, cash is required, and quality is variable. Remember, too, that auction purchases are subject to provincial and federal sales taxes, the auction's sales commission (3-5%), and, in some cases, an administration fee of $75-$100.

The best strategy with auctions is to take someone from the car business with you to help you pick, price, and bid for a vehicle. You'll find the vehicles in a compound, but your expert should have ample opportunity to inspect them and, in some cases, take a short drive around the property before the auction begins.

The Internet

The Internet is an excellent place to shop ads but a risky place to buy a used car. You don't know the seller, and you know even less about the car. It's easy for an individual to sell a car they don't own, and it's even easier to create a virtual dealership, with photos of a huge inventory and a modern showroom, when the operation is likely made up of one guy working out of his basement.

Used car predators troll the Internet. Here, Ziggy and Tigger, hunt for the scammers.

Rating systems are unreliable too. Ratings from "happy customers" may be nothing but ploys – fictitious postings created by the seller to give out five-star ratings and the appearance that the company is honest and reliable.

If you must use the Internet to buy a car, use it to protect your wallet, as well. Don't accept any of the seller's information as truthful. Instead, order a comprehensive online title and accident report from CarProof or some other similar service. Do this before wasting $100 or more inspecting the car by an independent mechanic.

If the car is located in the States, print out the tips found on eBay's website at *pages.ebay.ca/ebaymotors/explained/checklist/howtobuyUS.html*. The website takes you through each step in detail and will tell you if the vehicle is permitted in Canada and the likely modification requirements. If the vehicle needs alteration, you should check with a mechanic for an estimate. You will also need to get a recall clearance letter from the dealer or automaker in order to pass federal inspection. Additional information can be obtained from the Registrar of Imported Vehicles (1-888-848-8240 or *www.riv.ca*).

Beware of phony eBay solicitations that are sent via doctored e-mails selling out-of-province vehicles. In the e-mail the "owner" will even promise to deliver the car to you at no extra cost. Rather than paying through the relatively secure PayPal used in most legitimate transactions, you will be instructed to send payment through a Western Union or MoneyGram money transfer.

The most obvious indications these ads were placed by scam artists is that the same e-mail address keeps reappearing, or the listed phone number is a dummy. Local advertisers do little to police this fraud. Always use a search engine to look for other ads with the same phone number or e-mail address.

Most fraudulent advertisements are placed outside Canada, apparently without the knowledge of the online sites that published them. Nevertheless, it's hard not to suspect some complicity because the ads are quite easy to verify by the hosting site. For example, *Wheels.ca* staffers say they refuse advertisers with an IP address outside of Canada and the ad claims and contact information are constantly checked by the business office.

Dishonest sellers aren't your only Internet trap. There are also plenty of crooks who will steal your car by pretending to be honest buyers. These phonies will take the delivery of the car, pay for it with a forged cheque, and then disappear. It could be weeks before your bank returns the forged cheque and deducts the money from your account; by then the buyer and your vehicle will be long gone. Again, use PayPal or an independent third-party that can confirm payment has been received before releasing the vehicle.

There is some government help available to catch Internet used-car swindlers. PhoneBusters, the federal-provincial agency set up to deal with telephone and Internet scams (1-888-495-8501) has ties to the RCMP and OPP, and will investigate these high-tech crooks. File a complaint with your local police service and at the same time voice your concerns with the Internet service provider (ISP) hosting the offensive material. The Canadian Association of Internet Providers (*www. caip.ca*) would also welcome your comments or concerns relevant to Canadian ISPs.

Financing Choices

Financing a used car purchase for more than 3 years is *seldom* a good idea. Instead, pay as much cash as possible, purchase a less expensive vehicle, or downsize to simplifying your choices.

If financing is necessary, do this exercise to figure out how much financing you can afford. First deduct your recurring monthly expenses – living expenses such as groceries, rent, subscriptions, club memberships, etc. – from your monthly income after taxes. What's left over is your disposable income. Then calculate how much of that you can pay each month for a new or used car. Most financial planners recommend spending no more than 10% of take-home income for monthly car payments. Make sure you have enough left for emergencies and entertainment.

Now don't panic. Depreciation can be reduced by half if the car is bought used; insurance premiums will be less if coverage is part of a total package and the car has a good claims history (find out before the purchase); fuel expenses can be lowered by 20% with an economy car and using *gasbuddy.com* to find the cheapest gas stations around; and maintenance can cost 30% less if performed by independent repair shops.

By keeping the purchase price low, there is less money to lose in depreciation.

Credit Unions

A credit union is the best place to borrow money for a used car at competitive interest rates and with easy repayment terms. In fact, credit unions jumped into car financing in a big way when the major automakers pulled back, 5 years ago. Keep in mind, you'll have to join the credit union or have an account with it before the loan is approved. You'll also probably have to come up with a larger down payment.

Banks

Financing a car through a bank can mean either applying for a car loan or a line of credit. Right now, the line of credit is cheaper, typically in the range of 3-4% for good risks. A loan will require a lien on your car and fixed monthly payments until the end of the term. Interest rates on used car loans vary considerably from 5% to 12% – they can go much higher for subprime borrowers. Lenders provide healthy cash incentives to dealers who are able to "bump" a creditworthy customer into a higher interest rate bracket. For example, hiking a customer who is financing the entire value of a $20,000 car from the best 4.9% rate to 6.5% might earn the dealer an under-the-table kickback of $400 from the lender. And the lender could be your own bank.

You can get a good idea of the different car-loan interest rates through an online comparison of bank rates. For purchases in the States, go to *www.bankrate.com*; Canadian loan interest rates are updated by the individual banks and credit unions who mostly ask you to call toll-free to get a current quote. Currently the banks offer their best rates directly to dealers, in the range of 4.5-4.9% for new and late-model vehicle financing to the best credit risks.

A line of credit requires no lien and offers the ability to pay a minimum each month, or as much as you can afford. The rates are often lower than traditional bank loans and there are no penalties for paying it off early, making it the preferred route for car buyers with some liquidity and good credit ratings.

Banks generally offer the dealer better rates on an auto loan than what they will offer you at your branch.

If you don't have a preapproved loan, it wouldn't hurt to buy from a local dealer, since the dealer may be more negotiable on the price if they can count on the kickback for arranging the loan. The banks offer dealers quicker loan approval than your branch, and you won't have to face a banker, which some people find stressful.

Attractive used car financing rates, including near-zero interest rates (watch out for an inflated purchase price or hidden fees), are available from automakers through their dealers as part of Certified used luxury vehicle programs.

Dealers

Now that auto loans are easier to get than they were several years ago, dealers are financing everything in sight – especially used cars.

Dealer financing isn't the rip-off it once was, but there are some notable exceptions, as a CBC British Columbia television investigation concluded in January 2014. Reporters interviewed a couple who paid TD bank 25.44% in interest charges on a 5-year-old Dodge Avenger that was financed for a 7-year term – costing more than double the price of their car.

"We're paying $21,000 for the loan – then $23,000 in interest," said Angie Hauser of Kelowna. "They're making money off of people who have no money...

We've been robbed by a bank with the help of a car dealer. I mean, that's the only way I see it," said her husband Enzo Gamarra.

"Why would I want to pay $44,000 for a car that's now only worth $15,000?"

High-interest subprime loans are offered to buyers with poor credit by some of Canada's better-known financial institutions. *Canadian Auto World* magazine says subprime loans make up approximately 25% of all auto loans arranged by dealerships. Suprisingly, defaults on these high-cost loans are relatively low.

Dealers want to wring as much profit as possible from each loan contract, so be careful not to let the seller pencil in additional charges for sickness or unemployment protection insurance. Used car financing at rates far below the prime rate occasionally involves jacking up the vehicle price to compensate for the "bargain" loan rate.

DEALER SCAMS

One of the more common selling tricks is to not identify the previous owner because the vehicle was used commercially, was problem-prone, or had been written off as a total loss after an accident. Your best defence? Ask for the name of the vehicle's previous owner and run a VIN check through CarProof as a prerequisite for purchasing. In Ontario, your best record of previous ownership is the UVIP, or Used Vehicle Information Package.

It would be impossible to list all the tricks employed in used-vehicle sales. As soon as the public is alerted to one scheme, crooked sellers use other, more elaborate frauds. Nevertheless, under industry-financed provincial compensation funds, buyers can get substantial refunds if defrauded by a dealer.

Here are some of the more common fraudulent practices you're likely to encounter.

Declaring a False Price

Here's where your own greed will do you in. In a tactic used almost exclusively by small, independent dealers and curbsiders posing as private sellers, the buyer is told that he or she can pay less sales tax by listing a lower selling price on the contract. But what if the vehicle turns out to be a lemon? The hapless buyer is offered a refund based on the fictitious purchase price indicated on the contract. If the buyer wanted to take the dealer to court, it's quite unlikely that he or she would get any more than the contract price. Keep to the legal principle: "Come to the court with clean hands."

Misrepresentation

Used vehicles can be misrepresented in a variety of ways. A used airport commuter minivan may be represented as having been used by a Sunday school class. A defective sports car that's been rebuilt after a major accident may have plastic filler in the body panels, "stretched" and compromised structural members, heavy oil in the motor to stifle the clanks, and cheap tires to eliminate the thumps. Your best protection against these dirty tricks is to have representations about the vehicle written into the sales agreement or offer to purchase, and have the vehicle inspected by an independent mechanic before completing the sale. Of course, you can still cancel the sale if you learn of the misrepresentation only after taking the vehicle home, but your chances of successfully doing so dwindle if nothing was recorded in the agreement.

"Free-Exchange" ("You Got a Lemon? Here's a Greener One")

How nice. The dealer offers to exchange any defective vehicle for any other vehicle in stock. What really happens, though, is that the dealer won't have anything else selling for the same price and so will demand a cash bonus for the exchange – or you may get the dubious privilege of exchanging one lemon for another.

"Money-Back" Guarantee

The purchaser feels safe in buying a used car with this kind of guarantee. After all, what could be more honest than a money-back guarantee? Dealers using this technique may charge exorbitant handling charges, rental fees, or mechanical repair costs to the customer who bought one of these vehicles and then returned it. The APA recommends dealers in Toronto and Montreal who offer a real 30-day money-back guarantee (you'll pay a charge for use of the vehicle). Very few buyers actually ask for their money back but it gives them piece of mind.

"50/50" Guarantee

The devil is definitely in the details with this trick. Essentially, the dealer will pay half of the repair costs over a limited period of time. In most cases, the dealer inflates the repair cost to double their actual worth and then writes up a bill for that amount (a scam sometimes also used in "goodwill" settlements involving new car dealers). The buyer winds up paying more or less the full price of repairs at the dealer's commercial rate. The best kind of used-vehicle warranty is 100% with full vehicle coverage for a fixed time period and no deductible, even if that time period is relatively short.

"As Is" and "No Warranty"

Sellers insert these clauses much like parking lot owners or coat checkers at restaurants when they post warnings that they have no responsibility to indemnify your losses. In fact, when you pay for a custodial service or a used vehicle, the commission the seller of that service or product receives requires that you be protected.

Every vehicle carries a provincial legal warranty protecting you from misrepresentation and the premature failure of key mechanical or body components. Nevertheless, sellers often write "as is" or "no warranty" in the contract in the hope of dissuading buyers from pressing legitimate claims. Generally, when "as is" has been written into the contract or bill of sale, it usually means that you're aware of mechanical defects, you're prepared to accept the responsibility for any damage or injuries caused by the vehicle, and you're agreeing to pay all repair costs. To get around "as is" clauses it's usually necessary to prove the vehicle has been intentionally misrepresented. The courts have held that the "as is" clause is not a blank cheque to cheat buyers, and must be interpreted in light of the seller's true intent. Was there an attempt to deceive the buyer by including this clause? Did the buyer really know what the "as is" clause could do to his or her future legal rights? It's also been held that the courts may consider oral representations ("parole evidence") as an expressed warranty, even though they were never written into the formal contract. So, if a seller makes claims in their advertising or verbal representations as to the fine quality of a used vehicle, these claims can be used as evidence. Private sellers are usually given more latitude than dealers or their agents.

Odometer Fraud

Who says crime doesn't pay? It most certainly does if you turn back odometers for a living in Canada.

Odometer fraud is a pernicious crime that robs thousands of dollars from each victim it touches and hurts honest businesses. See, for example, *United States v. Whitlow*, 979 F.2d 1008 (5th Cir. 1992), at 1012 (under sentencing guidelines, the court affirmed the estimate that consumers lost $4,000 per vehicle). Victims of this fraud are commonly the least able to afford it, since buyers of the older high-mileage vehicles whose mileage is more likely to have been turned back include large numbers of low-income people. Most buyers never discover they were duped.

Odometer tampering involves several interrelated activities. High-mileage vehicles are purchased at a low price. The vehicles are "reconditioned" or "detailed" to remove many outward appearances of long use. Finally, odometers are reset, typically removing more than 100,000 km.

In addition to the cosmetic "reconditioning" of the car, the odometer tamperer "reconditions" the car's paperwork. Automobile titles include a declaration of mileage statement to be completed when ownership is transferred. To hide the actual mileage that is declared on the title when the car is sold to an odometer tamperer, the tamperer must take steps to conceal this information. These steps vary from simple alteration of mileage figures to creating transfers to fictitious "straw" dealerships to make it unclear who was responsible for the odometer rollback and title alteration. Alternatively, the odometer tamperers destroy original title documents indicating high mileage and obtain duplicate certificates of title from provincial or state motor vehicle departments, upon which the false, lower mileage figures are entered.

Odometer fraud is practiced by a variety of people, including:

- Organizations that roll back ("clock") the odometers on thousands of cars, wholesaling them to dealers who resell them to the public;
- Curbsiders who buy cars, clock them, and sell them through the classifieds, passing them off as cars of a friend or relative ("I'm selling Aunt Sally's Buick for her"); and
- Individuals who only clock their own car to defeat a lease penalty or cheat on a warranty. In this situation the rollback is much lower, usually less than 40,000 km.

Odometer scammers ply their trade in Canada because it seems as if no one cares what they do, and they stand to gain thousands of dollars of profit for each mile erased from the odometer on the resale value of a doctored car. Moreover, electronic digital odometers make tampering child's play for anyone with a laptop computer.

Think: When was the last time you heard of a Canadian dealership being charged with odometer fraud? Probably a long time ago, if at all. And what is the punishment for those dealers convicted of defrauding buyers? Not jail time or loss of their franchise. More than likely, it'll be just a small fine.

Not so in the States. Many victims can get compensation from dealers who sold cars with altered odometers, regardless of who was responsible for the alteration. For business and legal reasons, dealers frequently compensate consumers who purchased vehicles with altered odometers. U.S. federal law permits consumers to obtain treble damages or $1,500, whichever is greater, when they are victims of odometer fraud (49 U.S.C. section 32710). The courts have been hard-nosed in protecting consumers in these kinds of lawsuits against dealers.

How to spot a car that's been to a "spin doctor?"

- When calling a supposedly private seller, ask to see the car in the ad, without specifying which one.
- Ask the seller for a copy of the contract showing the name of the selling dealer and previous owner.
- Check the history of the car through CarProof.
- Examine brake and gas pedal wear as well as the driver's door sill, steering wheel rim and armrest. Does their wear match the kilometres?
- On old vehicles that don't use a digital odometer, check to see if the numbers on the odometer are lined up and not scratched.
- Contact a franchised dealer for that make of vehicle, and try to obtain a copy of the service records, noting the mileage each time the vehicle was serviced.

Odometer fraud could be stopped in its tracks through effective legislation and law enforcement.

PRIVATE SCAMS

A lot of space in this section is dedicated to describing dealer tricks used to cheat uninformed buyers. Of course, private individuals can be dishonest, too. In either case, protect yourself by getting as much information as possible about the vehicle you're considering. After a test drive, give as small a deposit as the vendor is prepared to accept, and write that the offer is subject to cancellation if the automobile proves unsatisfactory after its inspection. After you've taken these precautions, watch out for the following private sellers' tricks.

Dealers Disguised as Private Sellers

Called "curbsiders," these scammers lure unsuspecting buyers through lower prices, cheat the federal government out of tax money, and routinely violate provincial registration and consumer protection regulations. Bob Beattie, former Executive Director of the Used Car Dealers Association of Ontario (*www.ucda.org*), once estimated that about 20% of so-called private sellers in Ontario are actually curbsiders. This scam is easy to detect if the seller can't produce the original sales contract or show repair bills made out over a long period of time in his or her own name. You can usually identify a car dealer in the want ads section of the newspaper – just check to see if the same telephone number is repeated in many different ads. Sometimes you can trip up a curbsider by requesting information on the phone, without identifying the specific vehicle. If the seller asks you which car you are considering, you know you're dealing with a curbsider.

Legitimate car dealers claim to deplore the dishonesty of curbsider crooks, yet they are their chief suppliers. Dealership sales managers, auto auction employees, and newspaper classified ad sellers all know the names, addresses, and phone numbers of these thieves but don't act on the information. Newspapers want the ad dollars, auctions want the action, and dealers want someplace they can unload their wrecked, rust-cankered, and odometer-tricked junkers with impunity. Talk about hypocrisy, eh?

Curbsiders are particularly active in Western Canada, importing vehicles from other provinces where they were sold by dealers, wreckers, insurance companies, and junkyards (after having been written off as total losses). They then place private classified ads in B.C. and Alberta papers, sell their stock, and then import more.

Vehicles that Are Stolen or Have Finance Owing

Many used vehicles are sold privately without free title because the original auto loan was never repaid. You can avoid being cheated by asking for proof of purchase and payment from a private seller. Be especially wary of any individual who offers to sell a used vehicle for an incredibly low price. The best is to conduct a lien search in the applicable provincial registry. You can also check the sales contract to determine who granted the original loan, and call the lender to see if it's been repaid.

Place a call to the provincial Ministry of Transportation to ascertain whether the car is registered in the seller's name if this information is made available. Check the auto insurance policy to see if a finance company or leasing company is named as beneficiary. Still unsure? Contact the original dealer to determine whether there are any outstanding claims.

In Ontario, all private sellers must purchase a Used Vehicle Information Package at one of 300 provincial Driver and Vehicle Licence Issuing Offices, or online at *www.mto.gov.on.ca/english/dandv/vehicle/used.htm*. This package, which costs $20, contains the vehicle's registration history in Ontario; the vehicle's lien information (i.e., if there are any liens registered on the vehicle); the fair market value on which the minimum tax payable will apply; and other information such as consumer tips, vehicle safety standards inspection guidelines, retail sales tax information, and forms for bills of sale.

In other provinces, buyers don't have easy access to this information as readily. Generally, you have to contact the provincial office that registers property and then pay a small fee for a computer printout that may or may not be accurate. You'll be asked for the current owner's name and the car's VIN, which is usually found on the driver's side of the dashboard. Title protection is one of the major advantages of buying from a licensed dealer in provinces that have compensation programs.

Helpful Websites

Real Trade-in Values

If you intend to trade in your vehicle, it's important to find out its true value to decide whether selling it privately would put more money in your pocket than selling it to the dealer. Right now there is a shortage of good 3- to 5-year-old used cars on the market and private buyers are paying a premium for them.

Problem is, how do you find out how much your trade-in is worth? In the past dealers had a monopoly on this information because only they could afford the annual subscription fees charged by the publishers of *Black Book* and *Red Book,* the industry valuation guides. The Internet has changed all that. Now there's an excellent alternative to the traditional *Red* and *Black Book* price guides.

Go to *www.vmrcanada.com* for free listings of trade-in values for 1984 to 2015 cars and trucks, reliability predictions, and 3- to 5-year residual value projections. Better yet, subscribe to the publication in eBook format. A year's subscription for $9.95 U.S. is more comprehensive than either the *Black Book* or *Red Book* (although the other two publications give current new and used prices and are more popular with car dealers, insurance companies and government agencies). The *Black Book* gives used values online for free at: *www.canadianblackbook.com/*; *Red Book*: *www.canadianredbook.com/* gives values to online subscribers for an annual fee of $195.95.

VMR Canadian Used Car Prices delivers unbiased, market-based values in an easy-to-use format. The smart PDF has a simple, built-in menu system incorporated with the Table of Contents, allowing fast and easy navigation to anywhere in the publication. Download it once to your computer or device and access it anytime, anywhere – just like a book. Only $9.95 U.S. for a full year, published quarterly.

Other Helpful Websites

Recent surveys show that close to 80% of car buyers get reliability and pricing information from the Internet before visiting a dealer or private seller. This trend has resulted in easier access to confidential price margins, secret warranties and lower prices – if you know where to look.

Automobile companies have helpful – though self-serving – websites, most of which feature detailed sections on their vehicles' histories and research and development, as well as all sorts of information of interest to auto enthusiasts and bargain hunters. For example, you can generally find out the freight fee before you even get to the dealership; salespeople prefer to hit you with this charge at the end of the transaction when your guard is down. Manufacturers can easily be accessed through a search engine like Google or by typing the automaker's name into your Internet browser's address bar followed by ".com" or ".ca". Or for extra fun and a more balanced presentation, type the vehicle model or manufacturer's name into a search engine, followed by "lemon," "problems," or "lawsuits."

Consumer Allies

Automobile Protection Association *(www.apa.ca)*

A motherlode of honest, independent, and current car-buying information, the non-profit APA has been protecting Canadian motorists for over 40 years from its offices in Toronto and Montreal. This dynamic consumer group fights for safer vehicles for consumers and has exposed many scams associated with new-vehicle sales, leasing, and repairs. For a small fee, it will send you the invoice price for most new vehicles and help you out if you get a bad car or dealer. The APA also has a useful free online guide for digging out court judgments.

Canadian Legal Information Institute *(www.canlii.org)*

Be your own legal "eagle" and save big bucks. Use this site to find court judgments from every province and territory all the way up to the Supreme Court of Canada.

Car Help Canada *(www.carhelpcanada.com)*

Founded by former director of the Toronto APA, Mohamed Bouchama, the ACC's Car Help Canada website provides many of the same services as does the APA; the ACC is effective in Ontario and uses a network of honest garages and dealers to help members get honest and fair prices for vehicles and repairs. The ACC has been successful in getting new legislation enacted in Ontario and obtaining refunds for its members.

CBC TV's Marketplace *(www.cbc.ca/marketplace)*

Marketplace has been the CBC's premier national consumer show for almost forever. Staffers are dedicated to searching out scammers, airbag dangers, misleading advertising, and unsafe, poor-quality products. Search the archives for auto info, or contact the show's producers to suggest program ideas.

Class Actions in Canada *(www.classproceedings.ca)*

After successfully kicking Ford's rear end over its front-end thick film ignition (TFI) troubles and getting a million-dollar out-of-court settlement, this powerhouse Ontario-based law firm got a similar settlement from GM as compensation for a decade of defective V6 intake manifold gasket failures. Estimated damages were well over a billion dollars. The firm has also worked with others to force Liberty Mutual and other insurers to refund money paid by policy holders who were forced to accept accident repairs with used, reconditioned parts instead of new, original-equipment parts.

Class Actions in the U.S. *(www.lawyersandsettlements.com)*

This is a useful site if you want to use a company's class action woes in U.S. jurisdictions as leverage in settling your own Canadian claim out of court. If you decide to go the Canadian class action route, most of the legal legwork will have been done for you. The site is easy and free to search. Just type in the make of the vehicle you're investigating and read the results.

Canadian Competition Bureau *(www.competitionbureau.gc.ca)*

Imagine, consumers can file with the federal government an online complaint regarding misleading advertising or price fixing. The Competition Bureau's role is to promote and maintain fair competition so that Canadians can benefit from lower prices, increased product choices, and quality services.

This website includes a handy online complaint form that gives Ottawa investigators the mandate to carry out an official probe and lay charges. Most auto-related complaints submitted to the Bureau concern price-fixing and misleading advertising. After *Lemon-Aid*, the APA, and Mohamed Bouchama from the ACC submitted formal complaints to Ottawa against Toyota's Access pricing program a few years ago, the automaker settled the case for $2.3 million. The Bureau agreed to drop its inquiry into charges that the automaker rigged new car prices.

Consumer Affairs *(www.consumeraffairs.com/automotive/manufacturers.htm)*

Expecting some namby-pamby consumer affairs site? You won't find that here. It's a "seller beware" kind of website, where you'll find the scandals before they hit the mainstream press.

Consumer Reports and Consumers Union *(www.consumerreports.org/cro/cars.htm)*

It costs $6.95 (U.S.) a month ($30 a year) to subscribe online, but *CR*'s database is chock full of comparison tests and in-depth stories on products and services. The group's $29.95 New Car Price service is similar to what the APA offers.

Protégez-Vous (Protect Yourself) *(www.protegez-vous.qc.ca)*

Quebec's French-language monthly publishes dozens of test-drive results as well as articles relating to a broad range of products and services sold in Canada.

Auto Safety

Center for Auto Safety *(www.autosafety.org)*

A Ralph Nader-founded agency that provides free online info on model-specific safety- and performance-related defects.

Insurance Institute for Highway Safety *(www.iihs.org)*

A dazzling site that's long on crash photos and graphs that show which vehicles are the most crashworthy in side and offset collisions and which head restraints work best.

Transport Canada *(www.tc.gc.ca/eng/roadsafety/safevehicles-defectinvestigations-index-76.htm)*

No way as informative as the U.S.-based NHTSA or IIHS sites. You can access recalls for 1970-2017 models, but owner complaints aren't listed, and service bulletin summaries aren't provided. A list of used vehicles admissible for import is available at *www.tc.gc.ca/roadsafety/safevehicles/importation/usa/vafus/list2/menu.htm* or by calling the Registrar of Imported Vehicles (RIV) at 1-888-848-8240.

U.S. National Highway Traffic Safety Administration *(www.safercar.gov)*

This site has a comprehensive free database covering owner complaints, recall campaigns, crashworthiness and rollover ratings, defect investigations, service bulletin summaries, and safety research papers.

Information/Services

Alberta Government's Vehicle Cost Calculator *(www.agric.gov.ab.ca/app24/costcalculators/vehicle/getvechimpls.jsp)*

Your tax dollars at work! This handy calculator allows you to estimate and compare the ownership and operating costs for any business or non-business vehicles. Eleven types of vehicles can be compared and the ownership cost can be calculated by modifying the input values. Alternatively, you may select the same model if you wish to compare one vehicle but with variations in purchase price, options, fuel type (diesel or gas), interest rates, or length of ownership.

ALLDATA Service Bulletins *(www.alldatadiy.com/TSB/yr.html)*

Factory technical service bulletins (TSBs) are listed by year, make, model and engine option. You can take the TSB number to your dealer or repair shop, or access your vehicle's full bulletins online by paying the $26.95 (U.S.) subscription fee.

Car Complaints *(www.carcomplaints.com)*

Huge database of owner complaints about their vehicles for every make and model and year. The site uses bar graphs to help you hone in on the biggest problems. It incorporates complaints from the NHTSA website, too. Major recall announcements are posted quickly.

GM Inside News *(www.gminsidenews.com/forums)*

Kelley Blue Book and Edmunds *(www.kbb.com; www.edmunds.com)*

Prices and technical info are American-oriented, but you'll find good reviews of almost every vehicle sold in North America – plus there's an informative readers' forum. *Edmunds.com* has a robust collection of owners' feedback about their cars, good and bad. Canadian owners post there often.

True Delta *(www.truedelta.com)*

This site utilizes its membership base to gather model repair history by actual owners with data published quarterly. Sign up for free and create a file for your vehicle, then update with any repair details that aren't regular maintenance. In return, you gain access to a rich database of repairs reported by owners for almost every available model. Learn what's good and what's troublesome.

Summary

Don't treat your used-car negotiation like a World Wrestling Federation title bout. You are no Vince McMahon and most private sellers are simple, honest folk. Dealers, on the other hand, want to maximize their profit, but you will likely still get a good deal if the vehicle condition and inspection results are acceptable. You will end up with a reliable used car, truck, or minivan at a reasonable price – through patience and homework.

Here are the steps to take to keep your level of risk to a minimum.

1. Keep your present vehicle for at least 10 years. Don't get panicked over high fuel costs – depreciation is a greater threat to your pocketbook.

2. Sell to a dealer if the reduction in applicable taxes on your next purchase with that dealer is greater than the potential profit of selling privately.

3. Buy from a private party, rental car outlet, or dealer.

4. Shop for the best condition, not the best price. It always costs less to pay more up front for a clean vehicle, than to bring a below average vehicle up to clean condition.

5. Use the APA or ACC to help you find a vehicle from a reputable seller with a money-back warranty (Toronto and Montreal).

6. Buy a *Lemon-Aid*-recommended 3- to 5-year-old vehicle with some original warranty left that can be transferred. Or buy an older vehicle (120,000 km or less) that you have had checked out and obtained some information about.

7. Have the vehicle inspected before purchasing it.

8. If you're buying a vehicle that *Lemon-Aid* predicts has below-average reliability or expensive repairs choose an automaker warranty over an independent plan; they're more complete and accepted at all dealerships selling the brand.

9. Have maintenance repairs done at independent repair shops that know your model of vehicle.

10. Keep all the previous owner's repair bills to facilitate warranty claims and to let mechanics know what's already been replaced or repaired.

11. Upon delivery, adjust mirrors to reduce blind spots and adjust head restraints. Sit at least 30 cm away from the airbag housing.

12. Look for head protecting side curtain airbags.

13. Make sure that the automaker has your name in their computers as the new owner of record. Ask for a copy of your vehicle's history, which is stored in the same computer.

14. Go to *www.safercar.gov* and look up the free confidential service bulletins applicable to your vehicle and compare that to the free ALLDATA index of bulletins at *www.alldatadiy.com/recalls/index.html*. For true copies of all the recalls and U.S. service bulletins that are particularly significant to your needs from ALLDATA's site (*www.alldatadiy.com/buy*). The cost is $26.95(U.S.) for a 1-year subscription, or $44.95 for 5 years. A 1-year subscription for additional vehicles costs $16.95 per vehicle. Overnight, you will be sent an Internet download or data disc of all your vehicle's service bulletins going back to 1982. This will keep you current as to the recalls, and troubleshooting tips for correcting factory screw-ups. *Safercar.gov* can also give you details on all recalled vehicles and which ones have been fixed by the dealer.

3 Part Three
"ROBBERS" AND RECOURSES

Who Can You Trust?

Infamous gangster Clyde Barrow wrote to Henry Ford in 1934, two months before he was gunned down by police, "I have drove Fords exclusively when I could get away with one. ... What a fine car you got in the V8."

In June 2015, a $5 million (Cdn.) class action was filed against Treadz Auto Group Inc, the Minister of Service Alberta, and the Alberta Motor Vehicle Industry Council (AMVIC). The claim alleges that Treadz breached the Consignment Agreement by not honouring its contracts and that Treadz was unjustly enriched from monies received from the sale of the members' vehicles and not returned. The claim also alleges that a duty of care was owed by AMVIC and Service Alberta to the members and that both defendants, through negligent acts or omissions, breached this duty of care.

www.knightllp.com/services/class-action-litigation/

IT PAYS TO COMPLAIN

Canadians know that it pays to complain and studies show we do it just as much as Americans – but differently. Americans fight back hard – with small claims and class action lawsuits, with demonstrations, and with media manipulation. In Canada, we are, well, *Canadian*. Our grievances are bilingual, aired politely and, if they are not acted upon, we vow to take our business elsewhere, or delay doing anything. We eventually forge institutional solutions to problems, such as making healthcare available to everyone, but, individually, we tend to grumble passively.

This section of *Lemon-Aid* seeks to change all that. In the pages that follow, you will learn to see complaining in a new light and:

- Discover the many benefits of complaining, be inspired by the success stories of other complainers, and learn when complaints are justified.

- Be encouraged to follow step-by-step instructions for effective consumer complaining, enabling you to act individually to get a refund for a new or used car "lemon," or service that was incompetent, not needed, or covered by a "secret" warranty.

- Understand the benefits of collective complaining and the process through which effective outcomes can be achieved.

- Find tips for using the court system as a means to resolve customer complaints, get practical information about choosing an appropriate venue, anticipating costs, and handling the actual litigation.

- Access detailed information pertaining to safety- and performance-related defects.

When to Complain

First, let's be clear – there are times when you *should not* complain. Contrary to the popular adage, the customer is not *always* right. Sure, we have all been spoiled by retailers who will take back a shirt or dress, no questions asked. But that is just good public relations. We don't have the *right* to a refund or exchange credit if we change our mind, paid too much (unless there was misrepresentation), or can't find financing for the purchase. Actually, if the sale is cancelled by the buyer, the seller is entitled to charge a penalty to cover reasonable expenses caused by the lost sale.

Nonetheless, there are many times – particularly if you are faced with a defective product, an unsatisfactory service, or have been misled – when *you should complain*. I recommend that you claim a full or partial refund (damages) if any of the following allegations can be substantiated.

- **The product is unsafe or defective; service is inadequate, or incomplete:** This principle holds true even if the product was sold "as is" or "without warranty" if the buyer can prove the seller's bad faith.

- **The product or service does not meet the client's needs as expressed in the contract or promised in the sales representation:** For example, gas mileage is grossly less than represented; the voice-activated infotainment system doesn't respond to plain language instruction; navigation aids lead you into a lake; and dash gauges wash out in sunlight.

- **The warranty has been breached:** This comes into play when the guarantee wasn't honoured or differs in its application from what was promised. Since the warranty is considered to be an integral part of the contract, when it is breached (not honoured), a full or partial refund and sometimes punitive damages can be claimed from the seller, warranty company, or manufacturer. Prudent plaintiffs sometimes hold all parties equally responsible and let the presiding judge decide how to apportion blame.

- **A consumer protection law is violated:** Even if the seller is contravening only a technical requirement of the law, like not giving the buyer a copy of the contract, the contract may be voidable according to some statutes. In some used car cases, buyers who had paid too much were able to get their money refunded because the mileage written on the contract was incorrect or the warranty wasn't clearly stated. Judges take a dim view of clauses in standard-form contracts that don't comply with the law. In fact, consumer-protection laws may require that the judge give the consumer the edge when deciding responsibility in ambiguous circumstances.

- **The product or service doesn't last for a reasonable period of time:** A judge has the final say as to what is a reasonable period of time; the court's decision regarding implied warranties prevails over the contractual guarantee. This rule applies to all products and services, including a vehicle's durability and even possibly car repairs.

- **Delivery is delayed or the price is boosted:** The seller must respect the delivery date and price given verbally or written on the contract. If there is no promised delivery date, the court will decide what is a reasonable wait based upon the industry norm.

- **Parts availability or after-sales servicing is inadequate:** There is no specific legal time period for manufacturers to provide parts and service beyond the warranty period. However, judges could refund part of the purchase price and award damages, even if the warranty has expired, if a product becomes unusable due to unavailable servicing or an inadequate supply of replacement parts.

- **A "fix" doesn't fix the problem:** When the seller's corrective warranty repairs don't fix the problem indicated on the work order after repeated customer visits, the seller and/or manufacturer should either replace the product or pay for repairs done elsewhere. If the warranty period runs out during repeated repairs, coverage for the uncorrected problem must continue until it is fixed.

- **A secret or "goodwill" warranty extension isn't honoured:** Carmakers often extend their warranties long after the original warranty has expired. A problem occurs when the company applies the longer warranty in the United States only, or restricts its extension to specific regions. For example, Firestone/Bridgestone tried to limit its tire warranty extension to cars registered only in hot-weather states, until the courts showed this was impractical because cars registered elsewhere could have a catastrophic tire failure when driving through a warmer region, or after having moved to a warmer state. Incidentally, carmakers still routinely restrict their post-warranty free repairs. In Canada, showing a service bulletin (like the one shown for Honda, below) will often open the door to partial coverage or a free repair. (Current secret warranties and warranty extensions are in Part Two and in the Part Four vehicle reviews).

- **There has been a false representation or misinformation:** This applies when an important characteristic of the product or service was represented incorrectly (cost, size, warranty, performance, fuel economy, towing specs, is the wrong model year, etc.), or important facts were not disclosed (vehicle had transport or accident damage repairs, etc.).

Times have changed as our governments and courts become more responsive to consumer issues. Small-claims "people's courts" allow claims for as much as $25,000. We have multi-million dollar class actions, and more responsive regulators to ensure our rights are respected.

Two Warranties

Like new cars, used-vehicle defects are covered by two warranties. The *expressed* or *written* warranty, has a fixed time limit and lots of seller escape clauses; the *implied* or *legal* warranty is up to a judge's discretion to apply based upon the vehicle's cost, how it was maintained, manufacturer and dealer representations, the severity of the failure, the extent of that failure's consequences, and, I add only half-jokingly, the judge's own experience with car dealers.

Expressed

The expressed warranty given by the seller is often full of empty promises, and it allows the dealer and manufacturer to act as judge and jury when deciding whether a vehicle was misrepresented or is afflicted by defects they'll pay to correct. Rarely does it provide a refund or the replacement of a defective product or last beyond 5 years. As of October 1, 2015, though, Volvo Canada is offering a Lifetime Replacement Parts & Labour Warranty on all parts purchased and installed at an authorized Volvo retailer. Simply put, Volvo customers now pay only once and never pay again for Volvo Car replacement parts and labour, for as long as they own their vehicle.

Carmakers can use a lot of loopholes. Some of the more familiar lame excuses used in denying expressed warranty claims are "You abused the car," "It was poorly maintained," "It's normal wear and tear," "It's rusting from the outside, not the inside," and "It passed the safety inspection." The expressed warranty sometimes says there is no warranty at all other than what's written on paper, or that the any glowing verbal representations made to induce you to make a purchase are deemed never to have existed. Fortunately, courts usually throw out these exclusions by upholding two legal concepts.

1. The vehicle must be fit for the purpose for which it was purchased.
2. The vehicle must be of merchantable quality when sold.

Not surprisingly, sellers use the expressed warranty to reject claims, while smart plaintiffs mention the expressed warranty, and they argue for compensation under the implied warranty as well.

Implied

The implied warranty ("of fitness") is your ace in the hole. As clearly stated in the under-reported Saskatchewan decision *Maureen Frank v. General Motors of Canada Limited*, in which the judge declared that paint discolouration and peeling shouldn't occur within 11 years of the purchase of the vehicle, the implied warranty is an important legal principle. It is solidly supported by a large body of federal and provincial laws, regulations, and jurisprudence, and it protects you primarily from hidden defects that may be either dealer- or factory-related.

This warranty also holds dealers to a higher standard of conduct than private sellers because, unlike private sellers, dealers and auto manufacturers are presumed to be aware of the defects present in the vehicles they sell. That way, they can't just kick the can to the buyer and walk away from the dispute.

Dealers are expected to disclose defects that have been repaired. In British Columbia, provincial law (the *Motor Dealer Act*) says that a dealer must disclose damage that cost more than $2,000 to fix; in Ontario it's body damage over $3,000. These are good standards to cite in other jurisdictions. In spite of all your precautions, there's still a chance you'll buy a lemon.

1. It establishes the concept of reasonable durability, meaning that parts are expected to last for a reasonable period of time, as stated in jurisprudence, judged by independent mechanics, or expressed in extended "goodwill" warranties given by automakers in the past (examples: 10 years/ 193,000 km for catalytic converters; 7 years/200,000 miles for diesel injectors as expressed in one U.S. service bulletin; and 10 years/200,000 km for engines and transmissions).

2. It covers the entire vehicle and can be applied for whatever period of time the judge decides.

3. It can order that the vehicle be taken back, or a major repair cost be refunded. One *Lemon-Aid* reader writes:

   > I wanted to let you and your readers know that the information you publish about Ford's paint failure problem is invaluable. Having read through your "how-to guide" on addressing this issue, I filed suit against Ford for the "latent" paint defect. The day prior to our court date, I received a settlement offer by phone for 75% of what I was initially asking for.

4. It can order that plaintiffs be given compensation for supplementary transportation, inconvenience, missed work, screwed-up vacations, insurance paid while the vehicle was in the repair shop, repairs done by other repairers, and exemplary, or punitive, damages in cases where the seller was a real weasel. (Hello! VW diesel owners.)

5. It is often used by small claims court judges to give refunds to plaintiffs "in equity" (out of fairness), rather than through a strict adherence to the contract.

SUPPLEMENTARY WARRANTY SCAMS

The Automobile Protection Association (APA) has discovered that third party warranties offered by some dealers amount to a racket. During negotiations, the dealer extols the value of the warranty, say for an entire year on the powertrain, and claims your back is covered in the event of a problem. "That car must be good to qualify for that kind of coverage." During the selling process, you're given a pamphlet or directed to a poster that shows only the positive features of the warranty. You'll discover the tricks later after you go home with your new purchase. In some cases it may be a couple of weeks later than that, because the copy of the contract you signed at the dealership was sent to the warranty company for processing before it was sent to you. Here are the surprises:

- The maximum coverage is too low, limited to say $1,500 or $2,500. That's not enough for even one major powertrain repair. Replacing an engine or transmission can easily amount to double the claim limit.

- Oil leaks, parts that wear out without actually breaking, and starting troubles may not be covered.

- You'll have to pay a $75 "activation fee" to get your warranty coverage started, or risk losing everything you paid already.

- The oil change schedule or other maintenance is required more frequently than the manufacturer of the vehicle recommends. You have to keep all records or risk having your claim rejected, even if it's for a part that did not require any maintenance.

Some warranty companies in Ontario have the repair shop show one repair invoice to the customer at the retail rate (say $2,500 for a used engine), but the warranty company reimburses the repair shop at a lower commercial rate (say $1,500). The warranty company then tells the customer the repair exceeded the $1,500 claim limit on the warranty and so tells the customer to pay $1,000 to the repair company to top up the $2,500 retail price of the repair. Then instead of the warranty company contributing $1,500 toward the repair (the supposed claim limit), the warranty company only refunds the repair shop $500, because the warranty company is actually paying at the lower commercial rate. The consumer doesn't know any of this is going on behind the scene! The APA was told the practice is not uncommon in Ontario, which has large gaps in the oversight and regulation of warranty companies.

Reputable warranty companies *deplore* this sort of trickery. Most of them are insured. Unfortunately, most of them sell a warranty with a low claim limit and high deductible, like the one described above, to satisfy dealer demand for a cheap product, but they don't like it. Ideally you should look for full or major components coverage warranty, with a claim limit of $5,000 or higher (up to the price of the vehicle).

Automaker extended warranties generally offer more certainty. Most carry published suggested retail prices and dealer markups are limited to about 35%. Repair limits are rarely an issue. The list of parts included is usually more generous, and repairs can be performed at any dealership selling the brand, with breakdown coverage sometimes extended into the United States. For vehicles rated as one star or two stars in Part Four, extra cost warranty coverage is worth a look.

Auto warranty companies operating in British Columbia, Alberta, and Saskatchewan must be insured; Quebec has a hybrid system. If you're shopping in Ontario, here's a list of insured warranty companies prepared by the Used Car Dealers Association, current to October 2015.

- Coast to Coast Services
- Cornerstone United Warranty (XtraRide and AutoXtra)
- Coverage One Warranty
- D.I.S.C.C. Enterprises Ltd.
- First Canadian Protection

- Global Warranty
- Lubrico Warranty
- Peoples Choice Warranty

- INDS Canada Warranty
- Nationwide Auto Warranty
- Sym-Tech i-Select Coverage

SUPREME COURT TACKLES "FINE PRINT"

Canada's courts have made a full-court press against misleading advertising. The Supreme Court has ruled that the omnipresent misleading advertising that has bombarded us in print, over the airwaves, and on the Internet for what seems forever must stop. In two powerful decisions, originating from Ontario and Quebec, Bell Canada and *Time* magazine were exposed as flim-flam hypocrites and hit with a record-breaking fine and precedent-setting damages.

On June 28, 2011, Bell Canada consented to pay a $10-million settlement (the first time that the maximum penalty for misleading advertising has ever been imposed) and change its advertising after the Canadian Competition Bureau said its ads were contrary to the *Competition Act's* civil prohibition against making representations that are false or misleading (*www.ct-tc.gc.ca*).

Bell lied continuously in its ads for over five years about the prices at which certain of its services were available (including home phones, Internet, satellite television, and wireless services). Bell's representations gave the "general impression" that the advertised monthly price for the services was sufficient, when in fact Bell used a variety of "fine-print disclaimers" to "hide" additional mandatory fees that made the actual price paid by consumers higher than the advertised price (in one instance 15% higher than advertised). According to the *Competition Act's* misleading advertising provisions, the "general impression" conveyed by the advertisement to the average consumer, as well as its literal meaning, were considered in determining that the representations made were false or misleading.

As with most businesses caught scamming the public, Bell maintained it did no wrong. Nevertheless, the company paid the $10-million fine and agreed to drop all non-compliant advertising within 60 days. In particular, Bell agreed not to use small print or other ancillary disclosures that contradict the general impression of its price representations. Bell also agreed to pay the Competition Bureau $100,000 to cover the costs of the Bureau's investigation.

About *Time*

On February 12, 2012, Canada's Supreme Court threw the book at Time magazine for lying to readers in order to sell subscriptions. Yes, the same *Time* that pillories politicians for being untruthful has used its subscription sales department for years to give consumers false expectations that they have won a sweepstakes prize.

The ruling is a nail in the coffin to the "buyer beware" mindset. The precedent-setting judgment relating to false and misleading representations under the province's *Consumer Protection Act*, in *Richard v. Time Inc.* (*scc.lexum.org/decisia-scc-*

csc/scc-csc/scc-csc/en/7994/1/document.do), held that a representation should be judged simply by what a credulous and inexperienced consumer would believe to be true – a position long held by the courts in matters relating to misleading advertising charges filed under the federal *Competition Act*.

The Court also stated that if a prohibited business practice exists, there is no need to prove actual damages; an irrefutable presumption of prejudice exists. This opens the door to punitive damages, even where the circumstances do not justify a compensatory award.

Although punitive, or exemplary damages, can go as high as $1 million (Cdn.). *Time* magazine was ordered to pay the plaintiff (yippee!) only $15,000. Yet, the impact of this award has been far greater than the amount, as it serves as a reminder to business and government that advertising lies won't be tolerated by the court "just because we've always done it that way."

Auto Industry Fine Print

If qualifying information is necessary to prevent a representation from being false or misleading when read on its own, then that information should be presented clearly and conspicuously. "Fine print," which is the bread and butter of auto advertising, won't do.

The U.S. Federal Trade Commission issued strict guidelines for defining misleading advertising in *United States of America v. Billion* (*www.ftc.gov/system/files/documents/cases/141211billioncmpt.pdf*):

This Consent Order defines "clearly and conspicuously" as

A. In a print advertisement, the disclosure shall be in a type size, location, and in print that contrasts with the background against which it appears, sufficient for an ordinary consumer to notice, read, and comprehend it.

B. In an electronic medium, an audio disclosure shall be delivered in a volume and cadence sufficient for an ordinary consumer to hear and comprehend it. A video disclosure shall be of a size and shade and appear on the screen for a duration and in a location sufficient for an ordinary consumer to read and comprehend it.

C. In a television or video advertisement, an audio disclosure shall be delivered in a volume and cadence sufficient for an ordinary consumer to hear and comprehend it. A video disclosure shall be of a size and shade, and appear on the screen for a duration, and in a location, sufficient for an ordinary consumer to read and comprehend it.

D. In a radio advertisement, the disclosure shall be delivered in a volume and cadence sufficient for an ordinary consumer to hear and comprehend it.

E. In all advertisements, the disclosure shall be in understandable language and syntax. Nothing contrary to, inconsistent with, or in mitigation of the disclosure shall be used in any advertisement or promotion.

Look at the above Federal Trade Commission standards and read the car ads in any Canadian newspaper. Can you see, let alone understand, the cryptic abbreviations at the bottom of each dealer/automaker ad? Or, what about the blue lettering on a darker blue or other colour background? How many brave Canadian publishers would submit their own newspaper ads to the FTC, let alone the provincial order of opthamologists and lawyers to confirm readability and clarity?

Not the *Globe and Mail*, and, most certainly, not the "Wheels" section of the *Toronto Star*.

Television commercials are slicker. You get over 20 seconds of praise for the vehicle and then a scant few seconds of small type scrolled down the screen at breakneck speed telling you all of the exceptions to the foregoing. In effect, fine print that flashes, "Don't believe what we just said."

'98 SEDAN – IMPORT 160K, 1 Acdnt, flpd 14x ovr clff into rvr, elctrcl sys fried. Nvr fxd. Box #43587
Research before you buy.
www.VehicleSalesAuthority.com

Motor
Vehicle Sales Authority
of British Columbia

Carmakers have gotten more brazen in the lies they tell on TV. For example, Nissan ran a 30-second ad in 2011 extolling the prowess of its 2012 mid-size Frontier pickup. In the spot, the Frontier scoots up a steep dune to rescue a dune buggy stuck in the sand. Competitors cried foul, saying what was depicted couldn't be done. The U.S. Federal Trade Commission investigated and confirmed the actual truck couldn't pull off such a feat, cables were used to pull both vehicles, and the dune was "photo shopped" to look much steeper than it really was.

Nissan admitted its commercial was deceptive, and in an out-of-court settlement with the FTC the carmaker promised to henceforth tell the truth or face a $16,000 U.S. fine for each day a misleading commercial is run during the next 20 years.

The last time the FTC and an automaker settled such a case was with Volvo in 1992. That case involved an ad showing a monster truck crushing a lineup of cars, some of which secretly had their roof pillars weakened, but unable to damage a Volvo station wagon that had secretly been structurally reinforced! Volvo and their ad agency paid penalties of $150,000 each.

BROKEN PROMISES

New or used vehicles can turn out to be bad buys for various reasons. They were misrepresented by the seller, who covered up damage, turned back the odometer, inflated their fuel economy, lied about their previous use (former taxi or daily rental etc.), or they are afflicted with factory-induced defects like sudden acceleration or brake failures. In some cases, abusive driving or neglected maintenance by the previous owner can make a vehicle unreliable or dangerous to drive. Misrepresentation is relatively easy to understand. You have to show the vehicle doesn't conform to the oral or written sales representations made before or during the time of purchase. These representations include sales brochures and newspaper, radio, television, and Internet ads. Omission of key information can also fall under misrepresentation.

A sale can be cancelled if the vehicle's mileage has been turned back, if accident damage has been seriously misrepresented, or if the seller is really a dealer pretending to be a private seller ("curbsiding" covered in Part Two)). Even descriptive phrases like "well-maintained," "lady driven" (whatever *that's* supposed to imply), or "excellent condition" can get the seller into trouble if it amounts to an intentional misrepresentation with consequences for the purchaser is proven. It's harder to cancel a private sale, and there are additional hurdles: You may not be able to collect from the seller (no assets in their name), or they may have disappeared.

To get compensation or to have the car taken back, defects need to be confirmed by an independent garage examination that shows either that the deficiencies are premature, factory-related, or not maintenance-related or that they were present at the time of purchase. You can also make your proof by showing repetitive repairs for the same problem over a short period of time. Many small claims court victories against automakers relating to defective paint, engines, and transmissions were won by owners who bought their vehicles used and then sued both the seller and the automaker.

NEGLIGENCE

Automakers will sometimes plead they are not part of the chain of responsibility because they didn't sell the product to the plaintiff. Fortunately, as you will learn reading this section, Canadian judges do not buy that argument if the defect was design- or manufacturing-related and caused an injury or death. Cases involving these kinds of failures can be won in Canada under the doctrine of *res ipsa loquitur*, meaning "the thing speaks for itself," or in negligence cases, the liability is shown by the failure itself. Planes shouldn't fall and brakes shouldn't suddenly fail. Under *res ipsa loquitur*, you don't have to pinpoint the exact technical cause of the failure.

The July 1, 1998, issue of the *Journal of Small Business Management* compared product liability laws on both sides of the border (see "Effects of Product Liability Laws on Small Business" at *www.allbusiness.com*).

Although in theory the Canadian consumer must prove all of the elements of negligence (*Farro v. Nutone Electrical Ltd. 1990*; Ontario Law Reform Commission 1979; Thomas 1989), most Canadian courts allow injured consumers to use a procedural aid known as *res ipsa loquitur* to prove their cases (*Nicholson v. John Deere Ltd. 1986; McMorran v. Dom. Stores Ltd. 1977*). Under *res ipsa loquitur*, plaintiffs must only prove that they were injured in a way that would not ordinarily occur without the defendant's negligence. It is then the responsibility of the defendant to prove that he was not negligent. As proving the negative is extremely difficult, this Canadian reversal of the burden of proof usually results in an outcome functionally equivalent to strict product liability (*Phillips v. Ford Motor Co. of Canada Ltd. 1971;* Murray 1988). This concept is reinforced by the principal that a Canadian manufacturer does not have the right to manufacture an inherently dangerous product when a method exists to manufacture that product without risk of harm. To do so subjects the manufacturer to liability even if the safer method is more expensive (*Nicholson v. John Deere Ltd. 1986*).

The International Comparative Legal Guides website at *www.iclg.co.uk/practice-areas/product-liability/product-liability-2015/canada* confirms it is common practice for a claimant to bring proceedings against every party in a defective product's supply chain. This includes the designer, manufacturer, importer, distributor or retail supplier:

> At common law, every participant in the product supply chain has a duty to prevent harm arising from use of its product. This duty may include notification of risk and product recall in certain circumstances, not as a standalone duty, but as part of the 'duty to warn' jurisprudence… The duty to warn is a continuous one. The content of the warning must be adequate, understandable and clearly communicated. The scope of the warning must be commensurate with the degree of risk or gravity of the hazard presented. Evidence that a manufacturer complied with all relevant regulatory and/or statutory requirements is not a defence to a product liability claim, however breach of such requirements does not establish liability.

Let's put the legalese aside and use the simple definition outlined by U.S. Supreme Court Justice Sotomayor when she served on the Court of Appeal. In *Jarvis v. Ford* (United States Second Circuit Court of Appeal, February 7, 2002), she rendered a judgment in favour of a driver who was injured when her six-day-old Ford Aerostar minivan suddenly accelerated as it was started and put into gear. What makes this decision unique is that the jury had no specific proof of a defect. The Court of Appeal agreed with the jury award, and Justice Sotomayor gave these reasons for the court's verdict:

> A product may be found to be defective without proof of the specific malfunction:
> It may be inferred that the harm sustained by the plaintiff was caused by a product defect existing at the time of sale or distribution, without proof of a specific defect, when the incident that harmed the plaintiff:
>
> (a) was of a kind that ordinarily occurs as a result of product defect; and
>
> (b) was not, in the particular case, solely the result of causes other than product defect existing at the time of sale or distribution.

> Restatement (Third) of Torts: Product Liability §3 (1998). In comment c to this section, the Restatement notes:

> [There is] *no requirement that plaintiff prove what aspect of the product was defective*. The inference of defect may be drawn under this Section without proof of the specific defect. Furthermore, quite apart from the question of what type of defect was involved, the plaintiff need not explain specifically what constituent part of the product failed. For example, if an inference of defect can be appropriately drawn in connection with the

catastrophic failure of an airplane, the plaintiff need not establish whether the failure is attributable to fuel-tank explosion or engine malfunction.

The jury awarded Ms. Jarvis $24,568 in past medical insurance premiums, $340,338 in lost earnings, and $200,000 in pain and suffering. For future damages, the jury awarded $22,955 in medical insurance premiums, $648,944 in lost earnings, and $300,000 for pain and suffering.

Canada's Supreme Supreme Court has made similar rulings.

REASONABLE DURABILITY

You may be able to win a refund after the end of the written "express" warranty if the part does last as long as it normally should. You'll have to show that the components involved did not offer what the law considers to be "reasonable durability."

Below are some benchmarks that automakers or some court decisions have recognized over the years (see the Reasonable Part Durability chart).

REASONABLE PART DURABILITY			
Accessories		**Engine and Drivetrain**	
Air conditioner	7 years/no mileage	CV joint	6 years/120,000 km
Cruise control	7 years/140,000 km	Differential	7 years/140,000 km
Headlights (HID)	5 years/100,000 km	Engine (diesel) fuel pump	10 years/193,000 km
Hybrid battery	10 years/no mileage	Engine (diesel) NOx sensor	10 years/193,000 km
Power doors, windows	5 years/no mileage	Engine accessory power module	10 years/240,000 km
Radiator, transmission cooler	8 years/160,000 km	Engine block	10 years/no mileage
Tire sensor	5 years/no mileage	Engine drivebelt (tensioner)	4 years/no mileage
Body		Engine EGR bypass valve	10 years/193,000 km
Door handles	10 years/160,000 km	Engine fuel flex sensor	10 years/240,000 km
Liftgate struts	7 years/no mileage	Engine fuel pump, module	10 years/193,000 km
Paint (peeling)	7 years/no mileage	Engine oxygen sensor	10 years/193,000 km
Rust (perforations)	12 years/no mileage	Engine oil burning	10 years/193,000 km
Rust (surface)	5 years/no mileage	Engine supercharger	10 years/193,000 km
Water/wind/air leaks	5 years/no mileage	Engine turbocharger	7 years/140,000 km
Brake System		Engine water pump	10 years/240,000 km
		Transfer case	10 years/200,000 km
ABS computer	10 years/200,000 km	Transmission, ECM	10 years/200,000 km
Brake drum linings	35,000 km	Transmission oil cooler	10 years/240,000 km
Brake rotor	40,000 km	Thrust bearing (new)	4 years/no mileage limitation
Brake pads	30,000 km		
Master cylinder	10 years/no mileage	Torque converter clutch	10 years/193,000 km

REASONABLE DURABILITY (cont.)			
Exhaust System		**Steering and Suspension**	
Catalytic converter	10 years/193,000 km	Alignment	1 year/20,000 km
Exhaust manifold	10 years/193,000 km	Coil springs	10 years/200,000 km
Ignition System		Power steering	10 years/240,000 miles
Electronic module	5 years/100,000 km	Power steering hose	10 years/no mileage
Safety Components		Power steering (Saturn 2003-09)	life of vehicle
Airbag passenger sensors	15 years/no mileage		
Seat belts	life of vehicle		

NOTE: The above guidelines were copied from automaker service bulletins, owner notices, and product improvement programs that OK'd payouts to millions of customers over the past several decades.

Let's use Honda as an example. Honda has a warranty extension covering engine blocks up to 10 years with no mileage limit (TSB #10-048). Another little-known warranty extension applies to engine misfiring and defective piston rings for 8 years/unlimited mileage due to Honda's settlement in *Soto v. American Honda Motor Co. Inc.* (Case No.3: 12-cv-1377-SI (N. D. Cal.)). Honda also will pay for paint defects up to 7 years with no mileage limit and power steering failures up to 10 years or 150,000 miles on 2006-09 Civics and Fits (TSB #14-058). Finally, 2007-09 CRVs will get free door locks, even if the present ones aren't faulty with no time or mileage limitations (TSB #14-083).

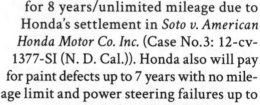

DON'T BE SILLY. THAT'S CAUSED BY BIRD DROPPINGS!

INADEQUATE PRIMER CAUSED MY PAINT TO PEEL!

If you bought a new or used 2006-2013 Honda Civic, 2007-2013 CR-V, 2009-2013 Pilot, or 2011-2013 Odyssey with cracked, chalking, or clouding paint, you may qualify for a free fix at your local Honda dealer, according to a series of technical service bulletins issued by Honda between January 2013 and June 2014.

CAMPAIGN – PAINT CHALKING, CRACKING, OR CLOUDING

SERVICE BULLETIN NO.: 14-034   DATE: JUNE 12, 2014

WARRANTY EXTENSION: 2006-13 Civic Paint Cracking, Chalking, or Clouding.

BACKGROUND: SB 14-034: Warranty Extension: 2006-13 Civic Paint Cracking, Chalking, or Clouding. Vehicles covered under this bulletin will have the warranty on their paint extended to 7 years from the original date of purchase with no mileage limit. The exterior paint on the hood and the leading edge of the front fenders may crack or look chalky or cloudy. Also the roof, trunk, upper portions of the quarter panel, and the upper portions of the doors may look chalky or cloudy.

CORRECTIVE ACTION: If necessary, repaint the entire affected panel(s) with an isocyanate two-part color and clearcoat paint after obtaining DPSM approval.

PARTS INFORMATION: If you need to replace any moldings or windshield clips, reference the parts catalog for the applicable part numbers, and submit them in your warranty claim.

With the exception of antilock brake systems (ABS), safety features generally have a lifetime warranty. Airbags that deployed in an accident – and the personal injury and interior damage their deployment will likely have caused – are covered by your vehicle insurance policy. However, if there is a sudden deployment for no apparent reason, the automaker should be responsible for all injuries and damages caused by the airbag. Front seat side airbag inadvertent deployments are covered on 2008 Honda Accords in another court settlement up to December 2016 (TSB #14-023, May 24, 2014).

SPECIAL COVERAGE ADJUSTMENT – ENGINE COOLING FAN MOTOR

SERVICE BULLETIN NO.: 14588A   OCT 2, 2015

2011-2015 Chevrolet Caprice and 2012-2015 Chevrolet Impala police patrol vehicles.

CONDITION: Idling the engine for extended periods of time can prematurely wear the engine-cooling-fan motor. In this condition, the motor may fail to operate or operate noisily. This condition can also damage motor-control relays in the vehicle's underhood bussed electrical center (UBEC).

SPECIAL COVERAGE ADJUSTMENT: This special coverage covers the condition described above for a period of 6 years or 100,000 miles (160,000 km), whichever occurs first, from the date the vehicle was originally placed in service, regardless of ownership.

THE ART OF COMPLAINING

Most Canadian consumers don't like to complain or get involved with the legal system. And, they have reason to be wary. Blood pressure rises, heated words are exchanged, and you always think of a better argument after the discussion is over.

Yet there are some complaint strategies that aren't hard to employ and can be successful.

163

"ROBBERS" AND RESOURCES

PART THREE

Cold-calling

Phone the seller or automaker, but don't expect to get much out of the call. Private sellers won't want to talk with you, and service managers will simply apply the dealership's policy, knowing that 90% of complainers will drop their claims after venting their anger.

Still, try to work things out by contacting someone higher up who can change the policy to satisfy your request. In your attempt to reach a settlement, ask only for what is fair and don't try to make anyone look bad.

Speak in a calm, polite manner, and try to avoid polarizing the issue. Talk about cooperating to solve the problem. Let a compromise emerge – don't come in with a rigid set of demands. Don't insist on getting the settlement offer in writing, but make sure that you're accompanied by a friend or relative who can confirm the offer in court if it isn't honoured or follow up with a friendly e-mail recapping any offer. Be prepared to act upon the offer without delay so that your hesitancy won't be blamed if the seller or automaker withdraws it.

Service manager help

Service managers have more power than you may realize. They make the first determination of what work is covered under warranty or through post-warranty "goodwill" programs, and they are directly responsible to the dealer and manufacturer for that decision (dealers hate manufacturer audits that force them to pay back questionable warranty decisions). Service managers are paid both to save the dealer and automaker money and to mollify irate clients – an almost impossible balancing act.

Nevertheless, when a service manager agrees to extend warranty coverage, it's because you've raised solid issues that neither the dealer nor the automaker can ignore. All the more reason to present your argument in a confident, forthright manner with your vehicle's service history and *Lemon-Aid's* "Reasonable Part Durability" table in hand (above). Also, bring any relevant technical service bulletins (TSBs) and owner complaint printouts as you can find from National Highway Traffic Safety Administration's (NHTSA) website and similar sources. It's important that they apply to your problem, as they can help establish parameters for giving out after-warranty assistance, or "goodwill."

Don't use your salesperson as a runner, since the sales staff are generally quite distant from the service staff and usually have less pull than you do. If the service manager can't or won't set things right, your next step is to convene a mini-summit with the service manager, the dealership principal, and the automaker's service rep, if you can get them to agree to meet with you. Regional service representatives are often technicians who are sent out by the manufacturer to help dealers with technical problems and warranty claims. By getting the automaker involved, you can often get an agreement where the seller and the automaker pay part of the repair cost.

Get an independent estimate

Try to make the case that the vehicle's defects were present at the time of purchase or should have been apparent to the seller, or that the vehicle doesn't conform to the representations made when it was purchased. Emphasize that you intend to use the courts if necessary to obtain a refund – most sellers would rather settle than risk a lawsuit with the potential expense and time lost. An independent estimate of the vehicle's defects and repair costs is important if you want to convince the seller that you're serious in your claim and that you stand a good chance of winning your case in court. Come prepared with an estimated cost of repairs to challenge a defendant who agrees to pay half the repair costs and then doubles the estimated cost so that you wind up paying the whole shot.

Send a written complaint you can use in court

If you haven't sent a written claim letter, fax, or e-mail, you really haven't complained – or at least, that's the auto industry's mindset, often upheld by the courts. If your vehicle was misrepresented, has major defects, or wasn't properly repaired under warranty, provide the seller a written summary of the outstanding problems or alleged misrepresentation and stipulate a time period within which the seller can fix the vehicle or refund your money.

If there are subsequent negotiations because a part isn't available or for other valid reasons, confirm the offer in a follow-up letter and issue another deadline. Should deadlines pass without a satisfactory settlement, take your "paper trail" of letters and file a small claims court lawsuit.

Use the format of the following sample complaint letters that mirror most things that may go wrong. Add additional court decisions that bolster your complaint.

You can ask for compensation for repairs that have been done or need to be done, towing charges, supplementary transportation costs such as taxis and rented cars, and damages for inconvenience. If no satisfactory offer is made, ask for mediation, arbitration, or a formal hearing in your provincial small claims court. Make the manufacturer a party to the lawsuit, especially if the emissions warranty, a secret warranty extension, a safety recall campaign, or extensive chassis rusting is involved.

Product Complaint Letter/Email/Fax

Without Prejudice

Date

Seller, Manufacturer, or Distributor Name and Address

Dear Sir or Madam,

Please be advised that I am dissatisfied with my _____
that I bought from you for the following reasons:

1. _____.
2. _____.
3. _____.

In compliance with Canadian consumer protection laws and the 'implied warranty" upheld by the Supreme Court of Canada in *Donoghue v. Stevenson and Kravitz v. GM*, I hereby request that these defects be repaired in the near future without charge, or the _____ taken back and my money refunded.

This product has not been reasonably durable, is not of merchantable quality, and is, therefore, not as represented to me.

Should you fail to repair these defects in a satisfactory manner and within a reasonable period of time, I reserve the right to have the repairs done elsewhere and claim reimbursement in court without further delay.

I also reserve my rights to punitive damages up to $1 million, pursuant to the Canadian Supreme Court's ruling in *Whiten v. Pilot* (February 22, 2002).

I believe your company wants to deal with its clients in an honest, competent manner and trust that my claim is the exception and not the rule.

A positive response within the next five (5) days would be appreciated.

Sincerely,

(signed with telephone number, email address, or fax number)

Fuel-Economy Misrepresentation

Without Prejudice

Date

Seller, Manufacturer, or Distributor Name and Address

Dear Sir or Madam,

Please be advised that I am dissatisfied with my _____ poor fuel economy. I bought this vehicle from you based upon your advertising that it would be fuel-efficient. It isn't. You indicated I could expect 12.7/8.3 L/100 km city/highway mileage but I am burning 14.7/10.3 L/100 km in careful, flat-highway driving.

I, therefore, seek $500 in compensation in compliance with *Sidney v. 1011067 Ontario Inc. (c.o.b. Southside Motors)* and provincial and federal misleading advertising statutes, upheld by the Supreme Court of Canada's recent award of punitive damages ($15,000) in *R. v. Time Inc.,* and ($10 million) in *R. v. Bell Canada.*

I also base my claim on the "implied warranty" of merchantability, and joint responsibility of automaker and dealer, also confirmed by the Supreme Court of Canada in *Donoghue v. Stevenson and Kravitz v. GM.*

This product is not as represented to me. Honda, in *Lockabey v. American Honda Motors,* Hyundai, and Kia have recently set up $200 owner refund programs and warranty extensions that compensate their customers misled by misrepresented fuel economy figures and faced with higher fuel costs. In *Paduano v. American Honda Motor Co., Inc.,* Honda later settled for $50,000, plus another $50,000 in attorneys' fees.

I also reserve my rights to punitive damages up to $1 million, pursuant to the Canadian Supreme Court's ruling in *Whiten v. Pilot* where an insurance settlement was unduly delayed.

I believe your company wants to settle these fuel-economy claims and move on. A positive response within the next five (5) days would be appreciated.

Sincerely,

(signed with telephone number, email address, or fax number)

Service Complaint Letter/Email/Fax

Without Prejudice

Date

Seller or Service Provider Name and Address

Dear Sir or Madam,

Please be advised that I am dissatisfied with the following service you provided, namely _____, for these reasons:

1. _____.
2. _____.
3. _____.

You have not fulfilled our contract for services as specified. This is a clear violation of Canadian consumer protection laws as upheld by both common and civil law statutes. I hereby request that you correct the deficiencies without delay and respect the terms of our contract. Failing which, I want my money refunded.

If my request is denied, I reserve the right under *Sharman v. Ford,* Ontario Superior Court of Justice, No. 17419/02SR, 2003/10/07, to have the contracted work done elsewhere. I shall then claim reimbursement in court for that cost, plus punitive damages for my stress and inconvenience, without further delay, pursuant to the Canadian Supreme Court's ruling in *Whiten v. Pilot.*

I am sure you want to deal with your clients in an honest, competent manner and trust that my claim is the exception and not the rule.

A positive response within the next five (5) days would be appreciated.

Sincerely,

(signed with telephone number, email address, or fax number)

Tire Defects or Premature Wear

Without Prejudice

Date

Seller, Manufacturer, or Distributor Name and Address

Dear Sir or Madam,

Please be advised that I am dissatisfied with my _____ that I bought from you for the following reasons:

1. _____.
2. _____.
3. _____.

In compliance with Canadian consumer protection laws and the "implied warranty" upheld by the Supreme Court of Canada in *Donoghue v. Stevenson, Kravitz v. GM,* Winnipeg Condominium v. Bird Construction *[1995] 1S.C.R.85* (negligence), and *Blackwood v. Ford Motor Company of Canada Ltd., 2006* (Provincial Court of Alberta, Civil Division; Docket: PO690101722; Registry: Canmore; 2006/12/08, I hereby request that the defective tire be replaced at no cost to me.

This product has not been reasonably durable, is not of merchantable quality, and is, therefore, not as represented to me.

Should you fail to deal with this claim in a satisfactory manner and within a reasonable period of time, I reserve the right to purchase a replacement from an independent retailer and claim reimbursement in court without further delay.

I also reserve my rights to punitive damages, pursuant to the Canadian Supreme Court's ruling in *Whiten v. Pilot* (February 22, 2002).

A positive response within the next five (5) days would be appreciated.

Sincerely,

(signed with telephone number, email address, or fax number)

Infotainment Device Failure

Without Prejudice

Date

Seller, Manufacturer, or Distributor Name and Address

Dear Sir or Madam,

Please be advised that I am dissatisfied with my car's Infotainment system _____ that I bought from you. This is what is wrong:

1. _____.
2. _____.
3. _____.

I want these defects repaired or my vehicle replaced and my money refunded under the "implied warranty" doctrine upheld by the Supreme Court of Canada in *Donoghue v. Stevenson, Kravitz v. GM,* and Winnipeg Condominium v. Bird Construction *[1995] 1S.C.R.85* (negligence). I also cite two pending class-actions: *Richards v. Ford Motor Co., Case No. 2:12-cv-00543 and Steven Rouse, et al. v. Ford Motor Company,* Case No. 11-CH-20581, Circuit Court of Cook County, Illinois, County Department, Chancery Division.

This product has not been reasonably durable, is not of merchantable quality, and is, therefore, not as represented to me.

Should you fail to satisfy my claim in a satisfactory manner and within a reasonable period of time, I reserve the right to have the repairs done elsewhere by an independent garage and claim reimbursement in court without further delay.

I also reserve my rights to punitive damages up to $1 million, pursuant to the Canadian Supreme Court's ruling in *Whiten v. Pilot* (February 22, 2002).

I believe your company wants to deal with its clients in an honest, competent manner and trust that my claim is the exception and not the rule.

A positive response within the next five (5) days would be appreciated.

Sincerely,

(signed with telephone number, email address, or fax number)

Mediation and Arbitration

If the formality of a courtroom puts you off, or you don't want to pay legal costs, consider using mediation or arbitration. These services are sponsored by the BBB and the Canadian Automobile Motor Vehicle Arbitration Plan (CAMVAP). Many small claims courts now require compulsory mediation as a prerequisite to going to trial.

Beware of mandatory arbitration clauses

The Supreme Court of Canada in *Seidel v. Telus Communications Inc.* (2011 SCC 15), struck down mandatory arbitration clauses in "contracts of adhesion" in a narrow 5-4 split decision. Seidel signed a cell phone contract with TELUS and she was being charged for connection time and ring time instead of just the actual talking time. Seidel claimed that TELUS engaged in deceptive and unconscionable practices contrary to the British Columbia *Business Practices and Consumer Protection Act*. She also sought certification to act as a representative of a class of allegedly overcharged customers under the *Class Proceedings Act*.

Contracts of adhesion are standard form contracts drafted by sellers and signed by customers without negotiation and usually without even being read. The arbitration clauses say that in the event of a dispute, the parties agree to submit their dispute to arbitration rather than to the courts. Some provincial legislatures, however, have enacted laws to invalidate these arbitration clauses thereby allowing consumers to pursue class actions. Also, lower courts in several provinces have made rulings that invalidate arbitration clauses where they would prevent consumers from pursuing class proceedings.

Dealers and automakers favour arbitration because it's relatively inexpensive, decisions are rendered more quickly than through regular litigation, there is a less formalistic approach to the rules of evidence, jurisprudence isn't created, and they can dodge bad publicity.

The disadvantages to binding arbitration are many and include the following: Loss of recourse to the courts, no appeals, no jurisprudence to guide plaintiffs as to the rules used in prior decisions (which often leads to quicker settlements or encourages litigants to stand by their principles), and the chumminess that often develops between arbiters and dealer/automaker defendants who may meet often over similar issues throughout the year – a familiarity that breeds complicity.

Automakers want binding arbitration because they can use them to oppose class actions related to their products and can more easily cover up design or production defects that are carried over year after year, since plaintiff's must file their cases individually and cannot pool their resources, or drum up media support.

Another drawback is that the defendant can refuse to take back the car or pay the cost of repairs simply by arguing that the arbitration process was flawed because the arbitrator exceeded his or her mandate. This objection puts the arbitration in the regular court system where each side has lawyers' fees and a final decision may take two years. This is what Ford of Canada did in refusing to take back a 2010

Focus that had abraded paint. Ford's appeal against the CAMVAP was tossed out of court.

Don't get the impression that binding arbitration is a useless tool to get redress. CAMVAP has worked fairly well with new car disputes where you want a repair rather than a refund of the purchase price. On the other hand it proved woefully ineffective in resolving the "death wobble" on Dennis Warren's 2007 Dodge Ram 2500 (see *www.cbc.ca/m/touch/news/story/2011/05/16/bc-dodgeproblem.html*).

SEEK OUTSIDE HELP

Ask government or trustworthy independent consumer protection agencies to evaluate how well you've prepared before going to your first hearing. Also, use the Internet to ferret out additional facts and gather support.

If there is no satisfactory response, *contact the media and register your complaint with the provincial government's consumer affairs ministry*. Ontario, for example, has a unique way of alerting businesses to your complaint by forwarding it with the government's own covering letter. In the government's letter the province's bureaucrats are careful to say they haven't initiated a *formal* investigation, yet – they are just passing on a consumer's complaint.

What is most likely to stick in the letter recipient's mind is this paragraph:

Where a Ministry investigation finds a violation of the Consumer Protection Act has occurred, charges may be laid. Successful prosecution under the CPA may result in fines of up to $50,000 for an individual or imprisonment for a term of not more than two years less a day or both and, if convicted, a corporation may be liable to a fine of not more than $250,000.

Ottawa will go one step further. The Competition Bureau's online form solicits citizen reports of dishonest business practices. One such complaint lodged by *Lemon-Aid* forced Toyota to settle a price-fixing investigation by giving $2 million to a Canadian charity, and a misleading advertising charge by the APA resulted in General Motors Canada paying a $20,000 fine after lying about its Firenza reliability.

Government investigators treat all information as confidential and look into allegations of price-fixing, misleading advertising, false weights and measures readings (such as car odometers), and a host of other prohibited activities – as described by the *Competition Act*, the *Consumer Packaging and Labelling Act*, the *Textile Labelling Act*, and the *Precious Metals Marking Act*. Such complaints are administered by the Competition Bureau (see *www.competitionbureau.gc.ca/eic/site/cbbc. nsf/frm-eng/GH%C3%89T-7TDNA5*).

But *what if you are ticked off about poor government service?* Well, the federal government has a bilingual free website for that, too. No kidding, it's called Service Canada (*www.servicecanada.gc.ca/eng/ocs*).

Pressure Tactics

It doesn't hurt to use independent, non-profit groups like the BBB, or other industry complaint agencies to get your claim resolved. Just don't expect rapid or consistent results. BBB offices throughout North America have come under fire over the years for being more a lap dog than a watch dog over business practices due to their close ties to business, as was the case in one television news expose that resulted in the closing of the Los Angeles (Southland) BBB office:

> The expulsion stems back to a pay-to-play scandal unearthed in 2010 by the ABC News show 20/20. The investigation showed extortion-type practices applied to local businesses: Those that paid annual dues to the BBB were handed accreditation and A ratings, while those that didn't play along were given subpar grades, even if they hadn't received complaints. Most disturbingly, investigators were able to get accreditation and an A- grade for a fake, totally nonexistent business after paying a $425 fee to the local BBB. (The name of the dummy business was Hamas—yep, the same as the Middle Eastern terrorist organization.)
>
> — business.time.com/2013/03/19/why-the-better-business-bureau-should-give-itself-a-bad-grade/

You can put additional pressure on a seller or garage by putting a lemon sign on your car and parking it in front of the dealer or garage, by creating a "lemon" website, or by forming a self-help group. Angry Chrysler and Ford owners, for example, received sizeable settlements in Canada by forming the Chrysler Lemon Owners Group (CLOG) and the Ford Lemon Owners Group (FLOG). But using your freedom of expression in this way, even if the allegations are true, can sometimes lead to heavy-handed cease and desist responses from car dealers, especially if your vehicle is visible from their premises.

And get this: Apple Inc. co-founder Steve Wozniak repeatedly called Toyota over the course of several months to report brake malfunctions with his Prius. Toyota officials ignored him. However, when he mentioned the problem in an aside during an Apple press conference, all hell broke loose. The company returned his call, apologized, fixed the car, and recalled thousands of others.

Use your website and social media (Twitter, Facebook, Yelp, etc.) to gather data from others who may have experienced a problem similar to your own. This can help you organize other auto owners for class action and small claims court lawsuits and it pressures the dealer or manufacturer to settle. Public demonstrations (picketing, decorating your car with lemons, etc.), websites and Twitter "buzz" often generate news stories that will take on a life of their own as others join the movement or add depth and breadth to the campaign.

Here's some more advice from this consumer advocate with hundreds of pickets and mass demonstrations under his belt. Keep a sense of humour, and never break off the negotiations. Flipping "the bird" to someone like Mercedes-Benz is counter-productive.

Dear Loyal Customers

Mercedes-Benz

When you shell out $35,000 to $80,000 for a Lexus, you expect a quality-manufactured vehicle that's safe and lives up to the express warranty that it came with. If there is a flaw with your Lexus that reduces its value or that is a safety concern and the manufacturer has been unsuccessful in fixing it, you are likely entitled to damages under state and federal Lemon Laws.

Gaulitics (*www.gaulitics.com/2015/06/mercedes-benz-settlement-rips-off.html*) was set up to protest an M-B engine settlement. Above is an "informational" protest site: *lemonlawexperts.com/lexus-repurchase-lemon-law/*. Courts generally rule that informational website are OK, while protest sites or signs that defame or interfere with customers' right to choose may be deemed illegal.

Finally, don't be scared off by threats that it's illegal to criticize a product or company. Unions, environmentalists, and consumer groups do it regularly (it's called informational picketing), and the Supreme Court of Canada in *R. v. Guinard* reaffirmed this right in February 2002 (see [2002] 1 S.C.R. 472). In that judgment, an insured posted a sign on his barn claiming the Commerce Insurance Company was unfairly refusing his claim. The municipality of Saint-Hyacinthe, Quebec, told him to take the sign down. He refused, maintaining that he had the right to state his opinion. The Supreme Court agreed.

This judgment means that consumer protests, signs, and websites that criticize the actions of corporations or government cannot be shut up or taken down simply because they say unpleasant things. However, what you say must be true, and your intent must be to inform, without malice.

Even if you do respectfully protest your treatment following a used car purchase from a dealer, on rare occasions that dealer may file suit against you for defamation or libel. Generally, Canadian courts take a dim view of consumers and non-government organizations, like unions and environmental groups, being sued for protesting, or even picketing. Nevertheless, some dealers will sue.

CONTACT THE RIGHT PEOPLE

Before we go any further, let's get one thing straight – a telephone call to a service manager or automaker may only be marginally effective. Auto manufacturers and their dealers want to make money, not give it back. Customer service advisors are paid to *apply* the warranty policy; don't expect them to *make* policy due to your claim's extenuating circumstances.

To get action, if you suspect a secret warranty applies or that your vehicle has an independently-confirmed factory-related defect, you have to kick your claim upstairs, where the company representatives have more power. This can usually be accomplished by sending your claim to the legal affairs department (typically found in Ontario). It should be a registered letter, fax, or e-mail – something that creates a paper trail and gets attention. What's more, that letter should indicate that you will take the matter further if no solution is forthcoming. Mention the implied warranty against the dealer and manufacturer and cite convincing jurisprudence to win your small claims court action.

TWENTY-ONE LEGAL "TIPS" YOU SHOULD KNOW

1. NO! is Just the Beginning

There are a number of situations where a defect is clearly the auto manufacturer's fault, yet, car owners are denied coverage by customer service until a lawsuit is filed. Sometimes the owner is told to make an insurance claim.

Don't do it!

Here are five common failures where the automaker is at fault due to poor design, or poor-quality materials and workship:

1. Airbag deploys when it shouldn't, or fails to deploy when it should.
2. Furry critters snack on engine compartment wiring and plastics.
3. AC condensor damaged by road debris because of unprotected placement.
4. Windshield cracks or sunroof explodes without impact.
5. Paint cracks, peels, or delaminates.

The manufacturer's or dealer's warranty is a written promise that a vehicle will be reliable, subject to certain conditions. Regardless of the number of subsequent owners, this promise remains in force as long as the warranty's original time/kilometre limits haven't expired. Tires aren't usually covered by car manufacturers' warranties; they're warranted by the tiremaker on a prorated basis. This may not be such a good deal, because the tiremaker may base the prorated calculation on the full list price that almost nobody ever pays. If you were to buy the same replacement tire from a tire store at the regular price, you might be able to pay less without the prorated rebate.

But consumers have additional rights as illustrated by Bridgestone/Firestone's massive recall in 2001 of its defective ATX II and Wilderness tires. Because of the confusion and chaos surrounding Firestone's handling of the recall, Ford's 575 Canadian dealers stepped into the breach and replaced the tires with any equivalent tires they had in stock, no questions asked. This is an important example that breaches the wall separating tire manufacturers from automakers in product liability claims. In essence, whoever makes and sells the product can be liable for damages. This liability is one of the reasons Honda replaced unsafe Takata airbags when the manufacturer dragged its feet – Honda had no choice.

This is particularly true now that the Supreme Court of Canada (*Winnipeg Condominium v. Bird Construction*, [1995] 1 S.C.R. 85) has ruled that defendants are liable in negligence for any designs that result in a risk to the public's safety or health. Sometimes automakers plead that their compliance with federal automobile safety laws immunizes them from product liability claims, but this argument has been shot down by the courts. (Type "auto safety standards liability" into an Internet search engine.)

In the U.S., safety restraints such as airbags and safety belts have limited warranty coverage sometimes extended for the lifetime of the vehicle. In Canada, however, some automakers have tried to dodge this responsibility, alleging that they are separate entities, their vehicles are different, and no U.S. agreement or service bulletin can bind them. That distinction is both disingenuous and dishonest and shouldn't hold up in small claims court.

Aftermarket products and services, such as gas-saving gadgets, rustproofing, and remote starters, may interfere with the manufacturer's warranty, so make sure you're in the clear before purchasing any optional equipment or services from an independent supplier.

How fairly a warranty is applied is more important than how long it remains in effect. Some new car dealers tell customers that they need to have original equipment parts installed in order to maintain their warranty. A variation on this theme requires that the selling dealer does routine servicing, including tune-ups and oil changes (with a certain brand of oil), or the warranty is invalidated. Nothing could be further from the truth. In Quebec, the *Consumer Protection Act* stipulates that whoever issues a warranty cannot make that warranty conditional on the use of any specific brand of motor oil, oil filter, or any other component, unless it's provided to the customer free of charge, or it's the only product available that will keep the vehicle running.

Sometimes dealers will do all sorts of minor repairs that don't correct the problem, and then after the warranty runs out, they'll tell you that major repairs are needed. You can avoid this nasty surprise by repeatedly bringing your vehicle to the dealership before the warranty ends. During each visit, insist that a written work order describes the problem as precisely as possible and mentions that this is the second, third, or fourth time the same problem has been brought to the dealer's attention. Write this down yourself, if need be. This allows you to show a pattern of non-performance by the dealer during the warranty period and establishes that the problem is serious or chronic. When the warranty expires, you have the legal right to demand that it be extended on those items consistently reappearing on your handful of work orders. *Lowe v. Fairview Chrysler* is an excellent judgment that reinforces this important principle. In another lawsuit, *François Chong v. Marine Drive Imported Cars Ltd. and Honda Canada Inc.*, a Honda owner forced Honda to fix his engine six times – until they got it right.

2. Don't Get "Cold Feet"

A judge can void unfair clauses in a sales contract or extend your warranty at any time, even though corporate lawyers spend countless hours protecting their clients with one-sided standard-form contracts. Judges sometimes look upon these agreements, called "contracts of adhesion," with skepticism. They know these loan documents, insurance contracts, automobile leases, and guarantees grant consumers little or no bargaining power. So when a dispute arises over terms or language, provincial consumer protection statutes require that judges interpret these contracts in the way most favourable to the consumer. Simply put, unequal bargaining power can be a good defence.

3. Compromise Can be a Victory

Winning litigants often end up losing their shirt after all the legal costs are included. This happens because once you are snared in the legal process, costs add up astronomically. Plus, the lawsuit can take on a life of its own and you may find yourself in too deep to drop the case. All the more reason to stay receptive to compromise offers from the other side. The old dictum that a fair compromise can be worth more than a winning judgment still holds true today.

4. Ask For "Fair" Compensation

Don't exaggerate or underestimate your claim. Pure economic losses are what can normally be recovered in cases involving misrepresentation, breach of contract, and warranty claims. Non-pecuniary damages for personal injury in Canada are generally capped at around $380,000 (Cdn.). Beyond that, plaintiffs can recover for past and future loss of income, and cost of care and medical expenses not paid by government programs. Family members may also get compensation for loss of care, guidance and companionship.

5. Sue as a Last Resort

If the seller you've been negotiating with agrees to make things right, give him or her a deadline and then have an independent shop check the repairs. Consider making the manufacturer a party to the lawsuit if the original, unexpired warranty was transferred to you; if your claim falls under the emissions warranty, a TSB, a secret warranty extension, or a safety recall campaign; or if there is extensive chassis rusting due to poor engineering and design, or cosmetic damage resulting from inferior paint or improper paint application.

6. Cast a Wide Net When Suing

We've mentioned before that civil liability means every link in the chain of production from design, manufacturing, marketing, and distribution can be sued for a product's failure or misrepresentation. This liability could include government regulators who don't act, are slow to act, or give incorrect, reckless advice. In Alberta, a $5 million class action has been filed against an auto broker/dealer and officials of the Alberta government, namely, the Minister of Service Alberta, and the Alberta Motor Vehicle Industry Council (AMVIC). The claim alleges that a duty of care was owed by AMVIC and Service Alberta to the car buyer and seller members of the class and that both defendants, through negligent acts or omissions, breached this duty of care.

Holding governments, professionals, and professional societies responsible for their negligence relating to your car complaint or other matters is not new.

7. It May Not Be Too Late to File

Limitation periods in Canada are usually two to six years depending on the province. However, the time to file can be extended according to the "discoverability" principle which applies if the plaintiff was unable to "discover" the claim until after the limitation period expired. This is especially effective in claims covered by a recall, a secret warranty, or an internal service bulletin advisory.

Because many factory-related deficiencies take years to appear, the courts have ruled that the reasonable diligence clock starts clicking only after the defect is confirmed to be manufacturer- or dealer-related (powertrain, paint, etc.). If there have been negotiations with the dealer or the automaker, or if either the dealer or the automaker has been promising to correct the defects for some time or has carried out repeated unsuccessful repairs, the deadline for filing the lawsuit can be extended.

8. Shop for Cheap Justice

The June 2009 issue of *The Canadian Lawyer* published a summary of average legal fees within Canada. From the following highlights of that article (*www.personal.umich.edu/~purzel/national_reports/ Canada.pdf*), it is easy to see how difficult it would be for many Canadians to pay to have their "day in court" going through the regular court system.

- The average hourly fee for an Ontario lawyer with ten years experience was $382 – though some fees were as high as $900 per hour.
- The hourly fee for lawyers in the western provinces was $467.
- In Quebec, 2% of the profession was charging more than $500 per hour, with a further 1% at more than $400 (*Le Journal du Barreau du Québec*, May 2009).
- In Ontario, one party's legal fees for a two-day trial would range from $18,738 to $90,404.
- The average cost (in Ontario) to each party in a two-day dispute would be $45,477.

Not surprisingly, litigants are fighting back by shunning lawyers and representing themselves, making contingency fee arrangements, asking for pay-as-you-go court costs, and searching out small claims courts where filing fees barely top $200 and lawyers are optional, or barred entirely (Quebec).

9. Use a Contingency-Fee Lawyer

Lawyers who see you are too poor to afford legal counsel but earn too much for legal aid will steer you toward a contingency-fee lawyer to help you through the regular court system. In Canada contingency fees vary from 20-45% of the proceeds awarded, and the client pays nothing unless and until there is recovery in the lawsuit. This fee arrangement particularly suits plaintiffs with serious injury claims who likely have little income. All contingency fee agreements are subject to court review; however, the agreement you signed in the lawyer's office will carry a lot of weight as to your intentions. Note, however that *most contingency-fee agreements provide that although there is no legal fee payable if the case is lost, the client remains responsible for reimbursing the lawyer for disbursements paid out.*

There are many ways to structure a contingency-fee agreement that is fair to both client and lawyer. For example, one could provide for a percentage fee that decreases (or increases) depending on the level of financial recovery. In some Canadian personal injury and malpractice matters, a higher percentage is due on the first $100,000 awarded and a lower percentage on compensation recovered in excess of $100,000.

Watch out for legal expenses like "Court Costs" that come at the end of the trial. Although filing fees are quite low, a successful litigant's disbursements may be charged to the losing party. These can include costs of effecting service; expenses for travel, accommodation, and photocopying; witness expenses; and experts' reports.

An unsuccessful party may also have to pay a self-represented successful party an amount as compensation for inconvenience and expense. If that plaintiff is represented by a lawyer, the court may award the winning side a reasonable representation fee at trial or at an assessment hearing

10. Mediation and Arbitration Slash Costs and Delays

If you have a dispute with a carmaker and are looking for a no-charge repair or refund of money spent on repairs, CAMVAP is worth a look. A CAMVAP arbitration is quick, inexpensive, and a relatively effective way to get money back for a repair or an order requiring the automaker and dealer to fix a vehicle.

Beware of standard form contracts containing forced arbitration clauses. The hearing process will likely be rigged in favour of whomever drew up the contract, arbitrators may be prejudiced or incompetent, and your recourse options could be severely limited. Nevertheless, mediation saves costs, shortens delays, and is more informal and convenient to litigants. Also, parties may agree to some form of alternative dispute resolution prior to, or at any time during, the course of a legal claim. Take note, in some provinces and cases, mediation before a recognized mediator is mandatory (especially in most small claims courts.).

Mandatory arbitration clauses in car sales contracts or on repair bills can be ignored, says the Supreme Court of Canada, which has held that the requirement for arbitration in consumer contracts of adhesion may be limited or curtailed by the courts. In fact, Ontario, Alberta and Quebec consumer protection legislation expressly prohibits mandatory arbitration clauses in consumer agreements.

Case law is also on your side. In *Seidel v. Telus Communications Inc.,* a consumer's contract with *Telus* prohibited her from filing a class action against the company. The court ruled the plaintiff could file her class action, notwithstanding the Telus arbitration clause. Ironically, franchised car dealers have also skirted around forced arbitration clauses that prevent them from suing automakers. In *Stoneleigh Motors Limited et al. v. General Motors of Canada Limited*, the Ontario Superior Court of Justice permitted various GM dealers to participate in a group action against GM despite the inclusion of an arbitration clause in their dealer agreement. This case centered on the 2009 federal auto bailout and the termination of approximately 240 GM dealers. Nineteen dealers sued GM, saying the arbitration clause in the dealer agreement was inapplicable. The Ontario Superior Court agreed and allowed the claim to proceed, citing concerns over the dealers' lack of resources as individuals.

11. Choose the Right Court

You must decide what remedy to pursue: A partial refund (*quanti minoris*) or a cancellation of the sale. To determine the refund amount, add the estimated cost of repairing existing mechanical defects to the cost of prior repairs. Don't exaggerate your losses or claim for repairs that are considered routine maintenance listed in the owner's manual. If it's not listed, it's not *routine*. A suit for cancellation of sale should be thought out carefully since it involves a number of practical problems non-lawyers often ignore.

First, the court requires that the vehicle be "tendered," or taken back to the seller, at the time the lawsuit is filed. This means that you are without transportation for as long as the case continues, unless you purchase another vehicle in the interim. Secondly, after two, up to seven, years the case is appealed, if you lose, you must then take back the old vehicle, pay storage and expert witness fees, and pay all of the monthly finance payments. You could go from having no vehicle to having two, one of which is a clunker. So, it's fair to ask – what did I really gain?

Generally, if the cost of repairs or the sales contract amount falls within the small claims court limit, file the case there to keep costs to a minimum and to get a faster hearing. Lawyers aren't necessary, filing fees are minimal (about $125), and, depending on the court's load, cases can be heard within a few months. CAMVAP is a good venue to use to recover money spent on repairs if your vehicle qualifies for their arbitration program.

Watch what you ask for. If you claim more than the small claims court limit, you'll have to go to a higher court, where court costs are deadly and hearings are frequently delayed.

12. Use Small Claims Court for Large Claims

Crooked companies scurry away from small claims courts like cockroaches from bug spray, not because the courts can issue million-dollar judgments or force litigants to spend millions in legal fees (they can't), but because they can award sizeable sums to plaintiffs ($25,000-$30,000) and make jurisprudence that other judges on the same bench are likely to follow. Plus, the possibility of losing a case could hurt their image in small communities, or encourage government to look more closely into some business activities.

Legal scholars look down their nose at small claims judgments, affirming that small claims decisions don't make "case law" or jurisprudence binding on other courts. It is *Lemon-Aid*'s experience, over 45-years, following thousands of lawsuits, that small claims judges discuss cases with their peers and develop a common perception relative to similar lawsuits. It happened with hundreds of premature rusting and paint delamination complaints, as well as Ford and Nissan's "redating" of year-old vehicles as new, current models. In fact, both of these small claims collective actions (rust and redating) were upheld in two separate judgements by our Supreme Court. How's that for jurisprudence?

Again, small claims doesn't necessarily mean "small" judgments. For example, in *Dawe v. Courtesy Chrysler* (Dartmouth Nova Scotia Small Claims Court; SCCH #206825; July 30, 2004), Judge Patrick L Casey, Q.C., rendered an impressive 21-page decision citing key automobile product liability cases over the past 80 years. He awarded $5,037 to the owner of a new 2001 Cummins-equipped Ram pickup that suffered from myriad ailments. The truck shifted erratically, lost braking ability, wandered all over the road, lost power or jerked and bucked, bottomed out when passing over bumps, allowed water to leak into the cab, produced a burnt-wire and oil smell as the lights would dim, and produced a rear-end whine and wind noise around the doors and under the dash. Dawe had sold the vehicle and reduced his claim to meet the small claims threshold.

Small Claims Courts in Canada

There are small claims courts in most counties of every province, and you can make a claim either in the county where the problem happened or in the county where the defendant lives and conducts business. Simply go to the small claims court office and ask for a claim form. Instructions on how to fill it out accompany the form. Remember, you must identify the defendant correctly, and this may require some help from the court clerk or a law student because some automakers name local attorneys to handle suits (look for other recent lawsuits naming the same party). Crooks often change their company's name to escape liability; for example, it would be next to impossible to sue Joe's Garage Inc. (2015) successfully if your contract is with Joe's Garage Inc. (2004).

Use the Maximum Limits for Small Claims Courts table to check your provincial or territorial court's website for specific rules and restrictions. Also, save time by downloading claim forms and other documents from the Internet (Google "small claims court Ontario," for example).

Claim Limits for Small Claims Courts

Province	Claim Maximum	Province	Claim Maximum
Alberta	$25,000	Nunavut	$20,000
British Columbia	$25,000	Ontario	$25,000
Manitoba	$10,000	Prince Edward Island	$8,000
New Brunswick	$12,500	Quebec	$15,000
Nova Scotia	$25,000	Saskatchewan	$20,000
Northwest Territories	$36,000	Yukon	$25,000

It is also important to note the following information:

- Plaintiffs with claims exceeding the maximum allowed may abandon the excess portion.

- Disputes involving title to land, slander, libel, bankruptcy, false imprisonment, or malicious prosecution must be handled in a superior court.

- In Quebec, people who appear before the Small Claims Division represent themselves, without a lawyer, and appeals are limited.

It wouldn't hurt to hire a lawyer or a paralegal for a brief walk-through of small claims court procedures to ensure that you've prepared your case properly and that you know what objections the other side will likely raise. If you'd like a lawyer to do all the work for you, there are a number of law firms around the country that specialize in small claims litigation. "Small claims" doesn't mean small legal fees, however. In Toronto, some law offices charge a flat fee of $1,500 for a basic small claims lawsuit and trial.

You're entitled to bring to court any evidence relevant to your case, including original copies of written documents such as contracts, letters, or bills of sale or receipts. If your car has developed severe rust problems, bring photographs (signed and dated by the photographer) to court. You may also have witnesses testify in court. It's important to discuss a witness's testimony prior to the court date. If a witness can't attend the court date, he or she can write a report and sign it for representation in court. This situation usually applies to an expert witness, such as an independent mechanic who has evaluated your car's problems. Remember, however, that signed documents presented without a witness to guaranty their authenticity or to submit to cross-examination can be easily set aside.

If you lose your case, some small claims court statutes allow a retrial, at a nominal cost, in very exceptional circumstances. If a new witness has come forward, additional evidence has been discovered, or key documents that were previously not available have become accessible.

Finally in small claims court where informality and mediation rule, don't be a smart-aleck, and, above all, don't mouth off to the judge. Although an award of costs in small claims court, other than disbursements, should not exceed 15% of the amount claimed, an irritated presiding judge may increase the costs to penalize a party or a party's representative for unreasonable behaviour during the proceeding. Stay cool and let the facts carry the day.

Justice Marvin A. Zuker's annual *Ontario Small Claims Court Practice 2017* (Carswell, 2016) serves as an excellent reference full of tips on filing, pleading, and collecting a judgment. Judge Zuker's annual publication is easily understood by non-lawyers and uses court decisions from across Canada to help you plead your case successfully in any Canadian court.

Alan MacDonald, a *Lemon-Aid* reader won his small claims court case by presenting important facts and jurisprudence. Here's how he describes the experience (*MacDonald v. Highbury Ford Sales Limited*, Ontario Superior Court of Justice in the Small Claims Court London, June 6, 2000, Court File #0001/00, Judge J. D. Searle):

> In 1999 after only 105,000 km the automatic transmission went. I took [my 1994 Ford Taurus wagon] to Highbury Ford to have it repaired. We paid $2,070 to have the transmission fixed, but protested and felt the transmission failed prematurely. We contacted Ford, but to no avail: their reply was we were out of warranty period. The transmission was so poorly repaired (and we went back to Highbury Ford several times) that we had to go to Mr. Transmission to have the transmission fixed again nine months later at a further $1,906.02. . . .
>
> My observations with going through small claims court involved the following: I filed in January of 2000, the trial took place on June 1 and the judgment was issued June 6.
>
> At pretrial, a representative of Ford (Ann Sroda) and a representative from Highbury Ford were present. I came with one binder for each of the defendants, the court, and one for myself (each binder was about 3 inches thick – containing your reports on Ford Taurus automatic transmissions, ALLDATA Service Bulletins, [and extracts from the following websites:] Taurus Transmissions Victims (Bradley website), Center for Auto Safety . . . Read This Before Buying a Taurus . . . and the Ford Vent Page . . . .

The representative from Ford asked a lot of questions (I think she was trying to find out if I had read the contents of the information I was relying on). The Ford representative then offered a 50 percent settlement based on the initial transmission work done at Highbury Ford. The release allowed me to still sue Highbury Ford with regards to the necessity of going to Mr. Transmission because of the faulty repair done by the dealer. Highbury Ford displayed no interest in settling the case, and so I had to go to court.

For court, I prepared by issuing a summons to the manager at Mr. Transmission, who did the second transmission repair, as an expert witness. ... Next, I went to the law school library in London and received a great deal of assistance in researching cases pertinent to car repairs. I was told that judgments in your home province (in my case, Ontario) were binding on the court; that cases outside of the home province could be considered, but not binding, on the judge.

The cases I used for trial involved *Pelleray v. Heritage Ford Sales Ltd., Ontario Small Claims Court (Scarborough) SC7688/91 March 22, 1993; Phillips et al. v. Ford Motor Co. of Canada Ltd. et al, Ontario* Reports 1970, 15th January 1970; *Gregorio v. Intrans-Corp.,* Ontario Court of Appeal, May 19, 1994; *Collier v. MacMaster's Auto Sales,* New Brunswick Court of Queen's Bench, April 26, 1991; *Sigurdson v. Hillcrest Service & Acklands (1977),* Saskatchewan Queen's Bench; *White v. Sweetland,* Newfoundland District Court, Judicial Centre of Gander, November 8, 1978; *Raiches Steel Works v. J. Clark & Son,* New Brunswick Supreme Court, March 7, 1977; *Mudge v. Corner Brook Garage Ltd.,* Newfoundland Supreme Court, July 17, 1975; *Sylvain v. Carroseries d'Automobiles Guy Inc. (1981),* C.P. 333, Judge Page; and *Gagnon v. Ford Motor Company of Canada, Limited et Marineau Automobile Co. Ltée. (1974),* C.S. 422–423.

In court, I had prepared the case, as indicated above, and had my expert witness and two other witnesses who had driven the vehicle (my wife and my 18-year-old son). As you can see by the judgment, we won our case and I was awarded $1,756.52, including prejudgment interest and costs.

13. Use Class Actions for Similar Claims

Class actions are used extensively to group a large number of people who have a similar claim against the same party or parties. A lawyer charges nothing up front, but exacts a 20-30+ percentage fee if the case is won or settled.

Be wary. Some lawyers get rich copying American lawsuits that have been settled and don't pursue the action vigorously themselves. Is this right? No. Can it be stopped? Yes. If presiding judges declare the lawyer fees excessive.

14. Avoid Hearsay and Annoying Courtroom Tactics

Judges have considerable latitude in allowing hearsay evidence if it's introduced properly. But it is essential that printed evidence and/or witnesses (relatives are not excluded) be available to confirm that a false representation actually occurred, that a part is failure-prone, or that its replacement is covered by a secret warranty or internal service bulletin alert. If you can't find an independent expert, introduce this evidence through the automaker reps and dealership service personnel who have to be at the trial anyhow. They more than likely know all about the service bulletins and extended warranty programs cited in *Lemon-Aid* and may contradict one another if they are excluded from the courtroom prior to testifying. Incidentally, you may wish to have the court clerk send a subpoena requiring the deposition of the documents you intend to cite, all warranty extensions relevant to your problem, and other lawsuits filed against the company for similar failures. This can make the fur fly in Oshawa, Oakville, Windsor or Toronto. Sometimes, the service manager or company representative will make key admissions if questioned closely by you, a court mediator, or the trial judge. Here are three important questions to ask:

1. Is this a common problem?
2. Do you recognize this service bulletin?
3. Is there a case-by-case "goodwill" plan covering this repair?

Automakers often blame owners for having pushed their vehicle beyond its limits. Therefore, when you seek to cancel the contract or get repair work reimbursed, it's essential that you get an independent mechanic to prove the vehicle was well maintained and driven prudently.

15. Exemplary, Punitive and Other Damages

Yes, you can claim for hotel and travel costs or compensation for general inconvenience. After a claim has been filed in small claims court, automakers sometimes up their out-of-court offer to include most of the owner's expenses because they know the courts will be far more generous. For example, a British Columbia court's decision gave $2,257 for hotel and travel costs, and then capped it off with a $5,000 award for "inconvenience and loss of enjoyment of their luxury vehicle" to a motorist who was fed up with his lemon Cadillac (see *Wharton v. Tom Harris Chevrolet Oldsmobile Cadillac Ltd. and General Motors of Canada Limited*; B.C. Supreme Court, Vancouver; 1999/12/02; Docket C982104). In the *Sharman v. Ford* case, the judge gave the plaintiff $7,500 for "mental distress" caused by the fear that his children would fall out of his 2000 Windstar equipped with a faulty sliding door.

Generally, damages are recoverable for personal and property damage and for both cost and loss of use of the product when reasonably foreseeable as a result of the wrongdoing. This includes non-pecuniary damages (for pain and suffering) and pecuniary damages (loss of income, of earning potential, business profits, dependency claims for the loss of care and companionship, out-of-pocket expense, etc.).

Unlike aggravated damages, which focus on the plaintiff's loss, punitive damages focus specifically on the defendant's conduct. Punitive damages may be recovered in rare cases where the conduct of the defendant was so egregious as to "shock the conscience" of the Court. Punitive damages, in addition to being rarely ordered, are usually for small amounts.

As of March 19, 2005, the Supreme Court of Canada confirmed that car owners can ask for punitive, or exemplary, damages when they feel the seller's or the automaker's conduct has been so outrageously bad that the court should protect society by awarding a sum of money large enough to dissuade others from engaging in similar immoral, unethical conduct. In *Prebushewski v. Dodge City Auto (1984) Ltd. and Chrysler Canada Ltd.* (2001 SKQB 537; QB1215/99JCS), the plaintiff got $25,000 in a judgment handed down December 6, 2001, in Saskatoon. The award followed testimony from Chrysler's expert witness that the company was aware of many cases where daytime running lights shorted and caused 1996 Ram pickups to catch fire. The plaintiff's truck had burned to the ground, and Chrysler refused the owner's claim, saying it had fulfilled its expressed warranty obligations, in spite of its knowledge that fires were commonplace. The plaintiff sued on the grounds that there was an implied warranty that the vehicle would be safe. Justice Rothery gave this stinging rebuke in his judgment against Chrysler and its dealer:

> In this case, the quantum ought to be sufficiently high as to correct the defendants' behaviour. In particular, Chrysler's corporate policy to place profits ahead of the potential danger to its customers' safety and personal property must be punished. And when such corporate policy includes a refusal to comply with the provisions of the *Act* and a refusal to provide any relief to the plaintiff, I find an award of $25,000 for exemplary damages to be appropriate. I therefore order Chrysler and Dodge City to pay: Damages in the sum of $41,969.83; Exemplary damages in the sum of $25,000; Party and party costs.

16. Make Dealers Honour Third-Party Warranties

It's often difficult to collect on supplementary warranties because independent companies go out of business or limit the warranty's coverage unreasonably. Provincial laws cover both situations. If the bankrupt warranty company's insurance policy won't cover your claim, take the dealer to small claims court and ask for repair costs or the refund of the original warranty payment. Your argument for holding the dealer responsible is that by making representations about the warranty or accepting a commission to act as an agent of the defunct company, the dealer has some obligations toward you.

17. Enforce "Secret" Warranties

The Ford Focus and Escape with steering issues, GM's biodegrable catalytic converters, Honda's overheating engines and paint delamination, Nissan's glitch-prone CVT transmissions, Toyotas needing new pistons and rings, and VWs that leak when it rains are only a few of the dozens of car models covered by service bulletin warranty extensions unearthed by *Lemon-Aid*.

Lawyers know manufacturers are reluctant to make free repair programs public because they feel that doing so would increase their legal liability. The closest they come to an admission is sending a "goodwill program," or TSB to dealers or "special policy" to first owners. Consequently, the only motorists who find out about these policies are the original owners who haven't changed their addresses or leased their vehicles. The other motorists who get compensated for repairs are the ones who read *Lemon-Aid* each year, ask to have TSBs stapled to their work orders, and yell the loudest.

Remember, vehicles bought used and repairs undertaken by independent repair shops could qualify for a reimbursement using these secret warranty programs. Large, costly repairs, such as blown engines, burned transmissions, and peeling paint, are often covered. Even little repairs are sometimes included. If you have a TSB but you're still refused compensation, keep in mind that the TSB may constitute an admission there is a defect.

18. Use Recall Compensation

Following the government bailout of Chrysler and GM in 2009 most auto industry pundits predicted that automobile quality would improve and safety-related defects would decline. They were half right. Although GM's quality did improve, almost half of the 30 million recall notices sent out to General Motors customers in 2014 involved vehicles made within the last few years rather than defects affecting GM's "old" pre-bankruptcy lineup – that's partly because GM implemented much tighter internal procedures around safety problems.

Vehicles are recalled for different reasons. They may be potentially unsafe or they don't conform to federal pollution control regulations, like Volkswagen's recent diesel emissions confession. Whatever the reason, recalls are a great way to get free repairs and other compensation – if you know which ones apply to you and you have the patience of Job. NHTSA says about 25% of the recalled vehicles never made it back to the dealership for repairs, because owners were never informed, didn't consider the defect to be that hazardous, or gave up waiting for corrective parts to come in.

If you've moved or bought a used vehicle, it's smart to pay a visit to your local dealership, give them your address, and get a report on which recalls, warranties, and free service campaigns apply to your vehicle. Simply give the service advisor the vehicle identification number – found on your registration, or on your dash just below the windshield on the driver's side – and have the number run through the automaker's computer system. Ask for a computer printout of the vehicle's history, and make sure you're listed in the automaker's records as the new owner. This ensures that you'll receive notices of warranty extensions and emissions and safety recalls.

In order to cut recall costs, automakers sometimes try to limit a recall to vehicles in a certain designated region. This practice may not make sense, since cars are mobile and an unsafe, rust-cankered steering unit can be found anywhere, not just in certain rust-belt provinces or American states. For instance, in 2001, Ford attempted to limit to five American states its recall of faulty Firestone tires. Public ridicule of the company's proposal led to an extension of the recall throughout North America.

Car companies hate to admit their mistakes because they know that lawsuits and bad publicity will inevitably ensue. Automobile manufacturers and dealers take a restrictive view of what constitutes a manufacturer safety or emissions defects and frequently charge for repairs that should be free under federal safety or emissions legislation. If you experience similar problems, insist that the automaker fix the problem at no expense to you.

Recall campaigns in the U.S. force automakers to pay the entire cost of fixing a vehicle's safety-related defect for any vehicle purchased up to eight years before the recall's announcement. In Canada, there is no specific time limit.

Monitoring recall campaigns is a real problem. The government devotes the barest minimum of resources to monitoring recall completions; automakers can drag their feet for a year of more before supplying replacement parts; dealers sometimes use recall visits to sell expensive work not covered by the recall; and the recall itself may leave out some vehicles that present the same defect.

19. "Black Box" Snitches

If your car has an airbag, it's probably spying on you. And if you get into an accident caused by a vehicle malfunction, you may be glad that it is.

Event data recorders (EDRs) have been hidden near the engine, under the seat, or in the centre consoles of airbag-equipped vehicles since the early '90s. To find out if your car or truck carries an EDR, read your owner's manual, contact the regional office of your car's manufacturer, or ask a dealer.

EDRs operate in a similar fashion to flight data recorders used in airplanes. They record data from the last few seconds before impact, including the force of the collision, the airbag's performance, whether the brakes were applied, engine and vehicle speed, gas pedal position, and whether the driver was wearing a seat belt.

EDRs are an excellent tool to determine what happened in the seconds leading up to a crash. Car owners who wish to dispute criminal charges, oppose their insurer's decision as to fault, or hold an automaker responsible for a safety device's failure (airbags, seat belts, or brakes) may find this data invaluable. Accessing EDR information requires special equipment and model-specific procedures that are beyond the capabilities of do-it-yourselfers and most mechanics.

In the past, some automakers hid their collected data from government and insurance researchers. This argument, however, has been roundly rejected by law enforcement agencies, the courts, and car owners who need the information (see *www.harristechnical.com/downloads/cdrlist.pdf*).

The police, rental agencies, and fleet administrators are also using EDR data to pin legal liability on drivers or automakers for accidents, including excessive speeding, inattention, and the failure of safety components, such as airbags that don't deploy when they should (or do deploy when they shouldn't).

20. Retrieving your Vehicle's Onboard Data

Access your vehicle's operating data using one of the smartphone Apps listed in Part One under "Helpful Automobile Apps," or browse through 50 of the most popular Apple or Android apps that are free or cost very little at *http://independentmotors.net/50-amazing-auto-apps/*. For do-it-yourselfers, OBD Auto Doctor is one of the best advanced OBD2 car diagnostics tools you can find. Among other things, this free Microsoft app will tell you why your check engine light or MIL keeps going on and shows you how to reset it. Google "Automobile diagnostic apps" for a comprehensive listing of other inexpensive or free applications.

21. Use "Internal" Service Bulletins for Settlements

In court each party has to show the other all documents in its possession, power, or control that may be relevant to the claim and make the documents available before trial. Each party is required by law to disclose the existence of any documents in its possession that are relevant to the proceeding if they have been requested. The obligation to disclose is ongoing throughout the trial.

In the United States, asking for a company's files scares the pants off corporations. In serious injury cases, out-of-court settlements are achieved by forcing an auto company to divulge owner complaints, or the amount of claim payouts for similar defects, or to disclose confidential service bulletins that show failure trends and fixes. Canadian subsidiaries of the same automakers usually argue that they are just a distributor of vehicles, with no information about their design, and not involved in their manufacturing. It usually takes a court order for them to provide the information.

*2011-2012 Chevrolet Cruze, equipped with a 1.8L engine
and 6-speed automatic transmission.*

CONDITION: Some models may be missing a shift-cable grommet at the transmission end due to contact with engine coolant from a leaking thermostat housing.

SYMPTOMS: an irregular or loose feel to the automatic transmission gear-selector lever; hard shifting; and the lever could bind or lock in one position.

SPECIAL COVERAGE ADJUSTMENT: 8 years or 120,000 miles (193,000 km), regardless of ownership.

This internal service bulletin included an admission of a defect that is GM's responsibility.

USING GOVERNMENT AGENCIES

Illusory consumer protection is created by legislation that defines consumer rights and obligations, but then sets up an enforcement mechanism that is ineffective for the purpose it was created. It is neither alive nor dead. It doesn't regulate nor deregulate. It's simply "there" – used as a "feel good" symbol of government's inactive action. Here's how a government "zombie" is created:

- Enact investigation and enforcement powers that are weak or unclear;

  - Ensure that investigation and enforcement are underfunded;

  - Keep civil penalties low and forego the use of criminal charges;

    - Choose staffers who were once employed by the industry to be regulated;

- Don't lay charges if a sizeable charitable donation is made;

- Channel settlement funds to lawyers and government, instead of to victims; and

- Set up a compliant advisory board with limited powers and little knowledge of what's going on.

- Select the majority of Board members from the regulated industry.

"Zombie" Consumer Protection

2007-2017 RATINGS "GOOD CARS, BAD CARS"

What Really Happened to Toyota?

Toyota executives had a number of warnings about its deteriorating quality. In early 2009, for example, before the massive recalls (for sudden unintended acceleration), Toyota disbanded a high-level task force that had been set up in 2005 to deal with quality issues. A Toyota manager explained the decision by saying that management had come to believe that quality control was part of the company's DNA and therefore they didn't need a special committee to enforce it.

In January 2008, Chris Tinto, Toyota's U.S. vice president in charge of technical and regulatory affairs, further warned his fellow executives that "some of the quality issues we are experiencing are showing up in defect investigations (rear gas struts, ball joints, etc...)." These and other early warnings were ignored. In a pattern not uncommon in large organizations, politically powerful executives shrugged off early warnings of lower-ranking executives.

MITSloan Management Review, June 22, 2011
Robert E. Cole
sloanreview.mit.edu/article/what-really-happened-to-toyota/

2016-2017: An Opportunity for Buyers

Despite the fact that our loonie lost almost 30% of its value against the U.S. dollar in the last couple of years, carmakers haven't increased prices proportionately. Evidently, their marketing people know that raising prices by almost a third would price them out of the market.

But, there is more.

Unrelenting demand, low fuel prices, and easy low-interest credit have resulted in another perfect alignment of the planets for buyers of new cars and trucks who took delivery of almost two million vehicles in 2016. Following last year's record sales, carmakers like Fiat Chrysler are over-reacting again and imprudently flooding the market with long 84- and 96-month auto loans. Furthermore, the market distortion caused by cheaper gas and very low interest rates makes "gas guzzlers," "luxo-cars," and all-dressed SUVs and trucks more attractive to consumers, even at higher prices, than discounted econoboxes, diesels, hybrids, and electrics.

Buick Drops 2017 Verano. The Verano compact sedan will be axed after an abbreviated 2017 model year, as GM concentrates on crossovers and SUVs. Now that it has been discontinued, you can expect the Verano's resale value to fall, making it an interesting used car for buyers looking for refinement in a small package.

The U.S. Department of Energy expects low gasoline pump prices to last beyond 2017. Moreover, fuel economy has improved so much that the fuel cost to operate a crossover or compact SUV is comparable to that of sedans from a decade ago. The public has fallen in love with the extra height that contributes to comfort and a better view of the road, along with the storage space that comes with an SUV's hatchback body.

Five Ways to Get a "Good" Car

1. **Treat the purchase as an investment:** Buy a vehicle that is reasonably priced, financed at a competitive interest rate, has a high predicted resale value, provides reasonable fuel economy, and can be serviced at most independent repair shops.

2. **Look for above-average reliability and durability:** Factory-related auto defects can't hide from the Internet or the Automobile Protection Association's (APA) public complaint hotlines. Thanks to information put out by government safety agencies, independent consumer groups, and private auto safety associations, you can separate the cherries from the lemons and purchase a vehicle that will last 12-15 largely trouble-free years – that's several years longer than the 6-8 years most first owners keep their vehicles.

3. **Load up on safety features:** This means getting a vehicle that has at least these four essential safety features: A high crash-protection test score, electronic stability control (all 2012 and later models), fail-safe accelerator override, and head-protecting side curtain air bags.

4. **Don't go overboard on performance and comfort:** More gadgets mean more glitches. Features should focus on functionality and interior amenities must be practical, comfortable, and convenient to access. Watch out for chin-to-chest head restraints.

5. **Be wary of infotainment features:** Unfortunately, the stampede for optimum "connectivity" has resulted in failure-prone in-dash systems like Ford's MyFord Touch on 2011-2017 models. Several years ago the Ford brand fell from 5th to 27th in J. D. Power & Associates' new-car quality survey, largely because of complaints with MyFord Touch. On the other hand, Chrysler's Uconnect touch screen infotainment system is ranked as one of the *best* in the industry. The better strategy is not to go overboard on in-dash features, and look for good connectivity with your smartphone instead. Your phone will likely get replaced every two to four years. The in-dash system will be obsolete long before the projected 15 year lifespan of your new vehicle is reached. When they are available and not free of charge, the price of automaker navigation system updates is exorbitant.

Infotainment Systems: All Not Created Equal

Well-rated infotainment systems include the Chrysler Uconnect, GM Buick/Chevrolet/GMC My Link, Hyundai Blue Link, Infiniti Connection, Kia Uvo, Nissan Connect, and the Volvo Sensus Connect system. Infotainment features drivers rate as poor are: Honda/Acura Link, Mazda Connect, Mercedes-Benz Comand, Subaru Starlink, Ford My Ford, Toyota Entune, and the Cadillac Cue system.

For 2016 or later models you can plug into your car's system using a smartphone app (Apple's CarPlay or Android Auto) that will give the infotainment system all the functionality of your smartphone, including quicker and more comprehensive free updates, current traffic reports, and points of interest, plus a screen with bigger icons, a more user-friendly menu, and voice-activated navigation.

Either the Android Auto or Apple CarPlay apps can be installed in minutes.

Also if your car's engine warning light suddenly comes on, you can pull over, attach the $50 U.S. 'Fixd' app and find out if you need to go slow or call for a tow (*https://www.fixdapp.com/buy*).

Fixd interprets your warning lights via a Bluetooth signal sent to your smartphone.

Best Model Choices

A car or truck should be kept ten years or longer to compensate for depreciation and assorted acquisition fees. A new well-equipped compact car or small SUV will run between $20,000 and $35,000; a four-year-old used version could sell for half as much. Add a couple more years and you can shave more than half from the original selling price.

New or used, the vehicle you buy should meet your everyday driving needs and have high crashworthiness and reliability scores. Average annual maintenance should cost no more than the CAA-and-DesRosiers-estimated average of $800 to $1,100. If you're buying a used vehicle more than three years old, the depreciation rate should have leveled off, so that subsequent years won't cut the car's price by more than a couple of thousand dollars. Parts and servicing costs shouldn't be excessive either. Ideally, you'll pay off your purchase before it's time to trade it for another vehicle; that way, you'll enjoy a couple of years of no car payments and have some equity for your next purchase.

South Korea: Boasting; Japan: Coasting; Volkswagen: Roasting

The most improved vehicles come from South Korea, which made an amazing quality/sales turnaround in the decade between 2005-2015. Toyota and Honda, the major Japanese automakers, rode on past glories during the same period and are now getting back on track. Among the European makes, Mercedes-Benz and Audi have improved their vehicles recently. Volkswagen is in disarray in the aftermath of the discovery that it cheated on diesel emissions certification for several years. Perhaps surprisingly, among the domestic automakers, General Motors has improved the most in the last few years. Fiat Chrysler is very uneven, and finally Ford continues to be trapped in its self-inflicted poor-quality funk.

In 2017, the compact car segment offers the most performance, safety, and reliability for the money. However, customers who were ready to buy smaller during the recession of 2008-2009, or consider a hybrid or electric vehicle, are now marching in tandem toward well-equipped compact and mid-size SUVs, pickups, and luxury vehicles. For buyers who are interested, there are plenty of well-priced fuel-efficient models on the market, including cars like Honda's Fit; Hyundai's Accent and Elantra; Subaru's Forester; the Mazda3, Toyota Corolla; and new Chevrolet Cruze hatchback.

If interior room is your paramount concern, nothing beats a minivan. Consider the Toyota Sienna or, if you're looking for a low price on a well equipped used van, one of the Fiat Chrysler products like the Town and Country or Grand Caravan. The smaller Mazda5 and Kia Rondo are good people movers that can carry more than five people, yet are often overlooked.

Luxury models and small-to-large Chrysler and Ford passenger cars represent the worst values among new vehicles. The best retained value among luxury vehicles are the BMW 3 Series, the X3, Acura RDX, and MDX, and the Lexus lineup. Luxury vehicles with rapid depreciation and uncertain reliability are those built by Cadillac, Jaguar, Land Rover, and Lincoln; it's probably best to lease them and let their manufacturers take the loss when it's time to turn them in.

Researchers at the University of Michigan publish an annual record, listing which automakers make the most and least satisfying vehicles. Called the American Customer Satisfaction Index (ACSI), the 2015 report pulls no punches in naming which manufacturers have the poorest owner satisfaction for different years. ACSI's most surprising conclusions confirm that there is no correlation between the cost of an automobile and owner satisfaction, although foreign makes generally have the most satisfied customers.

While it is true that all cars are now much better than they were 20 years ago, it is alarming that so many of them have quality problems. This is happening partly because of the rush to introduce new technology and has negative consequences for safety, costs and customer satisfaction. Here are some of the ACSI's 2015 findings.

- At the top of the industry overall, Toyota's Lexus plateaus at 84%, taking the lead from Mercedes-Benz, which falls 3% to 83%. After a sharp drop, Honda's luxury brand Acura appears to have turned a corner. One of only two brands to improve this year, Acura rebounds 8% to 83%, tied with Mercedes and Lincoln for second place.

- BMW – the other gainer – rises 3% to 82%. Also at 82% are Subaru and Toyota, the top-scoring mass market automakers. Volkswagen (pre-diesel scandal), Buick and Honda all slip into a tie at 80%. Cadillac and Mazda also score 80%. Meanwhile, the Ford nameplate and Chevrolet drop to 79% alongside Volvo, which returns to the ACSI near the bottom of the luxury category.

- The remaining automakers are below the industry average. GMC and Kia (each down 5%) match Audi at 78%, just ahead of Nissan and Nissan's luxury nameplate Infiniti, which debuts at 77%. Mitsubishi also posts its first ACSI score of 77%. BMW's MINI enters the Index at 76%, tying Fiat Chrysler's Dodge. At the bottom of the category are all four Fiat Chrysler brands: Dodge (-3% to 76%), Jeep (-5% to 75%), Chrysler (-9% to 74%) and Fiat (73%).

The charts that follow show five-year customer satisfaction trends for domestic automakers in comparison with international manufacturers, as well as individual results for Detroit's Big Three.

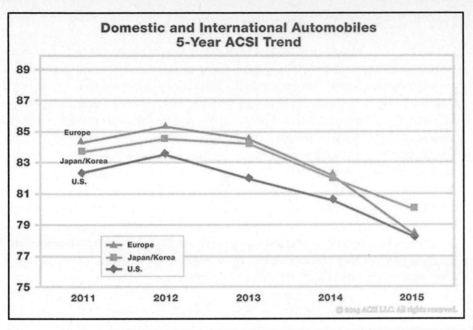

**Domestic and International Automobiles
5-Year ACSI Trend**

Europe
Japan/Korea
U.S.

Legend:
- Europe
- Japan/Korea
- U.S.

2011 2012 2013 2014 2015

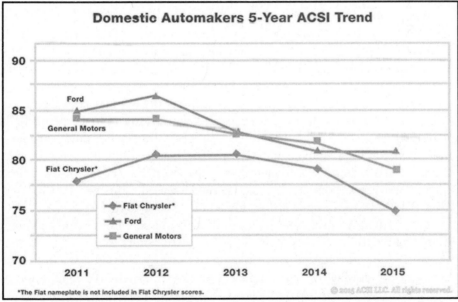

Domestic Automakers 5-Year ACSI Trend

Ford
General Motors
Fiat Chrysler*

Legend:
- Fiat Chrysler*
- Ford
- General Motors

2011 2012 2013 2014 2015

*The Fiat nameplate is not included in Fiat Chrysler scores.

Low owner satisfaction scores are due to the following three factors: Cost control, increased complexity, and a rush to introduce new technology on vehicles before all the bugs have been worked out.

Don't Believe in the "Fuel Fairy"

Ottawa is in cahoots with automakers in coming up with fanciful fuel economy ratings. It's not a conspiracy; it's just lazy complacency. Up to 2014, the Canadian mileage figures were "cooked" by as much as 22%, compared to the published fuel consumption ratings of the identical vehicles in the United States! In November of 2011, CBC News and the APA compared the Canadian and American fuel consumption ratings of various 2012 models. The survey showed that Canadian fuel-economy estimates were inflated by 16-22% compared to the U.S. estimates, for the identical vehicles.

More accurate U.S. fuel economy figures for 2014 and earlier models can be found at: *www.fueleconomy.gov*, while the puffed-up Canadian figures reside at: *oee.nrcan.gc.ca/transportation/tools/fuelratings/ratings-search.cfm*.

Fuel economy ratings are generated by the industry from standardized lab tests conducted with rosy assumptions, not under real-life road conditions. One objective is to encourage you to get rid of your current vehicle by dangling the mirage of dramatic fuel savings with a new model. The government test cycle becomes a fig leaf to protect the automaker from being fingered for its misleading misrepresentations.

Take our Part Four fuel economy estimates with a grain of salt and blame it on the feds, since the APA has discovered that even the new "restated" fuel consumption ratings introduced in Canada for 2015 are off between 0 and 20% compared to on-the-road fuel use (the 2L BMW turbo had the highest discrepancy in the APA's tests).

Ford, Hyundai, and Kia were caught advertising boosted mileage ratings and compensated owners through cheques and debit cards, while Honda extended its warranty. In 2015, VW and Audi were caught using "cheat" devices to give false emissions readings in government approved diesel certification tests. Then in 2016 Suzuki and Mitsubishi were caught using the wrong fuel economy test procedures on Japanese market vehicles. Suzuki claimed it was all a mistake. GM blamed their 2016 SUV mileage misrepresentations on a "clerical error."

These fraudulent schemes have resulted in massive fines by government regulators, hundreds of class actions filed by car owners in Canada and the U.S., and settlements by automakers that compensate owners. For example, GM U.S. announced last May that its compensation program will give 135,000 retail customers an average of $450 to $900 U.S. because the company overstated fuel economy by 1 to 2 miles per gallon on certain 2016 SUVs.

Customers who bought a 2016 Chevrolet Traverse, Buick Enclave, or GMC Acadia with incorrect fuel economy window stickers will be able to select a debit card or a 48-month/60,000-mile protection plan. The plan is on top of the automaker's bumper-to-bumper 36-month/36,000-mile warranty and includes additional features. The protection plan would begin after the factory warranty expires. Those leasing a vehicle will be offered the debit card, GM said.

What About the Electric Car?

Lemon-Aid doesn't recommend most of the current crop of electric cars for general use, although taxi companies and fleets can benefit through savings from operation over a known area that is within the range of current EVs. For personal transportation, the limited range, long charging times with some models, and the uneven charging infrastructure are limitations that would consign an EV to the status of a household's second or even third vehicle. Two EVs that could be viable primary vehicles are the Tesla Model S and new Chevrolet Bolt.

Among the gas-electric hybrids, the Prius line of cars has the best track record; reliability is assured, and you'll get a real payback from the fuel savings compared to a conventional compact car in six to eight years. Hybrid fuel sipping can save gas, especially in city driving – 5L/100km or less (Toyota Prius) – with some owners achieving a 40% reduction in fuel consumption. There is also a decent supply of used Prius compacts on the used car market, and their CVT transmission, batteries, and related systems have proven relatively trouble-free. Hybrid versions of other Toyotas like the Camry, RAV4, and Highlander use more fuel than a Prius but still deliver significant savings compared to their conventional gas counterparts. If you're looking for a plug-in hybrid, the Chevrolet Volt is a very good choice. Pundits are predicting the Volt may not survive the introduction of the all-electric Chevrolet Bolt this year, but whatever GM's decision, the dual-energy Volt is fully operable as a long-distance cruiser on its backup gas engine. Dual energy makes it a good play in an uncertain energy future, and it has been reliable.

Sales of most other hybrids and all EVs have been too limited for them to be a secure used car buy. *Consumer Reports'* April 2013 issue targeted the Honda Civic Hybrid as the worst of a bad lot:

> [It] has a big problem with the drive battery. The 2009 model was the worst: almost one in five owners needed a replacement hybrid battery in our 12-month survey period ... more than ten percent of owners of the 2003, 2004, and 2010 models also needed one.

Honda provided a software update to owners of 2006-2008 Civic Hybrids to help extend the life of the IMA battery and issued a technical service bulletin (TSB) for the States in late 2012 that extends the IMA battery warranty. Batteries that were once covered for 8 years/100,000 miles are now warrantied for 11 years/137,000 miles; vehicles covered for 8 years/80,000 miles are now covered for 9 years/96,000 miles; and replacement batteries are covered for 36,000 miles, or three years. The problem with the fix? Gas consumption increased to the point that the fuel savings compared to a regular gas Civic became insignificant. The used car market seems to have reacted to hybrids with a yawn and, the Prius excepted, the 8-year resale value of even a Toyota hybrid is no better than similar models with conventional power trains.

Vehicles depreciate at different rates. When buying new, you want a reliable model that depreciates slowly; when buying used, consider a vehicle that has prematurely lost much of its value but is still reasonably dependable and affordable to maintain. Fortunately, there are plenty of the latter on the market due to the increased longevity of vehicles. Lemon-Aid identifies the models that are better used car buys than new in the Strong Points section of its vehicle reviews.

During the last decade, rebates, subsidized leasing, along with poor reputations for quality depressed the residual values of most American cars, minivans and some SUVs. According to the Automotive Lease Guide (*www.alg.com*), Detroit-made vehicles barely keep 33% of their sticker values after 5 years, while the average Japanese make is predicted to keep 46% of its value after 4 years.

Below are some 2016 vehicles with high predicted retained values according to the Canadian Black Book. High retained value favours the original owner. The Black Book website also has a handy calculator to estimate the trade-in value of your current vehicle (see their home page at *http://www.canadianblackbook.com/*).

You may be surprised by some of the models the people at *Black Book* identified as having a high retained value. The takeaways: Among affordable vehicles, Toyota and Honda rank at the top because of their perceived reliability and limited new vehicle sales to daily rental fleets (this eventually floods the used car market, depressing prices). Cult classics with designs that change little over the years like the retro Jeep Wrangler, Toyota FJ Cruiser, and Dodge Challenger hold their values well. Among the luxury brands, Porsche is aspirational, with its SUVs basking in the halo of the 911 sports car. And then there are models on the Black Book and other highest retained-value lists that make no sense – vehicles like the Audi A7 and Q7 and Volvo XC70 that make you wonder "What are they thinking?"

Eight Ways to Maximize Resale Value when Buying a New Vehicle

1. Choose a vehicle that's popular but production doesn't exceed demand, which can drive down values. Vehicles with high fleet sales to daily rental companies or constant consumer rebates are cheapened, thus negating some of the upfront discount.

2. Choose features that buyers will want at resale time, such as air conditioning, power windows and locks, automatic transmissions, alloy wheels, Bluetooth, and cruise control. Adding upgraded sound systems or leather seating is worthwhile with higher-level models, not compact cars. A backup camera makes an SUV more appealing.

3. Factory-installed navigation systems are overpriced and require expensive updates.

4. Choose a colour that's popular with buyers, such as silver, white, or black. Don't experiment with unusual colours or excessive accessorizing.

Black Book Highest Retained Value by Vehicle Segment

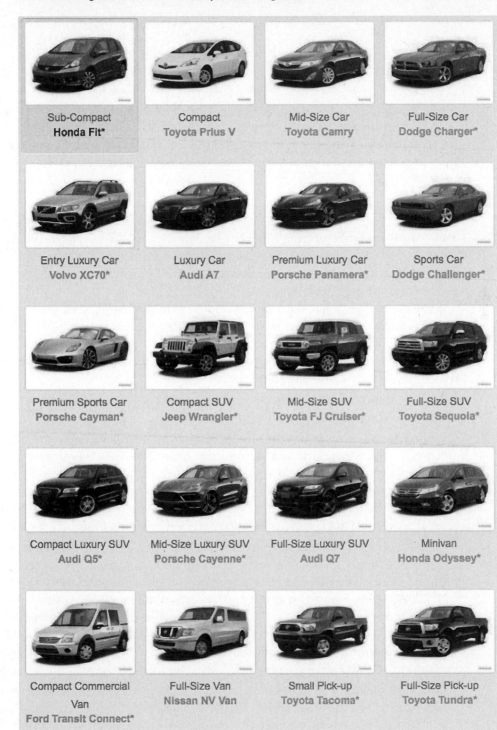

Sub-Compact **Honda Fit***	Compact **Toyota Prius V**	Mid-Size Car **Toyota Camry**	Full-Size Car **Dodge Charger***
Entry Luxury Car **Volvo XC70***	Luxury Car **Audi A7**	Premium Luxury Car **Porsche Panamera***	Sports Car **Dodge Challenger***
Premium Sports Car **Porsche Cayman***	Compact SUV **Jeep Wrangler***	Mid-Size SUV **Toyota FJ Cruiser***	Full-Size SUV **Toyota Sequoia***
Compact Luxury SUV **Audi Q5***	Mid-Size Luxury SUV **Porsche Cayenne***	Full-Size Luxury SUV **Audi Q7**	Minivan **Honda Odyssey***
Compact Commercial Van **Ford Transit Connect***	Full-Size Van **Nissan NV Van**	Small Pick-up **Toyota Tacoma***	Full-Size Pick-up **Toyota Tundra***

5. Invest in smart reconditioning. Wash and vacuum is essential.

6. Rotate tires; at resale time replace worn tires with good used ones if you can find them.

7. For trade-ins in rough condition, consider using brokers or the APA's used car appraisal service. A broker or industry contact working with the APA can send the vehicle to auction if necessary.

8. Market timing is influenced by the type of vehicle and region of the country. In general, vehicles put on the market in early spring and summer will sell more easily. 4x4s will sell well in the late fall and winter. Convertibles fetch a much better price in spring and early summer.

How Lemon-Aid Picks the "Best" and "Worst"

Lemon-Aid doesn't give a rating for every vehicle make sold in Canada. We focus on new and used vehicles sold in relatively large numbers going back a decade. Often, we may suggest buying a high-ranking used model that is similar to the new version, but sells for less.

If you have a question about a vehicle not found in *Lemon-Aid*, send us an e-mail at *lemonaid@earthlink.net* or write the APA at *www.apatoronto@apa.ca*. We will be glad to send you the information we have available at no charge.

Lemon-Aid has been giving honest, independent, and dependable auto ratings for over 45 years by following these simple rules.

- Ratings should be primarily comparative, and combine a road test with an owners' survey of past models.

- Failure trends should be compiled from owner complaints posted on the National Highway Traffic Safety Administration (NHTSA) *safercar.gov* site. It's a treasure trove of auto-failure anecdotes that show which cars have repeated failures or outstanding recalls, or are part of an ongoing safety probe, and which particular component is faulty. It also helps owners to get secret warranty repairs through the use of confidential service bulletins found on the site.

- Survey responses must come from a relatively large owner pool (over 1.1 million responses from *Consumer Reports* subscribers, for example). Survey findings should then be cross-referenced, and given depth and specificity through NHTSA's safety complaint prism and information from live consumer complaints (received by the APA on its consumer hotlines and experts in the repair industry). Responses must be checked against automaker internal service bulletins to determine the extent of the defect over a specific model and model-year range and to alert owners to problems likely to occur and the recommended fix.

- Rankings should be predicated on important characteristics measured over a significant period of time, unlike Car of the Year contests, or J.D. Power – "first impression" owner surveys carried out after only three months of ownership.

This is particularly important for first-year cars and models that have undergone a major redesign. As for awards given by auto clubs, car critics, and magazines like *Car and Driver* and *Motor Trend*, be on your guard. Any car can be Car of the Year – if the advertising payoff is big enough.

This includes the venerable 18 million member ADAC German Auto Club, founded in 1903 (*www.stuff.co.nz/motoring/news/9637705/Falsified-voting-tatters-award-reputation*):

> ADAC communications director Michael Ramstetter resigned in disgrace after conceding he manipulated the results of the car club's coveted Yellow Angel award for Germany's favourite car, which was won last week by the Volkswagen Golf.

- A vehicle will usually not be rated during the first six months it has come on the market or undergone a complete redesign. Look at the much heralded Honda Fit for example. It has always been a reliable, well-performing small car. But, the early-build 2015 model was not as good, due to its new design and relocation to another manufacturing plant in Mexico. 2016-2017 models are improved.

Honda Fit: Some model years are more reliable than others.

- Ratings must come from unimpeachable sources. There should be no conflicts of interest due to ties with advertisers or consultants. If they are used, results gathered from self-serving tests done under ideal conditions, like previous years' Transport Canada fuel economy tests, must be identified with a suggested correction factor. *Lemon-Aid* is wary of self-administered fuel economy ratings used by automakers.
- Automakers must be judged equally and not penalized if they refuse to "pay to play" in annual Car of the Year rankings handed out by car critics.

Ratings

Lemon-Aid rates vehicles on a scale of one to five stars, with five stars being our top ranking. Models are designated as "Recommended," "Above Average," "Average," "Below Average," or "Not Recommended." Ratings are correlated with specific model years when a vehicle's desirability varies according to its age or generation.

Recommended

Lemon-Aid doesn't award this rating very often, and is quick to drop it if safety, servicing, or overall quality control decline. We don't believe for one moment that the more you spend, the more reliable or durable the vehicle. For example, most Hondas are as trouble-free as Acuras, which cost thousands of dollars more for their luxury cachet. The same is true when you compare Toyota and Lexus. Even more surprising, some luxury makes, such as Jaguar and Lincoln, are "pseudo-luxe," because the older models may be merely dressed-up Fords sold at a luxury-car price. The extra money buys you nicer materials and more features including failure-prone electronic gadgetry. Because of their complexity, many luxury models are more likely to experience problems than cheaper vehicles.

In fact, the simplest choice is often the best buy. Ford's Mustang, Hyundai's Tucson, and the Mazda3 get positive ratings because they are easy to find, fairly reliable, and reasonably priced.

Above Average

Vehicles that are given an Above Average rating are good choices. The better European models fall into this group; most were knocked down a notch from a full five stars because of their predicted repair frequency and high servicing costs. In many cases, *Lemon-Aid* awards a high four-star rating to new vehicles from the European luxury carmakers because they are available at competitive lease rates and will be covered by full warranties. As used vehicles they may rank lower.

Average

Vehicles or model years with an Average rating are good second choices if a more highly rated vehicle isn't your first choice, isn't available, or isn't within budget. Sometimes you'll have a specific requirement that makes an Average vehicle the right model for you. When buying used, vehicle condition is very important; a vehicle rated Average with low mileage and a well documented history may well be a better choice than a more highly rated alternative that you can't get reliable information about. With the information on repairs and consumer complaints in the vehicle reviews, you'll know what to look out for after you buy the vehicle.

Below Average

Vehicles given a Below Average rating by *Lemon-Aid* are more likely be trouble-some; however, we also believe their low price and access to independent servicing may make them attractive to some buyers. Chrysler minivans, for example, are thousands of dollars cheaper than other minivans principally due to their reputation for poor reliability. But if you're on a tight budget, a clean Dodge Grand Caravan could be several model years newer than a Toyota Sienna or Honda Odyssey selling in the same price range. You can use the information in the reviews to anticipate trouble ahead, and to perform recommended preventive maintenance.

Not Recommended

Vehicles with a history of unforeseeable, recurring, and expensive defects are most likely to be given a Not Recommended rating. They are best avoided because they're so likely to suffer from performance and reliability problems that you may never stop paying for repairs. Sometimes, however, a Not Recommended model will improve after several model years and garner a better rating.

Incidentally, for readers who wonder how I can stop recommending model years I once recommended, let me be clear – as vehicles age, their ratings change to reflect new information from owners and from service bulletins relating to reliability and the automaker's warranty performance.

Reliability is defined as anything that causes one to return the car for non-maintenance repairs; it doesn't include most recalls, because recalls are not a consistent measure of quality. Rating data is compiled from a number of sources, including confidential technical service bulletins, owner complaints sent to us each year by *Lemon-Aid* readers, owners' comments posted on the Internet, and survey reports and tests done by auto associations, consumer groups like the APA, and government organizations. The results confirm *Lemon-Aid* has been mostly on the mark over the past four decades. This year's *Guide* has added Reliability and Road Performance information from the APA.

Lemon-Aid reviews and reliability rankings have nothing to do with how popular a vehicle is. Take a look at the 2015-2017 Jeep line. Many models are quntiessential lemons, fire-prone, and service-challenged, yet sales are "red hot" (pun intended).

Not all cars and trucks are profiled; those that are new to the market or less common may receive a more abbreviated treatment without owner or service bulletin information. Some vehicles aren't profiled at all due to page limitations.

Major Redesigns

This section outlines a vehicle's differences between model years, including over-hauls in design and other modifications. If a model is unchanged from one model year to the next, why pay a premium for it simply because it is one year newer? Or, if a vehicle was redesigned a few years ago, you may prefer to pass on the first year after the redesign, when many of the factory kinks were being ironed out.

Safety

How much crash protection can you expect? *Lemon-Aid* cites many NHTSA (*safercar.gov*) owner consumer complaints by model year, even though they aren't all safety related. These independent confirmations by other owners are key to proving your failure is factory related and widespread. Readers can use this corroboration to argue for free "goodwill" repairs. These complaints are also supportive in countering automaker/dealer dismissive responses like "We never saw that before," "No one else has complained," "It could be your driving or poor maintenance," "We couldn't duplicate the failure," and the most obnoxious rejection of all, "That's normal. They all operate like that."

NHTSA records list many common safety-related failures that include vehicles rolling away with the transmission in Park, power-operated sliding doors on minivans that don't open when they should or open when they shouldn't, or electronic computer controls that cause a vehicle to "lag and lurch." The vehicle won't accelerate from a stop for a few seconds, and then it will lurch out into traffic after the accelerator has been floored to get the vehicle out of harm's way.

Be wary and persistent in protecting your family. Heretofore, some automakers buried (literally) their mistakes, like Takata refusing to call its shrapnel-shooting airbags "defective," or Honda U.S.A. hiding thousands of accident reports from government investigators and waiting a decade to recall Takata airbags there was reason to suspect could kill as early as 2004.

If *Lemon-Aid* doesn't list a problem you have experienced (safety related, or not), go directly to the NHTSA website's database at *www.safercar.gov* for an update. Your vehicle may be currently under investigation, or may have been recalled since this year's guide was published. *Lemon-Aid* doesn't list most recalls because there are so many. In 2014 alone, over 600 recall notices were sent out in Canada covering 8 million vehicles, while the U.S. recalled almost 64 million vehicles with about 700 recall announcements over the same period.

Local dealers can also be helpful. They can easily run your car's Vehicle Identication Number (VIN) through their computers, since they hope to snag the extra recall repair dollars. Ask the dealer to also check for a "customer satisfaction program," a "service policy," a "goodwill" warranty extension, or a free emissions warranty service. The Transport Canada website has links to the automakers that offer real-time recall lookup capability. If proposed amendments to the federal *Motor Vehicle Safety Act* are passed (Senate Bill S-2, it has the support of all parties), all the automakers will have to offer this alternative.

Alert

The ALERT! points out information that could be a deal-breaker (like an uncomfortable head reastraint with no provision for adjustment). You won't find Alerts like this in other car guides.

Owner-reported Safety-related Failures

We list safety failures reported by owners, ensuing investigations, lawsuits, and court settlements.

Stonewall, then Recall

Don't be surprised if your vehicle is covered by a "phantom" recall where the defect is known but the remedy hasn't been approved, or the corrected parts aren't yet available. For example, in October 2014, Chrysler recalled nearly 500,000 2011 through 2014 cars and SUVs for faulty alternators that would make the 3.6L V6 engine stall unexpectedly. By early 2015 many owners were still waiting for a fix. Following that delay, Chrysler got hit last year with a $105-million fine in the U.S. for not issuing a recall in a timely manner. However, in Canada carmakers incur no penalty for late recall repairs. A proposed amendment to the *Motor Vehicle Safety Act* is supposed to fix that.

Last June, *Star Trek* actor Anton Yelchin, who played Pavel Chekov, was crushed to death after his parked 2015 Grand Cherokee rolled backwards and pinned him against a pillar. Apparently, Jeep had recalled the model earlier for that problem and is investigating the accident.

RECALLED

Blogspot.com and *allpar.com* say, "The 2014-15 Grand Cherokee was one of three models (alongside the Dodge Charger and Chrysler 300 sedans) recalled due to the roll-away risk. The problem was reported to have resulted in 41 injuries — and now possibly Yelchin's death, as well. No cars were fixed. There is nothing to fix. These are terrible shifters but the preliminary 'fix' was to send out a note saying 'hey, make sure you're in park before you open the door.' The recall is to have the vehicle shift into Park when you open the door."

Prices and Specs

The manufacturer's suggested retail price (MSRP) in the Prices and Specs box is a benchmark for new 2016 and 2017 models; *Lemon-Aid* usually lists the lowest and highest MSRP.

For used vehicles, the best way to determine the market value is to check current ads in your market on the Internet. Dealer asking prices usually leave some room to manoeuvre. If you're trading a vehicle in, it will be worth at least $2,000 less than the asking price in dealer ads.

Note that some options, such as a DVD/GPS infotainment system, paint protector, rustproofing, and tinted windows, have little worth on the resale market, though they may make your vehicle easier to sell. Other options, like a rearview camera, new brand name tires, and a supplementary warranty all add value. Electronic stability control has been a mandatory feature in Canada on vehicles built since September 1, 2011.

Reliability

Vehicle electronics and computer modules, transmissions, electrical systems, and brakes are the most troublesome components, manifesting problems over a vehicle's life. Other deficiencies that appear early, due to sloppy manufacturing and harsh environments, include failure-prone body hardware (trim, finish, locks, and glass), susceptibility to water leakage or wind noise, and peeling and/or discoloured paint. This year the APA provided information on preventive maintenance that can reduce the liklihood of paying for some expensive repairs down the road, as well as items to ask a mechanic to check during the inspection before you purchase a new vehicle.

Owners of vehicles with cracked or shattered windows or windshields are often told by dealers to make an insurance claim. If there is no evidence that the window was impacted by a foreign object, the window should be replaced by the automaker. Breakage may occur for all sorts of reasons not related to an impact: A change in temperature, shutting the car door, or passing over a bump in the road. VW recalled its 2013-2015 Beetles for just that reason: The sunroof glass panel may shatter when passing over a bump, particularly in cold weather. Smart owners are aware that making a glass claim to cover a manufacturing defect can lead to an insurance premium increase.

Internal Bulletins/Secret Warranties

The "Internal Bulletins/Secret Warranties" section provides details as to which specific model years pose the most risk and why. This compilation in summary form in a consumer guide is a unique feature of *Lemon-Aid*. It helps you foresee likely trouble spots before problems occur. It should also protect you from blank stares and the predictable "Never seen that before…" excuses from dealership personnel, in the event your vehicle does develop one of the problems covered in the service bulletins.

It's not enough to know which parts on your vehicle are likely to fail. You should also know which repairs will be done for free by the dealer on behalf of the automaker, even though you aren't the original owner and the manufacturer's warranty has long since expired. Welcome to the hidden world of secret warranties, found in confidential technical service bulletins (TSBs) published in *Lemon-Aid* or gleaned from owners' feedback on Internet auto forums.

Almost all automakers extend their standard new car warranty to cover components with a high rate of failure. Sometimes called a "special policy" or "warranty adjustment," under these programs, the manufacturer will pay for free repairs on vehicles with common problems, even after the warranty expires, in order to avoid a recall, bad press, or lawsuits. According to the Center for Auto Safety (*www.autosafety.org/secret-warranties*), at any given time there are approximately 500 secret warranty programs available through automobile manufacturers.

For years, the NHTSA declined to post on its website complete service bulletins from automakers about problems with their cars and about specialized warranty extensions that could save car owners thousands of dollars on repairs. Usually, what you will find on NHTSA's website (*www.safercar.gov*) is a cryptic reference to some service campaign or the bulletin itself.

How much money can be saved by knowing which secret warranties or special policies apply to your vehicle? Here are three recent examples where the savings could be significant.

- **BMW** – Sensors that detect the presence of a passenger in the front seat are getting 15-year warranties. A defective sensor will cause the airbag warning light on the dashboard to illuminate. TSB #010914 issued on Aug. 2, 2014, confirms that a 15-year warranty now applies to 2006-7 5 Series sedans and station wagons with the comfort seat option and to 2006-7 Z4 Roadsters and 3 Series sedans and wagons with either manual or power seats.

- **General Motors** – Warranty coverage for intermittent loss of power steering in large crossover models has been extended. In TSB #14329 issued on Sept. 16, 2014, GM said that premature wear in the power steering pump might be to blame and has extended the pump warranty up to 10 years or 193,000 km. Affected model years: 2008-11 Buick Enclaves, 2009-11 Chevrolet Traverses, 2007-11 GMC Acadias and 2007-10 Saturn Outlooks.

- **Lexus** – Repairs needed to stop engine oil cooler pipe leakage are covered by an extended warranty. Instead of the standard 4-year/50,000-mile warranty, the part will have an unlimited mileage coverage through Jan. 31, 2016, and after that a 10-year/193,000 km warranty. In TSB #SC-ZLC issued on Aug. 1, 2014, Lexus said the leak might develop in 2007-11 RX 350 and 2010-11 RX 450h models.

In addition to using *Alldatadiy.com* and *safercar.gov* there are other places where service bulletins can be found:

- *AutoMD.com* – This free site lists a summary of 1980-2015 model technical service bulletins in an easy-to-access format. Unfortunately, like the free *safercar.gov* bulletin summaries, the original bulletin isn't published. This makes it difficult to find out which other models are affected, what specific repairs are needed, and what is the automaker's admission of liability. ALLDATA's collection of original bulletins gives this information.

- Mitchell 1 DIY (*eautorepair.net*) – Like ALLDATA, Mitchell subscribers pay an annual fee per car model researched ($49.99 U.S.). This allows a free download of all pertinent TSBs throughout the year.

Real-Time Recall Lookups in Canada

Transport Canada maintains a complete list of vehicle safety recalls on its database. This database does not necessarily include emissions recalls, because Environment Canada and Transport Canada don't work together. The list includes all safety recalls but is not designed to perform a real-time check for open recalls on an individual vehicle. Some automakers now offer real-time vehicle recall lookups that will identify all open recalls using the 17 digit alphanumeric Vehicle Identification Number (VIN) marked on the vehicle driver's door opening and on your registration. Transport Canada has prepared the following page with links to the different automakers on its website "as a convenience for reference purposes only." That's code for saying Canada does not require an automaker to maintain a database consumers can use to look for open safety recalls (the compilation is the initiative of some individuals inside the bureaucracy). For emissions recall information, Canadians are able to look it up at the pleasure of the individual auto manufacturer.

If you just purchased a used vehicle, or if you've moved since taking delivery of a new vehicle, be sure to check this list. If there are open recalls for your vehicle, there's a good chance recall notices have been going to an old address for the vehicle still in the manufacturer's records. Contact the automaker or a dealer and have them update their recall record with current information for your vehicle.

Rustproofing

Most modern vehicles do not show visible signs of rusting until they are over five or six years old. Beyond that, in the high salt environments of central and eastern Canada, the vehicle will experience mechanical and body deterioration due to corrosion. By the seventh to tenth year in service, this deterioration will usually result in increased maintenance and repair costs, or a reduced market value for the vehicle upon resale. Repairs could include lower body panels like door bottoms and fenders, folded seams

---

on the hood, and mechanical parts like metal gas tanks, electrical connections, and brake, fuel and air conditioner lines. Unfortunately, most dealer-applied rustproofing leaves a lot to be desired. It's usually a one-time only application of a product that dries out and cracks as the vehicle gets older. A Canadian Automobile Association (CAA) study undertaken in the 1980s revealed that 85% of dealer-applied rustproofing left one or more high-risk areas of the vehicle unprotected.

When dealers offer a "lifetime" or "10 year" rust warranty, it's usually a well-hedged bet on their part. Profits are large on the initial application; total cost to the dealer is about $150 and the treatment is usually sold from $499 up to $795. Claims rarely succeed because the warranty will have been voided by the time rust becomes obvious, for one of a variety of reasons. First off, you may have to bring your car back every year for an inspection and they may ask you to pay for "touchups." If you miss just one appointment for an annual inspection, the dealer may void your rust warranty. Some warranties cover only a "perforation" so you may have to let the vehicle rust through before collecting — and then run the risk of the rustproofing company refusing the claim because of "neglect!" Some rustproofing warranties cover only defects in the product, but not in its application; if the dealer missed a vulnerable area, the warranty company won't cover eventual corrosion damage to that area. And some rustproofing warranties are not transferable if you sell the vehicle.

The APA has approved the following rustproofing treatments:

Across Canada
Krown Rust Control
Tel. 1-800-267-5744
www.krown.com

Annual rustproofing. The product is an excellent penetrant. It outperformed similar competing products in ASTM durability tests (ASTMB-117), and is used by the military and large commercial fleets. Krown recertifies technicians annually to maintain quality and provides excellent support from the head office. The application is thorough, with holes drilled using special bits to minimize damage. Most competitors cover about 10 areas on the vehicle; Krown does over 25. The cost is $110-$140 per year depending on the vehicle, and resprays are guaranteed against price increases for as long as you own your vehicle. APA members receive a $5 discount off the current regular retail price of a Krown application. The Krown warranty covers seam or crevice corrosion, and is honoured across Canada.

Montreal
Barry's Rustproofing
4066 Jean Talon West, Montreal
Tel. 514-344-1168

A small shop recommended by the APA for over 30 years. One-time grease application includes the inside of the floor in the front passenger area underneath the carpet. No holes are drilled. Barry's crew removes trim panels if necessary. Cost is

$450-$800 depending on the vehicle; $25 off the initial application for APA members. Retouching is recommended once or twice at three-year intervals and costs $120. For compacts and most used vehicles, the simpler "basic job" that involves no removal of interior trim panels will usually do the trick, and is significantly cheaper at $300 and up.

AMERICAN MODELS

Fiat didn't "rescue" Chrysler. Actually, Fiat is making money mainly
from strong Chrysler truck and SUV sales. Before he retires next year, FCA
prez Marchionne wants to "go for the gold" and close down Chrysler's
money-losing car division, while spinning off Jeep to another automaker.

From the early '70s until the 2009 bankruptcy of Chrysler and GM, American
automakers took every last dime out of their cars for profit, pushed junk out the
door, and made hapless owners unwilling victims of their poor designs and
quality control. Ford would have gone bankrupt as well, if it hadn't mortgaged
many of its fixed assets (including its Blue Oval logo) prior to the 2008 meltdown.

An entire generation of consumers ran to Asian and German products, while
American automakers showed an abject disdain for auto safety, reliable vehicles,
and honest transactions. All this became clearly apparent during Ford's stone-
walling over Firestone tire failures, GM's faulty ignition switch cover-up, and
Chrysler's multiple refusals and foot-dragging related to recalls, including its
fire-prone Jeeps.

American Car Quality

Going into the 2017 model year, a number of Detroit-made vehicles are safer and more dependable, but you need to know how to pick them out of the crowd. U.S. and Canadian auto recalls hit an all-time high in 2014. Both the number of recalls and the number of vehicles affected are significantly higher than in any other year, as carmakers cleaned the safety skeletons out of their closets. The longest delay to issue a recall goes to General Motors in 2014 ... for a defective ignition lock cylinder on the 1999 Grand Am, some 15 years after the car was put on the road! It took the exposure of the Cobalt/Pursuit ignition switch cover-up and possible risk of jail time for General Motors executives to compel the company to reform its safety culture.

Fiat Chrysler and Jeep

The Detroit Big Three became the Detroit Big Two-and-a Half, after Chrysler was taken over by Fiat and became part of Fiat Chrysler Automobiles NV (FCA), a Netherlands-based automotive holding company. As for the Chrysler corporate name, it is now *non grata*, having been ditched by Fiat in favour of a new moniker: FCA US LLC. The renamed group houses many other auto brands such as Alfa Romeo, Ferrari, Lancia, Fiat, and Maserati.

Chrysler is retaining the Dodge nameplate – can it be because the company has been "dodging" taxes for years by moving overseas? Called corporate "inversion," Fiat Chrysler's newly minted Dutch company pays minimal income taxes in North America and Italy where most of its income is earned and customers reside. This tax dodge is all the more shameful when one considers the architect of FCA's flight from North American and Italian taxes is Fiat CEO Sergio Marchionne – a Canadian/Italian dual national. Take note that this could be a prelude to the second time the Fiat brand abandons its North American customers. The company left Canadians with rust-bucket cars and worthless warranties in 1987, only to return 25 years later as Chrysler's self-styled financial saviour, feeding from Ottawa and Washington's bailout trough while marketing the mediocre Fiat 500. FCA warranty performance: Neanderthal.

Fiat Chrysler's accomplishments lately? Making huge profits with its trucks and SUVs, while letting its car divisions languish. FCA almost begged General Motors to acquire it, and it put Ferrari on the auction block. Ottawa rebuffed the company's request for a $700-million Canadian handout to retool its Windsor and Brampton, Ontario, plants. When the government grants and loans didn't appear, Mr. Marchionne withdrew his request and ponied up the money from Chrysler's profits.

His parting shot? "Canada was acting like 'a guppy in shark-infested waters'."

Chrysler's 2017 Pacifica minivan replaces the Town and Country and is one of the few all-new domestic products in the FCA pipeline. The minivan will be joined by a hybrid version next year. It looks sleek, and carries a new 9-speed automatic transmission – giving you nine ways to get stranded.

All three American carmakers are flush with money. Chrysler is a strong contender for sales gains, thanks to the resurgence of SUV and truck sales. Fiat Chrysler has its hugely popular Ram 1500 pickup; that's their best product, but it's not as well made as the competing Toyota Tundra or the Chevrolet and GMC pickups.

It is becoming apparent that Fiat Chrysler learned little from its 2009 bankruptcy and bailout. Fiat and Chrysler models continue to be among the least reliable and poorly-engineered. J. D. Powers' *Initial Quality Survey of 2016* models found both brands remained well below the industry average, as did Ram and Dodge. Fiat, which came in second to last, added 13 problems per 100 vehicles compared to 2015! After fawning over the 2014 Ram pickup as a Recommended Buy, *Consumer Reports* cut its rating a year later after receiving a flood of drivetrain, electronic, and electrical system complaints from readers. National Highway Traffic Safety Administration (NHTSA)'s *safercar.gov* website recorded 219 safety-related failures and TSBs for the 2014 model alone, compared to the normal frequency of about 50 safety complaints per model year.

The light-duty Ram 1500 Ecodiesel is a lemon. The VM Motori-sourced 3.0L turbo diesel engine has experienced numerous failures. Chrysler minivans and passenger cars will get hockey moms to a few games, but they may miss the playoffs while pacing in the penalty box at their dealer's service department. The minivans are heavily-discounted jack-in-the-boxes that have lots of sizzle (snap, crackle, and pop electronics), but less steak (drivetrain reliability, rust resistance).

The Jeep lineup is all about macho cachet, Tonka-inspired styling, superior off-road performance, electrical gremlins that can threaten your life and pocketbook, and unreliable powertrains. The Renegade, Jeep's latest entry has had surprisingly few safety-related complaints sent to NHTSA (64), but its Fiat 500X underpinnings are not promising.

Fiat Chrysler Advertising

Advertising placed by Fiat Chrysler and its dealers is among the most deceptive in Canada according to the Automobile Protection Association (APA). Fiat Chrysler doesn't appear to police deceptive advertising by its dealers. Fiat Chrysler takes advantage of gaping loopholes in provincial regulations that allow it to skirt advertising requirements that apply to its car dealers. APA secret shoppers were charged extra fees totalling hundreds of dollars at several Dodge dealerships shopped in the Vancouver, Calgary, and Montreal markets that did not appear anywhere in ads places by Fiat Chrysler.

Coquitlam Chrysler had the highest extra charges of the survey, adding $800 for a post-delivery inspection (on top of the $1,745 Freight and Delivery charge), and a $290 D.O.C. fee. Neither amount appeared in the Chrysler Canada ad, whose fine print states only that extra fees may be required, but doesn't say how much. That's not compliant with B.C. regulations governing car dealers. Fiat Chrysler's ad is tricky. The bold print promises "No payment for 90 days" but the fine print states that interest starts to accumulate after 60 days!

The image is of a Jeep Wrangler, but the ad from a Calgary area dealer is actually for the cheaper Dart! Although the car had only 47 kilometres on the odometer, it had been "pre-registered" four months earlier, and the warranty started to run from that date.

APA shoppers discovered pre-registering vehicles as already sold was common at Fiat Chrysler dealers in some markets. It's the result of pressure from the manufacturer to boost monthly sales numbers. By the way, to advertise the low $39 payment, the dealer is featuring a totally barebones car, with no air conditioning and a manual transmission.

The Chrysler dealers advertising "cashback" were not referring to a rebate on the price. Instead, the consumer would receive cash "back" by financing a loan for a larger amount than the actual price of the vehicle.

This loan from the consumer to him- or herself triggers additional sales tax as well as interest charges, because it is treated like part of the vehicle purchase. According to one dealer, lending institutions are well aware of the practice.

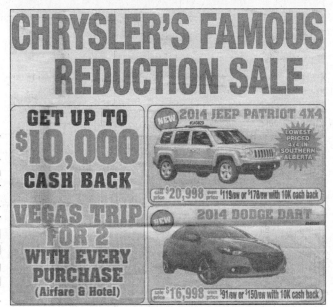

PART FOUR | AMERICAN MODELS

bad buy

FIAT 500

2012-2014 ★
2015-2017 ★★

RATING: Not Recommended (2012-2014); Below Average (2015-2017). When Fiat abandoned the North American market in 1984, I was in the trenches as President of the APA and remember only too well the many Fiat owners who were stunned that their rusty, unreliable, and unwanted pieces of garbage would never be fixed. Following its acquisition of Chrysler (now FCA), Fiat returned to our shores after three decades – perhaps long enough for past transgressions to be forgotten. Already four years old when it arrived in North America, the irresistibly cute 500 got some updates for its debut here, including revised suspension geometry for improved stability, as well as additional subframe bracing, different shocks, and more sound-deadening material. Being small but tall, the 500 felt roomy, although the stunted wheelbase left the footwells quite narrow. Fiat specified broader seats for North Americans (um, thank you) along with a driver's armrest. The back seat technically offered space for two humans, although they'd better not be adults. The cargo area was tiny, too. Independent auto critics throughout Europe and North America (U.K.'s *Which Auto, Consumer Reports,* J. D. Power, etc.) all concur that Fiat's models would be far from their first choice. The only Fiat *Lemon-Aid* can recommend is the one Pope Francis rides in, due to the possibility of divine intervention when it lets him down. **Road performance:** The base 1.4L 4-cylinder's 101 hp did not infuse the 500 with anything resembling espresso: Zero to 97 km/h came up in 9.9 seconds with the stick and 11 seconds with the automatic. The turbocharged Abarth was more befitting the Italian driving style, zipping to highway velocity in 6.9 seconds. Beyond acceleration, the 500 delivers a pleasing driving experience. The electric steering is quick and linear, especially when the Sport button is engaged. The handling is nicely controlled without the harsh ride endemic to short-wheelbase cars. **Strong points:** Buyers find the retro styling adorable inside and out, and the 500 is immensely qualified as an easy-to-park city car. The space for two adults up front is more than adequate, but the back seat is best suited to tots or small pets. Crash protection is good for such a small car. A well-designed and convenient convertible top is available for not much money. **Weak points:** Opt for the glass sunroof, and you'll lose valuable inches of headroom. This tiny lightweight is susceptible to crosswinds. Radio controls are diabolical, unless you get the Sport trim or cruise control, which adds radio controls on the steering wheel. Fuel economy is decent overall, but unimpressive for such a tiny car. Reliability fears are real and depreciation is steep. **Major updates:** 2013 more powerful Abarth turbo model. 2015 interior upgrades, adoption of a version of the Chrysler Uconnect infotainment system. **Best alternatives:** The MINI and VW Beetle are the obvious European-retro cross-shops, but both have reliability issues. Among more prosaic designs, there are the Chevrolet Sonic and Spark (2016-2017 only), Hyundai Accent, Kia Rio, and Toyota Yaris. The discontinued Mazda2 is also worth a look.

Prices and Specs

Prices (2016-2017): *500 Pop:* $18,995, *500 Abarth Cabrio:* $30,995 **Freight:** $1,795 **Powertrain (FWD):** Engines: 1.4L 4-cyl. (101 hp); 1.4L 4-cyl. turbo (135/160 hp). Transmission: 5-speed manual, 6-speed automatic. **Dimensions:** Passengers: 2/2; Length: 140 in., Wheelbase: 91 in., Weight: 2,366 lb. **Highway/ city fuel economy:** *1.4L:* 7.6L/100 km city, 5.9L/100 km highway; *1.4L turbo:* 8.5L/100 km city, 6.9L/ 100 km highway. **Assembled in:** Toluca, Mexico.

RELIABILITY: *2011-2012:* A lemon. *2013-2017:* Below average. FCA dealers find that the diagnosis and repair of the 500 can be a challenge; warranty support from FCA is deficient, toward both dealers and vehicle owners. The 500 is assembled in Toluca, Mexico, in the factory that used to build Chrysler's PT Cruiser, which had become one of Chrysler's better-assembled vehicles by the end of production. However, that didn't save early buyers of the 500 from experiencing quality hiccups. Common failures include short-lived clutches and other manual transmission components, noisy steering columns and rapid suspension

SAFETY	
IIHS 2016	
Small Front	Poor
Front	Good
Side	Good
Roof strength	Good
Head restraint and seats	Good
Child seat anchors	Not rated
NHTSA Overall 2015	★★★★

215

PART FOUR | AMERICAN MODELS

wear. Dealers have replaced the steering column, or the entire steering column, as well as struts, strut mounts, and jounce bumpers, often more than once on 2011-2012 models. Other reported issues include a leaking valve-cover gasket and other engine and turbo oil leaks, faulty ignition coils, worn wheel bearings, broken power-window regulators and seat belt retractors, frequently burnt-out headlights and bad radios. The driver armrest breaks easily and FCA charges $300 to replace this part that should be covered at no charge. The turbocharged engine is fond of oil and needs to be monitored. Check the rear hatch/trunk lid for corrosion. Despite work to hit its quality targets – indeed, newer 500s fare better – Fiat resides near rock bottom of the J.D. Power Dependability Study in the U.S. and also scores poorly in Europe. The Fiat factory warranty is three years/60,000 km in Canada and four years/50,000 miles (80,000 km) in the U.S.; Canadian consumers deserve parity. Purchase of an extended warranty from FCA with full coverage is recommended, even though it will add a lot to the price of the car; APA and ACC members may be eligible for a small discount on the price.

DODGE DART   *2013-2017* ★★

RATING: Below Average (2013-2017). The Dart was the first offspring of the Fiat Chrysler marriage assigned to fly the Dodge banner in the compact car class. To save time and money, Fiat supplied the platform from Alfa Romeo's well-received front-drive hatchback, the Giulietta. Engineers stretched the wheelbase and widened the track to American-friendly proportions. Electric power steering, MacPherson front struts, and a trailing-arm independent rear suspension provided handling talent. The car benefits from brazed roof seams, a process that dispenses with unsightly roof mouldings. Inside, soft-touch plastics contoured into pleasing shapes belie its budget mission. Higher trim levels feature a thin-film transistor (TFT) display in place of traditional instruments, along with a large infotainment touch screen positioned centrally. While the generous cabin is classified as midsize, some owners disliked the thinly padded seats, modest headroom, and the smallish rear bench that can only accommodate three adults for short trips. Three 4-cylinder engines are offered: Fiat's 160 hp 1.4L turbo, a 160 hp 2.0L, and a 184 hp 2.4L, along with three choices of 6-speed transmissions: a manual, an automatic, and a dual-clutch automated box. **Road performance:** Driving the Dart is a breeze, although the base 1.4L engine's turbo takes its time getting the car up to speed. Ride and handling are better than average, revealing the car's European heritage. The heavy but rigid chassis pays dividends; the steering is communicative and effort is linear. The Dart is fairly hushed at highway speeds. **Strong points:** Relatively fun to drive. The optional touch screen interface is quick and easy to use. Attractive styling. **Weak points:** The front seats are oddly contoured and mounted too high, compromising headroom. The thick rear pillars and tall trunk lid cut into rear visibility. Response is slug-like with the base engine. The dual-clutch automated transmission can be slow and unrefined; owners have complained of early transmission failures. Reliability concerns push the Dart off our recommended list, despite the promising design. **Best alternatives:** There's no shortage of attractive cars in this segment, including the Honda Civic, Mazda3, Hyundai Elantra (except 2011-2013), Kia Forte, and Subaru Impreza.

Prices and Specs

Prices (2016): *SE:* $19,195, *Limited:* $26,195 **Freight:** $1,795 **Powertrain (FWD):** Engines: 1.4L 4-cyl. (160 hp), 2.0L 4-cyl. (160 hp), 2.4L 4-cyl. (184 hp). Transmission: 6-speed manual, 6-speed automatic, 6-speed dual-clutch automated. **Dimensions:** Passengers: 2/3; Length: 184 in., Wheelbase: 106 in., Weight: 3,186 lb. **Fuel economy:** *1.4L:* 8.5L/100 km city, 5.8L/100 km highway; *2.0L:* 9.9L/100 km city, 7.0L/100 km highway; *2.4L:* 10.6L/100 km city, 7.5L/100 km highway. **Assembled in:** Belvidere, Illinois.

RELIABILITY: Below Average. The Italian-American Dart disappoints. One owner had his 2013 model towed back to the dealership with transmission issues four times before his first monthly payment; he finally got a new transmission the fourth time. The dual-clutch automatic is fragile and should be avoided. It comes tied only to the small 1.4L turbo engine, a drivetrain combo that responds unevenly in traffic. On the manual gearbox, the clutch slave and master cylinders can fail early, along with the clutch – why does making a durable clutch still confound Fiat after all these years? Turbocharger failures in the 1.4L engine are not uncommon, and the engine can overheat. Then there are the stalling engines and electrical failures that alarm drivers. Radio displays can go black intermittently. Other issues include prematurely worn spark plugs and ignition coils, fluid leaks, dead batteries, loose weatherstripping, and easily chipped paint. The Dart has been recalled for brake and transmission problems. The best bet if you're looking to buy a used example is the 2.0L or 2.4L 4-cylinder with the conventional 6-speed automatic, which is supplied by Hyundai. Purchase of a full coverage extended warranty from FCA is recommended, but buyers of cars in this segment are reluctant to pay the high prices charged by the manufacturer.

SAFETY

IIHS 2015

Small Front	Acceptable
Front	Good
Side	Good
Roof strength	Good
Head restraint and seats	Good
Child seat anchors	Acceptable
NHTSA Overall 2014	★★★★★

RATING: *200:* Below Average (2011-2017); *Avenger:* Below Average (2005-2014); *Sebring:* Below Average (2005-2010). Superior crashworthiness for an unreliable and sometimes unsafe car. The Chrysler 200 and its earlier incarnations, the Sebring and Avenger, are the automaker's entries in the hotly contested mid-size sedan segment. The Avenger is a Dodge twin of the Sebring/200 sold until the 2014 model year; it shares their ratings. All three models are generally a poor bet, despite their bargain prices. 2010 was the last year for the Sebring. The 200, a reworked Sebring with more fluid styling and nicely upgraded interior, arrived for 2011 along with a 6-speed automatic and powerful optional 3.6L V6. As of its 2015 redesign, the 200 is based on a platform derived from the Alfa Romeo Giulietta. Unfortunately, the usual Fiat Chrysler bugaboos crop up (engine, transmission, and electrical faults) that make these cars risky buys and depreciation disasters if you buy a new one. Fiat Chrysler CEO Sergio Marchionne has announced the 200 will be discontinued in the next year or so, which will impact the already poor resale value. Mounting repair bills make the cars expensive to keep in the long run. **Road performance:** Considerably improved as of 2011 with stiffened body mounts, a smoother suspension, upgraded rear sway bar, improved noise reduction, and a softened ride. The base 4-cylinder engine coupled to the Jurassic 4-speed tranny is a puny performer and lacks reserve power for passing and merging. **Strong points:** The Avenger and Sebring are cheap. 2015-17 models have vastly improved styling, a refined, comfortable ride and a classier, quieter interior with a well-designed infotainment system. 3.6L V6 engine gives plenty of power when it isn't stalling out. Brakes well. Dealers discount them heavily and the cars sell on price. **Weak points:** *2005-2010:* Sloppy handling. *2007-2009:* Mediocre fit and finish. Noisy 4-cylinder engine. *2015-2016:* The 9-speed ZF transmission can shift erratically. Mediocre fuel economy for a compact/mid-size car. Standard front seats have insufficient thigh room. Rear seating cramped for a mid-size car; it's inferior to some compacts. Smallish trunk. **Best alternatives:** New: Hyundai Sonata, Kia Optima, or Chevrolet Malibu. Used: Hyundai Elantra or Sonata; Kia Forte or Optima.

Prices and Specs

Prices (2016-2017): $22,345-$31,445 **Freight:** $1,795 **Powertrain (FWD/AWD):** Engines: 2.4L 4-cyl. (184 hp), 3.6L V6 (295 hp); Transmission: 9-speed automatic **Dimensions/capacity (sedan):** Passengers: 2/3; Wheelbase: 108 in.; H: 59/L: 192/W: 74 in.; Cargo volume: 16 cu. ft.; Fuel tank: 60L/regular; Tow limit: 2,000 lb.; Load capacity: 900 lb.; Turning circle: 39.2 ft.; Weight: 3,475 lb. **Fuel consumption:** *2.4L:* 10.2L/100 km city, 6.4L/100 km highway; *3.6L:* 12.4L/100 km city/7.5L/100 km highway. **Assembled in:** Michigan.

Available powertrains for 200, Avenger, Sebring

Engines:

- 2.4L 4-cyl. (150 hp 2005; 173 hp 2007-2013; 184 hp 2014-2017)
- 2.7L V6 (200 hp 2005; 189 hp 2007-2010) AVOID this engine, it's a lemon
- 3.5L V6 (235 hp 2007-2010)
- 3.6L V6 (283 hp 2011-2014; 295 hp 2015-2017)

Transmissions:

- 2005-2006: 4-speed auto
- 2007-2014: 4-speed auto or 6-speed auto
- 2015-2017: 9-speed auto

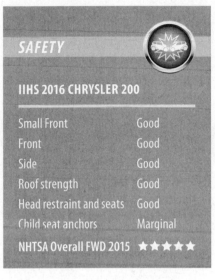

SAFETY

IIHS 2016 CHRYSLER 200

Small Front	Good
Front	Good
Side	Good
Roof strength	Good
Head restraint and seats	Good
Child seat anchors	Marginal
NHTSA Overall FWD 2015	★ ★ ★ ★ ★

Owner-reported safety-related failures: The NHTSA database shows over 460 safety-related complaints for the redesigned 2015 model (50 complaints would be normal). Compare with the 2014 model, the last year for the previous generation, which generated only 38 reported incidents. Interestingly, the 2016 model has very few reported safety complaints. The failure-prone 2015 model may suddenly lose power, making you a target on the highway:

> Without notice, my 2015 Chrysler 200 did not want to pick up speed going up hill. Almost got rear ended. Also when trying to stop the car – it jolts forward before slowing down. This is dangerous – I was told by an employee of the rental agency that 2 other people had the same incident happen to them and they returned the cars. I fear someone will get seriously injured or killed. Chrysler needs to recall these vehicles before precious lives are lost or permanently injured.
>
> • • •
>
> Chrysler's infamous Totally Integrated Power Module (TIPM) causes non-deployment of front airbags, hard starts and frequent stalling in traffic on cars equipped with the 3.6L V6. Chrysler recalled the 2011-13 Avenger, Sebring, 200, and Jeeps but owners say this didn't correct the stalling, starting problem. They want a recall that works and they want the 'fix' extended to 2007–2014 model years.

— carcomplaints.com

Replacing Chrysler's ubiquitous TIPM module may cost as much as $1,200 (US) A number of class actions are winding their way through the American courts. If no settlement or favourable decision is reached, use the small claims court to claim a refund for the TIPM replacement due to its "premature failure," or "lack of reasonable durability."

RELIABILITY: *Below Average* The optional 2.7L V6 is a lemon. The optional Pentastar 3.6L V6 offers excellent performance in the 200, but has seen its share of issues (early rod bearing failure due to debris in engine; faulty head gaskets). Owners complain about mysterious electrical issues and stalling engines. Many electronic glitches.

INTERNAL BULLETINS, SECRET WARRANTIES: 2007-08—Engine surge or gear hunting upon deceleration. Steering honk, moan, or grinding sound when making left turns (replace the power steering fluid reservoir). Broken transmission gearshift-lever interlock spring retainer hook "freezes" lever in Park position. Customer Satisfaction Notification Program K16, dated August 2010, says steel reinforcement clip will be installed for free, if needed. 2007-10—AC leaks water onto passenger floor. 2010—Cold start is followed by rough idle. Automatic transmission transfer gear beating noise. Rear-door glass may make a "shuttering" noise when raised or lowered. Trunk release operates even though vehicle is locked. 2011—RPM fluctuations and hard starting are addressed in TSB# 18-028-11, issued May 27, 2011. 2011-12—Hard shifting can be resolved by reflashing the PCM says TSB# 18-020-12. 2011-13—3.6L V6 engine cylinder leakage may require a new cylinder head covered by an extended warranty (Chrysler X56 Warranty Extension). This little-known program is confirmed by TSB #09-002-14 REV.8, published December 15, 2014. 2011-14—Headliner falls down. 2012-13—A poor upshifting automatic transmission is covered in TSB# 21-013-12, issued November 10, 2012. 2013—Fix for off-centre steering wheels. 2015—Silencing rear brake squeal in Reverse. Fifth to Fourth poor shift quality requires the replacement of the C-clutch snap ring. *Avenger* 2013-14—Silencing left front door wind noise. *200:* 2011—Poor upshifting automatic transmission is covered in TSB# 21-013-12, issued November 10, 2012. Tips on silencing rear door wind noise. 2014-15—To improve powertrain durability, Chrysler will update transmission and powertrain control modules free of charge, no matter if the car was bought used or its mileage (RO1 Customer Satisfaction Notification). Call: 1-800-465-2001, or email: *www.fcacanada.ca/en/contact_us.php*. For further review or a refund contact: FCA Canada Customer Care Centre, P. O. Box 1621, Windsor, Ontario, N9A4H6. *Avenger and 200:* 2014—An extended crank time (3.6L engine) may be caused by a faulty #1 bank position camshaft sensor. 2015—A variety of powertrain defects contribute to continual transmission failures.

CHALLENGER ★★★★

RATING: Above Average. In a nutshell, the Challenger is the premier muscle/pony car with a retro look. Introduced for 2008 as a spinoff of the successful Charger/ 300, it's built on a shorter version of the same platform, available with rear-wheel-drive. All Challengers are made in Brampton, Ontario. The Challenger offers a choice of a V6 or the Hemi V8. *Challenger Hellcat:* The most powerful, regular production muscle car ever made, combining 1970's styling and today's more refined driveline and suspension. It's powered by a supercharged 6.2L V8 engine. One novel feature: Owners get two key fobs to start the car. One – a black fob – limits power output to 500 hp. The other, a red fob, lets the driver access all 707 horses. **Road performance:** Early versions with the base suspension make the Challenger more of a Clydesdale than a "pony" car, but subsequent suspension and steering tweaks have made the car more responsive. Overall performance is better than average even with the V6. **Strong points:** A comfortable, spacious, and affordable big sports car; all V8 versions provide a healthy dose of muscle car flair, with an intoxicating soundtrack. The Challenger's bigger back seat and larger trunk give it an edge as a daily driver compared to the Camaro and snug 2015-2017 Mustang. Outward visibility is superior to the Camaro, making the car more enjoyable in the city. The infotainment system is first class. It's undeniable that the Challenger has exceptional styling, horsepower to burn (as in, "What do you mean the fuel tank is on empty again?"), and attitude. Bonus: The Challenger V8 depreciates more slowly than other FCA cars, due to strong buyer interest. **Weak points:** Handling that's comfortable but not particularly agile with the base suspension; R/T models with the upgraded sports suspension and gigantic tire and wheel package ride surprisingly well and handle predictably. Overly assisted steering requires constant correction on early models; difficult rear seat access is typical of cars in its class. **Major redesign:** 2015 Challenger received some styling tweaks along with an upgraded interior. The supercharged 707 hp SRT Hellcat arrived in the winter of 2014. **Best alternatives:** *New:* Chevrolet Camaro, Ford Mustang, Dodge Charger. *Used:* Hyundai Genesis Coupe (not kidding), or any of the above.

SAFETY

IIHS 2016

Small Front	Marginal
Front	Good
Side	Good
Roof strength	Acceptable
Head restraint and seats	Acceptable
Child seat anchors	Acceptable
NHTSA Overall 2015	★★★★★

RELIABILITY: *Average to Above Average* Weak alternator on V6 models has been the subject of a recall. The front seat airbag wiring electrical connectors may have an intermittent connection, which sets off airbag warning lamp. Electronic glitches may be traced to TIPM (Totally Integrated Power Module) faults that can cause the engine to stall while driving at speed, lose all electrical power, block the ability to start a car, cause the fuel pump to stay on and cause the airbags to fail. Early examples of the Pentastar 3.6L V6 have been recalled for rod bearing failure due to debris inside the engine; faulty head gaskets are another common complaint. A noisy 3.5L V6 at high mileage may signal worn rocker shaft assemblies, a substantial repair. Eight-speed automatic transmission may exhibit jerky or hard shifting. Chrysler's poor customer service, frequently backordered parts, and refusal to provide a loaner vehicle will make a repair experience worse.

For Internal Bulletins and Secret Warranty Information check the Chrysler 300 review.

CHARGER, MAGNUM ★★★★

RATING: Above Average. Developed during the period when Chrysler was owned by Daimler Benz, the four-door Charger, along with the Chrysler 300, arrived for the 2006 model year. The robust rear-drive platform borrowed several Mercedes components from earlier models, often with defects corrected; the 5- and 8-speed automatic transmissions are designed by ZF of Germany, a longtime suppler to Mercedes, and built under license in the United States. The steering column, dash wiring in early models, and independent front and rear suspension are from Mercedes. Engine offerings include a V6 in mainstream models and optional V8s with gobs of power and a great soundtrack. Optional 4WD beginning in the 2007 model year significantly increased the appeal of the model in Canada. The Magnum was a station wagon version of the platform whose introduction preceded the Charger; it sold in small numbers and was discontinued at the end of 2008. Both cars offer a choice of the Hemi V8 or a V6 in more popular mainstream models. **Road performance:** Performance of most versions is better than average; mainstream models improved significantly with the arrival of the 3.6L V6 and 8-speed automatic. **Strong points:** Affordable and comfortable cruisers; used examples command a small premium for a well-equipped car, compared to competing imports. The Charger depreciates more quickly than the Challenger and 300, so prices are more affordable for essentially the same mechanical components; the V8 is a used car bargain. The infotainment system is first class. Comfortable front seats and handsome interior on premium models with leather trim, improving after interior upgrades introduced for the 2013 model year. **Weak points:** Cheap interior finish on basic models before 2011. Rear seat room is unexceptional for an intermediate. Plenty of more modern front-drive sedans offer better fuel economy and space utilization, but lack the macho flair and feeling of heft at the wheel. **Major redesign:** 2011 models got a number of significant upgrades, including sharper styling with a slightly larger trunk, higher-quality interior materials, a more powerful 3.6L Pentastar V6 standard, retuned suspension, electric-assist power steering and a new electronic interface. **Best alternatives:** Ford Fusion, Infiniti G35/G37, Chevrolet Impala.

Prices and Specs

Prices (2016-2017): *Charger SE:* $35,295, *Charger SRT Hellcat:* $79,840 (Costa Nostra firm price)
Freight: $1,795 **Powertrain (Rear-drive/AWD):** Engines: 3.6L V6 (305 hp), 5.7L V8 (370 hp), 6.4L V8 (485 hp), 6.2L Supercharged V8 (707 hp); Transmissions: 6-speed manual (V8s only), 8-speed automatic.
Dimensions: Passengers: 2/3; *Length*: 198 in.; Wheelbase: 120 in.; *Weight:* 3,934 lb. **Fuel consumption:** 3.6L: 12.4L/100 km city, 7.7L/100 km highway; 5.7L: 14.8L/100 km city/9.3L/100 km highway. **Assembled in:** Brampton, Ontario.

ALERT! 68 injuries and 266 crashes have been blamed on a confusing electronic automatic transmission shifter in some 2012-14 Dodge Charger and Chrysler 300 sedans, and 2014-15 Jeep Grand Cherokees. The driver may exit without having the transmission in Park, increasing the risk of a rollaway. After a NHTSA investigation, Fiat Chrysler was compelled to recall 1.1 million vehicles in 2016 to update the transmission software and include more visual warnings and chimes that the vehicle is not in Park. All ZF-supplied 8-speed transmissions in the aforementioned models and model-years are recalled in the U.S., Canada, and elsewhere.

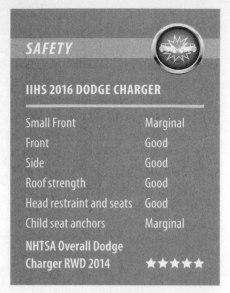

SAFETY

IIHS 2016 DODGE CHARGER

Small Front	Marginal
Front	Good
Side	Good
Roof strength	Good
Head restraint and seats	Good
Child seat anchors	Marginal
NHTSA Overall Dodge Charger RWD 2014	★★★★★

RELIABILITY: Average Powertrains, electronics, electrical shorts, and suspension/steering defects are the most common. Early models of Charger and Magnum exhibited short-lived front lower control arm and tension strut bearings; models from 2010 received better components (more info in the Chrysler 300 review). Beware of TIPM issues that can render the vehicle undrivable at any time. Eight-speed automatic transmission can be problematic. A noisy 3.5L V6 at high mileage may signal worn rocker shaft assemblies, a substantial repair. The 3.6L V6 has come under fire from owners of 2011-2012 models. Chrysler's poor after-sales supports, frequently backordered parts, and refusal to provide a loaner vehicle can make a bad situation worse:

Shifter in Park? "Do you feel lucky, punk?"

> My 2014 Charger's transmission started to slip/skip and shift roughly. After a few visits to dealer and after they kept my car for a week, it was determined that the tranny valve body needed replacing, and Chrysler won't provide a loaner due to my vehicle still being driveable. The part is on backorder and Chrysler doesn't know when they will have it in. So, now I am stuck with a $40,000 paperweight in my driveway until Chrysler gets off their sorry butts to get this problem resolved. This is obviously a common problem.
>
> *– safercar.gov posting*

For Internal Bulletins and Secret Warranty information check the Chrysler 300 review.

CHRYSLER 300 ★★★★

RATING: Above Average. Introduced in 2005, the 300 is a more upscale and refined model built on the rear-drive Chrysler LX platform shared with the Charger. Powertrains include V6 and V8 models, the latter carry the letter C after the model name, as in 300C. Interiors are elegant, even more so after 2011, and feature the convenient Chrysler infotainment package. Leather-trimmed vehicles feel and drive like a cross between the big domestic sedans of years gone by and a luxury German sedan – not surprising given the marriage of Mercedes-Benz and Chrysler underpinnings. The "gangsta" styling, with the high beltline, shallow glass area, and splashes of chrome, was initially very popular and nicely updated over the years, but it's beginning to date the car. Unfortunately, Fiat Chrysler has been too distracted making a fortune selling SUVs and pickups to invest in modernizing the 300. All-wheel drive, initially the Mercedes 4-Matic system, significantly increased the appeal for Canada. **Road performance:** Here's your dilemma: The Pentastar 3.6L V6 gives the car power and fuel economy the old V6 lacked, but less reliability; the V8 has much more power, but it guzzles fuel (not as much of a hardship with cheap gas). The Touring model with the V6 is smoother, with a more-comfortable ride than the 300C. **Strong points:** You will enjoy a remarkably quiet, luxurious, and spacious interior (up front), and a large trunk. Uconnect infotainment system works flawlessly and the Garmin-based navigation system is easy to master. **Weak points:** Rear seat dimensions don't match class standards in this segment. Hemi V8-equipped models are expensive and the resale value drops quickly – a negative for new-car buyers, but a plus if you're buying used. At just 1,000 lbs, towing capacity is oddly low. **Major redesign:** New landlord Fiat finally got around to refreshing the 300 for 2011, with a stiffer structure, electrically assisted steering, and recalibrated suspension. The cabin boasted higher-quality materials, more acoustic insulation and a more refined appearance. The exterior received some bling in the form of LED lighting and added chrome. **Best alternatives:** Chevrolet Impala (2014-2017), Honda Accord V6, Infiniti G35/G37 or Q50, Toyota Avalon.

Prices and Specs

Prices (2016-2017): *Touring:* $39,995, *300C Platinum:* $45,695 **Freight:** $1,795 **Powertrain (Rear-drive/AWD):** Engines: 3.6L V6 (292 hp), 5.7L V8 (363 hp). Transmissions: 8-speed automatic. **Dimensions:** Passengers: 2/3; *Length:* 199 in.; Wheelbase: 120 in.; *Weight:* 4235 lb. **Fuel consumption:** *3.6L:* 12.4L/100 km city, 7.7L/100 km highway; *5.7L:* 14.8L/100 km city/9.3L/100 km highway. **Assembled in:** Brampton, Ontario.

ALERT! Make sure the car is in Park before getting out of a 2012-14 Charger or 300. Poorly-designed shifter may fool you. NHTSA ordered Fiat Chrysler to recall 1.1 million vehicles, including some 300s, to update the transmission software. In addition, have an independent garage check the brakes, the steering assembly, and the transmission fluid. Also, ensure that the tilted head restraints aren't a pain in the neck.

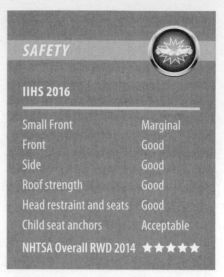

RELIABILITY: Average Mercedes-sourced electronics have had serious, head-scratching reliability glitches that defy correction. Airbag and engine warning lights are constant and not always meaningful. The recurring powertrain, electronic, electrical system, and steering/suspension failures are endemic to most of Chrysler's lineup. Brakes may need frequent replacement. Head gasket failures are common with the Pentastar 3.6L V6 engine, at least in 2011-2012. A noisy 3.5L V6 at high mileage may signal worn rocker shaft assemblies, a substantial repair. Upper ball joint wear that few shops check correctly can require replacement of both front suspension control arms up to the 2009 model year. That's an expensive job that could set you back $800; the replacement control arms introduced at the factory for later model years were modified.

Challenger, Charger, Magnum, and 300

INTERNAL BULLETINS, SECRET WARRANTIES: *Charger and Magnum:* Rear door wind noise; and light to moderate paint defects. 2009-12—TSB #P01 says that some 300s, Chargers, and Challengers with Hemi engines and automatic transmissions may develop a fracture in the engine timing chain. The timing chain, tensioner, and guide will be replaced free, regardless of warranty status. 2011-13—Chrysler trunk lids may pop open on some 2011-13 Chrysler 300s and Dodge Chargers when the vehicle is in Park and the keyless remote is nearby. Replacing the switch (a free repair for this safety hazard) should keep the lid shut. *Charger:* 2005-10—Inoperative door locks remedy found in TSB #08-061-12, issued Nov. 29, 2012. 2011-12—A front-end clunk can be silenced by replacing both the left and right side front tension struts (no-charge during the warranty), says TSB #02-005-12. Automatic transmission controls cause a shudder, shift concern; deck lid spoiler rattle, chatter; front door wind noise; battery drain; radio powers itself on with the ignition off; fix for the rear chime; false chime from the blind spot system; trunk won't open with passive switch; and coolant leaks. 2014—Rear shock absorbers with reduced performance or leakage should be replaced under warranty. *Challenger:*

2011-12—Intermittent no-start; automatic transmission malfunctions; booming noise at idle; battery drain; door handles inoperative; and deck lid and trunk can be opened without the key fob nearby. Incorrect ride height can be fixed by replacing the rear springs. *Charger and Challenger:* 2011-13—3.6L V6 engine cylinder leakage may require a new cylinder head covered by an extended warranty (Chrysler X56 Warranty Extension). See TSB #09-002-14 REV.8, published Dec. 15, 2014. 2013-14—Ways to reduce audio distortion. 2014—On vehicles carrying the 3.6L engine, extended crank time can be corrected by inspecting the Bank 1 position camshaft sensor and replacing it, if needed. Powertrain system improvements via reprogramming the powertrain control module (PCM). Remedy for a steering column squeak or moan. 2014-15—Silencing door wind noise. 2015—A loss of steering assist may require the free replacement of the pinion shaft cover retaining washer. Infotainment system, radio, and camera malfunctions. Headlamps that are too dim or appear yellow may have a defective body control module. 2016—Heated steering wheel suddenly shuts off.

DODGE JOURNEY

2009-2011 ★★
2012-2017 ★★★

RATING: Below Average (2009-2011); Average (2012-2017). Dodge entered the crossover SUV segment as a way to hedge its bet in the shrinking minivan market. Introduced early in 2008 as a 2009 model, the five-door Journey was a mid-size crossover built on the front-drive Avenger car platform. It sat lower to the ground and offered no off-road capability unlike the Dodge Durango and Jeep Liberty, but it had the looks of a genuine crossover that the public is in love with, unlike the Dodge Caravan it replaced. Engineers specified an aluminum hood, composite plastic tailgate and lots of high-strength steel to keep weight down, so it could be offered with a 4-cylinder engine, not seen on the Caravan since 1998. The Journey seats five in base trim and seven with the 50/50 split third-row bench in place. Seat rows are arranged theatre style, each one slightly higher than the one in front. Dodge applied some of its minivan expertise, sprinkling the interior with cupholders, power outlets and cubbies, an available beverage-chilling glovebox, and storage wells in the floor. The rear doors swing open 90 degrees for easy access. Base model uses a noisy and overtaxed 2.4L 4-cylinder engine tied to a four-speed automatic transmission driving the front wheels. Uplevel models featured a 235 hp 3.5L V6 with a six-speed automatic, available with either front-wheel drive or all-wheel drive. The Journey underwent a wholesale freshening for 2011 that included styling tweaks, a reworked suspension, a vastly improved interior, and a powerful V6 – the 3.6L Pentastar, making 283 hp. If you can afford it, the 2011 and later V6 is the way to go. As a new vehicle, this sport-ute competes on price; it's aging, while Jeep brand vehicles are receiving all the attention from FCA. It offers none of the latest safety technologies. **Road performance:** The Journey works best with a V6, and the Pentastar is the one to get. The rejuvenated 2011 versions are more composed and rewarding to drive, thanks to revised rear-suspension geometry, retuned shocks, and beefier steering links. **Strong points:** Available seven-seat configuration is a plus in this segment. All-wheel drive versions capable in foul weather. With the V6, the Journey is quiet, subduing both road and powertrain noises. The optional 8.4-inch infotainment system touch screen is feature-packed and easy to use. Bargain used vehicle prices are typical of Fiat Chrysler vehicles. **Weak points:** The base 4-cylinder engine is noisy when pushed. The four-speed automatic is outdated. Fuel consumption is high for the segment with both engines. **Best alternatives:** For three-row seating, the 2011-2016 Mazda5, 2013-2017 Kia Rondo or Fiat Chrysler's own Grand Caravan. Two-row alternatives that compete in this price range include the Chevrolet Equinox and Hyundai Santa Fe.

Prices and Specs

Prices (2016-2017): *Canada Value Package:* $21,995, *Crossroad AWD:* $33,895 **Freight:** $1,795 **Power-train (FWD and AWD):** Engines: 2.4L 4-cyl. (173 hp), 3.5L V6 (235 hp), 3.6L V6 (283 hp). Transmission: 4-speed automatic, 6-speed automatic. **Dimensions:** Passengers: 2/3/2; Length: 192 in., Wheelbase: 114 in., Weight: 3,818 lb. **Fuel economy:** *2.4L:* 12.7L/100 km city, 9.1L/100 km highway; *3.6L:* 14.5L/100 km city, 9.9L/100 km highway. **Assembled in:** Toluca, Mexico.

RELIABILITY: The worst model years were 2009-2010 following the launch, which took place just after Chrysler's insolvency bailout. Early models had an insatiable appetite for brakes and tires. Have the rear brake calipers serviced annually to postpone expensive brake repairs. Some reports of engines shutting off in the middle of traffic. Transport Canada recall # 2014-261 points to a Wireless Ignition

Node that may allow the ignition key to inadvertently move from the ON position to the accessory (ACC) position while driving, causing the engine to shut down. A no-start condition that cannot be attributed to a dead battery, since the accessories work, may point to a defective power control module (PCM) or replacement needed of the entire wiring harness. The optional 2011-2012 Pentastar V6, has a known problem with the left cylinder head, which can develop cracks; the U.S. warranty has been extended to 10 years/150,000 miles on a case-by-case basis. Other reported issues include hard-shifting and broken transmissions, worn axle seals, leaking transfer cases, air conditioner failures (common on

SAFETY	
IIHS 2016	
Small Front	Poor
Front	Good
Side	Good
Roof strength	Good
Head restraint and seats	Good
Child seat anchors	Marginal
NHTSA Overall 2014	★ ★ ★ ★

several FCA models), faulty window regulators (try them all and the door locks before you buy), electrical faults, peeling paint and flimsy interior trim. Wet carpets may be attributable to a water leak, most commonly caused by improperly sealed body seams. Don't try to save money by purchasing an older high-mileage example, because repair cost and frequency increase appreciably.

TIPM Units Faulty on Various Chrysler Products

The Jeep Grand Cherokee, Dodge Durango and Grand Caravan use the troublesome Totally Integrated Power Module (TIPM) that can prevent the vehicle from starting or, if it does start, to shut off without warning — sometimes at speed. The TIPM can introduce other issues, including running the fuel pump after the engine stops, wearing out the battery and alternator, and prompting other electrical quirks. A U.S. class action lawsuit compelled Fiat Chrysler to address faulty TIPM units on the 2011-2013 Durango and Grand Cherokee, but ignored the issue on several additional FCA vehicles:

> Our Durango will just completely go haywire (display screen, lights – interior, dash, and exterior lights, the 3rd row head rests will automatically go down, doors lock/unlock) and shut down while in motion. All power goes out and the vehicle becomes impossible to regain control.

Replacement modules are sometimes backordered and can take weeks to arrive. Replacement is not covered after the basic three-year warranty, even when the module fails a second time. Transport Canada lists recalls on the TIPM for various model-years of Chrysler products, but their limited scope is inadequate (the problem goes back to 2007 on some models).

For Internal Bulletins and Secret Warranty information check the Dodge Caravan/Grand Caravan/Chrysler Town & Country review.

DODGE CARAVAN/GRAND CARAVAN/ CHRYSLER TOWN & COUNTRY/ 2009-2012 VOLKSWAGEN ROUTAN

2005-2010 ★★
2011-2017 ★★★

2017 Dodge Grand Caravan

RATING: *All models:* Below Average (2005-2010); Average (2011-2017). These vans dominate their segment in Canada, thanks to relentless advertising, heavy discounting and considerable buyer loyalty. The practical short-wheelbase Caravan was axed at the end of 2007, replaced by the Dodge Journey crossover introduced for 2009. Sold from 2009 to 2012, the Volkswagen Routan is a clone of the Grand Caravan, assembled by Chrysler and sold through the VW dealer network to fill a gap in VW's North American lineup; it has the same rating as the Grand Caravan. Since 2008, all versions of the Grand Caravan except for base models with the Canada Value Package offer two rows of rear seats that fold into the floor – that's a unique innovation that's coveted by buyers. The 2008 redesign seemed promising, but it coincided with Chrysler's bankruptcy reorganization, and quality – never a strong suit at Chrysler – tanked. Refinements for 2011 corrected many past deficiencies and added new features, including the powerful Pentastar V6. A focus on cabin design put the interiors at the head of the class. Road performance: Spacious and comfortable highway cruisers, minivans in general and the Grand Caravan particularly, are ideal for road trips and families. *2011-2017:* Revisions to the suspension for the 2011 model year improved the ride and handling; the chassis is tighter and the steering is nicely weighted. The powertrain got a significant boost in 2011, when both the 3.3L and 4L V6 engines were superceded by the new 3.6L V6. Typically for Fiat Chrysler, the early Pentastar V6 tends to run roughly and suddenly lose power, and the standard 6-speed automatic can shift erratically on 2011-2012 models. **Strong points:** Priced for thousands less than the competing Toyota Sienna and Honda Odyssey on the used vehicle market; luxury Town & Country models offer especially good used value thanks to their rapid depreciation. Among the most comfortable vehicles if you need to cover a lot of highway miles. Spacious, with easy ingress and egress, good visibility, and good availability of wheelchair conversions. The ride is quiet. Lots of innovative convenience features, with user-friendly instruments, controls, and infotainment features. **Weak points:** Despite deep discounting, a new Town & Country or Grand Caravan often ends up with payments similar to the Toyota Sienna. Fuel consumption with all engines is a bit higher than for the Sienna, and Odyssey. Bargain hunters are drawn by the rapid depreciation on used models, and then payback can arrive in the form of an expensive air conditioner, transmission, or V6 repair. There's a history of chronic powertrain and electronic module (TIPM) failures at least up to 2014, along with short-lived air conditioners and frequent brake service. Chrysler Canada is super-hard-nosed when it comes to warranty coverage, almost never formally extending its warranty to cover parts with high failure rates, and dragging its feet on recalls. **Major redesign:** 2008 saw a wholesale redesign, adopting the current breadbox profile. The floorpan was carried over to accommodate the Stow 'n Go seating system. The 2011 models were substantially improved with a better suspension, engine and cabin furnishings. **Best alternatives:** The Toyota Sienna is good new alternative, and some new Sienna models actually compete well against the Grand Caravan on price or payments; a used Sienna with comparable mileage and age will cost a lot more than a Grand Caravan. If you can think small, look at the 2011 or later 7-passenger Kia Rondo.

Prices and Specs

Prices (2016-2017): *Grand Caravan Value Package:* $22,395, *Grand Caravan R/T:* $35,995 **Freight:** $1,795 **Powertrain (FWD):** Engine: 3.6L V6 (283 hp); Transmission: 6-speed automatic. **Dimensions:** Passengers: 2/3/3; Length: 203 in.; Wheelbase: 121 in.; Weight: 4,510 lb. **Fuel consumption:** *3.6L:* 13.7L/100 km city, 9.4L/100 km highway. **Assembled in:** Windsor, Ontario.

ALERT! Beginning in 2008, there were widespread malfunctions with the Totally Integrated Power Module (TIPM), which controls power to all of the electrical functions of the vehicle, including the safety and ignition systems. Seemingly random symptoms include hard starting, stalling (sometimes at highway speed!), a fuel pump that won't shut off, a dark instrument display, and a host of other electrical headaches. Dealers can charge well over $1,000 for a new TIPM – and some of those subsequently proved defective, too.

RELIABILITY: Incredibly, Fiat Chrysler has had recurring trouble supplying replacement parts for the 2008 and later minivans, even though the current generation has been on the market for nearly a decade and is widely sold. The 2005-2007 vans have average reliability, but their repair frequency is increasing now that they are older. In Central and Eastern Canada they are subject to severe rusting affecting the rocker panels and eventually the doors, hatch, and underbody. The APA recommends Krown Rust Control or Barry's Rustproofing in the Montreal market to protect the fragile rocker panels, rear fenders, and floor (contact information is in the Part Four Introduction). The ABS electronic braking system is unreliable on older vans and costly to repair. All years of these minivans have an appetite for brakes. *2008-10 models:* Check the coolant level and have a mechanic look for coolant leaks at the intake manifold, which are common on both the 3.3L and 4L engines. The brake pedal can feel mushy, and the brakes tend to heat up after repeated application, warping the rotors. Prematurely seized rear brake calipers can cause the rear brakes to drag and overheat; have the calipers de-seized and lubricated annually to postpone expensive brake repairs. (It's usually billed as 30 minutes to an hour of shop time.) 2008-2017: Have the calipers checked annually and serviced preventatively if required. 2011 and newer: The Pentastar V6 may develop cracks in the left-side cylinder head. Other weaknesses include faulty air conditioners, prematurely worn wheel bearings, electrical gremlins, bad thermostats, rattles, and that old Chrysler Achilles heel – transmission failures.

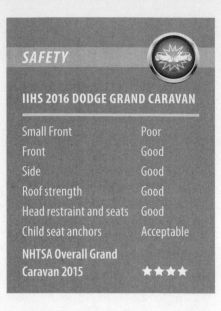

SAFETY

IIHS 2016 DODGE GRAND CARAVAN

Small Front	Poor
Front	Good
Side	Good
Roof strength	Good
Head restraint and seats	Good
Child seat anchors	Acceptable
NHTSA Overall Grand Caravan 2015	★★★★

Dodge Journey, Dodge Caravan/Grand Caravan/Chrysler Town & Country/Volkswagen Routan

INTERNAL BULLETINS, SECRET WARRANTIES: 2008-13— Sliding door rattle is caused by the door panel bowing and contacting the rear quarter panel when the door is opened. Battery may be drained due to a faulty Fold and Stow module that creates a continuous electrical draw. 2010—Silencing transfer-gear noise. Water leakage onto the front floor. 2010-12—Remedy for a water leak in the jack storage area. 2010-17—Diagnosis and correction for steering that pulls to the left or right when underway. 2011-13—3.6L V6 engine cylinder leakage may require a new cylinder head covered by an extended warranty (Chrysler X56 Warranty Extension). This little-known program is confirmed by TSB #09-002-14 REV.8, published Dec. 15, 2014. Erratic automatic transmission shifting may be corrected flashing the Powertrain Control Module (PCM) with new software covered by the 8-year

Emissions warranty. 2011-14—If the AC blows cold at any setting, flush the HVAC module. Cost is covered during the warranty. 2012-13—Sunroof opens but won't close; scratched glass. 2013-15—A fix for rear sliding door rattling may involve modifying the rubber bumper located at the rear end of the sliding door upper track. 2014—On the 3.6L engine, extended cranking time can be corrected by inspecting the Bank 1 position camshaft sensor and replacing it, if needed. Power liftgate won't close (passenger-side pinch sensor wire harness may be misrouted). Chrysler will reset the tire pressure monitor free of charge (Customer Satisfaction Notification P69). 2014-15—Water dripping from the sunroof signals that the drain tubes are clogged. Both tubes should be replaced. 2015—Fix for the front door dragging on the door striker, or high door closing effort. A hard-to-open power rear liftgate may require its replacement. Harsh shifts on hard acceleration may be due to low transmission fluid level. Also, try flashing the TCM. 2016—Manual sliding door may not open after the fuel filler flap is opened then closed; replace the latch assembly for the fuel fill door blocker. Heated steering wheel suddenly shuts off.

CHRYSLER PACIFICA NOT RATED (TOO NEW)

For 2017, Fiat Chrysler unveiled an all-new Pacifica minivan, but has hedged its bet by continuing production of the Grand Caravan for at least one more year. Here's why: The Pacifica starts at an ambitious $44,000, while the base Grand Caravan costs half the money and FCA believes that many Canadians will likely gravitate to the value play. The Pacifica looks like a brilliant design, but a good strategy would be to wait a year or two to see if Fiat Chrysler has worked out its traditional first-year bugs. A plug-in Pacifica hybrid is planned for the spring of 2017. Like the last Pacifica, *Lemon-Aid* predicts the new Pacifica will depreciate very quickly after its first couple of years on the market.

DODGE DURANGO	2005-2009 ★★
	2011-2017 ★★★
CHRYSLER ASPEN	2011-2017 ★★★
ASPEN AND DURANGO HYBRIDS	★

RATING: *Dodge Durango:* Below Average (2005-2009); Average (2011-2017); *Chrysler Aspen:* Average (2011-2017); *Durango and Aspen Hybrids:* Not Recommended. The Durango is a large, truck-based SUV that offers three-row seating. It's popular in the western U.S. and Canada where its heavy chassis and good towing ability are appreciated. The second-generation vehicle, with body-on-frame construction and a front end styled like a Dodge pickup was sold from 2004-2009. An update in 2006 saw the addition of optional electronic stability control, an important safety feature that reduces the likelihood of a rollover. The Chrysler Aspen, an upscale twin of the Durango, arrived for 2007. Both models were dropped at the end of 2009; their respective 385 hp hybrid versions had an abbreviated 2008-09 run before being dropped for good. The Durango returned for model year 2011 on an extended version of the Jeep Grand Cherokee's unibody platform, which brought new refinement; the additional length permits three-row seating, which is not available on the Grand Cherokee. *2011:* Arrival of the third-generation Durango related to the Grand Cherokee. Industry insiders predict the Durango will stick around until it's replaced by an upscale, resurrected 2018 Jeep Grand Wagoneer. This could put the Durango on a highway to nowhere and cause resale values to drop more. **Strong points:** *2011-2017:* Spacious, reasonably quiet, easy handling for the size with a decent ride, and a practical, easy-to-understand Uconnect infotainment system. Fuel economy improved with the advent of cylinder deactivation on the V8 and the 8-speed automatic transmission in 2014, but this is a heavy, thirsty vehicle whose popularity rides on low-cost gasoline. Performance is decent with the 3.6L V6, though it needs to be revved to get into its power band. The 5.7L V8 is impressive, as is handling with the R/T package. **Weak points:** Prices climb quickly for well-equipped versions, putting a new Durango in the range of luxury models from some European manufacturers. In theory, this is the ideal large truck-style SUV, capable of handling both bad weather and towing with aplomb. The problem is that it sometimes acts "possessed;" electronic module (TIPM) demons can wreak havoc upon vehicle safety and reliability. Shorter drivers may find that the view over the raised hood is partially obstructed. Limited rear visibility; consider investing in an aftermarket rearview camera if this is a concern. **Major redesign:** 2004, 2007 Aspen introduced, 2008 hybrids introduced, 2011. **Best alternatives:** The domestic makers produce lots of three-row competitors in this class, including the Chevrolet Tahoe and Suburban, GMC Yukon, GM's Acadia, Traverse, and Enclave, and the Ford Expedition. The Toyota 4Runner may also be a viable new vehicle to cross-shop; used 4Runners are in short supply and expensive. If you only need a five-seater, the Jeep Grand Cherokee is a possible cross-shop.

Prices and Specs

Prices (2016-2017): *Durango SXT:* $43,395, *Citadel:* $56,395 **Freight:** $1,795 **Powertrain (AWD):** Engine: 3.6L V6 (295 hp); 5.7L Hemi V8 (360 hp). Transmission: 8-speed automatic. **Dimensions:** Passengers: 2/2/3; Length: 200 in.; Wheelbase: 120 in.; Weight: 5,105 lb. **Fuel consumption:** *3.6L:* 12.8L/100 km city, 9.5L/100 km highway; *5.7L:* 16.7L/100 km city, 10.7L/100 km highway. **Assembled in:** Delaware and Michigan.

ALERT! The Dodge Durango uses a rotary dial-type gear selector to operate the 8-speed automatic transmission, and not the "monostable" stubby selector that has been recalled on certain model years of the Jeep Grand Cherokee, Dodge Charger, and Chrysler 300. Durango owners have reported a significant number of complaints on the NTHSA website where their vehicles rolled away after they thought they had put the selector in Park. If this happens to you, be sure to report the incident to Transport Canada and the APA:

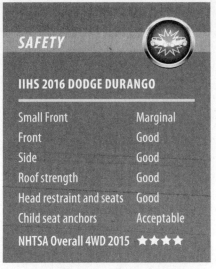

> I put the vehicle in Park at the end of my driveway so I could check the mail. While walking back to the vehicle from the mailbox, the vehicle starting backing up a hill on its own. I had to run next to the vehicle, hanging partially inside the cab, to attempt to shut off vehicle. Vehicle would not shut off. I had to push down emergency brake with my hand in order to get vehicle to stop.
>
> The contact owns a 2014 Dodge Durango. The contact stated that the vehicle was placed in the Park position, however the vehicle rolled forward and the contact became trapped between the vehicle and the garage door. The contact sustained three fractured ribs, which required medical attention.

– safercar.gov postings

RELIABILITY: The Durango has experienced a few bad transmissions, stubborn alignment issues, short-lived fuel and water pumps, and some fragile interior trim. Purchase of a full-coverage extended warranty from FCA is recommended; APA and ACC members may be eligible for a small discount. Many owner reports of mediocre braking. The 2004-2009 models are rust-prone; vulnerable areas include the rocker panels, door bottoms, hood, and rear quarter panels. The APA recommends Krown Rust Control or Barry's Rustproofing in the Montreal market (contact information is in the Part Four Introduction).

INTERNAL BULLETINS, SECRET WARRANTIES: 2006-08—Fuel spitback can be prevented by replacing the fuel filler tube under an extended warranty that has no time or mileage limitation.

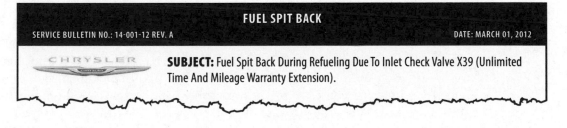

FUEL SPIT BACK

SERVICE BULLETIN NO.: 14-001-12 REV. A   DATE: MARCH 01, 2012

CHRYSLER

SUBJECT: Fuel Spit Back During Refueling Due To Inlet Check Valve X39 (Unlimited Time And Mileage Warranty Extension).

2011-12—Remedy for excessive transfer case noise when shifting from Drive to Neutral (TSB# 21-010-12). Noise from the instrument panel may be caused by an improperly adjusted hood hinge. 2011-13—3.6L V6 engine cylinder leakage may require a new cylinder head covered by an extended warranty (Chrysler X56 Warranty Extension). This little-known program is confirmed by TSB #09-002-14 REV.8, published Dec. 15, 2014. A rattle or clunk noise from the rear of vehicles equipped with Load Leveling suspension may mean the rear shock absorbers need to be replaced (a full-coverage extended warranty is a good idea if you're buying a vehicle with this feature). Front brake squealing when braking can be corrected by installing a front brake pad kit (68052370AC). 2011-14—Remedy for a rear suspension rattle and front brake squealing. 2012—Troubleshooting engine misfiring and power loss. Engine power sag; hesitation may be fixed by replacing the power control module. A shudder felt when accelerating, decelerating, or when coasting may require only the reflashing or changing of the drivetrain control module. Fix for a power liftgate that won't open or close. A rear shock absorber buzz, squeak, or rattle may signal the need to replace both rear upper shock mounts. Excessive exhaust noise can be corrected by replacing the exhaust pipe/catalytic converter assembly. Dealing with light to moderate paint imperfections. 2013—A second-row head restraint squeak or creak may require the replacement of the head restraint mechanism. 2013-14—A click, creak, or groaning sound near the C-pillar, Dual Plane sunroof may require the replacement of the rear sunroof glass or adding structural adhesive at the rear right corner. Rear brake rattling can be silenced by replacing the caliper adapter mounting bolts. 2014—Vehicles with the 3.6L V6: Extended cranking time can be corrected by inspecting the Bank 1 position camshaft sensor and replacing it, if needed. If the truck won't shift out of Park, the electronic shifter may need to be replaced. Replace it under warranty. Remedy for a rear suspension rattle, chuckle: Replace both rear shock upper mounts. 2015—Heated steering wheel suddenly shuts off.

DODGE & RAM 1500	2005-2011 ★★★
	2012-2017 ★★★★
	ECODIESEL
	2014-2017 ★
DODGE & RAM 2500/3500	2005-2008 ★★
	2009-2017 ★★★

RATING: *Light-Duty 1500 Series:* Average (2005-2011), Above Average (2012-2017); *Ecodiesel:* Not Recommended (2014-2017); *Heavy Duty 2500 and 3500 Series:* Below Average (2005-2018); Average (2009-2017). The full-size pickup market is vast, lucrative, and hotly contested by Detroit's three manufacturers. Late-model Ram 1500s are better than they used to be and compare well with their competitors. Ram continues to play the value card with a standard V6 engine that's priced better than competing V8 models and Ford's V6 EcoBoost engines. Reliability has

bad buy

improved and powertrain failures are less frequent. Fiat Chrysler's Ram pickups are unique: They are the only half-ton models with an available diesel engine, or a coil-spring 2500 heavy-duty pickup. Ram 2500s are capable daily drivers, even with their "death wobble" suspension/steering assemblies for which most of the models concerned have been recalled. **Road performance:** The newest Ram exhibits better handling and a more comfortable ride than ever. With the optional air suspension, it provides best-in-class ride quality. Mercifully, this may mean the end of the Ram "death wobble," where the truck loses steering control after passing over potholes or uneven terrain. **Strong points:** In a recent comparison test by the APA, the Ram beat the Ford F-150 and Toyota Tundra. The GM Silverado/Sierra twins scored almost as highly as the Ram. The test Rams were 4WD 1500 Crew Cabs, with the gas V6 and optional diesel. This gas engine provided seamless power along with good fuel economy; the diesel was remarkably fuel efficient but slower. The lockable "Ram box" storage compartment keeps items secure and out of the weather. **Weak points:** The 5.7 Hemi V8 is thirsty, despite the fact its cylinder-deactivation system can shut down 4-cylinders under light load conditions. Three other minuses: Unusually high step-up, a heavy tailgate, and premature corrosion of the undercarriage. Fiat Chrysler's aftersales support is in disarray, and replacement parts with high failure rates are often backordered – this makes the Ram Heavy Duty commercial pickups a less attractive choice for commercial users, who lose revenue when their trucks are sidelined. **Major redesign:** *2009 and 2013:* The Ram was redesigned for the 2009 model year, featuring bolder styling, a more decadent cabin and added muscle. Engineers abandoned the traditional leaf-spring rear suspension – an inexpensive and durable design, but a jerky one in terms of ride quality – in favour of a civilized coil-spring setup. The base-model 3.7L V6 was tied to an outdated 4-speed automatic. The 2013 models gained updated styling and equipment changes. Chief among them was the 3.6L Pentastar V6 with 305 hp as the new base engine – 42% stronger than the outgoing 3.7L. Combining the engine with a new 8-speed automatic transmission meant that many buyers didn't need a V8. In addition to the 2014 Ram 1500's EcoDiesel V6 – which is supplied by Fiat's VM Motori and not Cummins – there's also an all-new 6.4L Hemi V8 used with the 4500 and 5500 models. Giving heavy-duty truck buyers a plethora of horsepower and torque choices with the 6.7L Cummins inline-6 diesel engine and two V8 gasoline engines is what the market demands. Chassis cabs use reinforced steel frames to allow for much bigger payloads and trailer towing. **Best alternatives:** Which truck is best? It's a question as old as the hills, and everyone has an opinion. The Dodge Ram returned from near obscurity to carve out a sizable chunk of the North American pickup market after its 1994 resurrection; that's a testament to its appeal. Rivals include the GM twins – Chevrolet Silverado and GMC Sierra – as well as Ford's juggernaut, the F-150. The Toyota Tundra has the best long-term reliability, but it's more expensive and not nearly as appealing to drive. The Honda Ridgeline is a unibody pickup that performs very well as a daily driver, but most pickup buyers wouldn't consider it.

SAFETY

IIHS 2012 RAM 1500

Small Front	Good
Front	Good
Side	Good
Roof strength	Marginal
Head restraint and seats	Good
Child seat anchors	Not rated
NHTSA Overall Ram 1500 2015	★★★★

ALERT! The dash-mounted rotary transmission gear selector is easy to misapply. The mushroom-shaped gear selector in other Fiat Chrysler models has grabbed headlines for its confusing operation in other Fiat Chrysler models. The Ram's rotary gear selector is not yet the subject of a recall, but owners' experiences are equally chilling:

> Turned the transmission rotary knob on the dash of my 2016 Ram to R and backed out of the garage. The engine was still running and put my foot on the brake to go to Park. As I was getting out of the truck and taking my foot off the brake pedal, the truck starting moving forward, going back into the garage. It pinned me between the inside of the front and the garage door opening. I was able to reach for the knob again to put it back into Reverse. It smashed the left front door in and tore the side of garage door opening.

Owner-reported safety-related failures: Many owner reports of mediocre braking. Shorter drivers may not be able to see over the raised hood. Some 2015-16 model owners have gotten sick from exhaust fumes entering the cabin. Water may enter the cabin through the roof-mounted brake light. Many owners have complained of dim headlights:

> 2016 Ram Rebel has extremely dim headlights on low beam. Dangerous to drive on back roads. Headlights are projection type and I believe they are of poor design.

Acceleration lag is another safety-related problem affecting the 2014s:

> This truck has been to the dealership several times for the "dead pedal" issue. There is a 3-4 second delay from the moment you ask the truck to accelerate before there is any throttle

response. And then once it does respond, the power delivery is extremely slow. I have had several near accidents when I was attempting to turn left in front of oncoming traffic, and the truck does not respond to full throttle.

While leaving the lot I go to accelerate and the truck slowly increases speed and then starts to move. This happens all the time and I took the truck into the dealership and they stated this is Chrysler's torque management system. This system has almost caused me to get into a wreck twice. I know of one friend who has gotten into a wreck. I researched this issue and sure enough there are hundreds of members on Dodge and Cummins forums complaining of this issue and Chrysler will not do anything about it.

Here are links to some threads: *www.cumminsforum.com/forum/2013-general-discussion/ 1193537-quick-rant.html* and *www.cumminsforum.com/forum/2013-general-discussion/ 1179305-dead-pedal.html*.

Is your truck's axle misrepresented? Chrysler has been sued in a class action where a 2014 Ram 1500 wasn't equipped with the heavy-duty axle for which the owner had paid extra (*Beasly vs. FCA US*). A higher axle ratio usually gives more torque to the rear wheels, improving towing performance, though you will burn more fuel. Chrysler wouldn't say how many other Rams were misrepresented. Be wary of "pain in the neck" front head restraints on some model years. They could be a deal-breaker.

 RELIABILITY: Faulty Totally Integrated Powertrain Modules (TIPM) can affect all Ram pickups, as well as numerous other Fiat Chrysler models as far back as 2007, all the way up to 2014. A bad TIPM can lead to multiple hard-to-diagnose defects, including malfunctioning airbags, dashboard instruments that suddenly fail, random stalling at speed, and a host of electrical failures and bugaboos that can make the car or truck appear possessed. Fiat Chrysler did recall a few selected model years of the Dodge Durango, Nitro, and Jeep Grand Cherokee, while a U.S. class-action lawsuit forced the automaker to fix a bunch more. However, owners of Ram and Dodge pickups are often on their own. Budget well over $1,000 to have the module replaced:

I parked my 2004 3500 series Ram in a parking space in front of the office at about 7:30 and came out at approx. 4:45. Noticed the windshield wipers were on but the switch was off; then noticed the message center said air bag mat. required but then went away very quickly; then went to put on my seat belt then thought what I saw was smoke coming from the steering column; then saw a red seat belt light come on in the instrument cluster; then the air bag blew out in my face causing bruising and abrasions to my face and upper body area and stinging to my face.

. . .

I purchased my 2015 Ram 1500 Outdoorsman back in December. Salesman had just left my house. I go out to start it and would not start. Dealer replaced the TIPM, and I was told not to worry it is a common issue. The very next day I have the same exact issue this time it has a check engine light which said it had a bad (fuel pump control module). The tech informed me this is a new part for late model 15's and going to be placed in all of the 2016 model Rams. Now after I pick it up from the fuel pump control module being replaced, I get stuck in heavy traffic and the truck begins to sputter, shake, and misfire. As I get off the road it shuts off and will not start. Take it to the dealer for a 3rd time and misfire, and fuel control module codes come on again. Now they are replacing the PCM. Hope this is it.

3500 Series: By banishing live front axles on Ram 1500 models years ago and 2500 trucks more recently, "death wobble" is now limited to the 3500 Series trucks. Death wobble, which is described as severe shaking after passing over a pothole, is endemic to any live-axle vehicle whose suspension and steering have worn over time. Contact the APA for a referral to a shop in Southern Ontario or the Montreal area that can perform the necessary modifications to the suspension to correct the defective original design. Yes, it can be fixed, but it's usually better to pass on the ineffective Fiat Chrysler original components if you're paying the bill. Be prepared to open your wallet wide.

Vehicle is designed and constructed with non-adjustable camber for the front wheels. This is causing uneven wear to the front tires (outside edge bald while rest of tire tread is intact). The only known repair is using aftermarket parts and a proper alignment along with new tires costing the consumer $1000 and $1500 per vehicle.

The Ram 1500 EcoDiesel engine is supplied by a VM Motori, a Fiat affiliate in Italy. The camshaft gear on the fuel pump side of the engine can slip and cause a catastrophic engine failure. D&J Diesel in Midvale, Utah, has developed a process to permanently fix this problem. Here are a few links describing the engine failures:

- *http://www.pirate4x4.com/forum/general-chit-chat/2242010-real-world-ecodiesel-reliability-so-far-4.html*
- *http://www.edmunds.com/ram/1500/2014/long-term-road-test/2014-ram-1500-ecodiesel-back-in-service.html*
- *http://www.ram1500diesel.com/forum/ram-1500-diesel-general-discussion/2833-engine-blew-up-23.html*

INTERNAL BULLETINS, SECRET WARRANTIES: 2007—Automatic transmission torque converter shuddering. Transmission defaults to Neutral. **2009**—Steering wander may require installation of a steering shaft kit. Under a special warranty extension campaign, Dodge will replace free of charge torn seat cushion covers or seat cushions. Hood squeaking, creaking sound on turns or when passing over bumps. AC hissing noise. **2009-10**—Quad rear doors won't lock or unlock. Water leaks diagnostic tips. Under Customer Satisfaction Notification K23, Dodge will replace a corroded front bumper under warranty. Another campaign will tackle poor AC performance by replacing defective air door actuators free of charge. **2009-11**—Excessive steering wheel vibration on the 1500 model may require a new steering wheel assembly under warranty. Fuel filler housing pops out of opening. **2011-12**—Excessive transfer case noise when shifting from Drive to Neutral can be remedied by installing a revised separator plate into the transmission valve body (reimbursable under warranty, says TSB# 21-010-12). **2011-13**—3.6L V6 engine cylinder leakage may require a new cylinder head covered by an extended warranty (Chrysler X56 Warranty Extension). This little-known program is confirmed by TSB #09-002-14 REV.8. **2012-13**—A howl, and/or humming noise at speeds below 48 kph (30 mph) may be corrected by installing an insulating package onto the transmission cooling lines. **2013-14**—If the truck won't shift out of Park, the electronic shifter may need to be replaced. **2014**—A rear high-speed vibration can be corrected by replacing the rear propeller shaft (driveshaft assembly). Metallic rattle from the roof headliner area. Excessive tire wear. **2015**—Steering column noise and/or minor movement can be corrected by replacing the brake pedal bracket bolts. A lower instrument panel noise may be due to loose centre instrument panel fasteners. *2500, and 3500 Series:* **2015**—Free radio software upgrade available, per TSB# 08-031-15 REV. A transmission slip and premature wear under high engine load; replace the torque converter.

2017 Dodge Ram 2500

JEEP

Chrysler Fiat's Jeep division is proof positive that basement ratings published by *Lemon-Aid, Consumer Reports,* and J.D. Power don't mean a darn to buyers who will pay lots of cash for some *macho* cachet, even if that means taking home one of the brands with the lowest reliability ratings. Indeed, the Jurassic-era Wrangler is a perennial bestseller for off-roaders, and the Mercedes-designed Grand Cherokee continues to be a preferred model among luxury/performance SUVs. Then there is the Fiat-inspired, Dart-based Cherokee that manages to be both underpowered and unreliable, thanks to its 9-speed automatic transmission and wimpy 4-cylinder engine that are not ready for prime time. Bringing up the undistinguished rear is the Jeep starter set, the Compass, Patriot, and Renegade.

Most Jeeps are rated Below Average or Not Recommended buys. True, the Grand Cherokee offers an appealing combination of granite-like construction, luxury features, and go-anywhere capability, but the 2011 and newer models were wracked by electrical issues, as owners will attest. For the past several years, the Jeep line has been bedevilled by powertrain, fuel system, electrical system, brake, suspension, and body deficiencies. Depreciation? The Wrangler holds its value surprisingly well (thanks to a unique legacy, to be sure), but the Liberty, Compass, and Patriot all lose value quickly.

Several Jeep models have major rust issues, including structural corrosion affecting the undercarriage. The Automobile Protection Association (APA) recommends aftermarket rust protection either by Krown Rust Control for an annual application, or in the Montreal area for a lifetime grease application at Barry's Rustproofing (contact information is in the Part Four Introduction).

PATRIOT/COMPASS ★

2017 Jeep Patriot

RATING: Not Recommended. Spin-offs of the underwhelming Dodge Caliber, the compact Jeep Patriot and Compass arrived just before the Chrysler's bankruptcy reorganization; they proved to be a half-hearted effort to capitalize on Jeep's popularity with new entry-level offerings. Unfortunately, the pair has terrible reliability and corrosion problems. Initially there was one engine, a 2.4L 4-cylinder that sent power to the front or all wheels via either a 5-speed manual or a CVT automatic transmission. A 2.0L 4-cylinder became the new base engine in 2008. The interior was significantly upgraded the following year; mechanical changes included a quieter exhaust, revised suspension, and a new 2.4L front-drive model. Revised styling and upgraded interiors arrived for 2012, along with revised suspension and steering settings. The Freedom Drive II dual-range all-wheel drive system became newly available on the Compass. Changes for 2014 included a conventional 6-speed automatic transmission that replaced the previous CVT on all versions except the Freedom Drive II; standard seat-mounted airbags for both front occupants; and there were minor cosmetic updates inside and out. Incredibly, Jeep still continued to offer both the Compass and Patriot alongside the newer Renegade and Cherokee, though one or both of the former are scheduled to be discontinued by 2018. **Strong points:** These easy-to-maneuver, Jeep-badged crossovers provide good visibility and are not expensive to buy. The younger demographic appreciates the convenient infotainment system shared with other Chrysler vehicles. Rapid depreciation results in low prices on the used car market. **Weak points:** The coarse and sluggish 2.0L and 2.4L engines are especially noisy with the CVT automatic. High road and wind noise. Fuel economy is disappointing and interior materials look cheap prior to 2012. **Major redesign:** 2007 introduced, 2012 partial update, 2014 partial update. **Best alternatives:** Chevrolet Trax, Hyundai Tucson, Kia Sportage and Soul – and the list goes on. Virtually anything is better than this pair.

Prices and Specs

Prices (2016-2017): *Sport:* $14,745/15,745; *High Altitude:* $22,885/24,185 **Freight:** $1,795 **Powertrain (FWD/AWD):** Engines: 2.0L 4-cyl. (158 hp), 2.4L 4-cyl. (172 hp). Transmission: 5-speed manual transmission, continuous variable (CVT) automatic, 6-speed automatic. **Dimensions:** Passengers: 2/3; Length: 174 in. Wheelbase: 104 in.; Weight: 3,111 lb. **Fuel consumption:** *2.0L:* 10.8L/100 km city, 8.9L/100 km highway; *2.4L:* 11.7L/100 km city, 9.1L/100 km highway. **Assembled in:** Belvidere, Illinois.

ALERT! The Compass and Patriot are vulnerable to corrosion that attacks the front subframe and can require major chassis surgery to replace the rusted components. FCA has so far avoided issuing a recall that would pay for the required corrosion repairs. If damage to the undercarriage is not already severe, the APA recommends Krown Rust Control or Barry's Rustproofing in the Montreal market to protect the fragile rocker panels, rear fenders, and floor (see the end of Part Four's Introduction for contact information).

RELIABILITY: The Japanese-made CVT (supplied by Nissan subsidiary Jatco) didn't always function perfectly, with some drivers reporting a slipping transmission on steep grades. Owners report overheated CVTs, indicated by a dashboard warning lamp, and some expensive transmission failures. Other weaknesses include very short-lived ball joints and other steering and suspension parts, leaky struts, bad fuel tank sending units, and noisy brakes. Used-car dealers report having to spend $800 to $1,200 per vehicle in reconditioning costs to replace prematurely worn suspension and steering components. Rapid brake wear, electrical, and powertrain failures are common. The two-piece fuel tank uses a transfer tube between the two halves, which may have been manufactured incorrectly; dealers will replace the fuel transfer tube on affected vehicles. Rainwater can penetrate the cabin, often via the dome light on the ceiling. "Wear a raincoat," advised one frustrated owner online. Recommended is a check of all grommets and plugs, reseal roof seams, and replacement of the sunroof drain tubes if necessary. Compass and Patriot buyers who are usually very sensitive to monthly payments won't pay the additional $2,000 to $2,500 FCA wants for additional warranty coverage on a new vehicle.

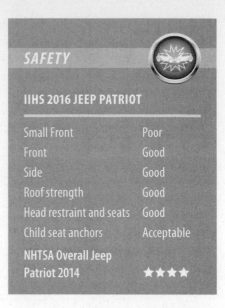

SAFETY

IIHS 2016 JEEP PATRIOT

Small Front	Poor
Front	Good
Side	Good
Roof strength	Good
Head restraint and seats	Good
Child seat anchors	Acceptable
NHTSA Overall Jeep Patriot 2014	★★★★

RENEGADE ⭐

RATING: Not Recommended (2015-17). During its first years on the market, especially because of its untested Fiat technology and spotty servicing, *Lemon-Aid* does not recommend this vehicle. Typically, Chrysler needs a couple of years to fix early-production defects; wait at least until the arrival of the 2018 models before buying a Renegade. While it's marketed as an American SUV, the Renegade is actually a Fiat sporting Jeep styling and logos. Currently competing with the Compass and Patriot in the ever-expanding Jeep line-up, the Renegade shares about 40% of its components with Fiat's 500X; both are built at Fiat's plant in Melfi, in central Italy. Designers imbued it with lots of character and there are Jeep cues called "Easter eggs" to find inside and out. Fiat Chrysler media flacks claim the 500X/Renegade is an amalgam of the best components of both companies; *Lemon-Aid* is not so sure after looking at long-term owner reviews in Europe, combined with safety-related complaints posted by NHTSA related to the Fiat 500's performance in the States. In J.D. Power's European Dependability Study (Germany), the Fiat 500 ranked at the very bottom of the rankings. How does this Italian company remain in business?

Two wrongs don't make it right. Fiat is combining the low-rated Fiat 500X SUV with the low-rated Jeep brand. Neither car is recommended. Only in algebra do two negatives make a positive.

For those who may think we're too concerned that Fiat's poor quality will afflict the new Renegade, take a look at the safety-related complaints posted by NHTSA. Here are just a few: Engine compartment fires; fuel tank leaks caused by road debris; airbag, engine, and transmission warning lights that come on repeatedly; persistent stalling in traffic and sudden unintended acceleration; automatic transmission-equipped cars that roll backwards when stopped on a hill; clutches that self-destruct; engines that cannot be turned on or off; and persistent wiper fluid leaks. Owners also give a failing grade for fit and finish, warranty service, and parts availability. On top of all that, the Renegade uses the same ZF-supplied 9-speed automatic transmission that causes jerky shifting, stuck gears, front-axle vibration, surging, stalling, and transmission-warning lights reported in other Jeeps, and even the Acura TLX. This is some heavy baggage for the new Jeep Renegade to carry. **Road performance:** Weighing in at up to 3500+ pounds, the Renegade is heavier than the Buick Encore, or Nissan Juke. It has a relatively quiet powertrain that's a bit on the rough side when pushed and the 9-speed tranny constantly "hunts" for the right gear to save gas. So the car lugs along, conserving fuel while fraying nerves. All 4WD Renegades have selectable drive modes for different terrains. The Renegade Trailhawk model has a more advanced 4WD system that has enhanced low-speed, off-road gearing, a rarity in this segment. Although the new 9-speed automatic is the most commonly ordered gearbox, a 6-speed manual transmission is also available (with the smaller engine). If you can live with a manual transmission, the APA found that it works very well with the turbocharged engine. **Strong points:** There's a nicely appointed cabin, a spacious interior up front, decent cargo room, and two available removable "My Sky" roof panels. Chrysler's Uconnect infotainment system works flawlessly and is easily mastered. The Garmin-based navigation system is one of the most intuitive available. **Weak points:** Owners report middling fuel economy with the 2.4L engine, and rear-seat legroom is tight. Seats warm up slowly. There's lots of wind and road noise. Then there's the potential "witches brew" of defects caused by the mismatch of Fiat and Chrysler componentry. **Best alternatives:** Chevrolet Trax, Honda HR-V, or Mazda CX-3.

Prices and Specs

Prices (2016-2017): *Sport:* $21,495, *Limited:* $32,795 **Freight:** $1,795 **Powertrain (FWD/AWD):** Engines: 1.4L Turbo 4-cyl. (160 hp), 2.4L 4-cyl. (180 hp); Transmission: 6-speed manual, 9-speed automatic. **Dimensions:** Passengers: 2/3; Length: 167 in., Wheelbase: 101 in., Weight: 3,045 lb. (base model). **Fuel economy:** *1.4L Turbo:* 9.9L/100 km city, 7.5L/100 km highway; *2.4L:* 11.2L/100 km city, 8.0L/100 km highway. **Assembled in:** Italy.

SAFETY

IIHS 2016

Small Front	Not Rated
Moderate Front	Good
Side	Good
Roof strength	Good
Head restraint and seats	Not Rated
Child seat anchors	Marginal
NHTSA Overall 2016	★★★★

ALERT! Be careful when refueling. One owner writes:

> Entire capless gas tank housing broke off and stayed attached to the gas nozzle at the pump.

During your test-drive, put the automatic transmission through its paces. Several reviewers and owners say it's not sufficiently responsive and could be dangerous if a quick manoeuvre is required. Also, make sure that the large side pillars don't obstruct your forward or rearward visibility too badly. **Owner-reported safety-related failures:** Engine suddenly lost power on the highway and caught fire; leaking fuel fittings; sudden unintended acceleration; loss of brakes; chronic transmission failures; engine replaced; door locks don't work; strong alcohol smell permeates the cabin from leaking windshield wiper fluid; passenger seat sensor doesn't always activate the airbag; and a plethora of electrical glitches:

> Forward collision warning inadvertently and randomly turns off, as does back up camera and camera guide lines. Additionally, Uconnect randomly indicating a malfunction. Seven trips to dealer have not corrected.

One owner reported his front windshield has shattered four times from small debris:

The windshield cracks as result of debris or simply because it will no longer retain support with such a long, 42" horizontal crack. Other owners have made similar complaints on the Internet.

RELIABILITY: The ZF-supplied 9-speed automatic has been problematic in other models. Renegade owners report clunky shifts, surging, and lunging. A transmission computer reflash at the dealer isn't always effective. The Renegade's manual transmission is a question mark, as Fiat clutches are reputed to wear rapidly or self-destruct. Interior trim squeaks and rattles reported in the first year. The APA strongly recommends purchasing a full-coverage extended warranty from the manufacturer. *Carcomplaints.com* gave the Renegade its Beware of the Clunker seal of disapproval.

INTERNAL BULLETINS, SECRET WARRANTIES: 2015—Erratic transmission shifting with the 9-speed requires a software patch. Excessive steering wheel vibration? Applying aluminum adhesive tape around the radiator anchoring pin may solve the problem. AC compressor won't switch on? Try changing the climate control module under warranty. A front brake squeak or squeal may need Pad Kit Number 68299399AA. Plugging a water leak coming through the door handle cable grommet may involve replacing the door latch cable assembly. 2015-16—If the key isn't recognized, reprogram the radio frequency hub module. 2016—If the electric parking brake doesn't work, update the electronic anti-lock brake system module software.

JEEP LIBERTY ★★

RATING: Below Average Introduced in 2002, the Jeep Liberty bucked the trend in compact SUVs by offering V6 power exclusively on a box-section steel frame so rugged it could do jail time. The Liberty involved compromises from the outset and never gained the following of the Cherokee it replaced. The second-generation Liberty debuted as a 2008 model with an improved suspension. Previously optional, the previous 3.7L V6 became the sole available engine. Command-Trac, a part-time 4WD system suited to off-road use or slippery surfaces, was standard. Full-time 4WD was optional. The interior is hard to access and narrow, plus the ride is very unsettled, though it improved somewhat as of the 2008 redesign. Cargo space goes from adequate with the rear seat up to good when it is folded down. Real-world fuel consumption is very heavy by compact SUV standards. The Liberty was discontinued in 2012. **Strong points:** Old-school design and construction allow the Liberty to "hack it" in the bush. Lots of towing capacity (5,000 lb.) for the low asking price. **Weak points:** The V6 engine burns a lot of fuel. The 4-speed automatic transmission was outdated by 2012 when the model was dropped, the ride is choppy, handling is sloppy, and cabin finish is subpar prior to 2008. Frontseat foot room is tight. Some owners complained about weak headlamps. **Major redesign:** 2002 introduced, 2008 redesigned. **Best alternatives:** Anything in the compact SUV class is likely to be more comfortable and easier on gas. Buyers choose a Liberty mainly for the price; for similar or less money, the Suzuki Grand Vitara is a better vehicle.

RELIABILITY: As with most Jeeps, poor reliability and poor corrosion resistance are the Liberty's most serious deficiencies. Premature brake disc and rotor replacements also figure prominently. The Check Engine warning may light when the temperature falls below freezing, requiring installation of an improved throttle body. Other reported weaknesses included bad water pumps, electrical glitches, worn suspensions, oil leaks from various drivetrain components, slipping transmissions (in small numbers) and malfunctioning air conditioners. Avoid models with the Sky Slider fabric roof. In addition to the cacophony you'll hear on the highway, the canvas roof sometimes allows water to infiltrate the seals and flood the cabin. Even without the fabric roof, owners caution water may find its way in to soak the carpets, most often through the back hatch and around the cargo lamp. Corrosion begins in the rear fender area, eventually attacking lower body panels and the undercarriage. If the vehicle is not too badly damaged already, the APA recommends Krown Rust Control or Barry's Rustproofing in the Montreal market to protect the fragile rocker panels, rear fenders, and floor (see the end of Part Four's Introduction for contact information).

CHEROKEE

2014-2015	★
2016-2017	★★★

RATING: Not Recommended (2014-2015); Average (2016-2017). The 2014 Jeep Cherokee marked the return of a familiar Jeep nameplate that last graced showrooms in 2001. It came back as an affordable, compact sport-utility vehicle. While it still offered good all-terrain capability, the new Cherokee was more noteworthy for its futuristic styling, spacious cabin, pleasant ride, and smooth optional V6 –

now becoming a rarity in the compact SUV segment. While it seemingly checked off all the boxes for consumers, the unsuccessful mishmash of Chrysler and Fiat components makes the early models a risky buy . Built on the same front-drive platform architecture as the Dodge Dart sedan (which originated with the European-market Alfa Romeo Giulietta), the technology transfer worked poorly initially. The German-designed 9-speed automatic was a dog, frustrating owners and dealer service departments alike, with its clunky shifts and poor reliability. Add to this the ongoing electronic faults with the TIPM – which can shut down the engine at highway speeds – and the Cherokee is a potentially awful ownership experience that has seen some early buyers turn theirs in early. Best is probably to avoid the 2014-2015 models. **Road performance:** The base 184 hp 2.4L 4-cylinder engine is overwhelmed by the task of lugging around the Cherokee's considerable mass, so acceleration is leisurely and real-world fuel consumption is higher than published ratings promise. The 271 hp V6 is the way to go, providing a welcome adrenalin boost. This Jeep's European roots are evident after a short time behind the wheel, as the ride quality and handling traits are very good. For those who actually need some Jeep-like agility in the rough, the Trailhawk version offers low-range gearing and an exclusive locking rear differential. **Strong points:** The Cherokee is roomy inside and has one of the most accommodating rear seats of any compact crossover in this price range. The cabin is very nicely finished and can be outfitted with Chrysler's convenient infotainment gear and available electronic driving aids. Driving refinement with the V6 is class-leading – vastly superior to the older compact Patriot/Compass twins. **Weak points:** With its emphasis on passenger accommodations front and back, cargo space gets short shrift. The Cherokee offers 10-15 fewer cubic feet than many segment competitors with the rear seatback up. Owners report unimpressive fuel economy with the 2.4L engine; the V6 is smoother and fuel consumption not much higher. The big drawback is the Cherokee's appalling reliability, which owners have complained about at length. **Best alternatives:** Mazda CX-5, Toyota RAV-4, or Chevrolet Equinox.

Prices and Specs

Prices (2016-2017): *Sport:* $26,695, *Overland:* $39,895 **Freight:** $1,795 **Powertrain (FWD/AWD):** Engines: 2.4L 4-cyl. (184 hp), 3.2L V6 (271 hp) Transmission: 9-speed automatic. **Dimensions:** Passengers: 2/3; Length: 182 in., Wheelbase: 106 in., Weight: 4,044 lb. **Fuel economy:** *2.4L:* 10.9L/100 km city, 7.7L/100 km highway; *3.2L:* 12.2L/100 km city, 9.0L/100 km highway. **Assembled in:** Toledo, Ohio, and Belvidere, Illinois.

RELIABILITY: The launch of the all-new 2014 Cherokee was delayed several weeks due to quality concerns with the ZF-supplied 9-speed automatic. This was a bad omen, and a flood of reports about issues with shift quality and reliability surfaced shortly after the Cherokee left showrooms. Both 2014 and 2015 models have a high number of consumer complaints on *safercar.gov* and *carcomplaints.com*,

SAFETY

IIHS 2016

Small Front	Marginal
Front	Good
Side	Good
Roof strength	Good
Head restraint and seats	Good
Child seat anchors	Acceptable
NHTSA Overall 2015	★★★★

with the vast majority being related to the transmission:

> With four visits to the dealership for transmission software upgrades and two tranny replacements later, I am now waiting on an arbitration decision for replacement or reimbursement. Very disappointed, as I loved taking this truck off road. It handled mud, hills and dirt trails with no issue. Highway driving, however, has been far more thrilling than it should be with "wobbling" between gears in downshifts and acceleration from standing position. Lurching forward in traffic is not fun…. Hoping to replace this with new SUV that works.

Fiat Chrysler released a few software updates for the 2014-2015 Cherokee transmission in the vain hope that the solution could be limited to software upgrades. However, as documented online by owners, Chrysler is repairing or swapping out the transmission; ZF, the transmission's German manufacturer, also maintains that the issue is with the software, but owners are reporting that software updates don't reliably resolve issues. In some instances, the autobox's "snap ring" has been replaced to address durability concerns. Add to this the ongoing issues with Fiat Chrysler's Totally Integrated Power Module (TIPM) found in the Cherokee and many other products:

> My husband and I are on the highway going 75 (mph) and the car completely turns off. OFF! I had my daughter in the backseat so that freaked me out even more. It turned itself back on and all these alerts kept dinging and then saying our 4WD no longer was working. We head to the exit ramp and the car shuts off once again bringing us to a complete stop. When my husband finally got the car to start back up he had to floor it so we could get home at 11mph. Once we arrived home, as soon as my husband let off the gas, the rpms shot up and made a terrible sound. He tried to turn it off by pushing the button and it wouldn't turn off. It was ridiculous.

Beyond the jerky, unreliable ZF transmission on 2014-2015 models (the only one available in this model) and the freaky electrical faults, owners have also reported some brake problems, drivetrain wobble and shaking, airbag warning lamps, faulty wiring harnesses and numerous issues with accessories. The Cherokee is selling well in Canada, but we expect to see this model enter the used-car market and prices to drop as soon as the factory warranty runs out. Buying new or used, you're well advised to purchase the best warranty coverage available from Fiat Chrysler for all components with a zero or small deductible. APA members may be eligible for a small discount.

RATING: Below Average (2005-2011); Average (2012-2017). Jeeps are all about *cachet* and cash. The cash is needed to pay for repairs and to correct the many designed-in-factory defects. Yet, in spite of its antiquated legacy design, or perhaps *because* of it, the Wrangler remains one of the most desirable Jeeps made. Like a Harley Davidson motorcycle, Mont Blanc fountain pen, or Zippo lighter, the Wrangler is more about nostalgia than functionality. America's original sport-ute falls a bit short when driven on-road, although the arrival of the four-door Unlimited model in 2007, and more powerful V6 in 2012, have certainly broadened its appeal. It's currently the only four-door convertible on the market. The new-generation 2007 models saw the introduction of the popular four-door Unlimited, the first Wrangler to seat five comfortably. All models benefited from a stiffer, fully boxed frame, and while the live axle remained intact up front, a new feature allowed the front anti-roll bar to disconnect by remote control to improve axle articulation off-road. Cabin materials were improved inside; power door locks and windows, and a navigation system were available for the first time. The 2012 Wrangler models adopted Chrysler's new aluminum 3.6L V6 DOHC Pentastar V6 engine, which provided more torque (260 lb-ft) and an 83 hp boost over the outgoing 3.8L pushrod V6. A 5-speed automatic transmission replaced the 4-speed box. The interior benefited from new technology and convenience features, added sound insulation, and better operating soft-tips in subsequent years. The upcoming 2018 redesign is reported to have an aluminum body and 8-speed automatic transmission. **Road performance:** The Wrangler's impressive off-road performance is eclipsed by its unstable jittery on-road performance, highlighted by the powertrain suddenly jumping out of gear when the outside temperature drops, or the steering and suspension going into a "death wobble" after passing over potholes or speed bumps. With the two-door, the short wheelbase, loud and porous cabin, and mediocre highway performance can make the Wrangler an annoying daily commuter. The four-door Unlimited model is better by virtue of its longer wheelbase, and engineers have made good strides in recent years to mitigate some of the noise and harshness. With the four-door, the old 3.8 L V6 engine is barely powerful enough, and fuel economy suffered. The 2012 and newer Wranglers employ the more powerful 3.6L Pentastar V6 as the sole engine offering. It's a big improvement with the automatic transmission. The clumsy handling is compromised by vague steering and low cornering limits (standard stability control is a plus), with a stiff and jiggly ride quality. Braking distances are long. Overall, the Rubicon is a better performer than the slightly cheaper Unlimited Sahara. Wranglers are not likely to be discounted by much due to strong buyer demand, and Fiat Chrysler raised prices recently. Fortunately, slow depreciation takes some the bite out of the price tag. **Strong points:** Superior off-road capability. Unique roof-off, doors-off driving experience. The four-door Wrangler Unlimited comes with a roomier cabin with plenty of headroom, much more legroom in the back, and more cargo space. The Wrangler offers the best resale value in the Jeep line; buyers line up for all years and mileages if the vehicle is in acceptable condition. **Weak points:** Obtrusive wind and tire noise. Getting in and out takes some acrobatics and patience. Two-door models are less comfortable, and there is barely room for two adults in the back while cargo room suffers, too. Soft-top is cumbersome to raise and lower. **Major redesign:** 2007 and 2012 (new powertrain). **Best alternatives:** Nissan Xterra, or Toyota FJ Cruiser (another nostalgia ride) or 4Runner; all are true off-roaders, but unlike the Wrangler none is a convertible.

Prices and Specs

Prices (2016-2017) (Firm): *Sport:* $27,695, *Unlimited Rubicon:* $44,295 **Freight:** $1,795 **Powertrain (Rear-drive /part-time/full-time AWD):** Engine: 3.6L V6 (285 hp) Transmissions: 6-speed manual, 5-speed auto. **Dimensions (base):** Passengers: 2/2 or 2/3 (Unlimited); Length: 164 in. or 173 in.; Wheelbase: 95 or 116 in.; Weight: *Sport:* 3,849 lb., *Rubicon:* 4,165 lb. **Fuel economy:** *3.6L V6:* 14.8L/100 km city, 11.7L/100 km highway. **Assembled in:** Toledo, Ohio.

ALERT! Soft-top models can permit water leaks throughout the interior; the cowl area is especially vulnerable. If you're looking at pre-2012 four-door Wrangler Unlimited, consider test driving a newer model with the 3.6L V6 to see whether you would prefer to pay more for the improvements. Be sure to lift up the carpet to check for water infiltration and check out the undercarriage for rust and off-road damage. Hosing down a Wrangler from outside with a dry interior may help you spot the location of water infiltration:

Roof leaks and soaks carpet on passenger side floor every time it is parked in the rain or snow and causes windows to fog up because of moisture in the cockpit and creates a safety problem not being able to see in our cold climate.

Stay away from heavily modified Jeeps. You can't tell the quality of the aftermarket parts that were used or how well the customizing was done. Pentastar 3.6L V6 models experienced early engine cylinder head and gasket failures covered by a little-known Chrysler extended warranty. Beware of windshield stress fractures. They are a common Wrangler defect and replacement should be covered by the warranty – not your vehicle's insurance policy:

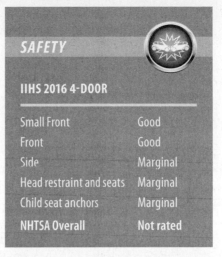

SAFETY

IIHS 2016 4-DOOR

Small Front	Good
Front	Good
Side	Marginal
Head restraint and seats	Marginal
Child seat anchors	Marginal
NHTSA Overall	**Not rated**

> I took the Jeep to the local dealer who said it was a stress fracture probably due to freezing conditions along with the heat from the defroster. The individual I spoke with conceded it was in all probability a manufacturing defect since he had heard of "a lot of other cases like mine" but would not be quoted on that. He contacted Chrysler who refused to cover the windshield damage because although I only had the vehicle for seven months, the mileage was over 12,000. I have continued to investigate incidences of stress fracture damage to front windshields in the Jeeps and have collected a significant amount of data through numerous complaint blogs that support the fact that either the Jeep windshields themselves are defective or some problem with the vehicle design itself makes it possible for considerable heat to be trapped between the windshield and dashboard to the point where stress causes the window to crack. Rather than address the issue, Chrysler is instead forcing owners to go through their private insurance for repairs.

Owner-reported safety-related failures: Jeep "death wobble" continues to unnerve drivers who've hit bumps at speed and felt the front end lift, setting off violent suspension tremors and sending calamitous vibrations through the steering wheel. The condition is endemic to solid front axles as suspension components wear with age. It's not a funny and endearing "Jeep thing," it's a serious design flaw that warrants caution. More recent Pentastar engines appear to have a faulty oil filter housing that can crack and leak motor oil onto hot engine components, with the risk of an engine fire. Loss of power while underway, especially when cresting a hill or driving on a level surface. Beginning with the 2007 redesign, some random electrical malfunctions can be traced to a faulty Totally Integrated Powertrain Module (or TIPM), including stalling, sudden acceleration, loss of steering, no brakes, inoperative locks, no horn or a delayed horn response, and malfunctioning lights and gauges:

At around 3:45 am, while I was sleeping, the horn started intermittently blaring. I looked out the window and the reverse lights were on (at full brightness). For the next hour, it would start and stop randomly. I finally disconnected the battery in frustration. Earlier the previous evening, the headlights came on and stayed on. I had not used the Jeep for the previous two days. This issue is clearly related to the totally integrated power module (TIPM), which has already been replaced once in this vehicle (which had caused my 2014 Jeep to stall — and completely die — several times). I am extremely concerned for my safety with this vehicle and this issue.

RELIABILITY: Below Average Purchase of an extended warranty backed by Fiat Chrysler is recommended if you plan to keep your Wrangler past the end of the manufacturer's warranty; APA and ACC members may be eligible for a small discount. Reportedly, owners have been finding *casting sand* in the cooling system, which can clog up the radiator, the water pump, oil cooler, heater core, and cooling passages of the Pentastar V6. Ongoing electrical issues related to faulty TIPM modules can affect drivability, as noted above. Other issues include short-lived clutches, leaky soft-tops and door seals (it's a Jeep thing), faulty air conditioners, failed sensors, and early rust. The Wrangler is highly susceptible to corrosion, which begins in the front fenders and footwells, eventually attacking the cowl, floor and rocker panels. If the vehicle is not too badly damaged already, the APA recommends Krown Rust Control or Barry's Rustproofing in the Montreal market to protect the fragile rocker panels, rear fenders, and floor (see the end of Part Four's Introduction for contact information).

INTERNAL BULLETINS, SECRET WARRANTIES: 2007-09—Excessive steering vibration when passing over rough surfaces. Difficult fuel fill. Wind noise and water leaks from the windshield/soft top header. 2007-10—Manual transmission pops out of First gear when upshifting. Hard starts, no-start or dead battery. Special Campaign #J34 for free replacement of the steering damper hardware. 2007-14—Remedy for cowl trim panel water leakage. 2008-10—Warranty is extended to 7 years/70,000 miles to cover the replacement of the automatic transmission cooler line on vehicles equipped with a 3.8L engine. 2007-16—Vinyl windows are susceptible to cracking in cold temperature below 41°F (5°C). Jeep says this problem is not warrantable. 2009-10—Transmission fluid may overheat; a chime will be installed to alert the driver when this happens. This is a Customer Satisfaction Program, not a safety recall. 2011-12—Countermeasures to eliminate engine misfiring. Manual transmission pops out of gear (TSB #21-002-12). Light to moderate paint imperfections. Inoperative front heated seats. Front water leak onto front floor. 2011-13—3.6L V6 engine cylinder leakage may require a new cylinder head covered by an extended warranty (Chrysler X56 Warranty Extension). This little-known program is confirmed by TSB #09-002-14 REV.8. 2012-14—Tailgate retaining strap over extends and breaks. This is a warrantable repair due to the premature failure. 2013—A cracked upper swing gate hinge cover should be replaced under warranty. Windshield wiper vibration may be caused by a faulty wiper module linkage bolt.

Replace the front windshield if it appears chipped along the bottom edge. 2014—Extended crank time can be corrected by inspecting the Bank 1 position camshaft sensor and replacing it, if needed. A rear high-speed vibration can be corrected by replacing the rear propeller shaft (driveshaft assembly). Intermittent cooler operation may be fixed by replacing the cooling fan module under warranty. Fix for a hard-to-adjust front passenger seat. 2015—Replace the hard top if it leaks at the rear seam. 2015—Change the front caliper slide pins under warranty, if the brakes rattle.

GRAND CHEROKEE

2005-2014	★ ★
2015-2017	★ ★ ★
ECODIESEL	
2014-2017	★

RATING: Below Average (2005-2014); Average (2015-2017); *Ecodiesel:* Not Recommended (2014-2017). The Jeep Grand Cherokee is a refined sport-ute that is midway between a domestic offering like the Ford Explorer and a luxury SUV from the European manufacturers. Prices for used vehicles increased significantly after the Canadian dollar dropped, and export brokers began snapping up Canadian models for their U.S. clients. The third-generation 2005 Grand Cherokee grew in every direction including its wheelbase, which improved the ride and legroom. Engineers replaced the solid axle up front with an independent suspension and introduced rack-and-pinion steering. The live rear axle remained, but was located by five links to improve control. A more powerful standard 3.7L V6 was under the hood, and the optional 4.7L V8 got a remapped power curve. Chrysler's 5.7L Hemi V8, making 330 hp, was a welcome option. All engines came with a 5-speed automatic transmission. Major changes for 2009 included 57 more horsepower for the V8, and the Mercedes diesel option was dropped. The redesigned 2011 model was based on the unibody Mercedes-Benz M-class, with an independent multilink suspension in place of the old live axle. It bristled with technology, including an optional air-suspension system and "Selec-Terrain" all-wheel drive that emulates the Land Rover system. Furnishings are decadent inside, every lever and switch moving with precision. Construction is vault-like, thanks to the Mercedes genetic coding, and the Cherokee became truly "Grand." The standard V6 engine has to work to move it with authority, but the exhaust is muted and distant. Jeep's 2011 redesign introduced a stouter platform, improved roadholding, an upgraded interior and a new, more efficient V6 engine. The powerful SRT8 sat out the 2011 model year. A diesel V6 engine returned for 2014, this time supplied by VM Motori, a Fiat subsidiary. An 8-speed automatic was new for the V6 and significantly improved response in city driving. The latest Grand Cherokee offers more performance and reliability than earlier models. **Road performance:** The Grand Cherokee is built on a proven unibody platform used by the Mercedes-Benz ML for years; when combined with updated front and rear independent suspension systems, the result is enhanced on-road handling and comfort. A small turning circle enhances maneuverability. The 3.6L V6 has to be pushed to move this heavy SUV, due to its lack of low-end torque. Response improved on 2014 and later models equipped with an 8-speed automatic; its electronic shifter takes some getting used to. Low-range gearing for off-road driving is available on some models. **Strong points:** The 290 hp Pentastar V6 boosts power with 80 horses more than the previous V6 engine. The cabin is quiet and well-appointed, with high-quality materials, comfortable seats, and good ergonomics. Fit and finish improved over the years. **Weak points:** The 2011 redesign spawned an incredible proliferation of factory-related defects that took four years to correct. **Major redesign:** 2005 and 2011. **Best alternatives:** The closest cross-shop is FCA's own Dodge Durango. The Honda Pilot, Hyundai Santa Fe XL, and Toyota Highlander are other alternatives. None of them can follow the Grand Cherokee far off-road and they don't project the same image, but on the other hand, they won't be following the Grand Cherokee into the repair shop as frequently, either. A European SUV may offer more perceived sophistication, but repair costs could be higher post-warranty.

Prices and Specs

Prices (2016-2017): *Laredo:* $40,395, *SRT:* $68,695 **Freight:** $1,795 **Powertrain (Rear-drive/part-time/full-time AWD):** Engines: 3.6L V6 (293 hp), 5.7L V8 (360 hp), 6.4L V8 (475 hp), 3.0L V6 EcoDiesel (240 hp) Transmission: 8-speed automatic. **Dimensions:** Passengers: 2/3; Length: 190 in. Wheelbase: 115 in.; Weight: 4,680 lb. **Fuel consumption:** *3.6L:* 12.8L/100 km city, 9.5L/100 km highway; *5.7L:* 16.7L/100 km city, 10.7L/100 km highway; *3.0L EcoDiesel:* 11.2L/100 km city, 8.4L/100 km highway. **Assembled in:** Detroit, Michigan.

SAFETY

IIHS 2016

Small Front	Marginal
Front	Good
Side	Good
Roof strength	Good
Head restraint and seats	Good
Child seat anchors	Marginal
NHTSA Overall AWD 2015	★★★★★

ALERT! Make sure the car is in Park before getting out of a 2014-15 Grand Cherokee; its poorly designed shifter can fool you. NHTSA ordered a recall of 2014 and 2015 Jeep Grand Cherokees and other cars that use the oddball electronic gear shifter because it sometimes does not go into (or does not remain in) the Park position, or owners may not realize the pushbutton starter has not turned off the engine. Actor Anton Yelchin was killed when his personal vehicle slipped out of Park and pinned him against a brick pillar, crushing him:

The 2015 I had just purchased with the V6 and 8-speed transmission, due to my 2014 Dodge Durango with the same engine and transmission being bought back by Chrysler, is exhibiting the same unsafe shifting and stalling conditions.

Owner-reported safety-related failures: 1993-2007 Jeeps may have fire-prone fuel tanks similar to the notorious Ford Pintos recalled in the 1970s. The solution? Chrysler will install a free trailer hitch, if needed (??!!). In 2015, a Georgia jury awarded $150 million to the family of Remington Walden, age four, who was burned to death when his family's 1999 Jeep Grand Cherokee was rear-ended. As of 2015, there were 395 fatal fire crashes of the 1993-2004 Jeep Grand Cherokee, 1993-2001 Jeep Cherokee, and 2002-2007 Jeep Liberty. Fiat Chrysler has recalled certain 2011-2013 Jeep Grand Cherokees and Dodge Durangos to replace wiring for the vanity lamp in the sun visor that may short circuit, causing a fire. Also, certain model year 2011 Dodge Durango and Jeep Grand Cherokee vehicles equipped with either a 3.6L or 5.7L engine are recalled due to the fuel pump relay inside the Totally Integrated Power Module (TIPM-7) that may fail, causing the vehicle to stall without warning. Some brake boosters have also been recalled to prevent water from getting inside and compromising braking performance. Try to determine if the headlights provide sufficient illumination during a night road test; some owners wish they had tested this before buying their vehicle.

RELIABILITY: During the past decade the Grand Cherokee has been beset with recurring automatic transmission, engine head gasket, brake, air conditioner, and electrical system defects. The engine, automatic transmission, and electrical system continue to be unreliable and expensive to diagnose and repair. Owners report engine surges when brakes are applied and that a soft brake pedal may not provide much stopping power until halfway through its travel. The VM Motori diesel option is both expensive and troublesome. The automatic transmission can shift erratically in and out of Second gear, suddenly downshifts, or leaks fluid. The 2005-2010 Grand Cherokee had an odd problem with water flooding the transmission. It turns out air conditioning condensation would dribble down the filler tube and compromise the fluid, turning it into a strawberry milkshake. Consider a transmission service if the fluid looks suspect. In addition, rainwater can breach the sunroof and A-pillar and pool on the floor. Other headaches include short-lived water pumps, starters and air conditioners, as well as a peculiar stalling problem that may be related to a WIN module recall for the keyless ignition. Faulty TIPM modules have also been identified in earlier pre-2011 modules. There's a NHTSA campaign (08V059000) to address unintentional shifting of the transfer case into Neutral. The previous CRD turbodiesel engine is susceptible to swirl motor failure due to oil contamination. A recurring complaint with the 2011 and newer Grand Cherokee involves the TIPM, which can introduce starting problems, as well as running the fuel pump after the engine stops, wearing out batteries and alternators, and prompting bizarre electrical quirks. Replacement modules are frequently backordered, cost a bundle ($1000+), and can fail again. The optional air suspension system experiences failures after the third year in service, the steering shaft may require replacement, the back-up camera can fail intermittently, radiators and water pumps may fail prematurely, as have a few transmission solenoids. In Central and Eastern Canada, the Grand Cherokee is prone to premature rusting in the wheel wells, doors, and rocker panels, eventually attacking structural members in the undercarriage. If the vehicle is not too badly damaged already, the APA recommends Krown Rust Control or Barry's Rustproofing in the Montreal market (see the end of Part Four's Introduction for contact information).

INTERNAL BULLETINS, SECRET WARRANTIES: 2011—A shudder or bump felt through the steering wheel under moderate braking and/or driving over rough roads may require a new intermediate steering column shaft. If the torque converter drive plate fasteners are loose, you will hear a knocking or rattling from the automatic transmission on vehicles equipped with the 3.6L engine. A rear shock buzz, squeak, or rattle may mean you need new rear upper shock mounts. Sloshing fuel tank; the remedy is to replace the fuel tank under warranty. 2011-12—Excessive transfer case noise when shifting from Drive to Neutral can be remedied by installing a revised separator plate into the transmission valve body (reimbursable under warranty, says TSB #21-010-12). 2011-13—3.6L V6 engine cylinder leakage may require a new cylinder head covered by an extended warranty (Chrysler X56 Warranty Extension). This little-known program is confirmed by TSB #09-002-14 REV.8. 2011-14—Remedy for a rear suspension rattle, chuckle. Front brake squealing when braking can be corrected by installing a front brake pad kit (68052370AC) under warranty. 2012—Troubleshooting engine misfiring and power loss. Engine power sag; hesitation may be fixed by replacing the power control module. A shudder felt when accelerating, decelerating, or when coasting may require only the reflashing or changing of the drivetrain control module. Power liftgate won't open or close. A rear shock absorber buzz, squeak, or rattle may signal the need to replace both rear upper shock mounts. 2013-14—A click, creak, or groaning sound near the C-pillar, Dual Plane sunroof may require the replacement of the rear sunroof glass or adding structural adhesive at the rear right corner. Rear brake rattling can be silenced by replacing the caliper adapter mounting bolts. 2014—On vehicles with the 3.6L engine, extended crank time can be corrected by inspecting the Bank 1 position camshaft sensor and replacing it, if needed. Excessive steering wheel vibration may signal the need to replace the wheel bearings. A rattle from the driver side instrument panel or steering wheel may require the replacement of the steering column lock control module wiring harness bracket. An exhaust system rattle or squeak may be caused by a loose heat shield. 2015—Heated steering wheel suddenly shuts off.

FORD

Ford took advantage of the 2009 Chrysler and GM bankruptcy bailout to successfully hype its "no bailout, better car quality" image and trounce the competition. Unfortunately, both parts of the statement turned out to be only half true. Ford, along with Chrysler and General Motors, got millions in "soft" grants from the Bush White House ostensibly to research the development of fuel-efficient vehicles, and Ford's quality tanked after the 2010 model year.

Like the other domestic automakers, Ford copied its more fuel-efficient European designs and transferred their production to North America. The theory of building and selling the same models worldwide is that the automaker can amortise costs more quickly, and offer better-performing, more fuel-efficient, and higher-quality vehicles. However, all of Ford's small cars are incurring large losses in North America, while the company's domestically designed high performance cars, SUVs, and pickups are enjoying record-breaking sales, as is the case with the other domestic automakers. The Mustang, Escape, and F-150 are selling very well, assisted by low-interest-rate financing and the return of auto leasing. Meanwhile, the affordable Fiesta, Focus, and Fusion stagnate in dealer inventories. Lincoln is on life-support.

Ford Quality from 2011-2014, A Bad Joke

J.D. Power and Associates' 2012 Initial Quality Study (IQS) fingered Ford for its poor quality and complicated MyFord Touch and MyLincoln Touch electronic systems and other controls. Ford's dual-clutch automatic transmission used in the Fiesta and Focus was also singled out as being balky and troublesome. Ford's C-Max and Fusion Hybrid fuel savings claims were no more believable than government budget forecasts.

Head restraints on some models are poorly designed, interior instruments and controls far from user-friendly, high-tech communication and navigation gizmos needlessly complicated, and quality control woefully inadequate (see the reports on "lag and lurch" self-destructing manual transmissions in the Mustang review and failure-prone automatics in the Fusion rating). In the past decade, powertrain defects, faulty suspensions and steering components, and premature brake wear and brake failures were the primary concerns of Ford owners. The company's engine and automatic transmission deficiencies affected many of its products, and have been a recurring challenge since the early '80s, judging by Lemon-Aid reader reports, National Highway Traffic Safety Administration (NHTSA) complaints, confidential Ford internal documents, and technical service bulletins (TSB).

Lemon-Aid noted a steady erosion of quality in Ford products after 2010, when the company's "Quality is Job 1" motto appeared to morph into "Quality is Job Gone." Consider one of the company's most popular cars and a *Consumer Reports* 2015 Recommended Buy – the mid-size Ford Fusion.

Normally, *safercar.gov* registered about 50 safety-related complaints per model year for most cars. For instance, a 2010 model would likely have a cumulative total of a few more than 250 registered safety-related complaints. Hold your breath. The 2010 Fusion has amassed more than 2,580 complaints and counting (the Fusion Hybrid generated a respectable 141 complaints), many involving a faulty electronic power-assisted steering system or a malfunctioning throttle body. Here's an example:

> I was turning left at a major intersection and all of sudden I lost power steering. On my message screen the words popped up "service power steering now" then another message popped up regarding traction control. I almost collided with another vehicle. I was able to muscle the car to the right and avoid the collision. If my wife was driving, she would have hit the other vehicle. This is very much a safety issue. When I heard the repair costs to get it fixed, I cannot afford to have it fixed and now I am making payments on a vehicle I cannot drive due to this safety issue.

Doors that Won't Latch

A safety defect has surfaced with a number of Ford models: Their doors may suddenly fly open due to faulty door latch. One Fiesta owner wrote on NHTSA's *safercar.gov*: "When I made a turn, one of the doors came flying open. I had to use a cargo strap to keep the door shut both times while taking it to the dealership for repair." A new expanded recall covers the following models:

- 2012 through 2015 Focus;
- 2013-2015 C-Max and Escape;
- 2014-2016 Transit Connect; and
- 2015 Lincoln MKC and Mustang

An earlier recall covers latches on the Fiesta, Fusion, and Lincoln MKZ.

Ford's overall quality finally began to improve significantly with the 2015 models, as infotainment systems were revamped and engine issues addressed, and the J. D. Power Initial Quality Survey for 2016 models shows a significant improvement. Sure, Ford makes some recommended vehicles and its quality control is currently better than Fiat Chrysler's, but that benchmark is way too low.

EcoBust?

EcoBoost Stalling

Ford Motor Co. is being sued by three vehicle owners in Ohio because of alleged defects in the automaker's six-cylinder EcoBoost engine. According to the lawsuit, the 3.5-liter V6 EcoBoost engine "contained serious latent design, manufacturing, or assembly defects" that cause vehicles to shake, misfire and rapidly lose power.

Ford knew of the problem, the suit says, because it published several technical service bulletins and suggested potential fixes covering the F150 to dealers. The problematic V6 EcoBoost was introduced in the 2010 Ford Flex crossover, Taurus SHO, Lincoln MKT crossover and MKS sedan, the 2011 pickups, and the 2013 Ford Explorer Sport. The National Highway Traffic Safety Administration has received nearly 100 complaints about the engine, the lawsuit states.

– Vince Bond Jr.
Automotive News, May 15, 2013

Ford is hyping its "EcoBoost" family of new turbochargers as an innovative attempt to provide fuel savings and added power throughout the automaker's lineup; disgruntled Ford owners call the technology "EcoBust." EcoBoost describes a new family of turbocharged and direct-injected 4-cylinder and 6-cylinder gasoline engines that deliver power and torque consistent with larger displacement power plants. Engines using this design are touted to be 20% more fuel-efficient than naturally-aspirated (non-turbo) engines. Ford says the EcoBoost's power output and fuel efficiency rival hybrid and diesel engine technology, and the company intends to use it extensively in future vehicle applications. This is a different direction than GM and Chrysler are taking for their pickups; they're sticking with more conventional engines, but adding features like cylinder deactivation and engine shut-offs at idle.

Independent testers like *Consumer Reports* say the EcoBoost engines don't live up to their promised fuel-savings and performance. Here's what they had to say about the 2L EcoBoost engine in the mid-size Fusion:

> Its 25 mpg overall places it among the worst of the crop of recently redesigned family sedans. The Toyota Camry, Honda Accord, and Nissan Altima, all with conventional 2.4- or 2.5-liter four-cylinder engines, get an additional 2, 5, and 6 mpg, respectively. And all accelerate more quickly.

Owners claim in several lawsuits that Ford knew the Fusion and C-Max hybrids would never match the glowing mileage figures hyped by the automaker (*editorial.autos.msn.com/2013-ford-c-max-hybrid-review*):

> I thought my 2013 C-MAX would be a Prius Killer? NOT! As a returning Ford buyer I feel deceived. I want to support US companies and US jobs. What was Ford thinking when they published 47/47/47 estimates? Based on the advertised EPA estimates, I would have been OK with low 40's but 28-33 mpg is not even in the ballpark. This is not an issue about EPA testing standards, but rather an issue about setting false customer expectations in order to promote sales. Ford's "47mpg" marketing campaign tarnished what should have been the roll-out of a truly remarkable vehicle, the C-MAX. Real world mpg estimates should have been promoted in the mid-30's.

In 2014, Ford cut the fuel-economy rating on six new models, most of them hybrids, and paid between $125 US and $1,050 US to owners of 4-cylinder versions of the 2014 Ford Fiesta, hybrid and plug-in hybrid versions of the 2013-14 C-Max and Ford Fusion, and the hybrid version of the 2013-14 Lincoln MKZ.

Technology Run Amok

Not since the bad old days in 1995-2001, when Ford's Taurus, Sable, Windstar, and front-drive Lincoln Continental generated thousands of complaints of self-destructing engines and automatic transmissions, has Ford's car product line been so bad. Back then, former Ford Canada President Bobbie Gaunt saw the problems, met with angry consumers, extended the powertrain warranty, paid off the outstanding customer claims, and set up a small group to respond to incoming complaints.

But, that's all gone.

Bobbie Gaunt retired from Ford in December of 2000 and Ford of Canada's integrity and honourable customer relations went with her. Ford staffers close their eyes to the veracity of owner complaints, and when confronted with evidence of secret warranties, they prevaricate and deny the obvious.

I know of no other company whose customer relations staff member had to take the company to court to fix his Windstar minivan. He was fearful his kids would fall out when the side door opened on turns.

Beginning in 2010, Ford introduced complex touch-screen menus and glitch-prone voice software; every Ford vehicle to receive these systems between 2011-2014, including the Focus, Fiesta, and Escape experienced recurring problems. Ford responded to owners' infotainment complaints with constant software updates that didn't work. Now the automaker has finally come to its senses and is rediscovering knobs and buttons; it's dumping the Microsoft-based MyFord Touch in favour of the Blackberry OS Sync 3 system expected by the end of 2016. Actually, the company had no choice. One senior analyst for *AutoTrader.com* says the five-year-old MyFord Touch feature was on a fast track to become "the modern-day equivalent of an Edsel."

Ford's 2010-2014 mid-size Fusion and F-series trucks are vulnerable to powertrain breakdowns, EcoBoost turbos that gulp fuel, stall out or suddenly lose power, plus there are steering, electronic, and infotainment failures. Two new features can scare the owners of late model Fords who are afraid they may be hit by other vehicles. Those features are the collision avoidance sensor and the Start/Stop feature:

> My truck's collision avoidance/adaptive cruise control has false sensing when passing large heavy duty trucks. At 50-75mph with someone right behind you, this can be very dangerous. If a heavy duty truck is one or two lanes to your right and you are passing them with no one in front of you, the radar sensor senses incorrectly and hits the brakes, flashes the red collision avoidance light and the tone goes off. I've had this happen at least 30 times since I bought the truck. 4-5 times I've almost been rear ended. Ford dealers attempted repairs at least 5 times. It's also not safe to let someone else drive who is unaware of the issue.

After coming to a rolling stop and then trying to accelerate into traffic the engine will bog down and then a split second later feel as if it is going to full throttle without me depressing the throttle further. The engine speed surges when attempting to lightly accelerate and maintain speed with the flow of traffic. Ford needs to give owners the option to turn off the auto stop/start permanently.

Overheated seats on the 2015-16s may also be a safety hazard:

Vehicles with climate controlled seats may have temperatures in excess of 132 degrees F on the rear of the front seats just above the magazine pocket. Children often store books and toys in the magazine pocket. Affected vehicles include the late 2015+ Ford F150, Ford Explorer, Ford Mustang, and other models with the same seat climate control system. Ford TSB 15-0154 says to add an additional sock to the seats, but this repair doesn't mitigate the safety risk to children.

Ford's Advertising

The Automobile Protection Association (APA) discovered that basic "S" models of the Fiesta and Escape advertised by Ford were not available at dealerships in markets where the ads were running. Ford dealers carried more equipped versions of those vehicles costing thousands of dollars more; that's a classic "bait and switch." Ford has since promised to feature vehicles that are actually available in its advertising.

Ford ads downplay the high prices of some vehicles with large down payments over $2,500, instead of zero money down, which is preferred by consumers and promoted by most of the competition. Ford dealers in some markets advertise a price they call "Costco-in" that includes a $1,000 rebate available to Costco members. The trick? Your Costco membership has to *predate* the promotion to qualify! APA believes that sort of price advertising belongs in the newsletter Costco sends to its members, but neither Ford nor any regulator has intervened to eliminate this practice.

The ad states "You pay $28,391." Fine print: All rebates incl. Costco.
The price in the bold print does not apply to the APA shopper who is not a Costco member; they will have to pay $29,391, plus a $725 admin. fee not mentioned in the ad.

FIESTA

WITH MANUAL TRANSMISSION

2011-2014	★ ★ ★
2015-2017	★ ★ ★ ★

WITH AUTOMATIC TRANSMISSION

2011-2014	★
2015-2017	★ ★

bad buy

Fuel economy at all costs. This includes a quirky transmission and infotainment malfunctions, a cramped interior, and poor overall reliability. Buy a Honda Fit, Kia Rio or Hyundai Accent instead of a Fiesta with an automatic transmission.

RATING: Not Recommended (2011-2014 with automatic transmission); Above Average (2015-2017 with manual transmission). Available as a five-door hatchback or sedan, the Fiesta was developed by Ford of Europe. Interestingly, Ford has rarely imported a European-derived vehicle that went on to become a success in North America (the German-made Mercury Capri was an exception). **Road performance:** Superior driving dynamics with responsive steering, and nimble, best-in-class handling. Engine is adequate but could use more low-end power, and the ride can get choppy on uneven roadways. The PowerShift automatic transmission shifts erratically and unexpectedly. The car performs better with the manual gearbox. Just adequate space for the driver and passenger in front. **Strong points:** Fun to drive, stylish, nicely assembled, with plenty of high-tech interior features and good gas mileage. Well-appointed cabin for this class. Tilt and telescopic steering wheel, height-adjustable driver's seat, and comfortable front seats. The relatively high ground clearance reduces "belly drag" in the snow (an inch higher than the Toyota Yaris and VW Jetta). **Weak points:** A brand new Fiesta carries a premium price for the small-car class. Misleading new-car advertising sometimes features the "S" model that dealers don't stock. The rear seat is snug. The cheaper Hyundai Accent and Kia Rio have more cabin space. The erratic automatic transmission should never have made its way into production; some owners of early model years report that the automatic cuts gas mileage by almost 15%. In-dash controls on 2011-2013 models take getting used to and can "freeze" or otherwise malfunction. Seats could use a bit more lumbar and thigh bolstering. Armrest is too far forward on the Fiesta's door. **Best alternatives:** Honda Fit, Hyundai Accent, Kia Rio, or Mazda2.

Prices and Specs

Prices (2016-2017): *S:* $15,365, *ST:* $23,588 **Freight:** $1,600 **Powertrain (FWD):** Engines: 1.0L 3-cyl. (123 hp), 1.6L 4-cyl. (120 hp), 1.6L turbo 4-cyl. (197 hp); Transmissions: 5-speed manual, 6-speed dual-clutch automated. **Dimensions:** Passengers: 2/3; Length: 160/174 in., Wheelbase: 98 in., Weight: 2,537-2,742 lb. **Fuel economy:** *1.0L:* 7.5L/100 km city, 5.5L/100 km highway; *1.6L:* 8.7L/100 km city, 6.4L/100 km highway; *1.6L turbo:* 9.0L/100 km city, 7.1L/100 km highway. **Assembled in:** Mexico.

ALERT! Brake and accelerator pedals are placed too close together. Some drivers find the head restraint design forces a chin-to-chest driving position that's very uncomfortable:

> The headrest is causing me to have headaches due to the forward leaning position of the headrest. I have tried all the situations of the seat and it is the same for all of them. I am 5'2" and in my research have found most other short people have the same issue.

Owner-reported safety-related failures: Other complaints: Airbags failed to deploy; rear seatbacks may not lock into position, allowing cargo to fly forward in a sudden stop; and fuel leaks under the car.

RELIABILITY: Well Below Average for the 2011-13 models, improved for 2014-17. Erratic-performing automatic transmissions are reprogrammed or repaired free under warranty. After that repairs are very expensive; some or all of the cost may be covered under various Ford Customer Satisfaction Programs. Owners report the following additional failures: Oil pan, coolant pump and front crank seal leaks; engine stalling and surging; electrical shorts; excessive steering-wheel vibration; noisy brakes; and various fit and finish deficiencies (door panels can fall apart). The manual transmission has also exhibited some early clutch wear and defective slave cylinders.

SAFETY	
IIHS	
Small Front	Marginal
Front	Good
Side	Good
Roof strength	Good
Head restraint and seats	Good
Child seat anchors	Poor
NHTSA Overall	★★★★

INTERNAL BULLETINS, SECRET WARRANTIES: All Years—"Paint Defects Warranty Information" is a confidential service guide used by dealer body shops to decide if your paint warranty claim is valid. **2011**—Customer Satisfaction Program 11B31 (secret warranty) calls for a free upgraded clutch replacement on the DPS6 automatic transmission. Engine stalling and surging along with poor transmission performance may be due to a malfunctioning transmission control module. Automatic transmission grind or rattle noise in Second, Fourth, or Reverse gear. Poor or no engine start, or transmission engagement. Engine block heater coolant leakage and spillover into the spark plug well. Some Fiestas may exhibit an oil leak at the cylinder head oil galley located behind the exhaust cam phaser. On Fiestas equipped with manual windows, the window glass may suddenly drop due to a defective window regulator (a warranty item, for sure). AC condensation may collect on the front passenger floor. **2011-12**—Automatic transmission fluid leak from the clutch housing will require a major repair covered by the base warranty (TSB #12-4-6). Steering column pop, clunk, knock during slow-speed turns. **2011-13**—Some cars may produce a thump, rattle in the fuel filler neck area. Ford will correct the problem free of charge under its emissions warranty. **2011-15**—Remedy for fluid leak, clutch shudder on acceleration. A lack of heat; blower motor frozen in cold weather. This may be caused by snow entering through the cowl top area. The snow melts and the water enters the blower motor and then refreezes overnight and/or when temperatures dip below freezing. The blower motor fuse at location F4 in the Power Distribution Box may also be open (repair covered under the base warranty). Vehicles equipped with air conditioning and built on or before Sept. 10, 2013, may leak water onto the front passenger floor area in high temperature and high humidity conditions. Remedies for clutch shudder or automatic transmission fluid leaks may include installing a seal kit, replacing the clutch, and reprogramming the PCM/TCM module. This is an expensive repair that's covered up to 7 years/100,000 miles under Ford's Customer Satisfaction Program #14M01, created July 21, 2014.

EXCESSIVE TRANSMISSION CLUTCH SHUDDER AND/OR AUTOMATIC TRANSMISSION FLUID LEAK

SERVICE BULLETIN NO.: 14-0131   DATE: 07/23/14

2011-14 Fiesta and Focus

ISSUE: Vehicles equipped with a DPS6 automatic transmission may exhibit an excessive transmission clutch shudder on light acceleration. Some vehicles may or may not exhibit transmission fluid leaking from the clutch housing.

2012-13—Various SYNC malfunctions are tackled (TSB# 13-9-22). **2012-14**—Vehicles equipped with 1.6L Twin Independent Variable Cam Timing (Ti-VCT) may exhibit a whirring, buzz, or saw-type noise from the engine after a cold start between 950-1200 RPM from the timing belt cover. Ford suggests changing the engine timing chain under warranty.

FOCUS

2005-2011	★★★
WITH AUTOMATIC	
2012-2013	★
2014-2017	★★
WITH MANUAL	
2012-2013	★★★
2014-2017	★★★★
ELECTRIC	★

bad buy

bad buy

RATING: Average (2005-2011); Not Recommended (2012-2013 with automatic); Below Average (2014-2017 with automatic); Average (2014-2017 with manual transmission); Electric: Not Recommended (2013-2016). Prior to the 2012 redesigned models arriving from Europe, the Ford Focus was a decent workaday economy car that had become dated. Model year 2007 was the last to offer a practical wagon body. The restyled 2008 Focus attempted to prolong its run in a very competitive segment using Ford's unremarkable 140 hp 2.0L 4-cylinder; it was a fairly reliable American-made econobox. Everything changed when Ford introduced the next version of the Focus, a "world car" designed in Germany, for the 2012 model year. It was fun to drive and a fairly good highway performer when the dual-clutch transmission was working properly. Developed by Ford and Getrag, the 6-speed automatic optimized fuel usage by employing two manual transmissions, each with its own clutch alternating shifting duty. One clutch acted on First, Third, and Fifth gear, and the other handled Second, Fourth, and Sixth gear. The auto-box relied on dry clutches and electric solenoid actuation to provide quick shifts without the hydraulic losses associated with torque converters. On paper, it looked promising. **Road performance:** Like the Fiesta's similar transmission, the actual performance is punctuated by stumbles and surges that spoil the driving experience. Get past that and the 2012 and newer Focus has a smooth, supple ride, superior handling and confident roadholding. Titanium models come with a sport-tuned suspension, which is too firm for some. Exceptional performance and handling with the Focus ST, but the Recaro-brand front seats are very tight – try them on before you buy. The all-electric Focus is basically a one-trick pony that will be retired or see its current technology superceded. **Strong points:** Stylish with a well-appointed interior and capable handling. The Focus now comes standard with a user-friendly rearview camera and Ford's SYNC3 voice-control system (excluding S and SE), with Bluetooth and a USB port. Available features include dual-zone automatic climate control, navigation, blind-spot monitoring, and the MyFord Touch infotainment system with an 8-inch touch screen. On recent models, Ford re-introduced conventional redundant controls for most HVAC functions. *Electric:* This plug-in electric car has an upscale interior and agile handling for an EV. **Weak points:** *2011-2013:* Jerky automated manual transmission hardly impresses even when it's working well. Backseat legroom is back of the class. MyFord infotainment controls are distracting, uncooperative and glitchprone.

Best alternatives: *2005-2011:* Chevrolet Cavalier/Pontiac Sunfire, Hyundai Elantra, or Kia Forte. *2012-2017:* Take a look at the Chevrolet Cruze, Honda Civic, or Mazda3. A new VW Golf offers comparable handling and predicted reliability with cabin space to comfortably seat up to five and better fuel economy. Hotshoes may want to look at the Golf GTI as an alternative to the Focus ST. A used gas engine Golf or GTI is likely to be too expensive to be an attractive alternative and repair costs are high as the car ages.

Prices and Specs

Price: *Sedan S:* $17,199, *ST:* $30,749, *Electric:* $31,999 **Freight:** $1,600 **Powertrain (FWD):** Engines: 1.0L 3-cyl. turbo (123 hp), 2.0L 4-cyl. (160 hp), 2.0L 4-cyl. turbo (252 hp), Electric motor (143 hp); Transmissions: 5-speed manual, 6-speed manual, 6-speed dual-clutch auto. **Dimensions:** Passengers: 2/3; Length: 172/179; Wheelbase: 104 in.; Weight: 2,919-3,622 lb. **Fuel economy:** *1.0L:* 8.5L/100 km city, 5.9L/100 km highway; *2.0L:* 9.0L/100 km city, 6.2L/100 km highway; *2.0L turbo:* 10.5L/100 km city, 7.7L/100 km highway. **Assembled in:** Wayne, Michigan.

SAFETY

IIHS 2016

Small Front	Acceptable
Front	Good
Side	Good
Roof strength	Good
Head restraint and seats	Good
Child seat anchors	Acceptable
NHTSA Overall	★★★★★

ALERT! Watch out for the driver head restraints pushing your chin to your chest, especially with the Recaro seats on the ST.

Owner-reported safety-related failures: Shuddering transmission, broken latches that allow the doors to swing open spontaneously (now covered by a recall), sunroof shattering spontaneously, as well as brake and electrical failures. Some owners have reported the engine stalling at speed:

> My 2013 Ford Focus almost got me killed. I was on the Bay Bridge in the middle lane, when I experienced extreme loss of power. I was moving with the speed of traffic, and all of a sudden no power. I had to cut across three lanes of traffic to get to the shoulder, just missed getting smashed by a Mack Truck. I had just gotten the car back from the dealer two weeks earlier for the same problem. They assured me that it was fixed and that what was going on was 'normal.' I am scared to drive it, I am scared to sell it to someone because they might hurt themselves or others...

— www.consumeraffairs.com/automotive/ford_focus.html

RELIABILITY: The current-generation 2012-13 Focus was teleported back into the lemony former state of the original North American Focus of the early 1980s. The car's deficiencies in its first two years are legion – related to the engine and transmission, steering, brakes, electronics (infotainment), and electrical systems. Reliability improved subsequently but durability of the dual-clutch automatic is still a question mark. Manual transmission models dispense with the troublesome Getrag automatic and are a safer bet. The 2000-2011 previous-generation models are well-known quantities that are easy to fix. Common problems include brake corrosion (check parking brake operation), suspension wear, and body rusting that starts with the rocker panels and door bottoms and spreads to the rear quarter panels. If rust damage is not advanced, the APA recommends Krown Rust Control or Barry's Rustproofing in the Montreal market to protect the fragile rocker panels, rear fenders, and floor (contact information is in the Part Four Introduction).

INTERNAL BULLETINS, SECRET WARRANTIES: 2008-10—Ignition key binds in the ignition cylinder. Some Focus models equipped with a 4F27E transmission may exhibit a 2-3 or 2-4 upshift flare, or lack of Third and/or Fourth gear along with burnt automatic transmission fluid and lit diagnostic trouble codes (DTCs) P0733, P0734, P0751, and/or P0972. A direct clutch repair kit is available under warranty to fix these malfunctions. Vehicles may exhibit a whine, howl, or groan type noise from the intermediate shaft bearing with the vehicle in motion. This maybe due to moisture getting past the bearing seals. An underbody squeak or creaking noise may be silenced by replacing the parking brake cables and routing eyelets (TSB #10-24-06). 2009-10—A fix for inoperative door locks. 2010-11—If the idle speed intermittently drops lower than desired and/or fluctuates, the throttle body may be the culprit. 2011—Ford says excessive road wander, steering drift, or uneven rear tire wear may require the installation of a new right rear lower control arm (TSB #11-1-1). 2012—Engine controls/drivability issues. Automatic transmission controls have various drivability concerns. Free transmission clutch replacement is available. Steering wander. Front-end crunching, creaking when passing over bumps. MyFord Touch glitches. Loss of electric power steering. Erratic fuel gauge readings. Fixing a caved-in hood. 2012-13—A crunching or creaking-type noise from the front suspension may be due to a worn strut bearing. Water leaking into the passenger side front footwell may be leaking condensate from the A/C. If the instrument panel cluster won't light up on startup, the body control module ISP may need rebooting after fuse #69 has been removed for a minute and reinserted. 2012-14—If there is early nozzle shut off, or a slow fuel fill, clean out the EVAP canister fresh air vent hose and the screen filter. Some vehicles may exhibit a clunk and/or rattle-type noise from the left and/or right front strut area at low speeds. Lubricate both front strut shafts. Another problem that falls under both the regular and Emissions warranty: Some vehicles may have inaccurate fuel gauge indication and/or inaccurate distance to empty readings. The Check Engine may also be lit. More infotainment failures: Some vehicles equipped with MyFord

Touch/MyLincoln Touch may screw up navigation data, voice recognition, call sound quality, phone pairing, clock, media indicators, WiFi pass code entry, rear-view camera guide lines, and other system features. Ford says troubleshooting the above problems should take no more than 20 minutes of electronic module tinkering (under warranty). **2012-15**—A clutch shudder or automatic transmission fluid leaks require a new seal kit, clutch, and reprogramming of the PCM/TCM module. This is an expensive repair that's covered up to 7 years/100,000 miles under Ford's Customer Satisfaction Program #14M01. Fix for a headliner that sags or rattles. **2013-14**—Erratic idling can be corrected by recalibrating the powertrain control module. **2013-15**—A pervasive fuel odour in the cabin may be coming from a poorly connected PCV hose. **2014**—No crank or electrical power? Body control module may need to be changed. **2015**—Reprogram the HVAC control module if there is no A/C airflow. **2016**—Stalling and erratic shifting. Shudders when rounding corners. Tire may separate on both sidewalls.

PAINT DEGRADATION/ROAD ABRASION

BULLETIN NO.: 10-15-6   DATE: AUGUST 16, 2010

2008–11 Focus

ISSUE: Some 2008–11 Focus vehicles may experience paint damage or road abrasion on the rocker panel and on the side of the vehicle located slightly ahead of the rear tires on both 2 door and 4 door models. Rocker Panel, 1/4 panel, dog leg and/or rear door, dependent on model. This has been reported in geographical areas that commonly experience snow and ice conditions and use various forms of traction enhancers.

ACTION: Follow the Service Procedure steps to correct the condition.

NOTE: Per the warranty and policy manual paint damage caused by conditions such as chips, scratches, dents, dings, road salt, stone chips or other acts of nature are not covered under the warraty. However, paint abrasion at the dog leg area due to the above circumstances is a unique condition on the focus and, as a result, repairs are eligible for basic warranty coverage.

Cheap gas and poor quality are driving buyers away from Ford econocars. Granted plummeting gas prices was a surprise, but Ford did nothing to fix its Focus paint problem (above) during four model years.

FUSION		2006-2012	★★★
		WITH 2.5 BASE ENGINE	
		2013-2017	★★★
		WITH ECOBOOST ENGINES	
		2013-2014	★
		2015-2017	★★
		HYBRID	★★★★
LINCOLN MKZ		2006-2012	★★★★
		2013-2017	★★★

bad buy

RATING: *Fusion:* Average (2006-2012); Not Recommended (2013-2014 with EcoBoost engines); Average (2013-2017 with 2.5L base engine). The Ford Fusion was an all-new nameplate introduced for 2006, slotted between the compact Focus and the full-size Five Hundred/Taurus, to compete in the mid-size segment dominated by the Honda Accord and Toyota Camry. Based on the Mazda6 sedan (Ford and Mazda were partners at the time), the Fusion adopted the 6's control-arm front suspension and multilink rear setup for good handling. The 4-cylinder engine was supplied by Mazda, while Ford provided the V6. Updates for 2010 improved the car; the Fusion Hybrid was also introduced that year. The Fusion was completely redesigned for 2013. The 2013 and later Fusion introduced a poor-shifting automatic transmission, a dysfunctional infotainment system, unreliable EcoBoost powertrains, and, on 2013-14 models, doors that could spontaneously fly open on turns – the latter now covered by a recall. *MKZ:* Above Average (2006-2012); Average 2013-2017). Lincoln got its own glossy version of the mid-size platform. The 2013 redesigned MKZ delivers adequate acceleration and fair handling, steering that is tight, precise, and vibration-free; the 4-cylinder and V6 engines are adequate, but not as thrifty or dependable as represented. The 2013 and later MKZ's controls, especially the pushbutton transmission gear selector resurrected from the 1950s, are a triumph of styling over ergonomics and safety. Road performance: *2006-12 Fusion and MKZ:* Good acceleration and handling; the 4-cylinder and V6 engines are competent, though they're fond of gasoline. Additional rigidity and chassis tweaking in 2010 improved comfort and handling. On 2013s, all-wheel drive is again available; a fuel-saving engine stop-start system is standard on 1.6L EcoBoost (turbo) models. Hybrids received a new 2.0L Atkinson-cycle 4-cylinder to replace the previous 2.5L. The high-performance Fusion ST uses a version of the troublesome EcoBoost 2.0L engine. Strong points: Both are good used buys due to their steep depreciation (the MKZ depreciates *very* quickly). *2013-2017:* Stylish. Weak points: Rear seating and tilted-forward head restraints in 2013 and later models can be pure torture. Some owners report the front seat backs are uncomfortable due to a hard block within the seat. Some owners report the knee airbag restricts brake pedal access and brake response is weak. Real-world fuel consumption with the 1.5, 1.6, and 2L EcoBoost engines is pretty much the same for all three, and disappointing. The automatic transmission sometimes shifts erratically. *Hybrid:* The brake pedal is mounted too close to the accelerator pedal. Hybrid and EcoBoost fuel economy ratings can't be trusted. **Best alternatives:** *Fusion:* Honda Accord, Toyota Camry (both will cost thousands more on the used car market), or a Hyundai Sonata or Kia Optima. *MKZ:* Lexus ES 350, Nissan Maxima, and Hyundai Genesis (all will cost thousands more used).

Prices and Specs

Prices (2017): *Fusion S:* $23,688, *Sport:* $42,288, *Hybrid S:* $28,888; *MKZ gasoline or hybrid:* $42,000 **Freight:** $1,650/$1,900 (Lincoln). **Powertrain (FWD/AWD):** Engines: *Fusion: 2.5L 4-cyl. (175 hp),* 1.5L 4-cyl. turbo (181 hp), 2.0L 4-cyl. turbo (240 hp), 2.7L V6 turbo (325 hp), 2.0L 4-cyl. hybrid (188 hp) and Energi plug-in electric; *Lincoln:* 3.7L V6 (300 hp), 3.0L V6 Twin-turbo (350-400 hp), 2.0L 4-cyl. hybrid (188 hp); Transmissions: 6-speed automatic or CVT (Hybrid). **Dimensions:** *Fusion:* Length: 192 in.; Wheelbase: 112 in.; Weight: 3,323-3,911 lb. **Fuel economy:** *Fusion:* 2.5L: 11.3L/100 km city, 7.5L/100 km highway; *1.5L turbo:* 10.0L/100 km city, 7.0L/100 km highway; *2.0L Hybrid:* 5.4L/100 km city, 5.7L/100 km highway; *Lincoln:* 3.7L V6: 12.8L/100 km city, 8.7L/100 km highway. **Assembled in:** Michigan and Mexico.

ALERT! Ford says bolts used in the assisted-steering system could rust and fracture, causing the 2013-15 Fusion or Lincoln MKZ to lose power steering. Affected cars will be repaired free of charge if the vehicle has been registered in a province that uses road salt in the winter, which may have accelerated the corrosion. Limiting liability to certain areas means some vehicles will not be fixed if they were driven in one area and sold in another. Logically, Ford should accept a warranty claim if the defect exists, no matter where the car was bought or registered. Automatic transmission may not hold the Lincoln on an incline. Sometimes the vehicle lurches forward in Park:

> I pulled into a parking space (space in front of a canal) and pushed buttoned into Park and the car then lurched forward, going into the canal (front half only, the back half was stopped by the sea wall). We see there was a recall for the same problem for 2013 Lincoln MKZ Hybrids (ours is not a hybrid).

SAFETY

IIHS 2016 FORD FUSION

Small Front	Acceptable
Front	Good
Side	Good
Roof strength	Good
Head restraint and seats	Good
Child seat anchors	Marginal
NHTSA Overall Ford Fusion 2016	★★★★★

Owner-reported safety-related failures: The 2010 Fusion amassed more than 2,500 safety complaints and counting, many involving a faulty electronic power-assisted steering system that can abruptly stop working, or a malfunctioning throttle body that can stall the car almost spontaneously. Ford's recall campaigns are incomplete. NHTSA has collected troubling owner reports of broken door latches, which can allow doors to open arbitrarily, sometimes when the vehicle is in motion. There's a recall on the latches, but on the Fusion and MKZ it is limited to 2013-2014 models. Owners have also documented intermittent loss of steering ability:

> While attempting to turn the vehicle, the power steering assist became difficult to operate. The steering wheel suddenly began to vibrate and the power steering assist warning light illuminated. The instrument panel also indicated many other warning lights and functions were being activated that were not in use. The vehicle was taken to a certified mechanic and dealer. Both stated that the power assist failed and there was also an electrical failure.

RELIABILITY: *Fusion and MKZ:* Average (2006-12); Below Average (2013-2017 except for base models with the old 2.5L engine, which are Average to Above Average). Overall the 2006-2012 generation Fusion had the potential to be the most reliable of the domestic mid-size sedans, if it were not for the malfunctioning electric steering systems and bad throttle bodies. The 4-cylinder and 3L V6 shared with the Mazda6 had fewer problems in the Fusion. *V6:* Check for valve cover and timing cover oil leaks. Check rear shock absorber struts, as well as the left-side axle shaft for leaks. Brake calipers and rotors will need replacing frequently if the brakes are not serviced; have the rear calipers de-seized and lubricated annually to prevent expensive rear brake repairs. *2013-2017:* 1.6 and 2L EcoBoost engines had plenty of problems in their first two years on the market, and fuel consumption is disappointing. Overheated engines and coolant leaks were common. Purchase an extended warranty from Ford if you are buying a Fusion or MKZ with an EcoBoost engine. Air filter replacement can cost up to $500 on the hybrid as you may have to change the housing. The battery pack in the Hybrid can prove troublesome. One Edmonton owner wrote this to his local TV station:

> My 2013 Ford Fusion vehicle has been in the service department for a total of 3 months (8 times) for the same issue and no dealership can fix it (I have had it to 2 different dealerships) with no luck currently it is being towed to Metro Ford for the 4th time (9 times total including this time). The issue is the hybrid system. The dealers have replaced the battery 3 times and now it is dead again. Ford Canada has been notified on several occasions and has done nothing to resolve these issues. This vehicle has only a little over 18,000 kms and is usually in the service dept. at least once a month (one time it was in for 33 days straight).
>
> It has also been in for "no key detected" at least 3 times, as well. When this happens the car is dead and the only way to get into it is by using a dummy key, which will open the doors but nothing else. These vehicles are not very good for the environment as they have been replacing batteries left and right over the last 18 months and can't fix the issues. Three weeks ago they replaced a main motherboard in the dash and it solved the problem for less than three weeks and it is dead again this morning.

INTERNAL BULLETINS, SECRET WARRANTIES: *Fusion:* 2012-13—SYNC malfunctions diagnosed. 2013—Fusion Hybrid and Fusion Energi models may make a noise that could be described as a ting, pop, or click from the front wheel area when accelerating from a stop or when shifting between Drive/Reverse and Reverse/Drive. 2013-15—Clearcoat peels off of black wheels. Free wheel replacement until July 31, 2017 (Customer Satisfaction Program 15B13). 2014-15—Heated steering wheel may not heat. 2015-16—If the car exhibits a rolling R to D shudder on acceleration, reprogram the powertrain control module. *MKZ:* 2012—More SYNC malfunctions addressed. 2013-16—An intermittently inoperative power decklid can be fixed by reflashing the rear gate trunk module. *Fusion, MKZ:* 2007-11—Vehicles equipped with all-wheel drive systems and built on or before Aug. 13, 2010, may exhibit a driveline vibration or a howl noise at highway speeds in cold temperatures. 2010—Vehicles equipped with all-wheel drive may exhibit a shudder/chatter/vibration driveline sensation during a tight turn, or a thump/clunk noise on light acceleration. 2010-11—Vehicles may experience a leaking/stuck canister purge valve. This condition may cause various intermittent drivability symptoms. The condition may also cause drivability symptoms with malfunction indicator light lit. 2010-12—Transmission fluid leak from the left-hand half shaft seal. 2011-12—Look out for an intermittent harsh 1-2 shift or harsh 5-6 shift regardless of temperature or soak time. Additionally, 4-5 shift flare may be experienced after an extended cold soak on the first few 4-5 shifts of the day. 2.5L-equipped vehicles with delayed 4-5 shift events and/or high RPMs may also benefit from a calibration of the PCM. SYNC infotainment functionality concerns. 2011-14—An extended warranty (Customer Satisfaction Program 14N02) applies to PCM reprogramming in the event of ABS brake communication failures. 2013—Vehicles that won't start may need to reprogram the radio transceiver module (RTM). 2013-14—Vehicles equipped with an HF35 transmission may exhibit a thumping, rubbing, or grinding noise coming from the transmission. Remedy is to replace the transfer shaft gear assembly, transmission assembly, and exhaust manifold gasket, per instructions in TSB #14-0176. Inoperative ambient lighting can be turned on by reprogramming the body control module. Some vehicles equipped with MyFord Touch/MyLincoln Touch may have problems with overall system performance. TSB #13-10-6, troubleshoots these failures. Windows may not work in freezing temperatures. 2013-15—Fuel odour emanating from the PVC hose. 2014-15—Headliner sags near the door openings. 2015—Heated steering wheel may not heat. An unpowered fuel pump module may be the cause of hard starting or chronic stalling.

2017 Ford Taurus

RATING: *Five Hundred:* Below Average; *Taurus:* Average. Ford's large front-wheel drive sedan is big on the outside, but an intermediate on the inside. Developed during the years when Volvo was owned by Ford, it is based on the previous-generation Volvo large-car platform. The Taurus name was reintroduced in 2008; it retained the body of the poorly received 2005-2007 Five Hundred, with significant powertrain and suspension updates. The 2008-09 Taurus offered a stronger V6, and the very unreliable CVT was dropped in favour of a Ford-GM 6-speed automatic used across the board. The redesigned 2010 Taurus made use of the same 263 hp 3.5L V6 and automatic transmission inside a sleek new body and cabin. EcoBoost engines arrived soon after, but the naturally aspirated V6 remained the way to go. A mid-cycle refresh for 2013 included an optional new 2.0L EcoBoost turbo 4-cylinder and some optional active safety features. The Taurus has been largely unchanged since 2013. **Road performance:** The 2008 and 2009 Taurus is a smooth, quiet, and exceptionally roomy car that was significantly improved compared to the mediocre Five Hundred it was based on. *2010 and later:* Strong performance from the quiet, non-turbo V6. Slick-shifting, responsive automatic transmission. The turbocharged V6 in the SHO furnishes blistering acceleration but is heavy on gas. Good handling and competent ride. Progressive braking despite mushy pedal feel. **Strong points:** Fit, finish, and materials are all very good. Precise, nicely weighted steering. Smooth, quiet ride. Big, clear gauges. Optional Haldex all-wheel drive system migrated from the Volvo XC90 and S80. **Weak points:** *2010-2017:* Despite its vast exterior size, cabin space is disappointing, inferior in some ways to the smaller pre-2013 Fusion. The swept-back dashboard is a dramatic piece of architecture but it consumes a lot of cabin space. Low-mounted front seats restrict rear seat passenger toe space. Weak air conditioning. Poor visibility, especially for reversing. **Major redesign:** 2005 Five Hundred introduced; 2008 models upgraded and renamed Taurus; 2010 redesign; 2013 partial redesign. **Best alternatives:** Chevrolet Impala, Dodge Charger, Chrysler 300, Toyota Avalon, Nissan Maxima, and Infiniti M37.

Prices and Specs

Prices (2016-2017): *SE:* $30,999, *SHO:* $48,499 **Freight:** $1,650 **Powertrain (FWD/AWD):** Engine: 3.5L V6 (288 hp), 2.0L 4-cyl. turbo (240 hp), 3.5L V6 turbo (365 hp); Transmission: 6-speed automatic. **Dimensions:** Passengers: 2/3; Length: 203 in.; Wheelbase: 112 in.; Weight: 3,969 lb. **Fuel consumption:** *3.5L:* 13.6L/100 km city, 9.8L/100 km highway; *2.0L turbo:* 11.8L/100 km city, 8.1L/100 km highway. **Assembled in:** Chicago, Illinois.

RELIABILITY: *Average* Avoid 2005-2007 Five Hundred models with the unreliable CVT transmission. *2008-09 Taurus:* The early models used Ford's "Duratech" V6 that provided middling power for such a large sedan. Standard CVT transmission is very unreliable and expensive to repair; at this point a failure would likely see the car written off. The Limited model used a conventional 6-speed automatic sourced from Toyota supplier Aisin. Quality lapses include noisy brake calipers, faulty throttle bodies, turbo fluid leaks, a few leaky sunroofs and paint/clearcoat issues. Like the Fusion, brakes wear quickly and calipers can seize; have the rear brake calipers serviced annually to postpone expensive repairs.

SAFETY

IIHS 2016 FORD TAURUS

Small Front	Not rated
Front	Good
Side	Good
Roof strength	Good
Head restraint and seats	Good
Child seat anchors	Acceptable
NHTSA Overall Ford Taurus 2016	★★★★★

Ford's 2011 rear-drive Mustang came with a better V6 engine and
other improvements that took a couple of years to perfect.

RATING: Recommended; Average (2016-2017 with EcoBoost 4-cylinder). The 2017
Mustang has been carried over without any significant changes. **Road performance:**
Fast acceleration and impressive handling and braking. The ride and cornering
on bumpy roads improved thanks to the introduction of independent rear suspension in 2015. The V8 is a rocket with a great soundtrack and surprisingly good
highway fuel economy. The manual transmission is responsive with crisp short-
throws. Introduced for 2015, the 2.3L EcoBoost 4-cylinder sounds flat and is no
lighter than the base V6 engine it competes with – *Lemon-Aid* doesn't see the point
of the four. The Shelby GT350 returned as a 2016 model with a new, 5.2L naturally-
aspirated V8 with a racing-style crankshaft and a more advanced cylinder head
and valvetrain. It also features lightweight aluminum body panels from the
A-pillar forward. **Strong points:** Most Mustangs come equipped with a host of
luxury and convenience features. Prior to 2015, access to the front seats is reasonable, and the comfortable, relatively upright front seating provides a good view of
the road for a pony car. Ford delayed the introduction of the MyTouch and Sync
systems in the Mustang, so it was spared the early, worst versions, and the Mustang
always retained some redundant conventional controls for heating and cooling. If
you're buying new, you'll be pleased to know that resale value is better than other
Ford cars. **Weak points:** Cabin space declined significantly with the 2015 redesign;
the two previous generations offered more comfort and better visibility. Limited
rear seat room. Unimpressive interior finish of base models. The 6-speed automatic
transmission can "hunt" for the proper gear. **Major redesign:** 2005, 2011, 2015. The
2005 redesign finally dispensed with the eternal "Fox" platform that dated back
to 1978, and adopted the rear-drive platform underpinning the Lincoln LS sedan.

As of 2011, the base Mustang got a huge horsepower boost that turned its ho-hum 210 hp V6 into a caffeinated 305 hp performer that's one of the best bargains around. Other goodies on the 2011-2014 and later Mustangs: A new limited-slip differential, larger brakes (taken from the 2010 GT), electronic power steering, a retuned suspension, stiffer rear anti-roll bars, and a convertible with less body flex thanks to a new shock-tower brace. Another welcome change: Fold-down rear head restraints to improve visibility. **Best alternatives:** The Camaro is the obvious cross-shop; the smaller Mustang offered better visibility and tidier dimensions that make it a better daily driver, at least until its 2015 redo. The Dodge Challenger is very entertaining with more interior space, but it's less nimble. Among the imports, the Hyundai Genesis and Infiniti G-series coupes are good rear-drive alternatives.

Prices and Specs

Prices (2017): *V6:* $26,398, *Shelby GT350:* $73,678 **Freight:** $1,650 **Powertrain (Rear-drive):** Engines: 3.7L V6 (300 hp), 2.3L 4-cyl. turbo (310 hp), 5.0L V8 (435 hp); 5.2L V8 (526 hp). Transmissions: 6-speed manual, 6-speed auto. **Dimensions:** Passengers: 2/2; Length: 188 in.; Wheelbase: 107 in.; Weight: 3,533-3,904 lb. **Fuel economy:** *3.7L:* 12.8L/100 km city, 8.9L/100 km highway; *2.3L turbo:* 11.0L/100 km city, 7.9L/100 km highway; *5.0L V8:* 15.6L/100 km city, 9.6L/100 km highway; *5.2L V8:* 17.2L/100 km city, 11.3L/100 km highway. **Assembled in:** Michigan.

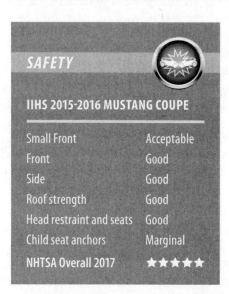

SAFETY

IIHS 2015-2016 MUSTANG COUPE

Small Front	Acceptable
Front	Good
Side	Good
Roof strength	Good
Head restraint and seats	Good
Child seat anchors	Marginal
NHTSA Overall 2017	★★★★★

ALERT! Inadvertently touching the push-button Start/Stop ignition can shut down the engine at speed, say owners:

> The ignition switch is located directly under the radio control buttons and it will shut the car off while in gear and in motion. This happened while I was in a parking lot, going about 5 mph. My husband accidently pushed the ignition button instead of the radio control button and shut the car off. Ford has no solution to this hazardous design flaw, and told me they can't re-engineer the vehicle to eliminate the risk of a serious accident.

Your Mustang may not have a spare tire:

> Ford has failed to make a spare wheel/tire available on all vehicles (a tire inflation kit is all there is) and the spare wheel/tire is on backorder for all dealerships because supply is low… Three different tire stores have told me they do not have a compatible spare available. (A recycler may be able to help with a compact spare, jack and tie-down from a Mustang taken off the road.)

Invest in an anti-theft system (one that includes an engine immobilizer) and tires recommended by the APA at *www.apa.ca or www.tirerack.com*. The notchy, erratic-shifting 6-speed Getrag manual transmission performed poorly on 2011-13 models and the jury's still out on the 2014s (see *mustangsdaily.com/blog/2011/11/09/ford-responds-to-nhtsasinvestigation-of-the-mustangs-mt82-6-speed-transmission*).

Owner-reported safety-related failures: Exhaust fumes enter into the cabin. Fuel tank may fall off due to the mounting bracket bolts failing. Engine throttle body frequently fails, preceded by stalling and drivability issues. Emergency brake doesn't hold on an incline. Steering constantly pulls to one side or the other.

RELIABILITY: The rugged rear-drive design is relatively easy to repair. *2005-2010:* These Models generated the fewest complaints (the Mustang benefited from Japanese assembly standards, since it came out of the Flat Rock, Michigan, factory shared with Mazda). Some complaints of failing rear ends and driveshafts on cars with manual transmissions. A "chattering" clutch when you let out the pedal slowly may point to severe usage and a pending clutch replacement. Some power steering failures. *2011-13:* Manual transmission can grind when upshifting, especially when engaging Fifth gear. The engine also sometimes shuts off when the car slows down with the clutch applied. *2011-2015:* Owners cite manual and automatic transmission failures and "shift lag," "unfixable" electrical shorts, electronic module malfunctions, and rattling door panels. *2009:* A wet carpet underneath the rubber mat on the front passenger side may indicate a leak at the firewall.

INTERNAL BULLETINS, SECRET WARRANTIES: Airbags fail to deploy. 2005-12—May have a major fluid leak from the rear axle vent. 2010-15— Driving with the windows down or the sunroof open may be unbearable, but Ford says too bad: The issue, related to aerodynamic design, is hardly limited to the Mustang or other Fords; many automobile designs introduce harmonic resonance at highway speeds when the windows/sunroof are opened – it's the price of higher efficiency. 2011-12— SYNC voice recognition system may ignore your voice. Manual transmission can be difficult to shift in cold weather. Front-end suspension may produce a grunt, creak, chirp, or squeak. Owners say the same noise affects 2013-14 suspensions. 2011-13—Mustangs that won't start, or are rough running, may simply have a blown #13 fuse in the battery junction box. 2011-14—Vehicles may have a delayed Park to Forward or Reverse transmission engagement. Ford suggests replacing the transmission pump assembly – a six-hour repair. This repair should not be needed. A refusal by Ford to pass this repair under warranty should prompt owners to haggle or file a claim in small claims court. Use TSB #14-0076 as proof of the company's responsibility (see TSB in F-150 Pickup *Internal Bulletins*). Mustangs equipped with a 3.7L, 5.0L DOHC and 5.0L DOHC SEFI with a rear axle vent located on the left axle tube may exhibit a fluid leak from the rear axle vent. Ford will install a vent kit under warranty (takes about a half-hour).

ISSUE: Some 2011-2014 Mustang vehicles equipped with a 3.7L, 5.0L 4V DOHC and 5.0L 4V DOHC SEFI with a rear axle vent located on the left axle tube may exhibit a fluid leak from the rear axle vent.

ACTION: Install a new vent kit following the instructions included in the kit.

A Mustang that grunts, chirps, creaks, or squeaks when passing over bumps may need a new lower control arm (about two hours for the job). 2012—Engine cold startup ticking noises with 3.5L and 3.7L engines; the repairs require installing a camshaft kit that takes two hours of labour. Automatic transmission fluid leak from the bell housing. 2012-13—Vehicles equipped with a 3.7L engine may produce a chirping or squealing noise from the accessory drive belt during idle and acceleration. You may need to replace the accessory drive belt and tensioner. 2013—Mustangs equipped with a MT-82 manual transmission may experience a hard to shift or grind condition during a 1-2 upshift, or a pop out of Second gear condition during acceleration. Ford says to check the clutch pedal reserve and replace the synchronizers, if needed (almost a six-hour job). 2013-14—Vehicles may make a growl or buzz noise coming from the transmission that occurs when shifting from Park to Drive or Park to Reverse most often after the vehicle has been parked and then restarted. Ford says the main control valve body separator plate may need to be replaced under warranty. 2014—Water that enters the front driver's side of the vehicle will be corrected under warranty. Vehicle may not decelerate when foot is taken off the gas pedal. 2015—Right side exhaust manifold guaranteed up to 7 years/70,000 miles in California and U.S. states that prohibit "secret" warranties. Everywhere else, Ford will charge for the repair. There may be a loss of rpms when the clutch pedal is depressed (5.0L). Reflashing the PCM should resolve the problem. A "hard" brake pedal may only require a recalibration of the PCM. Wind noise from the upper windshield area.

ESCAPE

RATING: Below Average (2005-14); Average (2015-17); *Hybrid:* Average (2005-2012). Introduced for 2001, the conventional gas Escape became a market leader, thanks to its attractive, off-road, truck-inspired styling, spacious interior, and available V6 engine. The Escape hybrid arrived for 2005, combining a 2.3L 4-cylinder with an electric motor for a total system output of 155 hp. Overall performance and economy of Ford's first hybrid were good and surprisingly it generated few complaints in its early years. The ride and assembly quality appeared to be superior to the conventional model. *2008:* The Escape that debuted for 2001 was moderately restyled and treated to a new interior. *2009:* Base engine grows from 2.3L to 2.5L. V6 engine gains 40 hp, to 240, and a 6-speed automatic transmission is new. *2013:* An all-new Ford Escape, based on the European Ford Kuga, goes on sale. Designed by Ford of Europe, the new Escape is elegant, with a superior ride and handling, and an attractive cabin. Ford replaced the previous V6 engine with a 2L turbo 4-cylinder belonging to the EcoBoost family, rated at 240 hp. The Escape also offered an EcoBoost 1.6L turbo four, as well as the proven 2.5L normally-aspirated 4-cylinder from the previous Escape, now limited to basic models. A 6-speed automatic transmission was offered on all models. Unlike the previous design, cabin space was now no more than adequate; the front seats are quite narrow and the rear seatbacks are upright and their cushions thinly padded. Cargo space is acceptable. *2017:* Mid-cycle refresh, including a new front fascia, revised cabin, a new 1.5L EcoBoost turbo 4-cylinder replaces the previous 1.6L four, and the slick-acting Blackberry-designed SYNC3 infotainment system supplants the previous recalcitrant one. Front seat padding is improved. **Road performance:** *2001-2012:* Unexceptional with the four; the V6 uses more fuel but is responsive and sounds nicer. By now the suspension on this generation Escape will likely be pretty worn. Good outward visibility. *2013-2017:* The Ford of Europe design combines great agility with a well-controlled ride that is on the firm side. The 1.6L turbo 4-cylinder is barely faster than the normally-aspirated 2.5L four; the 2L turbo is quick and flexible. Both turbo engines use more fuel in real-world use than the official fuel economy cycles would indicate, and the savings with the 1.6L are negligible compared to the 2L. **Strong points:** *2001-2012:* Large supply at almost every price point because the Escape was a best seller in its class for a long time. Four-cylinder and front-drive models are significantly less expensive, and will stretch your dollar. *2013-2017:* The well-finished interior provides lots of high-tech content and plenty of cargo space. *Hybrid:* Surprisingly, the Escape, which was Ford's first hybrid, was the one that best lived up to its promise. **Weak points:** *2001-2012:* Both engines use more fuel than import competitors from the same period. Wind and road noise at highway speeds are fairly intrusive. *2013-2015:* Non-intuitive inconvenient in-dash controls can "freeze." The new EcoBoost engines use up to 40% more fuel than promised. **Best alternatives:** *2001-2012:* Chevrolet Equinox, GMC Terrain, Hyundai Tucson or Santa Fe, Kia Sportage. *2013-2017:* Honda CR-V, Toyota RAV4, and Nissan Rogue.

Prices and Specs

Prices: *S:* $25,589, *SE 1.6L EcoBoost:* $28,089, *Titanium 4x4:* $34,089 **Freight:** $1,700 **Powertrain:** Engines (2016): 1.6L 4-cyl. (173 hp), 2.0L 4-cyl. (231 hp), 2.5L 4-cyl. (168 hp); Transmission: 6-speed automatic. **Dimensions:** Wheelbase: 106 in., 2689 mm.; L: 178. 4524 mm.,/W: 72 in., 1839 mm.; Weight (2017 1.5L AWD: 3,526 lb., 1599 kg. **Fuel Economy (2016):** *FWD, 2.5L:* 7.6/10.9 L/100 km. *AWD, 2.0L:* 7.9/ 10.9L/100 km. **Assembled in:** United States.

SAFETY

IIHS 2016

Small Front	Acceptable
Front	Good
Side	Good
Roof strength	Good
Head restraint and seats	Good
Child seat anchors	Acceptable
NHTSA Overall	★★★★★

ALERT! *2009 Escape:* The windshield washer nozzles may allow spray to accumulate in the cowl area, and drip onto the electronic module installed in the same area of the engine bay; the replacement part costs $1,400. Consider having the area checked and the module and its connectors protected.

Safety-related failures reported by owners: Airbags fail to deploy, driver's seat collapses, or seat belt latch pops open; spontaneous windshield cracks and sunroof/side window shattering; distorted windshields; and liftgate glass exploded. Chronic stalling affecting some 2013-2015 models:

Purchased vehicle 1/30/2015 and drove off lot with 3 miles on it. Less than a week later vehicle started stalling at traffic lights and hesitating upon acceleration. Vehicle was in Ford repair shop for 12 days with $1200 worth of parts replaced on transmission. Picked up vehicle with 810 miles on it and less than a week and 150 miles later the vehicle is again stalling at traffic lights upon acceleration. The vehicle is dangerous to drive!

– safercar.gov

RELIABILITY: *2001-2008:* Model years prior to the updated V6 and 6-speed automatic needed fewer repairs. *2005-2012:* Common faults include a knocking or loose steering column, worn ball joints and front suspension control arm bushings, noisy wheel bearings and broken suspension sway bar links. Check the level and cleanliness of the power steering fluid; if the steering pump is noisy, changing dirty fluid may prolong its life. A lit ABS light may indicate a faulty sensor assembly or wiring. Some alternator failures. The vehicle may fail to recognize the ignition key; reprogram. Check the rear differential for leaks at the pinion shaft and output seals. If fluid is low, the bearings may have become damaged; a repair kit is available for about $500. As of 2009, reliability dropped to well below average due to the powertrain changes. The 6-speed automatic experienced many failures. So did the uprated 2009-2012 V6, typically a thrown connecting rod or main bearing while towing, or in hilly country with a loaded vehicle; neither the V6 engine nor 6-speed gearbox is suitable for intensive use, even though the Escape was rated for towing. *Escape Hybrid:* For a vehicle that has such a complicated drive system, there haven't been many complaints on the first-generation Escape. Owners report some brake and steering issues. The 2008-2012 Escape is subject to severe rusting, which attacks the lower fender area, door bottoms, folded seams of the rear hatch and rocker rails. Many were repaired fairly extensively by Ford dealers under warranty and some have begun to rust out again. If rust damage is not advanced the APA recommends Krown Rust Control or Barry's Rustproofing in the Montreal market to protect the fragile rocker panels, rear fenders, and floor (contact information is in the Part Four Introduction). *2013-2015:* Expect the usual EcoBoost engine and turbo oil leaks, stalling and overheating covered in the reviews of other Ford models from this period. The dash can "freeze" or be slow to execute commands. The best bet with a 2013 and later vehicle is to purchase a vehicle with a full-coverage new or used vehicle warranty from Ford.

INTERNAL BULLETINS, SECRET WARRANTIES: **2008-09**—All instrument cluster warning lights come on intermittently. Uncommanded liftgate opening or closing. Exterior heated mirror glass cracking. **2008-10**—Special Ford fix for steering column pop or clunk. Ignition key binds in ignition cylinder. Washer nozzles leak fluid onto the hood. Poor radio reception. **2008-12**—Escapes equipped with electronic manual temperature control (EMTC) may find the AC blows warm air or lacks sufficient blower motor power. This may be due to a blower motor resistor damaged by water entering the heater core and evaporator core housing through the cowl. **2009**—Ford Customer Satisfaction Program #10B15100419-001 (secret warranty) was set up April 19, 2010, to cover the cost of reprogramming the Power Control Module to reposition the solenoid regulator valve and eliminate bore wear. Mechanics are also empowered to replace the valve body, overdrive, and forward clutch. Ford says these measures are needed to increase the transmission's durability. Automatic transmission fluid leaks from the dipstick tube. Exterior door handles may be hard to open and may not be flush. **2009-10**—Automatic transmission sticks in Fifth gear (reprogram the power control module). A harsh-shifting automatic transmission requires the same remedy. Harsh engagements, shifts, or starts in Fifth gear from a start signal; there's an open signal in the output shaft speed sensor or the main control lead frame connector. Automatic transmission axle shaft seal fluid leak. All-wheel drive models may produce a vibration, rumble, and/or excessive exhaust noise in cold temperatures. **2009-12**—An intermittent water leak originating from the liftgate glass/seal can be easily plugged says TSB #12-2-2. **2009-13**—Ford has extended the throttle body warranty up to 10 years/150,000 miles per Customer Satisfaction Program #13N03. **2012**—Transmission fluid leakage. Engine drone or rattle. 2.0L and 2.5L engines may constantly cause the MIL light to come on. Harsh or delayed shifts. Broken liftgate window. **2012-14**—Before spending big bucks, try simply lubricating the front strut shafts to eliminate a clunk or rattle from the front strut area. **2013**—Per TSB # 13-4-25, models with noisy front brakes may need to replace the front disc brake caliper anchor plates with new service parts. **2013-14**—Vehicles equipped with 1.6L or 2.0L gasoline turbocharged direct injection (GTDI) engines may be hard to start, run rough, lack power, or lose RPMs. These conditions may be caused by a wiring short in the signal return splices. Other vehicles equipped with a 1.6L or 2.0L may lose power in cold weather. It may be necessary to replace the charge air cooler (CAC) tube and screen assembly from the CAC to the throttle body. Some Escapes equipped with 1.6L or 2.0L gasoline turbocharged direct injection (GTDI) engines may exhibit a rattle/buzz noise or vibration from the right rear floorboard on acceleration between 1500-2500 RPM. The fuel pump may need to be replaced under warranty. Vehicles equipped with all-wheel drive may exhibit rear drive unit (RDU) whine at highway speeds of 64-88 km/h (40-55 mph). Ford says the RDU front bushings may need to be replaced under warranty. Excessive wind noise at highway speeds or whistle in crosswind conditions may be due to the windshield A-pillar moulding lip not staying retained tightly to the pillar. An extended warranty (Customer Satisfaction Program 14N02) applies to PCM reprogramming in the event of ABS brake communication failures. Use TSB #13-10-6 to troubleshoot a number of MyFord Touch/MyLincoln Touch failures with navigation, voice recognition, call sound quality, phone pairing, clock and media malfunction, WiFi pass code entry, rearview camera guidelines, and overall poor system performance. An intermittent lack of air conditioning and/or a loss of airflow from the vents may occur after extended driving in hot, humid conditions. This is likely due to the evaporator core icing. **2013-15**—A clunk noise may come from the left or right shock absorber when passing over a bump. A foul odour may emanate from the PCV hose connection. Gear whine at any speed. **2013-16**—Wind or whistle noise from exterior mirrors at highway speed. Remedy for cracked or damaged front seats. **2014**—Escapes equipped with a 1.6L EcoBoost engine may exhibit an illuminated malfunction indicator lamp (MIL) with a transmission overheat condition. Reprogram the powertrain control module to the latest calibration. **2015-16**—If the car exhibits a rolling R to D shudder on acceleration, again, reprogram the powertrain control module.

FORD EDGE	2007-2017 ★★★★
	WITH ECOBOOST ENGINES
	2011-2014 ★

RATING: Above Average (2007-2017); Not Recommended (2011-2014 with EcoBoost). A five-passenger wagon/CUV crossover introduced for 2007, the Edge comes in either front-drive or all-wheel drive. The original Edge is based on the platform that underpins the Ford Fusion and first-generation Mazda6. For 2011, the Edge underwent a comprehensive refresh, including exterior styling updates, revised cabin including new dash centre stack, additional sound insulation, as well as a new 2L turbo 4-cylinder EcoBoost engine option. Beginning in 2015, Ford brought back more conventional controls on the Edge, so that adjusting the radio or climate controls became easier than on 2011-2014 models. For 2017, three different engines are offered: a 2.0L EcoBoost 4-cylinder turbo with 245 hp; a 280 hp 3.5L V6; and a 2.7L turbocharged V6 that cranks out 315 hp. **Road performance:** The first-generation Edge is roomy and comfortable but has a choppy ride allied to distinctly unenthusiastic handling. Some drivers found the 6-speed automatic transmission shifts roughly. Avoid the larger wheel and tire options as they diminish ride comfort considerably. The current Edge has a well sorted suspension that reconciles ride and handling adroitly. The 2.7L moves the Edge along with authority. **Strong points:** Good performance with non-turbo V6 engines, exhilarating EcoBoost 2.7L turbo V6. Nicely-appointed cabin, comfortable seats, and plenty of space for people and cargo. **Weak points:** The previous SYNC infotainment system used from 2011-2014 was not user friendly but the new SYNC3 interface works quite well. The 2L turbo 4-cylinder is a gas guzzler. Long-term reliability of the available EcoBoost engines is a question mark. **Major redesign:** 2007 introduction; 2011 partial update; 2015 second-generation redesign. **Best alternatives:** Chevrolet Equinox and GMC Terrain with the V6 engine. Nissan Murano, Hyundai Santa Fe 2.0L T, and the Jeep Grand Cherokee.

Prices and Specs

Prices (2016): *SE 2L FWD:* $33,099, *Sport 2.7L AWD:* $46.399 **Freight:** $1,550 **Powertrains (FWD/AWD):** Engines (2016): 2L turbo 4-cyl. (245 hp); 2.7L V6 EcoBoost (335 hp); 3.5L V6 (280 hp); V6; 3.7L V6 (303 hp). Transmission: 6-speed auto. **Dimensions:** Passengers: 2/3; Wheelbase: 112 in., 2849 mm.; L: 188 in., 4,779 mm.; W: 76 in., 1,928 mm; Weight: 4,078 lb., 1850 kg. **Fuel Economy (2016):** *FWD, 2.0L 4-cyl.:* 7.8/11.5L/100 km. *AWD, 2.7 V6 turbo:* 3.8/13.6L/100 km. *3.5L V6:* 9.6/13.7L/100 km. **Assembled in:** Oakville, Ontario.

SAFETY

IIHS 2016

Small Front	Acceptable
Front	Good
Side	Good
Roof strength	Good
Head restraint and seats	Good
Child seat anchors	Acceptable
NHTSA Overall 2017	★★★★★

ALERT! The MyFord Touch infotainment system should be part of your test drive if you're shopping for a 2011-2014 model. Improved over the years, it can become tolerable once drivers are accustomed to it; vehicles from the early years with this system may experience a "frozen" screen that effectively blocks the functions it controls until the vehicle is restarted and the system reboots itself. When accelerating, the Edge can lose all power and stall:

> On April 11, 2015, the throttle body assembly on the engine of my 2011 Ford Edge failed while in heavy traffic at highway speed on a 6-lane highway. I was traveling in the inside lane when the failure occurred. There was no power to the engine, and I coasted quickly across two lanes to a right turn lane. Fortunately, everyone reacted positively to my emergency flashers as I decelerated. On Monday, April 13, the local Ford dealership repaired the car. After returning home, I checked the internet for information on this failure mode and was surprised to read that Ford had a couple years earlier settled a NHTSA complaint for several Ford models that exhibited the problem my car experienced. The Ford Edge was not part of the settlement. Further research revealed other Ford Edges with the same problem as mine. Apparently, Ford won a partial settlement on the throttle body issue...

Owner-reported safety-related failures: Electrical fires, possibly originating around the fuse box; airbags that fail to deploy; loss of power on the highway or when turning (throttle body sensor):

> Wife was driving the car 6-21-16 at approximately 55 mph when suddenly and unexpectedly the car lost power. She was able to get the car off the road without incident but could have been rear ended. Drivetrain malfunction/reduced power icon was displayed on instrument panel. Car was towed to nearest Ford dealership but no problem was found.

Collision warning alert sounded without any cars or objects nearby; car in Park rolled back and hit another parked car; brake failures (faulty brake booster); stop/brake/signal lights frequently burn out; windows fog up in cold weather and rear glass sometimes shatters suddenly for no apparent reason:

> The rear window of vehicle shattered simultaneous to turning the ignition switch. There was no impact to the window; it just shattered. Nothing dropped from the sky; the vehicle was parked in the driveway well away from traffic both vehicle and pedestrian. I repeat it just spontaneously shattered. There is only two thousand miles on this vehicle. This should not have happened.

For Reliability and Internal Bulletin information, check the Lincoln MKX review.

LINCOLN MKX   *2007-2017* ★★★
WITH TURBOCHARGED ECOBURST ENGINES ★★

RATING: Average (2007-2017); Below Average (with turbocharged EcoBoost). The MKX debuted for the 2007 model year; it's an upscale spinoff of the Edge with a plusher interior, a smoother ride, more soundproofing, and a slightly larger V6. The Lincoln benefits from the space efficiency of the Edge but adds a unique exterior and cabin with more luxury. Although the MKX offered the luxury accoutrements and high seating position that premium crossover buyers want, the original was too much like the cheaper Edge to justify the additional outlay. The second-generation cabin MKX went on sale as a 2016 model. Unlike its predecessor that shared a lot of exterior body panels and cabin elements with its Ford counterpart, the new MKX has a unique exterior and show-vehicle cabin design. The exterior, with flowing lines and more voluptuous surfacing, displays current Lincoln styling cues. The Lincoln is available with a 360-degree view camera, self-parking, self-braking, and an anti-collision feature. **Road performance:** Like the

Edge, the MKX now offers Ford's incredibly responsive 2.7L V6 EcoBoost turbo; its primary character flaw is an uninspiring, slightly gruff sound. The MKX is smoother and quieter than the Edge. Suspension compliance is superior to the Edge, but it's no magic carpet. **Strong points:** Luxurious and refined interior. Quiet. Prices not much higher than a well-equipped Edge on the used vehicle market. **Weak points:** Outward visibility is appalling. **Major Redesigns:** 2007 introduction, 2016 **Best alternatives:** Acura RDX, Buick Envision, Cadillac XT5, and Lexus RX 350.

Prices and Specs

Prices (2016): *AWD: Base:* $47,000, *Reserve:* $52,100 **Freight:** $1,900 (Lincoln). **Powertrains:** AWD 2.7L V6 EcoBoost (335 hp), V6; 3.7L V6 (Lincoln: 303 hp). Transmission: 6-speed auto. **Dimensions (Edge):** Passengers: 2/3; Wheelbase: 112 in., 2850 mm.; L: 190 in., 4826 mm.; W: 76 in., 1,928 mm.; Weight: 4,447 lb., 2017 kg. **Fuel economy:** *AWD 2.7 V6 turbo:* 9.7/14.1L/100 km. *3.7L V6:* 14.4/10.3L/100 km. **Assembled in:** Oakville, Ontario.

SAFETY

IIHS 2016

Small Front	Good
Front	Good
Side	Good
Roof strength	Good
Head restraint and seats	Good
Child seat anchors	Acceptable
NHTSA Overall 2017	★★★★★

Owner-reported safety-related failures: Fuel and exhaust fumes can leak into the interior through the air vents. Vehicle destroyed by fire while parked; car rolls away when parked on an incline; shuts down on the highway as dash control panel goes blank; sudden loss of brakes; faulty blind spot and cross-traffic sensors; often electronic keys are way too sensitive:

> The keys can be in a purse or backpack and the buttons can be pressed down. They are also easily pressed down if you have them in your pocket with another item. On multiple occasions we have walked out to our car and had the windows all down, the sun roof open and/or the tailgate up. We frequently will set off the alarm. One time it had started raining heavily and the windows had gotten rolled down. Consequently the interior of the car was soaked.

Edge, MKX

RELIABILITY: The normally-aspirated 3.5L V6 in the Edge, and the 3.7L V6 powering the MKX are the best bets for long-term durability. Check for oil leaks at the valve covers of the V6, oil leaks at the front and rear differentials, and rear shocks. Purchase of an extended warranty from Ford is recommended if you are considering a model with a turbocharged EcoBoost engine. Some automatic transmission failures (Reverse gear, Fifth and Sixth gear, and clutch); defective transmission power transfer unit (PTU) on all-wheel drives (commonly, Ford may contribute to the repair under a secret warranty); interior lights come on and shut off for no reason; radio can't be shut off; push-button starter takes several pushes to turn off the vehicle. *2007-2010 Edge:* The leading edge of the roof at the junction of the windshield, and lower body panels including the rocker rails, door bottoms and rear quarter panels are vulnerable to corrosion. If damage is not advanced, the APA recommends Krown Rust Control or Barry's Rustproofing in the Montreal market to protect the fragile rocker panels, rear fenders, and floor (contact information is in the Part Four Introduction).

Edge, MKX

INTERNAL BULLETINS, SECRET WARRANTIES: 2006-2011—*Ford Fusion, Lincoln Zephyr, and Lincoln MKZ:* The floor mats are secured by a single retention device, which could allow the driver's floor mat to move out of position and jam the accelerator pedal. Dealers will replace Ford all-weather floor mats with an updated design having two retention devices under a recall. 2007-10—Some Edge and MKX vehicles may exhibit a growl or howl type-noise coming from the left or right rear wheel area. Consider changing the hub assembly. 2009-11—Transmission and camera malfunctions may have a simple solution covered by the Emissions Warranty (see TSB in Flex *Internal Bulletins*). This bulletin also applies to the Lincoln MKS and MKX and the 2010-11 Lincoln MKT. 2010-13—Edge and Lincoln MKX brake booster warranty extension to 10 years/150,000 miles (Customer Satisfaction Program #13N02, Sept. 30, 2014). 2011—Some 2011 Edge Sport, Limited, and Lincoln MKX vehicles may exhibit a stress crack(s) in the front door window glass. Typical complaint is stress crack that originates from glass edge(s). Ford will replace the window during the warranty per TSB #12-1-5. 2011-13—Fluid leak from rear differential vent cap (2011-12 MKZ; 2011-13 MKT and MKX, and 2011-14 MKS). 2011-2013 Edge, MKX, 2013 Flex and MKT vehicles and 2013 Explorers may exhibit a door ajar warning light illuminated with all doors closed. Ford says new push pins will solve the problem. This is a major complaint of Ford owners who say the defect locks and unlocks the doors while the vehicle is in motion and costs $200+ dollars to fix. Ford should pay for this safety-related failure. Cite Ford TSB No. #14-0154, published Aug. 29, 2014. Intermittent power liftgate operation (Lincoln MKX). 2011-14—Edge and Lincoln MKX various infotainment upgrades. 2012-14—Edge and Lincoln MKX headliner sagging near roof opening panel. 2013—Exterior lights that flash on and off may need a new front lighting control module. 2014—Glass fogging, slow to clear with defroster. 2015—Transmission fluid leak from the converter housing area. Cabin may be assailed by a helicopter-like noise if the car is driven with the windows open. Front seat backrests may not cool sufficiently.

RATING: Above Average (2009-2017). Like its showroom mate the Explorer, the Flex three-row CUV is based on Volvo's old large car platform that was available to Ford when it owned Volvo. Available with either front-wheel drive or all-wheel drive, the Flex can seat six or seven people, depending on seating configuration. Power comes from a normally-aspirated 287 hp 3.5L V6 or a 365 hp turbocharged 3.5L EcoBoost V6. The sole transmission offered is a 6-speed automatic. *2010:* Turbo V6 becomes available. *2013:* A mid-cycle refresh includes a new front fascia, cabin revisions and optional new collision avoidance features, including radar cruise control and forward collision warning. *2016:* The Blackberry designed SYNC3 infotainment system, which mimics the successful Chrysler UConnect system, is introduced. **Road performance:** The standard V6 engine is smooth, quiet, and flexible. While the turbocharged V6 delivers prodigious power, engine failures have been reported. The 6-speed automatic transmission works well enough with either engine. The car handles confidently for a giant CUV, combining it with a smooth, quiet ride and precise, if numb, steering. **Strong points:** A large, well laid-out cabin with plenty of amenities. Compared to its Explorer platform mate, the Flex has more second-row legroom, and a more elegant, better finished cabin. Though not long from front to back, cargo space when the third-row seat is in place is very deep, allowing a surprising amount of luggage to be stacked there. **Weak points:** This is a large, heavy vehicle; fuel consumption is on the high side with both engines. **Major redesign:** *2007:* Introduction, *2013:* Mid-cycle refresh. **Best alternatives:** GM's Enclave, Acadia, Traverse trio, the Honda Pilot, Toyota Highlander, and Hyundai Santa Fe XL.

ALERT! The MyFord Touch infotainment feature needs to be part of your test drive.

Owner-reported safety-related failures: Airbags fail to deploy; sudden loss of power on the highway; vehicle goes forward when put into Reverse; liftgate glass shatters when it is closed; and brake failures when the car is parked on an incline:

> My 2014 Flex was parked on side of road, on an incline facing uphill, with engine running. Two adult passengers in vehicle. Without notice vehicle began rolling backwards. Passenger turned wheel in an attempt to stop vehicle on curb. Center console prevented passenger from being able to access vehicle brakes or parking brake. Vehicle ended up striking another vehicle before it came to rest. Luckily there were no injuries as hill ends in cul-de-sac with large drop off. I requested local Ford dealers inspect powertrain system as a car in park should not suddenly begin rolling. Two local dealers have refused to look at vehicle citing they do not want to get involved.

SAFETY	
IIHS	
Small Front	Acceptable
Front	Good
Side	Good
Roof strength	Good
Head restraint and seats	Good
Child seat anchors	Acceptable
NHTSA Overall	**Not Rated**

RELIABILITY: A surprisingly low number of owner complaints recorded since its introduction in 2009 as a replacement for the Ford Taurus X. It was rated the most reliable large sized CUV and Ford's most reliable vehicle by *Consumer Reports.* This positive reception by Ford owners is reinforced by NHTSA's *safercar.gov* website that shows few owner complaints from 2009 through the 2015 model year.

> The 'door ajar' switch is faulty on most Ford Flex and Edge models. While the door is completely shut, the door ajar light stays on resulting in the doors not locking. Even if you press the automatic lock they simply unlock. Ford is not willing to address the issue or fix the issue. The way the faulty part is built into the lock mechanism requires the owner to replace the entire lock mechanism. This part cost $230 and due to the number of failures was not available on the market currently. As a result of the safety issue, we were required to force the switch to ground itself out, meaning we grounded out the wires linked to the door ajar light so the light is no longer on and the doors were locked.
>
> *– safercar.gov*

INTERNAL BULLETINS, SECRET WARRANTIES: 2009—Water leaks from the rear of the roof opening panel. This may be more pronounced when parked with the front of the vehicle elevated. Likely cause is the headliner foam panels restricting the rear drain tubes for the roof opening panel. Some 2009 Taurus, Taurus X, Sable, Flex, and MKS vehicles equipped with an automatic transmission may have a moan or buzz type noise during upshifts. This may be due to the cooler lines grounding out on the vehicle body. **2009-10**—Owners of vehicles equipped with power folding second-row seats may find the seat not fully lifting and folding forward (tumble). The seat track riser assembly may need to be replaced. **2009-11**—Some 2009 Edge, MKX, and Flex vehicles built on or after May 4, 2009, 2010-2011 Edge, Flex, MKS, MKT, MKX, Taurus, and 2011 Explorer vehicles built on or before April 15, 2011, may have a sluggish acceleration or hesitation feel during a rolling stop 0-8 km/h (0-5 mph) followed by a harsh bump or slip on take-off from a stop followed by a harsh bump. Ford says you may need to change the valve body separator plate. Transmission and camera malfunctions may have a simple solution:

TRANSMISSION – SLIP/NEUTRAL OUT – 5TH GEAR START FROM STOP – BACKUP CAMERA ON IN DRIVE

SERVICE BULLETIN NO.: 13-5-27   DATE: 5/31/13

2009-2011 Taurus, Edge, Flex; LINCOLN: 2009-2011 MKS, MKX 2010-2011 and MKT.

ISSUE: Some 2009-2011 Edge, Taurus, Flex, MKS, MKX and 2010-2011 MKT vehicles equipped with a 6F50 or 6F55 transmissions and built on 3/13/2009 and through 6/30/2010 may intermittently exhibit one or more of the following concerns; transmission slipping or neutral-out, 5th gear start from stop, backup camera on in Drive, or speed control dropping out or inoperative. This may be due to high resistance in the digital transmission range (TR) sensor.

2009-13—A remedy for headliner scratching or rattling. **2010**—Some Taurus, Edge, Flex, Fusion, Milan, MKS, MKT, MKX, and MKZ vehicles equipped with all-wheel drive may exhibit a shudder/chatter/vibration driveline sensation during a tight turn, or a thump/clunk noise on light acceleration. These symptoms may also occur under 40 mph (64 km/h), when driving uphill, or towing under heavy acceleration. A faulty power transfer unit (PTU) may be the culprit, says Ford. **2010-14**—Some 2010-2014 Flex, MKS, MKT, and Taurus vehicles, and 2013-2014 Explorers equipped with a 3.5L Turbocharged engine with an aluminum valve cover may burn oil and/or produce excessive engine oil smoking from the tail pipe at idle during normal engine operating temperatures. Ford TSB #15-0086 published May 27, 2015, says the valve cover, crankcase vent oil separator, and upper manifold gasket may need replacing (see TSB in Explorer *Internal Bulletins*). **2011-13**—Fluid may leak from the rear differential vent cap. Some 2011-2013 Edge, MKX, 2013 Flex, and MKT vehicles and 2013 Explorers may exhibit a door ajar warning light illuminated with all doors closed. Ford says new push pins will solve the problem. This is a major complaint of Ford owners who say the defect locks and unlocks the doors while the vehicle is in motion and costs $200+ dollars to fix. Ford should pay for this safety-related failure. Cite Ford TSB No. #14-0154, published Aug. 29, 2014. *2013-14*—Vehicles equipped with a power liftgate that's inoperative, or produces a crunching noise, may have a faulty liftgate motor. A wind or whistle-type noise from the left and/or right A-pillar area at highway speeds in crosswind conditions may be due to the A-pillar window moulding not being fully seated.

EXPLORER ★★★
WITH TURBOCHARGED ENGINES ★★

RATING: Average; Below Average (with turbocharged engine). For 2006, Ford undertook a significant mid-cycle update of the old-school, body-on-frame Explorer that debuted for 2002. The 2006 model featured a revised chassis, a more powerful V8 hooked to a new 6-speed automatic transmission and a significantly improved interior. For 2011, an all-new unibody Explorer based on the same Volvo platform that underpins the Flex and Taurus brought the Explorer nameplate into the mainstream of the CUV market. *2016:* Late-cycle remake for Explorer. Updates included a new 2.3L turbo 4-cylinder that is compatible with all-wheel drive, minor exterior styling, and cabin trim updates. **Road performance:** Available with front-wheel drive and all-wheel drive. Starting from 2016, all-wheel drive is available with all models, including the 2.3L EcoBoost (the older 2.0L EcoBoost was limited to front-wheel drive). Downshifts can be slow and abrupt. **Strong points:** *2016-2017:* Average performance with the V6. The new 2.3L turbo 4-cylinder is quick, but sounds coarse and its durability is unproven. Like the related Flex and Taurus, the Explorer is pleasant to drive. **Weak points:** *2005-2010:* Cabin finish was rather grim, but improved considerably after 2011. *2016-2017:* Unimpressive middle-row legroom. The cabin is an adequate size, but it's not quite as roomy as what is offered by the Ford Flex, or GM's Traverse, Enclave, and Acadia trio. With the third-row seat up, the deep well at the rear of the cargo area allows a surprising amount of cargo to be stacked back there. **Best alternatives:** Ford Flex, GM's Traverse, Enclave, and (pre-2017) Acadia trio, Honda Pilot, Hyundai Santa Fe XL, and Toyota Highlander.

Prices and Specs

Prices (2017): *Base FWD 3.5L V6:* $33,999, Platinum AWD 3.5L V6: $59,599 **Freight:** $1,690 **Powertrain (FWD/AWD):** Engines: 2.3L 4-cyl. turbo (280 hp), 3.5L V6 (290 hp); 3.5L V6 turbo (365 hp); Transmission: 6-speed auto. **Dimensions:** Passengers: 2/2/2, 2/3/2; Wheelbase: 113 in., 2866 mm., L: 198, 5037 mm., W: 79 in., 2005 mm.; Weight (AWD V6): 4,633 lb., 2101 kg. **Fuel economy:** *2017 V6 AWD:* 14.8L 100 km city, 10.7L 100 km highway. **Assembled in:** United States.

294

SAFETY

IIHS

Small Front	Acceptable
Front	Good
Side	Good
Roof strength	Good
Head restraint and seats	Not Rated
Child seat anchors	Acceptable
NHTSA 2017	★★★★★

ALERT! Deadly carbon monoxide exhaust fumes can leak into the interior. NHTSA has received over 154 complaints of the toxic gas leaking into possibly 600,000 2011-16 Explorers' cabins, despite Ford sending two unsuccessful advisory "fixes" to dealers. Owners have never been told by Ford of the safety hazard, although many have told Ford:

> Burning exhaust smell entering into cabin of car when car is under hard acceleration/full throttle. Especially noticeable when accelerating onto a highway or climbing steep hills. This burning exhaust smell makes all passengers feel sick by affecting your respiratory passageways, leaving a lump in your throat, burning your eyes, giving you a headache,

and making you feel nauseous. The recent NHTSA investigation into 2011-2015 models should include 2016 models as well.

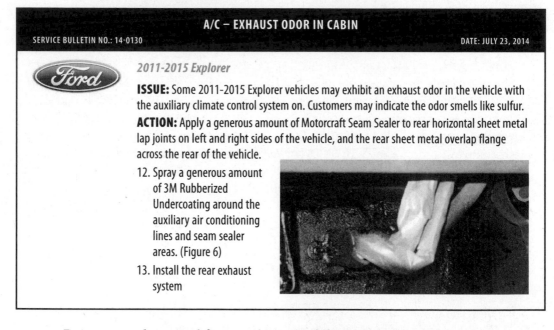

A/C – EXHAUST ODOR IN CABIN

SERVICE BULLETIN NO.: 14-0130   DATE: JULY 23, 2014

2011-2015 Explorer

ISSUE: Some 2011-2015 Explorer vehicles may exhibit an exhaust odor in the vehicle with the auxiliary climate control system on. Customers may indicate the odor smells like sulfur.

ACTION: Apply a generous amount of Motorcraft Seam Sealer to rear horizontal sheet metal lap joints on left and right sides of the vehicle, and the rear sheet metal overlap flange across the rear of the vehicle.

12. Spray a generous amount of 3M Rubberized Undercoating around the auxiliary air conditioning lines and seam sealer areas. (Figure 6)
13. Install the rear exhaust system

Driver says obstructed front and rear visibility is a deal breaker:

> I am going into the 5th month of leasing my 2015 Ford Explorer and I am not happy with this vehicle. Currently the odometer reads 2,100 miles and they were not enjoyable miles. I have to say that this 2015 Explorer has the worst design on the inside that I've ever seen. The outward visibility from the driver's seat for the front and rear of this vehicle is severely compromised by the huge C pillars which create blind spots within the vehicle.

The brake and accelerator pedals are mounted too close to each other; narrow, poorly cushioned seats lack sufficient thigh support; the small rear window cuts visibility; and the headlights don't light up enough of the road. Other criticisms: The head restraints are literally a pain in the neck and their close proximity can be dangerous if the airbags deploy; sunvisors are poorly designed; sudden power-steering failure; and worst of all, unintended acceleration accompanied by loss of brakes.

RELIABILITY: *2006-2010:* Some failures of the 5-speed automatic. *2009-2010:* Check the 4L V6 for coolant leaks; a noise from the front of the engine may indicate a defective crankshaft pulley. A vibration through the floor may indicate a worn driveshaft bearing. Front suspension ball joints and shocks wear quickly. Check the oil level in the rear differential and replace if it has not been serviced. Ford makes an additive that may quiet a noisy differential; if not a repair kit is available. Wheel bearings may be noisy. A lit ABS light is likely due to a malfunction at one of the sensors. Replace the power steering fluid if it is dirty or the pump is noisy. *2006-2014:* Poor corrosion resistance; rust-prone areas include the folded seams on the hood and hatchback, and the bottoms of the rear quarter panels. Pay special attention to aluminum hoods on 2011-2015 models to check for corrosion damage. If rust damage is not advanced the APA recommends Krown Rust Control or Barry's Rustproofing in the Montreal market to protect the fragile hood, tailgate, and rocker panels (contact information is in the Part Four Introduction). *2016-2017:* The most likely areas of concern for the redesigned Explorer are costly powertrain failures and vehicle electronics.

INTERNAL BULLETINS, SECRET WARRANTIES: 2011-12—There are a number of bulletins that address intermittent front brake squeal; a hard-to-open forward centre console storage bin door; interior rattle or buzz; and front bumper creaking. Troubleshooting power liftgate malfunctions. Countermeasures to silence a buzzing, howling, or rattle at higher vehicle speeds and/or cross winds coming from the windshield appliqués. 2011-13—Door ajar warning light comes on with all doors closed. Doors lock and unlock at any time and cost $200+ dollars to fix. Ford should pay for this safety-related failure. Cite Ford TSB No. #14-0154, published Aug. 29, 2014. If the front window glass jumps or chatters during up/down travel, replace the front window regulator motor. 2011-14—An inoperative all-wheel drive may be fixed simply by recalibrating the ABS module. Fixes for a host of infotainment failures are addressed in TSB #13-10-6 and TSB #12A04S4. 2011-15—Troubleshooting tips to get rid of an exhaust odour in the cabin with the auxiliary climate control system engaged (TSB #14-0130). Another TSB (#14-0118) shows an inexpensive way to free up the interior front console door when it sticks shut. 2012—Fixes for power liftgate malfunctions. 2013-14—Explorers powered by a 3.5L engine with an aluminum valve cover may burn oil and/or show engine oil smoking in the exhaust at idle during normal engine operating temperatures. TSB #15-0086, dated May 27, 2015, suggests changing the right-hand valve cover, upper intake manifold gasket, crankcase vent oil separator, valve cover, and PCV valve. Ford's admission of this defect makes the company responsible for its correction under an extended "goodwill" warranty.

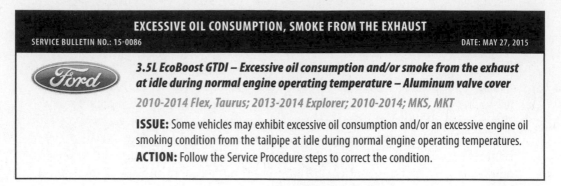

EXCESSIVE OIL CONSUMPTION, SMOKE FROM THE EXHAUST

SERVICE BULLETIN NO.: 15-0086   DATE: MAY 27, 2015

3.5L EcoBoost GTDI – Excessive oil consumption and/or smoke from the exhaust at idle during normal engine operating temperature – Aluminum valve cover

2010-2014 Flex, Taurus; 2013-2014 Explorer; 2010-2014; MKS, MKT

ISSUE: Some vehicles may exhibit excessive oil consumption and/or an excessive engine oil smoking condition from the tailpipe at idle during normal engine operating temperatures.

ACTION: Follow the Service Procedure steps to correct the condition.

Power transfer unit (PTU) fluid leaking is likely due to a missing or disconnected PTU vent hose. No audio output on startup during cold ambient temperatures or when abnormally low battery voltage levels are present. Take 20 minutes to reprogram the audio control module (ACM) to correct this problem. **2014**—A raw fuel odour that is most noticeable near the intake manifold can be eliminated by replacing the high-pressure fuel tube. **2016**—Front seat backrests may not cool sufficiently.

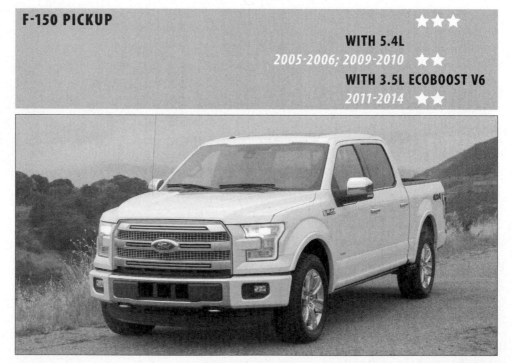

F-150 PICKUP   ★★★

WITH 5.4L
2005-2006; 2009-2010 ★★

WITH 3.5L ECOBOOST V6
2011-2014 ★★

2015 Ford F-150 with 3.5L Ecoboost

RATING: Average; Below Average (2011-14 with 3.5L EcoBoost V6); Below Average (2005-2006 and 2009-2010 with 5.4L V8). The F-150 is a perennial sales champ but the vehicle itself no longer outclasses the other domestic pickups, despite Ford's use of more advanced technology in the redesigned 2015-17 models. The F-150 still retains the pickup truck sales crown, although GM's two nameplates now sell almost as many vehicles combined as the F-150, and the Ram pickup is not far behind in Canada. Commercial customers appreciate the widely available parts and service for the F-150, that carry the promise of low downtime while waiting for repairs. And fleet customers have the option of propane and compressed natural gas with the 5.0L V8 engine. For the 2015 model year, Ford bet the farm with an all-aluminum bodied pickup; meant to be more fuel efficient, it was released at a time when fuel prices were at historic lows. It features an infotainment system that's more user-friendly and responsive, and excellent body assembly quality. **Road performance:** Ford offers four engines, two of them turbos marketed under the EcoBoost name. The standard, normally-aspirated 3.5L V6 delivers adequate power for light duty work but you will lose any purchase savings upon resale. The 5L V8 is smooth and flexible, and will suit the needs of the majority of users, but Ford is phasing it out. Two V6 turbos are offered, a 2.7L V6 with relentless energy, and a 3.5L V6 turbo that is stronger still. Long-term durability of the new 2.7L turbo is unknown, but the 3.5L V6 turbo, which arrived earlier, has been troublesome through the 2014 model year. Forget about the published fuel consumption ratings; the APA concluded that real-world consumption with the 3.5 EcoBoost V6 is comparable to the V8, and that neither is class leading. Ford has settled class-action lawsuits over false fuel economy claims and, more recently, false truck payload ratings. Towing will require either of the turbocharged V6s or the V8. *2015-2017:* The new aluminum F-150's suspension seems to have been calibrated by the same team that used to set up Detroit's 1970 luxo-barges. With just the driver on board, the truck has a soft ride and reasonably stable cornering, but adding a full complement of passengers and some cargo in the bed of a Crew Cab causes the truck to wallow on curves and hit its bump stops on large dips. In the APA's trailering comparison test, the 2016 F-150's soft suspension put it at a disadvantage compared to the Ram and Silverado/Sierra for hauling. **Strong points:** The best availability of any used pickup on the market over the widest range of price points. Expect to pay about $3,000 more for a used 2012 Double Cab, up to $5,000 more for a Crew Cab. Add $3,000 more for 4WD. Although it once commanded a large premium, prices for the 3.5L turbo V6 are now in the range of the V8. A nice array of powertrain combinations, lots of comfort and convenience features, good cabin space, and comfortable seats. **Weak points:** Cabin finish in recent years takes a back seat to Chrysler and even GM. Prior to 2015: An inconvenient and unreliable infotainment system (pre-SYNC3). **Major redesign:** 2004, 2009, 2011 partial redesign, and 2015 all-new aluminum body on a steel chassis. **Other opinions:** "GM dropped 825 pounds of concrete landscaping blocks from a height of five feet into the bare pickup beds of a Chevy Silverado and a Ford F-150.

The steel bed of the Silverado was scratched and dented, but the Ford aluminum bed sustained multiple punctures."–*forbes.com/sites/joannmuller*. **Best alternatives:** GM's Silverado and Sierra twins, the RAM pickup and the Toyota Tundra. GM's duo offer a reliable V8. The RAM has a richer interior and recent model years have one of the best infotainment systems around (Uconnect). Toyota's Tundra has a few rough edges but is durable.

Prices and Specs

Prices (2016): *F-150 XL Regular cab, 6.5 foot box, 3.5L, RWD: $25,799, F-150 Limited Crewcab, 5.5 foot box, 3.5L V6 turbo, 4WD: $75,999* **Freight:** $1,600 **Powertrain (Rear-drive/Part-time 4x4/AWD):** Engines: (2016): 2.7L V6 (325 hp), 3.5L V6 (282 hp), 3.5L turbocharged V6 (365 hp), and a 5.0L V8 (385 hp), Transmission (2016): 6-speed auto. **Dimensions (2016 Regular cab):** Wheelbase (6.5 foot box): 122.4 in., 3,109 mm, (8 foot box) 141.1 in., 3,584 mm.; L (6.5 foot box): 209.3 in., 5,316 mm., (8 foot box), 227.9 in., 5,787 mm.; W: 79.9 in., 2,029.; Wheelbase (Super cab 6.5 foot box): 145 in., 3,683 mm., (8 foot box), 163.7 in., 4,158 mm.; L (6.5 foot box): 231.9 in., 5,890 mm., (8 foot box), 250.5 in., 6,363 mm. Wheelbase (SuperCrew 5.5 foot box): 145 in., 3,683 mm., (6.5 foot box), 156.8 in., 3,983 mm. Weight: 4,486 lb., 2,036 kg (3.5L Regular cab, 5.5 foot box, RWD), 4,936 lb., 2,239 kg (3.5L turbo SuperCrew, 6.5 foot box, 4WD). **Fuel economy:** *3.5L V6 RWD: 9.8/13.5 L/100 km. 2.7L V6 turbo 4WD: 10.1/13.1L/100 km; 5L V8 4WD: 11.3L/16L/100 km.* **Assembled in:** United States.

SAFETY

IIHS 2016 SUPERCREW

Small Front	Good
Front	Good
Side	Good
Roof strength	Good
Head restraint and seats	Good
Child seat anchors	Moderate
NHTSA Overall 2017	★★★★★

ALERT! Headrests on some model years are uncomfortable and a potential hazard: Headrest forces driver's chin into the chest. Dealer stated that this is the new safety design. Headrests are non-adjustable. Also, they are very wide and, in conjunction with the frame post at the rear of the doors, create a blind spot on both sides of the pickup. Test-drive the head restraints before you spend $40,000 on a truck that's a pain in the … neck. Seat headrest protrudes too much out of the seat and it pushes forward head of some drivers. The only adjustments available (slide up and down, tilt top forward) do nothing to alleviate the issue. The lack of ability to "scoot" the entire headrest backwards causes back and neck pain while driving for as little as 10 minutes. One solution people are resorting to is to re-insert the headrest backwards, but (reversing) prevents the head from being stopped in the event of an accident. Another solution is to recline the seat back so much that your back is no longer supported.

Owner-reported safety-related failures: Ford's new EcoBoost engines have been heralded as providing plenty of turbo power and using less fuel than previous engines. This is half true (they are powerful but they guzzle fuel), but the 2011-2014 engines have a nasty habit of losing power when most needed and then lurching forward. Hundreds of owners have reported this behaviour:

> While taking off from T-intersection and turning left crossing oncoming traffic the truck started to take off then lost all power for approximately 3-5 seconds. This left my family and I sitting in the oncoming traffic lane on a blind corner. The truck did not die (I thought it did), I mashed the accelerator to the floor and the truck did not respond whatsoever. My wife was screaming frantically at me asking what I was doing while I attempted to get the truck to move out of the oncoming lane. After approximately 5 seconds the truck regained power and accelerated normally. This has occurred 3X now and I am afraid to drive the truck but do and my wife will not drive it at all.
>
> — *www.blueovalforums.com/forums/index.php?/topic/49606-f-150-ecoboost-shutter*

The owner of a 2014 F-150 describes his experience this way:

> As I accelerate, the truck seems to go into neutral for about three seconds. Then it re-engages and jerks violently. I have taken the truck to the dealership twice. The first time, they reprogrammed it but didn't repair the issue. This last time, the technician told me to pick up my truck because they couldn't recreate the issue I was experiencing. Another technician stated it was the EcoBoost but that Ford was side stepping the issue because they couldn't find how to fix it.

Aluminum Panels

The aluminum-clad 2015-2017 F-150 performed impressively in crash tests. Although crash safety doesn't seem to be a problem, accident repairs could be. Aluminum is harder to work with, and collision repairs can be expensive. F-150 panels are colour-coded, which can be confusing to an inexperienced bodyman; the rivets used to hold the panels together aren't all the same size, which requires extra time for rivet gun changes. (*https://www.youtube.com/watch?v=nulijDlH1Pl*).

The Insurance Institute for Highway Safety crashed a 2014 and 2015 F-150 (picture below) into each other at low speeds to simulate offset rear-ender accidents. More damage was sustained by the aluminum-bodied truck in all the tests. Repair costs for the aluminum truck were 42% higher for parts and 22% higher for labor, the IIHS said. In addition, one side of the aluminum truck's bed had to be replaced.

Source: IIHS

Other F-150 complaints: Sticking cruise control; unintended acceleration; and when parked on a down slope the truck won't start even though almost a quarter of a tank of gas remains. The front windshield and windows may crack for no apparent reason; if there is no evidence of an object hitting the windshield, Ford should accept your warranty claim:

> I was parked in my driveway when a section of the rear window exploded. The vehicle was warming up (auto start) for about 5 minutes before my daughter and I got in to leave when we heard a loud pop. I looked back and noticed the rear driver side window was shattered. There were little pieces of glass throughout the back of the vehicle and landed on my daughter's hair and clothes. The vehicle is a 2015 4x4 SuperCrew cab with the sliding 3 piece rear window.

Chronic stalling can be traced to defective throttle body and other components:

> My 2016 F-150 has less than 9000 miles. While traveling on highway, it suddenly lost acceleration and began to shudder. No response when pressing gas pedal. Vehicle dash warnings for descent assistance and collision avoidance appeared. The issue occurred on 4 other occasions including stalling in a busy intersection shortly after accelerating from a stop. Each time restarting the car results in shuddering and error messages on the dash. Dealership says it's a known issue and parts will take up to 3 weeks, plus repair time.

When reading the complaint below, look up Ford's confidential bulletin under Internal Bulletins, Secret Warranties, below, that confirms this dangerous defect:

> My 2016 F-150 Platinum with adaptive cruise control, runs up behind vehicles on occasions then brakes hard. If the other vehicle is a semi, as you attempt to pass it with adaptive cruise on, the pickup brakes hard and slows down… on at least one occasion I was almost rear ended by a semi that was coming up behind me when the brakes applied themselves.

Braking goes from "iffy" to "scary." Transport Canada recently issued an advisory asking for reports from the public to influence Ford to take some action on 2011-2012 that experience delayed power assist when braking *www.tc.gc.ca/eng/motorvehiclesafety/safevehicles-1478.html*:

> 2016 King Ranch Ford F-150 brakes recurrently fail. No accident but they currently have greatly reduced stopping power, super dangerous. Ford reports long backorder 3+weeks on master cylinder, makes me wonder if there is larger issue.

Headlights also may not be too your liking:

> 2014 F-150: When the vehicle is driven down a grade you lose all vision to the upcoming grade. Please, have someone drive one of these trucks at night in the hills.

RELIABILITY: *2005-2014:* The most reliable engines are the 3.7L V6 and 5L V8 shared with the Mustang. A lit engine service light could indicate a misfire resulting from defective spark plugs or ignition coils. If it is allowed to persist, further damage is possible to the engine and catalytic convertor. Ford stumbled badly in 2011-2014, with the introduction of the 3.5L EcoBoost V6 in the F-150. The same years also saw expensive failures of the 5.4L V8 related to the timing chain and variable cam timing; the APA recommends using synthetic oil exclusively with this engine, which may provide a better margin of safety for its marginal internal lubrication. An exhaust manifold may crack at high mileage (over 140,000 km) on the 5.4L. Other complaints include some reports of hard gear shifts with the 5.4L engine, and transmission failures. The Internet is full of F-series owners pointing out powertrain, steering, electronic module, and infotainment defects, all confirmed by confidential service bulletins, *safercar.gov*, NHTSA-posted owner complaints, and multi-million-dollar out-of-court settlements. Before you buy, check the oil pan (leaks), front suspension, including ball joints (wear), steering tie rod ends (wear), rear differential (noisy), and look for a driveshaft vibration that could be caused by a worn U-joint. *2015-2017:* Long-term durability of the aluminum redesign remains to be determined. Questions remain as to galvanic corrosion of the aluminum body, poor paint adhesion, more limited collision repair options, inexperienced repairers, repair delays, higher costs, and, perhaps eventually, increased insurance premiums. The current aluminum truck is now in its third year of production and a variety of initial bugs have been worked out. This is important, because the F-series pickups have periodically disappointed owners in the first year or two after major changes since the mid-80s.

INTERNAL BULLETINS, SECRET WARRANTIES: 2008-10—A service kit will assist in repairing the 4R75E transmission in 2008-10 F-150, E-Series, 2008-211 Crown Victoria, Grand Marquis, and Town Car vehicles that exhibit a grinding, whine-type noise, vibration and/or gear slippage while driving or a loss of Reverse resulting from a planetary gear assembly failure. *2009-2010:* Door latch could open in a collision; modify or replace door handle assembly under recall. 2009-11—F-150, 250, 350, and F-Super Duty vehicles equipped with a 4.6L 3V or 5.4L 3V engine may emit a low frequency engine knocking noise at hot idle. 6R80 transmission bulkhead connector sleeve leaking fluid. Install a seal kit. Shudder, vibration on moderate acceleration. Before springing for costly repairs, simply ask mechanic to adjust the rear axle pinion angle. Water stains the rear portion of the headliner due to the high mounted stop lamp assembly leaking water. Water leak at satellite antenna. Remedies for SYNC phone problems affecting most of Ford's lineup. The foam seal detaches between the instrument panel and the windshield glass (covered under a "goodwill" extended warranty on a case-by-case basis, but likely a winner in small claims court). Headline droops, sags at rear of roof opening panel. 2009-12—Trucks equipped with a 9.75 in Traction-Lok rear differential assembly may produce a shudder, chatter, and/or vibration during slow, tight turns. This concern may be more noticeable after cold start-up and less noticeable once the rear axle fluid warms up. Ford has a clutch pack replacement kit to fix the problem. Excessive vibration, a thump, or clunk noise from under the vehicle can be corrected by replacing the driveshaft assembly. Trucks equipped with a 2-piece driveshaft may exhibit a rear driveshaft slip/bump on light to moderate acceleration from a stop or when coming to a stop with light braking. Remedy: Replace the slip yoke. If the gear selector lever takes excessive effort to shift in cold weather, snow may have built up around the shift cable and lever. A snow shield kit will alleviate this problem. **2010-13**—Repair tips for a water leak at the rear glass sliding center panel. **2011**—Trucks equipped with a 6R80 automatic transmission may have transmission fluid leaking from the bell housing area. Install a pump kit. A harsh 1-2 shift at or below 24 km/h (15 mph), harsh downshifts, and/or a flare on upshifts can all be corrected by recalibrating the PCM module. **2011-12**—Vehicles equipped with a 3.5L gasoline turbocharged direct injection (GTDI) EcoBoost engine may exhibit an intermittent engine surge during moderate to light loads at cruise, stumble, and/or misfire on hard acceleration after an extended drive at highway speeds during humid or damp conditions. This could result in a steady or flashing malfunction indicator lamp (MIL). **2011-13**—Vehicles equipped with a 6R80 transmission may exhibit a transmission engagement in higher (Fifth) gear when starting. The wrench indictor and/or the seat belt minder may be illuminated, the speedometer reads zero and the odometer displays flashes while driving. Symptoms may clear after an ignition key cycle. Replace the moulded lead frame on the main control assembly to fix the problem. Engine misfiring on trucks equipped with a 3.5L turbo engine may need new spark plugs and coil boots. F-150s equipped with a turbocharged 3.5L engine that buck/jerk with the transmission in Sixth gear and experience engine lugging up grades at 1500-2000 RPM may simply need a PCM recalibration. **2011-14**—Vehicles may have a delayed Park to Forward or Reverse transmission engagement on start-up after parking several hours or overnight. Ford suggests replacing the transmission pump assembly – a six-hour repair. A refusal by Ford to pass this repair under warranty should prompt owners to file a claim in small claims court. Use TSB #14-0076 as proof of the company's responsibility. Trucks equipped with a 3.5L turbo engine may exhibit a hard start or no start condition after using the block heater when temperatures are below -15°C (0°F). Ford suggests installing an immersion block heater kit. An intermittent click or snap from the rear axle on initial light acceleration from a stop while in Drive or Reverse may occur on light acceleration after changing direction from Drive to Reverse, or Reverse to Drive. Ford suggests changing the rear pinion seal. If there is a delayed engagement when shifting between Park and Reverse, the transmission pump assembly may be defective.

2011-2014 Expedition, F-150, Mustang; LINCOLN: 2011-2014 Navigator.

ISSUE: Some 2011-2014 Expedition, Mustang, F-150 and Navigator vehicles may exhibit a delayed park to forward or reverse transmission engagement only on initial vehicle start up after parking several hours or overnight. The vehicle functions normally after the initial engagement has completed.

ACTION: It may be necessary to replace the transmission pump assembly.

Fixes for a host of infotainment failures are addressed in TSB #13-10-6, dated Oct. 4, 2013, and TSB #12A04S4. 2011-15—Some 2011-2015 F-150 and 2015 Expedition, Navigator, and Transit vehicles equipped with a 3.5L gasoline turbo-charged direct injected (GTDI) engine may exhibit diagnostic trouble codes and/or drivability symptoms, that may include surging or noises that may be described as an air rush, hiss, whoosh, whistle, grinding, growling or scraping. Tapping, ticking, or rattling from engine's top front cover area when starting up. 2012-13—Repair tips for headliner sagging along the windshield or rear window glass. 2013-14—Vehicles may make a growl or buzz noise coming from the transmission that occurs when shifting from Park to Drive or Park to Reverse most often after the vehicle has been parked and then restarted. Ford says the main control valve body separator plate may need to be replaced under warranty. No audio output on start-up during cold ambient temperatures or when abnormally low battery voltage levels are present. Take 20 minutes to reprogram the audio control module (ACM) to correct this problem. 2013-15—Remedy for 3.5L GTDI popping sound heard on start-up. 2014—Trucks equipped with a 3.7L engine may leak coolant at the rear of the engine at the heater hose. 2015—Troubleshooting, intake valve, throttle body, and air leaks as a cause of repeated on-road stalling; fix for cruise control module to prevent activation of forward collision warning with adaptive cruise control on, leading to reduction of speed when going under bridges or when passing semitrailers. (WHAT??) Yes, the pickup suddenly brakes under bridges, or when passing or being passed by other trucks. (YIKES!) 5.0L dual overhead camshaft engine coolant leak caused by a disconnected heater outlet hose; harsh 5-4 downshifts when coasting; inoperative or frozen door latches on the Super Cab; install a new door lower latch assembly or latch cable; stuck webbing in seat belt retractor; windows may not work in freezing temperatures; doors are hard to close, produce excessive isolated wind noise coming from door panel margins, driving at highway speed with an open window will produce a deafening, helicopter-type noise in the cabin, fit/flushness gaps; A-pillar and front windshield water leaks; steering wheel doesn't heat; seat backrests don't cool; improved tailgate step adjustment procedure; and replacement for a warped accessory tailgate liner.

General Motors

GM's Shaky SUVs

> Some full-size SUV owners are getting sick, thanks to a buffeting and vibration problem in 2015 model year examples of the Chevy Tahoe and Suburban, Cadillac Escalade, and GMC Yukon. According to owners' complaints to the National Highway Traffic Safety Administration, the issue can vary from an annoying vibration inside the cabin to an experience so severe that it leads to dizziness and headaches.
>
> *— autoblog.com/2015/12/30/fullsize-gm-suvs-making-owners-sick-report/*

The 2017 model year finds GM with the strongest new vehicle lineup of the Detroit Three. The Buick, Chevrolet, and GMC divisions have completed a major upgrade of their hybrid, electric car, and SUV offerings. The Volt plug-in hybrid was recently reworked, along with re-engineered Malibu and Cruze sedans, a new Cruze hatchback, an improved Camaro, and a Buick Envision crossover from China. The conservative Silverado and Sierra pickups have generated fewer complaints than the competing Ram and Ford pickups since their 2014 redesign.

GM's profits are healthy. The automaker had an exceptional 2016 second quarter with earnings that rose 11% to $42.37 billion, a record for any quarter since the automaker was bailed out of bankruptcy in July 2009. Profits increased in North America, Europe, and China as a result of improved cars, trucks, and most SUVs, with the company relying less on cut-rate fleet sales, and concentrating, instead, on higher-margin pickup truck and SUV retail sales. To keep sales strong through 2016-2017, GM will likely continue to offer discounts up to $10,000 on its Silverado/Sierra trucks. Sales aren't so rosy with GM's hybrids, electric vehicles, and luxury brands.

Cadillac

Like Ford's Lincoln division, Cadillac has a sombre future. Cadillac sales fell in North America last year at a time when sales of other luxury brands were booming. GM is playing catch-up to get decent luxury car sales as German automakers led by Audi, BMW, and Mercedes Benz run away with the market. Hyundai is also making inroads with its Genesis sedan, a more reliable and better-performing competitor that's a bit cheaper than the similarly-equipped $49,505 Cadillac CTS sedan. GM should drop or shrink the Cadillac division and use the savings to beef up its product line, and merge GMC into Chevrolet to save on marketing and distribution costs.

Cadillac dealers currently rely on the giant Escalade SUV to make their targets. Their only standout, it is really just a luxury version of the Yukon/Tahoe SUV. GM needs to trim sticker prices on its CTS and other models, and successfully launch its 2017 XT5 crossover. Among the brand's recent blunders was its wildly overpriced $82,000 Cadillac ELR plug-in hybrid. GM officials say the high price was meant to give the car a cachet of exclusivity, but it ended up driving customers away. Customers figured, "Why pay an extra $45,000 for a Cadillac with the drivetrain and chassis of the Chevrolet Volt?"

Quality: Promise vs. Performance

Generally, all-new and redesigned vehicles or those with the latest electronic gadgets tend to have more problems than carry-over models that undergo fewer design, engineering, and equipment changes. This is not the case, however, with the Impala and Silverado/Sierra pickups – three vehicles reworked as 2014 models that have proven to be better performers and more reliable than previous iterations.

The Chevrolet Impala was voted "best sedan tested" by *Consumer Reports* after it was redesigned in 2014, and is riding high, along with GM's pickups. It was recently joined by the redesigned 2016 Malibu, which is also significantly better than the outgoing model.

GM quality has definitely improved with other models, as well – not across the board, but in key areas like fit and finish, fuel economy, and infotainment features. Nevertheless, General Motors still lags behind the better Asian carmakers when it comes to long-term reliability, a five-decade-old problem shared with Ford and Fiat Chrysler. Now, all three automakers say those bad old days are gone and that the 2017 models will have first-class engines, transmissions, and fuel delivery systems.

Don't believe it!

GM still has some serious engine, electrical, emissions, and fuel system shortcomings that afflict its 2010-16 models; the company has responded to cover repair costs for some of the premature failures, as can be seen in the service bulletins, below.

ENGINE CYLINDER HEAD GASKET LEAK

CUSTOMER SATISFACTION CAMPAIGN #15638   DATE: OCT. 14, 2015

2015-2016 Escalade ESV; 2016 Cadillac Escalade; 2015 Silverado LD; 2016 Corvette; 2015 Sierra LD, Yukon Denali XL; and 2016 GMC Yukon Denali equipped with a 6.2L V8 engine

*****THIS PROGRAM IS IN EFFECT UNTIL NOVEMBER 30, 2017.*****

CONDITION: Some of the above-noted 2016 models may have engines built with cylinder head gaskets in which the head gasket stopper ring was off location. The gasket may fatigue over time leading to the possibility of a leak into the combustion chamber. Possible symptoms include: a check engine light for P0300 Misfire, possible combustion gas leaks to coolant resulting in overheating, over-flowed coolant bottle, milky-colored engine oil in the crankcase, piston scuffing and if the vehicle is continued to be driven in this condition, engine failure.

CORRECTION: Replace the left and right side engine head gasket.

2012-2013 Buick Enclave, LaCrosse; 2012-2013 Cadillac CTS, SRX; 2013 Cadillac ATS, XTS; 2012-2013 Chevrolet Camaro, Captiva, Equinox, Impala, Traverse; 2012-2013 GMC Acadia, Terrain. All Equipped with 6 CYL, 3.0L or 6 CYL, 3.6L.

CONDITION: Some customers may comment on an engine oil leak under their vehicle. Upon inspection, the Service Technician may observe an engine oil leak between the engine and transmission mounting surfaces.

CAUSE: This may be caused by the crankshaft # 3 thrust bearing wing separating from the thrust bearing, resulting in excessive crankshaft end play and damaging the crankshaft rear oil seal and housing.

This is a warrantable item inasmuch as this oil leak has more to do with mechanical failure than owner maintenance. Stand your ground.

GMC and Chevrolet continue to offer a high-mileage powertrain warranty for 5 years/160,000 km, and 2 years of no-charge scheduled oil changes in Canada. The base warranty is for 3 years/60,000 km, whichever comes first. Buick and Cadillac offer a 6 years/110,000 km powertrain warranty and a base warranty of 4 years/ 80,000 km. Furthermore, GM has softened its consumer-hostile attitude as of late (multi-million dollar fines help). Recently, when GM makes a major screw-up it is quicker to set things right by extending its warranty coverage or issuing a recall.

One recent example is the 2015 OnStar system that drained the battery when a vehicle was parked for four days or more. After learning of this problem, GM quickly sent out an owners' letter announcing that it would replace the OnStar® module free of charge until November 30, 2017. But, GM hasn't suddenly become "Generous Motors." The company recently tried to duck payment for replacing defective ignition switches on recalled vehicles built prior to its 2009 bankruptcy and got tossed out of court.

Hidden Warranties

All car companies occasionally make "lemons" and cars with safety defects – GM just builds more of them, and has been getting caught more frequently lately. GM just kicked its hypocrisy index up a notch with two secret warranty programs that should have been recalls.

The first "goodwill" program will replace ignition keys on trucks so the shift lever doesn't bump the key and shut off the engine. General Motors maintains this is not a safety defect because it occurs only when the driver has a foot on the brake and is shifting gears. GM issued a technical service bulletin (TSB) to dealers, instructing them to replace keys for customers who complain. The bulletin covers 2014-15 Silverado/Sierra 1500 pickups, and 2015 Suburban/Tahoe/Yukon/ Yukon XL SUVs. Trucks with keyless start buttons aren't covered by the bulletin.

The second secret warranty that should have been a recall is GM's warranty extension for the intermittent loss of power steering in large crossover models. In TSB #14329 issued on September 16, 2014, GM said that wear in the power steering pump might cause the problem in the 2008-11 Buick Enclave, 2009-11 Chevrolet Traverse, 2007-11 GMC Acadia, and 2007-10 Saturn Outlook. The pumps are now covered for ten years or 150,000 miles – a warranty extension unknown to many affected owners.

Quality

Since emerging from bankruptcy in 2009, most of GM's trucks, SUVs, and full-sized vans are better built than equivalent models made by Fiat Chrysler and Ford. However, suppliers said that GM's focus on cutting costs is what's compromising quality and safety and it's not limited to the Detroit Three (*insights.globalspec.com/article/165/global-study-on-automaker-supplier-relations*):

> For most volume carmakers, including VW, Fiat Chrysler, Ford, General Motors and Renault, cost pressures on the supply base are increasingly overriding the quality performance demanded of their suppliers.

What's particularly ironic about the "bean counter" culture at GM is that cheapening the product has turned out to be much more costly in the long run, due to recalls, lawsuits, and lost market share. The company's initial refusal to change its lethal ignition switches saved 90 cents (US) per vehicle, but cost GM several billion dollars with recall expenses and victim compensation.

GM Advertising

According to the Automobile Protection Association (APA), GM's new car advertising is better than the industry average, though still nothing to write home about. General Motors dealers were more likely to have their advertised vehicles in stock, and GM ads are more likely to feature reasonably-equipped models you might actually want to own, except for ads featuring base models of the Sonic and Trax with manual transmissions and no air conditioning. Like other brands, GM dealers add a little extra money for themselves to advertised weekly payments. Because there are so many payments when you pay weekly (364 payments over a seven-year loan, 260 payments with a five-year lease), even a small bump of say $3 or $4 a payment amounts to an increase of hundreds of dollars over the life of the loan.

The advertised Trax is a base model with a manual transmission and no air conditioning. The weekly payment of $58 with taxes works out to more than $1,200 above the advertised payment over the term of the loan.

2014 CHEVROLET TRAX AWD

- BLUETOOTH/ONSTAR
- 1.4L TURBO CHARGED ENGINE
- 6 SPD TRANSMISSION
- FULL POWER OPTIONS
- ALL WHEEL DRIVE URBAN UTILITY
- 24 TO CHOOSE FROM

AUTO 4 LIFE

NOW EVERY NEW VEHICLE SOLD BY SHAGANAPPI COMES WITH A 10 YEAR/160,000 KMS WARRANTY AT NO EXTRA CHARGE!

INCLUDES CHEVROLET COMPLETE CARE:

- COMPLIMENTARY OIL CHANGES — 2YR/40,000 KM†
- NEW VEHICLE LIMITED WARRANTY — 3YR/60,000 KM†
- POWERTRAIN WARRANTY — 5YR/160,000 KM‡
- ROADSIDE ASSISTANCE — 5YR/160,000 KM‡
- ONSTAR* — 6 MONTHS**

2014 CHEVROLET TRAX AWD

MSRP	$28,140
SALE PRICE	$25,680
FINANCING FOR	0% 84 MTHS
DOWN PAYMENT	$0

INCLUDES LOYALTY DISCOUNT OF $750*

$152 bw/84mo

The dealership has five vehicles that correspond to the Trax advertised in that day's newspaper in a selection of colours conveniently displayed right next to the showroom. Important information about the 10 year powertrain warranty is missing: it's conditional on all service being performed on schedule at the dealership (the ad doesn't say that.)

2013-2015	★
2016-2017	★★★
SPARK EV	NOT RATED

bad bu

RATING: Not Recommended (2013-15); Average (2016-2017); *Spark EV:* Not rated. A front-drive, four-door hatchback, the Spark is smaller than Chevy's previous smallest car, the Aveo subcompact. Like the Aveo, it's built by GM Korea (formerly Daewoo). The first-generation car was offered from 2013-2015. The original Spark was more whimsical looking than the current car, but slower and much noisier. The interior was surprisingly roomy for such a small car. A redesigned Spark with 17% more horsepower and a low entry-level price arrived for 2016. Once you accept the fact that this is a basic, tiny, four-passenger econocar you won't be disappointed with the redesigned 2016-2017 model. **Road performance:** *2013-2015:* The 1.2L 4-cylinder produces insufficient power and either howls or drones with the CVT automatic. The ride is rough, and there is lots of road and wind noise. The interior is surprisingly roomy, with some attractive avant-garde touches. Reasonable trunk space for such a small car. The 2016-2017 Spark introduced clear, conventional gauges, a large touch screen, and straightforward minor controls. Attractive fabrics and other cabin trim, especially for the price. The front seats are a bit on the small side, but they are acceptably padded and supportive. The rear seat is roomier than expected for such a small car. Trunk space is tall, regularly shaped but volume is modest; a spare is provided, which is no longer the case with several entry-level cars. The base car is equipped with Android Auto/Apple CarPlay. The 1.4L 4-cylinder is smooth, flexible and surprisingly zingy. While the clutch engagement point is a bit high, the clutch is light and easy to modulate. Overall gearing is a bit on the high side, which permits low-rev cruising but does require a downshift, even for modest hills. The steering is quick and nicely weighted. The brakes perform well but could offer more initial bite. The car leans a bit when cornering but handling is sound and is allied to a surprisingly supple ride for a car with such a short wheelbase. Driven briefly, the 2LT model was equipped with a CVT that works unobtrusively and kept revs low while cruising at highway speeds. Wind noise and road noise were much lower in the new Spark than its predecessor, but tire noise is noticeable. A rearview camera is standard on all models with Lane Departure and Forward Collision warnings standard on the 2LT model. The Spark EV was fleet-only until 2016, when sales to individuals commenced; sales have been negligible. It is one of the few lower-priced, battery-electric vehicles to offer DC quick charging as well as conventional 240-Volt charging. In a practical sense, this means 80% of the battery can be charged in under half an hour. **Strong points:** *2016-2017:* The car's low price is quite reasonable with the base model but can get pricey when better equipped. Big, clear LCD screen and easy access to the media and climate controls. Best-in-class MyLink infotainment unit is standard and offers convenient smartphone connectivity. **Weak points:** *2017:* The $9,995 base model lacks air-conditioning or a power group, even as options. A well-equipped new Spark costs almost as much as larger, more competent cars. *2013-2015:* A mediocre car, with unimpressive fuel economy; long-term reliability is a question mark. **Major redesign:** Gas models: 2013 first year, 2016. *2017:* The Spark EV will be replaced by the much better performing and roomier Bolt EV. That car will have a range rating of about 300 kilometres, and a price not much higher than the Spark EV. **Best alternatives:** Nissan Micra. A new Hyundai Accent or Kia Rio has a stronger engine and is more refined; it will cost about $1,000 more when similarly equipped to a non-base Spark.

Prices and Specs

Prices (2016): *LS man.:* $9,995, *2LT CVT:* $18,195 **Freight:** $1,500 **Powertrain (FWD):** Engines: 1.4L-4 (98 hp). Transmissions: 5-speed man., CVT. **Dimensions:** Passengers: 2/2; Wheelbase: 93.9 in, 2,385 mm.; L: 143.1 in., 3,636 mm.; W: 62.8 in., 1,595 mm.; Weight: 2,312 lb., 1,049 kg. **Fuel economy:** *2016 CVT:* 5.7/7.6L/100 km. **Assembled in:** South Korea.

ALERT! 2013-2015 model could shut down if the driver's knee jostles the ignition keychain. Avoid using large key fobs with a bundle of keys on the ignition switch; report any occurrence to Transport Canada.

Owner-reported safety-related failures: Owners say the front passenger-side airbag sensor doesn't recognize that the seat is occupied; engine lags and lurches when accelerating; engine loses power when merging with highway traffic; windshield wiper motor overheats and stops working; first-generation car doesn't come with a spare tire.

SAFETY	
IIHS 2016	
Small Front	Not Rated
Front	Good
Side	Good
Roof strength	Not Rated
Head restraint and seats	Not Rated
Child seat anchors	Acceptable
NHTSA	**Not Rated**

RELIABILITY: Insufficent data. GM products Made-in-Korea have previously been very unreliable, but reports on the 2013-2015 Spark are still incomplete. *2016-2017:* Too new to have established a reliability profile; troublefree launch.

INTERNAL BULLETINS, SECRET WARRANTIES: 2005-15—Reduced Engine Power: Repair Instrument Panel (IP) to Body Harness Connector. 2013—GM will replace broken engine mounts free of charge. 2013-14—GM repaired the AC also at no charge until April 30, 2016; it's an expensive repair, owners should haggle for some compensation. 2014-15—Intermittent stall in heavy traffic and/or driving down steep grades (recalibrate the engine control module). Drive quality degradation, or transmission harsh shifts. Warranty extension up to January 31, 2018.

SONIC ★★★

RATING: Average (2012-2017). The Sonic is the car that replaced the awful Chevrolet Aveo; it is a significantly better car. Unusual for a small car nowadays, the Sonic is assembled in the United States thanks to some concessions from the U.A.W. to reduce labour costs. The Sonic is fully competitive against other B-Segment cars like the Ford Fiesta, Hyundai Accent, Kia Rio, and Toyota Yaris. Compared to the Spark, the Sonic is roomier and much more refined. Chevrolet treated the Sonic that debuted for 2012 to a surprisingly comprehensive spate of late-cycle revisions for 2017. Updates outside include a restyled front and rear, new headlamps, and a restyled hood. Interior revisions encompass a revised dash that houses a new seven-inch touch screen for Chevrolet's MyLink infotainment system; it can now optionally support Apple CarPlay and Android Auto. Conventional gauges replace the previous quirky motorcycle-inspired gauge package. Active safety features making their debut for 2017 include optional forward collision and lane departure alerts, and a rear parking sonar. For 2017, the previous LTZ range topper has been replaced by the new Premier trim level. **Road performance:** Fairly responsive with the standard 1.8L 4-cylinder; the optional turbocharged 1.4L engine has similar horsepower to the 1.8L 4-cylinder but greater torque and delivers very satisfying performance. Steering is precise but some owners report some steering shake and vehicle wander. **Strong points:** Reasonably priced, refined, and well appointed. The interior is comfortable, practical, and quiet for its class. Sedans are about a foot longer than hatchback; like other hatchbacks with a trunk grafted on, cargo space is impressive. **Weak points:** The hatchback's load floor is quite high. The Honda Fit is more useful and versatile but significantly more expensive to buy used. Some drivers find the head restraints are intrusive and force the head downward. **Best alternatives:** Hyundai Accent, Kia Rio, Mazda2, Nissan Versa, and Toyota Yaris.

Prices and Specs

Prices (2016 hatchback): *LS man.:* $14,895; *RS auto.:* $23,795 **Freight:** $1,700 **Powertrain (FWD):** Engines: 1.8L 4-cyl. (138 hp), 1.4L 4-cyl. turbo (138 hp); Transmissions: 5-speed man., 6-speed man., 6-speed auto. **Dimensions (2016 hatchback):** Wheelbase: 99.4 in., 2525 mm.; Length: 159 in., 1735 mm.; Weight (LT Hatchback LT): 2,712 lb. 1230 kg. **Fuel economy:** *1.8L hatchback:* 8.3L/100 km city. **Assembled in:** U.S.A.

ALERT! Make sure the front head restraints are comfortable.

> The head restraint is terrible; it shoves my head forward, forcing me to either stare at the instrument cluster or raise my eyes in a Stanley Kubrick stare to see the road. It wasn't immediately apparent during the test drive, but after 200+ miles of driving in less than a week, my neck is stiff and shoulders feel like rocks.
>
> — *safercarcar.gov*

Owner-reported safety-related failures: Car rolls backwards when stopped on a hill, even though Hill Holder is engaged.

SAFETY	
IIHS 2016	
Small Front	Good
Front	Good
Side	Good
Roof strength	Good
Head restraint and seats	Good
Child seat anchors	Marginal
NHTSA Overall	★★★★★

RELIABILITY: Average, with relatively few major issues reported since its introduction for the 2012 model year. Owners report that the front passenger-side airbag sensor doesn't recognize that the seat is occupied; the transmission sometimes hesitates before shifting; and the front end of the vehicle is too low and scrapes the ground when passing over uneven terrain.

INTERNAL BULLETINS, SECRET WARRANTIES: 2012—The driver airbag module retainers may not be fully engaged in the steering wheel. A rattle or clunk noise during turns or over bumps may point to replacement of the stabilizer bars, whose ball joint boots may experience water and dirt intrusion. There is a free service campaign to replace the fuel pipe and quick connect on certain 2012 Sonics equipped with a 1.4L turbo engine and 6-speed manual transmission. A bump feeling, surge, or an engine vibration while stopped at idle with the transmission in Drive and the foot on the brake may be caused by the transmission Neutral Idle feature. 2012-14—Inoperative heated seats is a seat module software issue. 2012-16—Manual shifter may be difficult to shift or hard to get into gear. 2013-14—Oil leaks, high oil consumption, or blue exhaust smoke may be caused by an improperly seated exhaust manifold, or one with a missing non-return valve (see TSB in Cruze

Internal Bulletins). Malfunction Indicator Lamp (MIL) on and/or hard cold starts; changing to top tier fuels may correct this condition. GM says it's normal for a cold Sonic engine to be slow in providing adequate cabin heat.

CRUZE

2011-2012 ★ ★
2013-2017 ★ ★ ★ ★

2017 Cruze hatchback: lighter, stronger, and more high-tech.

RATING: Below Average (2011-2012); Acceptable (2013-17). This car could be a contender. Right size, right equipment, reasonably-priced. Launched two years after GM emerged from bankruptcy, the Cruze generated many recall notices in its first two years, but seems to have settled in with acceptable reliability over the long haul, and GM appears to have been more committed to correcting problems than it has been in the past after some small car launches. Used examples are plentiful and reasonably priced. Launched in mid-2016, the second-generation Cruze is handsome, performs well, and offers a number of high-end convenience and active safety features. Rear seat space improved. Like other recent GM redesigns, it is lighter than before to save fuel. **Road performance:** The peppy, smooth, and efficient turbocharged engine is well-matched to a conventional 6-speed automatic; the combo delivers good performance and economy. **Strong points:** *Both generations:* Good overall refinement, a serene highway cruiser and a conservative, elegant cabin with simple, logical controls. **Weak points:** *First-generation:* Snug rear seating with low seat cushions; limited storage area. **Best alternatives:** Some good alternative models include the Honda Civic, Hyundai Elantra (not 2011-2013), and the Toyota Corolla. The Cruze has been significantly more reliable than its principal domestic rival, the Ford Focus.

Prices and Specs

Prices (2016): *1LS:* $15,995, Premier: $23,895 **Freight:** $1700 **Powertrain (FWD):** Engines (first-gen): 1.8L 4-cyl. (136 hp), 1.4L turbocharged 4-cyl. (138 hp); 2.0L turbocharged diesel 4-cyl. (151 hp), (second-gen) 1.4L turbocharged 4-cyl; Transmissions: 6-speed man., 6-speed auto. **Dimensions:** Passengers: 2/3; Wheelbase: 106 in., 2700 mm.; Length: 181 in., 4666 mm.; Weight (LT auto) 2932 lb., 1331 kg. **Fuel economy (second-gen 2016):** *1.4L auto.:* 6.9 L/100 km. **Assembled in:** U.S.A.

ALERT! Think twice before you buy a used Cruze diesel. The model sold poorly and GM dealers and independent shops are unfamiliar with the diesel Cruze; parts and service could prove expensive if it experiences failures.

Owner-reported safety-related failures: Up to 350 incidents for some Cruze model years is astoundingly high; 50 complaints is the norm for most vehicles. The experiences described in this section have been taken from the first 90 complaints posted by 2014-15 model year owners. There are hundreds other equally harrowing postings covering 2011-15 models. Sudden stall out followed by unintended acceleration ("lag and lurch"), when accelerating:

SAFETY

IIHS FIRST-GEN 2016

Small Front	Marginal
Front	Good
Side	Good
Roof strength	Good
Head restraint and seats	Good
Child seat anchors	Acceptable
NHTSA Overall 2017	★★★★★

> My 2014 Cruze has a safety issue, so scary I am afraid of driving It now: the gas pedal has a delay in it and scared me to death several times, trying to come out of a stop light on a busy intersection as the car had a 2-3 second delay in responding to the gas pedal, and then whooshed out on top of incoming traffic!!! On the highway it happened several times that changing lanes becomes an issue as this delay in responding and sudden acceleration almost got me into an accident last week.

GM says a "sag or hesitation" on acceleration is a normal characteristic of most of its cars and trucks.

All 2008-15 Vehicles

CONDITION/CONCERN: Some customers may comment on a sag or hesitation when accelerating under the following conditions: When coasting at low speeds of less than 15 miles per hour with a closed throttle and then aggressively applying the throttle. Examples of this maneuver include a rolling stop or a lane change maneuver. In this type of maneuver, even though the accelerator is applied aggressively, the throttle blade is opened slowly for up to 0.7 seconds to help minimize drive-line lash and clunking. Also, in a vehicle equipped with a six speed automatic transmission when making a hard, complete stop with a closed throttle, immediately followed by an aggressive throttle opening the transmission down-shifts may not be completed by the time the throttle is opened. As a result approximately 0.5 seconds of "zero" torque may be commanded to allow the shift to first gear to occur.

RECOMMENDATION/INSTRUCTIONS: Both of the above conditions are a result of Torque Management and both of these conditions should be considered normal and no repairs should be attempted.

Additional safety related failures: Airbags fail to deploy when they're needed; frequent stall outs in traffic; ignition keyring may cause the ignition switch to shut off the car; brake/accelerator mounted too close together, they both can be applied at the same time, or the wrong pedal may be applied; accelerator pedal fractured; floor mats slide up under the pedals; loss of braking when backing up or underway (vacuum pump suspected).

> The driver owns a 2015 Chevrolet Cruze. While driving at an unknown speed, the brakes were engaged and failed to stop the vehicle. Driver had to stand on the brake pedal in order to stop the vehicle. He was able to turn off and restart the vehicle successfully. The failure recurred on 3 separate occasions.

Front axle shaft failure and wheel came off; chronic automatic transmission failures and malfunctions; rearview mirror blocks the view through the front windshield, reflects excessive headlight glare, and vibrates constantly; "sticky" power steering binds or fails completely (see *Internal Bulletins* below); exhaust, AC, and anti-freeze fumes leak into the cabin; extensive undercarriage rusting; dangerous doors suddenly slam shut:

> The doors should definitely be recalled. They are a safety concern. They slam back on you even if opened all the way, if on an uneven pavement or slight incline.

Headlights shut off; windows slow to defog and, don't clear completely; and in one incident, the steering wheel came off in the driver's hands.

> After 5 recalls and an accident caused by my brakes failing, I now have to replace the entire engine because of cracked pistons. This just doesn't make sense. How is this car still on the road? Someone is going to get killed driving one of these cars.

> — *www.consumeraffairs.com/automotive/chevy-cruze.html*

One family complained to CBC Calgary TV that their 2011 Cruze LT's "real" gas mileage is half what's touted by General Motors:

> The 20-percent improvement in fuel economy provided by diesel is quickly reduced, if not eliminated, by its higher price. Using Natural Resources Canada ratings, the 2014 Chevrolet Cruze will use about 1,200 litres of diesel fuel per year on average, compared to 1,520 for the gasoline version of the same car. However, Canada's most popular car, the Honda Civic in comparable EX trim, will use 1,220 litres of fuel per year, as will the Mazda3. Using recent prices in downtown Toronto, the Cruze diesel would consume $1,618 worth of fuel, and the Civic/Mazda3 $1,511 over a year. It makes diesels a pretty tough sell…

RELIABILITY: (2011-12) Below Average (2013-17) Average. Early 2011-2012 Cruze models were recalled many times with long wait times for some repairs; check for recalls if you purchase an early Cruze. Early exhaust manifold replacement; leaking engine head gasket; leaking engine, transmission and axle seals; hesitation when accelerating; heater and AC malfunctions; heater overheats, or can't be shut off; rear windshield water leaks (covered by a secret warranty); all dash lights suddenly come on for no reason; leaking water pump; key sticks in the ignition when in Park; SmartKey locks owners inside or out of their car; rear engine mount failures; "clunky" steering covered by a "secret" warranty.

INTERNAL BULLETINS, SECRET WARRANTIES: 2011-12—Uneven brake pedal feel. This bulletin provides a service procedure to reprogram the electronic brake control module. 2011-14—Coolant level decreases over time with no evidence of leaks. A free fix for a sticking, binding steering wheel that extends to new and used car owners (see TSB in Malibu *Internal Bulletins*). 2012—Engine hesitation at startup under high accessory loads requires reprogramming of the ECM under the Emissions Warranty. Stumbles, or hesitates when accelerating from a stop. Oil leaks, burning oil, and turbo failures are covered in the following service bulletin:

EXCESSIVE OIL CONSUMPTION – OIL LEAKS – BLUE EXHAUST SMOKE – MIL – OR FUEL TRIM CODES

SERVICE BULLETIN NO.: PIP5197   DATED: MAY 6, 2014

2012-2014 Chevrolet Cruze; 2013-2014 Buick Encore; 2013; 2014 Chevrolet Sonic; 2013; 2014 Chevrolet Trax (Canada Only) equipped with 1.4L.

CONDITION/CONCERN: You may encounter a customer concern of oil consumption, oil leaks, and blue smoke from the exhaust, MIL or fuel trim codes.

CORRECTION: Check for a missing or improperly seated intake manifold Non Return Valve that may have damaged the PCV orifice diaphragm. If the intake manifold Non Return Valve is missing or not properly seated, then replace the intake manifold assembly. Check the PCV orifice for leaking oil or drawing vacuum at idle thru its external port.

2013—On certain Buick LaCrosse, Regal, Verano, Cadillac SRX, and Chevrolet Cruze and Malibu vehicles an interference condition between the outside door handle and the door handle bracket assembly could cause the outside door handle to stick or bind in the open position when the door is opened from outside of the vehicle. To correct, dealers are to inspect and modify the front and rear outside door handles, free of charge. GM dealers will also repair, for free, vehicles that produce a steering clunking noise when turning. (The offer expired after May 31, 2015; ask for goodwill coverage.)

STEERING CLUNK NO POWER ASSIST

SERVICE BULLETIN NO.: 13101   DATE: APRIL 29, 2013

2013 Chevrolet Cruze

CONDITION: On certain 2013 model year Chevrolet Cruze vehicles, a possible tear in the passenger side steering gear boot may allow moisture and contamination to enter the boot. This could cause a clunking noise when making a turn. If this clunking noise is ignored and contamination continues to build, it could cause the loss of power steering assist.

CORRECTION: Dealers are to replace the passenger side steering gear boot on all vehicles. On customer vehicles, dealers are to also inspect the steering gear, and if signs of contamination are present, replace the steering gear.

2013-14—A notchy or stick/slip feel in the steering wheel when turning near center wheel position can be corrected by reprogramming the power steering control module. Also applies to same-year GM Verano and Malibu (TSB #P11239). Again, this GM admission makes the company responsible for the free correction of this defect. 2014—Incorrect door lock power switches will be replaced, gratis. Certain 2014 model year Chevrolet Cruze vehicles may have had an incorrect power switch installed on the driver door. Dealers are to inspect and, if necessary, install the correct door switch. This program is in effect until March 31, 2016. GM will also replace all door strikers on certain 2014 Cruze vehicles. The door striker may have been incorrectly plated, giving the appearance of "pitting." Rearview mirror bracket pulling away from the windshield may require a new windshield covered by the base warranty (Campaign #15655). Rear glass leak. Other water leaks may be covered under a "secret" warranty; if not, consider using small claims court:

CUSTOMER SATISFACTION PROGRAM – WET CARPET ON DRIVER'S SIDE

SERVICE BULLETIN NO.: #14490   DATE: AUGUST 11, 2014

2014 Chevrolet Cruze

*****THIS PROGRAM IS IN EFFECT UNTIL AUGUST 31, 2016.*****

CONDITION: Certain 2014 model year Chevrolet Cruze vehicles may not have an adequate seal on the driver's side lower windshield panel-to-cowl interface. This could allow water to enter the vehicle and moisten the front and rear carpet on the driver's side.

CORRECTION: Dealers are to reseal the windshield panel-to-cowl interface seam.

Cruze and Regal 2014-15—GM will replace, at no charge, sunroofs that shatter for no reason under Customer Satisfaction Campaign # 15224A (Jan. 26, 2016).

BUICK VERANO ★★★

RATING: Average. The 2017 model year will be the last for Buick's compact that debuted for the 2012 model year. Based on the same platform as the last-generation Chevrolet Cruze, the Verano has been a fairly good seller for Buick. Fronted by Buick's waterfall grille, the Verano's lines are tastefully conservative. Like the Cruze it is based on, rear seat legroom is tight. The cabin is quite luxurious, and quiet. **Road performance:** Expect brisk, linear performance from the large 2.4L EcoTec 4-cylinder that is well matched to a 6-speed automatic transmission. An available 2L turbo 4-cylinder is very quick. Stable handling, the car is biased toward a comfortable ride over sporty handling. Reasonable trunk space. For 2016, the Driver Confidence Package that includes blind spot, rear cross-traffic, lane departure and forward collision warnings became a new option. Expect deep discounting toward the end of the model run.

Prices and Specs

Prices (2016): *1SB auto.:* $24,190, *1ST auto.:* $32,235 **Freight:** $1,600 **Powertrain (FWD):** Engines: 2L-4 turbo (250 hp). 2.4L-4 (180 hp). Transmission: 6-speed auto. **Dimensions:** Passengers: 2/3; Wheelbase: 105.1 in, 2,685 mm.; L: 183.9, 4,671 mm.; W: 71.4 in., 1,841 mm.; Weight: 3,420 lb., 1,551 kg. **Fuel economy:** *2017 2.4L auto:* 7.6L/11.3L/100 km. **Assembled in:** U.S.A.

RELIABILITY: Not rated, insufficient data. Few complaints received thus far. Average reliability predicted.

SAFETY

IIHS 2016

Small Front	Not Rated
Front	Good
Side	Good
Roof strength	Good
Head restraint and seats	Not Rated
Child seat anchors	Poor
NHTSA Overall	★★★★★

CHEVROLET VOLT ★★★

Compared to the original, the second-generation version is more evolution than revolution. It will cost a bit less this year, and GM is mulling whether it will eventually be replaced by the Bolt. Rated at 85 km (53 miles) of electric range, and about 40 mpg when the battery pack has been depleted, this year's Volt has more standard equipment and now offers a fifth seating "position," which consists of a padded cushion on top of the battery pack in the centre of the rear seat — not suitable for long drives or adults.

RATING: Average. General Motors developed the Volt in an attempt to improve its reputation and create a new market for a revolutionary vehicle. The company assigned a head engineer who had worked on GM's original EV-1, a two–seat, electric-only vehicle developed in the 1990s that had turned out to be a dead end at GM (remember *Who Killed the Electric Car?*). GM continued to pour money into the Volt project even as it slid into insolvency. When the time came to make their bailout requests to the U.S. government, GM management, who had spent three decades fighting fuel economy standards, became EV true-believers; they promised to launch the vehicle of the future that would get America off its dependence on foreign oil. The bailout money came, and surprisingly, for an audacious new GM product developed in difficult times, the Volt turned out to be a fully-developed car. However, the Volt's modest sales did not meet projections. Although it was a more ambitious technical achievement than the 2004 Prius, the Volt did not elicit the same excitement with early adopters. In the end, the New GM was saved by its pickup trucks and SUVs, while the Volt was ignored by most of the buying public. The Volt went on sale for 2012 in Canada. It operates on an electric battery pack until it is depleted, when a gas engine takes over to extend the range of the vehicle. As of 2013, the range in full electric mode increased somewhat, to about 60 kilometres, and a new Safety Package with front parking sensors, forward collision alert, and lane departure warning became available. The second-generation Volt with a new 1.5L 4-cylinder and an all-new body and cabin went on sale in 2016 and promptly sold out. *2012-2015:* The Volt is quiet in normal driving, has precise, nicely weighted steering, and a supple ride; the regenerative brakes can require some adaptation to modulate. The cabin is fronted by a swoopy dash housing a bright, crisp, digital display package including a battery meter. The touch screen and multiple buttons on the prominent dash centre stack can be distracting. Adequate space and comfortable in front, but rear legroom is tight. Cargo capacity is acceptable, and the hatchback body adds some versatility. Power is furnished by a 149 hp electric motor drawing off a 16 kWh lithium-ion battery pack with a range of 50 to 80 kilometres. A full recharge takes four hours at 240 volts or ten to twelve hours at 120 volts. An 84 hp 1.4L gas engine takes over when the batteries are drained, extending the range to a possible 580 kilometres; the engine requires premium fuel. Very low running costs if the Volt is fully charged for its daily commute so it runs totally in electric mode. Overall, the Volt is a technical tour-de-force that functions relatively seamlessly. *2016-2017:* The second-generation Volt looks more mainstream. The interior, while functional, is less "special" and overtly futuristic. To address a purchase objection with the original Volt, three seat belts are now supplied in the rear to increase versatility a bit. That said, rear seat leg and headroom are tight for all seating positions, and access to the rear seat requires agility. The Volt's new gasoline "generator" is more powerful and now runs on regular-grade gas. The electric motors are more powerful and the car is 90 kg (200 pounds) lighter. **Road performance:** The new Volt moves off the line quickly and acceleration is effortless. Well sorted steering and suspension. The regenerative braking works well. **Strong points:** A relatively affordable plug-in that can meet both daily and long-distance driving needs. Good overall refinement. Low annual fuel cost of about $600 results in a savings of $1,200 to $1,500 a year. Very low emissions, particularly if you live in a province with abundant hydro-electricity. **Weak points:** Restricted visibility to the sides and rear due to multiple blind spots. Snug rear seating with seat cushions set too low; limited storage in the cabin. Compared to a compact car, payback will take the better part of a decade at current fuel prices, even when taking into consideration the Volt's higher resale value compared to other GM compacts. **Best alternatives:** The most practical "green" alternative is the conventional Prius 5-door, without the plug-in capability. Among plug-ins, if you're looking for a second vehicle, the all-electric Nissan Leaf or Kia Soul are good alternatives, but both will be outdated much sooner than the Volt with its hedge-your-bets dual-energy drivetrain. Among conventional compacts, the Chevrolet Cruze (it shares the same platform), or the Honda Civic.

Prices and Specs

Prices (2017): *LT:* $38,390, *Premier:* $42,490 **Freight:** $1,600 **Powertrain (FWD):** Engine: 1.5L-4 (101 hp), Electric motor: (149 hp). Transmission: None. **Dimensions:** Passengers: 2/3; Wheelbase: 106.1 in, 2,694 mm.; L: 180.4 in., 4,576 mm.; W: 71.2 in., 1,809 mm.; Weight: 3,543 lb., 1,607 kg. **Fuel economy:** N/A. **Assembled in:** U.S.A.

RELIABILITY: The Volt has not been trouble-free, but General Motors has been uncharacteristically diligent about addressing concerns. Owners of 2012 models reported hatchback supports detaching, poorly sealed taillights, spontaneous horn honking, front suspension problems and an overheating charging system. Any early issues related to the battery pack appear to have been resolved.

MALIBU/MALIBU HYBRID

2005-2012	★★
2013-2015	★★★
2016-2017	★★★★

RATING: Below Average (2005-2012); Average (2013-2015); Above Average (2016-2017). The rating for the 2016 and later mid-size Malibu went up a notch, as it has returned to the heart of the mid-size market it abandoned with the too-small Malibu that debuted for 2013. For 2017, the Malibu receives a new turbocharged 1.5L 4-cylinder, 160 hp engine coupled to a 6-speed automatic transmission. An optional 250 hp, 2.0L 4-cylinder engine comes with a new 9-speed automatic. The Malibu hybrid has a 1.8-L 4-cylinder gas engine that works with a two-motor electric drive unit from the 2016 Volt plug-in hybrid. An interesting addition for parents is Chevrolet's new Teen Driver system, which mutes the audio system when front seat belts aren't buckled, alerts occupants when the vehicle is exceeding a preset speed, and allows parents to monitor their teen's driving behaviour. **Road performance:** The 1.5L turbo 4-cylinder delivers smooth, flexible performance and works well with its 6-speed automatic transmission. The 2L is very quick. The hybrid is quick enough, but its gas engine is loud for this class. Nicely-weighted and geared steering. Handling is secure, if not sporting, but the ride is a bit firm. The new Malibu's cabin space is now fully competitive and it boasts clear instruments and logical controls. Big trunk. **Strong points:** Well-priced on the used vehicle market; quiet, with convenient controls. **Weak points:** The model that debuted for 2013 was downsized to avoid a perceived conflict with the Impala; cabin space is no roomier than compacts like the Honda Civic and Toyota Corolla. Chevrolet also botched the launch of the car as it was initially offered only as a hybrid that cannot operate in full electric mode. The complex hybrid with its tiny fuel economy benefit is a risky used car buy; the 2.5L 4-cylinder that followed is a better choice.

Major redesigns: 2004, 2008, 2013, and 2016. **Best alternatives:** The Ford Fusion, Hyundai Sonata, and Kia Optima have more usable back seats than the 2013-2016 Malibu. The 2013-2015 Honda Civic and Hyundai Elantra have roughly the same cabin space as a Malibu of the same years but don't equal the Malibu's refinement.

Prices and Specs

Prices (2016): *L man. S:* $21,745, *Premier:* $32,045 **Freight:** $1,750 **Powertrain (FWD):** Engines: 1.5L turbocharged 4-cyl. (160 hp); 2.0L turbocharged 4-cyl. (250hp); 1.8L Hybrid (182 hp). Transmission: 6-speed auto. (1.5L); 8-speed auto. (2L), None (Hybrid). **Dimensions:** Passengers: 2/3; Wheelbase: 111.4 in., 2829 mm.; Length: 193.8 in., 4922 mm.; W: 73 in., 1854 mm.; Weight: 3,126 lb., 1481 kg. **Combined overall fuel consumption:** *2016 1.5 L:* 7.6L/100 km. **Assembled in:** U.S.A.

ALERT! 2016 models may come with poorly-designed engine mounts;

> I believe that GM's motor mount designs and quality aren't in line with industry standards. I've tried to contact Chevrolet and they're not providing me with an avenue to start an investigation. I can currently demonstrate what I believe to be excessive powertrain movement on my current 2016 Malibu which I believe exists on other Malibus and other GM made models…
>
> . . .
>
> Downshifts cause the vehicle to suddenly propel forward, especially when cruising to slow down or while brake is depressed, causing an unsafe change in vehicle speed that requires a sudden need to brake or increase brake pressure to avoid striking a vehicle in front. Transmission also at times has an "engine miss" type jolt while at cruising speed on flat pavement 30-45mph that has at one time repeated for 3 minutes straight. Majority of time transmission behaves normally and without incident and then suddenly goes nuts.

SAFETY

IIHS 2016 (NEW-GEN)

Small Front	Good
Front	Good
Side	Good
Roof strength	Good
Head restraint and seats	Good
Child seat anchors	Moderate
NHTSA Overall	★★★★★

Owner-reported safety-related failures: 2016 rear windshield shattered spontaneously while vehicle was parked. 2015 and earlier Malibus are afflicted with a dangerous "lag and lurch" powertrain; No reports on later models. Excessive dash glare into the front windshield. Steering wheel binds, doesn't track straight, or jerks to one side; and the Stop-Start gas-saving feature can leave the car without power when stopped. Sudden engine failure; won't restart.

RELIABILITY: 2005-2007 Avoid; 2008-2011 Below Average; 2013-2017 Average. Pre-2012, you can count on the usual GM issues with emissions system malfunctions and worn suspension and steering. The steering system and ignition key are troublesome up to the 2007 model year inclusively. Premature wheel bearing replacement; trunk opens on its own.

INTERNAL BULLETINS, SECRET WARRANTIES: 2005-08—2005-06 G6, Malibu, and Malibu Maxx; 2008 G6, Malibu, Malibu Maxx, and Aura may have a sudden loss of steering power-assist. Under Special Coverage Adjustment #10183, GM will replace the failed components free of charge up to 10 years/100,000 mi. (160,000 km). 2006-07—TSB #10134A, published Aug. 24, 2011, says that cars with the 2.2L 4-cylinder engine and those with the 2.4L 4-cylinder with 4-speed automatic transmission may have a deteriorating catalytic converter, causing the engine light to illuminate. The warranty is extended to 10 years/192,000 km. for 2006-07 Cobalt, G4/G5, and Ion. 2010-14—Here is a free fix for a sticking, binding steering wheel. This warranty extension applies to new and used car owners:

SPECIAL COVERAGE ADJUSTMENT – POWER STEERING STICK-SLIP

SERVICE BULLETIN NO.: 14232   DATE: NOVEMBER 21, 2014

2012-2014 Buick Verano; 2011-2014 Chevrolet Cruze, Volt; 2010-2014 Chevrolet Equinox; 2013-2014 Chevrolet Malibu; 2010-2014 GMC Terrain.

CONDITION: Some vehicles may have increased friction in the steering system. This could cause the steering wheel to stick in the straight-ahead position after driving long distances on a straight highway. The steering wheel can be turned but it may require increased effort.

SPECIAL COVERAGE ADJUSTMENT: This special coverage covers the condition described above for a period of 10 years or 150,000 miles (240,000 km), whichever occurs first, from the date the vehicle was originally placed in service, regardless of ownership. Dealers are to 1) replace the steering gear on 2010-2012 model year vehicles; or 2) reprogram the power steering control module on 2013-2014 model year vehicles. The repairs will be made at no charge to the customer.

2011—Wet front or rear passenger-side carpet (this condition may be caused by a plugged HVAC evaporator drain). 2012-15—Driver's front seat moves, makes noise when turning. 2013—Some 2013 Malibu and Cadillac ATS models equipped with a 2.0L turbo engine may have a rough-running engine with a "check engine light" on, low compression, and misfiring. This condition may be caused by a cracked piston. 2013-14—Unwanted trunk opening. Water leaking from the AC can be remedied by repositioning the AC evaporator and blower module drain hose. 2013-14—Sudden loud engine noise or engine seizure:

2013-2014 Buick Regal; 2013-2014 Cadillac ATS; 2014 Cadillac CTS Sedan; 2014 Chevrolet Impala; 2013-2014 Chevrolet Malibu; Equipped with 2.0L Engine or 2.5L Engine.

CONDITION/CONCERN: Some customers may comment on a loud engine noise or that the engine is seized. In some cases, the engine will stop running and will not restart.

RECOMMENDATION/INSTRUCTIONS: This may be caused by one or more of the rod or main bearings being damaged or spun. The bearing material will enter the oil and be distributed throughout the engine. The damaged bearing material cannot be completely removed from the engine and may cause future damage. The only way to assure a complete repair is to replace the engine assembly. Replacing the crankshaft and bearings should not be attempted. Replace the engine assembly.

2013-16—Front seats may stick in the full-up position. 2014-15—Engine blows hot air when vehicle is decelerating. 2014-16—Multiple infotainment issues. 2016—STOP/START malfunctions.

CHEVROLET IMPALA	2006-2013 ★★
	2014-2017 ★★★★★
BUICK ALLURE	2005-2009 ★★

2017 Chevrolet Impala

RATING: *Impala:* Below Average (2006-2013) Recommended (2014-2017); *Allure:* Average (2005-2009). The 2017 Impala is carried over virtually unchanged. Based on GM's Epsilon II platform, the 2014-2017 Impala is roomy, comfortable, smooth, and quiet. The 2006-2013 Impala and the Buick Allure are based on an ancient

GM platform that first saw the light of day in the late 1980s; they're examples of mediocre GM designs that contributed to its 30-year slide into insolvency. **Road performance:** *2014-2017:* The 3.6L V6 on the current Impala provides smooth acceleration and works well with the 6-speed automatic transmission. Pleasing ride and handling for a family sedan. For 2017 the Impala continues to get high marks for peppy acceleration, agile handling, a comfy ride, a spacious cabin, and large trunk. The 2006 to 2013 is soft riding and with good highway fuel economy; component quality is appalling be it the engine gaskets, computerized engine controls, steering or suspension. **Strong points:** *Impala:* With its 2014 transformation, the Impala won the top spot among popularly-priced sedans recommended by *Consumer Reports.* Prices for pre-2014 models are extraordinarily low, so pick the newest, lowest mileage car that fits your budget. The 3.5L and 3.9L V6 engines offer impressive fuel economy, especially in highway driving. **Weak points:** *2005-2013 Impala:* Cheaply finished interior; inferior seat comfort in earlier years. Repair intensive. *Allure:* Tight rear legroom. **Major redesigns:** *Impala:* 2006 (partial), 2014. **Best alternatives:** *2005-2013 Impala and Buick Allure:* Hyundai Sonata, Ford Fusion pre-2012, and Dodge Charger. *2014-2017 Impala:* Chrysler 300, Honda Accord V6, Nissan Maxima, and Toyota Avalon.

Prices and Specs

Prices (2016): *Base Impala 1LS:* $29,295, *2LZ:* $40,495 **Freight:** *Impala:* $1,750 **Powertrain (FWD):** Engines: 2.4L eAssist hybrid (182 hp), 2.5L (195 hp), 3.6L V6 (305 hp), 3.9L V6 (230 hp), 5.3L V8 (303 hp); Transmissions: *Impala:* 4-speed auto, 6-speed auto. **Dimensions Impala (2016):** Passengers: 2/3; Wheelbase: 112 in., 2837 mm.; L: 201.3, 5113 mm.; Weight: LT V6: 3,800 lb, 1723 kg. **Fuel economy:** *2016 Impala 2.5L:* 7.5L/100 km highway, 10.6 L/100 km city. **Assembled in:** Canada and U.S.A.

SAFETY

IIHS 2016 IMPALA

Small Front	Not Rated
Front	Good
Side	Good
Roof strength	Not Rated
Head restraint and seats	Not Rated
Child seat anchors	Acceptable
NHTSA Overall 2017	★★★★★

BUICK LACROSSE

RATING: Above Average (2011-2016); the all-new 2017 is not rated. **Road performance:** Redesigned for 2010, the LaCrosse was a totally redesigned car built on the then-new Epsilon II architecture that subsequently underpinned the 2014 and later Impala. Good performance with the V6; the 4-cylinder hybrid is not particularly economical and its performance and refinement are disappointing for a car marketed as a luxury product. A luxurious cabin and Buick's "Quiet Tuning" system make for a serene environment. The available "on demand" all-wheel drive system sends power to the rear wheels when it determines the front wheels are slipping. The all-new 2017 LaCrosse, based on the same architecture as the new Malibu, is an elegant car with a chic, roomy cabin. **Strong points:** LaCrosse is elegant, luxurious, and refined. LaCrosse has a better reliability record than the pre-2014 Impala. **Weak points:** Limited outward vision on the LaCrosse. **Major redesigns:** 2010, 2017. **Best alternatives:** With new Buicks sold as luxury cars, new alternatives would be the Lincoln MKZ and Chrysler 300C, and imports like the Acura TLX and excellent Lexus ES. Comparable used imports will cost a lot more, because the Buicks depreciate rapidly.

Prices and Specs

Prices (2017): *Base:* $35,345, *Premium AWD:* $47,400 **Freight:** $1,750 **Powertrain (FWD/AWD):** Engines: 2.4L 4-cyl eAssist hybrid (182 hp), 3.0L V6 (255 hp), 3.6L V6 (305 hp); Transmissions: 6-speed auto. **Dimensions (2017):** Passengers: 2/3, Wheelbase: 114.4 in., 2905; L: 197.5 in., 5017 mm.; Weight: N/A. **Fuel economy:** *2017 FWD:* 11.2L/100 km city, 7.5L/100 km highway. **Assembled in:** U.S.A.

ALERT! 3.6L V6 twin-cam engine: Timing chain and tensioner failures reported. Check for excessive noise when starting engine.

Owner-reported safety-related failures: Chronic stalling; car can be left in Park, and roll away; wheel lug nut studs snap off; and large tires and wheels on the redesigned Impala (2014) susceptible to blowouts:

> I can deal with the poor visibility headlamps, the front camera that keeps flagging "service front camera" and camera false alarms, but the huge 19 inch wheels and tires with hardly any sidewall to absorb rough roads are a recipe for disaster and dangerous. I live in

SAFETY

IIHS 2016

Small Front	Not Rated
Front	Good
Side	Good
Roof strength	Good
Head restraint and seats	Good
Child seat anchors	Marginal
NHTSA overall	★★★★★

the northeast and it is loaded with potholes. When I hit one yesterday the tire blew causing a very dangerous situation.

Other failures: Airbags may fail to deploy in a collision; loss of brakes; loss of steering; inadequate headlight illumination; and visibility is obstructed by the tall, wide rear-seat head restraints. Says one owner of a 2012 LaCrosse:

> The "Blind Spots" on this vehicle are outrageous. The front seat head restraints are so big it is not possible to look out the driver's side rear window when backing up. I would remove the headrests to make the car safer for others (the ones you can't see), but they cannot be removed. The decklid is so high that the rearview mirror shows only one half of the outside – the rest of the mirror shows the interior of the car. The pillar between the rear side windows and the back window is so wide this also obscures the view when backing up.

The collision warning system can give false alerts, possibly causing an accident, as this driver told NHTSA:

> On about a half dozen occasions the vehicle's early detection system has engaged without any vehicles in front. These occurrences seem to be on days when it is raining and there are reflections off the road, or very sunny days (again causing reflections). The flashing light, loud alarm, and interruption with regular audio is very jarring (scary). On one occasion I applied my brakes very hard because of the alarm (but there was no car in front) – this almost caused the car behind to hit me.

CHEVROLET IMPALA, BUICK ALLURE, BUICK LACROSSE

RELIABILITY: *Impala:* Below Average (2005-2013), Average to Above Average (2014-2017); *Allure:* Below Average (fewer complaints than the contemporary Impala); *LaCrosse:* Average. Typical General Motors issues with the emissions control system (yellow engine service light on dash), and premature wear of the suspension, steering, and brakes. Ignition key and anti-theft security defects through 2007. The 3.5L, 3.8L, and 3.9L normally-aspirated V6 engines are the most reliable. Check for intake manifold and head gasket leaks on the 3.5L engine. Avoid the supercharged 3.8L V6. The 3.0L and 3.6L V6s can experience expensive timing chain issues; some years were covered by a special program from GM that has now expired. The V8 is too powerful for the chassis and can cause the transmission to fail. Steering rack and brakes lack durability. Faulty electronic sensors and ABS issues as well. The V8 engine is too strong for the automatic transmission. Some ABS and stability control problems can be fixed under by the powertrain warranty in the first five years, with the help of a sympathetic dealer. Some 4-speed transmission failures reported starting from 100,000 km. Check for corrosion damage on door bottoms and folded seams in the hood. *2011-2012:* Some complaints about a partial lack of power and hesitation; contact Transport Canada if the issue is not a result of neglected maintenance. *2014-2017 Impala:* Few complaints recorded in the first three years.

INTERNAL BULLETINS, SECRET WARRANTIES: All model years—General Motors says it's "normal" for your automatic transmission to "clunk" when changing gears. No wonder GM went bankrupt with this attitude:

2-3 UPSHIFT OR 3-2 DOWNSHIFT CLUNK NOISE

SERVICE BULLETIN NO: 01-07-30-042H   DATE: JAN 14, 2014

2014 and Prior GM Passenger Cars and Light Duty Trucks Equipped with 4L60-E, 4L65-E or 4L70-E Automatic Transmission (RPOs M30, M32, M70)

IMPORTANT: Some vehicles may exhibit a clunk noise that can be heard on a 2-3 upshift or a 3-2 downshift. During a 2-3 upshift, the 2-4 band is released and the 3-4 clutch is applied. The timing of this shift can cause a momentary torque reversal of the output shaft that results in a clunk noise. This same torque reversal can also occur on a 3-2 downshift when the 3-4 clutch is released and the 2-4 band applied. This condition may be more pronounced on a 4-wheel drive vehicle due to the additional tolerances in the transfer case.

This is a normal condition. No repairs should be attempted.

This is NOT a normal condition. GM has been sending out this bulletin for decades, rather than fix these transmissions. Owners with this problem can ask small claims court to refund part of the price they paid for their vehicle under the *quanti minoris* doctrine. ("I would have paid this much less (your claim amount) if I knew I'd be getting less performance.").

2005-11—Reduced power, as MIL alert lights up (see bulletin). 2008—Power steering leak may require the replacement of the steering gear cylinder line. 2008-09—Poor AC performance. Inaccurate fuel gauge readings. V8 engine oil leak from the rear cover assembly area. 2009—V8 engine valve tick noise remedy (replace the valve lifters). *Impala:* 2006-08—GM bulletin #08-06-04-039, says that if the car cranks but won't start, the likely culprit is a blown fuel pump fuse. 2012-13—Engine oil leak between the engine and transmission mounting surfaces. This may be caused by the crankshaft #3 thrust bearing wing separating from the thrust bearing, damaging the crankshaft rear oil seal and housing. GM and the dealer should pay the repair bill (see TSB in General Motors Introduction). Provincial consumer laws say vehicles should be "reasonably" durable. 2014-16—Front seats may stick in the full-up position. *Impala:* 2014—Sudden loud engine noise or engine seizure (see TSB in Malibu Internal Bulletins). 2014—Another repair that should be free involves water leaking into the trunk; here's the "secret" warranty that will cover some of the repair cost, if you haggle:

CUSTOMER SATISFACTION PROGRAM – TAIL LAMP GASKET SEAL

SERVICE BULLETIN NO.: 14047   **DATE: MAY 8, 2014**

TAIL LAMP GASKET SEAL

2014 Chevrolet Impala

**********THIS PROGRAM IS IN EFFECT UNTIL MAY 31, 2016.**********

CONDITION: With heat and age, the tail lamp gasket on certain 2014 model year Chevrolet Impala vehicles may lose the ability to seal. This could allow water to leak into the trunk area.

CORRECTION: Dealers are to replace the tail lamp gaskets and inspect the trunk for water damage or odor.

CADILLAC ATS ★★★

RATING: Average. This compact-size performance sedan arrived for 2012 to compete against European cars in the segment that have seen their sales increase for more than a decade. **Road performance:** Equipped with a 2L turbo 4-cylinder – the choice of most buyers – and automatic transmission, the ATS is fast, flexible, and quite refined except when pushed hard, when it takes on a sporting bark. Quick, lively, communicative, beautifully-weighted steering. A firm, yet never harsh ride is allied to near-cerebral handling. Quiet. Very good driving position. Sleek, contemporary design, lavish materials and rigorous assembly combine to make for a luxurious interior. The dashboard features crisp, clear instrumentation, but Cadillac's touch-sensitive CUE (Cadillac User Interface) interface is supremely irritating. Firm yet resilient seats front and rear. Cabin space is a bit less than the comparable German-branded competitors, the rear being tight. Trunk space is sufficient, but no more. Predicted resale value is much lower than the competing 3-series BMW. Updates for 2016 included a revised 3.6L V6, direct injection for the 2L four, an 8-speed automatic transmission for all models and the addition of Apple Car Play and Android Auto. **Strong points:** The APA actually rated the handling superior to the contemporary BMW sedan in a comparison test. Handsome interior. **Weak points:** Limited sales means parts and service are limited to GM dealers and a few specialist shops. Frustrating controls. **Best alternatives:** The Audi A4, BMW 3-Series, and Lexus IS.

Prices and Specs

Prices (2016): *ATS Sedan 2.5L RWD:* $36,380, *3.6L V6 AWD Premium Collection:* $55,685 **Freight:** $1,950 **Powertrain (FWD, AWD):** Engines: 2L-4 turbo (272 hp), 2.5L-4 (202 hp), 3.6L V6 333 hp); Transmission: 6-speed man., 8-speed auto. **Dimensions (Sedan):** Passengers: 2/3; Wheelbase: 109.3 in, 2,775 mm.; L: 182.8 in., 4,643 mm.; W: 71.1 in., 1,806 mm.; Weight: *2L AWD Sedan auto:* 3,542 lb., 3,542 kg. **Fuel economy:** *2016 2L turbo AWD:* 7.8L/10.8L/100 km. **Assembled in:** U.S.A.

RELIABILITY: Some complaints received regarding some engine shake at idle and steering maladies. Repair costs for most Cadillacs are high as the vehicles get older; purchase of a full-coverage extended warranty from GM is recommended.

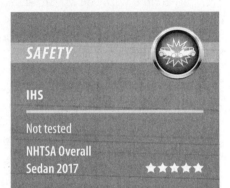

SAFETY	
IHS	
Not tested	
NHTSA Overall Sedan 2017	★★★★★

CADILLAC CTS

2014-2010	★
2010-2017	★★★

bad buy

2017 Chevrolet Impala

RATING: Not Recommended – Avoid (2004-2010); Average (2010-17). The third-generation Cadillac CTS, which debuted for the 2014 model year, is a mid-size luxury car intended to compete against the Audi A6, BMW 5 Series and Mercedes E-Class. While the car itself is competitive against the German brands in terms of performance, luxury, and features, Cadillac doesn't have the market appeal of its rivals, and offering the CTS at the same price point has doomed it to also-ran status as buyers opt for the European brands for the same money. Cadillac will need several more years of creative marketing to get luxury buyers back to even look at the car; in the interim, look for significant incentive money during the year when the inventories pile up. **Road performance:** Competent and secure handling, a pleasant ride and precise steering. The 2L turbo 4-cylinder is more than quick enough, the normally-aspirated V6 delivers brisk acceleration and the supercharged V8 in the CTS-V high performance model endows the CTS with Corvette performance in a 4-door body. All-wheel drive, a virtual necessity in Canada, is available with the 2L turbo 4-cylinder and normally-aspirated 3.6L V6, but is not offered with the 3.6L V6 turbo, nor with the supercharged V8 in the CTS-V. An 8-speed automatic transmission is offered on all variants. GM's Performance Data Recorder gadget offers up to 30 channels of performance data and real-time audio and video. Cadillac boasts that the front-view camera will capture each curve and straightaway and, when parked, let you watch and analyze your driving performance on the Cadillac CUE screen. The footage can be saved on an SD card to share later when you are sentenced to Driver Rehab school. **Strong points:** Stylish cabin featuring attractive components; pleasing to drive. **Weak points:** Cadillac User Experience touch-sensitive control interface will drive you to distraction. Rear-seat access on the coupe requires some acrobatics due to the low rear roofline, and the rear seatback could use additional bolstering. The trunk is small and its narrow opening can make loading bulky items more difficult. Optional Recaro seats may be too firmly padded for some. **Major redesign:** 2003, 2008, 2014. **Best alternatives:** Acura TL SH-AWD, BMW 5 Series, Hyundai Genesis, and Infiniti G35 and G37.

Prices and Specs

Prices (2016): *CTS 2.0L RWD (1SC):* $49,405, *CTS-V:* $92,135 **Freight:** $1,950 **Powertrain (Rear-drive/AWD):** Engines: 2.0L turbo (272 hp), 3.6L V6 (333 hp), 3.6L V6 turbo (430 hp), 6.2L Supercharged V8 (640 hp); Transmissions: 8-speed auto. **Dimensions (CTS Sedan):** Passengers: 2/3; Wheelbase: 114.6 in., 2910 mm.; L: 195.5 in., 4966 mm.; W: 72.2 in.,1835 mm.; Weight (3.6L AWD): 3,889 lb, 1764 kg. **Fuel economy:** *2016 2.0L-4 turbo-auto. AWD sedan:* 7.8/10.8L/100 km. **Assembled in:** U.S.A.

ALERT!

The auto stop/start cannot be safe. I almost got T-boned in my first several hundred miles in my 2016 CTS. I was at a complete stop and needed to make a left across traffic. I did not realize the delay would be that great and almost got T-boned turning across traffic.

RELIABILITY: If buying used, look for a car with the balance of its factory warranty or buy a full-coverage extended warranty offered by General Motors. Frequent electronic malfunctions; consider checking for codes to ensure the seller hasn't recently cancelled a lit Engine Service or ABS warning light. Excessive oil consumption possible with the 3.6L V6; check for noisy timing chains and/or camshafts on earlier models; shoppers should be especially vigilant with 2008 and 2009 models. The brake system and rear differential are also prone to expensive repairs. Some automatic transmission failures reported; check for rough shifting or a slipping transmission. Power seats, the navigation system and radio are potential trouble areas. The ABS brake pump can fail and electrical problems are fairly common. A hard to diagnose vibration may point to a defective driveshaft joint; a reconditioned driveshaft can cost up to $1000 as the part is not offered separately. *2011-2014 Coupe:* Interior squeaks and rattles, especially from the rear parcel shelf, and weather stripping that creates wind noise. You may want to take a pass on the panoramic sunroof in view of reports that sunroofs often crack or implode for no apparent reason.

SAFETY	
IIHS 2016	
Small Front overlap	Marginal
Moderate Front overlap	Good
Side	Good
Roof strength	Good
Head restraints/seats	Good
Child seat	Marginal
NHTSA 2017	★★★★★

INTERNAL BULLETINS, SECRET WARRANTIES: All models/years—Reverse servo cover seal leak. Paint delamination, peeling, or fading. *CTS: 2005-15*—Loss of engine power may be caused by water intrusion into the instrument panel (TSB #07-06-04-019D). *2008-09*—Clunk noise while turning, and automatic transmission extension housing leaks. Front door window drops incrementally. Rear door windows may go down by themselves. *2008-10*—Front door window is slow or noisy when activated. *2008-12*—Front seat lateral movement/clunking noise. *2008-13*—Clunk noise heard when shifting out of Drive to Reverse or Reverse into Drive.

CLUNK NOISE AFTER SHIFTING FROM REVERSE TO DRIVE OR DRIVE TO REVERSE AND THEN ACCELERATING

SERVICE BULLETIN NO.: PIP4554K   DATE: JUNE 10, 2014

2007-2009 Cadillac SRX; 2007-2011 Cadillac STS; 2008-2013 Cadillac CTS; 2010-2014 Chevrolet Camaro RWD only, equipped with an Automatic Transmission.

CONCERN: Some customers may comment on a clunk noise after shifting from Reverse to Drive or Drive to Reverse and then accelerating, this noise typically does not occur during the Reverse to Drive or Drive to Reverse shift, but is heard after the shift when the vehicle is accelerated. The noise may sound like it is coming from the rear drive axle.

Customers may also comment on a driveline bump, clunk or thud on heavy acceleration or upon braking. This condition is more likely to be duplicated in low gear on acceleration or deceleration.

RECOMMENDATION: This condition may be caused by the torque on the propeller shaft flange nut or movement between the flange and the transmission output shaft. Apply thread locker to the transmission output shaft flange splines and a new front propeller shaft flange nut.

This is a 90-minute job. GM dealers are authorized to cover it up to a year after the powertrain warranty on a "goodwill" basis.

2011—The airbag warning light comes on intermittently. An easy, inexpensive way to eliminate a chatter-type noise or rear axle clunk. **2012-13**—Crankshaft rear seal oil leaks (see TSB in General Motors Introduction). **2012-14**—Remedy for a water leak or wind noise from passenger front door glass according to TSB #PI0748A. **2013-14**—Sudden loud engine noise or engine seizure (see TSB in Malibu *Internal Bulletins*). **2014**—GM bulletin #13429 says software in the hazard warning switch may cause the activation of the hazard warning lamps when the vehicle has been turned off, and drain the battery. **2016**—GM TSB #15-NA-087 troubleshoots various STOP/START failures. Inoperative gauges at startup.

CAMARO ★★★★

Camaro: The 2017 Camaro performance car enters into its second year with many of last year's redesign glitches corrected. Like Ford's Mustang, it is likely to give drivers high-performance thrills without the bills.

RATING: Average to above-average buys; owner reports on the redesigned 2016-2017 models are still incomplete. After an eight-year break, the Camaro returned to GM's lineup for 2010 on a platform developed by GM's Holden division in Australia. Styling was inspired by the original late 1960s model, but was a less overt retro copy than the Challenger. The Camaro was redesigned for 2016 on a vehicle platform borrowed from the Cadillac ATS. Last seen in the mid-1980s, a 4-cylinder engine became available on a Camaro again that year. There are currently three engine choices: A 2.0L 270 hp turbocharged in-line 4-cylinder; an optional 3.6L 330 hp V6; and a high-performance 6.2L 450 hp V8. All three engines can be coupled to either a 6-speed manual or an 8-speed automatic. Weight dropped by almost 300 pounds as of 2016, but the Camaro remains a big, heavy car. The cabin of the current generation is still tight for rear seat occupants, but it uses nicer materials. The V8 commands a large premium on the used car market. Until its recent redesign, the Mustang ranked higher in APA comparison tests, partly due to its more livable interior and better visibility. **Road performance:** All versions of the V8 offer exhilarating performance and a pulse-quickening soundtrack; the harder you drive, the better they appear to run. The V6 is quick and also sounds nice. The 2L is smooth, quick, and flexible. The redesigned 2016-17 models are a bit lighter and more nimble. **Strong points:** The premium architecture results in a seriously solid, crisp handling car. Impressive acceleration with both the V6 and V8 engines, surprisingly good highway fuel economy, and competent steering/handling. Powerful braking. **Weak points:** Very poor outward visibility to the sides and rear; test drive in the city to determine if you can live with the poor sightlines. Interior design and materials on the pre-2016 Camaro are disappointing. The interior is tight for the overall size of the car, and access to the back seat is a chore. If you are taller than average, your head will be constantly brushing up against the headliner; rear seating is a "knees-to-chin" affair; not much cargo room; small trunk and trunk opening. Owners report and *Consumer Reports* confirms that fit and finish glitches were everywhere through 2015. Fuel sloshes in the gas tank. **Other opinions:** "The 2016 Camaro still makes you feel like you're sitting in a bunker, looking out of a gun slit." – *Aaron Bragman, cars.com.* **Major redesign:** 2010, 2014 minor restyling, and 2016. **Best alternatives:** The Dodge Challenger and Mustang are the obvious alternatives; the Hyundai Genesis Coupe may be worth a look.

Prices and Specs

Prices (2016): *1LT man.:* $29,095, *2SS convertible:* $54,455 **Freight:** $1,650 **Powertrain (Rear-drive):** Engines: 2L-4 turbo (270 hp), 3.6L V6 (330 hp), 6.2L V8 (440 hp). Transmissions: 6-speed man., 8-speed auto. **Dimensions:** Passengers: 2/2; Wheelbase: 110.7 in, 2811 mm.; L: 188.3, 4784 mm.; W: 74.7 in., 1897 mm.; Weight: N/A. **Fuel economy:** *2016 3.6L V6-auto. coupe:* 8.5/12.3L/100 km. **Assembled in:** U.S.A.

ALERT! Convertible tops on 2011-15 Camaros are known for water leaks. Check for this during your pre-purchase inspection. A class action was authorized in March 2015 in Louisiana under *Cain v. General Motors LLC* (Civil Action #14-1077). The lawsuit alleges that the plaintiff purchased a 2011 Chevrolet Camaro Convertible on April 14, 2011, and had the vehicle in the repair shop on 12 separate occasions for a cumulative total of 125 days due to the water leaks caused by the convertible top design.

Owner-reported safety-related failures: Passenger-side airbag doesn't recognize the seat is occupied; 2010 through 2015 models can stall suddenly on the highway:

> I was driving my 2014 Camaro at approximately 70 mph. I slowed to get off the exit and as I did the engine died and the power steering and brakes were inoperative. Luckily I didn't hit anyone. The engine failed again later in the same evening and twice 2 days later.

SAFETY	
IIHS	
Small Front overlap	Good
Moderate Front overlap	Good
Side	Good
Roof strength	Acceptable
Head restraints/seats	Good
Child seat	Not Rated
NHTSA Overall 2015	★★★★★

RELIABILITY: Above average for most years; the 2010-2011 models appear more troublesome. Some oil consumption complaints with the 2010 V8. *V8 all years:* Check for leaking oil cooler lines or connections. Expect the usual GM electronic and sensor issues on older models; consider checking for trouble codes as part of your pre-purchase inspection in the event the previous owner cancelled an engine service, airbag, or traction control warning light. The huge tires wear quickly and are expensive to replace. Stone chips on the hood and front bumper.

INTERNAL BULLETINS, SECRET WARRANTIES: 2005-15—Intermittent malfunction indicator lamp (MIL) illuminated with reduced engine power (repair instrument panel to Body Harness Connector). **2007-14**—Excessive oil consumption, fouled, cracked spark plugs, and a rough running engine may need ten hours of work and the replacement of key engine parts (see TSB in Cadillac Escalade *Internal Bulletins*). If this repair is premature, it should be covered. **2008-14**—Troubleshooting tips for front and rear windows that bind, fit poorly, are misaligned, rattle or squeak, move slowly or don't move at all. Tips on silencing a chatter noise from the rear of the vehicle that occurs when making low speed turns. **2009-14**—Some vehicles may not crank or start, caused by excessive leakage from cylinder past exhaust or exhaust intake valve, low static compression, sensor is disconnected, or while cranking, valvetrain fails to move. **2010-13**—Clunk noise heard when shifting out of Drive to Reverse or Reverse into Drive (see TSB in Cadillac CTS *Internal Bulletins*). **2011**—Automatic transmission makes a clunk sound when shifted. Recalibration of the electronic brake control module to improve cold weather braking performance. Likely causes of power-steering fluid leaks; lower rear window seal loose or missing. Side window glass won't clear moulding. Door light bar inoperative or loses intensity. Noisy six-way power front seats. Rear bumper fascia contacting body/paint peeling. Door and quarter panel paint appearance.

Convertible top spots, indentation/damage. **2011-12**—Convertible top headliner tears near the support brackets; excessive wind intrusion. **2012**—The correction for an airbag warning light that stays on for no reason. **2012-13**—Crankshaft rear seal oil leaks (see TSB in General Motors Introduction). **2012-14**—When trying to shift into First or Second gear, the manual transmission may bind and a clunk/grind/rattle noise may be heard. **2013-15**—GMC/Cadillac/Chevrolet: After shifting into Park, the vehicle rolls when brake pedal is released (TSB: #380746, dated: Nov. 1, 2014). **2014-15**—When braking or accelerating, a clunking or a popping sound noise can be heard from the rear of the vehicle. The upper control arm ball joint may be loose.

CORVETTE ★★★

RATING: Average. A bulky sport coupe that has evolved into a more refined machine. The Corvette does deliver high-performance thrills – along with an automatic transmission that tends to overheat, suspension hop, and numb steering. Overall, get the quieter and less temperamental base Corvette; it delivers the same cachet for a lot less money. The seventh-generation Stingray that debuted for 2014 is faster, more fuel-efficient, more refined, and offers a nicer interior, with a smaller steering wheel and better seats. The base 6.2L V8 coupled to a 7-speed manual transmission produces 455 hp and offers cylinder deactivation. Standard features include a good audio system, rearview camera, satellite radio, and GM's easy-to-use MyLink infotainment system. A key-controlled lockout feature discourages joy riding by cutting engine power in half. Cars equipped with manual transmissions get a Performance Traction Management system that modulates the engine's torque output during fast starts. This feature also manages engine power when the driver floors the accelerator coming out of a corner. **Road performance:** Powerful and brawny powertrain that responds quickly to the throttle; the gearbox performs well in all ranges and makes shifting smooth, with short throws and easy entry into all speeds. Stable handling for the level of performance available, with no oversteer, breakaway rear end, or nasty surprises, thanks in part to an effective electronic stability control system. Strong brakes that are easy to modulate and fade free. Some optional features aren't worth the extra money. For example, the Performance Data Recorder, which you can use to record driving videos and collect performance data isn't as useful as some smartphone apps. Also, the Competition Sport bucket seats are more about cachet than support and comfort. Beware of classic car dealers who tout recent Corvettes as an investment "vehicle." **Strong points:** Supercar performance; V8 power and soundtrack. The Corvette has relatively user-friendly controls, clear instruments, and lots of convenience features. Comfortable and supportive bucket seats. **Weak points:** A large, heavy car with limited luggage space. *2014-2017:* Luggage capacity, never a strong point on Corvettes, decreased significantly. Popular with car thieves. Quality control continues to be uneven, and powertrain, suspension, and body deficiencies are common. NHTSA recorded this 2015 Corvette owner's lament, "Water leaking into rear cargo hold area. Accumulating and not draining out. Don't know why." The car is so low that its front air dam scrapes over the smallest rise in the road. Expect lots of visits to the body shop. **Other opinions:** "Drivers are blown away by its incredible acceleration, agile handling and ride comfort." – *U.S. News & World Report.* "In spite of the marketing claims, the paint on the newest cars, along with fit and finish of the body, along with a variety of mechanical and electrical problems plus an eye opening number of engine and transmission failures rendered the newest Corvette a certifiable piece of shit and overall failure." – *corvettec7fiasco. blogspot.com/.* **Major redesign:** C6 Corvette 2005, C7 Corvette Stingray 2014. **Best alternatives:** Other sporty models worth considering are the Porsche 911 or Boxster, or a Nissan 350/370Z. The Camaro is less high-strung, and provides comparable Chevrolet V8 overkill for much less money.

Prices and Specs

Prices: *1LT Coupe:* $64,395, *Z06 3LZ convertible:* $107,510 **Freight:** $2,000 **Powertrain (Rear-drive):** Engines: 6.2L V8 (455 hp), 6.2L V8 Supercharged (650 hp); Transmissions: 7-speed man., 8-speed auto. **Dimensions:** Passengers: 2; Wheelbase: 106.7 in., 2,710 mm.; L: 176.9, 4,493 mm. W: 73.9 in., 1,877 mm; Weight (coupe): 3,298 lbs., 1,499 kg. **Fuel economy:** *2016 6.2L V8-auto. coupe:* 8.1/14.6L/100 km. **Assembled in:** U.S.A.

SAFETY: Not crash tested by either the IIHS or NHTSA.

Owner-reported safety-related failures: Worried about low-flying drones? Low-flying Corvette roofs may be a greater safety hazard. According to the December 31, 2009, *New York Times article,*

General Motors recalled 22,000 Corvettes [2005-07 Corvettes and 2006-07 Z06], because the roof might fly off. What do you think kicked the company into action? Complaints on the National Highway Traffic Safety Administration website from owners? Was it the safety agency itself, worried about the complaints? Concerns raised by the Federal Aviation Administration? Nope. It was the Japanese Ministry of Land Infrastructure and Transport, unhappy about the problem on imported Corvettes.

Vehicle rolls away when parked on an incline; Goodyear Eagle F1 tires hydroplane on wet roadways; leaking fuel pump; both headlights suddenly shut off and limited rearward visibility. Complaints posted at *safercar.gov* point out that through 2015, the 8-speed transmission often sticks in Second gear, shifts erratically, and lags and lurches when shifting:

> It always shifts erratically when starting out cold (lazy shift, slow shift, etc.) And occasionally does not downshift when car comes to a stop, only to slam hard into 1st when gas pedal is pressed to resume travel. Dealer says GM claims this is "normal," but no car I've ever owned behaved like this.

> ...

> Shifter sticks in Park intermittently. Defective solenoid on shifter that cannot be replaced. Need to replace entire shifting unit to repair. Defective solenoid on new shifters fail also. $700 to $1,000 U.S. to repair.

Jerky acceleration blamed on bad fuel, yet continued after driver went to a half dozen different gas stations. The suspension is unstable when passing over uneven roads and can make the car suddenly hop about on turns:

> There are reports of the 2014 Corvette skipping and hopping at low speeds when the wheels are locked all the way left or right while turning. It feels like the front end is going to fall off.

The car may self-start when gassing up:

> My 2015 Corvette was being filled at a gas station. The engine was off and I was 25 ft. away with my keys in my jacket pocket. The engine started by itself. No one was in the car, or near it.

> — *safercar.gov*

 RELIABILITY: Complex electronic suspension and powertrain components have a low tolerance for real-world conditions. The Camaro is easier to diagnose and much less finicky. In addition to the problems listed already, owners of 2005-2013 C6 Corvettes have reported random airbag malfunction warnings, Active Handling and traction control system electronic malfunction warnings, and the predictable GM Engine Service warning light on. Window and door locks can operate erratically; the convertible top can experience problems. Independent automobile journalists have been critical of the Active Fuel Management System and C6 Z06's valve guide failures:

Due to the lack of effective vibration suppression measures that are typically used in four-cylinder engines, such as a balance shaft, the Active Fuel Management (AFM) literally wreaks havoc on the engine, under the best scenario obliterating the under designed hydraulic serpentine belt tensioner and in more drastic situations, shuttering the thrust bearing and destroying the crankshaft and ultimately the entire engine.

On top of it, the excessive oil consumption directly related to AFM and specifically, oil getting pushed by the rings on the deactivated cylinders is becoming the norm as well, forcing owners to check the oil frequently.

Add to it the ill thought out direct injection system and flawed PCV system and the ownership of the Stingray can easily turn into a big nightmare, making old Lancias and Fiats look like a Honda Accord.

– corvettec7fiasco.blogspot.com/

• • •

The LS7 that powers the mighty, high-performance, super-cool C6 Z06 is subject to valve guide failure. GM claims that the problem affects a small percentage of LS7s built before Feb 2011, when a new inspection procedure "100% eliminated" the failure. The problem is that some mechanics report excessive valve guide wear on all LS7 engines regardless of age. There's even a suggestion that the faulty head design continues into the Camaro Z/28, which would be a shame.

– www.thetruthaboutcars.com/2014/09/fixed-abode-holding-corvette-standard)

Owner complaints about an overheating centre console:

Lift up a suitcase or put arm on the console storage area and you would burn your arm or hand. Heat inside storage area exceeded est. of 130 deg and burned spots in cell phone screen and computer in suitcase melted hard drive and ruined computer.

INTERNAL BULLETINS, SECRET WARRANTIES: 1997-2013—Front or rear composite springs may crack or break for no apparent reason. **2005-12**—Be wary that the top doesn't lift off while driving. Snap, pop, creak, or rattle noise from lift-off roof panel while driving. **2005-13**—Brake rotor may have surface cracks. Folding top contacts stowage compartment lid (tonneau) and/or tonneau contacts rear window during top operation (verify condition and perform appropriate adjustments). **2006-14**—TSB #09-04-20-001D addresses a chatter noise during low speed tight turn conditions (i.e. parking lot, driveway, etc.) primarily during cooler ambient temperatures. The condition can be experienced in all directions: Right, left, Forward, Reverse. **2006-15**—GM service bulletin #PIP4112P says "lag and lurch" acceleration is "normal." **2008-13**—When the engine is warm, the underhood bussed electrical center (UBEC) housing will expand, causing the headlamp low-beam relay control circuit routed wire to bend slightly. After the wire is repeatedly bent, it can fracture and separate. When this occurs, the low-beam headlamps will not illuminate. Dealers are to install a jumper wire. **2008-13**—Window malfunctions explained. **2009-14**—Some vehicles may not crank or start, caused by excessive leakage from cylinder past exhaust or exhaust intake valve, low static compression, sensor is disconnected, or while cranking, valvetrain fails to move. 2011—Wheel hop and differential chatter, under-hood rattle, engine tapping noise, and automatic transmission clunks. Power-steering and shock absorber fluid leakage. Airbag warning light comes on intermittently. Cracks in transparent removable roof panel. Convertible headliner frayed at outer edges. Troubleshooting tips for eliminating various noises from lift-off roof while driving. 2012-13—Campaign allows for the free replacement of the air inlet grille panel. 2012-15—GM bulletins confirm poor shifting into all gears; clutch pedal clunk, grind, or rattle. 2013— Low engine oil pressure, no oil pressure, and/or engine noise could be the result of a sticking oil pump pressure relief valve. 2013-15—When gear is in Park, it may fail to hold the vehicle when the brake is released. 2014—An engine that ticks or runs hot, may have a faulty head gasket. Vehicle may have a cooler outlet connector pipe on the auxiliary transmission cooler that may not be properly sealed to its mating connection. The improper seal may cause transmission oil to leak or, under certain conditions, the connector pipe to disconnect from the mating connection. This may result in a stall out, and leaking transmission oil could cause smoldering if it contacts the heated intake exhaust pipes or mufflers. GM bulletin says manual transmission may not shift from Sixth to Seventh gear. Another TSB says Performance Traction Management feature may fail. 2014-15—If car cranks, but won't start, GM says the camshaft position actuator solenoid valve may need to be replaced (TSB #PIP5130E). Hard cranks and a persistent fuel odour may require fuel injector servicing or replacement in addition to a new fuel injector oil ring seal. Sierras, Silverados, Suburbans, and Yukons are also affected (see Silverado section). Oil drips out of the air filter box. 2014-16—Engine misfire/tick noise. 2015—Fuel odour, fuel leaks or hard starts. 2015-16—Rattle heard from the engine bell housing area. 2016—Engine cylinder head gasket extended warranty for 6.2L V8 engines (see TSB in General Motors Introduction).

BUICK ENCORE ★★★

RATING: Average. Designed at the GM operation in South Korea, these micro-CUVs were introduced for the 2013 model year. They are based on the Chevrolet Sonic platform. The Encore is built in South Korea and the Trax is assembled in Mexico. The vehicles are the same mechanically, but exterior and cabin styling are unique to each model. A new Encore is much more expensive than a Trax. Both offer reasonable accommodation for four adults and acceptable cargo space. For 2017 the Encore is treated to minor restyling with Buick's new "wing" grille motif and new headlamps (L.E.D. on top models); cabin updates include a new dash centre stack, highlighted by an eight inch touch screen. Keyless Go and touch-activated entry are now offered on all models. Apple CarPlay and Android Auto are part of an updated IntelliLink infotainment system. **Road performance:** The tidy overall dimensions make them very easy to manoeuvre in the city. The 1.4 turbo delivers solid acceleration and is nicely matched to its 6-speed automatic transmission. Good ride-handling compromise for small family haulers. Few buyers are cross-shopping the two vehicles. **Strong points:** Last year, saw the arrival of a more powerful Encore Sport Touring model. The Buick is more luxurious than the Chevrolet and, due to what Buick refers to as Quiet Tuning, more refined as well. If you want a used all-wheel drive version of these vehicles, the Trax will be harder to find, but about half of all Encores sold were all-wheel drive. A used Encore is the better value if you want the additional features or luxury, because it doesn't retain the premium it commanded over the Trax when it was new. **Best alternatives:** Kia Soul and Nissan Juke.

For Safety and Reliability discussion, see under Chevrolet Trax.

Prices and Specs

Prices 2016: *FWD auto.:* $28,505, *Encore Premium AWD auto.:* $35,475 **Freight:** $1,600 **Powertrain (FWD/AWD):** Engines: 1.4L-4 turbo (138 hp., 153 hp., Encore 2016-2017) Transmissions: 6-speed auto. **Dimensions:** Passengers: 2/3; Wheelbase: 100.6 in, 2,555 mm. **Fuel economy:** *2017 AWD-auto:* 7.7/ 9.8L/100 km. **Assembled in:** South Korea.

CHEVROLET TRAX ★★★

RATING: Average. For discussion, see Buick Encore, above. Updates for 2017 include minor front styling with Chevrolet's new "dual port" grille, and new head and tail lamps. Cabin updates comprise a revised dash with a new seven inch touch screen, new instruments and revised trim. Advanced active safety features, including forward collision alert, blind spot detection, rear cross traffic alert, and lane departure warnings are now optional. **Road performance:** For discussion, see Buick Encore, above. **Strong points:** Apple CarPlay and Android Auto are now available as part of an updated MyLink infotainment system. The Premier trim level replaces the 2016 LTZ range topper. **Weak points:** The cabin looks plasticky on basic models. **Best alternatives:** Kia Soul, Nissan Juke, Mazda CX-3, and Honda HR-V.

Prices and Specs

Prices (2016): *1LS FWD man.:* $19,975, *LTZ AWD auto.:* $31,295 **Freight:** $1,600 **Powertrain (FWD/AWD):** Engines: 1.4L-4 turbo (138 hp.) Transmissions: 6-speed man. (Trax FWD only), 6-speed auto. **Dimensions:** Passengers: 2/3; Wheelbase: 100.6 in, 2,555 mm.; L: 168.5, 4,280 mm.; W: 69.9 in., 1,776 mm.; Weight: 3,208 lb., 1,455 kg. **Fuel economy:** *2017 Trax AWD-auto.:* 7.7/9.8L/100 km. **Assembled in:** Mexico (Trax) and South Korea (Encore).

Trax and Encore

RELIABILITY: Not rated due to insufficient data. Possible trouble points could include the turbo engine, electronics, and suspension.

SAFETY	
IIHS 2016 TRAX	
Small Front overlap	Good
Moderate Front overlap	Good
Side	Good
Roof strength	Good
Head restraints/seats	Good
Child seat	Acceptable
NHTSA 2017 Trax	★★★★

RATING: Average. The Equinox and Torrent were introduced for the 2005 model year. GM opted for an in-between size that was larger than prevailing compact SUVs at a compact SUV price. The Torrent was dropped at the end of 2009, with the demise of Pontiac. The 3.4L V6 in the first-generation vehicles was a U.S. design made in China. The redesigned 2010 Equinox was joined by the GMC Terrain, a new twin to replace the Pontiac. **Road performance:** The second-generation models offer nice performance with the smooth V6; the 4-cylinder engine and automatic are acceptable. The V6 was replaced by a stronger 3.6L for the 2013 model year, with no loss in fuel economy. The Terrain is more expensive to buy new than the Equinox with little to show for it, but maintains a price premium as it ages, with used examples priced up to 15% more than an equivalent Equinox. The Torrent sells for less than either of the other variants, because it is an orphaned Pontiac; all its mechanical components are shared with the Equinox. **Strong points:** Generous passenger room for this class; a reasonably quiet interior; most controls are well laid out, and seating is comfortable. 2016 and 2017 models feature the convenient MyLink infotainment system and onboard WiFi. Used prices are lower than for competing Japanese imports and reliability since 2013 has been superior to the competing Escape and all the compact Jeeps. Look for heavy discounting on end-of-run new 2017s as GM switches over to a redesigned 2018. **Weak points:** At nearly 3,800 pounds these are rather heavy vehicles, and the 4-cylinder engine gets noisy when pushed. Relatively high fuel consumption compared to published ratings suggests that GM "gamed" the fuel consumption test. Head restraints cut rear visibility; some cheap interior touches; and some controls are difficult to reach. **Major redesign:** 2005 introduction, 2010 major update, 2016 late-cycle update, 2018 pending third-generation redesign. **Best alternatives:** Ford Escape up to 2012, Hyundai Tucson or Kia Sportage new or used, or a used Santa Fe. Among the major Japanese brands only a used Nissan X-Trail or Rogue are anywhere near the low price point of a used Equinox or Terrain. Suzuki Grand Vitara or XL7.

Prices and Specs

Prices (2016): *Chev. LS FWD:* $27,170, *GMC Denali AWD:* $42,470 **Freight:** $1,700 **Powertrain (FWD/AWD):** Engines: 2.4L 4-cyl. (182 hp), 3.6L V6 (301 hp); Transmission: 6-speed auto. **Dimensions:** Passengers: 2/3; Wheelbase: 112.5 in., 2,857 mm.; L: 187.8, 4,770 mm.; W: 72.5 in. 1,841 mm.; Weight (2.4L AWD): 4,020 lb., 1,823 kg. **Fuel economy:** *2016 Equinox 2.4L-4 AWD:* 8.2/11.5L/100 km. **Assembled in:** Ingersoll and Oshawa, Ontario, Spring Hill, Tennessee.

ALERT! V6 engines suffer from timing chain issues, particularly the 3L. Have your mechanic check for timing chain noise coming from the front of the engine on start up.

Owner-reported safety-related failures: Outward visibility is obstructed by thick rear pillars.

RELIABILITY: Below average to 2011; overall reliability improved thereafter and parts and service are reasonable. The transmission, suspension, steering, electrical, and fuel systems are trouble areas. Expect the usual lit Engine Service warning from GM. ABS sensor and defective wheel bearings were more common through the 2011 model year.

INTERNAL BULLETINS, SECRET WARRANTIES: *Acadia, Enclave, Equinox, Outlook, Terrain, Torrent, Traverse, and VUE:* 2007-12—Transfer case fluid leak. 2010-11—Excessive oil consumption may be due to premature engine piston wear; replace the piston for free up to seven years and six months or 120,000 miles (193,000 km.). *Avalanche, Escalade, Sierra, Silverado, Suburban, Tahoe, and Yukon:* 2007-13—Tapping/clicking/ticking noise at windshield area. *Avalanche, Equinox, Escalade, Sierra, Silverado, Suburban, Tahoe, Terrain, Yukon, and Yukon Denali:* 2010-12—Roof panel flutters/rattle noise when doors close. 2010-14—*Troubleshooting various front end noises on bumps. Euqinox, Terrain:* Power steering sticks or slips (see TSB in Malibu *Internal Bulletins*). 2010-15—Power steering noise or hose leaks are addressed in TSB #13-02-32-001C. Steering shudder during slow speed maneuvers:

SAFETY

IIHS 2016 EQUINOX AND TERRRAIN

Small Front	Good
Front	Good
Side	Good
Roof strength	Good
Head restraint and seats	Good
Child seat anchors	Acceptable
NHTSA Overall 2017 Equinox and Terrrain	★★★★★

STEERING SHUDDER (VIBRATION) DURING SLOW SPEED MANEUVERS

SERVICE BULLETIN NO.:#PI0814D   DATE: APRIL 15, 2014

GM

2010-2015 Chevrolet Equinox; 2010-2015 GMC Terrain.

CONCERN: Some customers may comment they are experiencing a steering vibration, felt through the steering wheel and vehicle structure, combined with a moan type noise. This condition is most noticed during low speed parking lot maneuvers or when the vehicle is stationary and the steering wheel is turned.

IMPORTANT: The following repair will make noticeable improvements to the shudder (vibration) condition. However, in most cases it will not completely eliminate a common hydraulic power steering system noise. This condition can be corrected by replacing the following components: power steering gear inlet hose assembly, generator (alternator) assembly and the emission evaporative hose. The revised power steering hose assembly is longer and provides a dampening quality. The revised generator has an isolation pulley and the revised evaporative hose is designed to clear the revised power steering hose.

AMERICAN MODELS

PART FOUR

2011—Automatic transmission clunks when shifting. Trouble-shooting tips to plug transfer case fluid leaks. Power steering, shock absorber leaks. Tire-pressure monitor system free update for Canadians only. *Equinox, LaCrosse, Malibu ECO, Regal, Terrain, Verano: 2012-13*—Voice recognition feature inoperative. *Equinox: 2013*—The flexible fuel sensor may fail prematurely; a "secret" warranty covers the replacement cost (see Silverado section). GM will replace a defective starter motor for free under its base warranty. Crankshaft rear seal oil leaks (see TSB in General Motors Introduction). *Equinox, Terrain: 2013-14*—Power steering "secret" warranty (see TSB, above). *Trax: 2013-14*—Oil leaks, burning oil, and turbo failures (see TSB in Cruze *Internal Bulletins*). *2013-16*—Front seats stick in the full-up position. *2014*—Water leaks on front carpet. Creak or pop from right front of body. *2014-16*—Troubleshooting various infotainment malfunctions. *2015-16*—Fuel door won't pop open.

BUICK ENCLAVE 2008-2017/CHEVROLET TRAVERSE 2009-2017/GMC ACADIA 2007-2017/SATURN OUTLOOK	*2007-2010* ★ *2007-2016* ★★★

RATING: *All models:* Below Average (2007-10); Average (2007-16). These are practically identical seven- and eight-passenger crossover SUVs; the Acadia and Outlook arrived first, followed by the Enclave a year later and finally the Traverse in 2009. The Outlook was dropped in 2010 when GM axed the Saturn brand. These vehicles performs reasonably well, and offers three-row seating. They're large, ponderous vehicles with good people-carrying ability. The downsides are high fuel consumption, and they're unsuitable for heavy towing. The discontinued Saturn Outlook and Chevrolet Traverse are the least expensive variants of this platform, with the Buick being the most expensive. That said, mid-range versions of these three vehicles are similarly equipped and priced. Some Outlook-specific body parts could become increasingly hard to find as time progresses. For 2017, GMC introduced an all-new second-generation Acadia. The vehicle has abandoned its former unique "supersized" positioning and is now sized against mainstream rivals like the Ford Explorer, Honda Pilot, and Toyota Highlander. The new Acadia is powered by GM's ubiquitous 3.6L V6, with 4-cylinder power available for the first time. GM is once again following a staged release strategy for the second-generation versions of the trio, with the next-generation Traverse and Enclave to follow. **Road performance:** The smooth 3.6L V6 has plenty of power for most chores and isn't as fuel-thirsty as some of the large body-on-frame SUVs in the same class. Comfortable ride and reasonably responsive handling for large, overweight vehicles. The automatic transmission sometimes hesitates when shifting. **Strong points:** A quiet and spacious interior; good towing capability. Being larger than mainstream vehicles, GM's giants have more third-row legroom and cargo space with the third-row seat in place than any other competitor. A used Enclave offers plenty of luxury for a small premium over the other versions. **Weak points:** Poor reliability of early models.

Used prices jumped after the Canadian dollar dropped, because of competition from pickers working for U.S. dealers. Middle-row passenger windows vibrate and make a loud noise when partially rolled down; excessive interior creaking and squeaking. **Major redesign:** *2007: Acadia and Outlook introduced; 2008: Enclave introduced; 2009: Traverse introduced; 2010: Outlook discontinued; 2017: Acadia redesign; 2018: Traverse and Enclave pending redesign.* **Best alternatives:** Smaller three-row alternatives include the Explorer and Flex from Ford, the Honda Pilot, Mazda CX-9, and the Toyota Highlander.

Prices and Specs

Prices (2016): *Enclave FWD Leather:* $48,935, *AWD Premium:* $56,435; *Traverse FWD LS:* $34,530, *AWD LTZ:* $51,170; *Acadia (2017): SLE-1:* $34,995, *AWD Denali:* $55,695 **Freight:** $1,700 **Powertrain (FWD/AWD):** Engine: 2.5L 4 (193 hp/2017 Acadia only), 3.6L V6 (281-288 hp); Transmission: 6-speed auto. **Dimensions:** *Traverse:* Passengers: 7/8; Wheelbase: 118.9 in., 3021 mm.; L: 203.7 in., 5173 mm., W: 78.5 in., 1993 mm.; Weight (2016 Enclave AWD): 4,922 lb., 2,233 kg. **Assembled in:** U.S.A.

ALERT! Again, those pesky head restraints can make your driving a living hell if you are not the ideal size.

Owner-reported safety-related failures: Passenger side window may spontaneously explode, accelerator sometimes "sticks", smell of fuel inside the car, side airbags sometimes fail to deploy, vehicle may stall on the highway, side panels create a huge blind spot, and there's limited rear visibility.

RELIABILITY: The 2007-2010 models are risky buys. Reliability improved afterward, as GM corrected several recurring engine and transmission deficiencies. Engine timing chain and internal failures reported to 2010

SAFETY	
IIHS 2016 ACADIA	
Small Front overlap	Not Rated
Moderate Front overlap	Good
Side	Good
Roof strength	Good
Head restraints/seats	Good
Child seat	Moderate
NHTSA 2017	★★★★★

and on some higher mileage versions of more recent engines. Transmission oil leaks and failures to 2010. Fuel-pump module fails, making the engine run rough or stall; inaccurate fuel gauges; a noisy, failure-prone suspension; defective wheel bearings and ABS sensors; Engine Service light on; check for excess condensation in the headlights and taillights, and burnt headlights.

INTERNAL BULLETINS, SECRET WARRANTIES: 2007-10—"Secret" warranty coverage on the water pump shaft seals up to ten years or 120,000 miles. In TSB #13091 issued on May 20, 2013, GM said the seal might fail and cause coolant leaks. Affected models: 2007-10 GMC Acadias and Saturn Outlooks; 2008-10 Buick Enclaves; and

2009-10 Chevrolet Traverses. Should the leak develop, a new water pump will be installed. **2009-16**—Clunk noise from rear suspension in cold weather. **2011**—Electrical/water issues. Troubleshooting tips to plug transfer case fluid leaks. Power-steering, automatic transmission clunks. Second-row "Easy Entry" seats may not work. Engine won't shut off or start. **2012-14**—Windshield popping or creaks in cold weather. **2012-13**—Crankshaft rear seal oil leaks (see TSB in General Motors Introduction). **2013-14**—Faulty door locks. Intermittent radio shut off, instrument cluster gauges inoperative, and blind spot indicator flashing. **2014**—Inaccurate fuel gauge readings. **2014-15**—Airbag warning light comes on for no reason. **2015**—Trouble-shooting delayed upshifts, firm upshifts or downshifts, and shift flare. Intake air heater fires on diesel-equipped models.

CADILLAC SRX

2010-2011 ★
2012-2016 ★★★

bad buy

RATING: Not Recommended (2010-2011); Average (2012-2016). Introduced for the 2010 model year, the second-generation SRX was replaced by the XT5 for 2017. 2010 and 2011 models could be powered by either a 2.8L V6 turbo or a normally-aspirated 3L V6, both of which were replaced by a better 3.6L V6 starting in 2012. Cadillac's irritating CUE interface took control of the dashboard in 2013. The very angular Cadillac styling of the SRX attracted a fair number of admirers, and over 4000 were sold in 2014. The same angular styling reappears inside the cabin. Comfortable seats, front and rear, but rear seat legroom is no more than average. Reasonable cargo space, but total volume is hampered by a shallow cargo bay and the slope of the tailgate. Since 2012, the 3.6L V6 has been the sole engine offered; it delivers more than adequate performance to the front, or optionally, all wheels, via a 6-speed automatic transmission.

RELIABILITY: If buying used, look for a vehicle with the balance of its factory warranty or try to purchase a full-coverage extended warranty offered by General Motors. Frequent electronic malfunctions; consider checking for codes to ensure the seller hasn't recently cancelled a lit Engine Service warning light. Excessive oil consumption possible; check for noisy, worn or stretched, timing chains and/or camshafts on high mileage vehicles. The 2.8 and 3L engines are less reliable than the later 3.6. The brake system is prone to needing expensive service. The ABS brake pump can fail and electrical problems are common.

SAFETY

IIHS 2016

Small Front overlap	Not Rated
Moderate Front overlap	Good
Side	Good
Roof strength	Good
Head restraints/seats	Good
Child seat	Moderate
NHTSA Overall 2016	★★★★★

CADILLAC ESCALADE/CHEVROLET SUBURBAN/CHEVROLET TAHOE/ GMC YUKON

★★★★

HYBRID
2007-2013 ★

2015 GMC Yukon

RATING: Above Average; *Hybrid:* Not recommended (2007-2013). The Hybrid was dropped in 2013 because it was "the right airplane at the wrong airport" according to *Los Angeles Times* car critic, Dan Neil. These vehicles, based on GM's large pickup line, were all new for the 2015 model year with little change for 2017. These large SUVs are for those who need rugged, truck-like capabilities for towing boats, horse boxes, or large travel trailers. The Tahoe, Yukon, and Escalade are built on a shorter wheelbase, with the Yukon XL, Suburban, and Escalade ESV underpinned by a longer frame. Only the long-wheelbase variants have the passenger capacity and cargo space of GM's own Enclave, Traverse and (pre-2017) Acadia trio. The chief difference between the Chevrolet and GMC versions and the Cadillac is a plusher cabin and a much higher price tag. These SUVs have been flying out of dealer showrooms since fuel prices plummeted and new-generation models were introduced for 2015. Based on GM's large pickups that went on sale the year before, upgrades included greater refinement, aluminum hoods and liftgate panels, and more-efficient powertrains. Also new is the addition of fold-flat second- and third-row seats and greater legroom for second-row passengers. The prices of these "carriage class" SUVs are such that fuel economy is not a factor for potential new vehicle buyers. However, prices for used examples are sensitive to gasoline prices; resale values are strong when fuel prices are low, dropping when fuel prices cross about $1.30 per litre. **Road performance:** Surprisingly confident handling for SUVs this large. Comfortable highway cruisers and relatively manageable in suburbia. **Strong points:** Robust acceleration with either engine and a comfortable ride and quiet interior. Good towing capacity (Tahoe up to 8,600 lb., 3900 kg.). The square-rigged styling offers outward visibility that is superior to many smaller vehicles. **Weak points:** Mediocre fuel economy; small third-row seat sits too low and the seats on pre-2015 versions don't fold into the floor; long braking distances to 2014; and spotty fit and finish. **Major redesign:** 2007 and 2015. **Other opinions:** Reviewers call the all-new Tahoe "one of the best large SUVs on the market, pointing to its gentle ride, strong acceleration, refined cabin and favorable fuel economy."– *U.S. News & World Report.* **Best alternatives:** The Ford Expedition/Lincoln Navigator twins, the Toyota Sequoia, and the Nissan Armada/Infiniti QX80 duo are the other vehicles in this boat/Airstream hauling segment. If you don't require the towing capacity, GM's own Acadia, Enclave, Traverse trio offers virtually the same passenger and cargo space. Of course, a minivan beats all of these vehicles handily when it comes to people carrying and their luggage, but most buyers in this segment wouldn't be caught dead owning one.

ALERT! Used prices have climbed substantially because of competition from U.S. buyers taking advantage of favourable exchange rates on the Canadian dollar.

Owner-reported safety-related failures: The headlights don't sufficiently illuminate the roadway:

> The contact owns a 2015 Chevrolet Tahoe. While driving various speeds at night, the exterior lighting was too dim because of an invisible line above the dashboard.

Also, keep a wary eye on the rear hatch when loading or unloading cargo warns this Escalade owner in his *safercar.gov* posting:

> 2011 Cadillac Escalade power rear cargo door is a serious safety hazard. Son was seriously hurt at airport luggage claims when a power rear cargo door was closing, came down on his head and face without warning of any kind that this door was closing. The door is so large and heavy as it comes down, it's fast and does not retract back up when it hits something.

SAFETY

IIHS 2016 TAHOE	
Small Front overlap	Not Rated
Moderate Front overlap	Not Rated
Side	Not Rated
Roof strength	Not Rated
Head restraints/seats	Not Rated
Child seat	Acceptable
NHTSA 2017 Tahoe	★★★★

RELIABILITY: Fewer reliability problems since the last redesign in 2007. Problem areas include poor front brake durability (improved aftermarket components are available and reasonably priced); faulty powertrains, suspension, and climate controls; chronic electrical shorts; and various body glitches. Expensive HID headlight failures on the Escalade and some Yukon models. Avoid the hybrid as too few were sold and service expertise is scarce. Parts are easy to find, many are reasonably priced in the aftermarket, and repairs can be performed at independent shops. Five-year/160,000 km powertrain warranty is a plus. Aftermarket rust-proofing is recommended to extend the service life and resale value of these rugged vehicles; buyers line up for clean vehicles at every price point. The APA recommends Krown Rust Control for an annual application or Barry's Rustproofing in the Montreal market for a lifetime grease treatment to protect the fragile rocker panels, rear fenders, and floor (contact information is in the Part Four Introduction).

INTERNAL BULLETINS, SECRET WARRANTIES: 2007-13—Inoperative cruise control; inoperative or unwanted activation of radio controls; backlighting flashes, flickers, or inoperative due to possible short to ground on steering wheel coil connector. 2007-14—Excessive oil consumption, fouled, cracked spark plugs, and a rough running engine may need ten hours of work and the replacement of key engine parts says TSB: #10-06-01-008M, dated Nov. 26, 2014. If this repair is premature, it should be covered.

ENGINE OIL CONSUMPTION ON ALUMINUM BLOCK/IRON BLOCK ENGINES WITH ACTIVE FUEL MANAGEMENT (AFM) (INSTALL AFM OIL DEFLECTOR AND CLEAN CARBON FROM CYLINDER AND/OR INSTALL UPDATED VALVE COVER)

SERVICE BULLETIN NO.: 10-06-01-008M   DATE: NOVEMBER 26, 2014

2007-2014 Cadillac Escalade; 2007-2013 Chevrolet Avalanche, Silverado; 2007-2014 Chevrolet Suburban, Tahoe; 2010-2012 Chevrolet Colorado; 2010-2015 Chevrolet Camaro; 2007-2013 GMC Sierra, Sierra Denali; 2007-2014 GMC Yukon; 2010-2012 GMC Canyon; 2008-2009 Pontiac G8 GT; Vehicles Built Prior to February 1, 2011 Require Updated Valve Cover and October 2010 Require AFM Shield; Equipped with Any of the Following Engines: Aluminum Block V8 Engine with Active Fuel Management (RPOs LH9, L94, LZ1, L99, LC9, LH6, L76, L92, LFA (Hybrid); Iron Block V8 Engine with Active Fuel Management (AFM) (RPOs LMG, LY5).

CONDITION: Some customers may comment about engine oil consumption of vehicles with higher mileage (approximately 48,000 to 64,000 km. (30,000 to 40,000 mi) and a service engine soon light being on and/or rough running engine. Verify that the PCV system is functioning properly. If the customer understands that some oil consumption is normal and still feels the consumption level is excessive, more than 1 quart per 2000 to 3000 miles of driving, perform the service indicated in this bulletin. It is no longer necessary to have the customer return multiple times to have the usage verified.

CAUSE: This condition may be caused by two conditions. Oil pulled through the PCV system or oil spray that is discharged from the AFM pressure relief valve within the crankcase. Under most driving conditions and drive cycles, the discharged oil does not cause a problem. Under certain drive cycles (extended high engine speed operation), in combination with parts at the high end of their tolerance specification, the oil spray quantity may be more than usual, resulting in excessive deposit formation in the piston ring grooves, causing increased oil consumption and cracked or fouled spark plugs (# 1 and/or # 7). Refer to the latest version of Corporate Bulletin Number 12-06-01-001.

NOTE: When installing the updated valve cover or reinstalling a used valve cover, verify that the baffles can hold water and do not leak. If any leaks are found, seal with RTV if possible or replace the valve cover. Thoroughly clean and dry the valve cover before installation.

2007-16—Owners report a clunking noise originating from the front of the vehicle when traveling over bumps. Likely cause is a damaged stabilizer bar frame bracket. There have been some cases on older vehicles of corrosion affecting the bracket, as well. *Suburban, Tahoe, Yukon:* **2009-14**—Some vehicles may not crank or start, caused by excessive leakage from cylinder past exhaust or exhaust intake valve, low static compression, sensor is disconnected, or, while cranking, valve train fails to move. **2011**—Engine knocking on a cold start (GM says, "Don't worry, be happy"). Power-steering, shock absorber leaks. Airbag warning light comes on intermittently. Airbag isn't flush with the dash. Exhaust leak, rattle, and rumble noise. Tapping, clicking, and ticking noise at windshield area. Sun visor fails to stay in the up position. Sticking, binding door mounted seat switches. Front-door window regulator squeaks. Third-row seat hard to remove and install. Front seat cushion cover becomes detached and warped. Wavy front or rear fender liners. **2012-13**—4WD fails to engage as Service alert lights up. What to do if the blower motor is noisy or doesn't work properly. **2014-15**—Shift lever hits ignition key: Truck shuts down (see TSB in Chevrolet Silverado/GMS Sierra *Internal Bulletins*). An engine that ticks or runs hot, may have a faulty head gasket. If the vehicle cranks, but won't start, GM says the camshaft position actuator solenoid valve may need to be replaced (TSB: # PIP5130E). **2015**—TSB #PIT5288A gives tips for troubleshooting electrical malfunctions: Dead battery, no entry/start, no audio, and an inoperative touch screen, rear wiper, rear power windows, and tire pressure warning device. Hood fluttering. **2016**—Engine cylinder head gasket extended warranty for 6.2L V8 engines (see TSB in General Motors Introduction).

CHEVROLET COLORADO/GMC CANYON

2004-2012 ★★
2015-2017 ★★★

2015 GMC Yukon

RATING: Below Average (2004-2012); Average (2015-2017). These GM pickups are an alternative to the expensive and sometimes hard to find used Toyota Tacoma;

most budget buyers choose the Ford Ranger instead because of its lower prices and wider availability. Introduced in 2004, they received improved engines in 2007. The base engine is a 4-cylinder, with an unusual inline five being optional. Unsettled ride. Mediocre interior finish. After having been discontinued at the end of 2012, the Colorado and Canyon returned for the 2015 model year. In 2016, a 2.8L 4-cylinder turbodiesel arrived – it's the only diesel available in a compact pickup – as well as Apple CarPlay and Android Auto. Unlike Ford, which dropped its compact Ranger pickup and bet the farm on a lighter, full-size F150, GM opted to return to a two-platform strategy, using conventional engine technology and steel bodies for both its small and large pickups. Available body styles include an extended cab, with rear flipper doors and vestigial rear seats, and a crew cab with four forward hinged doors. The crew cab body style is offered in two different cargo bed lengths. Three engines are offered, a 200 hp version of the proven 2.5L Ecotec four, a 305 hp 3.6L V6, and a 2.8L turbodiesel 4-cylinder with 181 hp and an impressive 369 lb-ft of torque. A 6-speed manual transmission is available on extended cab models but a 6-speed automatic is standard with the crew cab and optional on the Extended Cab. Rear-wheel drive is standard, with all-wheel drive optional with all engines. **Road performance:** Driven with the 2.8L diesel and automatic transmission, the truck was quick enough, but very noisy when accelerating (it calms down at constant speed). Ride, handling and steering were all well sorted. **Strong points:** *2015-2017:* Well designed, practical cabin that is carefully assembled from attractive components. Roomy, comfortable front seats and those in the second row of crew cab versions have competitive legroom for the class. **Weak points:** The brakes stop the truck well, but pedal effort required to engage the brakes is too high. **Best alternatives:** A new Toyota Tacoma, or used Ford Ranger or Nissan Frontier.

Prices and Specs

Prices: *Extended cab 2.5L RWD manual 6.2 foot box base model:* $21,340, *Crew cab Z71 AWD 3.6L V6:* $37,580 **Freight:** $1,695 **Powertrain (Rear-drive, AWD):** Engines: 2.5L 4 (200 hp), 2.8L 4 turbodiesel (181 hp), 3.6L V6 (305 hp). Transmissions: 6-speed man., 6-speed auto. **Dimensions (Extended Cab):** Wheelbase: 128.3 in., 3,258 mm.; L: 212.7 in., 3,258 mm. W: 74.3 in., 1,886 mm. *(Crew Cab) 5.2 foot box:* Wheelbase: 128.3 in., 3,258 mm., L: 212.7 in., 3,258 mm., W: 74.3 in., 1,886 mm; Weight (Crew Cab 5.2 foot box) 4,310 lbs., 1,955 kg.). **Fuel economy:** *2016 Crew Cab V6:* 9.2L/13L/100 km. **Assembled in:** U.S.A.

RELIABILITY: *2004-2012:* Below average, improving to average. Check for lit ABS and engine service lights. *2015-2017:* Incomplete data. Complaints relate to erratic automatic transmission performance. Five-year/160,000 km powertrain warranty is a plus; the first four oil changes are now included. (Also see TSB in Cadillac Escalade *Internal Bulletins*.)

CHEVROLET SILVERADO/GMC SIERRA 1500 AND 2500

2005-2013	★★★★
2014-2017	★★★★★
HYBRID	
2009-2013	★★

Silverado/Sierra and Chrysler Ram have the edge over Ford's F-150 until we see how Ford's aluminum body and redesign hold up long term.

RATING: Recommended (2014-2017); Above Average (2005-2013). General Motors introduced its first pickup truck in 1930. Since then, GM has marketed its pickups under two brand names while Ford and Fiat Chrysler market under a single brand name. Ford always snags the pickup truck sales crown even though the combined total of Silverado/Sierra sales can exceed those of the F-150. There is little difference between the two nameplates; the Denali version of the Sierra is a bit fancier than a top-of-the-line Silverado. Sold from 2009 to 2013, the Silverado 1500 Hybrid has a 6.0L V8 that pairs with an electric motor to produce 332 hp. It can run on one or both of its power sources depending on driving demands, and doesn't need to be plugged in. The Hybrid sold in paltry numbers and is not recommended. GM's pickup quality and performance improved considerably with the 2014 redesign. The 2014 re-engineered 1500 model gets better fuel economy, is impressively refined, and has a well-conceived cabin assembled with attractive materials. Unlike the F-150 and Ram pickup, which are styled to intimidate, GM's pickup duo are sleeker and built to a more human scale. GM's pickups are easier to get into and the tailgate sides are low enough for people to see into, which is not possible on the Ford or Ram unless you are tall. **Road performance:** Post-2014 models handle much better, offer more usable power, provide a controlled ride, and have attractive cabins. Some annoying powertrain glitches:

I have had a recurring problem with my new 2012 Chevrolet Silverado 1500 LT (5.3L engine) going into "Reduced Engine Power Mode" which also results in the disabling of stability control and traction control. This is a dangerous condition in that it results in a loss of power while operating the vehicle upon the roadway. An authorized repair facility has replaced the number one and two throttle sensors, the accelerator pedal assembly, the throttle body, the alternator, the computer, and a large ground wire behind the dash. A GM engineer has flown in and now the repair center is replacing the engine wiring harness. The vehicle (which was purchased less than three months ago) has been out of service for approximately 30 days. In researching this matter I have found that Chevy has had an ongoing problem with this in various vehicles in its product line since 2003. Although several service bulletins have been produced there does not seem to be a consensus regarding the cause of this problem. All of the parts associated with trouble codes C0242, P2127, and P2138 have been replaced without result. This condition could result in the affected vehicles being rear-ended, or, because of the loss of stability and traction control, result in a rollover. Transmission shifts hard from a complete stop as 1st gear was being engaged. The transmission body and valves were replaced. Now getting more problems with the transmission shifting between gears at a speed of 35-45 mph [56-72 km/h]. Transmission disengages and I have no power going to the wheels for 5-10 seconds.

Strong points: *2014-2017 1500:* Comfortable front seating; a quiet interior; lots of storage capability; generally good crashworthiness scores; and best-in-class V8 fuel economy with the 6-speed automatic transmission coupled to the 5.3L V8. *2500:* These are heavy-duty work trucks. The standard engine is a powerful 360 hp 6.0L V8, with an optional 397 hp 6.6L turbodiesel. Both engines feature 6-speed auto. transmissions, with the diesel hooked up to the Allison 1000 unit. **Weak points:** Least inviting back seat and smallest rear head restraints of the large domestic pickups. Introduced for 2016, the new 8-speed automatic doesn't appear to improve fuel economy. *2500 series:* GM Duramax-equipped pickups need diesel exhaust fluid (urea) refills every 8,000 km. (5,000 mi.). Furthermore, the urea-filling process can be costly when done by the dealer, versus buying the product off the shelf and pouring it yourself. **Major redesign:** *Silverado/Sierra 1500:* 2007 and 2014. **Other opinions:** "The rear headrest of the crew cabs are too small and do not raise up high enough to protect the head of anyone in the rear seat. There is also no centre head rest for the rear seat." – *safercar.gov.* **Best alternatives:** The Ford F-150 and Ram pickups. If you don't need the truck to earn a living, a Toyota Tundra is more reliable but less comfortable and uses more gas; same-day parts availability is superior with Ford and GM.

ALERT! *1500:* Complaints of excessive vibration at moderate speed:

> I have what has been deemed "the Chevy shake." Tires have been replaced and balanced. But at highway speeds 70 mph and above there is a very noticeable vibration in the truck. I just read a report describing this problem in the '14 & '15 models but GM hasn't fixed the problem yet in '16.

Owner-reported safety-related failures: 2013 models may surge suddenly and the accelerator sometimes sticks when "floored."

RELIABILITY: Improved after the 2007 redesign. *2007-2013:* The 5.3L Vortec engine can burn oil and has marginal crankcase ventilation that can permit internal sludge buildup; don't skip oil changes. Some 6-speed transmission failures to 2013; slipping or a knock or shudder when going through the speeds may point to an impending repair. Lit Engine Service and ABS warning lights are fairly common. Top of dash can crack. Check the front suspension control arm bushings, ball joints, rear shocks and springs. The five-year/160,000 km powertrain warranty is a plus; it now includes the first four oil changes. Aftermarket rustproofing is recommended to extend the service life and resale value of these rugged vehicles. The APA recommends Krown Rust Control for an annual application or Barry's Rustproofing for a lifetime grease application in the Montreal market to protect the fragile rocker panels, rear fenders, and floor (contact information is in the Part Four Introduction).

SAFETY

IIHS 2016 SILVERADO CREW CAB

Small Front overlap	Moderate
Moderate Front overlap	Good
Side	Good
Roof strength	Good
Head restraints/seats	Good
Child seat	Poor

NHTSA 2017 Silverado Crew Cab ★★★★★

INTERNAL BULLETINS, SECRET WARRANTIES: 2001-16—Silencing diesel engine noise. 2002-15—Leakage of EGR engine coolant into the combustion chamber of the 2002-15 Silverado, Sierra; 2004-09 Kodiak, C4500-C5500, Topkick C4500-C5500; 2006-15 Express, and Savana. By admitting this defect, GM admits liability. GM should pay the estimated $3,000 repair when the engines fail prematurely. 2007-13—Inoperative cruise control; inoperative or unwanted activation of radio controls; backlighting flashes, flickers, or inoperative due to possible short to ground on steering wheel coil connector. Excessive oil consumption, fouled, cracked spark plugs, and rough running engines may need ten hours of work and the replacement of key engine parts says TSB: #10-06-01-008M. This repair is premature and should be covered after the manufacturer warranty expires (see TSB in Cadillac Escalade *Internal Bulletins*). Fractured leaf springs are covered by a secret warranty up to five years/160,000 km. 2007-16—Owners report a clunking noise originating from the front of the vehicle that is more predominant during turns or traveling over bumps. Likely caused by a damaged stabilizer shaft frame bracket. There have been some cases on older vehicles of corrosion affecting the bracket. Power steering noise or leak in cold temperatures. 2009-13—Brake-induced pulsation/vibration felt in steering wheel, rumble noise from underbody during downhill descent (verify condition and replace front brake pads). GM admits this is a factory goof-up. *Silverado, Sierra, Savana, Express:* 2009-14—Some vehicles many not crank or start, caused by excessive leakage from cylinder past exhaust or exhaust intake valve, low static compression, sensor is disconnected, or while cranking valve train fails to move. 2010-15—A fuel odour in the cabin may be caused by a leak at the bottom of the flywheel housing. 2011—Airbag light comes on intermittently. Side roof-rail airbags may not deploy as designed, says GM Customer Satisfaction Campaign Bulletin #11288 (shh…it's a "secret warranty" – the fix is free). Automatic transmission clunks when shifted. Rear suspension clunk and squeaks. Rattle noise from wheel or hubcap. Underbody pop, clunk when turning. Rear leaf-spring slap or clunk noise. Exhaust leak, rattle, or rumble. Front-door regulator squeak. Tapping, clicking, or ticking at the windshield area. Shock absorber and power-steering leaks. Sun visor won't stay up. Water leaks through the headliner near the sunroof. Tires may slowly go flat. Warped or wavy fender liners. Rearview mirror shake. Front brake vibration. *Sierra, Silverado, Express, Savana, Suburban, and Yukon XL:* 2011-12—Free fix to correct a rear axle grinding noise/vibration. Program was in effect until April 30, 2014; an extension can be requested through small claims court. Right side roof-rail airbags may be improperly mounted; GM will remount the airbags free of charge. 2012-13—4WD fails to engage as Service alert lights up. What to do if the blower motor is noisy or doesn't work properly? 2013—Starter motor may short out after wearing through insulation. 2014—Some 2013 model year Buick LaCrosse and Regal; Cadillac ATS and SRX; Chevrolet Caprice, Captiva, Equinox, and Impala; and GMC Terrain vehicles; and 2014 Chevrolet Silverado 1500 and GMC Sierra 1500 vehicles, equipped with E85 flex fuel capability. The flexible fuel sensor may become inoperative during normal operation due to an electrical failure caused by road salt and other environmental contaminants. Special Coverage Adjustment: Dealers are to replace the fuel flex sensor, free of charge. This special coverage covers the condition for a period of ten years or 150,000 miles (240,000 km.), whichever occurs first. Water leak under back glass from power sliding window. The power sliding rear glass regulator may need to be replaced if the power window doesn't work. Want a laugh? Another TSB (#14002A) outlines a free "service procedure to inspect and, if necessary, repair the appearance of underbody components on our pickups that may not meet GM appearance requirements for new vehicles. These vehicles may exhibit signs of premature surface degradation on certain underbody components." Surface degradation is GM-speak for rust. 2014-15—Hood fluttering (TSB #PIT5288A) gives tips for troubleshooting electrical malfunctions: Dead battery, no entry/start, no audio, and inoperative touch screen, rear wiper, rear power windows, and tire pressure warning feature. An engine that ticks or runs hot may have a faulty head gasket. If the truck cranks, but won't start, GM says the camshaft position actuator solenoid valve may need to be replaced (TSB # PIP5130E). In some trucks, various diagnostic trouble codes are displayed and panel cluster warning lamps and/or malfunction indicator lamp (MIL) illuminating diesel exhaust fluid (DEF) and engine may crank, not start, and runs rough or misfires. Trailer hitch may have defective welds; free replacement until February 28, 2018. Shift lever hits ignition key: Truck shuts down.

SHIFT LEVER CONTACTS IGNITION KEY

SERVICE BULLETIN NO.: 14-00-89-005   DATE: NOV 6, 2014

GM

2014 Chevrolet Silverado 1500; 2015 Chevrolet Silverado, Suburban, Tahoe; 2014 GMC Sierra 1500; 2015 GMC Sierra, Yukon, Yukon XL – Without Keyless Engine Start Switch (Push Button).

CONDITION: Some customers may comment that if the tilt steering column is in the full-up position and the shift lever is moved between gears, the shift lever contacts the head of the ignition key. Some contact force may rotate the ignition key and shut the engine off.

CORRECTION: A new design ignition key has been released. Technicians should replace the ignition key with the latest design. Refer to the pictures below for identification of the old key (1) versus new key (2).

2015—In response to owner complaints of dead batteries, GM will modify the OnStar feature, *gratis,* because it could be draining the battery. Fuel tank may be hard to fill. 2015-16—Delayed transmission shifting after sitting with engine off. 2016—Troubleshooting excessive shake or shudder, a recurrent problem throughout the years. Engine cylinder head gasket extended warranty for 6.2L V8 engines (see TSB in General Motors Introduction).

JAPANESE AND KOREAN AUTOMAKERS

ACURA

Automobile magazine called Acura "a lost brand" – a sobering judgment of the first Japanese nameplate to take on the U.S. luxury market (four years before Lexus) with its popular 1986 Legend and Integra. Acura was also the first Japanese luxury brand to arrive to Canada. Acura copied its U.S. distribution network, selling through standalone dealerships, a model that both Toyota (Lexus) and Nissan (Infiniti) avoided when they came here. Along with marketing gaffes like discontinuing the popular Integra, and some lacklustre products, luxury vehicle volume in Canada has not been sufficient to sustain the Acura dealer network. Acura was compelled to release Acura-branded Civic spinoffs like the EL and CSX compacts to keep dealerships viable. Acura luxury-cruisers like the RL have no customer following here, and are essentially vanity products marketed regardless of any possible return on investment. One of Acura's best moves was to create the MDX, a luxury three-row sport utility vehicle, which has become a popular mainstay; the current RDX luxury sport utility combines existing components from various Honda products with unique exterior styling and an appealing cabin. It also appears to be on target.

Like Infiniti, Acura seems perpetually stuck in a junior prestige rut. Its vehicles are not compelling enough in their own right to draw enthusiasts. The German carmakers can bank on their prestige, and have made life more difficult by introducing entry-level models that sell for Acura prices (without Acura reliability). Acura needs a reboot to successfully re-establish itself in Canada, and that will come only if Honda commits to making a line of compelling, no-excuses vehicles. Without brand cachet, Acura's well-thought-out, reliable, reasonable-to-maintain products are sometimes slow sellers; if you wait until the end of the model year, impressive incentives may be available.

2017 Acura ILX

RATING: *CSX:* Recommended (2006-11); *ILX:* Recommended (2012-17). A used CSX or ILX are viable alternatives to a well-equipped Civic, but few used car buyers consider them. One extra year warranty compared to the Civic. For a review of the CSX take a look at the nearly identical Honda Civic. **Road performance:** *ILX:* The ILX is currently Acura's smallest sedan. Based on the previous-generation Honda Civic, a new ILX is an underwhelming value proposition. A 2L 4-cylinder was the standard engine until 2015; it's smooth with acceptable power, but needs to be revved to get into its power band. Optional previously, and standard since 2016, the 2.4L 4-cylinder has more punch, but its exhaust note can become tiresome. Steering weight and gearing are particularly well judged, but it could be more communicative. Strong brakes with good pedal feel. Wind noise is well suppressed but road noise is greater than expected from a car in this price bracket. The large outside rearview mirrors are a necessity, as vision for lane changes is impeded. Comfortable, supportive front seats. Excellent driving position; leg and headroom may be tight if you are tall. Elegant dashboard. There is nothing fundamentally wrong with the cabin design but the materials used are ho-hum at this price point. Reasonable trunk space. Unimpressive audio system. **Strong points:** Balanced performance and nice ride and handling. Unlike the previous CSX that was obviously a gently amended Civic, the ILX has a unique exterior and cabin. Clear conventional instrument panel and convenient controls. Lowest-in-class running costs. **Weak points:** Buyers pay a premium for a model that is in some ways no more than a dressed up Civic. The Civic, which shared this platform until 2015, has more rear seat room. A current Civic is built on a platform that debuted as a 2016 model and offers most of the same attributes for less money. **Best alternatives:** Honda Civic Si or Touring, Mazda3 GT, and Hyundai Elantra Sport.

RELIABILITY: *CSX:* Refer to the Civic review. *ILX:* Incomplete data, predicted reliability is very good.

SAFETY

IIHS 2016 ILX

Small Front	Good
Front	Good
Side	Good
Roof strength	Good
Head restraint and seats	Good
Child seat anchors	Acceptable
NHTSA Overall 2017	★★★★★

TL ★★★★

RATING: Above Average (2009-14). *2009-14:* Based on the Honda Accord, the fourth-generation TL debuted for the 2009 model year. **Road performance:** Engine performance resembles a V6-engined Accord; the car feels more substantial than an Accord, with a more luxurious cabin environment. Road noise is noticeable, but the TL is quieter than the Accord. Noticeable torque steer with the standard front-wheel drive, and the steering wheel tugs to one side when accelerating hard. A good all-wheel drive system is available, using Acura's sophisticated SH-all-wheel drive system; it adds about $2,500 to the market value. Nicely assembled with generous cabin space and comfortable seats; the back seat is more accommodating than competing vehicles from the European automakers. The dashboard is festooned with buttons and requires some adaptation. Exterior styling lost the restrained elegance of the TL prior to 2009. High resale value typical of used Acuras; a bargain price usually indicates prior collision damage or or someoneter issue with the vehicle history. **Strong points:** Roomy, comfortable and well-finished. Strong acceleration and good refinement. **Weak points:** Visibility is less than panoramic. Brutish styling. **Major redesign:** 2009. **Best alternatives:** Infiniti G37, Lexus ES 350 or IS, BMW 3-series or Mercedes C-Class.

Powertrain (2009-14: FWD/AWD): Engines: 3.5L V6 (280 hp), 3/7: V6 (305 hp); Transmissions: 6-speed man., 6-speed auto. **Dimensions:** Passengers: 2/3; Wheelbase: 109.3 in., 2,776 mm.; L: 194 in., 4,928 mm.; W: 74 in., 1,880 mm.; Weight: 3,948 lb., 1,791 kg. **Fuel economy:** 8.5 L/12.2 L/100 km. **Assembled in:** U.S.A.

For Safety and Reliability information check TLX review.

TLX ★★★★

RATING: Above Average (2015-17). The TLX combined the previous TL and TSX, as Acura consolidated its model range due to weak sales of the TSX. Engine offerings include a 4-cylinder from the TSX, and V6 from the TL. **Road performance:** The 3.5L V6 is smooth, quiet, and quick, with a delicious wail at high revs. Though its gear selector takes some getting used to, the 9-speed automatic delivers smooth shifts and relaxed cruising. Unlike some "sports-luxury" cars that veer too much toward a "sport" suspension, the TLX has a reasonably absorbent ride. Steering is pleasant, nicely weighted, with good directional stability. The interior comes up a bit short. The dashboard houses crisp instrumentation and looks uncluttered, primarily because so many functions, including the ventilator fan speed, are accessed through a touch screen with multiple menus – it's less than ideal. Cabin trim doesn't match the opulence of the European brands in this class. All seats are comfortable with more than sufficient space for those in front, but access to the back seat is not the easiest and legroom is more limited than the old TL. Reasonable trunk space. Powerful heating and ventilation observed during early winter testing are an Acura hallmark. Very good audio system. **Strong points:** Strong, quiet V6 allied to a slick-shifting 9-speed automatic transmission. Good ride-handling compromise for a luxury car. **Weak points:** Uninspired exterior design and a prosaic looking cabin for a luxury class vehicle; too many touch screen controls. Given that the TLX is based on the roomy Honda Accord, it's odd that the cabin is so much smaller. **Major redesign:** 2015. **Best alternatives:** Honda Accord V6, Infiniti G35/37, Q50, Lexus ES350, and the BMW 3-series sedan.

Prices and Specs

Prices (2017): *Base FWD 2.4L:* $35,690, *Elite Sh-AWD:* $48,190 **Freight:** $2,045 **Powertrain (2015-17 FWD/AWD):** Engines: 2.4 L 4 (206 hp), 3.5L V6 (290 hp); Transmissions: 6-speed auto (2.4 L), 9-speed auto (3.5 L). **Dimensions:** Passengers: 2/3; Wheelbase: 105.7 in., 2,685 mm.; L: 184.4 in., 4,685 mm.; W: 73.7 in., 1,872 mm.; Weight: 3,926 lb., 1,781 kg. **Fuel economy:** *2016 V6:* 7.5 L/11.2 L/100 km. **Assembled in:** U.S.A.

RELIABILITY: Much more reliable with lower running costs than competing sedans from the European carmakers. The large high-speed-rated tires can wear quickly and are expensive; do not neglect tire rotation. *2009-2011 TL:* some reports of excessive oil consumption with the V6. Above 150,000 km an unstable idle may be due to a small air leak in the intake. Check for an oil leak at the right-side driveshaft seal and oil pressure switch on the engine block. Check constant velocity joints for wear on high-mileage models.

SAFETY	
IIHS 2016	
Small Front	Marginal
Front	Good
Side	Good
Roof strength	Good
Head restraint and seats	Good
Child seat anchors	Marginal
NHTSA Overall 2017	★★★★★

RDX   *2007-2012* ★★★★
2013-2017 ★★★★★

good buy

RATING: Above Average (2007-12); Recommended (2013-17). *2007-12:* The first RDX, a much-massaged luxury spin-off of the Honda CR-V, debuted for the 2007 model year. The lack of underhood space for a V6 dictated the use of a turbocharged 2.3L 4-cylinder to furnish the power expected to match the premium price tag. **Road performance:** *2007-12:* The RDX performs well enough but lacks the sonic polish customers expect and gas consumption is heavy. Handling, steering, and braking are all quite pleasing but the ride is turbulent for this class of vehicle. The cabin is quite elegant and with high assembly quality; the dash centre stack has too many buttons. Comfortable seats and good interior space for the size of the vehicle combine to keep a quartet of adults happy on a long trip. Good cargo capacity. *2013-17:* Honda raided their parts bin to combine proven components from existing vehicles into the new model. The "reactive" all-wheel drive system, which runs in front-wheel drive most of the time and sends power to the rear when slip is detected, is less sophisticated than the SH-all-wheel drive system used in the TLX and MDX. The eager, sweet-sounding V6 delivers swift acceleration, impressive flexibility, and relaxed cruising. Fuel economy in APA comparison testing is superior to competing Mercedes and BMW models with turbo 4-cylinders. The 6-speed automatic is very well matched to the V6, and delivers imperceptible upshifts and downshifts. The electric power steering is nicely weighted and geared but it is numb. Handling is steady and the RDX tackles corners with little lean for such a big machine. The high window line limits outward visibility for lane changes. While the air-conditioner is powerful, its temperature varied annoyingly on the test day. Very good audio system. The navigation system features an intuitive control set-up and works well. The dash centre stack is dominated by a touch screen that looks very clean but requires concentration to manipulate. The large, comfortable front seats locate occupants well without confining them. The driver's seat is multi-adjustable, but the low-mounted, fixed-height front passenger seat left some occupants feeling buried because of the high window line. The rear seat is comfortable for two and holds three in a pinch. Rear legroom is ample and the rear floor is flat. The cabin features abundant padded surfaces, matte finishes, attractive leather seating, is carefully assembled, and looks more upscale after its 2016 facelift. Despite a high cargo deck, cargo space is ample and the trunk is both wide and long. The 60/40 split rear seat can be folded by pulling release handles conveniently located near the wide-opening rear tailgate. Though the rear seats don't fold flat, the RDX has a substantial cargo hold when they are folded **Strong points:** *2007-12:* Good space efficiency, crisp handling. *2013-17:* Spacious cabin, smooth, creamy V6 engine, and well sorted ride and handling. **Weak points:** *2007-2012:* Coarse engine for this class, turbulent ride, and heavy fuel consumption for a Honda product. *2013-2017:* Limited visibility to the side and rear. **Major redesign:** 2007, 2010 update, 2013, 2016 update. **Best alternatives:** Lexus RX350, Nissan Murano, Buick Envision, Cadillac XT5, and Ford Edge/Lincoln MKX.

Prices and Specs

Prices (2017): *Base:* $42,190, *Elite:* $46,795 **Freight:** $2,095 **Powertrain (AWD):** Engine: 3.5L V6 (279 hp); Transmission: 6-speed auto. **Dimensions:** Passengers: 2/3; Wheelbase: 105.7 in., 2,685 mm.; L: 184.4 in., 4,685 mm.; W: 73.7 in., 1,872 mm.; Weight: 3,926 lb., 1,781 kg. **Fuel economy (2016):** 8.6 L/ 12.4 L/100 km. **Assembled in:** U.S.A.

RELIABILITY: *2007-2012:* Partial data, due to limited sales. Few complaints on the turbo engine to date. *2013-2017:* Proven or improved powertrain components from other Honda vehicles carry the promise of superior durability and low repair frequency. The few faults mirror Honda's, and generally relate to infotainment malfunctions, and accessories like the navigation, climate control, and sound systems.

SAFETY	
IIHS 2016	
Small Front	Good
Front	Good
Side	Good
Roof strength	Good
Head restraint and seats	Good
Child seat anchors	Acceptable
NHTSA Overall 2017	★★★★★

MDX	
2004-2006	★★
2007-2011	★★★★
2012-2017	★★★★★

2017 Acura MDX

RATING: Below Average (2004-2006); Above Average (2007-2011); Recommended (2012-17). **Road performance:** Good highway performance with commendable acceleration and nice handling for its class. As a big, fast, heavy vehicle with garden shed aerodynamics, the MDX was never going to be a fuel sipper, but the V6 is smooth and fuel efficient. Steering is reasonably responsive and the automatic transmission delivers a good balance between acceleration and low-rev cruising. Braking was upgraded in 2014; pedal "feel" and braking distance are a weakness on some earlier models. *Redesigned 2014-2017 model:* Powertrain improvements reduced fuel consumption, particularly in city driving, and the handling is sharper. The longer wheelbase added a bit of middle-row legroom at the expense of some cargo capacity. The dashboard has far fewer buttons and a cleaner look than its predecessor, because many features have been incorporated into a touch screen, which takes some time to get to know; it will never be as easy to use as conventional knobs and buttons. For 2017, the MDX enjoys a mid-cycle refresh, including Acura's new "Pentagon" grille set in a new front fascia incorporating restyled headlamps, front fenders, and hood. Acura announced a Hybrid version using the powertrain from the slow-selling RLX. **Strong points:** The MDX is a refined machine, among the cheapest to run and lest troublesome of the three-row luxury SUVs. Loaded with goodies: Lane Keep Assist, Adaptive Cruise Control with Low-Speed Follow, Blind Spot Information, and a Collision Mitigation Braking System are available, as are a wide variety of comfort and convenience features such as GPS navigation and a large sunroof. The roomy interior is stylish, carefully assembled, and comfortable. High resale value compared to other luxury SUVs. **Weak points:** The rear third seat is class competitive but doesn't compare with a true minivan like the Honda Odyssey. **Major redesign:** 2007, 2014, and 2017 update. **Other opinions:** *2014-2017 generation:* "Dual-screen infotainment system's mediocre graphics and distracting interface; modest cargo space behind the third row." – *Edmunds.com.* **Best alternatives:** GM's Buick Enclave and Infiniti QX60. If brand image is not an issue, the Honda Pilot or Toyota Highlander. The Audi Q7, BMW X5, and Volvo XC90 are similarly-sized but considerably more expensive when new; prices for used models drop into MDX territory, but service requirements will be much more intensive.

Prices and Specs

Prices (2017): *Base:* $53,690, *ELITE:* $65,790 **Freight:** $2,095 **Powertrain (AWD):** Engine: 3.7L V6 (290 hp); Transmission: 9-speed auto. **Dimensions:** Passengers: 2/3/2; Wheelbase: 111 in., 2,820 mm.; L: 196.2 in., 4,984 mm./W: 77.8 in.,1,975 mm.; Weight: 4,300 lb., 1,950 kg. **Fuel economy (2016):** 9.1/ 12.7 L/100 km. **Assembled in:** U.S.A.

RELIABILITY: An epidemic of transmission failures on MDX models to 2006 makes them a risky buy; after foot dragging and some duplicity, Honda finally extended the warranty formally, but coverage has now expired. Acura extended the warranty on some of its 2007-2011 models to cover an automatic transmission judder (shake) that may also damage the transmission's torque converter (below). Owners of older MDXs report noisy brakes and premature brake wear; erratic cruise control; brake shimmy; windshield cracks for no obvious reason; and malfunctioning power accessories and entertainment systems. Models with early versions of the cylinder deactivation feature may experience high oil consumption and expensive valve train failures.

INTERNAL BULLETINS, SECRET WARRANTIES: 2007-09—Acura will cover the cost of replacing the transmission torque converter up to 8 years/160,000 km 105,000 miles. 2007-10—Warranty extension for a steering wheel that's hard to turn. Acura is extending the warranty on the power steering pump to 7 years/160,000 km, whichever comes first. A water leak at the rear of the moonroof signals the need for a moonroof drain channel seal. 2007-11—With a normal

engine oil level, a "check engine oil level" message appears on the MID or the navigation screen. The low oil pressure indicator on the instrument panel may also be on. Acura will replace the engine oil pressure switch. 2007-13—Silence a squeaking, screeching window by removing the lower seal from the glass outer weatherstrips on each of the four doors. 2010-11—If the front or rear seat stays hot after the seat heater is turned off, the heater switch has to be replaced. 2010-13—A steering vibration/moan while turning at low speeds may be caused by a faulty alternator pulley. 2012—The master key won't lock in the extended position. 2013—The front brakes may squeal when applied. In TSB #13-020 issued on April 13, 2013, Acura says the noise is caused by glazed brake pads. 2014—A second-row passenger seat rattle may be caused by the cable link contacting the seat frame. If the engine "chirps" when warmed up, chances are the timing belt is contacting the back edge of the crankshaft pulley. A grinding, rattling, vibrating, fluttering, or buzzing noise coming from the front of the vehicle under light acceleration may signal that the bulkhead cover fasteners (latches and strikers) are loose. 2014-15—Warm timing belt chirping. A steering buzz or grunt may be heard from shifting out of Reverse. Navigation feature flashes or flickers. 2014-16—Erratic operation of the antitheft system. Homelink feature may have limited range. 2016—The transmission end cover leaks on vehicles with 9-speed A/T; replace the end cover sealing gasket.

HONDA

For over three decades Honda earned top scores for reliable, well-performing, and fuel-efficient vehicles. However, during the past decade the company hid some secrets – its life-saving airbags could be life-taking grenades and the company's quality control was slipping; a system of "secret" warranties swept production goofs under the carpet and concealed safety defect reports from U.S. official regulators.

Honda is air bag manufacturer Takata Corporation's biggest customer, and has been for well over a decade. Regulators believe that Honda failed to report cases involving defective Takata airbags that are linked to six deaths in Honda vehicles and hundreds of injuries. In February and June 2007, Honda informed Takata about additional airbag ruptures that year. But the automaker did not initiate a recall nor provide information about the ruptures to federal regulators. In late 2014, Honda acknowledged failing to tell NHTSA about 60% of its safety defect reports in the United States, or 1,729 incidents involving injuries or deaths in its automobiles since 2003. Honda explained it missed the safety implications due to inaccurate data entry and computer coding errors, as well as a "narrow interpretation" of what incidents it was required to report to regulators... This explanation didn't wash with U.S. federal investigators. U.S. federal safety regulators subsequently fined Honda $70 million – the maximum allowed – for failing to report deaths and injuries involving its vehicles in a timely manner. In addition to levying a precedent-setting U.S. fine, Honda signed a consent order giving the American government increased oversight over what Honda reports, and mandates third-party audits to ensure that required reporting is undertaken with integrity.

Lemon-Aid cast a wary eye at Honda's lowered quality ratings in the period from 2005-2012 and concluded the automaker had been "coasting" on its previous high rankings. The Nikkei Asian Review, in its December 1, 2014, issue concluded the company has pursued expansion at the expense of product quality since 2012, after getting its marching orders from Honda President Takanobu Ito. The redesigned Fit, Civic, and new HR-V appear to indicate that those days are over, and Honda is once again aiming for best-in-class.

New Products

Honda vehicles have a reputation for having few first-year problems and tolerating minimal vehicle maintenance. However, Honda is investing heavily in turbocharging its small-displacement engines, and introducing dual-clutch transmissions, conventional 9-speed automatics, and continuously variable transmissions (CVTs). Keep in mind that these innovations have as many detractors as boosters due to their complexity and repeated inability to meet both fuel-economy and long-term durability objectives.

And speaking of innovations that may be more trouble than they are worth – Welcome to Honda head-restraint hell! The Marquis de Sade head restraints used by some penny-pinching automakers are a literal "pain in the neck."

RATING: Recommended. Honda's entry-level car in North America, the Fit is a very good choice among small cars; however, the poor front seat design on the pre-2009 model can be a deal-breaker for some drivers.

2007-2008

Road performance: Smooth, adequate power, with either the manual or automatic transmission. Low gearing on the manual delivers snappy performance around town but makes it very buzzy at highway speeds. If you do a lot of highway driving, the automatic is quieter. Steering is light; the car gets pushed around by strong crosswinds. Handling is steady and the brakes are effective.

2009-2014

Road performance: Good blend of performance and fuel economy. The engine in the second-generation seems louder and sounds coarser. Like the original, engine noise is more noticeable with the manual on the highway; the Fit is a more relaxed highway cruiser with the automatic. Ride, handling, and steering all improved slightly over the first Fit and the car feels a bit more substantial. Cabin space and versatility are once again extraordinary, and the front seats are improved. Clear gauges and logical controls return for the second-generation Fit, but cabin design and finish were a step backward from the original. To save money, Honda Canada sourced 2013-2014 model year vehicles in ... China! The Fit has the distinction of being the first vehicle entirely assembled in China to be sold in our market.

Road performance: Once again, the Fit offers a lot of cabin space and excellent fuel economy. The Fit is priced at the top of its segment, but returns your outlay in the form of best-in-class resale value and enough space to serve as the only car for a household with four adults. While the direct injection system used on the third-generation Fit is a bit loud, the engine is smooth and works very well with its continuously variable transmission (CVT). Dynamically, the car is no longer class-leading, but like many Honda vehicles the lack of irritants moves it to the head of the B-segment class. The car feels less sporty and tossable than older Fits, but the ride is more poised and the chassis feels more substantial. The third-generation Fit is once more a paragon of space efficiency and cargo versatility. Cabin space is almost as good as a mid-size car but without the bulk. Like the two previous Fits, the driving position on the current car is a bit odd – perhaps a consequence of the gas tank location under the floor. Front seat comfort on the third Fit would make first-generation Fit owners weep. Elegant cabin design and impressive materials especially for the small car class. Visually appealing instrumentation is a highlight, but the inept, inconvenient Honda touch screen interface, is not. Big, square cargo area.

Strong points: Small on the outside but big on the inside, this mini-car sips fuel and performs reasonably well in both city and highway driving. Along with the Yaris, it offers the best fuel economy on the market of any contemporary vehicle short of a hybrid. Placing the fuel tank under the front seats liberates the full depth of the rear of the cabin for passengers and cargo. The very clever rear seat can be configured in a number of ways for unparalleled versatility – an ideal small car to load sporting equipment or camping gear. *2007-2008:* Clear gauges, simple, logical controls, and attractive cabin materials make for a nice interior. Excellent outward visibility is a throwback to cars from the 1990s. *2009-2014:* Its 1.5L engine delivers sufficient urge and superior fuel economy. *2015-2017:* Elegant, practical interior. Can be the sole car for a family of four adults. Superior visibility. **Weak points:** Selling prices for used Fits are high due to very slow depreciation. *2007-2008:* The engine can feel strained with a full load when passing. The ride is a bit firm for some, partly a consequence of the short wheelbase. Odd seating position, and front seat support is lacking; the seats can become seriously uncomfortable after a few hours. Tall drivers would like more seat travel. The bottle holders in the rear doors can infringe on the outboard calves of some rear passengers. Some owners complain about weak headlight output. *2009-2014:* Noisy. Unimpressive cabin materials. *2015-2017:* Direct-injection engine is noisy, especially around town. **Major redesign:** 2007, 2009, and 2015. **Best alternatives:** The Hyundai Accent, Kia Rio, and Toyota Yaris, but no other car in the B-segment class offers the extraordinary cabin space or versatility of the Fit.

Prices (2016): *DX Manual:* $14,790, *EX-L Navi CVT:* $22,890 **Freight:** $1,595 **Powertrain FWD:** Engine: 1.5L 4-cyl. (130 hp); Transmissions: 6-speed man., CVT auto. **Dimensions:** Passengers: 2/3; Wheelbase: 99.6 in., 2,530 mm.; L/160 in., 4,064 mm.,W: 64.7 in., 1,694 mm.; Weight: 2,648 lb., 1,201 kg. **Fuel economy (2016):** *Man.:* 6.4/8.1 L/100 km. *Auto.:* 5.7/7.0 L/100 km. **Assembled in:** Japan (2007-2011), China (2012-2014), and Mexico (2015-2017).

ALERT!

The head rest pushes my head forward and strains my neck to the point that I either have to sit upright away from the seat or stretch my neck far out in pain. Either way it is not safe, whether in case of accident or generally for my health. I ran Google search for Honda head rest complaints and found out that customers have been complaining about Honda's new head rests for the very same reason since 2007 through 2015 for most of their models – from the Accord and Odyssey to the Fit.

— *safercar.gov*

SAFETY	
IIHS 2016	
Small Front	Acceptable
Front	Good
Side	Good
Roof strength	Good
Head restraint and seats	Good
Child seat anchors	Marginal
NHTSA Overall 2017	★★★★★

Owner-reported safety-related failures: Barely a handful of complaints per model year are logged by NHTSA, whereas 50 would be the norm. Owners of 2009-2014 models report airbag failures; some transmission seal leaks; a weak AC; windshield stress fractures; paint chipping/delamination and premature cosmetic rusting; and a fuel sloshing noise heard under the front seats. Some drivers report that the design with a small triangular fixed front side window obstructs their view:

This car has a major blind spot out the driver's window due to its design. On a winding road, I can lose sight of an oncoming car based on the angle of the curve. There are also times traffic coming at the driver perpendicularly is not visible.

Other safety concerns include engine undertray shield may fall off due to inadequate plastic screws; insufficient legroom that leads long-legged drivers to apply the brakes and accelerator at the same time; side wind sensitivity; broken seat belts; and a tire jack that can bend sideways when lifting the car.

RELIABILITY: The Fit has proven to be a very durable, easy to maintain car. *2007-2008:* Road debris can destroy the A/C condenser – an expensive repair not covered under warranty, says one owner in this NHSTA-logged complaint:

There are "vents" which lie below the license plate holder near the road, wide enough to fit a fist and the length of the front bumper. This allows all kinds of road debris to enter and hit the A/C condenser only inches behind the opening. This damage has been reported on a number of websites since model year 2008. A similar issue has also been reported in a number of other Honda car models, including the CR-V and the Odyssey, which resulted in a successful class action lawsuit.

INTERNAL BULLETINS, SECRET WARRANTIES: 2007-08—A warranty extends the electric power steering warranty to 10 years/240,000 km and covers repairs. The steering will feel heavier than normal, or is hard to turn. 2009-12—The windshield may have a vertical crack starting at the bottom, above the cowl, near the middle. Honda should replace the windshield as a "goodwill" gesture. Cite TSB #12-006, published Jan. 21, 2012. Fix for a fuel filler door that won't open. 2009-13—The rear cargo area and/or spare tire well may be wet or damp; replace the AM/FM antenna base and apply Konishi Bond to the seal prior to installation. 2014-15—Measures to correct rearview camera malfunctions. 2015—The 2015 front bumper beam was changed to improve narrow offset (also known as small overlap) front crash test protection. Honda will provide owners with the updated front bumper beam. Excessive water buildup in the taillights. 2015-16—Free replacement of door handle brackets.

CIVIC

2006-2015	★★★★
2015-2017	★★★★★
HYBRID	
2015-2017	★★

RATING: Above Average (2006-2015); Recommended (2015-2017); *Civic Hybrid:* Below Average. After General Motors discontinued the Cavalier and Sunfire twins in 2005, the Civic became Canada's best selling compact car, a position it has retained over the last decade. Strong resale value makes the Civic among the most expensive of used compact cars. Sold in small numbers, the Civic Hybrid did not deliver the promised fuel savings and some years were bedeviled by electronic issues.

2006-2011

Road performance: The spacious 2006 model with its futuristic digital dash was a revelation when it arrived. Smooth engines, well-calibrated transmissions and a comfortable ride make the 2006-2011-generation Civic a very good all-rounder that won an impressive number of vehicle comparison tests. The high-power Si model is entertaining. The Civic can easily house four adults over long distances. The dual plane instrumentation isn't universally appreciated but looks cool at night and the speedometer is easy to read. Comfortable seating. Spacious trunk for this size of car.

2012-2015

Road performance: The 2012 Civic generated extraordinary volumes of negative press decrying how bad the car had become, but the public wasn't influenced and the car sold in huge numbers. Terrified, Honda resorted to rebates and interest-rate promotions they hadn't felt the need to offer previously. The 2012 Civic looked like a cheapened, less precise version of the 2006 model. The exterior was poorly detailed and the cabin materials were dowdy. Typical Civic virtues, like a roomy and comfortable cabin, remained. The car drove competently, but most of the fun factor had been distilled out. Honda rushed a facelift that debuted for 2013. Better detailing outside and an updated cabin that boasted nicer fittings delivered the car Honda should have released in 2012. Detail suspension changes in 2013-2014 improved the driving dynamics and refinement a bit as well. The updates, combined with the inherent goodness of the 2006-2011 model on which this generation was based, resulted in a class-leading car.

2016-2017

Road performance: Stung by criticism of the 2012-generation car, Honda pulled out all the stops to produce the 2016 Civic, which is a total reboot for the nameplate. While over-styled to some eyes, the current Civic is dramatic; the exterior encloses a spacious, comfortable interior with extraordinary style and refined materials. Honda didn't scrimp on the chassis either, as it replaced the front MacPherson struts used since 2001, with the more expensive double wishbone design used on Civics prior to 2001. The base engine is a normally-aspirated 2L 4-cylinder, with fancier trims powered by a 1.5L turbo meant to deliver strong power along with good official scores in government-mandated fuel economy tests. The current Civic is a refined machine that delivers a premium experience for a mainstream price. Except for interior width for a third rear passenger, there is little benefit in terms of utility in spending more money for the Honda Accord. 2017 updates include a four-door hatchback, an available 6-speed manual for the 1.5 L turbo, and the promise of a high-power Si.

Strong points: *2006-2011:* Competent powertrains and superior fuel economy. Good cabin space and comfortable seats. Low running costs. *2012-2015:* Competent all-rounder that can handle most duties. *2016-2017:* Solid-feeling, precise driving, refined, roomy and comfortable, the 2016 and newer Civic is an impressive car. The strong resale value should return any extra money paid over competing brands for a new car. **Weak points:** *2006-2015:* Low sloping roofline makes the cabin harder to access than many other cars in this class. Noisier than most compacts. The dual plane instrumentation is not to all tastes. *2016-2017:* With no knobs, even for audio volume, Honda's touch screen infotainment system is inconvenient and unsuited for on-road use. Some drivers find that the 1.5L turbo engine tends to drone excessively on light throttle applications. **Major redesign:** 2006, 2012, and 2016. **Best alternatives:** Hyundai Elantra, Mazda3, Kia Forte or the Toyota Corolla. All cost less than a used Civic.

Prices and Specs

Prices (2016): *DX Sedan man.:* $16,155, *Touring Sedan CVT:* $27,155 **Freight:** $1,595 **Powertrain (FWD):** Engines: *2015:* 1.5 L 4-cyl Hybrid (110 hp combined), 1.8L 4-cyl. (140-143 hp), 2.4L 4-cyl. (201-203 hp); Engines: *2016:* 1.5 L 4-cyl turbo (174 hp), 2 L 4-cyl. (158 hp). Transmissions (2015): 5-speed man., 6-speed man., CVT auto. Transmissions (2016): 6-speed man., CVT. **Dimensions:** *Sedan (2016):* Passengers: 2/3; Wheelbase:106.3 in., 2,700 mm.; L: 182.3 in., 4,631 mm.;/W: 73.9 in., 1,878 mm.; Weight: 2,778 lb., 1,260 kg. **Fuel economy (2016):** *1.5 turbo 4-cyl., CVT:* 5.8/7.8 L/100 km., 2 L 4-cyl., CVT: 5.8/5.8 L/100 km. **Assembled in:** Canada and U.S.A.; Hybrid assembled in Japan and U.S.A.

ALERT! More front-seat head restraint complaints:

> I have tilted the seat back as far as I safely can and still be able to drive. I am [a] 53-year-old female, 5'3" tall, and wear bifocals. I am having difficulty focusing from tachometer to speedometer to road because I cannot [move] my head to use the right part of my glasses to see. I cannot tilt my head back at all because of the headrest. I also experienced a headache that evening as well due to eye strain.

Other deficiencies to check for during your test drive: Headlights may be too dim; uncomfortable front seats:

> I bought a 2016 Honda Civic LX Sedan. The seats do not hold my body in place while driving. Left knee hits driver door when turning, right knee hits console when turning left, short bottom seat, thighs are unsupported, back of seat hard/painful, arms and legs go numb within first 10 minutes of driving.

SAFETY

IIHS 2016 CIVIC SEDAN

Small Front	Good
Front	Good
Side	Good
Roof strength	Good
Head restraint and seats	Good
Child seat anchors	Acceptable

NHTSA Overall 2017

Civic Sedan	★★★★★

Owner-reported safety-related failures: The airbag warning light stays lit even though an adult passenger occupies the seat; inadvertent side airbag deployment, or airbags failing to deploy in collisions. Sometimes, the driver's door cannot be unlocked from inside:

> Upon viewing an accident in front of me, I parked on side of road, applied emergency flashers, called 911 (hand held – not attached to car) and was removing keys from ignition & trying to open driver side door & exit car to render aid. Car door would not open. I unlocked door manually at handle. Still would not open. I re-inserted key, turned engine on, pushed door open button. Door not open. (I was dialling & talking with the 911 operator during this time). I was getting excited about need to get to victim(s) of accident, but couldn't get out of my car. I eventually climbed over middle console to exit car from passenger's door.

Windshield wipers freeze in their housing; windshield cracks easily and replacements for 2016s on backorder; sudden loss of power steering; fractured front tie rods, causing complete steering loss; acceleration or surging when the AC or heater is engaged, or when the steering wheel is turned sharply; car veers sharply to the right when braking; the brake and accelerator pedal are mounted too close together; and premature replacement of brake pads and discs. It's easy to press the Start/Stop button by accident, as it is located near the flasher button. Hesitation when accelerating from a stop, especially when in ECON mode, or engine surges when exiting an off-ramp or when the brakes are applied:

> Car suddenly stops dead while accelerating to make left-hand turn. It will resume acceleration only after a 4-second pause. Turning into oncoming traffic with a dead vehicle is going to cause an accident... This is the third time that this incident has occurred to my vehicle. The Honda dealer cannot find the cause.

RELIABILITY: Above average. Problems increased with the 2006-2011 generation, and Honda extended the warranty on several troublesome components. The 2012-2015 and redesigned 2016-2017 Civic have been mostly troublefree to date. Cracked engine blocks: 2006 to early 2009 models are covered by a warranty extension for 8 or 10 years with no mileage limit. Air conditioner failures common on 2006-2009 models. Check the clutch on the air conditioner compressor, a $130 part, before replacing the entire compressor, which is a much more expensive proposition; the warranty on the clutch was extended to 7 years/160,000 km. On 2006-2009 models, failure of the electric power steering assist is covered by a warranty extension for 10 years/240,000 km. The warranty for a defective sun visor on 2009 models has been extended to 7 years/160,000 km. A lit engine service light could indicate a defective exhaust gas oxygen sensor or coolant temperature sensor. Check for broken front suspension springs on 2006-2011 models. *2009-2011 Hybrid:* Honda USA extended the warranty on failure-prone battery packs to 10 years/150,000 miles. *2006-2011:* Sound of fuel sloshing in the tank when braking or going over bumps; paint delaminates and is easily scratched (see "Internal Bulletins" below). A-pillar, dash, or sunroof rattles; doors and trunk lids are hard to close; fuel-door handles don't work; door locks and power windows malfunction, windows bind or come off their tracks; (another "Internal Bulletins" item); the trunk cannot be opened from inside the cabin; rear interior brake light cover comes off; lousy radio speakers; water leaks from the tail light into the trunk, and into the driver-side footwell; trunk springs fail; exterior and interior lights dim; heated side mirrors gradually lose their reflective ability; and the A/C condenser is easily destroyed by road debris.

> I own a 2007 Honda Civic LX. Went to dealership regarding terrible paint fading, broken visor (which had been replaced once already for being defective). They stated engine mount breakage is normal wear and tear issue ... now I read numerous reports of this problem from 1992-2010 – repairpal.com/bad-engine-mounts-may-cause-vibration-roughness-and-rattle-964.

INTERNAL BULLETINS, SECRET WARRANTIES: All models/years: Several Honda TSBs allow for special warranty consideration on a "goodwill" basis, even after the warranty has expired or the car has changed hands, but Honda Canada keeps the cost of claims down by not sending out owner notifications. Tips for submitting a successful paint claim can be found in TSB #10-002, published Jan. 20, 2010. **2006-09**—Engine overheats or leaks coolant because the engine block is cracking at the coolant passages. Honda will install a new engine block assembly free of charge up to 10 years, with no mileage limit as stated in TSB #10-048, issued Dec. 9, 2014. **2006-13**—Roof and trunk paint cracking, chalking, or clouding. Cite Honda TSB #14-034, issued Sept. 23, 2014. This TSB is critical as a benchmark by Honda for any paint claims targeting other models, colours, model years, or automakers. Again, the legal principle of "reasonable durability" and negligence applies. Worn engine mounts cause a rattle or a knock coming from the right front of the vehicle when driving over bumps at 15-20 mph (24-32 km/h). It is likely the passenger's side hydraulic side engine mount is cavitating, or is torn and making a knocking sound. Cite Honda TSB #06-060, issued Dec. 24, 2010. **2006-09**—The warranty on the electric power steering warranty is extended to 10 years/ 240,000 km miles and covers all repairs, including the replacement of the EPS control unit. The steering will feel heavier than normal, or hard to turn. **2006-11**—Trunk lid repaint warranty extension. Dissimilar metals in the chrome trim and the trunk lid, along with road salt, may create a very low electrochemical reaction that forms corrosion, rust spots, or stains on the trunk lid. Honda is extending the warranty on the trunk lid to 7 years from the original date of purchase says TSB #13-004, issued Jan. 3, 2013. **2012-13**—More free paint jobs: Honda will repaint any Civic up to 7 years if the roof or trunk paint has a chalky appearance or the paint is cracked. This free repair is available to all owners, whether their vehicle was bought new or used. (A copy of Honda's authorization letter is kept by the NHTSA at *safercar.gov* under "2013 Honda service bulletins"). Incorrect fuel gauge readings. Front windows may not go up due to lack of clearance between the window motor pinion and plate hole. 2013—Rocker arm may need to be replaced. Remedy for front brake squeaking, squealing, or grinding. Honda confirms inner door handles or latches may pop or stick. 2013-15—Faulty infotainment audio and screen features. 2014—Tire pressure alert may come on for no reason. 2014-15—Faulty fuel gauges. Troubleshooting tips for rearview camera, or audio malfunctions.

HR-V ★★★★★ *good buy*

RATING: Recommended. The HR-V is Honda's entry into the swiftly-growing micro-SUV segment also occupied by the Chevrolet Trax/Buick Encore, Jeep Renegade/Fiat 500X and the Mazda CX-3. With a wheelbase only marginally shorter than that of the CR-V, the HR-V provides a lot of room for passengers, and because it shares the Fit's ingenious use of space, surprising cargo space as well. Some drivers find the seating position not entirely comfortable, a fault the HR-V shares with the Fit upon which it is based. While the HR-V is priced fairly, its manufacturer incentives are not generous. **Road performance:** Good overall performance and fuel economy. The 1.8L 4-cylinder engine used in the previous Civic is mated to a CVT automatic or a manual transmission. The HR-V is a relaxed cruiser, and the ride and handling are well sorted for this type of vehicle; the steering is accurate, but a bit light and could be more communicative. In other words, it is a bit "numb." Strong braking. **Strong points:** The HR-V is the roomiest, most practical vehicle in its segment, with impressive space for passengers and cargo for a vehicle of its size. Very good predicted resale value. **Weak points:** Honda's touch screen infotainment system is inconvenient and unsuited for on-road use. The engine can get loud when accelerating strongly. Fairly high payments for a vehicle in the micro-SUV segment; compare with payments for a base CR-V before making your final decision. **Major redesign:** *2016:* All-new segment for Honda. **Best alternatives:** The Chevrolet Trax-Buick Encore twins from GM or the Mazda CX-3. If you're financing or leasing a new HR-V, you might be able to get a CR-V for not much more money per month.

Prices and Specs

Prices (2016): *LX FWD man:* $20,790, *EX-L AWD CVT:* $30,090 **Freight:** $1,725 **Powertrain (FWD/AWD):** Engine: 1.8L 4-cyl. (141 hp); Transmission: 6-speed man (FWD only), CVT. **Dimensions:** Passengers: 2/3; Wheelbase: 102.7 in., 2610 mm.; L: 169 in., 4294 mm./W: 70.6 in., 1794 mm; Weight: 2,921 lb., 1,325 kg. **Fuel economy (2016):** 7.4/8.7 L/100 km. **Assembled in:** Mexico.

ALERT! In your test drive, check the driver's seat:

I've owned my 2016 HR-V for a little over a week. I've tried nine ways to Sunday to make the seat comfortable – to no avail. It causes unbelievable pain in my neck, shoulder and jaw. It causes me extreme pain. I ordered a neck support and lumbar support which have helped slightly but not enough. I've found countless forums online for many Honda models complaining of the same issues.

. . .

I noticed a pressure point in my mid-back. It got to the point where it would take as little time as my seven minute commute to cause my back to go numb. This numbness would persist for several hours after getting out of the vehicle.

Owner-reported safety-related failures: Loss of brakes; premature tire wear; infotainment system crashes with software patch delayed a year; and windshield wiper fluid freezes and wipers sit too low to be helped by the defroster.

RELIABILITY: Proven powertrain components imported from other Honda vehicles carry the promise of superior durability and low repair frequency. Predicted reliability is similar to the Fit, which has been excellent.

INTERNAL BULLETINS, SECRET WARRANTIES: 2016—Free replacement of door handle brackets.

CR-V ★★★★★

RATING: Recommended. The CR-V is a competent all-rounder with low running costs and good fuel economy for a compact SUV. Best in class resale value; you can stretch your dollar by opting for a basic model with front-wheel drive. The redesigned 2007 model dropped the swinging rear door with a spare tire on it, which was a favourite with shorter people, in favour of a conventional hatchback. The split-rear seatback went from the versatile 40/20/40 to the more conventional 60/40 design. Redesigned again for 2012, cargo area volume grew a bit; the powertrain was a carryover. The powertrain was updated to save gas for 2015, with the arrival of direct fuel injection and a CVT automatic. **Road performance:** A smooth-running 2.4L 4-cylinder engine balances acceleration and fuel economy nicely. Acceptable ride-handling compromise for a mainstream family hauler. The steering, while a bit numb on models with electric power assist, is nicely weighted. The CR-V is a serene and relatively economical highway cruiser. **Strong points:** Even the base LX is nicely equipped for 2017, including heated front seats. Good blend of performance and fuel economy. Supportive seats and abundant cabin space. Large, regularly-shaped cargo hold. **Weak points:** The no-knob infotainment system on fancier models is the polar opposite of user-friendly and not really suitable for use while on the move. To minimize distraction, set your own radio presets and use the steering wheel controls to scroll through the various audio modes to switch stations and adjust volume. **Major redesign:** 2007 and 2012. An all-new CR-V was released for 2017. **Best alternatives:** The most likely new and used cross-shops are the Subaru Forester, Toyota RAV4, and Mazda CX-5; all of them sell for less than a used CR-V. For less money, GM's Equinox and Terrain twins are acceptable used alternatives and are available with V6 power for buyers wanting more performance. As a new vehicle alternative, if you are prepared to downsize a little, consider the current Hyundai Tucson or Kia Sportage.

Prices and Specs

Prices (2016): *LX FWD:* $26,290, *Touring AWD:* $37,090 **Freight:** $1,725 **Powertrain (FWD/AWD):** Engine: 2.4L 4-cyl. (185 hp); Transmission: CVT. **Dimensions:** Passengers: 2/3; Wheelbase: 103.2 in., 2,620 mm.; L: 179 in., 4,557 mm.; W: 72.6 in., 1,844 mm., Weight: 3,569 lb., 1,619 kg. **Fuel economy (2016):** 9.5/10.7 L/100 km. **Assembled in:** Canada and U.S.A.

ALERT! Uncomfortable front seats and head restraints for some drivers, through 2016:

The head restraint pushes my head forward. There is no position in which an anatomical posture can be achieved. In order to be comfortable I either sit away from the back of the seat with essentially no back support, sit sideways on the seat so my head can clear to the side of the neck restraint, or turn the head rest around. This however is also unsafe.

• • •

Upon driving the vehicle 30-40 miles I get leg cramps and my toes get numb. I tried several seat positions to relieve the pain to no avail. I researched the web for this problem and found it to be pervasive. I hate the vehicle and want to return it. It is causing severe leg and back problems.

• • •

Vibration at idle in gear. I found the vibration on the second day I got my 2016 CR-V with only about 100 miles on it. It vibrates at idle in gear. It only happens when the car is at 600-700 rpm. When I turn on the heater to max so it goes to 800 rpm, the vibration stops. But once the heater is off and it drops back to 600-700 rpm, the vibration comes back.

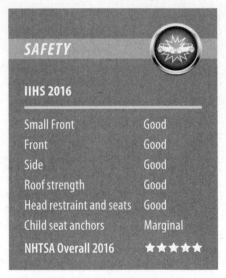

SAFETY

IIHS 2016

Small Front	Good
Front	Good
Side	Good
Roof strength	Good
Head restraint and seats	Good
Child seat anchors	Marginal
NHTSA Overall 2016	★★★★★

A 2015 Honda CR-V vibration lawsuit alleges the cars are dangerous to drive. Plaintiffs say the CR-V was modified to include a direct-injection engine called "Earth Dreams" that causes excessive vibration that doesn't exist in previous model years. See: *Vivian Romaya v. American Honda Motor Co. Inc. and http://www. girardgibbs.com/wp-content/uploads/2016/04/CRV-Filed-Second-Amended-Complaint. pdf* for a full engineering analysis.

Owner reported safety-related failures:

> Just bought a Honda CR-V 2015 EX-L. After driving it for one day experienced serious vibrations in driver and passenger seat while driving and even more intense when idling… I cannot drive in this car. Some dealers have actually refunded customers and exchanged cars to customer satisfaction. It's the right thing to do. They should be applauded. Not mine. They won't exchange or refund. I will be miserable every day in this car. Saw there is a potential class action suit since so many customers from 2015 have been affected and Honda has acknowledged the defect.
>
> – *www.carcomplaints.com/Honda/CR-V/2015/.*

When the accelerator is pressed hard, there is a loss of power and downshifting is delayed, just when extra power is needed. Sudden unintended acceleration when cruise control is engaged. Seat height adjuster fails when driving: Traction control has also been a problem with earlier models. Sun visors fall out of their mounting.

RELIABILITY: Very good overall. There was a bump in complaints beginning with the 2015 model year. Some owners of 2015 models reported dead batteries because charging system output is insufficient when making short trips. *2007-2014:* Check the timing cover and oil pan for leaks, which are fairly common with the 2.4L engine. A metallic noise coming from the engine when cranking could indicate a repair costing about $400 to the variable valve timing system. Some air conditioner failures reported; check the AC compressor clutch, a $130 part, before replacing the much more expensive compressor. A lit engine service light may point to a defective exhaust gas oxygen sensor. Repair shops neglect to check the rear differential oil level, and perform the required gear oil change; ask for it. *2008-2012:* Low oil level could indicate an engine that is burning oil; engine oil pan leaks; and windshield washer nozzles may be prone to freeze up in cold weather. On pre-2015 models, a vibration coming through the floor at speed may indicate a worn driveshaft joint; the Honda replacement part is expensive ($800), as it includes the entire driveshaft assembly. Check the aftermarket for a less expensive repair using a rebuilt driveshaft (if you are in Ontario or Quebec, the APA can refer you to a shops). 2007-2010 models are covered by a transmission recall to address a potential vibration problem.

INTERNAL BULLETINS, SECRET WARRANTIES: 2008-09—Headliner sagging near the liftgate. 2010-11—Fluid leaks from rear of vehicle. Low power on acceleration requires only a software update, says Honda. High oil consumption due to sticking rings will be remedied by a warranty extension on the pistons and piston rings up to 8 years/125,000 miles, says TSB #12-089. 2011-12—An engine oil leak at the rear of the cylinder head cover may be caused by a defective No. 5 rocker shaft holder. The left rear wheel well doesn't have enough seam sealer, which may allow water to leak into the interior under the rear seat. 2012-14—Excessive vibration at highway speeds caused by the propeller shaft and the dampening system not adequately supporting vibrations. A front brake judder may be caused by a mis-aligned brake pad, disc, or caliper. Install new brake pads. 2013-14—Engine rattles at cold startup due to a defective variable valve timing control. 2015—False low tire pressure warnings.

In Honda TSB 15-046, titled "Vibration While Driving and/or Stopped in Gear," the company lists three driving "modes" that can produce excessive vibrations. In Mode 1, the vibrations occur while the CR-V is stopped in gear. In Mode 2, the vibrations are felt when accelerating. And in Mode 3, the CR-V will shake while traveling 60-90 kph with the engine at 1,800 to 2,200 rpm. Repairs depend upon which mode a driver can feel the vibration.

One of the repairs can reduce fuel economy by about 1 mpg and Honda wants a record of the owner giving their approval to make the repairs.

- Mode 1 repairs will consist of installing new radiator lower cushions, a new transmission mount and new front head restraints.

- Mode 2 requires the installation of a tailgate damper kit and a software update to the (PCM).

- For Mode 3 repairs, dealers will update the PCM software only.

ACCORD ★★★★
CROSSTOUR ★★★★
HYBRID ★★★★

RATING: Above Average (2010-17). *Accord:* A perennial family car favourite, the Accord's 2008 redesign added a bit more content but was less reliable. The Accord was last redesigned for the 2013 model year and given a mid-cycle remake for 2016. The current-generation Accord retains its roomy cabin, with more elegant styling. No changes of note for 2017 other than the return of the Hybrid, which was not offered in 2016. **Road performance:** Good acceleration with all engines. The Accord has a very good ride-handling compromise for a mainstream family car. The Accord offered sharper handling than its chief competitor, the Toyota Camry, until the arrival of the 2015 Camry that has pretty much closed the gap. **Strong points:** The 4-cylinder engine combines good performance with fuel economy that is near the top of the class. The V6 is fast and sounds good; its fuel economy is commendable for the high performance level. Responsive handling. Pre-touch screen the Accord's controls were among the more convenient on the market. High resale value is a plus for new vehicle buyers. The Accord offers something for everyone. **Weak points:** Road noise intrudes into the cabin; it's long been a Honda irritant. The thief-friendly trunk sometimes opens on its own when parked – a problem known for over 7 years that also affects some Acuras. Trunk struts won't hold the lid up when parked on a hill. Interior design and materials used are uninspired. Excessive wind noise. **Major redesign:** 2008 and 2013, with a 2016 update. **Best alternatives:** Hyundai Sonata, Kia Optima, and Toyota Camry. All are less expensive on the used car market than the Accord – the Sonata and Optima cost thousands less.

Crosstour

RATING: This 5-door hatchback is based on the platform of the 2008-2012 Accord. The Crosstour is billed as a "Crossover Utility Vehicle," which is Honda-speak for a high-riding hatchback/station wagon available with all-wheel drive. Except for the 2013 model year when a 2.4L 4-cylinder engine was offered, all Crosstours are powered by the same strong 3.5L hp V6 offered in the Accord. Front-wheel drive was standard, with all-wheel drive being optional except for 2014, when it was standard. Launched as a large hatchback, the Crosstour was refocused for 2013 with an "Outback" like makeover, featuring a higher ride height and various SUV accents. **Road Performance:** Equipped with the V6 (as most Crosstours are), the Crosstour is quick and quiet unless you really hammer it, when it sounds intoxicating. Precise, nicely weighted steering. Impressive ride-handling compromise. Small side windows and a rising beltline combine to restrict outward vision. The dashboard is overscaled for the car and its controls for climate and audio functions are less than ideal. Crosstour occupants relax on large, supportive seats and enjoy plenty of space. The versatile hatchback tail can accommodate a large amount of luggage but the rear suspension towers intrude into the cargo area and the sloping tailgate reduces vertical height. **Best alternatives:** Toyota Venza (2016 was the last year of production).

Hybrid

RATING: A car that can run exclusively on electric power under certain conditions, the Hybrid harnesses the combined power of a 2L four and an electric motor, sending power to the front wheels via a CVT. The Hybrid was offered in 2014, 2015 and again in revised form for 2017. The 2017 Accord Touring Hybrid is priced roughly $4,000 higher than its gas 4-cylinder equivalent; if fuel savings is your only criteria, breakeven will take 6-7 years.

Prices and Specs

Prices (2017): *Accord LX man:* $24,590, *Touring V6 auto:* $36,390 **Freight:** $1,695 **Powertrain (2017):** *Accord FWD: Engines:* 2.4L 4-cyl. (185-189 hp), 3.5L V6 (278 hp); Transmissions: 6-speed man., CVT, 6-speed auto., *Crosstour (2010-2014) FWD/AWD: Engines:* 2.4L 4-cyl. (192 hp), 3.5L V6 (271 hp 2010-12), (278 hp 2013-14); Transmission: 5-speed auto (2010-12), 6-speed auto (2013-14). **Dimensions:** *Accord Sedan (2017 2.4L CVT):* Passengers: 2/3; Wheelbase: 109 in., 2,775 mm.; L: 193 in., 4,907.; W: 73 in., 1,856 mm.; Weight: 3,322 lb., 1,507 kg. **Fuel economy:** *2016 4-cyl.:* 6.5/8.8 L/100 km. **Assembled in:** U.S.A.

ALERT! Rear windshield distorts the view (makes objects wavy). The effect is magnified in rainy weather and at night. Four other things to check out during the Accord's test drive: Low-beam headlights that may give insufficient illumination; and poor seat and head restraint design that causes severe neck, back, and leg pain (a complaint over the past several years). Be careful where you put your knee when driving:

> My car stopped when the start button was pressed while driving. The start button is near my knee and an accidental press caused my moving car to shut down – fortunately I was just starting and only going 5 mph. Can you imagine what would happen if my knee hit the start button while going 65 in traffic? The dealer said that is normal!!

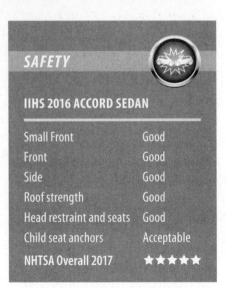

SAFETY

IIHS 2016 ACCORD SEDAN

Small Front	Good
Front	Good
Side	Good
Roof strength	Good
Head restraint and seats	Good
Child seat anchors	Acceptable
NHTSA Overall 2017	★★★★★

Owner-reported safety-related failures: Airbags may explode for no reason or fail to deploy; brake and power steering failures:

> All of a sudden steering cut out on me in the middle of my turn. I narrowly missed oncoming traffic and stopped right before I hit the curb and a parked car. When I did stop and got my composure back I looked down and there was a steering wheel light on and a buzzing

noise. All this while going no more than six miles an hour. At this current moment my car is less than two years old.

Horn honks on its own and drains battery, sunroof shatters for no discernible reason, soya-coated wiring and fuel line is "Kibble" for rodents.

RELIABILITY: Above average; 2008-2010 models elicited a higher number of complaints, a sign of the slide in quality at Honda from 2006-2012; quick-wearing brakes topped the list. Check for scored rear brake discs and have the brake calipers freed up annually if necessary. Replacement brake pads from Honda and parts available in the aftermarket are improved. Oil consumption possible with both the 4-cylinder and the V6 to 2012; Honda Canada extended the warranty on the 4-cylinder to 7 years/160,000 km, but Honda dealers were instructed to delay repairs until oil consumption reaches a very high 1L/1,500 km. *Four-cylinder engine:* Check for oil leaks at the valve cover, timing cover, crank seal and oil pressure switch. A metallic noise coming from the engine when cranking could indicate a repair costing about $400 to the variable valve timing system. *V6:* High oil consumption on some early engines with Honda's Variable Cylinder Management, which shuts off up to three cylinders. Some other owner complaints.

> Last night, my 2014 Honda Accord's windows and sunroof automatically opened; there have been other random electrical problems. The opening of the windows occurred during a rain storm and my brand new Honda is filled with water.

The driver's door collects and leaks water. Excessive side door wind noise; faulty tire pressure monitoring sensors; annoying windshield dash reflection; distorted windshields; and damage to the AC condenser:

> Air conditioner condenser damaged due to road debris. Vehicle design is poor leaving the condenser unprotected from road debris. Grill opening is large with no screen or mesh in front of the condenser. Repair cost is $786.

INTERNAL BULLETINS, SECRET WARRANTIES: 2003-15—V6-equipped models may leak oil from the rear cylinder head cover gasket. 2008—Court settlement relative to side airbag deployment. Excessive oil consumption. Road debris continues to damage expensive AC compressors. Blower motor noisy or inoperative. Carpet on the passenger's side pulls out from under the door sill trim. 2008-09—Troubleshooting an engine whining noise and a steering clicking. Fix for an engine that ticks or knocks at idle. 2008-10—Supplementary restraint system warranty extended to 15 years with no mileage limitation. 2008-12—High oil consumption due to sticking rings will be remedied by a warranty extension on the pistons and piston rings up to 8 years/125,000 miles, says TSB #13-078 (later extended to 2013s):

2008-12 Accord V6 A/T

BACKGROUND: American Honda is announcing a powertrain warranty extension as a result of a settlement of a class captioned, Soto et al. v. American Honda Motor Co., Inc., Case No. 3:12-cv-1377-SI (N.D. Cal.). The piston rings on certain cylinders may rotate and align which can lead to spark plug fouling. This can set DTCs P0301 through P0304 and cause the MIL to come on. **American Honda is extending the powertrain warranty to cover repairs related to engine misfire (that triggers DTCs P0301 through P0304) to 8 years with unlimited mileage from the original date of purchase and has settled a class action based on this remedial measure.**

2008-12—A clunk is heard in the front suspension while driving over irregular surfaces and in hot weather. You may need to replace both of the front lower ball joints with updated service parts made to address this specific symptom. If the ball joints were previously replaced, then replace both front knuckle assemblies. 2011-12—Bulletin confirms leakage from the driveshaft seals. Windshield wind noise may be caused by deformed hood seal. Engine rattles on cold start-up. 2011-13—Honda will change the spark plugs, clean pistons, and replace the piston rings for free, if the MIL light stays on under *Soto et al.* 2013—Engine oil leaks. Troubleshooting front and rear wheel bearing noise and rear head cover gasket oil leaks. Honda bulletin confirms some cars surge, hesitate, or judder. Driver airbag rattles and not centered; horn goes off by itself, measures to silence front door wind noise. 2013-14—Delayed CVT shifting. Judder on light acceleration from a stop. Some vehicles produce a pop or clicking sound when turning the steering wheel. 2014-15—A front suspension clunk or rattle (see Hybrid, below). Front suspension clunks or rattles heard when driving over bumps or when turning may mean at least one self-locking nut at the top of the front damper spring assembly is loose. Repair tips to silence wind noise from the driver's or front passenger's side window. 2015-16—Wind noise from the front windows. *Hybrid:* 2006-07—Hybrids that lose power when accelerating need three different software updates. Honda's 2006 Civic software update caused a dramatic drop in fuel economy and Accord Hybrid owners say they also get poor gas mileage, since the revised engine/IMA battery software was installed in their Hybrids to extend IMA battery life.

ODYSSEY

RATING: Above Average (2007-2017); Below Average (2005-2006). The Odyssey outclasses Toyota's Sienna in driving enjoyment but older models have been less reliable. A redesigned Odyssey appeared in 2005, offering a split folding rear seat to increase versatility. It was partially updated in 2008, including new active head restraints for the front seats. A redesigned fourth-generation Odyssey arrived in 2011; it was updated in 2014 with partial restyling and improved in-dash connectivity; the 5-speed automatic was dropped and the 6-speed automatic became standard across the board. A new Odyssey is expected during 2017. **Road performance:** The punchy, sonically compelling V6 mates nicely with Honda's automatic transmission. The V6 engine on the EX-L and Touring features variable cylinder deactivation to increase fuel economy; the engine's ability to switch automatically between 6-cylinder and 3-cylinder activation, depending on engine load, can reduce gas consumption by up to 10%. Nicely weighted and geared steering, and a well-developed ride-handling compromise. Very comfortable seats and abundant legroom make occupants in all three rows comfortable. Substantial cargo capacity even when the third row seat is up for occupants. An expensive used vehicle; a used Odyssey sells for more than the Sienna and much more than the Dodge Grand Caravan or Chrysler Town and Country. **Strong points:** Attractive for a box. Large interior for passengers and cargo. Great powertrain. Fuel consumption is better than a large three-row SUV, impressive on the highway (it's fairly high in town). **Weak points:** When the ECO function is engaged, the 6-speed automatic can make a rattling noise and the drivetrain can vibrate a bit. The second-row seats are heavy and it takes muscle to remove them if maximum cargo space is required. Inconvenient audio controls on recent high-end models. **Major redesign:** 2005, 2008 update, 2011, 2014 update, 2017-2018 redesign pending. **Best alternatives:** The Toyota Sienna is the obvious cross-shop; it costs less used and is a bit more reliable, but it lacks the Odyssey's flair. The Chrysler Town and Country offers comparable elegance, but most Honda buyers wouldn't consider it because of its inferior reliability.

Prices and Specs

Prices (2016): *LX:* $30,790, *Touring:* $48,890 **Freight:** $1,725 **Powertrain (FWD):** Engine: 3.5L V6 (248 hp); Transmission: 6-speed auto. **Dimensions:** Passengers: 2/3/3; Wheelbase: 118.1 in., 3,000 mm.; L: 202.1, 5,153 mm.; W: 79.2 in., 2,011 mm.; Weight: 4,487 lb., 1,996 kg. **Fuel economy:** 8.5/12.3 L/100 km. **Assembled in:** U.S.A.

SAFETY

IIHS 2016

Small Front	Good
Front	Good
Side	Good
Roof strength	Good
Head restraint and seats	Good
Child seat anchors	Acceptable
NHTSA Overall 2016	★★★★★

ALERT! Make sure the head restraint is comfortable. Some drivers regret not having done so before their purchase:

> My neck must bend forward about 15 degrees to conform to the headrest of my 2016 Odyssey. Any bumps in the road result in the headrest tapping and pushing the back of my head. I feel like a bobble-head!

Owner-reported safety-related failures: The Odyssey's size, weight, and higher minivan seating position make it very safe in a collision. A few safety-related complaints have been recorded:

> The automatic side door accidentally closed and squeezed on a 7-year-old child's fingers, and could not be opened by any method. We (as parents) tried all door open/close switches, door remote controls, as well as the door's manual handle in order to open the door to release the child's hand.

On older model years, the third row cup-holder panel area gets hot enough to burn passengers; driver-side mirrors can reflect a blurred, distorted image; sunroofs are prone to shatter, even when parked in the garage; the side sliding door frequently malfunctions by closing unexpectedly, opening when the vehicle is underway, and failing to retract when closing on an object; the headlights can blind oncoming drivers, and low beams are poorly designed:

> The low beam headlights illuminated vision is very bright on the road close to the vehicle but there is a line midway up the windshield above, which it is totally black.

RELIABILITY: The Odyssey suffered a bit from the general decline in Honda quality in the period from 2005-2012; it's the Honda model with the most body-related complaints. If you can live without them, the electric sliding doors may be worth a pass when buying a used Odyssey, or look for a vehicle with full warranty coverage from Honda, including the electric doors. Brake complaints were common, with reports of premature front brake wear, excessive noise; mushy braking; apparent loss of or reduced braking after the Vehicle Stability Assist light comes on (some dealers suggest unplugging the VSA); brake pedal sometimes sinks to the floor; and shimmying when the brakes are applied. *2005-2008:* Automatic transmission breakdowns; transmission slams into gear or suddenly locks in low gear while the vehicle is underway. *2005-2010:* Some power steering pump and rack failures. Owners say the A/C will come on and not shut off, the A/C-heat blower randomly increases in power, and road debris can destroy the A/C condenser. Rain water leaks through windows and out of the electrical conduit entering into where the sliding door mechanism is located. Electronic problems on recent models include a malfunctioning rearview camera, power lock faults, sliding doors that are slow to respond, and issues that cause the security alarm to sound randomly. The fuel pump is covered by a recall. *2008-2009:* Models with an electric rear hatch door: Defective hatch struts to be replaced free under a recall. *2011-2012:* A warped driver air bag cover is covered by a recall.

INTERNAL BULLETINS, SECRET WARRANTIES: All years—Honda TSBs allow for special warranty consideration on a "goodwill" basis by the company's District Service Manager or Zone Office. There's an incredibly large number of sliding-door problems covered by various recalls, and a plethora of service bulletins too numerous to print here. Honda has a secret warranty extension that covers paint defects up to 7 years, says TSB #08-031, issued Jan. 8, 2010. This service bulletin is specifically for blue metallic paint defects; coverage can be extrapolated to cover other colours, as indicated in TSB #10-002 "Paint Defect Claim Information," issued Jan. 20, 2010. **2005-06**—Noise remedy for the power steering, front brakes, front wheel bearings, windshield, sliding door, and exhaust system. **2005-09**—Engine timing belt chirp. Sliding door doesn't open all the way. Power door locks continually lock while driving. **2005-10**—If the steering wheel is hard to turn at low speeds, Honda will replace the steering pump for free up to 7 years/100,000 miles (TSB #11-039). **2008-09**—Water accumulates in the inner tail lights . **2008-10**— Powertrain coverage is extended to 8 years/unlimited mileage as part of an out-of-court settlement in *Soto v. American Honda Motor Co.* Apparently, engine misfires due to spark plug fouling can damage the engine. Dealer may have to clean the pistons, and replace the piston rings in the affected cylinders. If the service manager looks at you quizzically, cite TSB #13-080. **2008-12**—Remedy for engine ticking at idle. **2010-12**—Engine oil leaks in the B-cap side bolt area. **2011-12**—Honda extends the warranty on stained or corroded tailgates and chrome trim. Troubleshooting complaints that vehicle hestitates when shifting into higher gears . **2011-14**—A rear suspension clunk or squeak may indicate lower spring seat deterioration.

Replace the lower suspension arm and spring seat. **2011-15**—Remedy for roof rack and tailgate rattling. **2014**—Troubleshooting tips for a power sliding door that sticks in the unlocked position. **2013**—Remedy for power sliding doors that detach from their rollers. **2014-15**—Brakes may grind, rub, or screech due to the front brake caliper bracket contacting the brake rotor. Dealer must replace the brake caliper brackets and refinish or replace the affected disc. A Honda service bulletin confirms the power sliding doors may detach from their rollers.

> Drivers side sliding door on my 2016 Odyssey would not close by pushing the "open/close" buttons. Tried multiple times. Upon attempting to close door manually, the entire door fell off the van.

PILOT ★★★★

2016 Pilot: A minivan on steroids.

RATING: Above Average. Honda cleverly took the MDX/Odysssey platform and designed a truck-style vehicle to capitalize on the public's craze for SUVs. The Pilot shares the sparkling V6 of the Odyssey and MDX. While it is usually the last of the trio to be updated, this can be a good thing as it allows the bugs to be worked out. The 2009-2015 Pilot looks deliberately "trucky" on the outside, and interior finish trends to utilitarian. The Pilot was all-new for 2016 and is unchanged for 2017. The new body is about 150 kg lighter, and the V6 features direct injection. A 6-speed automatic is standard; the Touring features a 9-speed automatic. **Road performance:** The third-generation 2016 Pilot has grown into a large people carrier that offers good power for highway cruising, tidy handling, and a comfortable ride. A new one-touch system slides the split-rear seat forward to ease third-row access. The exterior looks less industrial. Its popularity has overwhelmed Honda

Canada's ability to satisfy demand, leading to delivery delays and inflated transaction prices. **Strong points:** Both the current and previous-generation Pilots are roomy, comfortable, and pleasant to drive. The current model is stylish with a cabin that now matches class expectations. **Weak points:** Typical intrusive Honda road noise on pre-2016 models. Honda's knob-free audio touch screen in 2016 and later models is not really suitable for use when the vehicle is moving. Heavy fuel consumption characteristic of a large, powerful vehicle that is shaped like a brick. Honda's much-heralded cylinder deactivation system doesn't appear to save as much fuel as Honda thinks it does in this vehicle. The cabin design and materials on the 2009-15 Pilot are disappointing. **Major redesign:** 2003 introduction, 2009, 2012 minor restyle, 2013 interior update, and 2016. **Best alternatives:** The Hyundai Santa Fe XL and Toyota Highlander top the list of alternatives, as does 2014-2017 Kia Sorento V6. The Santa Fe XL and Sorento sell for less on the used car market.

Prices and Specs

Prices (2016): *LX FWD:* $35,590, *Touring AWD:* $50,790 **Freight:** $1,725 **Powertrain (2016: FWD/AWD):** Engine: 3.5L V6 (280 hp); Transmission: 6-speed auto., 9-speed auto. (Touring only). **Dimensions (2016):** Passengers: 2/3/3; Wheelbase: 111 in. 2,820 mm.; L: 194.5 in., 4,941 mm./W: 79.9 in., 2,029 mm.; Weight: 4,336 lb., 1,967 kg. **Fuel economy:** 9L/13.1 L/100 km. **Assembled in:** U.S.A.

Owner-reported safety-related failures: Owners reported only 92 safety-related complaints to NHTSA during the past 3 years (most vehicles average 50 reports a year); some incidents implicate electronic systems added in recent years:

> Adaptive cruise control fails to detect vehicles in odd situations, such as a truck where the rear of the body protrudes out from the rear wheels. After an empty stretch, upon coming up to a slower car, the Pilot will get very close to the car and then suddenly brake, causing drivers to nearly rear-end me. Plus, I am constantly put in danger by lane keep assist false alarms taking over the steering.

SAFETY	
IIHS 2016	
Small Front	Good
Front	Good
Side	Good
Roof strength	Good
Head restraint and seats	Good
Child seat anchors	Acceptable
NHTSA Overall 2016	★★★★★

Other complaints include fuel leak under the vehicle; loss of power while underway affecting 2012-13 models (*www.piloteers.org*); long hesitation when accelerating; vehicle pulls to the right; when shifting from Park to Drive vehicle lurches forward; transmission also hunts back and forth between Fourth and Fifth gear; transmission doesn't hold when the Pilot is parked on an incline:

I had put my car in Park, it was still running, I reached in and turned the key off and the car immediately started to roll. I attempted to get in the car to brake, but was unable to do this and then was thrown away from the vehicle, hitting my head on my rock driveway. There was a slight incline where I parked but when it started to roll it reached a steeper incline and rolled down my driveway and hit a tree. (Use the parking brake.)

Several owners warn that unprotected wiring in the undercarriage area could be a hazard if damaged:

Wheel sensor wires on 2011 Honda Pilots are exposed and unprotected under the vehicle which when damaged, disable anti-lock braking system (ABS), vehicle stability assist (VSA), and the variable torque management (VTM-4) systems.

Other owner complaints include rear tailgate window exploded while vehicle was parked in a garage and the moonroof exploded while underway; the key won't turn the ignition; and the driver's seat height adjustment lowers on its own while the Pilot is underway. Pilot dealer servicing has also been found wanting:

Spontaneous star crack in lower center windshield, spontaneous rear hatch and passenger door opening while driving with my young child in the rear passenger seat (with "locked" doors), transmission rattle upon slow acceleration or coast at Second and Third gears… Honda dealer said call insurance about windshield, something must have "hit" windshield without me knowing it, said "found no abnormal noises" and "cannot duplicate" rattle noise because different people have different driving patterns, said "cannot duplicate" doors opening while driving, dealer did not "fix" any of these safety issues, just told us to pick up the car…. After research on Internet, I believe these to be manufacturer defects.

RELIABILITY: Overall reliability has been better than average. *2003-2015:* Owners report premature brake wear; long braking distance; mushy brakes with reduced effectiveness. Some owner complaints about excessive engine vibration, especially, when Variable Cylinder Management is engaged, and some owners of the 2009-2015 Pilot have reported engine mount wear leads to vibrations felt in the driver's seat when the vehicle is running in 3-cylinder mode. Shuddering and vibration when shifting gears; automatic transmission fluid leaks; whining and clicking noise from the power steering. Water leaks into the passenger compartment have been reported. Persistent rattling and grinding noise from the rear engine mounts when the A/C compressor is running. *2016-2017:* The new 9-speed transmission on the Touring is a ZF design that has caused grief to owners of Chrysler products that use it. The rear A/C can elicit a loud rushing wind noise inside the dashboard. Long waits for recall repair parts. *2016:* The battery can sometimes lose its charge when parked a few hours or overnight.

INTERNAL BULLETINS, SECRET WARRANTIES: 2008-13— Powertrain coverage extended to 8 years/unlimited mileage as part of an out-of-court settlement in *Soto v. American Honda Motor Co.* Apparently, engine misfires due to spark plug fouling can damage the engine. Dealer may have to clean the pistons, and replace the piston rings in the affected cylinders. If the service manager looks puzzled, cite TSB #13-080. **2009-11**—Honda will repair and repaint the tailgate for free, up to 7 years, if it is damaged or stained by rust (June 2014 Honda memo to owners). Another Honda service bulletin confirms the vehicle pulls to the right on a straight road, but offers no fix. **2009-14**—Front suspension rear lower arm rubber bushings may crack resulting in a leak or suspension noise. Honda extended the warranty of the front suspension rear lower arm bushings to 7 years from the original date of purchase or 100,000 miles, whichever comes first. **2010**—Honda bulletin admits the company is investigating inexplicable sunroof shattering (exploding). **2010-12**—Engine oil leaks from the B-cap side bolts. **2011-12**—Engine ticking or knocking at idle (see Odyssey). **2012-15**—Excessive engine vibration between 60 and 100 kHz: Update the PCM module and replace the propeller shaft (4WDs). **2014-15**—Honda bulletin confirms there is excessive brake travel when applied and that brakes feel spongy. **2015**—Honda is investigating customer complaints of "sticking" door handles. **2016**—The instrument control module adds mileage to the odometer each time the ON mode is selected. When the ignition is turned to OFF, the module clears the auto door lock personalized settings and resets them to the default factory settings.

RIDGELINE ★★★★★

RATING: Recommended. A unique top-performer that is well-appointed and reliable, too. Like a Swiss Army knife, the Ridgeline is designed to suit a wide variety of needs and does it well… for a price! Unfortunately, the public has mostly ignored Honda's excellent design in favour of conventional full-size pickups that have improved over the decade the original Ridgeline was on the market. *2017:* The redesigned Ridgeline continues to use a unibody, offers a smooth car-like ride and handling, and shares the Pilot's capable 3.5L V6 hooked to a 6-speed automatic transmission. **Road performance:** Sustained and quiet acceleration; a smooth-shifting automatic transmission; and secure handling and good cornering control, thanks to communicative, direct steering and well-tuned shocks that provide a comfortable, supple ride for a pickup. Even if you paid more than expected for a new Ridgeline, you will recoup a lot of the difference. **Strong points:** The Ridgeline mixes performance with convenience. It's an ideal truck for most jobs. Its long wheelbase and independent rear suspension provide a nice ride and road manners that are superior to other pickups. It has a friendly cabin environment where everything is easily accessed and storage spaces abound. There is a unique lockable trunk beneath the cargo bed; the tailgate opens either vertically or horizontally. Reliability and overall dependability are very good, and crashworthiness is exemplary. **Weak points:** High prices, both new and used. Limited sales volume makes it rare on the used vehicle market. **Major redesign:** 2006 introduction and 2017. Honda skipped the 2015-2016 model years. **Best alternatives:** GM's Canyon and Colorado duo, the Toyota Tacoma, or Nissan Frontier.

Prices (2017): *DX:* $34,990, *VP:* $36,690, *EX-L:* $41,490, *EX-L Navi.:* $43,690 **Freight:** $1,395 **Powertrain (FWD/4WD):** Engine: 3.5L V6 (250 hp); Transmission: 5-speed auto. **Dimensions:** Passengers: 2/3; Wheelbase: 122 in.; H: 70.3/L: 207/W: 69 in.; Headroom F/R: 6.5/4.5 in.; Legroom F/R: 42/28 in.; Fuel tank: 83.3L/regular; Tow limit: 5,000; lb.; Load capacity: 1,554 lb.; Turning circle: 42.6 ft.; Ground clearance: 7.5 in.; Weight: 4,504 lb. **Fuel economy:** 9.5L/12.8 L/100 km. **Assembled in:** U.S.A.

RELIABILITY: Incomplete data due to limited sales in Canada. Early models can experience transmission issues similar to other large Hondas. Some complaints regarding powertrain surging or hesitation: "Upon accelerating from a stop and turning to either the left or right the throttle control would hesitate and not be responsive to the gas pedal. It was like a dead zone as the vehicle was moving." – *safercar.gov.*

INTERNAL BULLETINS, SECRET WARRANTIES: 2006-07—Automatic transmission is hard to shift into Fourth gear. Vehicle pulls, drifts to one side. Drivetrain ping, squeal, or rattle upon light acceleration. Rear differential noise, judder on turns. 2006-09—Parking brake won't release in cold weather because of water infiltration. Noise and judder when turning. 2006-10—Steering column clicking when turning. 2006-11—Rear seat leg doesn't fold flat. 2006-14—Rear pop or clunk heard when passing over bumps in cold weather. Correct by applying a small amount of adhesive to the upper surface of the bump stop. 2009-10—Headliner vibrates or rattles. Whistling from the front door windows. Gap between the front bumper and the fender/headlamp. 2009-11—Tailgate won't open in swing mode; handle is stiff. Front seats squeak and creak. 2010-12—Engine oil leaks in the B-cap side bolt area.

SAFETY

IIHS 2014

Small Front	Not Rated
Front	Good
Side	Good
Roof strength	Good
Head restraint and seats	Good
Child seat anchors	Acceptable
NHTSA Overall 2016	Not Rated

Hyundai

Hyundai racked up impressive sales increases across Canada over the last decade thanks to leading edge designs introduced from 2006 onward, good value, and relentless promotion of low-interest-rate financing. Hyundai and Kia offer a more comprehensive warranty than all competing makes except for Mitsubishi. Sharing platforms and components delivers economies of scale, and Hyundai and Kia vehicles that share the same platforms do look and drive differently – even more than an Oldsmobile, Chevrolet, and Pontiac did in the 1960s, during the heyday of brand marketing at General Motors. Hyundai, with Kia close behind, copied the marketing strategy employed by Japanese automakers since the early '70s: Secure a solid beachhead with an inexpensive vehicle, and then branch into increasingly more expensive and profitable segments.

Hyundai now has an extensive lineup of fuel-efficient cars, minivans, and SUVs, and is increasingly targeting upscale customers. With its new Ioniq sub-line, Hyundai now offers a compact car with a conventional hybrid, plug-in hybrid, or full electric drivetrain. On the popularly-priced end of the spectrum, Hyundai and Kia have retained their magic touch, with mainstream small and compact cars that deliver commendable features and comfort. Hyundai built some sporty street cred with the Mustang-Camaro-stalking Genesis Coupe. The first-generation Genesis sedan was a fine luxury car kneecapped by its rear-wheel-drive-only powertrain. Hyundai corrected this misstep with the second-generation Genesis sedan by offering it exclusively with all-wheel drive. Among Hyundai's rare marketing flops, the Equus was a Korean market super-luxury car that borrowed some components from the Genesis; its styling was undistinguished, and it couldn't overcome a prestige deficit against European premium brands. Buyers looked elsewhere, and many of the cars ended up as personal transportation for Hyundai dealers and their spouses.

After the 2008 financial crisis, the two South Korean carmakers snagged dealerships dumped by Chrysler and General Motors. General Motors' ruthless decision to drop its Canadian Pontiac dealers overnight resulted in a lot of experienced old hands jumping to Hyundai and accelerating sales of their strong product line. GM's Canadian market share never rebounded to previous levels after this dealer elimination.

Pilfered Quality?

Hyundai car quality has gone from risible to reliable, thanks to better-made vehicles and perhaps a bit of corporate espionage.

Over two decades ago, Hyundai hired away a handful of Toyota's top quality-control engineers – and got a satchel full of Toyota's secret quality-control documents in the bargain. Following a cease-and-desist letter from Toyota's lawyers in 2006, Hyundai returned the pilfered papers and swore to Toyota's lawyers that they never looked at the secret reports stolen from the company (wink, wink; nudge, nudge).

"The $4,750 entry-level 1984 Pony was undoubtedly cheap and generally 'craptastic,' but it was a beginning. I knew a guy who drove one — and to say it was less than reliable would be an understatement." (See "Hyundai Pony, 1984-87" at *www.autos.ca/forum/index.php?topic=73546.0.*)

Whatever the real story is, Hyundai's reliability improved extraordinarily from 2002 to 2010. Industry insiders say the privileged information may well have helped Hyundai move up from the bottom of reliability rankings to the top third.

Has the Quality Bubble Burst?

As of the 2010 models, Hyundai's reliability began to decline measurably. The redesigned 2011 Sonata offered breakthrough styling and great performance, but reliability declined compared to the relatively troublefree 2008-2010 model years. Owners of 2011s have reported engine failures, steering "wander," and knocking suspensions requiring new struts or control arms. Steering malfunctions can drive the Sonata to one side of the road or the other:

> 2012 Sonata will not drive straight, it pulls to the left mostly but also to the right. Basically the car swerves all over the road, especially at higher speeds. I took it back to the dealership and they told me all foreign cars drive like this. They adjusted the tire pressure but that did not solve the problem. I do not feel safe driving the car. Hyundai issued a service campaign to fix the 2011 Sonatas for this exact problem, why can't they just do the same for the 2012s?

The 2011-2013 Elantra has been plagued with a major engine defect, and Hyundai has made consumers wait weeks for replacement engines; Hyundai occasionally rejects engine warranty claims because paperwork is incomplete or the owner followed the longer "normal" oil change interval posted on the Hyundai U.S.A. website.

Rocks on Your Roof

Both Hyundai and Kia take top prize for shattered sunroofs, a problem also shared with other domestic and imported, mid-level to luxury models, like the Audi A8 and S8, BMW 3-Series, Honda, and Toyota/Lexus. Here's what happens, while underway, or when parked: The sunroof explodes like a shotgun blast; pieces of glass fly through the cabin if the protective interior lining isn't closed; and afterwards the dealer or manufacturer refuses to cover the $1,500 to $3,000 warranty claim for a replacement under the pretext that the glass shattered after "being struck by an object."

This is a bogus excuse and automakers know it because the theory of "rocks on the roof" just doesn't fly with an exploding sunroof. Here's a report of what happened when a local TV station took up this story:

UC PROFESSOR SOLVES SHATTERED SUNROOF PROBLEM

MARCH 21, 2011

Michael Finney of "7 On Your Side," ABC News

FINNEY: A San Jose woman had a frightening experience when her sunroof suddenly shattered above her head while she was driving. Michelle Park asked BMW to cover her sunroof under warranty but the carmaker refused. That's when 7 On Your Side got involved.

PARK: It was like a little mini-explosion going right above your head and then you think, 'Oh my God, what just happened.

FINNEY: The explosion left a huge hole in her sunroof. Only the jagged edges remain.

Park brought her new 2010 328i into Stevens Creek BMW in Santa Clara for inspection. The service manager wrote in an email to BMW corporate saying, "The shop foreman found no signs of impact damage. The client is requesting this to be repaired under warranty."

An hour later, BMW replied saying, "I have picked up more rocks in the last three months and this is not a product issue. She will need to contact her insurance company."

PARK: He should have requested for pictures, he should have said, he'll send somebody out to inspect it, that was it, in 3 minutes he said it was a rock issue, how would he know.

FINNEY: Park searched the internet and found that car owners of various makes reported their sunroofs also suddenly shattered.

7 On Your Side then discussed this incident with Tarek Zohdi, a professor of mechanical engineering at UC Berkeley. He calculated a rock lofted into the air by a vehicle tire would reach a height of 10-15 feet and would have to come down at 70-80 miles an hour to break the sunroof.

ZOHDI: There is not a chance in the world that an unintentional rock that is lofted by a vehicle would ever break a sunroof panel.

FINNEY: Zohdi says the maximum velocity of a rock coming down would be 25 miles an hour, well short of the needed 70 miles an hour. He said it is more likely the sunroof broke due to the stress caused by changes in temperatures or from fatigue.

ZOHDI: In both cases I would say in my opinion the car manufacturer has the problem; basically it's a manufacturers defect.

FINNEY: 7 On Your Side called BMW corporate. It agreed to replace the sunroof free of charge even before we informed it of the professor's finding.

Tarek says it is possible a rock could break a windshield with a direct hit, but the same scenario is not true for a sunroof since the rock would have to be first lofted into the air.

RATING: Above Average (2006-11); Recommended (2012-17). For 2012, Hyundai transformed its entry-level Accent into a larger, more upscale car that is one of the best all-rounders in the subcompact class. Base models offer many standard features usually found only on more expensive cars such as a height-adjustable driver's seat, four-wheel disc brakes, active front head restraints, a tilt steering wheel, and power door locks. **Road performance:** *2012-2017:* Smooth, zingy 1.6L engine in combination with the optional slick-shifting 6-speed automatic provides good performance and fuel economy for the subcompact class. The clutch and gear change of the manual transmission work well. Nicely-weighted steering and a good ride-handling compromise set standards for a car in its segment. Front seat comfort is acceptable and legroom is abundant for a small car. Good trunk space on the hatchback, with the sedan having an enormous trunk for a car of its size. **Strong points:** *2012-2017:* Best-in-class cabin comfort with crisp instrumentation and simple, logical controls; matte-finish plastics and chic fabrics make for an inviting interior. Affordable. *2016-2011:* Very low prices; this generation Accent is a better alternative than GM Daewoo junk like the Chevrolet Aveo, Pontiac Wave, and Suzuki Swift that compete in its price range. **Weak points:** Last renewed for 2012, the 2017 Accent betrays its age by lacking active safety equipment that is becoming more commonplace in this segment. Small rear window on the hatchback. The rear seat backrest is a bit too upright. *2011-2016:* Mediocre suspension. **Major redesign:** 2006 and 2012, 2018 pending. **Best alternatives:** Kia Rio, Mazda2, or Toyota Yaris.

Surprisingly, the similar Rio performed much better in the small overlap frontal collision test because of a different engine mount breakaway design.

ALERT! Several models come with no spare tire – just an inflator and a can of sealant, which may have been removed or used up by the previous owner; check with a wrecker before you sign, as the dealer price for a compact spare, jack, and related tools is exorbitant.

Owner-reported safety-related failures: Driver's airbag deployed when vehicle was started; driver injured. Sometimes, airbags don't deploy when they should, or there's a sudden loss of power, or the steering locks up. Headlight bulbs burn out because of a voltage spike apparently caused by a faulty voltage regulator. Keep the car in the garage if you live in a woodsy area – rodents treat your yummy wiring insulation like a Tim Hortons' drivethrough. One owner reported that groundhogs love to snack on cables in the car's undercarriage, thereby disabling the transmission and important dash instruments:

> I put down moth balls and fox scent to ward them off, but they love Accent wires; losing the transmission and speedometer can make driving a little dangerous.

RELIABILITY: *006-2011:* Check for suspension wear including worn or leaking shock absorbers, broken sway bar links, and worn ball joints. Fluid leaks are common at the power steering hoses and transmission cooler lines. A lit Check Engine light likely indicates a defective engine or transmission sensor. *2012-2014:* Unstable idle or misfire may point to a need for cleaning of the direct fuel injection system, which tends to be more finicky than conventional port injection. Broken sway bar links are covered up to 5 years/100,000 km under the standard warranty. A stain in the door paint underneath the rearview mirrors can be cleaned using a special product; if damage is not too advanced, it may be possible to apply corrosion protection.

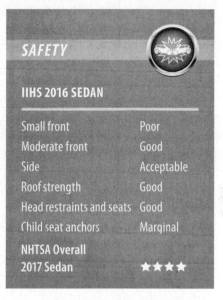

SAFETY

IIHS 2016 SEDAN

Small front	Poor
Moderate front	Good
Side	Acceptable
Roof strength	Good
Head restraints and seats	Good
Child seat anchors	Marginal

NHTSA Overall 2017 Sedan ★★★★

INTERNAL BULLETINS, SECRET WARRANTIES: 2008-11—Some 2008-11 Accents may have a rattle noise coming from under the vehicle near the front muffler pipe assembly. This bulletin provides a procedure to replace either the front muffler pipe hanger assembly or the front muffler assembly. **2011-13**—Harsh delayed shift diagnosis on the 6-speed automatic. Reducing wind noise from the front door mirror area. **2012-13**—A persistent spark knock on heavy acceleration may be due to incorrect canister purge valve flow. **2012-15**—An improperly adjusted or improperly operating inhibitor switch (range switch) may result in one or more of the following conditions: Malfunction indicator light (MIL) illuminated, or intermittent no engine crank/no engine start in Park or Neutral. Troubleshooting tips for shift lever concerns. Some Hyundai vehicles may experience brake noise due to improperly adjusted parking brakes. A maladjusted parking brake may cause floating brake shoes that, in turn, may create squealing and judder. Brake noise can be reduced by adjusting the parking brake cable to 0.5mm freeplay at the adjusting nut, then adjusting the rear shoes.

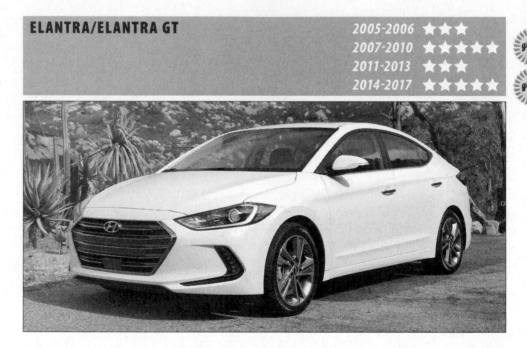

ELANTRA/ELANTRA GT	
2005-2006	★ ★ ★
2007-2010	★ ★ ★ ★ ★
2011-2013	★ ★ ★
2014-2017	★ ★ ★ ★ ★

RATING: Average (2005-06); Recommended (2007-2010); Average (2011-2013); Recommended (2014-17). Rapid depreciation and a plentiful supply makes the Elantra a good used car buy, with the possible exception of the 2011-2013 models. **Road performance:** *Redesigned 2017 Sedan:* Except when pushed hard, the 2L 4- and 6-speed automatic transmission combination delivers impressively smooth performance, especially in traffic and at normal operating speeds. The steering is very light. The ride-handling combination is good for a mainstream family hauler without any sporting pretensions. The front seats are not ideally shaped but provide adequate comfort once you are used to them. The rear seat is supportive, legroom is competitive. Good climate control system and pleasant sounding audio in the GLS model evaluated. Good trunk. *2011-16 Sedan:* Stylish. The redesigned 2011 Elantra was set-up to feel sporty and impress on a short test drive, but more time at the wheel revealed that the suspension suffered from a lack of development and copes poorly with anything other than smooth pavement, especially on premium models with bigger wheels and tires. Suspension calibration improved after 2012. Nicely-weighted steering. The interior is features crisp gauges, logical controls, and a class-leading design. The front seats are a bit too flat but provide acceptable comfort. The rear seat has enough space but headroom is short and there is little toe room under the front seats, reducing actual legroom for those in the back. Good trunk. *2007-2010 Sedan:* A good all-rounder, with a nicely finished cabin for the compact class and low prices. **Strong points:** *2017 Sedan:* Smooth 2L 4-cylinder and slick shifting 6-speed automatic transmission make the Elantra a pleasant all-round vehicle, especially in urban-suburban driving. Superior fuel economy. The cabin is classy with simple, logical controls, and attractive plastic trim. *2011-16 Sedan:* Stylish inside and out. Lower prices than competing compacts from Toyota and Honda. **Weak points:** *2017 Sedan:* Rear suspension could be smoother. Soft brake pedal. *2011-16 Sedan:* Excessive wind and road noise; and the dash vents would be more effective if they were mounted higher. Poorly calibrated suspension on 2011-2012 models. **Major redesign:** 2007, 2011 and 2017. **Best alternatives:** The Honda Civic, Mazda3, or Toyota Corolla.

Elantra GT

RATING: Made in Korea, the GT is a version of the I30 hatchback Hyundai builds in Slovakia. The car shares no exterior panels or cabin elements with the Elantra. The GT is stylish inside and out, with good rear seat headroom and better rear legroom as well. The GT's ride and handling are much better than the sedan. Versatile hatchback body.

Prices and Specs

Prices (2017): *L Sedan manual:* $15,999, *Limited Ultimate auto.:* $28,799 **Freight:** $1,695 **Powertrain (FWD):** Engine (2017): 2L 4-cyl. (147 hp); Transmissions: 6-speed man., 6-speed auto. **Dimensions:** *Sedan:* Passengers: 2/3; Wheelbase: 106.3 in., 2,700 mm,; L: 179.1 in., 4,550 mm.; W: 70.9 in., 1,800 mm.; Weight: 2,810 lb., 1,275 kg. **Fuel economy:** *2016 2L auto:* 7.0/9.8 L/100 km. **Assembled in:** Korea or U.S.A.

ALERT! One feature missing on some basic models of the sedan – a spare tire and jack. Check the trunk before you buy; the dealer price for a compact spare, jack, and hardware is exorbitant.

Owner-reported safety-related failures: Sudden engine shutdown on the highway; hood flew up while vehicle was underway; dangerous airbag deployment:

SAFETY

IIHS 2017 ELANTRA SEDAN

Small front	Good
Moderate front	Good
Side	Acceptable
Roof strength	Good
Head restraints and seats	Good
Child seat anchors	Acceptable
NHTSA Overall 2017 Sedan	★★★★

Drivers side airbag deployed and metal bracket deployed with airbag from headliner area, also. It sliced my ear in half… Could have been my neck…

At other times, both airbags deployed for no reason; the airbag warning light came on; the cruise control reset itself to a higher speed; throttle sensor sticks when cruising; automatic transmission jumps out of gear; complete electrical shutdown; faulty electronic stability control; car idles roughly, then refuses to shift into Drive; steering lock-up (possibly a loss of power assist); the car continually pulls to the right or left. History of front windshield cracks; windshield glare; sunroof implosions; can't trust the fuel gauge.

RELIABILITY: Above average to 2010, dropping to below average in 2011-2013. The 2014 and later cars are better. The GT has been more reliable than the sedans after 2011. *Up to 2010:* Check to see if the timing belt service was performed; it's an expensive maintenance item that is sometimes overlooked. *2007-2010:* Check for oil leaks at the timing cover, power steering hoses, and steering rack seals, and automatic transmission oil cooler lines to the radiator. A noisy accessory drive belt tensioner may require replacement. *2011-2013:* Elantra sedans with the 1.8L engine are a risky buy. Defective piston rings can lead to excessive oil consumption requiring a major teardown and reassembly, or replacement of the engine block; replacement engines from Hyundai are covered by a lifetime warranty. Hyundai dealers sometimes deny claims arbitrarily, by asking second owners for the previous owner's service records, or claiming the engine is low on oil (obviously… it's burning oil!). The best bet with a 2011-2013 sedan may be to choose a car whose engine has already been replaced. *2011-2016:* Premature rear brake wear. Check for noisy or rusted rear brakes; have the rear brake calipers serviced and lubricated once or twice a year to prevent expensive brake repairs.

INTERNAL BULLETINS, SECRET WARRANTIES: 2007-12—Troubleshooting hard shifts. 2010—Some Elantra and Elantra Touring vehicles may exhibit a noise originating from the front struts when passing over bumps. 2011-12—Rear door harness and centre muffler rattle noise repair. Excessive driveshaft noise (creaking or popping). Troubleshooting an automatic transmission that stays in Third gear, goes into "failsafe mode," or has an illuminated MIL alert. Touch screen new recalibration. 2011-13—Hard starts may signal the need to clean the electronic throttle control (ETC) throttle body.

SONATA

RATING: Recommended. *Hybrid:* Average (2012-2013); Above Average (2014-2016). There have been few owner complaints since the Sonata's 2015 redesign. **Road performance:** *2006-2010:* Smooth and peppy V6; the 2.4L 4-cylinder delivers solid performance. Hyundai never truly sorted out the suspension on the V6 models; the 4-cylinder version rides and handles more competently. The elegant, conservative interior is fronted by a dashboard with clear gauges and simple controls. Comfortable seats and plenty of space for four adults; the trunk is big enough to haul their luggage on a week-long vacation. *2011-2014:* The 2.4 L 4-cylinder works very well with the 6-speed automatic but can get loud on full acceleration; exceptional fuel economy for a mid-size car with owners reporting 7.5L/100 km on the highway and over 750 km on a tank of fuel. The 2L turbo is fast but unnecessary, and turbo models ride harder. Low seating, and swoopy styling of the 2011-2014 impede visibility for some drivers. The dramatic instrument panel looks like it belongs in a more expensive car and works very well. Good legroom front and rear but the front seats aren't completely comfortable; spacious rear seat but its support is not universally appreciated. *2015-2017:* A more conservative design, the interior is less flamboyant, but the materials are a bit richer. Despite the multiplicity of features on high-end versions, the controls are relatively straightforward. The newest Sonata is very spacious and has large, supportive seats front and rear. While a bit shallow, the trunk is large. On the road, the 2.4L normally aspirated Sonata is strong, smooth, flexible, and very well mated to a 6-speed automatic transmission that impresses because it operates without being noticed. The 2L turbo 4-cylinder is very quick but booms around 1500 rpm, a range in which it runs a lot of the time. Absorbent ride combined with steady handling make this generation Sonata one of the best balanced mid-size cars available. Quieter than the previous-generation car. **Strong points:** *2006-2010:* Smooth V6 engine. Comfortable cabin with good room and seating position. *2011-2014:* Quick, economical 2.4L engine with very good highway range. Good interior space, handsome design. Large trunk. *2015-2017:* Smooth, flexible performance from the base 2.4L engine, excellent fuel economy, good ride-handling compromise and a comfortable, well-finished cabin. Low prices on the used vehicle market for all generations; you'll get comparable performance and save thousands compared to a recent Camry or Accord, especially for deluxe models with a leather interior. **Weak points:** *2006-2010:* Suspension wallows over big bumps and is harsh over small impacts – the worst of both worlds. Fuel consumption higher than class leaders; it improved somewhat after 2009. *2011-2014:* More road noise than average for the segment. Some drivers of 2011-2012 models report poor highway directional stability. *2015-2017:* Nothing to report. **Major redesign:** 2006, 2011, and 2015. **Best alternatives:** A Honda Accord, Kia Optima, or a Toyota Camry; the Accord and Camry cost much more on the used car market.

Hybrid

RATING: Sonata's Hybrid debut in 2012 and provided little real benefit and a lot of complexity compared to the regular gas engine model. The claimed fuel economy was fanciful. The 2014 and later models were improved with a smoother-shifting transmission. Braking is more confidence-inspiring; the battery has a higher capacity and is smaller, freeing up some cargo space, and the car can reach highway speeds on battery power alone. *2016-2017:* The hybrid version of the newest Sonata works very well. Low prices on the used car market – with early hybrids, there is almost no premium compared to a fully equipped gas Sonata because potential buyers are put off by the complex technology.

> ### Prices and Specs
>
> **Price (2016):** *GL:* $24,749, *Hybrid Ultimate:* $37,499 **Freight:** $1,795 **Powertrain (FWD):** Engines: 2L 4-cyl. turbo (245 hp), 2L 4-cyl. hybrid (154 hp gas and 38 kW electric/50 kW for plug-in). 6-speed auto, 2.4 L 4-cyl., (185 hp). **Dimensions:** Passengers: 2/3; Wheelbase: 110.4 in., 2,805 mm.; L: 191.1 in., 4,855 mm.; W: 73.4 in., 1,865 mm.; Weight: 3,466 lb., 1,572 mm. **Fuel economy (2016):** *Auto. 2.0L turbo:* 7.4/10.4 L/100 km. *2.0L hybrid:* 5.3/5.9L/100 km, *2.4L:* 6.5/9.4 L/100 km. **Assembled in:** Korea and U.S.A.; Hybrid assembled in Korea.

ALERT! Check out the car's directional stability and headlight performance if possible.

Low beams did not project adequately when driving up and down hills and driving around curves. The low beam headlight projection decreased up to 50% and sometimes more than 50% depending on the size of the hill or curve.

Owner-reported safety-related failures: Cruise control resets itself to a higher speed; hybrid engine failure due to water intrusion in rainy weather:

> Engine can easily become hydro-locked in heavy rain and road splash-back from other vehicles due to the design of the direct air intake of the Sonata Hybrid. With its design, it does not have any water baffles to prevent water from entering the air filter and once it enters the air filter box, there are no drain holes for it to drain out. This forces the water through the engine. This could lead to damage of the HEV system and battery pack.

SAFETY

IIHS 2016 SONATA

Small front	Good
Moderate front	Good
Side	Acceptable
Roof strength	Good
Head restraints and seats	Good
Child seat anchors	Marginal
NHTSA Overall 2017	★★★★★

Prior to the 2011 model's redesign, only an average number of owner complaints appeared on NHTSA's safety database each year. Complaints spiked in 2011-2012 with the new model, settling down afterward: Electrical shutdown; passenger side airbag disabled when a normal-sized adult occupies the seat; side curtain airbag deploys inadvertently; left tail light fell out of its mounting inside the trunk due to the plastic mount crumbling; rear windshield exploded after door was closed; trunk opens spontaneously; the horn is weak; and hard starts, no-starts:

> The only reliable solution for starting the car is to depress the brake pedal and depress the Engine Start button for a minimum of 10 seconds. I've placed the key fob in several locations in the car (dashboard, cup holder, smart key holder) with no repeatable success. After a visit to the dealership, they cannot find a problem. However, a search on the Internet shows other owners experiencing the same problem.

Loss of power due to a faulty engine cam advance sensor; sunroof implosions, erratic downshifting with the automatic.

RELIABILITY: Above average for most years. *2006-2010:* Check the front subframe and rear strut area for excessive corrosion. Engine service light may point to a defective sensor. *2011-12:* Hyundai reluctantly extended the warranty on nearly a half-million Sonatas equipped with 2.0L or 2.4L engines to replace engines that may fail prematurely because metal debris may not have been fully removed from the crankshaft area at the factory. The prematurely worn connecting rod bearing will make a cyclical knocking noise, and it also could cause the oil pressure warning light to illuminate. In other cases, engines experience catastrophic valve timing failure. The engine warranty has been extended up to 10 years or 200,000 km. Dealers will inspect the cars and replace defective engines at no cost to owners. Hyundai may ask for oil change receipts going back several years, even though the defect predates delivery of the car to its first owner. *2011-2107:* Free up and lubricate the rear brake calipers once or twice a year to prevent expensive repairs later on.

INTERNAL BULLETINS, SECRET WARRANTIES: 2006-08—Engine hesitation and misfire repair tips. Remedy for seat creaking, squeaking. 2006-09—Correction for a rough idle or display of the MIL warning light on vehicles equipped with the 3.3L engine. The oil temperature sensor may leak. 2006-10—Steering squeaks when turning. 2007-10—Troubleshooting hard starts or a rough idle. 2008—Correction for a steering wheel shimmy/vibration. 2009-10—A cold weather no-start condition may require a new starter solenoid. Water leaking onto the passenger side front floor is likely due to a kinked AC drain hose. 2009-13—If the engine spins, but doesn't crank, replace the starter motor says Hyundai TSB #13-EE-001, issued Feb. 2013. Automatic transmission malfunctions caused by faulty solenoids and other electronic failures. The transmission may shift harshly, drop into a "safe" default mode, or hesitate between shifts. Consider replacing the driveshaft, if the transmission produces a grinding noise, won't move into Drive or Reverse, or the vehicle rolls away with the parking brake applied.

GENESIS SEDAN ★★★★★

RATING: Recommended. Hyundai launched its first luxury car, the Genesis sedan, as a 2009 model. (The coupe is a competitor for sporty cars like the Mustang and is covered separately.) The Genesis sedan is conservative outside and elegant and very nicely finished inside. Hyundai's 3.8L V6 powered most cars, but a 4.6L V8 was also offered. The car fulfilled its luxury mission nicely, but was undermined by offering only rear-wheel drive; by 2009 this had become a deal breaker for a luxury sedan in snowy Canada. Introduced in early 2012, the 2013 model received a mid-cycle remake, with updated styling, a 43 hp boost to the 3.8L V6 thanks to direct fuel injection and a 59 hp increase for the V8, which grew to 5L. A new 8-speed automatic also appeared across the board, and the suspension improved. *2015-2017:* The second-generation Genesis sedan built on the strengths of the original. **Road performance:** *2009-2014:* Powered by the 3.8L V6, the first-generation Genesis sedan is very quick and beautifully smooth. There is absolutely no practical need for the V8, but it is delightful. Smooth, transparent automatic transmission. Ride and handling are well sorted for a luxury sedan; the V6 rides more smoothly. The cabin is roomy, comfortable, beautifully finished, and quiet. Good trunk. Splendid sound systems. *Second-generation:* Once again, the Genesis sedan is an exemplar of conservative elegance inside and out. The cabin design is a delight, with chic two-toning, supple leathers and attractive wood and bright accents. The interior is enhanced by large, supportive seats and abundant space. The 3.8L V6 is near silent unless pressed hard, when it emits a symphonic bark. The V8 is smooth and very strong, but superfluous. The 8-speed automatic transmission impresses with its seamless gear changes. Standard all-wheel drive makes this Genesis a viable four-season car in Canada. A major improvement is the availability of advanced and effective collision avoidance features and vehicle guidance systems. **Strong points:** Both generations of the Genesis sedans are well-appointed with first-class interior fit and finish and smooth operation. Lower prices, both new and used, compared to the European prestige brands, with the promise of superior reliability. **Weak points:** The lack of all-wheel drive makes the first-generation Genesis sedan a three-season car for many Canadians. Some complaints about the first-generation car not being compatible will all cell phones. **Major redesign:** 2009 and 2015. **Best alternatives:** Infiniti Q70 and Lexus ES or GS. If you plan to lease a new vehicle, the BMW 5-series and the Mercedes-Benz E-Class.

Prices and Specs

Prices (2016): *3.8L Premium Sedan:* $43,600, *5.0L Ultimate:* $62,600 **Freight:** $1,995 **Powertrain (AWD):** Engines: 3.8L V6 (311 hp); 5.0L V8 (420 hp); Transmissions: 8-speed automatic. **Dimensions:** Wheelbase: 118.5 in. 3,010 mm,; L: 196.5 in., 4,990 mm.; W: 74.4 in. 1,890 mm.; Weight: 4,561 lb., 4,561 kg. **Fuel economy (2016):** *AWD 3.8L V6:* 9.4/14.4L/100 km. **Assembled in:** South Korea.

Owner-reported safety-related failures: Less than 100 safety-related complaints posted during the past six model years – 300 would have been average. Cruise control malfunctions; and a prolonged hesitation when accelerating after slowing down:

> Multiple times I have accelerated the car to get onto the highway, change lanes quickly, and make right turns on reds, only to have it literally do nothing. At times it takes 2 to 3 seconds before it accelerates and then seems to have a tough time shifting through the gears. At low speeds the car seems to hesitate and shift poorly.
>
> *— safercar.gov*

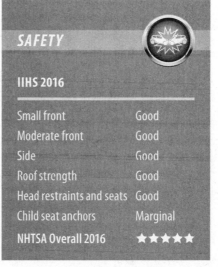

SAFETY

IIHS 2016

Small front	Good
Moderate front	Good
Side	Good
Roof strength	Good
Head restraints and seats	Good
Child seat anchors	Marginal
NHTSA Overall 2016	★★★★★

Random ESC and Bluetooth malfunctions; steering tracks to the right or left; turn signal continues blinking after it is no longer needed; and the GPS and rear camera malfunction intermittently.

RELIABILITY: V6 reliability is above average; insufficient data on the V8. Some transmission failures on early models.

For Internal Bulletins and Secret Warranty information, check the Genesis Coupe review.

GENESIS COUPE ★★★★

RATING: Above Average (2010-16). Based on the rear-wheel drive architecture of the first-generation Genesis sedan, the Coupe was marketed as an alternative to the brawny Chevrolet Camaro, Ford Mustang, and Nissan 370Z. The car debuted as a 2010 model with either a 2L turbo 4-cylinder or a 3.8L V6. There were few changes until the 2013 mid-cycle remake when power on the 2L turbo increased from 210 to 274 hp and a new 8-speed automatic transmission arrived. The 2L 4-cylinder was dropped at the end of 2014. Hyundai introduced the second-generation Genesis sedan but has shown no interest in renewing the coupe. **Road performance:** The V6 powered coupe is a fast, bellowing brute. Prodigious thrust is allied to a thrilling soundtrack. Precise gear change, but the clutch is so heavy that stop and go driving in traffic is tiresome. The shift lever is too close to the driver unless you have long legs. Most drivers will conclude that the automatic is a better choice. Handling is secure, and the ride firm. Precise, nicely-weighted steering and strong brakes. Though it corners predictably and has high limits, the Genesis Coupe is too big and heavy to feel truly agile. The dashboard is stocked with big, clear gauges and straightforward controls. Comfortable front seats grip occupants without pinching them. Access to the rear seat is awkward but seat comfort and legroom are adequate for occasional use. **Strong points:** Strong performance, seating for four in a pinch. Well-priced. **Weak points:** Heavy clutch and oddly placed gear change. The low seating position and high body sides inhibit outward vision. Rear-wheel-drive makes the coupe a three-season proposition for some buyers. **Major redesign:** 2010. **Best alternatives:** The Chevrolet Camaro, Dodge Challenger, and Ford Mustang; Nissan 370Z (if you don't need a back seat).

Prices and Specs

Prices (2016): *R-Spec man.:* $29,749, *GT auto.:* $39,249 **Freight:** $1,795 **Powertrain (Rear-wheel drive):** Engines: 3.8L V6. (348 hp); Transmissions: 6-speed man., 8-speed manumatic. **Dimensions:** Passengers: 2/2; Wheelbase: 111 in., 2,820 mm.; L: 182.3 in., 4,630 mm.; W: 73.4 in. 1,865 mm.; Weight: 3,629 lb., 1,646 kg. **Fuel economy (2016):** *Auto.:* 9.5/14.4L/100 km. **Assembled in:** South Korea.

SAFETY: Genesis Coupe was not rated.

RELIABILITY: Manual transmission knocking while the clutch is disengaged and the transmission is in Neutral; inaccurate fuel gauge (confirmed by Hyundai service bulletin), rattling caused by broken frame spotwelds.

INTERNAL BULLETINS, SECRET WARRANTIES: 2001-12—Remedy for engine ticking at idle. A faulty transmission solenoid may activate the Check Engine alert and send the transaxle into "Fail-Safe" limp mode. Troubleshooting tips for a harsh, delayed automatic transmission shift. Introduction of a new touch screen recalibration. *Coupe:* Free sunroof switch replacement campaign. *Sedan:* Troubleshooting speed sensor malfunctions (replace the valve body assembly). **2009-12**—An inoperable or noisy A/C may require an A/C pulley disc limiter (Equus included). **2010**—No start in Park or Neutral. **2012**—Shift lever can't be moved out of Park. **2012-14**—Erratic or unresponsive fuel gauge. **2013**—Service Campaign #938 provides for the free replacement of the fuel feed tube assembly if the Check Engine light comes on; there's a hesitation upon acceleration; or the transmission shifts erratically. **2013-14**—4-cylinder coupe: Hyundai TSB #12-EM-007, issued Nov. 2012, says an engine rattle or buzzing sound "results from the required tolerances in the waste gate pivot point and the waste gate valve. This normal operating characteristic will not affect the performance or durability of the vehicle." Despite what Hyundai says, other turbo-equipped cars don't produce this noise. **2015**—Hyundai will replace free of charge the lower cowl to prevent water intrusion into the cabin (Service Campaign TX1, TSB #15-01-016). Power window malfunctions are addressed in TSB #15-BE-007.

TUCSON

2005-2010 ★★★
2011-2017 ★★★★

RATING: Average (2005-10); Above Average (2011-17); Unrated with 1.6L Turbo (2016-2017). *2016-2017:* The all-new third-generation Tucson is marginally larger than its predecessor and looks better. Impressively finished cabin for an entry-level SUV. Comfortable seats, good legroom front and rear, and plentiful cargo space. The 2L 164 hp engine and the optional 175 hp 1.6L turbo 4-cylinder provide similar outputs on paper, but the turbo has more torque so it feels stronger. **Road performance:** Hooked up to the conventional 6-speed automatic transmission, the base 2L 4-cylinder delivers good performance and quiet cruising. The 1.6 turbo and 7-speed dual clutch automatic powerteam is eager, and feels more lively. Steering, ride, and handling are quite nicely sorted, and much superior to previous models. Good cargo capacity. *2005-2009:* Smooth V6 engine is not particularly frugal, but unique in this segment. *2010-2015:* This generation was reliable and roomy for its size but performance was unenthusiastic. Side curtain air bags became standard as of 2010. Direct fuel injection arrived in 2014, with a small improvement in fuel economy. **Strong points:** *2016-2017:* The Tucson is elegant outside and, roomy, versatile, and nice to drive. *2005-2015:* Well-priced used models are the best entry-level solution for many buyers. **Weak points:** *2016-2017:* Gear changes with the new 7-speed automatic are not nearly as smooth as a conventional hydraulic transmission. *2011-15:* Limited visibility due to small windows. Odd suspension that neither rides nicely nor handles well. Rear seat not ideally shaped. Fairly noisy. **Major redesign:** 2005, 2010 and 2016. **Best alternatives:** The similar Kia Sportage. Japanese models sell for more. A used Escape pre-2012 sells for similar money but is a riskier purchase, as are the Jeep Compass and Patriot.

Prices and Specs

Prices (2016): *2.0L GL FWD:* $24,799, *1.6 turbo Ultimate:* $38,599 **Freight:** $1,795 **Powertrain (FWD/AWD):** Engines: 2.0L 4-cyl. (165 hp), 2.4L 4-cyl. (176 hp); Transmissions: 6-speed automatic, 7-speed dual clutch automatic. **Dimensions (2016):** Passengers: 2/3; Wheelbase: 105.1 in., 2,670 mm.; L: 176.2, 4,475 mm.; W: 72.3 in., 1,850 mm.; Weight: 3,629 lb., 1,634 kg. **Fuel economy (2016):** *2L AWD Auto:* 9/11 L/100 km. **Assembled in:** South Korea.

Owner-reported safety-related failures: Firewall insulation caught fire; rear window shattered spontaneously; key can be taken out of the ignition and transmission placed in Park and the Tucson rolled downhill; loss of brakes for a couple of seconds after passing over speed bumps or small potholes; when accelerating to merge with traffic, the vehicle hesitates and then decelerates while the gas pedal is fully depressed; power steering seized (likely a loss of power assist); vehicle sways left and right while cruising; rear-tire lock-up; and speed sensor wires are vulnerable to road debris:

SAFETY

IIHS 2016

Small front	Good
Moderate front	Good
Side	Good
Roof strength	Good
Head restraints and seats	Good
Child seat anchors	Acceptable
NHTSA Overall 2017	★★★★★

Wires are located behind the tires and are fully exposed to road debris. They can be easily severed, thereby affecting ABS and traction control. The wire sticks out 3 inches in open air of the undercarriage and are located close enough to the tires that if they kick up any debris, it is in the direct path of the wire.

RELIABILITY: *2005-2009:* Light knocking when starting from cold is fairly common with the 4-cylinder engine. Before undertaking major exploratory work, check or replace the PCV valve if oil consumption is excessive. *2005 4-cylinder:* Check for a loose crankshaft pulley; tighten bolt if loose. *V6:* Check for coolant leaks at the hose connections. *2010-2015:* Check for oil leaks at the valve cover and timing cover, leaking or worn suspension struts, broken sway bar links, front differential leaks, noisy wheel bearings. *2016-2017:* Durability of the optional turbo engine and 7-speed dual-clutch transmission is unknown. Owners report the transmission can go into Neutral if it overheats in traffic forcing you to sideline the car until it cools down a bit. Hyundai has issued a TSB.

> Sudden downshifting with loud clunk and lurching of vehicle at 35 mph [55 km/h]. Felt as if I had been hit from behind by another vehicle. Instinctively hit the brakes and pulled over to check for exterior damage, and found none. Continued down the road and experienced unusual increases in rpms. When I arrived at my destination, the vehicle would not go in Reverse. Owned vehicle only 11 days. Incident occurred at 500 miles [800 km].

INTERNAL BULLETINS, SECRET WARRANTIES: 2005-09—No movement in Drive or Reverse. Fluid may leak from the area around the automatic transmission torque converter or between the transaxle and the transfer case. Correcting harsh gear engagement. Tips on silencing a rattling sunroof. 2008-12—Remedy for engine ticking at idle. 2010—Troubleshooting harsh, delayed shifts by the automatic transmission. Incorrect operation of the transmission solenoids will cause the transmission to perform erratically and the Check Engine warning to light up. 2010-15—An improperly adjusted or improperly operating inhibitor switch (range switch) may result in one or more of the following conditions: Malfunction indicator light (MIL) illuminated, or intermittent no engine crank/no engine start in Park or Neutral. Troubleshooting tips for shift lever concerns. Some Hyundai vehicles may experience brake noise/vibration due to improperly adjusted parking brakes.

SANTA FE/SANTA FE SPORT

WITH 3.3L V6

2006-2008	★ ★ ★
2009	★
2009-2012	★ ★
2013-2017	★ ★ ★ ★

SANTA FE XL

2014-2017	★ ★ ★ ★

RATING: *Santa Fe and Santa Fe Sport:* Average (2006-2008); Not Recommended (2009 with 3.3L V6); Below Average (2009-2012); Above Average (2013-2017); *Santa Fe XL:* Above Average (2014-2017). New for 2017: A mid-cycle remake includes revised styling inside and out. The 2L turbo 4-cylinder loses 25 hp after it was retuned for better mid-range acceleration and increased economy. Standard rearview camera and newly available optional active safety features. **Road performance:** *2013-17 Santa Fe Sport:* The base 2.4L 4- and 6-speed automatic combo delivers pleasing performance. The 2L turbocharged 4-cylinder engine and a 6-speed automatic transmission combine to deliver smooth, flexible power and good urge while using little more fuel than the base 2.4L 4-cylinder. The ride is absorbent but can wallow over big bumps and the Santa Fe leans in corners taken at speed. Numb steering. The upscale cabin could be mistaken for a Lexus if there were no logos inside. Clear gauges and simple, logical controls. Large, enveloping front seats; outboard rear seat occupants are pampered with a supportive, reclining seat and generous legroom. Good cargo space. *2014:* Introduction of the Santa Fe XL with available three-row seating and smooth standard V6 power. **Strong points:** A competitively priced SUV that provides an extra dose of style and luxury over the competition selling in its price bracket. Good interior space. **Weak points:** Poorly calibrated suspension leads to bouncing over large bumps and more lean than necessary in curves. Outward visibility could be better. **Major redesign:** 2007 and 2013. **Best alternatives:** *Santa Fe and Sport:* Honda CR-V, Mazda CX-5, or the Toyota RAV4. More luxurious versions of the 2L turbo Santa Fe Sport could actually substitute for a used Acura RDX Turbo. *Santa Fe XL:* Toyota Highlander.

Prices and Specs

Prices (Firm): *2.4 Sport FWD:* $28,599, *2L Turbo Ultimate:* $44,599 **Freight:** $1,895 **Powertrain (FWD/AWD):** Engines: 2.4L 4-cyl. (185 hp), 2.0L 4-cyl. turbo. (240 hp). **Dimensions:** Passengers: 2/3; Wheelbase: 106.3 in., 2,700 mm.; L: 185 in., 4,700 mm.; W: 74.4 in., 1,880 mm.; Weight: 4,107 lb., 1,863 kg. **Fuel economy:** *2.4L AWD.:* 9.3/12.5 L/100 km. **Assembled in:** U.S.A.

ALERT! Take a night test drive; low-beam headlight illumination may be insufficient.

Owner-reported safety-related failures: When accelerating, vehicle pulls sharply to the side; and often stalls out:

> Plaintiffs in a California class-action claim 2010-2012 Santa Fe SUVs have a stalling defect and Hyundai waited years to admit the problem. The lawsuit quotes a dealer service bulletin that admits the SUVs can stall because the alternator can't take the extra load and drops the engine rpms. Plaintiffs claim the vehicles shut off completely without warning, particularly when driven at low speeds, turning or coming to a stop. Some owners have also reported experiencing unexplained loss of power resulting in deceleration or stalling while driving at highway speeds. The case was filed August 8, 2014, in the U.S. District Court for the Northern District of California (see *Reniger v. Hyundai Motor America* or *HyundaiSantaFeProblem.com*).

SAFETY

IIHS 2016 SANTA FE SPORT

Small front	Good
Moderate front	Good
Side	Good
Roof strength	Good
Head restraints and seats	Good
Child seat anchors	Acceptable
NHTSA Overall 2017	★★★★★

Raw gas smell both inside and outside the vehicle; Santa Fe shuts down when underway; a loud knock and transmission jerk occurs whenever the vehicle is first started; when shifting, the jerkiness of the transmission feels like someone is hitting the rear end; and loss of brakes, as the pedal descended to the floor.

RELIABILITY: Acceptable reliability to 2008. Reliability nose-dived for the 2009-2012 model years; common problems include fuel pump failures, alternator failures on the V6 caused by oil leaking into it from a defective engine valve cover gasket (a service fix from Hyundai provides an alternator shield, but not necessarily free replacement of the leaky gasket!). The 3.3L V6 can knock and burn oil excessively due to a design defect; Hyundai did not extend the warranty. Starter failures also recorded with this engine. *2007:* A defective windshield seal can permit water infiltration and eventually a stress crack of the windshield glass. *2010-2011:* Many failures of the 6-speed automatic transmission; replaced transmissions are more durable. *2010-2012 with 3.5L V6:* Excessive oil consumption, rough running. *2013-*

2017: Reliability improved significantly. *All years:* Have the rear brake caliper guide pins de-seized and lubricated annually or more often to postpone expensive brake repairs. Check for blown sway bar bushings and broken sway bar links. Weak corrosion resistance for all years to 2012. *2005-2006:* Check the floor, door bottoms, rocker panels, rear wheel housings and rear suspension cradle as well as the front subframe (for structural corrosion). The APA recommends aftermarket rustproofing (Barry's Rustproofing in Montreal (Tel: 514-344-1168) for a lifetime application, or Krown Rust Control (*www.krown.com* or 1-800-267-5744) for an annual application) for all model years up to 2012 inclusive.

INTERNAL BULLETINS, SECRET WARRANTIES: 2008-12—Tips on reducing excessive driveshaft noise (creaking or popping). 2010—This bulletin provides an extended warranty to cover the replacement of the intermediate shaft on some 2010 Santa Fe 2.4L 2WD vehicles with automatic transmissions (CAMPAIGN 102). 2010-15—An improperly adjusted or improperly operating inhibitor switch (range switch) may result in one or more of the following conditions: Malfunction indicator light (MIL) illuminated, or intermittent no engine crank/no engine start in Park or Neutral. Troubleshooting tips for shift lever concerns. Some Hyundai vehicles may experience brake noise/vibration due to improperly adjusted parking brakes. 2013—Free front and rear door latch replacement under CAMPAIGN TS0. 2013-14—Cold start misfires with a 2.0L turbo engine can be corrected through an ECM upgrade. 2013-15—Some all-wheel drive vehicles may experience a buzzing or scraping noise from the transmission area when accelerating at slow speeds. The crank position sensor wheel plate may need to be replaced under warranty. 2015—19-inch Hankook tires may produce road noise and vibration (TSB #March 2015). These tires continually show up in owner complaint reports.

INFINITI

Toyota launched its Lexus division with the formidably capable LS400 that went head-to-head with the large Mercedes sedans on quality at a lower price, and with better service and reliability. Nissan took a different road with the Infiniti brand. Its big Q45 sedan stressed performance over opulence, and offered buyers some cutting-edge features at what were initially very reasonable prices. Infiniti's first ads did not focus on the cars, but showed images of rocks, trees, and other natural elements. The campaign did little to inform the public about the new brand and Infiniti's "zen" advertising contributed to the brand stumbling out of the gate, which it continues to do 25 years later.

Like Acura, Infiniti is mired in a Junior Prestige netherworld. Over the years, Infiniti introduced some interesting vehicles, like the Jaguar-esque J30, but none seemed to find a solid place in the Canadian market. Infiniti dealers, who needed more sales, began offering upmarket versions of Nissan vehicles like Pathfinder-based QX4 sport-utility-vehicle and the Maxima-based I30 and I35. Infiniti continued to wander aimlessly until it introduced the 2003 G35 sedan and coupe. Based on the Japanese Nissan Skyline and aimed squarely at the popular BMW 3-series, the G35 brought some respectability back to the franchise.

After the 2009 global recession, Infiniti's lineup went into retail freefall and Nissan was ready to shut it down after 24 years on the market. Nissan/Renault CEO Carlos Ghosn was adamant, "We don't need Infiniti, we just don't need that brand." But Infiniti got a reprieve and is now fighting to put performance and style into its vehicles. And it's working, almost. Infiniti currently sells a variety of vehicles in Canada but the only two models selling in any volume are the Q50 sedan and the QX60, a spinoff of the Nissan Pathfinder SUV. High-tech components in recent Infiniti models drive up servicing costs by making dealer servicing mandatory and electronic/mechanical complexity practically guarantees higher failure rates.

One bright spot, the company recently focused on improving quality control and performance of its 2015-2017 models. Infiniti was so successful, that the brand leaped from 23rd place in 2014 to 13th place in the 2016 J.D. Power Initial Quality Study ranking. The company raised its quality score principally by correcting software snags on the Q50 sedan's InTouch telematics system; enhancing shifting with the QX60 SUV; and giving the Q70 sedan a quieter interior and smoother steering.

G25/G35/G37 ★★★★

2013 Infiniti G37

RATING: Above Average. Marking Infiniti's rebirth, the 2003 G35 was based on Nissan's FM (front-midship) platform that underpinned the Japanese-market Skyline as well as the Nissan 350Z. **Road performance:** The first-generation G35 sedan featured a roomy cabin, with a strong V6 engine and rear-wheel drive handling at a reasonable price. The coupe was essentially a slightly larger and better finished Nissan 350Z. The sedan was distinctively styled; the coupe was sublime. All-wheel drive, marketed as the G35x, was introduced for the 2004 model year. The second-generation G37 sedan was introduced for 2007, while the second-generation coupe followed a year later. The new car was built on a stiffer platform, and Infiniti paid closer attention to panel fit and paint finish, as well as crafting the cabin with nicer materials. Styling was only a slight evolution from the previous generation. The sedan was renamed G37 for the 2009 model year due to its larger 3.7L V6. That same year, the 5-speed automatic transmission was replaced by a new 7-speed unit. A rare retractable hardtop convertible debuted for 2009. *2011-2012 G25:* This entry-level G-series sedan is fitted with a smaller 218 hp 2.5L version of the V6 that has less power and offers a small fuel savings. Interior finish is more basic and fewer options were available; it was perceived as cheapening the range and discontinued after two years on the market. **Road Performance:** The G-series sedans feature a very responsive engine, firm ride, steady handling, and nicely-weighted steering, combined with some "surprise and delight" cabin features. Depending on your tastes, the rumbling exhaust may be music to your ears, or a bit too loud. Cabin space is acceptable for four adults. *G37:* The new power train combines impressive performance and relaxed cruising. The more frequent gear changes are noticeable. The G37 was renamed Q50 when the model was redesigned in 2014. **Strong points:** An enjoyable luxury/sports car experience. Well-priced compared to the competing BMW 3-series and Mercedes models. **Weak points:** The trunk is small and its small lid can make loading large bags a chore.

With the coupe and convertible, trying to put anyone in the back seat is an interesting exercise. Noisy exhaust. Harder ride and suspension wear on models with oversized rims and low-profile tires. The convertible has some body shake. **Major redesign:** 2003 introduction, 2007 sedan, 2008 coupe, 2009 convertible, 2014 Q50 introduction. **Best alternatives:** The key competitor is the BMW 3-series. Other alternatives are the Lexus IS series, Mercedes-Benz C-Class and perhaps even the Cadillac ATS and CTS. A G35/G37 will likely cost less in repairs than the German cars and the two Cadillacs.

Specs for 2013 (last year of production)

Powertrain (Rear-drive/AWD): Engines: 3.7L V6 sedan (328 hp); coupe (330 hp); convertible (325 hp); Transmissions: 6-speed man., 7-speed auto. **Dimensions (G37 sedan):** Passengers: 2/3; Wheelbase: 112.2 in., 2,580 mm.; L: 187, 4,750 mm.; W: 69.8 in., 1,773 mm.; Weight: 3,818 lb., 1732 kg. **Fuel economy:** G37x (AWD) 3.7L 7-speed auto.: 9.4/13.3 L/100 km. **Assembled in:** Japan.

ALERT! Why can't Nissan … er … Infiniti … make powertrains that don't jerk you around, stall, or lag and lurch?

Owner-reported safety-related failures: NHTSA files show the G35 elicits few owner safety-related complaints. Driver's airbag failed to deploy; passenger-side airbag is disabled for no reason; stalling; clutch sticks until it warms up; warped brake rotors and prematurely-worn brake pads; traction control acts up in rainy weather; doors won't lock or unlock due to faulty door actuators; and defective tire pressure sensors. 2011 G37 models also generated only a handful of complaints. When the convertible top automatically folds into the trunk it doesn't stop if there is an object in the way, causing damage to the top; seat belt failed to lock in an emergency stop; long hesitation before accelerating:

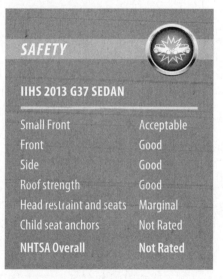

SAFETY	
IIHS 2013 G37 SEDAN	
Small Front	Acceptable
Front	Good
Side	Good
Roof strength	Good
Head restraint and seats	Marginal
Child seat anchors	Not Rated
NHTSA Overall	**Not Rated**

> As I was waiting to cross a major highway junction, I almost had a collision after crossing the highway due to what I suspect was a faulty transmission with hesitation in shifting. There was an SUV waiting to turn and while I had the right of way, they pulled off and as I had my chance to cross the 2-lane highway, they did too. I punched the gas and in the middle of the road, the engine took a few seconds to get into gear so I literally was in the road of oncoming traffic that was driving at speeds in excess of 55 mph. It happened within 5 seconds but after I crossed avoiding a front and side collision, I pulled off the road because I was shaking.

Side mirrors become distorted; and gas station automatic fuelling nozzles shut off after a few seconds. *2012 G37 owner complaints:* Head restraints cause driver to sit in a chin-to-chest position; hip pain caused by bolstering of the driver's seat; clutch pedal sticks; engine surges when braking (confirmed by TSB #ITBO7-048), or car is slow to brake. *G25:* Only a handful of owner complaints posted on the NHTSA (*safercar.gov*) website.

RELIABILITY: Above average reliability until the fifth year, declining to average as the cars age; repairs cost less than its closest European competitor, the BMW 3-series. The most frequent complaint concerns expensive brake service resulting from warped brake rotors and prematurely-worn rear pads; have the brake calipers and parking brake assembly freed up and greased annually to postpone expensive brake repairs. The optional Brembo brake system is expensive to renew; shop the aftermarket to price replacement parts before you approve a major brake job. The V6 is shared with several Nissan/Infiniti models, and uses four expensive oxygen sensors; a lit engine service light after the fifth year may indicate that one or more sensors is defective. Some electrical and electronic failures, defective tire pressure sensors. Check for a noisy timing chain upon starting the 3.5L V6; this engine is oil sensitive so don't neglect changes. *G35:* unreliable manual transmission on the 2007 model. *G37:* Luxurious and sexy to drivers; tasty and succulent to rodents:

> The Infiniti G37 has electrical wiring insulation made of soy-based polymer. Soy-based polymer is apparently biodegradable. The problem is that it is also attractive to rodents, who eat the wiring, creating electrical safety hazards. It also creates an economic stress on consumers and insurers who have to pay for repairs done to these automobiles, which Infiniti claims are not covered under any existing warranty.

INTERNAL BULLETINS, SECRET WARRANTIES: All models—Troubleshooting multiple transmission problems. Tips on reducing excessive driveshaft noise (creaking or popping). Steering pull/drift. Steering wheel is off-centre. Automatic transmission shifter boot may come loose. Drivebelt noise. Navigation screen goes blank (2010-12 models). Paint chipping off the edge of the trunk lid (2007-12 models). Steering noise on left turns (2012s). The warranty is extended under Campaign PO308 in relation to the radio seek function. *G25:* Shift issues (2011 models) Campaign PO385 relative to reprogramming the G25's engine control module (ECM). *G37:* Shift responsiveness issues (2009-12 models). Low battery, or no-start (2008-10). Bluetooth voice recognition. Convertible top water leak at windshield header. AC blows warm air at idle. Door accent garnish replacements.

2016 Infinity Q50

RATING: Average. The Q50 replaced the G37 sedan. The 3.7L V6 from the earlier car was retained; a new high-performance hybrid put out a combined 360 hp from its gasoline V6 and electric motor. The Q50 looks contemporary but the styling is not a standout. In 2016, a new Mercedes-Benz 2L turbo 4-cylinder as well as a new 3L turbo V6 in two states of tune replaced the previous V6. For 2017, a new-generation coupe built on the same platform and called the Q60 coupe has been introduced. **Road performance:** Driven with the 3.7L V6, the Q50 is quick, quiet, and solid with a well-honed ride-handling balance. Steering feel is decent considering it is a new "drive by wire" system but the driving experience is less involving than the G37. The cabin is tasteful and nicely assembled, with competitive space for a car in this segment. Small trunk. **Strong points:** Strong V6 power. Decent ride-handling compromise. **Weak points:** Touch screen controls are inconvenient. Small trunk. The hybrid power train, Mercedes-Benz-supplied 2L turbo 4-cylinder, and new turbo V6 are all unproven. **Major redesign:** 2014 introduced. **Best alternatives:** Acura TLX, Lexus IS or ES, BMW 3-Series, or Mercedes C-class.

Prices and Specs

Prices (2016 Q50): *2L Turbo 4:* $39,900, *3.5L-V6 Hybrid:* $56,400 **Frieght:** $1,995 **Powertrain (AWD):** Engine: 2L turbo 4 (208 hp), 3L V6 turbo (300 hp, 400 hp. Sport), 3.5L V6 hybrid (360 hp combined), 3.7L V6 (328 hp); Transmission: 7-speed automatic. **Dimensions:** Passengers: 2/3; Wheelbase: 112.2 in., 2,850 mm.; L: 188.3, 4,783 mm.; W: 71.8 in., 1,824 mm.; Weight: 3,937 lb., 1,786 kg. **Fuel economy (2016):** *3 L turbo V6 7-speed auto.:* 8.5/12.8 L/100 km. **Built in:** Japan.

RELIABILITY: The drive-by-wire steering on the first-year 2014 model is troublesome and the car is best purchased with a full coverage warranty. *All years:* Predicted trouble spots are the steering rack and brakes. *2016-2017:* It's probably best to pass on the unproven hybrid and Mercedes-supplied 2L turbo 4-cylinder engine. The 3.7L V6 is the best long-term bet. Purchase of an extended warranty from Nissan is recommended. APA members may be eligible for a small discount.

EX35/EX37	*2008-2013*	★★★★
QX50	*2014-2017*	★★★★

2012 Infiniti EX35

RATING: Above Average. The EX/QX is essentially a tall wagon based on the second-generation Infiniti G sedan. Although the EX is taller than the sedan, the extra height does not translate into more cabin space. The EX has a versatile hatchback body, but cargo space is disappointing. For 2013, the EX35 became the EX37 when its engine grew from 3.5L to 3.7L. Its name changed to QX50 for 2014 to reflect Infiniti's new naming regime. The biggest change arrived for 2016, when a 4.5 inch (113 mm.) wheelbase stretch finally delivered the rear legroom expected of a luxury SUV in this class. **Road performance:** Abundant power and a responsive automatic transmission combine to deliver vivid acceleration. Nicely-weighted, precise steering and a firm but resilient ride; the driving dynamics are pleasing overall. Exhaust rumble is noticeable. Comfortable seats, though rear passengers may feel snug on pre-2016 models. Occupants feel pampered inside. **Strong points:** Strong V6 power. Good ride-handling compromise. Comfortable front seats in an elegant cabin. **Weak points:** Poor visibility to the rear. Limited rear legroom makes the pre-2016 EX/QX a tighter fit for four adults. Small cargo area. **Major redesign:** 2008 introduced, 2013 updated powertrain, 2016 stretched wheelbase. **Best alternatives:** A flamboyant, luxury quasi-SUV with the cabin space of a compact hatchback, the EX/QX is in a league of its own; the Nissan Murano and perhaps the BMW X3 or X5 are possible cross-shops.

Prices and Specs

Prices (2016 QX50): *AWD (base):* $37,900, *Premium navigation with technology:* $47,800 **Frieght:** $1,995 **Powertrain (AWD):** Engine: 3.7L V6 (325 hp); Transmission: 7-speed automatic. **Dimensions:** Passengers: 2/3; Wheelbase: 112.2 in., 2,850 mm.; L:182.3, 4,631 mm.; W: 71 in., 1,803 mm.; Weight: 3,955 lb., 1,794 kg. **Fuel economy (2015):** *3.7L 7-speed auto.:* 9.7/13.7 L/100 km. **Built in:** Japan.

Owner-reported safety-related failures: Almost no safety-related complaints posted at NHTSA relative to the 2008-13 EX. Right-rear visibility is compromised by right-rear head restraint and side pillar and some drivers find the accelerator and brake pedals are too close together. Be wary of the Distance Control Assist or DCA. It creates a distracting "safety zone" around the vehicle and may apply the brakes or buzz an alert that could make matters worse. One owner did mention the following brake/transmission failure to NHTSA:

SAFETY

IIHS 2013 EX37

Small Front	Not Rated
Front	Good
Side	Good
Roof strength	Good
Head restraint and seats	Good
Child seat anchors	Not Rated
NHTSA Overall	**Not Rated**

2012 Infiniti EX35 ... The consumer stated she parked the vehicle in the driveway on a moderate slope covered with light snow. The consumer went back outside and stood by the vehicle, when all of a sudden it popped out of Park and started rolling down the hill. The consumer managed to catch up with the vehicle, opened the door and put her foot on the parking brake, and the vehicle stopped.

RELIABILITY: Canadian reliability data is incomplete due to the limited number sold. Expect brake wear and oxygen sensor issues, similar to the G35/G37 sedans. Defective tire pressure sensors were likely replaced at least once on early models; they may be ready for a second replacement. The oversized tires are expensive and must be rotated to wear evenly.

INTERNAL BULLETINS, SECRET WARRANTIES: 2009-10—Some vehicles may experience water entry into a wiring harness that could cause an engine no-start condition or a warning light to illuminate when no warning issue exists. Infiniti will repair any damage and install a cover to protect the harness from water entry. This service will be performed at no charge for parts and labour. 2010-13—Various navigation malfunctions. 2011-12—Steering pull/drift, or steering wheel is off centre. Bluetooth voice recognition issues. Door accent garnish replacements.

JX35/QX60   *2013-2017* ★ ★ ★

2012 Infiniti EX35

RATING: Average. The JX35 is Infiniti's spin on the Nissan Pathfinder model that debuted for 2013. Conforming to Infiniti's new naming system, the JX35 became the QX60 for 2014. The QX was treated to a mid-cycle refresh for 2016, including gently altered exterior styling, cabin updates and a fiendishly complex hybrid version powered by a 2.5L supercharged 4-cylinder combined with an electric motor. The JX/QX is flamboyant, fully embracing Infiniti's current rounded, arc-laden styling. **Road performance:** Hooked up to a CVT, the JX/QX's 3.5L V6 delivers acceleration that is beginning to trail the competition but it is a relaxed cruiser. Steering is numb but nicely geared. Unlike some luxury SUVs that veer too far into the sporty end of the performance spectrum, the JX/QX is a steady handler that doesn't beat passengers up on patchy tarmac. Overall refinement is not up to the standards expected of a vehicle with such a high price tag. The cabin features an elegant gauge package and acceptably intuitive minor controls. The front seats are very supportive but the middle row seat is too close to the floor for adults to be comfortable and legroom is unimpressive. Good cargo capacity. **Strong points:** Flexible V6. Good ride-handling compromise. **Weak points:** Styling not to all tastes. The cabin seems upscale at first look, but materials aren't class leading. Unsupportive second row seat that also lacks legroom. Uncertain long-term durability, especially the hybrid. **Major redesign:** 2013 introduction. **Best alternatives:** The Acura MDX is the only Japanese-branded alternative to the JX/QX but if you don't need a junior prestige key fob, you could look at the related Nissan Pathfinder, Honda Pilot, Hyundai Santa Fe XL, or the Toyota Highlander. GM's Acadia, Enclave, and Traverse triplets are reasonable alternatives but they do not age well.

Prices and Specs

Prices (2017 QX60): *AWD (base):* $47,400, *Hybrid Premium:* $66,900 **Freight:** $1,995 **Powertrain (FWD/AWD):** 2.5L 4 supercharged hybrid (2016: 250 hp combined), 3.5L V6 (265 hp); Transmission: CVT. **Dimensions:** Passengers: 2/3/2; Wheelbase: 114.2 in., 2,901 mm.; L: 196.4, 4,989 mm.; W: 77.2 in., 1,961 mm.; Weight: 4,516 lb., 2,048 kg. **Fuel economy (2016):** *3.5 V6 CVT AWD.:* 8.9/12.2 L/100 km. **Built in:** U.S.A.

RELIABILITY: Based on the service history of the related Nissan Pathfinder, reliability should be average to below average. The hybrid, with a supercharged 2.5L 4-cylinder teamed with an electric motor is too complex to consider, unless you're a lease customer.

SAFETY

IIHS 2016 QX60

Small Front	Good
Front	Good
Side	Good
Roof strength	Good
Head restraint and seats	Good
Child seat anchors	Marginal
NHTSA Overall 2017	★★★★★

Kia

What an amazing ten-year turnaround by Kia from a quality, performance, and reliability perspective.

We can't talk about Kia's tremendous gains without first mentioning the company's false horsepower ratings and gas mileage claims. Kia, along with its parent company Hyundai, made bogus claims to promote their vehicles for many years. In 2014, a class-action lawsuit was settled in Ontario against Hyundai and Kia Canada after the automakers were found to have overstated their vehicles' fuel mileage.

Kia and Hyundai are owned by the same Korean parent company and share vehicle platforms and technology. Under the direction of Peter Schreyer, a former designer at Audi, Kia's spins on Hyundai-supplied technology have often proven to be even more stylish, and sometimes a bit nicer to drive too. Like Hyundai, Kia's reliability has risen from bottom-of-the-barrel in the mid-2000s to upper tier today. The Kia warranty for major components is 5 years/100,000 km as opposed to the more common 3 years/60,000 km. However, Kia's after-sales support is weaker than Hyundai's, and Kia Canada usually runs and hides when consumers or the media pursue legitimate complaints. Dishonest dealers in the Kia network appear to have a free rein to prey on customers, and Kia will almost always wait for Hyundai to take the lead on extending a warranty or issuing a safety recall. Kia advertising also leaves something to be desired; the low prices and payments in Kia's small car ads frequently apply to a base car with a manual transmission and no air conditioning that dealerships may not have in inventory.

RIO/RIO5

2006-2011 ★★★★
2012-2017 ★★★★★

good buy

2016 Kia Rio

RATING: Above Average (2006-2011); Recommended (2012-2017). The 2017 Rio will have a short run, as the next-generation model goes on sale in spring 2017 as a 2018 model. **Road performance:** *2012-2017:* The Rio's 1.6L 4-cylinder delivers an appealing blend of acceleration and fuel economy, with both the 6-speed manual and 6-speed automatic transmissions. Tall gearing allows for serene cruising with both transmissions; the manual allies a docile clutch with a pleasant gearchange. Nicely-weighted, precise steering and a well-sorted ride and handling for such a small, inexpensive car. Though it uses the same mechanical components as the related Hyundai Accent, the Rio handles a bit more precisely. The dashboard and interior are black (the Accent is grey) and stocked with crisply marked gauges and excellent HVAC and radio controls. The front seats are reasonably comfortable; rear seat legroom is adequate for the size of car but not abundant. Large trunk in the sedan; adequate in the hatchback. **Strong points:** Well equipped for an entry-level small car; the cabin is impressive at this price point as are available features on top-end models such as navigation and a heated steering wheel. Good interior space for the footprint of the car. Nice to drive and reasonably quiet for the class. Affordable. The 2011-2016-generation of the Accent is available at very low prices; it's a good alternative to GM Daewoo junk like the Chevrolet Aveo, Pontiac Wave and Suzuki Swift that compete in its price range. **Weak points:** Kia Canada's head office organisation is less mature than that of Hyundai, so customer service is not as good. *2012-2017:* The rear seatback is a bit too upright. Limited rear visibility with the hatchback; the sedan is better. *2006-2011:* Mediocre suspension. **Major redesign:** 2006, and 2012. **Best alternatives:** The Chevrolet Sonic, Hyundai Accent, Mazda2, or Toyota Yaris.

Prices and Specs

Prices (2016): *Rio LX sedan manual:* $14,095, *Rio5, SX UVO Navigation Auto:* $21,895 **Freight:** $1,485 **Powertrain (FWD):** Engine: 1.6L 4-cyl. (137 hp); Transmissions: 6-speed man., 6-speed auto. **Dimensions:** *Rio5:* Passengers: 2/3; Wheelbase: 101.2 in., 2,570 mm.; L: 159.4 in., 4,050 mm.; W: 67.7 in., 1,720 mm.; Weight: 2,844 lb., 1.298 kg. **Fuel economy:** *Auto.:* 6.3/8.7 L/100 km. **Assembled in:** South Korea.

ALERT! Beginning in 2012, several models come with no spare tire – just an inflator and a can of sealant, which may have been removed or used up by the previous owner; check with a wrecker before you sign, as the dealer price for a compact spare, jack, and the related tools is exorbitant.

Owner-reported safety-related failures: Airbags failed to deploy in a collision. Fuel hose vent line may leak fuel into the back seat area; tie rod and ball joints broke away from the chassis while vehicle was turning; and the rear window shattered when the driver's door was closed.

RELIABILITY: *2006-2011:* Check for suspension wear including worn or leaking shock absorbers, broken sway bar links, and worn ball joints. Fluid leaks are common at the power steering hoses and transmission cooler lines. A lit Check Engine light likely indicates a defective engine or transmission sensor. *2012-2014:* Unstable idle or misfire may point to a need for cleaning of the direct fuel injection system that tends to be more finicky than conventional port injection. Broken sway bar links are covered up to 5 years/100,000 km under the standard warranty. A stain in the door paint underneath the rearview mirrors can be cleaned using a special product, if damage is not too advanced. It may be possible to apply corrosion protection. *2012-2017:* Brittle paint chips easily and Kia Canada doesn't like to pay for repairs; problem areas include the front bumper, hood, rearview mirrors, lower fenders around the wheel openings, door bottoms and rocker rails. If the paint is not already damaged, contact the Automobile Protection Association for a referral to an installer who can apply transparent plastic film onto most of these areas at a lower price than charged by new car dealers.

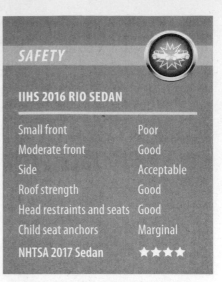

SAFETY

IIHS 2016 RIO SEDAN

Small front	Poor
Moderate front	Good
Side	Acceptable
Roof strength	Good
Head restraints and seats	Good
Child seat anchors	Marginal
NHTSA 2017 Sedan	★★★★

INTERNAL BULLETINS, SECRET WARRANTIES: 2009-10—How to silence a rear strut creaking noise. 2010-13—Poor windshield wiper performance can be fixed by replacing the washer pump inlet filter. 2011-12—Troubleshooting instrument panel noise. Fixing an outside mirror cover gap. Steering-wheel noise and vibration repair tips. 2011-15—A defective inhibitor switch may cause intermittent no crank and no start; erratic or harsh shifting; and a slight engine stumble when placed into Park position after a long drive. This condition occurs more often following a heat soak, after long periods of driving in regions with high ambient temperatures or during the summer months. 2012—A remedy for a noisy, vibrating steering wheel is detailed in TSB #084, Issued: Nov 2011. 2012-13—An easy fix for AC water leaks onto the front passenger side floor. 2012-14—DTC P0711, P0712, and P0713 can be set due to a faulty PCM, an open circuit, or a bad transaxle oil temperature sensor.

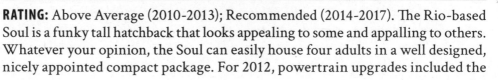

SOUL

	2010-2013	★★★★
	2014-2017	★★★★★

RATING: Above Average (2010-2013); Recommended (2014-2017). The Rio-based Soul is a funky tall hatchback that looks appealing to some and appalling to others. Whatever your opinion, the Soul can easily house four adults in a well designed, nicely appointed compact package. For 2012, powertrain upgrades included the arrival of a nice 6-speed automatic, improved responsiveness and better fuel economy. The second-generation Soul that debuted for 2014 has a better ride and more upscale cabin – it's a significant step up for the model. As of 2016, a pre-collision warning system became optional on the SX; that's a desirable feature that is unusual for a vehicle in the Soul's class. For 2017, the Soul is treated to a mid-cycle remake with a few mild exterior and interior tweaks. The main engine is a 2L 4-cylinder, but a full electric version is available. A 1.6L turbo and 7-speed dual clutch automatic are also new. **Road performance:** *2014-2017:* The 2L 4- and 6-speed automatic combination delivers acceptable performance and smoothness for a compact car. Steering, braking, ride, and handling are all competent. The Soul has comfortable seats and a lofty driving position that provides good forward visibility. **Strong points:** Good space utilization. Attractive gauges, logical controls and a surprisingly well finished interior. **Weak points:** *All years:* Rear visibility could be better. Good cabin space but the cargo area is limited with the rear seatback up. *2010-2013:* Jittery ride. Noticeable wind and road noise. Fragile or prematurely worn interior trim. Fuel economy is overstated. **Major redesign:** 2007, 2014. Mid-cycle remake for the 2017 model year. **Best alternatives:** The few vehicles that competed in the segment include the Scion xB and Nissan Cube; neither is available new anymore. The Nissan Juke, another funky hatchback on stilts, is also a possible cross shop.

Prices and Specs

Prices (2016): *LX manual:* $17,195, *Urban Special Edition auto.:* $26,395 **Freight:** $1,665 **Powertrain (FWD 2016):** Engines: 1.6L 4-cyl. (130 hp), 2.0L 4-cyl. (164 hp), Electric (109 hp). Transmissions: 6-speed man., 6-speed auto. **Dimensions (2016):** Passengers: 2/3; Wheelbase: 101.2 in. 2,570 mm.; L: 162.9 in., 4,140 mm.;W: 70.9 in., 1,800 mm.; Weight: 3,100 lb., 1,400 kg. **Fuel economy:** *2L auto.:* 7.5/9.8 L/100 km. **Assembled in:** South Korea.

ALERT! What? No spare tire? Make sure the can of aerosol and inflator are present:

Most Kia Souls don't come with a spare tire; instead they come with a can of Fix-A-Flat and an air pump. There is no jack either. The flat may be fixed if the damage is on the tread and the hole is under 1/4 inch in diameter. If the damage is on the sidewall or greater than 1/4 inch, the vehicle has to be towed. For those people that have no cell phone or are in an area that gets no reception they will be stranded until another motorist comes along, and these days most motorists don't stop for other drivers. Kia offers roadside assistance with the vehicle, but if you are traveling in a

SAFETY

IIHS 2015-2016

Small front	Good
Moderate front	Good
Side	Good
Roof strength	Good
Head restraints and seats	Good
Child seat anchors	Good
NHTSA Overall 2017	★★★★★

remote area, in the southwest (like Death Valley for example) what do you do without a spare? If your cell phone quits, you're done. Even if you have AAA, their driver will have to tow the vehicle as he won't have a spare either.

Owner-reported safety-related failures: Engine compartment fire; door locks cycled from unlock to lock while passengers were being pulled out of the cabin:

> I should note that while we left the car unlocked when we got out, the doors locked themselves during the fire, and the key fob was inoperable (lock electronics in the car were fried). Had a person or pet been in the car, they would have been trapped.

Airbags failed to deploy; front seat belts allow only a slight body movement before they lock up and don't retract; brake pedal is too small; car hesitates when accelerating from a stop; sometimes the transmission suddenly downshifts for no reason; when parked on an incline, with the emergency brake engaged, vehicle rolled down driveway into a house; fuel spews out when refueling; glass shatters when the rear hatch is closed; driver's door fails to latch; the steering column came off while the car was cruising on the highway; the electronic stability control may engage for no reason and power steering fails intermittently:

> The steering wheel could only be turned if considerable force was applied to it. The Kia dealer service shop ultimately had to replace the entire steering column to "fix" the problem. About two months later I was driving down the interstate and attempted to do a lane change. Again the electronic stability control falsely activated and caused me to collide with the vehicle directly in front of me. When the ESC activated, the steering wheel locked up and caused a sudden loss of control, resulting in the accident.

RELIABILITY: Average to above average for 2010-2013 models: The defroster may not clear the windshield; excessive condensation in the headlights, chips in the glass and paint, and door panels that scratch easily. Steering wheel noise and vibration. Oil leaks at the engine timing cover and power steering hoses. *2014-2017:* Very few complaints. *2017:* The 7-speed automatic is best avoided until Hyundai/Kia resolves its teething problems, and long-term durability is confirmed.

INTERNAL BULLETINS, SECRET WARRANTIES: 2010-13—A steering column clicking noise may require the replacement of the flexible coupling in the MDPS. Poor windshield wiper performance can be fixed by replacing the washer pump inlet filter. 2011-15—A defective inhibitor switch may cause intermittent no crank and no start; erratic or harsh shifting; and a slight engine stumble when placed into Park position after a long drive. This condition occurs more often following a heat soak, after long periods of driving in regions with high ambient temperatures or during the summer months. 2012—A remedy for a noisy, vibrating steering wheel is detailed in TSB #084, Issued: Nov. 2011. 2012-14—DTC P0711, P0712, and P0713 can be set due to a faulty PCM, an open circuit, or a bad transaxle oil temperature sensor. When either of these codes is set, the default value for the transaxle oil temperature sensor is 176°F (80°C). Prior to replacing the temperature sensor, perform a component and wire harness inspection after confirming proper connections, circuits, and PCM simulation checks.

FORTE, FORTE KOUPE, FORTE5

2010-2013 ★★★
2014-2017 ★★★★★

good buy

2017 Kia Forte

RATING: Arriving in 2010 and based on the Hyundai Elantra, Kia's Forte compact was a significant improvement over the outgoing Spectra. The Forte was introduced as a sedan and unusually, a two-door coupe. For 2011, a five-door hatchback called the Forte5 arrived, along with a new 6-speed automatic. SX models featured a larger 2.4L engine shared with the then current Rondo. *2014-2017:* Improved second-generation Forte, available with two conventional 4-cylinders of 1.8 and 2L, and a 1.6 L turbo. All three body styles are classy with some attractive bright accents. Comfortable seats, front and rear. While legroom is class competitive, rear seat headroom on the sedan and coupe is just adequate; the hatchback is more spacious. **Road performance:** The 2L engine and 6-speed automatic offer good performance and refinement. The 1.6L turbo is quick, flexible, and smooth. Ride is on the firm side, coupled with stable handling and accurate steering. **Strong points:** *All years:* Elegant class-leading interior, with clear gauges and straightforward controls – only higher versions of the current Honda Civic, VW Golf, and Mazda3 rival the Forte. Low used car prices compared to the likely alternatives. **Weak points:** *2010-2013:* Fairly hard ride, noticeable road noise. **Major redesign:** 2010, 2014. **Best alternatives:** *Sedan:* A new Honda Civic, Hyundai Elantra or Mazda3. A gas VW Golf or Jetta are also a possible cross shop. A used Civic is not price-competitive with the Forte. The Forte5 uses the same components as the Elantra GT hatchback. Other alternatives include a new or used Mazda3 Sport, and for 2017 the Honda Civic hatchback and Toyota Corolla iM.

ALERT! Can you say "Tire Mobility Kit?" Check for presence of a spare; if it's missing, try to find a jack, compact spare, and tools at a wrecker, to avoid paying Kia's exorbitant charge:

> 2014 vehicle lacks a spare tire, and it was not disclosed at time of purchase, nor does it state this fact in any of its published sales literature or website publications. Kia customer service was contacted and claimed there was not any need for a spare. Customer service indicated that a 'donut spare,' as provided on their other vehicles, is not available, yet, and has no delivery date scheduled. Their mobility kit (tire inflation) will not work on tire cuts and blowouts. The kit's usefulness date is one year. In addition, use of the kit will ruin the tire pressure monitor installed in the tire and void the tire warranty. Kia delivers a full-size spare tire, rim and tool kit in other markets, namely Australia and New Zealand, at no extra cost.

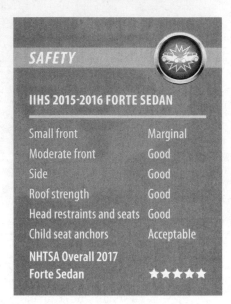

SAFETY

IIHS 2015-2016 FORTE SEDAN

Small front	Marginal
Moderate front	Good
Side	Good
Roof strength	Good
Head restraints and seats	Good
Child seat anchors	Acceptable

NHTSA Overall 2017 Forte Sedan ★★★★★

Owner-reported safety-related failures: Lousy recall treatment; engine compartment fire; force of airbag deployment broke driver's wrist; steering seized and brakes failed after driving through water; engine loses power when accelerating (the fuel pump was ruled out). Stalling on turns; broken drive axle; car lost all power and wouldn't start due to a blown fuel pump fuse; rear window shattered for no reason; defogger doesn't clear the windows sufficiently and frequent taillight failures. Some windshields may not be installed securely at the factory:

> Our technician was able to push most of the windshield out without having to cut the urethane bead. The urethane bead pulled right off the windshield, and was only adhered to about 1/3 of the windshield perimeter. This vehicle was not involved in an accident, but had it been, the windshield would not have remained intact. The safety of the vehicle occupants due to this factory-installed improper installation was compromised.

RELIABILITY: *2010-2013:* Check for oil leaks at the timing cover, power steering hoses, and automatic transmission oil cooler lines to the radiator. *2.4L engine:* A metallic noise upon starting can indicate a defective timing chain tensioner, an expensive repair. 2011-2013 sedans with the 2L engine may experience excessive oil consumption requiring a major teardown and reassembly, or replacement of the engine block. The warranty has been extended to 10 years/200,000 km. Kia dealers sometimes ask for full service records since Day One and then deny claims arbitrarily if one oil change is missing. *All years:* Check for noisy or rusted rear brakes; have the rear brake calipers serviced and lubricated once or twice a year to postpone expensive brake repairs. Some cracked headlights, leaking sunroofs reported. Fragile paint on some vehicles chips easily.

INTERNAL BULLETINS, SECRET WARRANTIES: 2009-13—Poor windshield wiper performance can be improved by replacing the washer pump inlet filter. 2011-12—An ECM software upgrade to address the MIL warning light coming on for no reason. 2011-14—DTC P0711, P0712, and P0713 can be set due to a faulty PCM, an open circuit, or a bad transaxle oil temperature sensor. When either of these codes is set, the default value for the transaxle oil temperature sensor is 176°F (80°C). Prior to replacing the temperature sensor, perform a component and wire harness inspection. 2012-14—A steering column clicking noise may require the replacement of the flexible coupling in the MDPS; the cost of this repair should be claimed from Kia. 2012-15—An improperly adjusted or improperly operating inhibitor range switch may result in one or more of the following conditions: Malfunction indicator light (MIL) illuminated, or intermittent no engine crank/no engine start in Park or Neutral. 2014—Some 2014 Forte vehicles equipped with a Kia accessory spoiler may exhibit a gap forming between the adhesive tape on the spoiler and the trunklid. Kia will inspect and correct this condition, free of charge.

OPTIMA ★★★★

RATING: Sharing its platform with the Sonata, the redesigned 2011 Optima was a design tour de force for Kia under the direction of Peter Schreyer; the car looked like it came from Europe and should sell for more money. For 2016 a redesigned gas engine Optima arrived; the hybrid was unchanged and is still assembled on the previous-generation platform. Advanced collision-avoidance features became available optionally on the new-generation car, including adaptive cruise control, pre-collision warning, and blind spot detection. **Road performance:** *All years:* The base 2.4L engine performs well and is very economical with owners reporting fuel consumption under 8L/100 km in highway driving. The optional turbocharged engine is strong, but not as smooth and not necessary. The ride is on the firm side; handling is secure. *2016-2017:* The 1.6L turbo 4-cylinder is mated to a 7-speed dual clutch automatic versus the conventional 6-speed automatic used with the other engines – shifting with this transmission is rougher than with the Hyundai/Kia's very good 6-speed conventional automatic. **Strong points:** Gorgeous design, nicely appointed cabin with some classy Audi touches and plenty of space. Supportive seats and lots of space, front and rear. Large trunk. Low prices on the used car market compared to competing Japanese-brand vehicles, especially for well-equipped models. **Weak points:** Mediocre braking; average rear headroom; oddly shaped rear seatback. Big rear roof pillars reduce visibility for lane changes. *Hybrid:* Few sold and most dealers lack the expertise to troubleshoot the car. **Major redesign:** 2011 and 2016. **Best alternatives:** Consider the related Hyundai Sonata or a new Honda Accord or Toyota Camry. A used Accord or Camry will cost thousands more.

Prices and Specs

Prices (2016): *LX:* $23,495, *SXL Turbo:* $37,595 **Freight:** $1,485 **Powertrain (FWD):** Engines: 1.6L turbo 4 (176 hp), 2.0L turbo 4 (245 hp), 2.4L 4-cyl. (185 hp); Transmissions: 6-speed auto, 7-speed dual clutch automatic. **Dimensions:** Passengers: 2/3; Wheelbase: 110.4 in., 2,805 mm.; L: 191.1 in., 4,855 mm.; W: 73.2 in., 1,860 mm.; Weight: 3,219 lb., 1,460 kg. **Fuel economy:** *2.0L turbo auto.:* 7.4/10.9 L/100 km. *2.4L auto.:* 6.5/9.4 L/100 km. **Assembled in:** U.S.A.

ALERT! Many complaints that the headlights don't provide enough light; check this out during a test drive at night. While you are at it, also check for excessive steering wander.

Owner-reported safety-related failures: Panoramic sun roof shattered; the front passenger seat is too low for some; and limited rear visibility:

> I purchased this new car in January and have had a difficult time adapting to the blind spots out of the rear window. The rear headrests of this car were designed too large. Even in the down position, these headrests block nearly two-thirds of the rear window visibility.

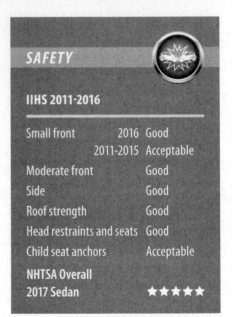

SAFETY

IIHS 2011-2016

Small front	2016	Good
	2011-2015	Acceptable
Moderate front		Good
Side		Good
Roof strength		Good
Head restraints and seats		Good
Child seat anchors		Acceptable
NHTSA Overall		
2017 Sedan		★★★★★

As with the related Sonata, some complaints have been received about the Optima pulling sharply to one side:

> Vehicle hard to control and steer straight, especially at highway speeds. Severe pull to the left, though occasionally it drifts to the right. If you let go of the steering wheel, then the car swiftly moves across to the left lanes (see: *www.arfc.org*).

Other complaints: Airbags failed to deploy; vehicle suddenly loses power when accelerating from a stop or when slowing down to make a turn:

If I press the gas pedal to increase my speed, whether from a stopped position, or to pull into a busy roadway, or to increase my speed to pass another vehicle, the car will start to go then choke, so that no matter how hard I press the gas pedal, the rpm stay the same and my 2014 Optima loses power and will not speed up…I have seen other people with different Optima vehicle years complain about this… I have had numerous near misses because of this problem. I also see many people saying Kia is telling them this is the way the vehicle is supposed to behave – really???

. . .

For 3 to 5 seconds, no response from engine at idle when accelerator depressed and the car is stopped (e.g., for traffic signal). Then, without warning, the engine went from idle (about 800 rpm) to rapid (surging) acceleration, often with screeching tires. This occurred each time I started from a stopped position.

Catastrophic transmission failure; driver-side floor mat bunches up around the brake pedal; brake warning light comes on for no reason; side-view mirror fell off while driving along the freeway.

OPTIMA HYBRID   *2012-2016* ★★★

RATING: Kia's Optima Hybrid can be driven on battery power alone, or in blended gas-electric mode. When the car is stopped, the engine shuts off to save fuel. It uses a lithium polymer battery that will hold its charge up to 25% longer than hybrids with nickel metal hydride batteries. The Hybrid also is one of the first full hybrid systems to use a conventional automatic transmission. An external electrically driven oil pump provides the pressure needed to keep the clutches engaged when the vehicle is in idle stop mode.

RELIABILITY: *2011-12:* Kia extended the warranty on vehicles equipped with 2.4L engines to replace engines that fail prematurely because metal debris may not have been fully removed from the crankshaft area at the factory. The prematurely worn connecting rod bearing will make a cyclical knocking noise, and it also could cause the oil pressure warning light to illuminate. In other cases, engines experience catastrophic valve timing failure. The engine warranty has been extended up to 10 years or 200,000 km. Dealers will inspect the cars and replace defective engines at no cost to owners. Kia may ask for oil change receipts going back several years, even though the defect predates delivery of the car to its first owner. *All years:* Free up and lubricate the rear brake calipers once or twice a year to prevent expensive repairs later on. Some power steering failures, suspension knocking from the rear of the car, stalling and surging when accelerating, and imploding sunroofs reported (see Hyundai introduction, under Rocks on Your Roof).

INTERNAL BULLETINS, SECRET WARRANTIES: 2006-10—Poor windshield wiper performance can be improved by replacing the washer pump inlet filter. 2011-12—An ECM software upgrade to address the MIL warning light coming on for no reason. Kia says the tire pressure monitor can be affected by radio signals. Remote Start system module software upgrade. Remedy for vehicles that stick in Park. TSB #040 outlines Kia Campaign #SA150, which covers the free replacement of both corroded rear lower control arms on vehicles driven where heavy amounts of road salt are used. Corrosion will cause a knocking or clunking noise from the affected lower control arm. 2011-13— Malfunction indicator light (MIL) illuminated with the ECM (Electronic Control Module) system-related DTC P0087. To correct this concern, follow the procedure outlined in Kia's TSB #026, issued Sept. 2013, and, if necessary, replace the high pressure fuel pump, fuel delivery pipe, and mounting bolts. 2011-14—DTC P0711, P0712, and P0713 can be set due to a faulty PCM, an open circuit, or a bad transaxle oil temperature sensor. Prior to replacing the temperature sensor, perform a component and wire harness inspection after confirming proper connections, circuits, and PCM simulation checks. 2011-15—An improperly adjusted or improperly operating inhibitor range switch may result in one or more of the following conditions: MIL illuminated, or intermittent no engine crank/no engine start in Park or Neutral. 2012-14—Remedies for rearview camera issues. 2014—A steering column clicking noise may require the replacement of the flexible coupling in the MDPS; this repair should be claimed from Kia.

RONDO

2007-2012 ★★★
2013-2017 ★★★★★

good buy

RATING: While the practical compact-size van has proven popular elsewhere, it is essentially dead in North America as people move to more expensive, less versatile compact SUVs. For 2017, the Rondo enjoys a late-cycle update including mildly revised exterior styling, cabin trim updates and Apple CarPlay and Android Auto phone interfaces. The 2013-2017 Rondo is the best of the small people carriers, ranked higher than the Mazda5 and Chevrolet Orlando in APA comparison testing. **Road performance:** All years offer good comfort, with available seating for up to seven, and superior cabin versatility. Generous cargo capacity when in two-row mode but luggage space is limited when all three rows of seats are open. *2007-2012:* The 4-cylinder engine sounds a bit coarse, and is thirsty. Nicely finished, comfortable cabin, with decent visibility. For a small premium, you can upgrade to a smooth V6 engine and classy cabin on luxury versions – a much better choice than a used Mercedes B200 if you're looking for a small luxury van. The second-generation 2013-2017 Rondo is offered exclusively with a 4-cylinder engine that is reasonably quick and quite smooth. The ride, handling and steering are nicely sorted for a family hauler, and a cut above the previous model. The cabin has crisply-marked gauges, straightforward controls and attractive materials. Supportive seats and good room in the first two rows. **Strong points:** Good all-rounder in a compact format. **Weak points:** Third-row seat is best suited for children and limber adults. The redesigned Rondo that arrived in 2013 is not sold in the United States; a breakdown there shouldn't be a problem as it uses mechanical components common to vehicles sold in the U.S. Those who regularly travel deep into the U.S. beyond the point where the car can be repatriated to Canada may want to consider something other than a 2013-2017 Rondo, as collision repairs could be tricky. **Best alternatives:** Mazda5; the competing Chevrolet Orlando, also made in Korea, sold in very small numbers and has been taken off the market.

Prices and Specs

Prices (2016): *Rondo LX 5-seat (manual):* $21,495, *EX Luxury 7-seat Navi:* $32,595 **Freight:** $1,715 **Powertrain (FWD):** Engine: 2L 4-cyl. (164 hp); Transmissions: 6-speed man., 6-speed auto. **Dimensions:** Passengers: 2/3, 2/3/2; Wheelbase: 108.3 in. 2,750 mm.; L: 178.1 in., 4,525 mm.; W: 1,805 mm.; 67.7 in.; Weight: 2,844 lb., 1,503 kg. **Fuel economy:** *Auto.:* 7.6/10.1 L/100 km. **Assembled in:** South Korea.

RELIABILITY: *2007-2012:* Below average reliability. Check for a fuel odour, which may indicate a leaking gas tank. The repair costs over $1000 as the repair shop will have to disassemble the rear suspension to replace the tank. If you have a V6 powered Rondo, make sure to replace the timing belt at 140,000 km, as failure to do so could lead to belt failure and expensive engine repairs. Some reports of a light knocking when cold and oil consumption with the 2.4L 4-cylinder

SAFETY

IIHS 2016

Not Rated

Euro NCAP 2013 Sedan ★★★★★

engine. Check for oil leaks at the timing cover, differential output seals, and steering rack and power steering hose connections. Front and rear brakes are frequently rusted; have the rear brake calipers freed up and lubricated annually to postpone expensive repairs. Check for broken sway bar links and worn suspension struts. Failure of the brake light switch on 2007-2012 models is covered by a recall. Poor corrosion resistance; check for structural corrosion in the undercarriage; also lower body panels and the windshield header. The APA recommends aftermarket rust protection using Krown Rust Control or in Montreal, Barry's Rustproofing for a grease treatment (contact information is in the Part Four Introduction). *2013-2017:* Few complaints to date. Check for broken sway bar links and an engine oil leak at the timing cover.

SPORTAGE

2005-2010 ★ ★ ★
2011-2017 ★ ★ ★ ★

RATING: Average (2005-2010); Above Average (2011-2017). The 2017 Sportage is marketed with a more sporting focus than its twin, the Hyundai Tucson. The base engine is a 181 hp 2.4L 4-cylinder that is stronger than the 2L engine featured in the Tucson and the Sportage's optional engine is a 2L turbo with 237 hp compared to the 175 hp produced by the 1.6L turbo on the Tucson. With its Porsche-inspired front end and clean side profile with bright accents, the Sportage offers champagne taste on a beer budget. The cabin impresses, with clear gauges, logical controls and high-end looking materials. Comfortable seats and good room for passengers combines with a versatile, roomy cargo area to make the Sportage a practical proposition. The previous-generation 2011-2016 Sportage was similar to the current model in many ways, but less refined. The rating for 2005-2010 is lower, as the suspension was unsophisticated and interior noise levels quite high. **Road performance:** *2017:* The available 2L turbo delivers an optimal blend of quick acceleration, flexibility and quiet operation. However, at 12.7L/100 km overall during hot summer weather, the Sportage is not that economical. Ride, handling, steering and braking are all competent and at or near the top of the segment. The base 2.4L is strong and furnishes effortless, flexible power and works very well with the 6-speed automatic transmission most buyers will specify. The 2011-2016 Sportage drives pretty much the same as the current one, with less refinement and driving precision. The 2L turbo, with 260 hp, is fast once moving but is peakier than the current Sportage that has been reconfigured for more torque and greater flexibility. **Strong points:** Competent powertrains, good all-round performers, space efficient and reliable. A very good value proposition. **Weak points:** Rear visibility compromised by styling; fairly hard riding; noisy; mediocre fuel economy prior to 2017. **Major redesign:** 2005, 2011 and 2017. **Best alternatives:** The related Hyundai Tucson and, though a half-class up, the Honda CR-V, Mazda CX-5, and Toyota RAV4.

Owner-reported safety-related failures: Unstable on the highway; wanders all over the road; stall and surge acceleration; ineffective brakes; early rust through of the lower control arms:

> I slowly pulled my car onto the Taconic to get out of the massive traffic. I looked under the rear of the car and saw that the control arm of the strut on the driver's side had rusted through completely and broken. The control arm on the passenger side was also rusted through and would have broken as well.

Snow and ice collects on the "running board" and makes it impossible to open the doors; persistent raw gasoline smell in the cabin; sunroof implosions continue (see Hyundai introduction, under Rocks on Your Roof); and windshield cracking without any object hitting it:

> My 2014 Sportage's sunroof exploded. I had just entered the highway (there was no overpass near me) merging into traffic. I heard a loud pop like a gunshot and glass rained down on me. I immediately called my dealership and drove it in. There was no determination as to the cause. Dealership had to completely replace the sunroof. Had to claim on my insurance and pay the deductible – total repair cost was roughly $1200.

SAFETY

IIHS 2017 SPORTAGE

Small front	Good
Moderate front	Good
Side	Good
Roof strength	Good
Head restraints and seats	Good
Child seat anchors	Acceptable
NHTSA Overall 2017 Sportage	★★★★★

RELIABILITY: *2005-2009:* Light knocking when starting from cold is fairly common with the 4-cylinder engine. Before undertaking major exploratory work, check or replace the PCV valve if oil consumption is excessive. *2005 4-cylinder:* Check for a loose crankshaft pulley; tighten bolt if loose. *V6:* Check for coolant leaks at the hose connections. *2010-2016:* Check for oil leaks at the valve cover and timing cover, leaking or worn suspension struts, broken sway bar links, front differential leaks, noisy wheel bearings. Some complaints about the rubber brake pedal pad falling off; windshields cracking; minor problems with the audio system; and some clunks and rattles and excessive road noise. *2016-2017:* Durability of the optional turbo engine and 7-speed dual-clutch transmission is unknown. Owners report the transmission can go into Neutral if it overheats in traffic forcing you to sideline the car until it cools down a bit. Hyundai has issued a TSB.

> Sudden downshifting with loud clunk and lurching of vehicle at 35 mph [55 km/h]. Felt as if I had been hit from behind by another vehicle. Instinctively hit the brakes and pulled over to check for exterior damage, and found none. Continued down the road and experienced unusual increases in rpms. When I arrived at my destination, the vehicle would not go in Reverse. Owned vehicle only 11 days. Incident occurred at 500 miles [800 km].

INTERNAL BULLETINS, SECRET WARRANTIES: 2006-13—Poor windshield wiper performance can be improved by replacing the washer pump inlet filter. 2011-12— Outside radio signals may cause the tire-pressure monitoring system to malfunction. Steering-wheel noise and vibration repair tips. 2011-13—Vehicle may experience a malfunction indicator lamp (MIL) illuminated with the ECM (Electronic Control Module) system-related DTC P0087. To correct this concern, follow the procedure outlined in Kia's TSB #026, issued Sept. 2013, and, if necessary, replace the high pressure fuel pump, fuel delivery pipe and mounting bolts. 2011-15—DTC P0711, P0712, and P0713 can be set due to a faulty PCM, an open circuit, or a bad transaxle oil temperature sensor. When either of these codes is set, the default value for the transaxle oil temperature sensor is 176°F (80°C). Prior to replacing the temperature sensor, perform a component and wire harness inspection after confirming proper connections, circuits, and PCM simulation checks. 2012—A remedy for a noisy, vibrating steering wheel is detailed in TSB #084, issued Nov. 2011.

SORENTO

2002-2009	★
2011-2015	★★★★
2016-2017	★★★★★

RATING: Below Average (2002-2009); Above Average (2011-2015); Recommended (2016-2017). The Sorento is Kia's spin on the component set of the Hyundai Santa Fe XL. The latest Sorento debuted as a 2016 and is unchanged for 2017. It is slightly bigger than the 2011-2015-generation vehicle it replaced. The exterior is a clean design accented with just the right amount of bright trim. Cabin materials and assembly exceed class expectations, comparing favourably with some vehicles selling for $20,000 more. The interior is a paragon of conservative good taste, with clear instruments and convenient controls, the latter particularly welcome on high-spec vehicles equipped with a wealth of features. The Sorento has comfortable seating and lots of room in the first two rows; like most other three-row SUVs, the third row is for the small and agile. Cargo space is ample with the third-row seat folded but less generous when the third-row seatback is up. Three engines are offered, a base normally-aspirated 2.4L 4-cylinder, a 2L 4-cylinder turbo, and a 3.3L V6. Power reaches the wheels via a 6-speed automatic transmission in all cases. A full complement of luxury, convenience and active safety features, like active cruise control, and pre-collision warning is available. You can still find some examples of the original 2002-2009 Sorento on used car dealer lots; although later versions boast impressive towing ability, the genesis of this generation goes back to the old Kia, before quality improvements. It's a gas guzzler with serious mechanical and chassis deficiencies that is likely best avoided. The 2011-2015 Sorento is a good all-round vehicle that is often overlooked by used SUV shoppers. This generation Sorento switched from a truck-style body-on-frame design to unibody construction and lost about 500 pounds in the process. Although overall length was about the same, better space utilization allowed for the addition of a third row seat, which the Santa Fe (pre XL) lost the same year. Few people ordered the manual transmission, which was dropped in 2012. **Road performance:** *2011-2017:* The V6 is quick and deliciously smooth. Virtually soundless in normal driving, it emits a muted, high precision snarl when extended. The 6-speed automatic shifts seamlessly. The powertrain is quiet and road and wind noise are virtually absent, making the V6 Sorento a mobile serenity chamber. The 2L turbo 4-cylinder works well but the V6 is such a delight that not having it would be a loss. The base 2.4L non-turbo 4-cylinder may feel a bit low on power in so large a vehicle. *2016-2017:* Steering is nicely weighted and geared and the suspension has an excellent ride-handling balance for a family hauler. **Strong points:** *2011-2017:* Luxury and refinement well beyond its price point. **Weak points:** *2002-2009:* Headed for the junkyard. *2011-2017:* Impeded outward visibility typical of current "bulked up" SUVs. *2016-2017:* Too much pedal travel before the brakes engage; brake pedal too soft. **Major redesign:** 2002, 2011 and 2016. **Best alternatives:** The related Hyundai Santa Fe XL, and the slightly larger Honda Pilot and Toyota Highlander or smaller Mitsubishi Outlander V6.

Owner-reported safety-related failures: Car stalls out when cruising; transmission hesitates or fails to upshift:

> On three occasions during the first month I owned the vehicle, I have experienced uncommanded downshift from Sixth gear to Fourth gear at speed. Transmission then locks in Fourth gear until shut down and restarted. Very violent event when it occurs, with an instantaneous bang and corresponding immediate loss of speed.

SAFETY	
IIHS 2016-2017	
Small front	Good
Moderate front	Good
Side	Good
Roof strength	Good
Head restraints and seats	Good
Child seat anchors	Acceptable
NHTSA Overall 2017	★★★★★

Vehicle jerks, stutters, and stalls when accelerating:

> Almost immediately started experiencing the occasional hesitation problem when pulling into traffic from a stop. On a couple occasions it put us in a very dangerous situation as we were crossing 2 lanes of traffic. Took the vehicle to dealer four times, they could not duplicate the problem. Finally they got us a 2012 near identical Sorento V6, and on the 3rd day had the same experience w/50 miles [80 km] on the vehicle. We now have 500+ [800 km] on it and have had a total of 7 similar situations.

RELIABILITY: *2002-2009:* Vulnerable to serious chassis corrosion that can require scrapping the vehicle; check the undercarriage, lower body panels, rear axle, and fuel and brake lines for corrosion before you buy. The APA recommends aftermarket rustproofing (Barry's Rustproofing in Montreal, or Krown Rust Control) for all model years up to 2009 inclusive (contact information is in the Part Four Introduction). Lit warning lights are common, and troublesome electronics include the engine sensors and antilock brakes. Check all window switches, the rear wiper and all fan speeds. Worn suspension parts can include the struts, sway bar bushings and sway bar links. Multiple oil leaks possible from the engine, transmission and transmission cooler lines, differential and power steering. A defective stop lamp warning switch on 2007-2011 models is covered by a recall. *2011-2013:* Chrome bezel instrument panel creates an annoying reflection; sunroof shatters for no apparent reason (see Hyundai introduction, under Rocks on Your

Roof) (2011-2013 models are covered by a recall); headlight illumination is too short. *2013-2017:* Reliability improved significantly. *All years:* Have the rear brake caliper guide pins de-seized and lubricated annually or more often to postpone expensive brake repairs. Check for broken sway bar links.

INTERNAL BULLETINS, SECRET WARRANTIES: 2011-12—Transmission shift improvement. Steering wander or pull troubleshooting. **2011-13**—Vehicles equipped with the 3.5L engine may produce a loud engine chatter during initial start-up after sitting for several hours. Kia TSB #140, issued Feb. 2014 says the best way to silence the noise is to replace both intake CVVTs and camshafts with upgraded parts. Oil leakage and/or noise coming from the front struts may require new struts and strut dust covers. New front strut bearings may be needed on some Sorentos that make a creaking noise from the front of the vehicle when turning the wheel, quickly, at slow speeds. This noise is likely caused by front strut bearing corrosion due to water or debris entry into the component. Troubleshooting tips for a difficult-to-release or inoperative second row seat. **2011-15**—DTC P0711, P0712, and P0713 can be set due to a faulty PCM, an open circuit, or a bad transaxle oil temperature sensor. When either of these codes is set, the default value for the transaxle oil temperature sensor is 176°F (80°C). Prior to replacing the temperature sensor, perform a component and wire harness inspection after confirming proper connections, circuits, and PCM simulation checks. An improperly adjusted or improperly operating inhibitor range switch may result in one or more of the following conditions: Malfunction indicator light (MIL) illuminated, or intermittent no engine crank/no engine start in Park or Neutral. **2012**—A cheap fix for a noisy, vibrating steering wheel is detailed in TSB #084, Issued: Nov. 2011. **2012-14**—There are various remedies for rearview camera issues outlined in service bulletins. Vehicle may experience a malfunction indicator lamp (MIL) illuminated with the ECM (Electronic Control Module) system-related DTC P0087. To correct this concern, follow the procedure outlined in Kia's TSB #026, issued Sept. 2013, and, if necessary, replace the high pressure fuel pump, fuel delivery pipe, and mounting bolts. **2013-14**—A parasitic drain on the battery may be caused by a faulty power window switch found on vehicles equipped with Integrated Memory System (IMS) seats.

STEERING/SUSPENSION – PULL OR DRIFT CONCERN

BULLETIN NO.: CHA 033   DATE: JULY 2011

SUB-FRAME AND SUSPENSION ADJUSTMENT FOR DRIFT CONCERN

This bulletin provides information related to a drift condition and adjusting/settling the suspension components under load as assembly variation can remain on the suspension. Camber and Caster may need slight adjustment depending on actual road conditions. To improve this condition the dealer is requested to first follow the TSB CHA 032 (Drift/Pull Diagnosis and Best Practices Tips) for specifications and if they are outside the parameters then perform the instructions as directed in this TSB.

Luxury Fever*

Unlike Acura, Infiniti, Cadillac, and Lincoln, Lexus is seen as the epitome of luxury and comfort, with a small dab of performance thrown in. Lexus executives know that no matter how often car enthusiast magazines say that drivers want "to feel the road," "responsive handling," and "high-performance" thrills, the truth of the matter is that most luxury car buyers simply want vehicles that look good, are comfortable, and give them bragging rights. They want to travel from point A to point B, without big repair bills in vehicles that are more than fully-equipped Honda Civics, warmed-over Nissan Maximas, or thinly disguised Ford Fusion or Flex-derived Lincolns. Lexus executives figure that hardcore, high-performance aficionados can migrate to its sportier models and the rest will stick with the ES sedans and RX SUVs.

Although the high-end Lexus cars and SUVs do attain high benchmarks for quality control in most cases, they're not perfect. And, yes, cheaper luxury cars from Acura, Hyundai, Kia, Nissan, and Toyota give you lots of comfort and are almost as reliable, but they don't have the luxury cachet and laidback refinement of Lexus.

No one had heard of Lexus vehicles suffering from sudden, unintended acceleration with attendant brake loss – until a few years ago. At that time, Toyota, the owner of the Lexus luxury brand, insisted the accidents and deaths were due to driver error. After some delay the automaker did a turnabout and in late 2009 recalled almost its entire lineup (4.4 million vehicles) to better secure floor mats and fix a sticky throttle. Technical Service Bulletins (TSBs) show that Lexus is grappling with the same technology challenges that bedevil other makes. Problems covered include powertrain and electrical malfunctions, faulty emissions-control components, computer module miscalibrations, and minor body fit and trim glitches. To Lexus' credit, many owners haven't heard of these problems because Lexus dealers have been adept at fixing defects early.

Speaking of resale values, let's be real. Most luxury models hemorrhage value pretty quickly, but Lexus is better than the rest because used car buyers perceive, correctly, that a used Lexus won't cost much more to run than a mass-market sedan or SUV.

Hybrids

Toyota has been a leader in hybrid sales since the Prius was first launched in 2001. Lexus hybrids have gotten good marks for reliability and fuel consumption. However, since gas prices dropped, the breakeven for fuel savings on a new Lexus

---

*Heading inspired by economist Robert Frank's book, *Luxury Fever: Why Money Fails to Satisfy in an Era of Excess.*

hybrid is now at 6-8 years. Toyota's proven technology makes a Lexus or Toyota the safest hybrid bet on the used car market.

ES 300/330/350/300H — *2007-2012* ★★★★★

2012 Lexus ES 350

RATING: Recommended. A comfortable front-wheel drive luxury sedan that shares its platform with the Camry. The 2007-2012-generation was impressively quiet, soft riding and nicely finished. Handling was predictable but not sporty. The 2013 redesign came with a firmer suspension, and more complex controls. Model year 2016 ushered in a slightly restyled exterior, additional structural reinforcements, and more insulation for the already quiet interior. There are no significant changes for 2017. The ES 300h hybrid is distinguished by different 17-inch alloy wheels, a rear decklid spoiler, and a frugal 2.5L Atkinson-cycle 4-cylinder engine working in combination with an electric motor and battery pack. The fuel consumption savings with this combo borrowed from the Camry is an impressive 35%. **Road performance:** Very smooth engine and transmission. Predictable everyday handling, but steering feedback is muted and the ES is less responsive than rear-wheel drive and all-wheel drive rivals in this class. A driver-selected knob on the centre console can be dialed to Normal, Eco, and Sport modes to tailor the steering and throttle response, but the difference is not that significant. **Strong points:** Comfortable and very quiet, with a well-appointed interior; good fuel economy for this segment; and low running costs for a luxury car. **Weak points:** Some torque steer – the car can pull to one side when accelerating hard; that's typical of powerful front-wheel drive vehicles. Headroom is inadequate for tall occupants; the trunk could be larger (low liftover, though). Visibility to the rear is hampered by the high window line. **Major redesign:** 2001, 2007, and 2013. **Best alternatives:** Other choices include the Acura TL, Mercedes C-class, Infiniti G35/G37/Q50, and, of course, the Toyota Camry XLE. A used ES is a recommended buy that will give less trouble than the alternative European and domestic luxury cars.

ALERT! Owners say the automatic power window can be a bone crusher:

> Dangerous when right front passenger grasps top of door frame to close door. Driver closes window but is unable to stop window from closing. Once it starts it can't be stopped nor is there a safety stop such as that found in garage or elevator doors. Window crushes finger of passenger and flesh is torn. Flesh retrieved and sewn in emergency room but hospital surgery required 3 weeks later on right ring finger… Imagine if it closes on a child, a dog, or object.

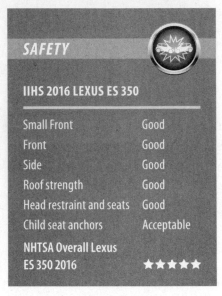

SAFETY

IIHS 2016 LEXUS ES 350

Small Front	Good
Front	Good
Side	Good
Roof strength	Good
Head restraint and seats	Good
Child seat anchors	Acceptable

NHTSA Overall Lexus
ES 350 2016 ★★★★★

Owner-reported safety-related failures: Dashboard melts from the heat of the sun causing a high shine and glare on the windshield. This bizarre defect is covered by a secret warranty and affects most of the Lexus lineup from 2003-09. (See "Internal Bulletins" below). Plastic tabs that hold the front (side) window in place break and the window falls down. A few reports of hesitation when throttle applied, more common prior to 2013:

> Vehicle has the "hesitation on accelerating" or "throttle lag" problem, which is documented on many models of both Toyota and Lexus vehicles. Vehicle hesitates when accelerating from stoplight, slowing to make a turn, or in traffic when slowing and then accelerating. It is unresponsive for 1-2 seconds then accelerates fast. This is especially dangerous when crossing a busy uncontrolled intersection. Occurs routinely when driving everyday. This hesitation is dangerous, not normal, and is a safety issue that needs addressing by the manufacturer.

Stuck accelerator (may or may not be related to improper floor mats); automatic transmission shifts erratically, suddenly accelerates, or slips and hesitates before going into gear; car lurches forward when the cruise control is reengaged.

RELIABILITY: Lowest servicing and repair costs in the luxury vehicle class. Predicted reliability is similar to the Camry V6 which shares many of its components. Above average dealer service for a luxury vehicle, typical of the Lexus dealer network. *2007-2010:* Automatic transmission can hesitate when shifting at city speeds, or appears to be confused about which gear to select.

INTERNAL BULLETINS, SECRET WARRANTIES: 1990-2013—Lexus service bulletin says the seat belt pre-tensioner devices "may, or may not, perform as expected." 2003-09—In a Dec. 10, 2014, letter to dealers, Lexus says it will reimburse owners, or replace free of charge melted, sticky dashboards on most of its model lineup. 2003-13—Troubleshooting tips to silence a creaking, or ticking windshield noise. 2007—Engine oil may leak from the front timing cover. The front passenger airbag Disable light may come on for no reason. Idle may fluctuate when the AC is turned on. Steering intermediated shaft noise. 2007-08—The oil supply hose degrades prematurely and leaks oil. Lexus will replace the hose free of charge until Dec. 31, 2021 (see RX350 "Internal Bulletins" for more information). Some models may experience a torque converter shudder. 2007-09—A rear seat "popping" may be caused by insufficiently torqued nuts. Silencing an engine ticking noise. 2007-14—Some vehicles may find the HVAC Evaporator Drain Hose obstructed with an insect nest. An insect repellent drain hose tip (ARINIX(R) Tip) is now available to help minimize future occurrences. For some models a new drain hose is required to properly fit the ARINIX Tip. Note: Lexus says "The ARINIX(R) Tip is not registered or labeled for sale or use outside the United States or Puerto Rico." 2008-10—When the heat is turned on there may be a large variation in temperatures between the vents. 2008-11—Vehicles that have sat in sub-freezing weather may not shift from Park to Drive, or multiple warning lights may come on. A new relay and wire harness may be needed. 2011—A faulty charcoal canister may activate the Malfunction indicator light (MIL) warning light. Check it first, before spending a bundle on other repairs. 2011-12—Steering wheel noise and vibration repair. Transmission shift improvement. Steering wander or pull troubleshooting. 2013—Bluetooth connection may suddenly cut off.

IS ★★★★

RATING: Above Average. Lexus initially went in the compact-luxury direction with the IS sedan. It did not sell well, as traditional Lexus buyers figured out they could supersize their purchase to the larger ES for about the same money. The 2014 redesign introduced more aggressive styling and sportier suspensions to follow the herd of European cars in the segment that were seeing increased sales. The result is a European sport sedan wannabe. The 2014 car received an 8-speed automatic transmission, a stiffer suspension, and electrically assisted power steering. For 2017, the IS receives mid-cycle styling updates, including standard LED headlamps, and an available 10-inch touch screen display inside. **Road performance:** The IS 350 has a strong 3.5L V6; the IS 250's smaller V6 needs to be revved more for good power. *2006-2013:* Quiet, reasonably soft riding, very nicely finished, with excellent assembly quality. Cabin dimensions are smaller than some compacts, which limited the appeal in North America. The basic car with rear-wheel drive sells for thousands less because it is not popular for winter. *2014-2017:* Interior amenities were upgraded for 2014, including an optional navigation screen that is more easily read. The new IS 200t uses a 241 hp turbo 4-cylinder. The suspension is stuck in the middle: it's too firm for many traditional Lexus buyers, yet isn't as sharp as competing European sedans. A lower beltline improves the view and the high-quality interior is relatively quiet. The previous IS-F ups the ante with a 416 hp 5.0L V8 powerplant. **Strong points:** All years feature low running costs. *2006-2013:* A jewel, refined, reliable. *2014-2017:* Good V6 powertrain. **Weak points:** Cramped rear seating and limited trunk space; convertibles lose almost all their trunk space when the top is lowered. So-so gas consumption; the ES uses less fuel. Although the 2014 is wider and longer than previous models, some owners still feel the interior is small. *2014-2017:* Trackpad controller less convenient than the better touch screen designs or the conventional controls on the older IS. The Vehicle Dynamics Integrated Management feature can perform erratically. Requires premium fuel (admittedly, almost every luxury vehicle demands premium, but the similar V6 in Toyotas does not). **Major redesign:** 2006 and 2014. **Best alternatives:** Try the Acura TL, a post-2011 Audi A4, BMW 3 Series, or Infiniti G37.

Prices and Specs

Prices (2017): *IS 200t:* $40,150, *IS 350 AWD:* $55,300 **Freight:** $2,045 **Powertrain (Rear-drive/AWD):** Engines: 2.0L Turbo 4-cyl. (241 hp), 3.5L V6 (255 hp or 306 hp); Transmissions: 6-speed automatic and 8-speed automatic. **Dimensions:** Passengers: 2/3; Length: 180 in.; Wheelbase: 108 in.; Weight: 3,814 lb. **Fuel economy:** *2.0L Turbo:* 10.6L/100 km city, 7.2L/100 km highway; *3.5L V6:* 12.6L/100 km city, 9.2L/100 km highway. **Assembled in:** Japan.

ALERT! A significant number of owners report spontaneously shattered sunroofs and their astronomically high replacement cost. (For more information on shattering sunroofs, see Hyundai introduction, under Rocks on Your Roof). The dealer may direct you to claim repairs from your insurer, which is not always correct.

Owner-reported safety-related failures: Electric seat warmer shorted out and burned through the seat cushion. Engine surges when the vehicle is stopped. The car can veer to one side when the brakes are applied. Automatic rearview mirror dimmer takes up to

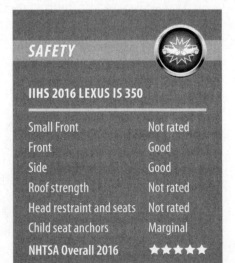

SAFETY

IIHS 2016 LEXUS IS 350

Small Front	Not rated
Front	Good
Side	Good
Roof strength	Not rated
Head restraint and seats	Not rated
Child seat anchors	Marginal
NHTSA Overall 2016	★★★★★

7 seconds to dim trailing headlights and won't dim at all on roads with brightly lit overhead lighting. Poor instrument visibility:

> The visual displays on the center dashboard console indicating HVAC and audio information for the Lexus IS 250 C are so light as to be virtually invisible to the driver, particularly in bright sun and when the driver is wearing sunglasses.

RELIABILITY: Owner reports are mostly positive, except for engine complaints (2006-09), some electrical system issues, and expensive brake service; have the rear brake calipers freed up and lubricated annually to postpone expensive brake repairs. Heating can be slow to come on pre-2010 models; check the thermostat. The navigation touch screen can shut off:

> There is a faulty connector on the 2008 IS 250 touch panel screen. The touch panel is a 4-wire resistive panel, taped to the LCD display. There's a four wire ribbon cable that is improperly bonded to the touch panel. Lexus quoted me $2,800 to fix this problem that is a common problem and a defect in their manufacturing.

INTERNAL BULLETINS, SECRET WARRANTIES: 1990-2013—Lexus service bulletin says the seat belt pre-tensioner devices "may, or may not, perform as expected." 2008-12—Lexus has extended the warranty on 2008-12 IS F models to replace free of charge faulty engine cooling fan motors or screws, and the cooling fan assembly, to prevent the engine from overheating. The extension (#LSC ELE) is in effect through Nov. 30, 2017. 2011-12—Fuel gauge indicates Empty when there is gas in the tank. Bubbled HID headlight housing. 2014-15—IS 250 models with squeaking rear brakes will be given a free brake kit to silence the noise under TSB #L-SB-0105-14, issued Nov. 21, 2014.

RX 330, 350/400H, 450H ★★★★★

RATING: Recommended. Lexus invented the luxury crossover segment with the RX series in 1998, and since then the RX has been the perennial bestseller in the segment. Buyers continue to give the RX series high marks for luxury, comfort and reliability. *2010-2015:* A good all-rounder with a plush interior. Overall length and cabin space increased from the second-generation model. Minor restyling for 2012 saw the addition of a more aggressive grille. *2016-2017:* The restyling job for 2016 is automotive paella with a soupcon of Nissan Murano, Jeep Cherokee, and Toyota Highlander mixed in with the clams and fish. The body is larger and the wheelbase grew 2 inches. The 3.5L V6 gained about 30 more horses, and the 6-speed automatic transmission was replaced with an 8-speed. The RX 450 Hybrid returned with more than 300 hp. Some new safety features were added: Lane-departure warning, lane-keeping assist, rear cross-traffic alert, and adaptive high beams. *RX 400h and 450h hybrids:* Recommended New, Above Average Used Buy. Essentially a more fuel-frugal RX model with plenty of horsepower and full-time all-wheel drive. There have been fewer safety-related complaints with hybrids and fuel savings are significant. New Lexus hybrids are expensive in Canada (they cost less in the U.S.). **Road performance:** Smooth suspension, and the progressive electronic power steering is speed-sensing for enhanced feel. Quiet, carlike ride and confident braking. The RX isn't as agile as its competition and steering gives little road "feel;" but buyers in this segment don't care. **Strong points:** Impressive safety and reliability ratings, lots of luxury in a spacious cabin, and plenty of back-seat legroom. Among the luxury crossovers with the lowest fuel consumption. **Weak points:** Rearward visibility is limited by the sloped styling and the rear camera view may be obscured by messages on the screen during startup. The mouse pad infotainment screen is outdated, not user-friendly and distracting. No third-row seating; expensive options packages; and modest cargo capacity. **Major redesign:** 2004, 2010 and 2016. **Best alternatives:** BMW X5, GM Acadia or Traverse, Honda Pilot, Hyundai Santa Fe Limited or Veracruz SE, Nissan Murano, and the Toyota Highlander Limited. Don't overlook the Acura MDX. It seats seven, has comfortable second-row seats, uses high-grade cabin materials, and provides strong acceleration with reasonable fuel economy.

Prices and Specs

Prices: *RX 350:* $55,800, *RX 450h:* $70,250 **Freight:** $2,045 **Powertrain (All-wheel drive):** Engines: 3.5L V6 (295 hp), Hybrid: 3.5L V6 (308 hp); Transmissions: 8-speed automatic, CVT. **Dimensions:** Passengers: 2/3; Length: 193 in.; Wheelbase: 110 in.; Weight: 4,387 lb. **Fuel economy:** *3.5L V6:* 12.2L/100 km city, 8.9L/100 km highway; *3.5L Hybrid:* 7.7L/100 km city, 8.2L/100 km highway. **Assembled in:** Cambridge, Ontario.

ALERT! Pay attention to how the RX 450h "On Demand" all-wheel drive and regenerative brakes perform; the vehicle can appear to surge forward when the brakes are applied.

I wanted to alert you that other hybrid models that were manufactured with the same braking system as the Prius suffer the same issue. I have a 2010 Lexus 450h RX and its brakes disengage when I am driving on bumpy roads and over potholes. I live in a northeastern city with many bumps and my brakes stop working often and as a result I have to slam them on much more quickly.

SAFETY

IIHS 2016 LEXUS RX 350

Small Front	Good
Front	Good
Side	Good
Roof strength	Good
Head restraint and seats	Good
Child seat anchors	Good
NHTSA Overall Lexus RX 350 2016	★★★★

The all-wheel drive (AWD) system may perform unpredictably:

> The RX 450h powertrain can be downright dangerous. The 4-wheel drive does not switch "on demand" as the advertising says. I live in snowy Massachusetts and do not need permanent 4 wheel drive, but it is essential when the roads are full of snow or ice. I was puzzled at first that the 4-wheel drive only actuated under 25 mph [40 km/h]. I tested it on sharp corners in the snow: The back slid out; and on faster, gradual corners: The car side slipped. Never did the 4-wheel drive switch on and correct the slide. I looked in the manual for the method to manually activate 4-wheel drive but couldn't find it. I contacted Lexus. They said that I should use the snow switch. This is a menu item which annoyingly [must] be switched on every time you drive. It didn't work, as it only changes the gear and acceleration characteristics like any other winter/summer switch. They also said that it should work at high speeds when more power is needed. I tried that and found that at 60 mph [95 km/h] if I absolutely floored the accelerator on a steep hill the 4-wheel drive would switch on briefly.

Owner-reported safety-related failures: Unfortunately, over a decade ago, Lexus followed Toyota's example of cost cutting to keep prices low and reach sales targets, with the result that safety was compromised. At that time, *Lemon-Aid* alerted readers to Lexus safety hazards and our ratings were lowered. Readers' comments, internal service bulletins, and owner complaints revealed airbags that failed to deploy, engine surging and automatic transmission delayed shifts ("lag and lurch"), sudden acceleration, unreliable brakes, inadequate and theft-prone headlights, and weak rear hatches that kept falling on people's heads. Despite reassurances from Toyota and Lexus, and millions of dollars in fines and out-of-court settlements, some unintended acceleration reports continue to come in. This accident reconstruction specialist believes sudden, unintended acceleration could result from interference near an electrical plant:

> I'm writing to you on behalf of the owner of this vehicle. They have contracted me as a vehicle accident reconstructionist in Puerto Rico. I need to know if you have made any inquiries in the fuel delivery and propulsion system. My concern is that the Toyota, Lexus and Honda vehicles that I know of so far are having some kind of sudden acceleration issues and the computer does not catch the problem. This acceleration surges that I have found out about, all have occurred around high electricity areas. So far that I know of, three of these surges have occurred next to the electrical plant center in Palo Seco Puerto Rico and one caused two deaths. The other one is the one I'm representing which occurred in their home twice ... my theory is that electric surges from this high intensity cables interfere with the throttle control and accelerate this vehicles. It is the only logical explanation.

RELIABILITY: Very good reliability overall; the V6 drivetrain is shared with the Toyota Highlander. The Adaptive Cruise Control can operate erratically and is costly to troubleshoot and repair. Some reports that excessive dust/powder blows from the AC vents; tire monitor system malfunctions; inoperative moonroofs; leaky shocks; the vehicle pulls to the right; and audio system glitches. *2015 and*

earlier Hybrid 2015: The steering takes more effort to turn; and the Remote Touch multifunction joystick and screen are distracting.

INTERNAL BULLETINS, SECRET WARRANTIES: All models/years—Dozens of bulletins address the correction of various squeaks and rattles found throughout the vehicle. **2003-09**—Cracked, sticky, or melted dashboards (instrument panels) will be replaced at no charge under Lexus Warranty Enhancement Program – ZLD, issued Dec. 10, 2014. **2003-10**—Windshield ticking fix. **2004-06**—Rear door-stay improvement. Unacceptable power back door operation. Fuel tank shield rattle. **2004-07**—Troubleshooting dash rattles. **2004-08**—Front power seat grinding, groaning. **2004-09**—Transmission fluid or gear oil leaks from the transfer case vent. Plugging water leaks at the liftgate area. **2004-10**—Remedy for brake rattle, buzz heard near the driver's side dash. Power back door noise. **2006-09**—Multiple warning lights; can't shift out of Park. Moonroof auto-close function inoperative. **2007**—Engine timing cover oil leaks. Engine squealing. Moonroof rattle. **2007-09**—Oil leak from the engine camshaft housing. Replace the engine VVTI oil hose for free until 2021 under a Lexus secret warranty extension #LSC9LH. Driver's door rattle fix. **2007-10**—Engine ticking noises. **2007-11**—An oil control valve will be replaced under warranty to stop a seeping oil leak from the engine oil cooler pipes. **2008-09**—Transfer case fluid leak. **2010**—Steering groan when turning the steering wheel. Front seat track noise. **2010-11**—Steering column rattle. **2010-12**—RX 350 and RX 450h vehicles may have a rear end squeak when going over an uneven road surface. In addition, the rear shock absorber(s) may leak oil. TSB #L-SB-0013-13, issued Feb. 28, 2013, addresses these issues. **2010-14**—The HVAC Evaporator Drain Hose may be obstructed with insect nests. An insect repellent drain hose tip (ARINIX(R) Tip) will help minimize future occurrences. A new drain hose may be required to properly fit the ARINIX Tip (see ES 350 "Internal Bulletins" for more details). *450h:* **2010**—Free replacement of the oxygen sensor wiring harness up to May 31, 2018. Fix for a steering groan when turning the steering wheel. **2011-12**—Fuel gauge indicates Empty when there is gas in the tank. Bubbled HID headlight housing. Inoperative SmartKey. Insufficient charging.

HVAC EVAPORATOR DRAIN HOSE CLOGGED DUE TO INSECT INTRUSION	
SERVICE BULLETIN NO.: #L-SB-0018-14	ISSUED: MAY 12, 2014

LEXUS   **MODELS:**

2011-2014	CT200H
2013-2014	ES300H
2007-2014	ES350, LS460
2010-2014	GX460, RX350, RX450H
2010-2012	HS250H
2012	LFA
2008-2014	LS600H

Lexus says "The ARINIX(R) Tip is not registered or labeled for sale or use outside the United States or Puerto Rico." Apparently, Canadian Lexus owners will have to live with Lexus-bred spiders, wasps, etc., and their nests.

Lithe and Frugal

It's not easy being a small player in the global automotive industry, but Mazda is back on track. Ford saved Mazda from bankruptcy in 1996 by buying a controlling interest in the company and sharing platforms. Mazda soon turned profitable thanks to better cost control and a popular range of small cars and trucks made in conjunction with Ford. During the past decade, Mazda and Ford ended their partnership and Mazda improved the quality of its lineup; Mazda's specialty is peppy, economical small cars, and compact SUVs. Its larger family sedans and SUVs don't sell as well. And let's not forget the MX-5 Miata roadster, the world's bestselling sports car. Quebec is Mazda's best market in Canada, second only to Australia in market share.

Mazda's product lineup was augmented by two new models in 2016. The new CX-3 subcompact crossover appeared, joining other small-but-tall crossovers like the Buick Encore, Nissan Juke, and Honda HR-V. Also new for 2016 was the redesigned CX-9 three-row crossover. A Mazda differentiator is its *unlimited* mileage warranty of three years for comprehensive coverage and five years on the powertrain; it's standard on every model sold since 2015.

MAZDA3

WITH 2L ENGINE
2004-2008 ★★

WITH 2.3L ENGINE
2004-2008 ★
2008-2010 ★★★★
2011-2017 ★★★★★

MAZDASPEED3
2007-2010 ★
2011-2013 ★★

RATING: When it arrived in 2004, the Mazda3 was a breakthrough car in the compact segment. It was stylish, available with a practical hatchback body, and had an upscale interior for its segment. Dynamically, only the VW Golf was comparable. Unfortunately the early cars aged very badly in Eastern Canada; they were rustprone; the 2.3L engine self-destructed, and defective door locks made the contents inside the cars a target for thieves. For 2007 side curtain air bags became standard, and the MazdaSpeed3, a high performance model was introduced. Most of the original defects were corrected with the 2008.5 mid-year model. The second-generation car arrived in 2010 and built on the strengths of the original. The first of the 2L SkyActiv 4-cylinder engines arrived in 2012. The unreliable and slow selling MazdaSpeed3 was dropped at the end of 2013. The regular Mazda3 was redesigned again for 2014 which saw the introduction of a large multimedia screen above the dash and a rotary knob on the console; the concept is similar to the Audi Multi Media Interface. The car is shorter, and has an interior that looks like it came out of a more expensive car. Power assist for the steering became entirely electric. High-end models offer some advanced collision avoidance features. The 2017 models are little changed, beyond a few styling and steering tweaks. **Road performance:** *All years:* The Mazda3 impresses with its responsive handling, precise steering, and well-appointed interior. The 2L SkyActiv engine is peppy and fuel-efficient; fuel consumption with the older engines is middling for a compact; some owners report fuel consumption increases markedly in cold weather. The optional 184 hp, 2.5L 4-cylinder provides more power but is not necessary; real-world fuel consumption is 5-10% higher than the base engine. Mazda stayed with a conventional 6-speed automatic on the current-generation car, which replaced a 5-speed automatic introduced on some models as of 2006; shift characteristics and reliability are superior to the dual-clutch and CVT automatics used by several competitors. **Strong points:** Available in a versatile hatchback body for $500-$1,000 more than the equivalent sedan on the used vehicle market. Easy, predictable handling; good steering feedback; small turning radius; and the nicely calibrated suspension contribute to driver enjoyment. Nice cabin design. Resale value that is lower than Toyota and Honda makes it a good used buy. **Weak points:** Rotary touch screen controller will take some getting used to unless you're a gamer. Rear seat legroom inferior to class leaders, small trunk; road noise is fairly intrusive. Advertised fuel economy of the SkyActiv powertrains is overblown; it's among the best-in-class with the 2L engine, but the Corolla and Civic are similar and their manufacturers don't make as much noise about it. **Major redesign:** 2004 introduced, 2008.5 update, 2010 and 2014. **Best alternatives:** The Golf is the closest driver-focused alternative, but costs more to buy and run. Other alternatives include the Civic, Elantra, and Forte. The Corolla is perceived correctly as too dull by many Mazda intenders.

ALERT! The Mazda3 is a theft magnet. The 2004-2007 models are subject to a recall to reinforce the door locks. Consider antitheft marking; the APA recommends Sherlock in Quebec. Check headrests before you buy a 2010 or later model, as they may be tilted too far forward for you.

Owner-reported safety-related failures: Normally, a new car would get at least 50 safety-related defect reports posted each year by the NHTSA. Surprisingly, the 2015 Mazda3 has only recorded seven incidents; the 2014 generated 22 safety failures (75 would have been normal). On vehicles with keyless starting, the engine may keep running if the driver leaves the car. This is common to vehicles with this design:

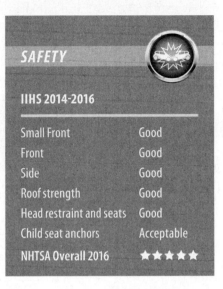

SAFETY

IIHS 2014-2016

Small Front	Good
Front	Good
Side	Good
Roof strength	Good
Head restraint and seats	Good
Child seat anchors	Acceptable
NHTSA Overall 2016	★★★★★

> There was no built-in safety mechanism to prevent the car engine from running while the "key fob" was nowhere near the car. Imagine the safety concerns associated with this? If the car were parked in a residential garage, why doesn't the engine automatically cut off when the key fob is a certain distance from the vehicle?
>
> • • •
>
> My car is equipped with a push to start/stop (keyless) "feature." I pulled my car into the garage last night (with the radio off), pressed the start/stop button to stop the engine, and went inside. When I woke up this morning, the car was still running, all night inside my attached enclosed garage.
>
> • • •
>
> I am a fire investigator with Lexington fire department. I responded to a structure fire on the listed date. It was determined that the fire originated in the engine compartment of the vehicle and spread to the building. The vehicle belongs to Hertz rental car. The individual renting the vehicle reported that he had experienced problems shutting the engine off and that the vehicle had turned on after he turned it off.

These complaints are inherent to the imprudent design of keyless ignitions, and involve an element of foreseeable operator error (no physical key to remove, driver doesn't hear the engine running, thinks car is turned off). Other complaints: Flickering headlights when braking; a high deck cuts rear visibility; design of the door posts creates a blind spot.

RELIABILITY: 2004-2005, and to a lesser extent, the 2006-2008 models had a lot of problems including 2.3L engine failures, engine mount failures, some automatic transmission failures, prematurely worn alternators, lit warning lights, and rapid rear brake wear and failed air conditioners. A clunking noise from the rear of the car could be due to blown rear suspension bushings. A corroded radiator fan cable could result in fan failure leading to engine overheating After 100,000 km, a noise heard when idling could signal a worn throttle butterfly in the air intake ($360). The 2.3L engine is a lemon; it was the only choice on the hatchback until 2008.5. *2010-2011:* Some reports of premature clutch failure on manual transmission Mazda3s. Some oil consumption problems reported with the 2.5L engine. A partially plugged catalytic converter and oil consumption between changes are signs of bigger problems to come. The later 2008.5-2010 series of the first-generation cars are significantly better. *MazdaSpeed:* Turbo failures, excess oil consumption as well as electrical problems. Mazda extended the warranty on the turbo and valve train of 2009-2010 models but coverage has now expired. *2004-2013:* Check sway bar links (rattling, broken), wheel bearings (noisy, not replacing them at $80 apiece could lead to hub failure ($250), air conditioning compressor (noisy), ignition (misfires), heater fan (defective resistors, check that all fan speeds are working). *All years:* Rear suspension (knocking, blown bushings), rear shock absorbers (worn after four years), front and rear brakes rusted or worn (clean and lubricate the rear brake calipers and check the parking brake mechanism twice a year to postpone expensive brake repairs). *Rust 2004-2008:* Poor paint adhesion: very vulnerable to rust at welded joints, rear wheel openings, lower body areas and the roof pillars. Drain holes on the lower doors can freeze in the winter, retaining salt and water. The APA recommends aftermarket rustproofing if the vehicle is not already damaged excessively; Krown Rust Control for an annual application or, in Montreal, Barry's Rustproofing for a lifetime grease treatment (contact information is in the the Part Four Introduction).

INTERNAL BULLETINS, SECRET WARRANTIES: 2004-11—Remedy for intermittent no starts in Park. 2004-12—Correction of brake judder, or dragging. 2007-10—In a January 2012 memo to dealers, Mazda unveiled a Special Service Program (SSP) #87 to extend the warranty to address variable valve timing (VVT) noise and/or timing chain noise on certain 2007-2010 CX-7 vehicles equipped with a L3T engine; 2007-2010 MazdaSpeed3 vehicles equipped with L3T engines; and 2006-2007 MazdaSpeed6 vehicles equipped with the same engine. The warranty coverage is extended to 7 years (84 months) from the original warranty start date or 140,000 km, whichever comes first. 2006-13—Troubleshooting a clunk, bang, or jolt from the front of vehicle upon takeoff. Fuel gauge indicates Empty when there is gas in the tank. Bubbled HID headlight housing. Inoperative Smart Key; insufficient charging. 2010-12—Corrective measures relative to cleaning rust on the bottom of the rear door guide. 2010-14—A rear windshield or window creaking noise is addressed in TSB #09-025-14. 2012-13—Mazda will repair or replace under warranty sticky or warping dash panels. 2012-13—Mazda service bulletin confirms engine may rev above 3,000 rpm with just a slight tap on the accelerator pedal. 2012-14—Engine drain plug oil leak requires a new oil pan covered by warranty. Troubleshooting engines that have a rough idle or low oil pressure. High pressure fuel pump may not be generating required fuel pressure. Troubleshooting automatic transmission whining. 2012-15—Manual transmission hard shifts, or jumping out of Third gear may need a new clutch hub. 2013—Excessive condensation in the headlamp assembly requires the replacement of the assembly under warranty. 2014—Repair procedure for an AC that won't blow cold (Mazda says it may be due to a factory-related glitch). Fix for a buzzing dashboard. 2014-15—Repairing squeaky front brakes and addressing groove marks on the front brake disc plate. Remedy for master warning light, charging alert, and instrument display coming on for no reason. How to silence a tapping noise from a full fuel tank. What to do when the fuel gauge reads Empty, but there is fuel in the tank? Active Driving Display vibrates and/or cannot be adjusted to a viewable position. Seat warmer malfunctions.

MAZDA5

2006-2008	★★
2009-2011	★★★
2011-2016	★★★★

RATING: Below Average (2006-2008); Average (2009-2010); Above Average (2012-2017). A practical compact people carrier that is popular in Quebec, which accounts for about half the Canadian sales. Based broadly on the Mazda3, the Mazda5 carries six passengers in three rows of two seats. Designed for other markets where roads are narrow, this small minivan is relatively tall and narrow. A manual transmission has always been available and may appeal to driving enthusiasts; you'll stretch your dollar with a used manual transmission Mazda5 as they are slow sellers. From 2006-2008, it featured the troublesome 2.3L engine from the Mazda3. *2008:* An improved 5-speed automatic replaced the 4-speed used previously; side-curtain airbags arrived. Cruise control did not arrive on the base GS trim level until 2009. The Mazda5 skipped the 2011 model year. The redesigned 2012 model saw the introduction of a slightly stronger 157 hp 2.5L 4-cylinder engine hooked to a standard 6-speed manual transmission (a rarity) or optional 5-speed automatic. Mazda doesn't offer its SkyActiv engine on this model. Road performance: Agile handling, a breeze to park and easy to maneuver, with a tight turning radius and direct steering – it's the best handling compact van. The engine doesn't have much reserve power for heavy loads or hill climbing, and towing isn't recommended. Some body roll when cornering. **Strong points:** Large, dual sliding side doors make this an ideal vehicle for installing child restraints and carpooling children. Fuel expense is much lower and it's easier to manage than a conventional van in the city. Very reasonably priced on the used car market, because the buying public in Canada and the U.S. hasn't appreciated the virtues of compact vans. **Weak points:** Fairly noisy; the third row seats are snug for adult passengers, and seating is on the firm side. Very limited cargo space with all seatbacks raised. Low-profile tires on the GT are noisier and make the ride harder. Legroom with the seat set at its furthest position may be insufficient for long-legged drivers. The Mazda5 did not score well in IIHS crash tests. **Major redesign:** 2006, 2008 update, and 2012. **Best alternatives:** The Kia Rondo and short-lived Chevrolet Orlando are the only direct competitors. Some shoppers may prefer to migrate to a more fashionable SUV with 3-row seating like the Nissan Rogue, Mitsubishi Outlander, and Suzuki XL-7. You'll give up the convenience of the sliding doors and superior space efficiency.

Prices and Specs

Prices (Firm): *GS:* $21,995, *GT:* $26,795 **Freight:** $1,895 **Powertrain (FWD):** Engine: 2.5L 4-cyl. (157 hp); Transmissions: 6-speed man., 5-speed auto. **Dimensions:** Passengers: 2/2/2; Length: 182 in.; Wheelbase: 108 in.; Weight: 3,465 lb. **Fuel economy:** *2.5L:* 10.8L/100 km city, 8.2L/100 km highway. **Assembled in:** Japan.

ALERT! Mazda head restraints can be pure torture:

> Mazda headrests tilt too far forward. We were ready to buy a Mazda5 but when my wife got behind the wheel in the test drive the headrest pushed her head forward; cannot adjust tilt. She got a headache after the test drive… Worst headrest I have ever seen… Customers will (and do) turn these around, providing no support and little protection.

Owner-reported safety-related failures: Very few owner complaints recorded by NHTSA, except for the suspension, brakes, and the fuel system (fuel pumps, mostly):

> The vehicle again suddenly shut down while driving on the highway. During this incident, not only was I about 80 miles [130 km] away from home, but I was traveling with 5 children in the vehicle!

SAFETY

IIHS 2014-2015

Small Front	Poor
Front	Good
Side	Marginal
Roof strength	Good
Head restraint and seats	Acceptable
Child seat anchors	Not rated
NHTSA Overall 2015	Not rated

Airbags failed to deploy; sunroof exploded; locks and doors freeze shut; parking brake won't hold vehicle parked on an incline.

RELIABILITY: The early 2006-2008 models share many of the weaknesses of the Mazda3, including an unreliable engine that is prone to burning oil, some automatic transmission failures and corrosion. *2006-2010:* Check the wheel bearings (noisy), air conditioning compressor (noisy), ignition (misfires). *All years:* Check sway bar links (rattling), rear suspension (knocking, blown bushings), rear shock absorbers (worn after four years, the right-side strut usually starts leaking first), front and rear brakes rusted or worn (clean and lubricate the rear brake calipers and check the parking brake mechanism twice a year to postpone expensive brake repairs). A lit engine service light can signal a small leak in the evaporative emissions system; the airbag and Traction Stability Control (TSC) warnings can light up intermittently, seemingly randomly. *Rust 2006-2010:* Vulnerable to rust at welded joints, rear wheel openings, and lower body areas. The APA recommends aftermarket rustproofing if the vehicle is not already damaged excessively; contact Krown Rust Control for an annual application or Barry's Rustproofing for a lifetime grease treatment available in Montreal (contact information is in the Part Four Introduction).

INTERNAL BULLETINS, SECRET WARRANTIES: 2006-10—Water entering the crash sensor connector may cause the airbag warning light to come on. 2008-12—Bluetooth hands-free troubleshooting. Headlights don't come on with parking lights. 2010—Repair tips for condensation/fogging inside the front and rear combination lights. Fix for a steering wheel that has a slight in or out movement when pushed or pulled. 2013—Troubleshooting passenger side airbag deactivation warning light that comes on for no reason. Remedy for excessive headlamp condensation or water accumulation.

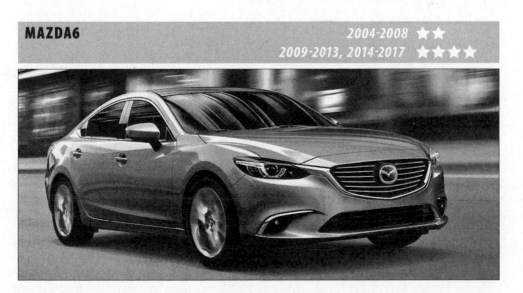

MAZDA6

2004-2008 ★★
2009-2013, 2014-2017 ★★★★

RATING: Below Average (2004-2008); Above Average (2009-2013 and 2014-17). A car enthusiast's front-wheel drive family sedan. The Mazda6 replaced the 626 for 2004; it was offered in three body styles: a sedan, a practical wagon, and a 5-door hatchback. Prior to 2014, the Mazda6 was assembled in a Ford plant in Michigan – one of the very few Japanese cars made in a unionized UAW plant. The V6 engine was a version of Ford's 3L Duratec engine with reworked Mazda cylinder heads. In 2006 and 2007, a low-volume turbocharged all-wheel drive performance model called the MazdaSpeed6 was offered; side curtain air bags and ABS became standard in 2007. For 2009 an all-new unique-to-North America second-generation Mazda6 debuted. The engines grew a bit; only the four-door sedan remained. Electronic stability control and Bluetooth became standard as of 2011. The 2014 redesign resulted in a handsome sedan that achieves better fuel economy, and adds more refinements. The V6 engine was dropped. Mazda's large infotainment screen and console-mounted rotary controller arrived for 2016. **Road performance:** *All years:* Good powertrains; agile, with responsive handling and precise steering; and effective braking. Ride quality is relatively firm. All generations feature nice-looking instrument displays. **Strong points:** Comfortable seating, and nicely finished. Low prices; pre-2014 models are just a little more expensive than a Mazda3 and thousands of dollars cheaper than the Accord, which is its closest competitor. **Weak points:** *2004-2013:* Fuel consumption is higher than competing mid-size Japanese cars. *2014-2017:* The low roofline restricts access to the interior. The navigation system can be difficult to use and the touch screen interface isn't user friendly. **Major redesign:** 2003, 2009 and 2014. The Mazda6 diesel promised for Canada has been delayed again. **Best alternatives:** Honda Accord, Hyundai Sonata, Kia Optima, Toyota Camry and Chevrolet Malibu.

Prices and Specs

Prices (2016): *GX:* $24,695, *GT:* $32,895 **Freight:** $1,695 **Powertrain (FWD):** Engine: 2.5L 4-cyl. (184 hp); Transmissions: 6-speed manual, 6-speed automatic. **Dimensions:** Passengers: 2/3; Length: 192 in.; Wheelbase: 111 in.; Weight: 3,232 lb. **Fuel economy:** *2.5L:* 9.1L/100 km city, 6.7L/100 km highway. **Assembled in:** Michigan and Japan.

Owner-reported safety-related failures: Premature front brake pad wear and rear door locks inoperative in freezing temperatures. Tire pressure monitoring system (TPMS) may detect annoying leaks – or false alarms.

RELIABILITY: Overall repair frequency and costs are higher than for the Accord and Camry after the vehicle passes the seven-year mark. *2004-2008:* A lit service engine light could indicate an ignition misfire or a defective computer sensor. *2.3L four:* Oil burning is common and can lead to connecting rod failure, especially on cars equipped with a manual transmission. *V6:* If the starter motor stays engaged for a long time, it needs to be replaced ($425 from Mazda or $250 in the aftermarket). A Mazda technical service bulletin outlines how to eliminate a small steering column knock. *2016-2017 MazdaSpeed6:* Unreliable engine and turbo, with high fuel consumption. Check for engine oil leaks, timing chain (if noisy, it's expensive to replace), turbo (leaks). *2004-2008:* Power steering fluid return line (leaks possible after 100,000 km), wheel bearings (premature wear), 3L-V6 (water pump (leaks), timing chain (noisy). Radio antenna (broken). *2009-2013:* 2.5L timing chain cover (oil leaks), cam cover (oil leaks). *V6:* Timing chain cover (oil leaks at the rear), transmission (leaks), transmission oil cooler lines (leaks), front and rear struts (worn, leaks, especially on V6 models). *2004-2013:* Sway bar bushings and links (worn). *Rust 2004-2008:* Check lower body; the folded seam at the leading edge of the hood is vulnerable to rust; apply grease or oil-based rustproofing if the hood is undamaged. Visit *www.apa.ca* for the name of a shop that can correct this problem. *2009-2013:* The lower body and rear wheel openings are vulnerable areas. An oil or grease-based rust treatment is recommended. Some paint delamination, blistering, and surface rusting. *2014-2017:* Factory-supplied Dunlop tires may wear prematurely; recommend switching to another brand.

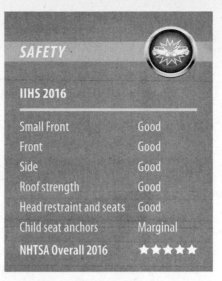

SAFETY	
IIHS 2016	
Small Front	Good
Front	Good
Side	Good
Roof strength	Good
Head restraint and seats	Good
Child seat anchors	Marginal
NHTSA Overall 2016	★★★★★

INTERNAL BULLETINS, SECRET WARRANTIES: 2003-12—Corrective repairs for brake judder or dragging. 2003-13—Tips on eliminating excessive sulfur odours. 2007-11—Excessive water/condensation in headlamps. 2009—Excessive manual transmission noise when shifting. Transmission servo-cover fluid leaks. Inaccurate fuel gauge. 2009-10—Engine runs hot, poor A/C performance. Manual transmission hard to shift into Third or Fourth gear. Diagnosing why the automatic transmission defaults to a "limp home" mode. Silencing drivetrain squeak noises. Front door speaker rattling. An electrical short circuit may cause the horn to intermittently self-activate. Rear taillight heat deformation. 2009-11—Fix for front brakes that click or pop when applied. Repair tips for an inoperative sunroof. 2009-12—Bluetooth hands-free troubleshooting. Improving poor A/C performance. 2010—Free fix for A-pillar water leaks. 2011-12—Headlights may not come on with the parking lights. 2012—Plugging water leaks from the left A-pillar/cowl area. 2014—Troubleshooting automatic transmission whining. Tips on freeing up a hard-to-move automatic transmission shift lever. 2014-15—Manual transmission hard shifting, or jumping out of Third gear may need a new clutch hub. Repair procedure for an A/C that won't blow cold (Mazda says it may be due to a factory-related glitch). Repair procedure to stop wind noise from door window edges. Fuel gauge reads Empty when there is fuel in the tank. Audio screen and touch screen lock up (black screen). Seat warmer malfunctions. Driver seat gradually moves down by itself.

Fun-to-drive quotient of an old British convertible sports car with modern Japanese manufacturer reliability

RATING: Recommended. For almost three decades, the Miata has proven to be an exceptionally fine-performing, time-tested and affordable modern roadster. It's still a stubby, lightweight, rear-drive, two-seater convertible that combines new technology with a salute to old English cars like the Lotus Elan, MGB and various Triumphs. The third-generation Miata arrived for 2006 with a more rigid body, slightly increased engine power, a larger interior, and more interior amenities. Still offering telepathic steering and handling, it was softened a bit and weight increased to improve occupant protection and comfort. Electronic stability control and traction control became standard – good safety features for a short-wheelbase car. The engine grew to two litres and a 6-speed automatic with paddle shifters became optional. Contrary to most other contemporary cars, manual transmission cars continued to predominate. A brilliantly designed optional retractable hardtop arrived in 2007. Minor restyling arrived in 2008 along with engine tweaks that saw the redline climb to 7,300 rpm. The fourth-generation 2016-2017 Miata is nearly a half-inch lower and is styled to look more aggressive. Mazda managed to reduce the weight of the previous-generation car, already light, by a substantial 150 pounds. The 2.0L 155 hp 4-cylinder engine works well with the 6-speed manual gearbox, and handling is extraordinary –even sharper than the earlier car. New for 2017 is the MX-5 RF, which features fastback styling that cleverly incorporates a trick hideaway roof. All models come with a heated glass rear window. **Road performance:** Well-matched powertrain provides better-than-expected acceleration when you let the revs climb. Balanced handling that puts all the classic affordable British sports cars to shame, with the exception of the Lotus cars. **Strong points:** It's amazing how well the MX-5 performs, considering that it adheres to the 1990 formula of the original Miata, and that many parts are borrowed from other Mazda models; for example, the engine is derived from the Mazda3's and the suspension design is from the old RX-8. A fun car to drive that costs less than other convertibles. Impressive braking. Mirrors are large and effective; instruments are driver focused and controls are convenient; powerful heater encourages top-down motoring when the weather turns cold; very good fuel economy for a sporty car; the manual top is easy to operate; and resale value is high. Prices for used Miatas drop significantly in the fall and winter, and bounce back when the good weather arrives in spring. **Weak points:** Noisy, the cabin is cramped for tall drivers, difficult entry and exit, tiny trunk, and a can of tire sealant instead of a spare. **Major redesign:** 2006 and 2016. **Best alternatives:** The new Fiat 124 Spider, Fiat's version of the Miata, uses the 500's 1.4L turbo 4-cylinder with different characteristics than Mazda's powertrain. But, hey, it's a Fiat made in Japan. If you want sharp handling but don't need a convertible, the Subaru BRZ or Toyota/Scion FR-S twins, or perhaps the MINI. If you're willing to go way back in model years, a used Porsche Boxster could be purchased on a similar budget, but it will cost much more to operate.

Prices and Specs

Prices (2016): *GX:* $31,900, *GT:* $39,200 **Freight:** $1,795 **Powertrain (Rear-drive):** Engine: 2.0L 4-cyl. (155 hp); Transmissions: 6-speed manual, 6-speed automatic. **Dimensions:** Passengers: 2; Length: 154 in.; Wheelbase: 91 in.; Weight: 2,332 lb. **Fuel economy:** *2.5L:* 9.1L/100 km city, 6.7L/100 km highway. **Assembled in:** Japan.

ALERT! The car's a neon sign saying "come and get me" to thieves. An engine disabler and GPS tracker are your best antitheft devices. Vehicle etching may help but it could affect the originality of the car if you are a collector. Forget about lights, alarms, and steering-wheel locks.

Owner-reported safety-related failures: Headlight beams that lack adjustment capability may blind oncoming drivers:

SAFETY

2016 MAZDA MX-5

Not crash tested

> I have to apply tape over the driver side headlight to "fix" the problem and now I get zero bright beam flashes from oncoming cars. Affixing an ugly piece of tape to my car is not what I expected when I paid $34,000 for this automobile.

RELIABILITY: Mazda's most consistently trouble-free vehicle. Some minor driveline and fuel system complaints.

INTERNAL BULLETINS, SECRET WARRANTIES: 2006-12—Brake judder or dragging. 2006-13—Differential whine may require a new differential; the Mazda powertrain warranty applies, says TSB #03-004/14, issued 09/09/2014. A clunk, bang, jolt from front of vehicle at takeoff is considered "normal" by Mazda. Dealing with excessive sulfur odours. 2007-12—Silencing hardtop rattles at the windshield header. 2009-12—Bluetooth hands-free troubleshooting tips. 2012-13—Attend to leather seat wrinkles.

CX-5 ★★★★★

The Mazda CX-5.

RATING: Recommended. The CX-5 is a late arrival to the crossover jamboree; it's a replacement for the Mazda Tribute (a clone of the Ford Escape, check the review for Escape to learn more). The CX-5 a compact SUV that uses Mazda's inventory of fuel saving refinements, including a rigid, lightweight steel unibody and SkyActiv engines. The interior was freshened in 2016 with upgraded materials; the console received the Mazda rotary controller and a large infotainment screen was mounted on top of the dashboard. An electric parking brake was added. No changes of note for 2017. **Road performance:** The base front-wheel drive versions are well-priced tall wagons that offer good ground clearance for winter with the convenience of a 5-door body. The 2L engine is adequate, but customers and the automotive press wanted more low-end response, which the larger 2.5 offers. **Strong points:** Best-in-class driver enjoyment, along with the Toyota RAV4 and VW Tiguan. Impressive fuel economy, a relatively roomy cabin with a convenient 40/20/40 rear seatback on GS and GT models. Simple convenient controls until the 2016 update. Higher trim levels available with active collision avoidance features. **Weak points:** Some inexpensive interior trim on the 2013-2014 models – look at that thin carpeting.

Partially opening a rear window immediately changes the air pressure inside the cabin and produces a headache-inducing loud thumping noise. Infotainment screen can be hard to read in direct sunlight. Mediocre speakers. Not the quietest in its class. **Major redesign:** 2013 introduced. **Best alternatives:** The Ford Escape, Honda CR-V, 2016-2017 Hyundai Tucson, Subaru Forester, Toyota RAV4, and VW Tiguan.

Prices and Specs

Price: *CX-5 GX FWD:* $22,995, *GT AWD:* $34,895 **Freight:** $1,895 **Powertrain (FWD/AWD):** Engines: 2.0L 4-cyl. (155 hp), 2.5L 4-cyl. (184 hp); Transmissions: 6-speed manual, 6-speed automatic. **Dimensions:** Passengers: 2/3; Length: 179 in.; Wheelbase: 106 in.; Weight: 3,272 lb. **Fuel economy:** *2.0L:* 9.0L/100 km city, 6.8L/100 km highway; *2.5L:* 9.8L/100 km city, 7.9L/100 km highway. **Assembled in:** Japan.

ALERT! The A/C compressor is vulnerable to road debris damage (a $1,500 U.S. repair); the defect seems to have been carried over all model years:

> I pulled out of the parking lot, drove one block in no traffic, and when parked at the stoplight, noticed a bit of smoke/steam coming from under the hood. The next day I pulled out of my driveway and noticed the A/C wasn't cooling. The dealership showed me a small pinhole in my A/C compressor and informed me that a rock must've flown through my grill area and left a hole in the compressor, causing the refrigerant to leak. It would cost around $1500 to fix and isn't covered because considered "road debris." The biggest issue I have is that the design of the grill is so open, I can fit my arm in there. What's to prevent this from happening again? Every time it happens, the passengers breathe in Freon and it's released into the environment. Clearly the grille is designed far too openly to prevent large debris, let alone a pebble, damaging the A/C condenser. Something needs to be done to retrofit the opening and prevent this from happening time and time again. I did research and discovered it's not uncommon for this vehicle and one person reported it happening on the 2nd day of her ownership and then again a year later.

SAFETY	
IIHS 2014-2016	
Small Front	Good
Front	Good
Side	Good
Roof strength	Good
Head restraint and seats	Good
Child seat anchors	Acceptable
NHTSA Overall 2016	★★★★

Owner-reported safety-related failures: Loss of power on the highway, and unintended acceleration. The automatic "Smart City Braking" feature may malfunction and make the car come to a dead stop in traffic. Be wary of the "Smart" braking feature:

Our vehicle is equipped with the "Smart City Braking" feature that automatically prevents collisions at low speed. This system triggers the brakes and brings the vehicle to a stop when an object is detected in front of the vehicle. This system has been triggered by steam clouds coming out of sewer grates and has brought the car to a complete and very unexpected stop several times.

RELIABILITY: No long-term data; the CX-5 has enjoyed very good reliability to date. Like other Mazdas, the warranty is for unlimited mileage as of the 2015 model year.

INTERNAL BULLETINS, SECRET WARRANTIES: 2013-14—Engine drain plug oil leaks require a new oil pan covered by warranty. Troubleshooting automatic transmission whining. Noisy front suspension struts may plague some CX-5 crossovers. In TSB #0200513 issued on May 24, 2013, Mazda says the knocking or squeaking noise is likely caused by a damaged strut bearing that will be replaced under warranty. Front glass rattling while underway is covered under warranty by TSB #09-17-14. 2013-15—Manual transmission hard shifts, or jumping out of Third gear may need a new clutch hub. Fuel gauge reads Empty when there is fuel in the tank. Audio screen and touch screen lock up (black screen). Seat warmer malfunctions. The seat warmer will be replaced under warranty, says TSB #09-033/14, issued Aug. 18, 2014. Driver seat gradually moves down by itself. Warranty repairs for an A/C that won't blow cold air. Repair instructions for a rattling instrument panel, or creaking noise from the A-pillar area. Mazda says it will repaint the liftgate area under warranty after removing paint blisters or rust spots. Cite TSB #09-018-15 as your reference for a free paint job in other parts of the vehicle that show up at a later date. 2014-15—"Chirping" rear shock absorbers will be replaced under warranty, says TSB #02-003/14, issued Oct. 23, 2014.

CX-7	TURBO		
	2007-2010 ★		
	WITH 2.5L NON-TURBO		
	2009-2010 ★★		
	2011-2012 ★★★★		

RATING: Not Recommended (*with 2.3L turbo* 2007-2010); Below Average (with 2.5L non-turbo 2009-2010); Above Average (2011-2012). The CX-7 is a five-passenger SUV built using a modified Mazda5 platform and the MazdaSpeed 2.3L engine. It debuted as a 2007 model and sold fairly well initially, on the strength of its classy interior, super-sized compact dimensions and competitive price. Mazda couldn't drop a V6 into the engine bay, so a turbo 4-cylinder from the MazdaSpeed6 was offered instead, coupled to a 6-speed automatic. A mid-cycle remake in 2010 included a mildly restyled front end, cabin updates and a new front-wheel drive base model. A more reliable and less expensive base engine also arrived in 2010; it's a non-turbo 161 hp 2.5L 4-cylinder, tied to a 5-speed automatic. 2012 was the last model year. **Road performance:** The turbo engine is strong but noisy. The non-turbo engine is smoother. A capable handler, with responsive steering. Firm ride bordering on jarring now that the suspension has aged. **Strong points:** Terrible reputation caused prices to crater; the best deal is a non-turbo model from 2010-2012 with a nice level of equipment. Handsome cabin, with plenty of space for occupants. **Weak points:** Hard ride, the sloped rear hatch cuts into cargo space. The turbo gulps fuel and likes a diet of premium; its published fuel consumption rating is fanciful. Fuel consumption is also relatively high with the non-turbo engine. **Major redesign:** Launched in 2007, the CX-7 only lasted for one generation with a modest update in 2010. Replaced by the CX-5 for 2013. **Best alternatives:** *Turbo:* Almost anything, including a transit pass or a bicycle. *Non-turbo:* The closest near-luxury competitor is the contemporary Acura RDX; it costs thousands more. The usual compact cross shops from the Japanese vehicle makers also all cost more, especially the premium versions that compete with the GS and GT trim levels of the CX-7.

Specs

Powertrain (FWD/AWD): Engines: 2.3L 4-cyl. Turbo (244 hp); 2.5L 4-cyl (161 hp) Transmissions: 6-speed automatic, 5-speed automatic. **Dimensions:** Passengers: 2/3; Length: 184 in.; Wheelbase: 108 in.; Weight: 3,929 lb. **Fuel economy:** *2.3L turbo 12.2/100 km city, 8.7L/100 km highway, 2.5L:* 10.4L/100 km city, 7.2L/100 km highway. **Assembled in:** Japan.

ALERT! The CX-7 turbo has Mazda's most unreliable drivetrain offered in North America in a decade. Mazda made changes in 2010 and extended the warranty on the timing chain and turbo to 7 years/140,000 km, but coverage has largely expired by now and Mazda makes it hard to collect if you are a second owner.

RELIABILITY: Change the oil every 5,000 to 8,000 km and keep your receipts. Check the turbo engine for a rattling noise upon start-up which is indicative of a worn timing chain or impending failure of the variable valve timing system. If allowed to continue, the eventual result will be engine self-destruction. Mazda does not recommend synthetic oil for this engine; regular mineral oil in a 5W-30 or 5W-40 weight can reportedly reduce wear on some internal components. Badly designed catalytic converter can become partially restricted, causing eventual engine oil consumption

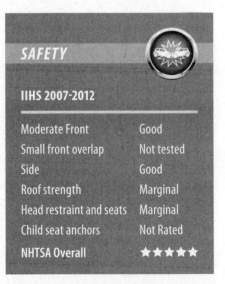

SAFETY	
IIHS 2007-2012	
Moderate Front	Good
Small front overlap	Not tested
Side	Good
Roof strength	Marginal
Head restraint and seats	Marginal
Child seat anchors	Not Rated
NHTSA Overall	★★★★★

issues. Mazda extended the EGR valve warranty on 2007-2009 models to 7 years/ 140,000 km. A lit check engine light (EVAP code) could be the result of a failed EGR valve; don't fill the gas tank past the first click to prevent Mazda denying a warranty claim. White smoke from the exhaust is a possible indication of EGR failure, which is often followed by failure of the turbocharger. The turbo engine is expensive to rebuild. Check for multiple fluid leaks (engine, transfer case, rear differential), turbo (leaks, blue smoke), lit "check engine" light (code 455, defective ignition coils or their circuits), steering rack (leaks), rear shocks (leaks), battery (weak output), front and rear brakes (seized calipers, scored rotors). Have the brake calipers de-seized and lubricated annually to postpone expensive brake repairs. Tire pressure sensors from Mazda cost only $35. Check the headlights for excessive condensation. An extended warranty is strongly recommended if you buy a used CX-7 turbo; make sure that the warranty provides comprehensive coverage with a repair limit in excess of $5,500.

CX-9 ★★★

RATING: Average (2007-2015); 2016-2017 New. Introduced in 2007, the original CX-9 enjoyed a long nine-year model run – that's unusual for a Japanese automaker. The seven-passenger platform is shared with the popular Ford Edge and adds a better interior. The engine derived from Ford grew from 3.5L to 3.7L in 2008. Comfortable and quiet. Competent road manners for the big heavy vehicle it is. The redesigned 2016-2017 CX-9 is completely new and no longer relies on donor parts from Ford. According to Mazda it was designed using the SkyActiv philosophy of lightweight but rigid construction, along with a complement of fuel-saving technologies. However lightweight it isn't. The smooth V6 has been dropped, and a 227 hp turbo 4-cylinder is the only available engine. **Road performance:** *2007-2015:* The Ford-sourced 273 hp 3.7L V6 delivers good power and is quiet. *2016-2017:* The 2.5L turbo 4-cylinder is rated at 227 hp and a useful 310 lb.-ft. of torque. Handling is better than average, and the ride is well controlled and quiet over bad roads. **Strong points:** *All years:* Nicely finished, roomy, with ample headroom, legroom, and storage space. Instruments and controls are nicely laid out and not hard to master. Third-row seating is surprisingly accommodating. **Weak points:** *2007-2015:* Gas consumption is relatively high even by the standards of the behemoths in its class. Poor outward visibility to the sides and rear in close quarters, typical of large SUVs. **Best alternatives:** Buick Enclave, GMC Acadia, Ford Edge, Hyundai Veracruz.

Prices and Specs

Price (2016): *CX-9 GX FWD:* $35,300, *Signature AWD:* $50,100 **Freight:** $1,895 **Powertrain (FWD/AWD):** Engine: 2.5L 4-cyl. Turbo (227 hp); Transmissions: 6-speed automatic. **Dimensions:** Passengers: 2/3/2; Length: 199 in.; Wheelbase: 115 in.; Weight: 4,054 lb. **Fuel economy:** *2.5L turbo:* 11.2L/100 km city, 8.8L/100 km highway. **Assembled in:** Japan.

RELIABILITY: Few complaints recorded. Brakes can wear rapidly; some audio system malfunctions covered under warranty. Limited sales in Canada means some parts are dealer only.

INTERNAL BULLETINS, SECRET WARRANTIES: 2006-12—Bluetooth hands-free troubleshooting tips. Silencing Bose speaker noise. Removing excessive sulfur odours. First-aid for wrinkled leather seats. A remedy for excessive vibration from the floor or steering wheel during acceleration; front brake squeaking. *CX-7:* 2007-12—Fixing a partly detached rear spoiler. 2010-12—Door armrest trim peeling. *CX-7 and CX-9:* 2007-11—These Mazdas may leak oil from the rear differential seal. In TSB #0300411 Mazda says the differential breather was placed too low and could easily become clogged by snow or water. A new differential with a raised breather covered by the breather boot will be installed for free on a case-by-case basis. *CX-9:* 2007-15—Inoperative or noisy power windows usually need the window motor replaced. This repair should be gratis under "reasonable durability" guidelines. 2011-13—Correcting engine surge and/or shift lock by recalibrating the transmission control module (TCM) under the more generous emissions warranty. 2013-15—Audio screen and touch screen lock up (black screen).

SAFETY

IIHS 2010-2015

Small Front	Poor
Front	Good
Side	Good
Roof strength	Marginal
Head restraint and seats	Marginal
Child seat anchors	Marginal
NHTSA Overall Mazda	
CX-5 2015	★★★★

Mitsubishi's Mirage econobox: Even less than meets the eye?

Mitsubishi Motors is a giant Japanese conglomerate involved in everything from banking to aviation, but subsidiary Mitsubishi Motors sinks or swims on the merits of its automobiles. Unfortunately for Mitsubishi, it came to Canada under its own name only in 2002, after the arrival of Hyundai and Kia. It used to be that a second-tier Japanese automaker like Mitsubishi (and Mazda, Subaru, Suzuki and Isuzu at one time) could trade on its Made in Japan reputation and slightly undercut the prices of the major Japanese brands or offer a unique feature to reach sales objectives in North America. That changed in the 2000s when the quality of the Korean makes began to improve. Hyundai and Kia undercut everyone else, and seemed to have unlimited product development budgets, completely redesigning models every four years and aggressively expanding their model ranges into new segments.

Mitsubishi's reputation for corporate integrity is in tatters, most recently for faking fuel economy ratings. In spring 2016, Nissan which had a distribution agreement to sell small Mitsubishi cars as Nissans in the Japanese market, revealed that it was unable to duplicate their published fuel economy ratings in its labs. Mitsubishi's deception unravelled and the stock cratered. Nissan bought a 34% interest controlling share in the company, with the opportunity to name directors on the Mitsubishi board – essentially a bloodless coup. Later in the year, in September 2016, the Japanese Ministry of Transportation identified additional Mitsubishi models with fuel consumption errors, including the Outlander and RVR. According to Japanese authorities, Mitsubishi's overstating of Japanese-market fuel economy ratings goes back to 1991 and averages 4.2%.

More integration between Mitsubishi and Nissan could go two ways in markets like Canada. On the one hand, Mitsubishi's product range could improve with a basket of Nissan or jointly-developed vehicles to choose from; on the other, the partners could decide to rationalise distribution networks in countries where one of them is much stronger than the other. Mitsubishi executives told the APA that the automaker has never pulled out of a country.

In Canada, Mitsubishi offers a unique five-year comprehensive factory warranty and 10 years/160,000 km warranty on the powertrain. It's a selling feature that speaks to new car buyers and helps retain the value of used Mitsubishis. A tip for used car buyers: If you don't have full service records from the previous owner, consider performing scheduled maintenance at a Mitsubishi dealer for your first couple of services, and retain your records going forward. That will make it harder to refuse a potential future warranty claim on the basis of a lack of maintenance.

MIRAGE ★

RATING: Not Recommended. The Mirage is an import from Thailand that uses a tiny 1.2L 3-cylinder engine that delivers a paltry 74 hp (up to 78 hp for 2017) to the front wheels through a standard 5-speed manual or an optional CVT automatic transmission. Mitsubishi introduced the 2-year-old Mirage to Canada in 2014, seeing a niche in the market for cars smaller than available subcompacts like the Accent and Rio. That market got a whole lot more crowded when Nissan introduced the Micra; assembled in low-cost Mexico and promoted relentlessly at a deceptive $9,998 starting price, the Micra quickly dominated the segment. Mitsubishi had to drop the price of the base Mirage by almost $2,500 to stay in the running. There was no 2106 model. For 2017, the Mirage receives some powertrain, suspension and interior upgrades to address deficiencies the automotive press has delighted in pointing out. The five-door hatchback now has a running mate: the four-door G4 sedan, which uses a 10-cm longer wheelbase for more room and a better ride. The 2017's larger brakes, suspension changes, recalibrated power steering, and available touch screen with Apple CarPlay will improve the car, but are unlikely to move the needle enough to impact its low overall ranking. **Road Performance:** Noisy, gutless engine. The CVT transmission allows the engine to rev constantly, increasing cabin noise even more; the manual is better. Surprisingly compliant suspension over bumps, but the Mirage rolls like a sailor in corners. The Spartan interior would have been normal in an entry level car sold in Canada about 20 years ago; assembly quality is good. **Strong points:** Tight turning circle and tidy dimensions make city maneuvers a breeze. Efficient utilization of the available cabin space. Good visibility. **Weak points:** Unstable, very noisy. Unless driven very gently, fuel consumption is not as low as expected, because the engine has to work hard. Poor collision protection. **Major redesign:** 2014 introduced, 2017 new sedan, hatchback refresh. **Best alternatives:** New: Chevrolet Spark or Nissan Micra. Used: Hyundai Accent or Kia Rio, Nissan Micra. If you can afford one, a used Mazda2 or Toyota Yaris.

Prices and Specs

Price (2017): *ES:* $12,698; *G4:* $14, 498; *SEL:* $18,298 **Freight:** $1,450 **Powertrain (FWD):** Engines: 1.2L 3-cyl. (78 hp); Transmissions: 5-speed manual, CVT automatic. **Dimensions:** Passengers: 2/3; Length: 149 in.; Wheelbase: 96 in.; Weight: 2,073 lb. **Fuel economy:** *1.2L:* 6.4L/100 km city, 5.5L/100 km highway. **Assembled in:** Thailand.

RELIABILITY: Incomplete data, the Mirage generated few reports in its first three years in Canada, partly because cars are still under warranty. The front brakes wear quickly; improved replacement pads are available. Long-term durability of the 3-cylinder engine is a question mark; 3-cylinder engines have generally held up poorly in Canada. The CVT transmission occasionally performs erratically, but the low power and light weight Mirage should be kinder to the transmission than other vehicles with CVTs. Given the limited sales, major parts are likely to be dealer-only. Replacement parts from Mitsubishi can be expensive after the warranty expires.

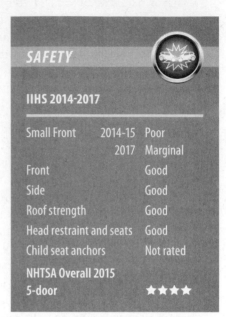

SAFETY

IIHS 2014-2017

Small Front	2014-15	Poor
	2017	Marginal
Front		Good
Side		Good
Roof strength		Good
Head restraint and seats		Good
Child seat anchors		Not rated
NHTSA Overall 2015		
5-door		★★★★

LANCER ★★

RATING: Below Average. The current Lancer compact sedan was introduced as an early 2008 model; the Lancer shares its platform with the Outlander crossover, as well as duds like the Dodge Caliber and Jeep Compass. Its claim to fame in the compact segment is an available all-wheel drive system, which benefits from some sophisticated technology that is also used by the celebrated Lancer Evolution high-performance sedan. Most Lancers are front-wheel drive economy cars that get the job done with an aluminum 2.0L DOHC 4-cylinder engine, good for 152 hp (now 148 hp). The motor is tied to an Aisin 5-speed manual gearbox or optional continuously variable automatic (CVT) supplied by Nissan's Jatco subsidiary. An optional 168 hp 2.4-L 4-cylinder appeared in 2009. It gives the Lancer a sportier character, aided by a tuned suspension and larger 18-inch tires on sportier wheels, at the expense of somewhat higher fuel consumption. To do battle with Subaru's WRX, the Ralliart also debuted in 2009, packaged with all-wheel drive and a 237 hp 2.0L turbo 4-cylinder – and a mandatory 6-speed, dual-clutch automatic transmission. The full-on Lancer Evolution, or Evo, uses a more highly tuned 291 hp version of the same engine. The Evo's sophisticated four-wheel-drive system includes three electronic programs for the centre differential, yaw control and a trick rear that splits power side to side. A practical five-door "Sportback" hatchback joined the range in 2010. Buyers balked at its high price, and Mitsubishi responded with a decontented Sportback for 2011 with the smaller 2.0L engine. Equipment and styling tweaks have made up the rest of the changes since then, and the Lancer is just marking time. The Lancer is most popular with a young male contingent that understands its connection to the Evo model, and with new Canadians who grew up in countries where Mitsubishi has a large market presence. **Road performance:** The Lancer represents a sport-flavoured alternative to the usual econobox fare, but refinement has fallen behind compact car standards. Zero to 97 km/h comes up in about 8 seconds in base models with the 5-speed stick, while the slow-acting CVT adds a full second. The 2.4-L GTS is quicker, at just over 7 seconds with a stick. The ride and handling are better than the class average. In APA comparison testing in 2010, the Evo and Subaru WRX scored closely; the Evo felt a bit more nimble. **Strong points:** Owners like the Lancer's quick reflexes and styling. Decent visibility. The practical Sportback is largely overlooked. **Weak points:** Noisy and unresponsive with the CVT. Basic cabin finish is typical of Mitsubishi vehicles. **Major redesign:** None to speak of. **Best alternatives:** Mazda3, Honda Civic, Hyundai Elantra, Toyota Corolla, Kia Forte. For the Evo the obvious cross-shop is the Subaru WRX.

Prices and Specs

Price: *ES:* $17,998; *GTS AWD:* $26,298 **Freight:** $1,600 **Powertrain (FWD and AWD):** Engines: 2.0L 4-cyl. (148 hp); 2.4L 4-cyl. (168 hp); Transmissions: 5-speed manual, CVT automatic. **Dimensions:** Passengers: 2/3; Length: 182 in.; Wheelbase: 104 in.; Weight: 2,877 lb. **Fuel economy:** *2.0 L:* 9.6L/100 km city, 7.0L/100 km highway; *2.4 L:* 10.2L/100 km city, 7.8L/100 km highway. **Assembled in:** Japan.

RELIABILITY: Engineered and assembled in Japan, the Lancer has generated very few reports, partly because owners benefit from long five- and ten-year warranties. The Ralliart and Evolution models come with a shorter 3-year/60,000 km base warranty and 5 years/100,000 km on the powertrain, likely because of their complex all-wheel drive powertrains and turbochargers, and more severe usage. Some early CVTs required replacement; later units appear durable. The manual transmission is known for its fast-wearing clutch.

OUTLANDER

4-CYLINDER ★★★
V6 ★★★★

RATING: Below Average (4-cylinder); Above Average (V6). Mitsubishi redesigned its compact crossover for 2007, giving the second-generation Outlander crisp styling, a V6 engine and available third-row seating for up to seven occupants. This looked like a winning combination. Sharing its platform with the new-generation Lancer, the Outlander's wheelbase grew 5 cm and it overall length by 9 cm. Base models came with front-wheel drive or optional all-wheel drive, which lacked low-range gearing but could be set for front-wheel drive only, all-wheel drive, or locked for a 50/50 power split. The all-wheel drive system's electronically controlled clutch aided handling by dispatching power to the rear axle before the front tires began to slip. Initially only a 3L V6 was offered with 220-230 hp, depending on the model and year, coupled to a 6-speed automatic with a manual shift gate. Antilock brakes and traction/antiskid control were standard, along with active front headrests, front-side airbags and curtain airbags. Mitsubishi brought back a 4-cylinder engine for 2008. Rated at 166 hp, the 2.4L 4-cylinder was mated to a continuously variable transmission (CVT) rather than the better conventional hydraulic automatic. Mitsubishi introduced a novel headliner that acted as an odour fighter, and gave the Outlander a two-piece tailgate – the lower segment dropped down to aid loading while the glass hatch swung skyward. The Outlander was updated extensively for 2014 with new sheet metal, an overhauled interior and more high-tech electronic features. **Road performance:** The standard 2.4L 4-cylinder with the CVT is noisy and could use more sparkle. The V6 transforms the Outlander, and is a significant plus. Steering and handling are good for this class, at the expense of a firm ride and significant road noise. The 2014-2017 models are better. The second-row seatbacks recline and the split seat cleverly slides fore and aft to maximize either passenger or cargo space. The third-row jump seat (kids only) folds neatly into a well in the cargo floor. The interior loses marks for its finish, including the felt-like carpet. **Strong points:** V6 power for towing. Sophisticated all-wheel drive system. Cabin space. Warranty. **Weak points:** Underwhelming and noisier with the the 4-cylinder. Some cheap touches inside the cabin. **Major redesign:** 2007, 2014. **Best alternatives:** Lots to choose from. For their handling, the Mazda CX-5, and Toyota RAV4. For V6 power, the RAV4 prior to its 2013 redesign, Suzuki Grand Vitara (most years of the Escape V6 are too troublesome). For the third row seat, the 2006-2012 Toyota RAV4, or 2014-2007 Nissan Rogue with optional three-row seating.

Prices and Specs

Price: *RVR ES:* $19,998; *Outlander ES FWD:* $25,998; *GT S AWD:* $36,498 **Freight:** $1,700 **Powertrain (FWD and AWD):** Engines: 2.0L 4-cyl. (148 hp); 2.4L 4-cyl. (166 hp); 3.0L V6 (224 hp). Transmissions: 5-speed manual (RVR only); CVT automatic. **Dimensions:** Passengers: 2/3 or 2/3/2; Length: 185 in.; Wheelbase: 105 in.; Weight: 3,252 lb. **Fuel economy:** *2.0L:* 9.6L/100 km city, 7.6L/100 km highway; *2.4L:* 9.2L/100 km city, 7.5L/100 km highway; *3.0L:* 11.9L/100 km city, 8.5L/100 km highway. **Assembled in:** Japan.

RELIABILITY: An extra-long warranty, no turbo, and a design that has been around more than long enough to work out the bugs all contribute to a low incidence of problems reported with the Outlander. Early models with the CVT automatic are now reaching the end of their warranties, so that may be something to watch out for.

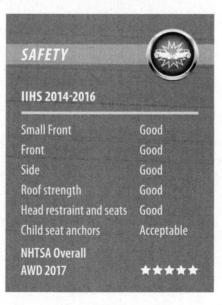

SAFETY

IIHS 2014-2016

Small Front	Good
Front	Good
Side	Good
Roof strength	Good
Head restraint and seats	Good
Child seat anchors	Acceptable
NHTSA Overall	
AWD 2017	★★★★★

The Cube (2010-2013) melted away after four years.

NISSAN

What's wrong with Nissan? Inconsistent quality control, poor reliability and oddball designs have hurt the brand considerably during the past decade. Why are there so many humdrum cars now, after cultivating an enviable reputation for making some extraordinarily good products, highlighted by run-forever 6-cylinder engines? One reason is Nissan's Jatco subsidiary, which builds continuously variable transmissions (CVTs), favoured for their fuel savings. Nissan is hell-bent on stuffing virtually every car and truck with the device, which doesn't provide the reliability or response of a conventional automatic.

It's hard to believe that the same automaker created the iconic 240Z sports car in the '70s, sold millions of cheap and reliable Hardbody and Frontier pickups, and developed the Leaf electric car. Sure, the 370Z, and GT-R supercar have helped the brand's image, but it's too little. Some examples of disappointing products include the mediocre Sentra and Versa small cars, and off-putting Quest minivan. Additionally, the bizarre Cube, Maxima full-size sedan, Armada SUV, and Titan full-size pickup haven't achieved much success either.

There is some reason for optimism in 2017, with a few redesigned and restyled models that may succeed; notably, the stylish entry-level Versa Note hatchback, the new Maxima and the Murano mid-size SUV. Nissan still has a few models that defy description, but there are other new vehicles like the NV200 Compact Cargo commercial van, and the Rogue compact SUV that provide glimmers of hope. We've seen the next-generation Micra and it's handsome.

Nissan pinches pennies when it comes to its "goodwill" extended warranties used to correct factory-related defects. Judging by the last few years of complaints sent in by *Lemon-Aid* readers and reports received by government and private agencies, Nissan quality control has picked up a bit in the last two years, though owners still complain about fuel-delivery systems, brake and original-equipment tire durability, climate controls, and fit and finish. Among Nissan's high volume vehicles, the Rogue continues to have the fewest complaints.

What's really wrong with Nissan? Answer: Excessive cost-cutting and hard-nosed top-down management. It all comes down to this: The lowest ranked Japanese automaker in the 2016 J.D. Power Dependability Study is Nissan, with 173 reported problems per 100 vehicles, placing it in the company of Volkswagen, Fiat, and Jeep.

Nissan Advertising

Nissan's advertising is among the most deceptive on the market – and it works! Under Canadian CEO Christian Meunier, Nissan sales are way up, and Nissan's advertising integrity is way down. Take a look at this ad for the Nissan Micra:

Nissan's manufacturer advertising was the most misleading shopped by the Automobile Protection Association (APA). The ad photo, price, and available discounts are a collage that mixes up two Micra models with different equipment, prices, discounts, and financing. The image shows a loaded Micra SR that sells for about $15,000 with an automatic transmission next to the $9,998 price of a base Micra S. The discount in the ad of up to $3,250 on the SR is not available on the Micra S.

To obtain a base Micra at the advertised $9,998, you have to take Nissan financing at a relatively high interest rate of about 5%, compared to 2.49% that Nissan charges for its other models. By doing that, a buyer ends up paying almost $1,000 in additional interest.

To arrive at the advertised price of $9,998 for the base Micra S, the fine print in Nissan's ad explains that the price includes $1,150 Nissan Canada Finance (NCF) standard finance cash, $650 non-stack cash (which includes a contribution from the dealer that APA secret shoppers discovered was not always forthcoming) and $500 bonus cash. Who can understand this?

Nissan charges extra for paint. Every colour except one or two on the Nissan vehicles shopped by the APA incurred a paint surcharge of $135 or $300 – but most Nissan ads don't tell you that.

Nissan Double CVT Warranty

Nissan has doubled the powertrain warranty on the Continuously Variable Transmission (CVT) to 10 years/200,000 km on 2003 to early 2010 models. Introduced on the 2003 Murano, the transmission migrated to other Nissans in following years; the Versa and Rogue have always had a CVT. Be sure to perform the required transmission fluid change *using the Nissan fluid and preferably at a Nissan dealership* and retain your records if your vehicle is covered by this warranty extension. The transmission service isn't cheap, but you'll need it to ensure an eventual transmission claim isn't rejected.

MICRA ★★★

RATING: Average (2015-2017). Nissan made headlines when it announced its sub-compact Micra was returning to Canada for the 2015 model year with a nostalgic opening price of $9,998. The five-door Micra S hatchback came with cloth seats, a 5-speed manual transmission, roll-your-own manual windows, manual-adjust outside mirrors and manual air conditioning (you can stick your head out the window and catch the breeze in your face). It also came with features that the 1991 Micra – the last year it was marketed in Canada – buyer could only dream of, including six airbags, ABS brakes, traction control, electronic stability control, a tilt steering wheel and an AM/FM/CD player with auxiliary audio input. Engineers modified the car a bit for Canada by adding larger wheels and tires, rear-seat heating ducts, and a rear stabilizer bar. The advertised price is a lowball. With the features almost every buyer will be looking for when you try to sell your Micra second-hand – automatic, air conditioning, cruise control, and power windows – the price leaps to more than $13,000, which is Hyundai and Kia territory. Still, the Micra caught on with Canadians looking for a basic new car with a full warranty, especially in Quebec, where cheap and cheerful manual-transmission cars still roam the roads outside major metropolitan areas. Like many other small cars sold in North America, the Micra is assembled in Mexico. **Road performance:** The 1.6L 4-cylinder engine from the Versa is reasonably lively in this application because the Micra is tiny and light. The conventional 4-speed automatic may appear dated, but durability is superior to the CVT transmission in other small Nissans and it shifts nicely. Handling is responsive, thanks to a well-sorted suspension (the Micra had received a mid-cycle refresh for the European market, which benefited Canadian buyers). Noticeable cabin noise, especially on the highway above 110 km is a given in the Micra's segment. With good suspension travel, the Micra doesn't punish riders much. The car is sensitive to strong crosswinds. Since it's not sold in the

U.S. a major breakdown or collision there could complicate repairs. **Strong points:** The Micra comes only as a five-door hatchback with a split-folding rear bench – the best configuration to maximize utility. The front seats offer plenty of room, in part because the roof is tall and even NBA players could find a comfortable position. Visibility is great all around. **Weak points:** Fuel consumption is acceptable, but higher than most small and even many compact cars. Rear seat legroom is tight. The cabin appears dated, but it looks durable. Misleading advertising; savings are overrated when equipment many buyers want is added to the price. **Major redesign:** 2015. **Best alternatives:** The obvious competitors are the Chevrolet Spark and Mitsubishi Mirage. For a bit more money than a new Micra with options, the Hyundai Accent and Kia Rio offer significantly more refinement and better fuel economy.

Prices and Specs

Prices: *S:* $9,998; *SR:* $15,998 **Freight:** $1,600 **Powertrain (FWD):** Engine: 1.6L 4-cyl. (109 hp); Transmissions: 5-speed manual, 4-speed automatic. **Dimensions:** Passengers: 2/3; Length: 151 in.; Wheelbase: 97 in.; Weight: 2,363 lb. **Fuel economy:** *1.6L:* 8.6L/100 km city, 6.6L/100 km highway. **Assembled in:** Mexico.

SAFETY: The Nissan Micra is not sold in the U.S., so no crash testing has been conducted by the IIHS and NHTSA. The Micra scored four out of five stars in Europe's NCAP crash tests.

RELIABILITY: Predicted reliability is very good. The suspension and rapid front brake wear are possible weak areas. The few Canadian complaints reported online mention engine vibration and squeaky brakes, the latter also common to some other Nissans. Owner comments in the U.K, where the Micra is popular, reveal complaints about short-lived wheel bearings, and some steering column replacements.

VERSA/VERSA NOTE ★★★

RATING: *Sedan:* Below Average (2007-2011), Not Recommended (2012-2014); *Hatchback:* Below Average (2007-2011), Average (2011-2013); *Versa Note:* Above Average (2014-2017). Nissan's nomenclature is confusing.

- The Versa was offered in two body styles, a 4-door sedan and a 5-door hatchback.
- There are two generations of the Versa sedan, but only one Versa hatchback.
- There is only one Versa Note, a hatchback still in production.
- The hatchback and sedan started in the same year, but were renewed or discontinued in different years.

Introduced for 2007, the original Versa was available as a hatchback or a sedan, slotted below the Sentra, which is Nissan's standard bearer in the compact car class. The Versa sedan was redesigned for 2012; it was immediately obvious that Nissan was back to its old cost-cutting ways. The base Versa S was an advertising bait-and-switch, as it wasn't available with an automatic transmission or air conditioning, even optionally. *2014:* Nissan spent a little money to improve the suspension and cabin finish on the sedan, and factory Bluetooth became available on most models. It was a case of too little and too late. The hatchback was redesigned and renamed the Versa Note (a name it already carried in overseas markets). For 2015, the Versa sedan was replaced by the Micra. Air conditioning and Bluetooth became standard on the Versa Note hatchback. The 2016-2017 Versa Note is unchanged. **Road performance:** *2007-2011 sedan and 2007-2012 hatchback:* Adequate power and response, but the engine/transmission combo doesn't feel lively. Soft ride, predictable non-sporty handling. The cabin is surprisingly spacious, with comfortable, well-padded seats, and finished to a level higher than the price of the car. The quietest generation of these cars. The hatchback offers more versatility and outclassed the more expensive Sentra. *2012-2014 Versa sedan:* Cheap interior, sloppy handling, lifeless steering, droning engine. *2014-2017 Versa Note:* Buyers get a stylish exterior and a comfortable interior, though the plastic trim doesn't quite rival the original Versa. Very roomy, with space for four and some standard features that would cost extra on competing models. The 1.8L 4-cylinder engine provides acceptable response but doesn't sparkle. Handling is sharper than on the sedans and old hatchback; tight, power-assisted steering. **Strong points:** The Versa/Versa Note offer a lot more interior room than other subcompact cars. A tall roofline and large front doors contribute to easy entry and exit particularly on the Versa Note. Visibility is good. Low prices on the used car market will stretch your dollar. **Weak points:** *2007-2011 sedan and 2007-2012 hatchback:* Fuel consumption was higher than the contemporary entry-level Toyota Yaris and Honda Fit. *2012-2014 sedan:* Weak points? Where do we begin? *Versa Note:* Unusual relationship between the seat, steering wheel, and pedals. The "sit-up-and-beg" style driving position is best suited to people with short legs. Some people like it, others don't. **Major redesign:** 2007, 2012 sedan, and 2014 hatchback. **Best alternatives:** Hyundai Accent, Kia Rio, Mazda2, and Nissan Sentra. The Honda Fit, another "space" machine in the small car segment, is too expensive to compete directly with the Versa.

Prices and Specs

Prices: *1.6 Note S:* $14,498, *SL:* $19,748 **Freight:** $1,600 **Powertrain (FWD):** Engines: 1.6L 4-cyl. (109 hp), 1.8L 4-cyl. (122 hp); Transmissions: 5-speed manual, 6-speed manual, CVT, 4-speed automatic. **Dimensions:** Passengers: 2/3; Length: 164 in.; Wheelbase: 102 in.; Weight: 2,414 lb. **Fuel economy:** *1.6L CVT:* 7.5L/100 km city, 6.0L/100 km highway. **Assembled in:** Mexico.

ALERT! Early models (2007-2008) experienced some transmission failure; reliability improved on later vehicles. Have the dealer check the fluid at the recommended interval; replace with Nissan fluid to maintain warranty coverage.

RELIABILITY: 2007-2010 models were well below average, improving to average after 2011. Check for light knocking on the 1.8L engine. At this point, the car would be past the Nissan warranty; many aftermarket used car warranties would exclude correction of this issue, arguing that it's "normal wear and tear" on a Versa. A lit engine service light could indicate a defective crank sensor. CVT transmission failures, or performance issues. Long cranking times before

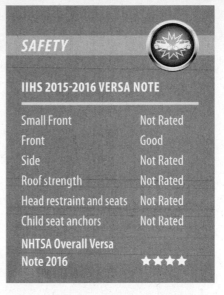

starting may signal a malfunctioning fuel pump. Exhaust system rusts out on 2007-2010 models and Nissan charges a lot to replace it. Defective front suspension coil springs that can corrode and break, puncturing a tire are covered by a recall on 2007-2012 models (Nissan took a L-O-N-G time to fess up to this). Power window regulator failures (check them all), car has to be turned off to unlock the doors; key sticks in the ignition. Water can leak into the cabin and contribute to mediocre defrosting and electrical issues; check the cabin and trunk for humidity, and find the source of the leak or risk issues with the electrical system down the road. Some cars are missing their cabin air filter (a Nissan cost-cutting trick; the filter is "recommended," not mandatory!). Check to see if a filter is present, and replace or install for the first time if necessary.

INTERNAL BULLETINS, SECRET WARRANTIES: You won't believe this, but Nissan service bulletin #EL09-010A, Reference NTB09-019A, issued Aug. 27, 2012, says, "[C]ar's rain sensors (windshield wipers) may operate, intermittently or unexpectedly, when exhaust gas, moisture, fingerprints, dirt, or insects are near or around the rain sensors." Lock on door handle doesn't respond or lock/unlock feature won't respond to "intelligent" key. Seats may not move, or adjust, either backwards or forward, or will have some slight movement from side to side. Repairs needed to fix a rear hatch that won't shut in cold weather. 2007-12—Guidelines for fixing water leaks that wet the floor carpets. 2009-11—Odometer racks up more miles than actually driven due to a faulty computer chip. If warranty repairs were refused due to an inaccurate mileage readout or a leased/rented car incurred extra charges, Nissan says it will offer restitution under its Customer Service Campaign #2508. Fix for a horn that doesn't work when pressed. 2011-12—Troubleshooting a rear hatch that is difficult to close in cold weather. Diagnosing CVT oil leaks. Rear brake squealing. Front axle clicking. Front seat creaking. Key sticking in the ignition, even though vehicle is in Park and shut off. Drivebelt noise troubleshooting tips. Repair tips for a malfunctioning fuel gauge. There's also a voluntary service program (campaign #PM053) involving the free replacement of the instrument panel cluster and a free correction for seatbacks that won't recline. *2012-14*—In hot weather, vehicle will hesitate when accelerating from a stop. Loose fuel cap warning light comes on for no reason. Windshield is fragile and can crack easily. *2015*—A low-speed vibration felt when decelerating can be corrected by recalibrating the transmission control module (TCM).

SENTRA ★★★

RATING: Average. Nissan's bread-and-butter compact trades on its low price, features and financing. *2007:* An all new larger Sentra with class-competitive cabin space and new CVT transmission arrives. *2009:* ABS becomes standard on all models. *2010:* Refreshed exterior and cabin. Electronic Stability Control and traction control standard on 2L SL and 2.5L models. *2013:* Next generation supersized Sentra arrives, with class leading cabin space. Compared to the previous car, Nissan's cost cutting is evident all over. *2016:* Dashboard updated, collision avoidance technology becomes optional on higher trim levels. For 2017, a sportier SR model with a 1.8L turbo joins the lineup. **Road performance:** *2007-2012:* Hooked to a well-calibrated continuously variable transmission (CVT), the Sentra's 2L 4-cylinder accelerates and cruises serenely. The CVT is one of the best of its type, with less of the annoying high-rev buzz during acceleration than most contemporary rivals. The 2.5L 4-cylinder from the Altima provides lots of power. Nicely weighted and geared steering and a well-judged ride-handling balance for a non-sporty sedan. Clear gauges, logical controls and good fit and finish. Comfortable seats and a roomy trunk. Good availability on the used car market at attractive prices. *2013-2015:* One step forward, two steps back, the Sentra is no longer among the contenders in this segment. Interesting styling explores Nissan rounded themes – not for everyone. Acceptable power, but the engine is noisy when you step on the gas. An uninvolving driving experience; the suspension becomes unsettled on bumpy roads. Some road wander; light steering. Flat seats with mediocre padding and cushions that are short for long-legged drivers. Rear seat space rivals intermediate-class cars. Huge trunk. **Strong points:** Used Sentras generally have more features for the price than the comparable Corolla, Civic and Mazda3, and the premium for moving up to a higher trim level is smaller. Roomy interior. Smooth ride. *2013-2017:* Plenty of cabin space; the rear seat cushion can be folded forward, permitting the split rear seatback to fold flat with the floor; the locking glove box could hold a small laptop. A good family car if you're not looking for something dynamic. **Weak points:** No zest. **Major redesign:** 2007 and 2013. **Best alternatives:** Honda Civic, Mazda3 or Hyundai Elantra.

Prices and Specs

Prices: *S:* $15,898, *SL:* $25,998 **Freight:** $1,600 **Powertrain (FWD):** Engine: 1.8L 4-cyl. (130 hp); Transmissions: 6-speed manual, CVT automatic. **Dimensions:** Passengers: 2/3; Length: 182 in.; Wheelbase: 106 in.; Weight: 2,866 lb. **Fuel economy:** *1.8L CVT:* 8.0L/100 km city, 6.1L/100 km highway. **Assembled in:** Mexico and U.S.A.

SAFETY

IIHS 2013-2016

Small Front	2015-2016	Good
	2013-2014	Poor
Front		Good
Side		Good
Roof strength		Good
Head restraint and seats		Good
Child seat anchors		Marginal
NHTSA Overall 2016		★★★★

ALERT! Early models (2007-08) experienced some CVT transmission failures; reliability improved on later vehicles. Have the dealer check the fluid and replace it with Nissan fluid at the recommended interval to maintain warranty coverage.

Owner-reported safety-related failures: Airbags failed to deploy; gas pedal is mounted too close to the brake pedal; defective computer module causes the vehicle to shut down; car can be started without driver's foot on the brake; the windshield pillar obstructs the driver's view. Premature wearout of rear tires due to factory suspension misalignment; sudden brake loss; and brakes are hard to modulate, resulting in abrupt stops; and power-steering failures.

RELIABILITY: *All years:* Noisy brakes; seized calipers are common, have them serviced annually. Vibration when braking. *2007-2012 generation:* "Piston slap" when starting a cold engine is not uncommon up to the 2011 model year; it's a precursor to high oil consumption starting after 100,000 km. Head gaskets can leak. Noisy accessory drive belt tensioner (as early as 50,000 km). *2007-2015:* Other reported failures: Oil-pressure sensor can leak; unstable front seats; driver's sun visor obstructs the rearview mirror; bottom of the windshield may be distorted. *2013-2015:* Fuel, climate, electrical, and audio systems, in addition to assembly deficiencies (a misaligned trunk lid and malfunctioning trunk locks, for example) that contribute to rattles and water leaks into the interior. SE-R and Spec-V models wear out their suspensions more quickly; check ball joints (worn) and springs (broken); a knocking sound when going over bumps can indicate a strut with a worn top plate.

INTERNAL BULLETINS, SECRET WARRANTIES: 2007-12—Reduced speed due to the CVT transmission over-ride. Troubleshooting an oil leak from the upper end of the oil cooler. Front seats may have a slight movement, or won't adjust. 2011-12—Correcting instrument cluster that may be too dim. 2013-14—If the engine RPM intermittently drops very low while stopped (idling) or the engine stops running while coming to a stop, diagnosis and repair costs may be covered by Nissan under Campaign ID P3212/NTB13-022. Another bulletin gives repair tips when the engine overheats, the AC doesn't cool, and the radiator fan is inoperative. A clunking, popping, or bumping when the steering wheel is turned may require a spacer in the front strut assembly. 2014—A low-speed vibration felt when decelerating can be corrected by recalibrating the transmission control module (TCM).

ENGINE – OIL LEAK FROM UPPER END OF OIL COOLER

CLASSIFICATION: EM10-002A — DATE: SEPTEMBER 6, 2011

ALTIMA SEDAN AND COUPE, SENTRA, AND ROGUE WITH FOUR-CYLINDER ENGINE OIL LEAK

2007-12 Altima Sedan; 2008-12 Altima Coupe; 2007-12 Sentra; and the 2008-12 Rogue.

IF YOU CONFIRM: Oil is leaking from the upper end of the engine oil cooler.
ACTION: Reseal the oil cooler.

CUBE ★★★

RATING: Average (2009-13). What would Dr. Seuss and SpongeBob SquarePants drive? Most likely the Nissan Cube. This five-passenger front-wheel drive compact is a competent, though odd-looking, small car. The Cube has extraordinary interior volume for its small footprint, but it looks strange. Originally targeted at young hipsters, the surprising outcome is that older drivers like the Cube for its ease of entry and egress. The Kia Soul, another reasonably-priced "out there" vehicle was embraced by the market, while the Cube was largely ignored and it was discontinued at the end of 2013. Its virtues may one day be rediscovered in the used car market; that happened to the Honda Element, another box on wheels that lost the favour of new car buyers, but has become a sought-after used vehicle. **Road performance:** The Sentra's 1.8L 4-cylinder engine provides leisurely acceleration. Clearly, the Cube was built for comfort, not speed, as the ride is creamy smooth for such a short car due in part to the long suspension travel. Body roll in the corners is pronounced. The CVT transmission is tuned to work seamlessly with the small engine. The manual transmission gearshift works well. Unfortunately, the car is geared low to extract the best possible performance from the engine, which means highway noise is prominent. Whimsical touches abound in the interior; the headliner features concentric ripples emanating from the dome light moulded into it, like the ripples in a pond. **Strong points:** The Cube delights with its roomy, otherworldly interior, great visibility and excellent maneuverability. It's easy to get in and out of, which is a boon for mobility-impaired drivers and passengers. **Weak points:** Power-challenged engine and mediocre fuel economy compared with other small cars. The upright windshield and square body generate lots of wind noise. Sensitive to crosswinds. Annoying cabin reflections off the vertical side glass at night; you can literally read the gauges in the side windows (in mirror image). **Major redesign:** 2009. **Best alternatives:** Kia Soul, Honda Element, Scion Xb.

Prices and Specs

Price (used): $11,000-13,000 (2013); $6,000-8,000 (2009) **Freight:** N/A. **Powertrain (FWD):** Engine: 1.8L 4-cyl. (122 hp); Transmissions: 6-speed manual, CVT automatic. **Dimensions:** Passengers: 2/3; Length: 157 in.; Wheelbase: 100 in.; Weight: 2,846 lb. **Fuel economy:** 7.5L/100 km city, 6.3L/100 km highway. **Assembled in:** Japan.

ALERT! Vehicles built until early 2010 are covered by a 10 year warranty on the CVT automatic. Have the dealer check the fluid and replace it with Nissan fluid at the recommended interval so Nissan doesn't deny coverage if you have trouble later on.

RELIABILITY: Limited data due to the small number sold. Reliability should be similar to the Versa, as the 1.8L engine and transmission are shared. Problems recorded in small numbers include squeaky brakes, faulty rear-wheel alignment, interior ventilation fan quits, and broken door handles.

SAFETY	
IIHS 2009-2014	
Small Front	Not rated
Front	Good
Side	Good
Roof strength	Good
Head restraint and seats	Good
Child seat anchors	Not Rated
NHTSA Overall	**Not Rated**

RATING: Average (2011-2017). This funky-looking small crossover makes no attempt to blend into the crowd. The five-door Juke crossover was designed by Nissan's U.K. studio – and immediately became a hit with European and Japanese buyers. That it even came here for 2011 might have something to do with the success of the Kia Soul. Like the Soul, the Juke targets young consumers who want a nice-performing car with a unique look. The Juke uses a peppy direct-injection, turbo-charged 188 hp, 1.6L 4-cylinder engine coupled to a 6-speed manual or an optional CVT automatic transmission. **Road performance:** The Juke feels agile, even tossable, thanks to a well-sorted chassis. The steering is light and communicative. All-wheel drive models are especially fun to drive due to the torque-vectoring system that assigns the correct amount of power to each rear wheel. Firm ride; rough pavement taken at speed upsets the chassis, revealing the car's econobox roots. **Strong points:** Good acceleration; agile, with steering that is quick and sensitive; decent seating in front and back; a well-appointed interior. **Weak points:** The Juke is decidedly small: the sloped roof cuts into rear headroom significantly and three adults in the rear seats will become very close friends. The split-folding bench expands the meagre cargo hold somewhat. The published fuel consumption ratings are fanciful; some owners report barely exceeding 9.5 L/100 km (30 mpg) on the highway using the recommended premium fuel. Turbo engines – especially small ones – sip gas only when the lightest of throttles is applied. There's also a lot of cabin noise. **Major redesign:** 2011. **Best alternatives:** Mazda CX-3, Honda HR-V and Chevrolet Trax – but none of these offer the zip of the Juke.

RELIABILITY: The timing chain may wear prematurely and break without warning, destroying the engine. Nissan is replacing the chains on 2011-2013 models. Engines that become noticeably noisier may be exhibiting a loose or worn chain and should be brought in for inspection. The turbocharged engine needs a diet of synthetic oil. Juke owners have reported failed turbochargers (bearings shot). Other reported issues, in small numbers, include some no-start conditions, prematurely rusted exhaust systems and a few manual gearboxes that broke. A recall addresses the fuel pressure sensor on the engine's fuel delivery rail, which may not have been sufficiently tightened at the factory, leading to a fuel leak.

SAFETY	
IIHS 2011-2016	
Small Front	Poor
Front	Good
Side	Good
Roof strength	Good
Head restraint and seats	Good
Child seat anchors	Acceptable
NHTSA Overall 2016	★★★★

LEAF ★★★

RATING: Acceptable. The world's bestselling all-electric car was part of Nissan CEO Carlos Ghosn's great gamble. After Nissan spent billions to develop and market the Leaf, Tesla stole the show with the model S electric supercar. Suddenly, the Leaf and all the other electric vehicles seemed old. *Lemon-Aid* believes we are on the verge of another EV or plug-in hybrid breakthrough, which accounts for the lowered Acceptable rating on the Leaf. It's virtually guaranteed that a new 2017 Leaf will be dated within your first couple of years of ownership. The Leaf's front-wheel drive platform is a clean-sheet design, required to accommodate the 24 kWh lithium-ion battery pack arranged on the floor and under the seats for a low centre of gravity. A conventional 12-volt battery lives under the hood, which powers the computers and accessories, such as the audio system, LED headlights, windshield wipers and airbags. The tall greenhouse makes for an airy interior about the size of a Toyota Prius with comfortable seats. The futuristic design features digital displays and a gear selector modeled after a computer mouse. Informative graphics coach the driver to use the available energy wisely and monitor the range.

For 2013, production moved from Japan to the U.S. and a new base model was introduced to combat price sensitivity with buyers. *2014:* The high line SL gets leather seating, a backup camera and improved audio. *2015:* Hands-free voice activation on SV and SL. *2016:* SV and SL receive a higher capacity 30 kWh battery and every model features a quick-charge port. **Road performance:** The quiet-running 107 hp electric motor provides good acceleration in city traffic. Although it leans in the corners, the softly sprung suspension is good for city streets. The brakes have frequently been described as "grabby," though there's a software upgrade (what else?) to address that. Depending on the model, the Leaf is advertised as being able to travel up to 160 kilometres without stopping to recharge. However, "Battery capacity decreases with time and use. Actual range will vary depending upon driving/charging habits, speed, conditions, weather, temperature, and battery age." The APA discovered that the range drops significantly in winter, and if speed increases above 105 km/h. **Strong points:** The Leaf feels swift because of the electric motor's instant torque, making quick sprints to 60 km/h, before the motor starts to run out of whiz. The ride is comfortable, with spacious seating front and back. The Leaf is cheap to run. Its estimated energy cost to run is only 2.2 cents per kilometre, partly because EV users don't pay the road taxes built into the price of gasoline. Driving an electric car brings other benefits, including free charging at some retailers and college campuses, and access to highway commuter lanes. Sales have been high enough for dealers and fleets to develop some expertise in their maintenance and repair. **Weak points:** Light steering, excessive lean when cornering. Long charging times; allow eight hours on a 220-volt circuit (the same one your clothes dryer uses). Double that if you're limited to a standard 110-volt outlet. **Major redesign:** 2011. **Best alternatives:** A new or used Volt plug-in hybrid offers more versatility. Among EVs, a new Kia Soul EV or Chevrolet Bolt. Short of a Tesla model S, the Leaf is the safest bet in a used EV on the market.

Prices and Specs

Prices: *S:* $32,698; *SL:* $40,548. Note: There are provincial incentives that kick back $8,000-12,000 to new-car buyers. **Freight:** $1,990 **Powertrain (FWD):** Engine: AC electric motor (107 hp); Transmission: Single-speed reduction gear. **Dimensions:** Passengers: 2/3; Length: 175 in.; Wheelbase: 106 in.; Weight: 3,347 lb. **Fuel economy:** N/A. **Assembled in:** Japan.

RELIABILITY: Maintenance is almost non-existent: There are no oil changes and other fluids to worry about. With no transmission, emissions controls, gasoline delivery system, and other old-school technology, the Leaf's reliability has been exemplary. A common concern among owners, understandably, is battery life. The pack is warrantied for eight years or 160,000 km, but it isn't covered for gradual capacity loss, which inevitably occurs. Nissan took its time admitting that the quick-charge feature on the Leaf really shouldn't be used (until the arrival of the latest model). If you're buying used, ask the seller to show you the charging history, which should provide a good idea of current battery life. As the lithium-ion battery pack ages, the range erodes to half of what it was when new. A new pack is projected to be required somewhere between 120,000 and 160,000 km. Nissan currently charges $6,500. If you're buying a new Leaf, the aftermarket will have developed cheaper solutions by the time the battery needs replacing. Repair issues reported include malfunctioning power windows, worn struts, leaky A/C lines, "grabby" brakes and, (ironically) short-lived 12-volt batteries.

SAFETY

IIHS 2011-2016

Small Front	2013-2016	Poor
	2011-2012	Not Tested
Front		Good
Side		Good
Roof strength		Good
Head restraint and seats		Not Rated
Child seat anchors		Marginal
NHTSA Overall Nissan Leaf 2016		★★★★

ALTIMA ★★★

RATING: Below Average (2005-2006); Above Average (2007-2012); Below Average (2013-2014); Above Average (2015-2017). The Altima is a nicely styled, roomy sedan that has the performance features that drivers and techno-philes want. The car's base 4-cylinder engine is more powerful than the competition's, and the optional 270 hp 3.5L V6 has few equals among cars at this price and market segment. When you consider that the Altima is also lighter than most of its competitors, it's obvious why this car produces spirited acceleration with best-in-class fuel economy. (The

CVT transmission helps.) What the car lacks, however, is consistent year-over-year quality and reliability. This conclusion contradicts J. D. Power and *Consumer Reports'* high ratings for the model, but accurately reflects owner complaints and Nissan internal service bulletins obtained by *Lemon-Aid.* The CVT transmission in the 2013 and newer models is performing poorly. The best-made vehicles can generate up to 50 NHTSA-registered owner complaints per model year. Yet, the reported safety-related incidents for the 2013 Altima was 718 complaints and counting! The model history follows. *2007:* Fourth-generation Altima introduced, with an elegant cabin. It features a CVT automatic for the first time. The 4-cylinder and V6 engines are retained. *2008:* Altima coupe and hybrid introduced. *2010:* ESC becomes standard on all models. Minor updates inside and out. *2012:* The slow-selling hybrid is dropped. *2013:* All-new fifth-generation car; Nissan cost cutting affects engineering, cabin finish, suspension. The old coupe continues for one more year, offered exclusively with the 2.5L 4-cylinder. *2014:* Updated infotainment and backup camera on most models. *2015:* Changes to V6 lower fuel consumption. *2016:* Nissan puts some quality back in the car; chassis upgrades, better sound insulation. **Road performance:** *2013-2017:* The 4-cylinder engine delivers good performance and best-in-class fuel economy. The V6 provides scintillating acceleration with higher fuel consumption. The car drones at some speeds because of the CVT transmission programming. Handling is only so-so, and the car can wander, requiring frequent steering corrections on the highway (much better after 2015). Ride comfort is best with the soft-sprung 2.5 S; the 3.5 SE V6 is equipped with a firmer suspension and wider tires. **Strong points:** Low fuel consumption, good highway cruiser, well-priced as a used car. Distinctive coupe body provides exclusivity with the running costs and repairability of the sedan. **Weak points:** Quality control declined after 2013, and interior finish is not as elegant. Limited sales of the Hybrid; finding parts and service could be tricky. **Major redesign:** 2007, 2008 hybrid and coupe, and 2013. **Best alternatives:** New: Honda Accord, Toyota Camry Used: Hyundai Sonata, Mazda6 and Chevrolet Malibu.

Prices and Specs

Prices: *2.5:* $23,998, *3.5 SL:* $35,498 **Freight:** $1,750 **Powertrain (FWD):** Engines: 2.5L 4-cyl. (182 hp), 3.5L V6 (270 hp); Transmissions: CVT automatic. **Dimensions:** Passengers: 2/3; Length: 192 in.; Wheelbase: 109 in.; Weight: 3,177 lb. **Fuel economy:** *2.5L:* 8.7L/100 km city, 6.0L/100 km highway; *3.5L V6:* 10.3L/100 km city, 7.4L/100 km highway. **Assembled in:** U.S.A.

Owner-reported safety-related failures: The CVT automatic transmission, supplied by Nissan's Jatco division, was re-engineered to cut friction and boost fuel efficiency in the redesigned 2013 models – and possibly sacrificed performance and durability in the process. "The CVT transmission shudders and shakes and (the car) dies at low speeds or when put into Park. I've talked to others that have replaced them two or three times," reads one post online. Post-warranty, replacement transmissions are more than $4,000 apiece. There are hundreds of complaints logged on the NHTSA website regarding failed CVT transmissions. Keyless ignition allows car to be left with the engine running; there is no automatic shut-off:

> I went back and opened the garage door. A rush of hot air hit me in the face. To my horror, I realized that I did not shut the car off. Garage temperature had to be about 120 degrees. Who knows what could have happened, had the car run all night … I'm just thankful that my garage was detached. Carbon monoxide deaths via keyless ignition are easily avoidable.

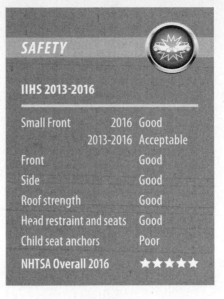
Defective fuel-pump fuse makes it impossible to shut off the engine; vehicle may jerk when accelerating; shifts into Neutral, without warning; abrupt downshifts; premature clutch failure; car "drifts" constantly; while cruising, or suddenly veers to the right as the steering freezes; loss of power steering; loss of brakes; headlights don't cast a wide enough beam. And the ignition key may inadvertently start the car:

> If you leave the key outside the vehicle and it is touching the vehicle, the push-button ignition will acknowledge the key and start the vehicle. According to the manual the key must be with you (inside) in order for the vehicle to start. There is no warning stating otherwise.

BRAKE MASTER CYLINDER

BULLETIN NO.: NTB12-001A   DATE: APRIL 3, 2012

VOLUNTARY SERVICE CAMPAIGN
2007–12 Altima Sedan & Coupe Brake Master Cylinder

INTRODUCTION: Nissan is conducting a Voluntary Service Campaign on Model Year 2007–12 Nissan Altima Sedan and Coupe vehicles to inspect the brake systems in vehicles with an illuminated brake warning lamp. If no leak is present, the reservoir will be topped off. If a leak in the brake master cylinder is identified, the brake master cylinder will be replaced for free.

ALERT! In your test drive of an Altima, check out these four design deficiencies reported by other owners to NHTSA:

1. **Painful front head restraints:**

   The contact owns a 2013 Nissan Altima. The contact stated that the headrest caused the contact back pain, headaches and numbness in the arm. The contact took the vehicle back to the dealer where the dealer turned the headrest around. The contact stated that after the headrest was turned, there was no more pain.

2. **A crooked driver's seat:**

   The driver's seat is crooked – both across the back and across the seat. This means one's shoulders and torso are twisted and facing the center console, not the steering wheel. Hips are uneven with the right side significantly lower than the left. This is a very uncomfortable and painful position to be in. I have been informed by the dealership that all 2012 Altimas are like this and therefore it is not a warranty item! I have been able to determine the back of the seat is in fact crooked in the more than two dozen examples.

3. **Brake and gas pedals are mounted too close together:**

   My husband complained of this a few weeks ago when he drove my car because his shoe got caught on the brake pedal as he was lifting his foot off the gas pedal. Then, yesterday, the same thing happened to me. I nearly drove my car through the front of the daycare where I was dropping off my son.

4. **Blind spot warning feature gives false alerts:**

   When it was raining or the roads were wet, the BSW would give false alarms that a car was next to me. I was handed a bulletin that shows the issue. I was told by the dealer to contact Nissan customer support for resolution. I just heard back from them on 12/30/14 and their response was that it was working as designed. How can a safety feature that is part of a $1000 package be designed to give false alarms when the roads are wet?

RELIABILITY: *2007-2012:* Reliability improved over the previous-generation car and is Average to Better than Average. The most expensive repair risk is a CVT transmission failure. Nissan extended the warranty out to ten years (see Nissan introduction, under Nissan Doubles CVT Warranty) on cars manufactured until early in the 2010 model year. Transmission hesitation may be resolved with a software update at the dealership. A lit Check Engine warning could signal one or more defective oxygen sensors in the emissions system, or a catalytic converter that is on the way out. A lit ABS warning likely indicates a defect at one of the rear wheel sensors. Check the disc brakes on all four wheels for binding calipers; Altimas from this generation often have one or more seized brake calipers. Service the calipers at least annually to postpone expensive brake repairs. *2013-2017:* Quality control nosedived on the 2013-2014 models. The passenger-side airbag can be disabled even though the seat is occupied. Other issues include faulty back-up camera displays, leaky sunroofs, squealing brakes and whining power-steering:

Power steering was very noisy at all times. Like a high-pitched dentist's drill that only gets worse when wheel is turned. Not sure how long electric power steering system will last. After three weeks, dealer agreed to accept car back and swap it for another one.

Windshields can crack spontaneously. Owners have parked their cars overnight in a locked garage, only to discover a large crack spreading across the windshield in the morning. Insurance often pays the tab, when in fact it should be a warranty claim. Some AC, electrical, and fuel system failures; sulfur odour can invade the cabin intermittently. *All years:* Rust perforation in the driver and passenger-side floor is an old Altima problem:

I lifted the carpet and noticed a hole on the passenger side floorboard. The hole is as big as my foot. Just yesterday my wife was seated there and felt the floor soft. I went over to the driver's side and noticed that the floor is so rusty that I could put my foot right through.

To reduce the risk of damage to the floor, the APA recommends large deluxe winter style rubber mats, and checking the carpet periodically and drying it out when necessary. The APA recommends aftermarket rustproofing to protect the rust-prone undercarriage. Barry's Rustproofing is the only shop the Association knows that will apply rustproofing to the inside of the floor, underneath the carpet and insulation (contact information is in the Part Four Introduction).

INTERNAL BULLETINS, SECRET WARRANTIES: 2007-12—Front seats bind, won't move fore or aft. Inoperative driver power seat lumbar support. 2008-12—Buzzing wind noise from the A-pillar/mirror area. 2008-13—Oil cooler leakage. 2009—Nissan set up a special Campaign (#PCO 44) to prevent the front windshield wipers from scraping the windshield. Parts and labour are Nissan's responsibility. Another Campaign (#PC005) provides free replacement of the rear suspension knuckle. 2011-12—Oil may leak from the upper end of the engine oil cooler (see the Sentra profile). Steering/suspension drift. Sunroof water leak. Rear end clunking. Knocking on turns. Brake master cylinder may slowly leak fluid. If the ignition push button doesn't respond, the body control module (BCM) may need recalibrating. 2013—Shuddering at moderate speeds could indicate problems with the transmission torque converter in certain Altimas and Pathfinders. TSB #13-064A issued on June 13, 2013, says the shaking in 2013 V6-equipped models could be a sign that the torque converter is defective and needs to be replaced. The bulletin only covers a shudder occurring at 18-35 mph. 2013-14—Light acceleration shuddering with V6-equipped Altimas and Pathfinders may be corrected by recalibrating the transmission control module. 2013-15—Excessive right rear brake pad wear is covered by TSB #BR15-001 and NTB15-047. 2015—Under a voluntary service campaign (PC346), Nissan will pay for the replacement of the transmission torque converter on Altimas equipped with a 4-cylinder engine.

VOLUNTARY SERVICE CAMPAIGN REAR SUSPENSION REPLACEMENT/BUSHING REPLACEMENT AND SEALING

On some model year 2002–05 Nissan Altima and 2004–05 Nissan Maxima vehicles, there is a possibility that corrosion of the rear sub-frame may occur. Corrosion is most likely in cold climates where heavy salting of roads is common practice in freezing conditions.... In severe cases, cracking of the rear sub-frame may occur, which may result in a knocking noise coming from the rear of the vehicle.... On most vehicles, Nissan will replace the rear sub-frame assembly. On some 2005 Model Year vehicles, where sub-frame replacement is not necessary, Nissan will replace and seal the front bushings and seal the rear bushings.

WARRANTY EXTENSION: To ensure the highest levels of customer satisfaction, Nissan is also extending the warranty for cracking of the rear sub-frame due to corrosion to a total of 13 years with unlimited mileage on all model year 2002–05 Nissan Altima and 2004–05 Nissan Maxima vehicles. Vehicles included in the Service Campaign (as described above) are also covered by the Warranty Extension.

MAXIMA ★★★★

RATING: Average to Above Average. Except for a couple of early model years, Nissan's redesigns of the Maxima didn't produce more than a handful of complaints. Could it be that Nissan has finally shaken the poor-quality Quest and Altima monkeys off its back? Not really. In fact, one month after the 2016 Maxima's debut, Nissan issued a rarely used "stop-sale" order to fix some quality problems. In 2004, a new clean-lined Maxima based on the same platform that underpinned the 2002-2006 Altima, debuted. It was assembled in the U.S for the first time. The car continued to stress performance, with a strong engine and firm ride for a luxury sedan. The Maxima was significantly updated for 2007, with refinements to the 3.5L V6 and a CVT for the first time. The redesigned 2009 Maxima, once again arriving a couple of years behind a new Altima platform, projects a bulky, multi-surfaced exterior. Cabin design has avant-garde touches with good room front and rear; class standards for the interior had eclipsed the Maxima by the time this generation went out of production. The Sport and Premium option groups feature rear bucket seats that can't be folded forward to enhance trunk space. For 2016, the redesigned front-wheel drive carries an upgraded 300 hp 3.5L V6 (a 10 hp gain) that is still coupled to the problematic CVT automatic transmission. The car is a little longer (by 2.2 inches) and 1.3 inches lower. You get plenty of horsepower, comfort, and gadgets, but less refinement than some competitors. **Road performance:** As always, the powerful V6 engine provides impressive acceleration, and performance of this year's CVT is slightly improved. Handling is also better. Steering takes some getting used to: It's overboosted at low speeds and then suddenly firms up. The 18-inch original equipment tires are noisy. **Strong points:** *All years:* Brawny engine with lots of power and a gruff exhaust note. Decent gas mileage for the level of performance. Flamboyant cabin design. User-friendly controls and instrumentation are easier to master than European brands.Well-priced new and used. **Weak points:** Fairly noisy, engine and road/tire noise are audible. Torque steer (the steering wheel will pull to one or both sides coming out of a corner) that is typical for a powerful front-wheel drive car when you press hard on the gas. Artificial power steering assist. Tall occupants may find rear seating a bit cramped. **Major redesign:** 2004, 2009 and 2016. **Best alternatives:** Acura TL, TLX, BMW 3 Series, Honda Accord V6, Nissan G35/G37, or a Toyota Camry SE V6.

Prices and Specs

Price (Negotiable): *S:* $34,400, *Platinum:* $43,900 **Freight:** $1,750 **Powertrain (FWD):** Engine: 3.5L V6 (300 hp); Transmission: CVT automatic. **Dimensions:** Passengers: 2/3; Length: 193 in.; Wheelbase: 109 in.; Weight: 3,471 lb. **Fuel economy:** *3.5L V6:* 11.1L/100 km city, 7.8L/100 km highway. **Assembled in:** Tennessee, U.S.A.

ALERT! Vehicles from model years 2007 until early 2010 are covered by a 10 year warranty on the CVT automatic. Have the dealer check the fluid and replace it at the recommended interval so Nissan doesn't deny coverage if you have trouble later on.

Owner-reported safety-related failures: Front airbags failed to deploy or the passenger-side airbag is disabled when the seat is occupied:

> The passenger side airbag does not activate with my wife in the seat. She is well over the 80 pound limit for activation. Seat was changed but did not change. Dealer service department says there is no fix.

SAFETY		
IIHS 2009-2016		
Small Front	2016	Good
	2009-2014	Acceptable
Front		Good
Side		Good
Roof strength		Good
Head restraint and seats		Good
Child seat anchors		Acceptable
NHTSA Overall 2017		★★★★★

This problem represents the majority of owner complaints affecting Nissan's entire lineup over the past 5 years. C'mon Nissan, replace those sensors, as other automakers have done when faced with the same problem. *Other negatives:* Sometimes, the Maxima won't shift into Drive; the CVT automatic transmission can be truculent and may require replacing. Engine surges when brakes are applied; drivers must constantly fight the steering wheel to keep from veering to the left or right; car would not shift out of First as the Check Engine warning light came on; electrical problems knock out the interior lights, door locks, and other controls; headlights may provide insufficient illumination; head restraints obstruct rear visibility, particularly when backing up; and the adjustable steering wheel may stick in its highest position.

RELIABILITY: Reliability has been less uneven than the Altima's, likely because Nissan gets a couple of extra years' experience with a new platform before it migrates up to the Maxima. The Maxima has similar issues with the brake calipers and ABS warning light signaling a defective rear wheel sensor. Some of the same quality control issues reappear over several years: Malfunctioning sunroofs; engine knocking from the front crankshaft bearing; the passenger-side airbag that's disabled when an average-sized occupant is seated; power steering failures; and driver seats that wobble, or won't move fore or aft. The SkyView roof can shatter spontaneously. Heated seats can leave occupants cold. Check for coolant leaks (a little pipe on the right side of the engine block). If the rear suspension is noisy, lubricating the bushings could slow down the need for replacements, which is expensive. Check all the fan speeds to make sure they are working.

INTERNAL BULLETINS, SECRET WARRANTIES: 2000-06—Oil leaks from oil-cooler oil seal. 2002-06—How to silence an engine ticking noise. 2004-05—Exhaust rattle/buzz when accelerating. Voluntary service campaign entails the free replacement of the rear suspension and bushing sealing for 13 years. If the subframe is too corroded, Nissan will buy back the car. 2004-06—Erratic fuel gauge, AC operation. Front power-seat malfunction. Hard-to-move shifter. 2004-07—ABS activates when it shouldn't. Noisy driver's power seat. 2004-08—Tire-pressure-monitor sensor may leak fluid. Inoperative power-door mirrors. Heat shield rattles. 2007-08—Front suspension rattling. Inoperative lumbar support. 2007-09—If the vehicle has low power accelerating to 80 km/h, the likely cause is a defective wheel speed sensor. Sunroof is inoperative or operates erratically. 2007—A loose fuel filler cap may be the cause of emissions alert. 2007-12—Loss of power between 0-70 km/h. 2009—Sunroof glass chatter, creaking, or popping. Sunroof wind noise. Power window "Up" and steering column adjustment may both be inoperative. Loose headliner. Front passenger seat shakes at highway speeds. Voluntary Service Campaign #PC005 to replace the steering knuckle for free. 2009-10—Transmission "booming" countermeasures. Front power seats won't move. Driver's seat is wobbly. Can't turn ignition to the On position. Fuel gauge issues. 2009-11—Silencing a rear-end squeak or clunk heard when passing over bumps. 2009-13—Steering wheel switch may need replacing. 2010—Slower than normal acceleration. Lock/Unlock button on outside handle doesn't respond. 2009-14—Number one crankshaft bearing noise. Rain sensor may activate intermittently. 2011-12—If the ignition push button doesn't respond, the body control module (BCM) may need recalibrating. Steering pull/drift; door panel looks faded, discoloured. Rear-end squeak, clunk when driving over bumps. Driver's seat bottom shifts or rocks slightly.

350Z/370Z   ★★★★★

RATING: Recommended. Nissan does have a pair of genuine sports cars that are worth considering. The V6-powered 370Z is available as a two-door coupe or as a roadster (convertible), seating just two people. Is either model worth the price? Yes. Both are speedy and attractive alternatives to the Chevrolet Corvette, which costs much more. The fifth-generation 350Z, released in mid-2002, was a bold re-imagining of the original "Z" car at a lower price than the 300ZX it replaced. It made use of Nissan's rear-drive FM platform, or "front midship," which situated the engine behind the front wheel centre line to enhance weight distribution and balance. Some 20 cm was excised from the FM's wheelbase to make the Z-car more agile. The sophisticated independent suspension used multilink components all around, forged in aluminum to pare unsprung weight. Ride height was set lower than in other FM applications, with more negative camber dialed in. The 350Z was replaced by the 370Z in 2009. Almost every component of the 370Z has been redesigned, with a further wheelbase reduction of 4 inches (100 mm) to enhance handling. Weight was reduced with the use of a front aluminum subframe, aluminum-alloy engine cradle, and aluminum door panels, hood and hatch. For 2016 Nissan introduced a decontented base model at a ludicrously low starting price just under $30,000 (actually more like $32,000 with the "upcharge" for freight and delivery). If that car has the features and focus you are looking for it's an exceptional opportunity. **Road performance:** Brutal acceleration and soundtrack. The VQ-series V6 engine does exhibit some coarseness, inherent to its design – it's in keeping with the character of the car. The chassis is rigid and balanced, permitting the Z-car to carve and brake with poise. The ride is fairly stiff in keeping with the character of the car, and grip is tenacious. **Strong points:** The 350Z and 370Z offer drivers an intoxicating mixture of wicked power, a well-sorted chassis and avant-garde styling for their money. The Z is also unusually reliable and unfussy about maintenance for a car with so much performance. Nissan fortunately chose a conventional automatic transmission (a 6-speed manual transmission is standard). A 370Z Coupe will accelerate to 60 mph in under 5 seconds. **Weak points:** H-E-A-V-Y clutch on the manual transmission 370Z tested by the APA could be a dealbreaker; consider the automatic. Very poor visibility to the rear. Cargo space is in short supply; the hatchback design incorporates a cross brace in the 350Z that forces owners to use soft luggage, such as gym bags. The 370Z dispenses with the brace on most models (it is below the floor), but the shallow cavity still doesn't accept much luggage. Four winter tires or a beater for winter are mandatory. **Major redesign:** 2003, 2009. **Best alternatives:** Chevrolet Corvette, Hyundai Genesis Coupe, Porsche Cayman or Boxster, BMW Z4 (used), Ford Mustang GT.

Prices and Specs

Prices: *Coupe:* $29,998, *Roadster Touring Sport:* $54,998 **Freight:** $1,750 **Powertrain (Rear-drive):** Engine: 3.7L V6 (332 hp); Transmission: 6-speed manual, 7-speed automatic. **Dimensions:** Passengers: 2; Length: 168 in.; Wheelbase: 100 in.; Weight: 3,343 lb. **Fuel economy:** 13.3L/100 km city, 9.3L/100 km highway. **Assembled in:** Japan.

SAFETY: Not crash tested by the IIHS and NHTSA.

RELIABILITY: *350Z:* Owners of early models have complained about short-lived front tires that feather and cup, indicating a problem with camber and toe alignment. Dealers can correct toe-out during alignments, but the problem can persist if the adjustment is done incorrectly. Owners of 6-speed manual cars with the special 300 hp engine (2006) have reported excessive oil consumption; some engines were replaced. Other deficiencies include bad clutch slave cylinders (a recall item), faulty window regulators, noisy brake pads, short-lived wheel bearings and batteries, and sundry rattles. *370Z:* Steering lock unit notorious for failing, preventing car from starting. Owners reported mechanical issues involving a seized steering column, and starting issues – both likely due to a steering-lock solenoid failure. Towing to dealer is often required. There was a recall on the same part for 2009 GT-R models – yet there is no recall for 370Z models that use the same defective part. In manual transmission cars, clutch pedal can suddenly go limp, affecting driveability. Problem can be traced to leaking master cylinder or slave cylinder – a longstanding Z-car issue that goes back some 15 years.

ROGUE

RATING: Above Average (2008-2009). Recommended (2010-2016). Nissan's compact SUV crossover is loosely based on the Sentra platform and provides car-like handling and good fuel economy. It's currently the strongest product in Nissan's lineup, accounting for more than a third of the sales at some dealerships. Power comes from Nissan's familiar 2.5L 4-cylinder driving the wheels (front or all four) via a continuously variable transmission (CVT). The 2008 Rogue replaced the X-Trail in Canada and provided Nissan a conventional car-based compact cross-over to sell in the United States. For 2011, a mid-cycle update included minor exterior changes and standard Bluetooth. In 2012 a new "Sport mode" switch changes engine/transmission mapping for more engaging performance; an all-round monitoring system became standard on the SL. The 2014 second-generation Rogue is built on a platform from Nissan partner Renault; 3-row seating became optional for the first time. The Rogue largely avoided the overt cost-cutting that compromised some other Nissan products over the last decade. **Road performance:** *2008-2013:* The Rogue delivers a pleasing blend of performance and fuel economy, ride comfort and handling precision, and passenger room within a tidy exterior envelope. *2014-2017:* Cabin size grew and the interior finish is more elegant with nicer materials. **Strong points:** Well-crafted interior, comfortable front seating and impressive braking. CVT delivers on its promise of reasonable fuel consumption, too. *2008-2013:* Good supply of used models on the market at prices that are significantly lower than the CR-V and RAV4; better selection of well-equipped models. **Weak points:** Engine sounds like a diesel when accelerating at some speeds. *2008-2013:* Cargo space is reduced by the sloping hatch, and rearward visibility is impaired. **Major redesign:** 2008 and 2014. The 2017 is due for a mid-cycle refresh that should be revealed very early in the new year. **Best alternatives:** Honda CR-V, Toyota RAV4, Mazda CX-5, GMC Terrain and Chevrolet Equinox.

(see Nissan introduction, under Nissan Doubles CVT Warranty). *2008-2013:* Check the timing cover at the front of the engine (leak), rear struts (wet, noisy), front struts (knocking, defective top plate), and ball joints and tie rod ends (wear). Fragile door release handles; pull on them C-A-R-E-FULLY in cold weather and have the mechanism lubricated if possible. Check all fan speeds; a dying blower will pull excess current and burn the speeds out progressively. Parts for this repair cost $400. A refrigerant leak in the air conditioning may involve only sealing a connection; check before replacing the compressor. Lower ball joints are now available in the aftermarket for about $90 so it's no longer necessary to replace the entire suspension control arm assembly. A lit Check Engine warning may indicate a fault in the EVAP emissions system; the repair costs about $200. *2014-2017:* The launch was more successful than the Altima's from the previous year. Incomplete data. Some climate control complaints taken care of under warranty.

 INTERNAL BULLETINS, SECRET WARRANTIES: 2007-12—A leak from the oil cooler may be a problem on some Nissans. In TSB #NTB11015A, Nissan says the leak is from the upper end of the oil cooler. Door locks inoperative with Keyless Entry. 2008-12—Troubleshooting a grinding, knocking noise from the rear on turns. 2008-13—Oil cooler leakage. 2008-14—A quick fix for a rattling heat shield (TSB #NTB 14-018, issued March 20, 2014). 2011-12—Inaccurate ambient display temperature. Troubleshooting water vapour in the exterior lights. Steering/suspension pull or drift diagnosis. Oil may leak from the upper end of the engine oil cooler (see Sentra profile). Noise when turning the steering wheel. 2014—Free replacement of the engine On/Off button:

CAMPAIGN #PC311 TO REPLACE ENGINE ON/OFF PUSH BUTTON

SERVICE BULLETIN NO.: NTB14-082   DATE: AUGUST 28, 2014

 2014

INTRODUCTION: Nissan has a Voluntary Service Campaign covering the free replacement of the engine ON/OFF push-button. Dealers are to correct each vehicle falling within the range of this campaign.

Water leaking onto the driver or front passenger floor may be coming in through the kick panel and/or the cowl end area. 2014-15—Vehicle may lose power due to snow entering into the air cleaner case. In TSB #BT14015a and #NTB14-069a, issued Dec. 15, 2014, Nissan admits responsibility for sunshades that may bind or come apart. 2015—Under a voluntary service campaign (PC346), Nissan will pay for the replacement of the transmission torque converter.

MURANO

2004-2006	★★
2007	★★★
2009-2016	★★★★

RATING: Below Average (2004-2006); Average (2007); Above Average (2009-2016). The mid-sized, five-seater Murano features expressive styling and is loaded with many standard safety, performance and convenience features. **Road performance:** Nicely equipped with a refined, responsive powertrain that includes a strong V6, a comfortable and quiet, though sometimes bouncy, ride and car-like handling. Passing/merging power is lethargic; the ride stiffens with 20-inch wheels. The 2015 redesign dumbed down steering feel and response, but ratcheted up the styling. **Strong points:** A plush, comfortable, roomy and easily accessed interior; easy-to-use tech features, and good fuel economy for its class. Flamboyant styling. **Weak points:** Space utilization could be better; there is less cargo space behind the second row than many compact SUVs; limited rear visibility; the sloping windshield and hood make it hard to judge distance; and premium fuel is required. Recommended optional active collision avoidance features are tied to the purchase of a troublesome sunroof. Centre rear seat passengers' legs uncomfortably straddle the centre console. **Major redesign:** 2003, 2009 and 2015. **Best alternatives:** The Ford Edge is the likely cross shop. Other alternatives include the Hyundai Santa Fe, Honda Pilot and the Jeep Grand Cherokee.

Prices and Specs

Prices: *S:* $29,998, *Platinum:* $43,998 **Freight:** $1,795 **Powertrain (FWD/AWD):** Engine: 3.5L V6 (260 hp); Transmission: CVT automatic. **Dimensions:** Passengers: 2/3; Length: 192 in.; Wheelbase: 111 in.; Weight: 4,021 lb. **Fuel economy:** *AWD:* 11.2L/100 km city, 8.3L/100 km highway. **Assembled in:** Mississippi.

ALERT! The driver's view of the road can be compromised by the sloped front windshield, sitting position being too far back, and poor hood design (2015 model):

> The inclination of the hood near the wipers reflects the sunlight directly onto the driver's eyes and obstructs vision … the driver may not asses the distance of braking before the impact in emergency situations.

Muranos experience typical Nissan CVT "lag and lurch" performance:

> At low speeds on a slight incline will not accelerate with input to gas pedal rpms will [increase but] vehicle will not respond then suddenly drivetrain will [respond] and engage (a slipping action) vehicle will suddenly launch forward with a slight bang and bucking.

SAFETY	
IIHS 2015-2016	
Small Front	Good
Front	Good
Side	Good
Roof strength	Good
Head restraint and seats	Good
Child seat anchors	Acceptable
NHTSA Overall **AWD 2016**	★★★★★

Owner-reported safety-related failures: Airbags failed to deploy when needed; passenger-side airbag may be disabled when an average-sized occupant is seated; airbag warning light comes on continually, even after multiple resets by the dealer; vehicle rolls down incline when stopped in traffic; faulty transmission body causes the powertrain to vibrate when cruising; Check Engine light comes on after each fill-up (cap must be carefully resealed); headlights may suddenly switch off; the blind spot warning indicator is just a flicker; the Start/Stop ignition button can be accidently pressed, and this can suddenly shut down the vehicle in traffic; steering wheel turns with no effect:

> Adaptive steering failed at below freezing temperature. Lost ability to steer in a curve and hit another car. After, car could not be driven, as steering was totally inoperative. Steering wheel actually turns 360 degrees over and over with no effect on the front wheels. Front wheels actually ended up in a "pigeon toe" alignment and the car could not be towed.

Remote-controlled door locks operate erratically; the rearview camera image may be fuzzy and distorted:

> I agree with the complaint about the backup camera visibility problem with excessive glare and distortion. My 2006 Murano was somewhat blurry so I was looking forward to my 2013 Murano having a much improved camera similar to my friend's 2013 Honda Accord, but to my dismay my camera visibility is even worse than before, especially in the rain when it is needed the most for safety.

The sunroof may shatter suddenly:

> Driving 30 mph [48 km/h] on open asphalt road, no cars ahead of me, no cars behind me, when I heard a loud explosion, similar to a shotgun blast. The moon roof had exploded. Appeared to be an upward explosion. Damage was not caused from any flying objects.

RELIABILITY: The principal repair risk with the Murano is a transmission failure after the end of the warranty. The Murano was the first Nissan to receive a CVT in North America, and it's a heavy powerful vehicle that tends to be driven harder than Nissan's sedans by the extroverts who own them (see Nissan introduction, under Nissan Doubles CVT Warranty). Brake service is expensive; like other Nissan models the calipers can bind, and the Murano's heavy weight and powerful engine are hard on the brakes; have the calipers freed up and lubricated or risk an expensive brake renewal on all four wheels every couple of years. Excessive vibration can sometimes be reduced/resolved by reducing tire pressure about 4 psi; inoperative sunroof; faulty sun visors suddenly flop down blocking the view forward; and power windows open and close erratically.

INTERNAL BULLETINS, SECRET WARRANTIES: 2003-12—Troubleshooting a grinding, knocking noise from the rear on turns. 2009-12—Cold weather hard starting countermeasures. 2009-14—Powertrain transfer assembly oil leaks may require the replacement of the transfer assembly (TSB: #NTB11-017b, March 24, 2014). 2011-12—Intermittent power-steering noises; steering/suspension pull or drift diagnostics; Bluetooth voice recognition issues; and possible reasons for a faulty navigation screen. If the ignition push button doesn't respond, the body control module (BCM) may need recalibrating.

NAVIGATION SYSTEM – SCREEN GOES BLANK

BULLETIN NO.: EL12-010   DATE: MARCH 16, 2012

2010-12 370Z Coupe and Roadster; 2011-12 Murano and Cross Cabriolet; and the 2011-12 Quest.

IF YOU CONFIRM: The customer states the navigation display turns off, goes completely blank, or "blacks out" in DRIVE or REVERSE intermittently, and all functions of the audio system and heater/defroster/air conditioning work normally.

ACTION: Replace the AV display unit (also referred to as monitor or screen).

FRONTIER ★★★★

RATING: Above Average. Nissan's compact pickup truck – essentially the only one left on the market – has bones that can be carbon-dated back to the original Datsun Lil' Hustler and the Hardbody models. Fans will remember these Japanese trucks almost never broke (if only they didn't rust so badly). The 2017 models march on virtually unchanged since the latest generation was unveiled for 2005. **Road performance:** A gutsy pickup that offers a powerful V6 with towing horsepower to spare, or a 4-cylinder engine that's acceptable for light duty work. Handling is responsive, though steering is a bit slow. **Strong points:** It's the only truly compact pickup truck left on the market. An accommodating interior, especially with the Crew version; plenty of storage in the centre console; and easy to repair. **Weak points:** Ride is stiff and jiggly; cabin looks and feels cheap; rear seat room is tight; and you'll need to eat your Wheaties before attempting to lift the tailgate on earlier models. The 4.0L 6-cylinder is a gas hog. The 4.0L V6 models between 2005 and 2010 are cursed with a poor radiator that can fail, forcing coolant into the automatic transmission through the transmission cooler lines, and causing the transmission to self-destruct in as little as 60,000 km. There is an extended warranty to cover this to 130,000 km. **Major redesign:** 2005. Reportedly, the next Frontier will be redesigned with a new body, higher ground clearance, more cargo space, increased fuel efficiency, and revised styling. A Cummins diesel engine may be on the way. **Best alternatives:** Honda Ridgeline and Toyota Tacoma. A used Ford Ranger is more plentiful and costs less.

Prices and Specs

Prices: *King S 4x2:* $23,298, *Crew SL 4x4:* $38,498 **Freight:** $1,795 **Powertrain (Rear-drive/AWD):** Engines: 2.5L 4-cyl. (152 hp), 4.0L V6 (261 hp); Transmissions: 5-speed man. 6-speed man., 5-speed auto. **Dimensions:** Passengers: 2/3; Length: 206 in.; Wheelbase: 126 in.; Weight: 4,312 lb. **Fuel economy:** *2.5L 4-cyl.:* 13.6L/100 km city, 10.4L/100 km highway, *4.0L V6 AWD:* 15.7L/100 km city, 11.3L/100 km highway. **Assembled in:** Tennessee and Mississippi.

ALERT! Check the front head restraints on some models:

> The contact owns a 2012 Nissan Frontier. The front driver's seat headrest could not be adjusted. The headrest was positioned downward, causing the driver's head to be forced to look down. The dealer was made aware of the failure and advised the owner that the headrest was designed in that manner and they could not compromise the design of the vehicle.

Owner-reported safety-related failures: Passenger-side front airbag is disabled when an average-sized adult occupies the seat. Also, airbags may deploy for no reason:

SAFETY	
IIHS 2010-2016	
Small Front	Not Rated
Front	Good
Side	Good
Roof strength 2016	Not Rated
2010-2015	Good
Head restraint and seats	Acceptable
Child seat anchors	Marginal
NHTSA Overall	**Not Rated**

Myself and one passenger were off-roading in my 2012 Frontier PRO-4X going over a bumpy surface and without warning the side airbags went off! Luckily no one was injured, but we both got quite a scare due to the noise and lack of visibility. There is no damage to the front end nor were we at any degree of an angle. Yes it was bumpy but when you pay for a vehicle that states clearly off road on the side you expect it has the suspension to support the ride.

Delayed acceleration; faulty fuel-level sending unit sensor:

I went online to nissanhelp.com after performing a search. I came across many others who have experienced the same problem. Apparently it has something to do with the fuel sending unit. A similar problem was found on the 2000–2004 Xterra models and a recall was performed when the vehicle would stop after not getting any fuel.

 RELIABILITY: Nissan extended the radiator warranty on 2005-2010 Frontiers, Pathfinders, and Xterras to eight years or 130,000 km (80,000 mi) to fix a coolant-leak problem, caused by "a cracked oil cooler tube." Nissan assured owners it would cover "damage, repairs, replacement, and related towing resulting from this issue." What Nissan doesn't mention is that the radiator cooler tanks are rupturing in the 4.0L V6 models, which forces the coolant into the transmission through the transmission cooler lines, causing the transmission to self-destruct in as little as 60,000 km. Nissan insiders say the company is settling claims for transmission replacements on a "case-by-case basis." Nissan SUV and truck owners faced with $6,000 U.S. repair bills want the 8-year extended warranty extended further to cover transmission damage.

 INTERNAL BULLETINS, SECRET WARRANTIES: 2005-11—Correction for a water leak onto passenger-side floor when the AC is on. 2007-12—Front seats bind, won't move fore or aft. Inoperative seat lumbar support. 2008-12—Buzzing wind noise from the A-pillar/mirror area. 2011-12—Oil may leak from the upper end of the engine oil cooler (see the Sentra profile). Steering/suspension drift; sunroof water leak. Rear end clunking, knocking on turns. Brake master cylinder may slowly leak fluid. 2013—Nissan will replace the front air control assembly with a new one, free of charge, under "Campaign 239" outlined in TSB #NTB13-092, issued Oct. 28, 2013. 2013-14—A fuel tank that is hard to fill will likely need a new vent tube that connects the charcoal canister to the fuel tank. This correction should be free under the emissions warranty. 2015—Fix for a sunroof that won't close from the tilt-up position.

RATING: Average (2005-2016). The Titan is a full-sized truck designed to compete with its domestic competition. Nissan was the first importer to challenge the American full-size pickup market with its Mississippi-built Titan in 2004 (Toyota was selling a smaller Tundra at the time). The Titan is more reliable and durable than many of its rivals. It has a roomy cabin and handles well, though the ride is a bit busy over irregular roadways. Powerful V8 engine and transmission work smoothly. The truck is available in only the most common configurations to limit production costs. Surprisingly, the Titan hasn't changed all that much since its introduction – until the launch of the heavy-duty XD in 2016, and regular half-ton Titan for 2017. The XD offers an optional Cummins diesel engine, considered the gold standard in trucking, although it is a V8 turbodiesel and not the straight-six classic. **Road performance:** *2005-2014:* Strong acceleration from the standard 317 hp V8 engine (pre-2016), loud engine, high fuel consumption compared to current pickups. Transmission shifts well. Compared to current domestic full-size pickups the Titan is noisy, hard riding and feels primitive. **Strong points:** The rack-and-pinion steering is nicely weighted and the truck tracks well and is easy to drive. **Weak points:** The Titan's V8 is a gasoholic. Fit and finish are mediocre, and the cabin layout lacks some of the helpful storage space found in the Ram and others. When the armrests are down it is practically impossible to latch or unlatch the seatbelts. **Major redesign:** 2016/2017. **Best alternatives:** The closest competitor in terms of overall performance is the Toyota Tundra. The Ram 1500, Chevrolet Silverado and GMC Sierra are good new buys. The Ford F-150 is the most plentiful used pickup on the market.

Prices and Specs

Prices (Firm): *Crew S 4x2:* $44,650, *Crew Platinum 4x4:* $65,800 **Freight:** $1,795 **Powertrain (Rear-drive/AWD):** Engine: 5.6L V8 (390 hp); Transmissions: 7-speed automatic. **Dimensions:** Passengers: 2/3; Length: 228 in.; Wheelbase: 140 in.; Weight: 5,685 lb. **Fuel economy:** *5.6L V8:* 15.2L/100 km city, 11.1L/100 km highway. **Assembled in:** Mississippi.

RELIABILITY: Early Titans were rife with brake problems, blamed on undersized rotors that were prone to overheating and warping. Nissan upgraded the brake hardware in response. Rear axle seals can leak; factory bulletin advises to replace the axle shaft assembly with a newly designed assembly. Leaking gear oil can drip on the rear brakes and compromise their performance. Rear differential failure is not uncommon in older trucks. Transmission cooler lines are prone to leaking. Owner-reported problems include: Excessive vibration when underway linked to propeller shaft U-joint, which may be replaced for free under a Nissan voluntary service campaign; fractured exhaust

SAFETY

IIHS 2012-2015

Small Front	Not Rated
Front	Good
Side	Not Rated
Roof strength	Acceptable
Head restraint and seats	Good
Child seat anchors	Not Rated
NHTSA Overall	**Not Rated**

manifolds, also sometimes replaced *gratis*, as "goodwill." Inadequate heaters are covered by a Nissan "voluntary service campaign;" leaking wheel seals can affect braking; premature brake rotor repairs; early rust-out of the exhaust flange, and strut tower bracket may separate from the frame.

PATHFINDER ★★★

RATING: Average. Nissan redesigned its five-door mid-size sport utility for 2005, switching back to stout body-on-frame construction like the 1986 original, and unlike the unibody 1996 second-gen model. Underpinning it was a modified version of Nissan's F-Alpha truck frame, which it shared with the Frontier and Titan pickups, and Xterra, Armada and Infiniti QX56 sport-utes. The pre-2013 Pathfinder had a few problems, including a radiator that disgorged its coolant into the transmission, effectively killing it. Nissan changed direction radically for 2013, and adopted the Altima's unibody platform for the redesigned 2013 model. The Pathfinder's fuel-economy, handling and interior amenities improved; however, service bulletins and owner complaints confirm that reliability and overall performance were initially inferior to the outgoing model. The big concern is using a fragile CVT automatic transmission in a heavy vehicle that will conceivably be used for towing. **Road performance:** *2013-2017:* The 260 hp, 3.5L V6 provides good power. This generation is significantly lighter. Front-wheel drive is standard; the optional all-wheel drive system apportions power between the front and rear axles as needed, or permits the driver to lock in a 50/50 split. Imprecise handling when pushed; the ride is tuned for comfort above all, which is what most buyers in this segment want. **Strong points:** Attractive cabin with lots of technology and comfort features. Quiet composure. Good tow rating. Strong name recognition. Consider this Nissan's family hauler in place of the invisible Quest minivan. **Weak points:** The Pathfinder's biggest drawback is poor predicted reliability. **Major redesign:** 2013. **Best alternatives:** Honda Pilot, Toyota Highlander, Hyundai Santa Fe, GMC Acadia, Buick Enclave, Ford Explorer, Dodge Durango or Mazda CX-9.

Prices and Specs

Prices: *S FWD:* $32,498, *Platinum AWD:* $48,398 **Freight:** $1,795 **Powertrain (FWD/AWD):** Engine: 3.5L V6 (284 hp); Transmission: CVT automatic. **Dimensions:** Passengers: 2/3/2; Length: 199 In.; Wheelbase: 114 in.; Weight: 4,449 lb. **Fuel economy:** *3.5L V6:* 12.1L/100 km city, 8.9L/100 km highway. **Assembled in:** Tennessee.

RELIABILITY: *2005-12:* The pre-2011 models feature a radiator that introduced coolant into the transmission, creating a "milkshake" that spells certain death for the transmission. Transmission shudder is often the first symptom. The web is full of chilling stories:

> Mine was at 142,000 km when antifreeze filled up the transmission. When I took it to the transmission shop, there were another five Pathfinders with the exact same problem.

Nissan's warranty extension covers 2005 to 2010 models for up to eight years. Some owners have routed the transmission lines to an aftermarket transmission cooler pre-emptively, rather than risk the radiator disgorging its contents. Other mechanical flaws include noisy secondary timing chains (requiring replacement), faulty fuel gauges and fuel pumps, bad catalytic converters, worn U-joints, squeaky brakes and tire-pressure monitor issues. *2013-16:* The present-generation Pathfinder is also beset by transmission problems, this time of the CVT kind. Lots of complaints about the automatic transmission jerking or slipping or not permitting the truck to move. Some mistake it for an engine issue. Other mechanical issues include lit airbag warning lamps, fast-wearing brakes, drooping sun visors, and windshields that seem to crack too easily. Still, the transmission issues take the cake. Best would be to lease the Pathfinder or purchase an extended warranty from Nissan. Have you noticed that what was a common nameplate on Canadian roads 15 years ago has all but disappeared?

XTERRA ★★★

RATING: Average (2005-2015). The second-generation Xterra arrived for 2005 built atop Nissan's F-Alpha chassis that's shared with the Frontier pickup and previous Pathfinder. The Xterra retained the original's unique visual cues; namely, a stepped roof with an integrated rack, a liftgate compartment with an optional first-aid kit, and enough cubbies, nets and tie-downs to excite any camper. It had legitimate off-road credibility for use on the street. The 2005 retained a solid rear axle and leaf springs, rather than the Pathfinder's independent rear suspension. An exceptional body-on-frame SUV that's almost as good off road as the Jeep Wrangler, but more reliable. Acceptable off- and on-road performance, a spacious cabin and adaptable cargo area, distinctively aggressive looks, adequate power and acceleration. **Road performance:** The 4.0L V6 engine had enough muscle to propel the Xterra from 0 to 60 mph in just 7.0 seconds. The XTerra is bouncy on uneven pavement – you can't take the truck out of it. And with its high centre of gravity, don't expect it to grip well in fast corners. **Strong points:** The part-time four-wheel-drive system included genuine low-range gearing, but it could not be left engaged on dry pavement. Appealing cabin with lots of headroom, thanks to the tall roofline. Unique styling and standard roof racks won points with the weekend crowd (but bring a foot stool). Tidy size helped with parking and visibility is reasonably good. Manual transmission available to the very end. **Weak points:** Cabin space is tight for five with a rear bench that offers little legroom, but good cargo space when folded down. The dashboard is cast in fifty shades of grey and is prone to scratches. The ride is fairly rough and noisy, in part due to the big, off-road tires. Fuel economy is very poor. Too tall for many indoor garages on account of the roof rack. Model discontinued at the end of 2015. **Major redesign:** 2005 and 2009 update. **Best alternatives:** Toyota FJ, Jeep Wrangler and Unlimited.

Prices and Specs

Price (used): $28,000-29,000 (2015); $10,000-16,000 (2009) **Freight:** N/A. **Powertrain (4x4):** Engine: 4.0L V6 (261 hp); Transmissions: 6-speed manual, 5-speed automatic. **Dimensions:** Passengers: 2/3; Length: 179 in.; Wheelbase: 106 in.; Weight: 2,846 lb. **Fuel economy:** 7.5L/100 km city, 6.3L/100 km highway. **Assembled in:** Tennessee and Mississippi.

RELIABILITY: Early examples of the Xterra, especially 2005 to 2007, were afflicted with cooling problems that led to transmission failure. Avoid these model years. From a reliability perspective, the 2008-2015 models are relatively trouble free. Minor issues with the powertrain and fuel delivery systems. There have been a few engine timing chain tensioner issues, as well as oil leaks. Overall, the Xterra has fewer problems reported than the Nissan Pathfinder, and comes in third only to the Toyota 4Runner and FJ Cruiser as a relatively problem-free vehicle with off-road potential.

SAFETY	
IIHS 2009-2015	
Small Front	Not Rated
Front	Good
Side	Good
Roof strength	Acceptable
Head restraint and seats	Marginal
Child seat anchors	Not Rated
NHTSA Overall	**Not Rated**

An Extraordinary Ordinary Car

Despite the marketing bluster, there is nothing remarkable about Subaru's lineup beyond the inclusion of standard all-wheel drive in its models, with the exception of the rear-wheel drive BRZ sports coupe. If you don't require all-wheel drive capability, you're wasting your money. Studies show that most owners don't need off-road prowess; only 5% will ever use their Subaru off paved roads. The other 95% just like knowing they have the option of going wherever they please, whatever the weather. All-weather capability? A front-wheel drive car wearing four snow tires can't go everywhere a Subaru can go, but it will easily handle the conditions on most public roads unless it's a day you really should have stayed home. As one retired Quebec mechanic told me, "All-wheel drive simply means that you will get stuck deeper, further from home. It's no replacement for common sense."

Subaru is one of the smaller automobile companies, although it has seen its sales grow tremendously over the past 20 years as consumers clamour for the benefits of all-wheel drive. Subaru's marketing strategy uses all-wheel drive to appeal to fans of the outdoor lifestyle and its safety record to appeal to sensible types who want a safe vehicle. Subaru has been so good at selling safety that former Volvo owners have migrated into its vehicles. Because it is small (Toyota does own a stake in it), Subaru uses only a few engines and drivetrains across all of its models. The advantage is it keeps development and production costs down; the disadvantage is any engine problems will appear across a lot of the lineup.

A Reliable Supplier for Rebuilt 2.5L Subaru Engines

The Automobile Protection Association (APA) has located a reliable engine supplier for rebuilt 2.5L engines and turbochargers. The SWAP Shop is a Subaru rally car facility that also rebuilds engines for the street because of the strong demand from customers. The Swap Shop is located at 740, boul Industriel, Blainville QC J7C 3V4 Tel: 450-420-0991, *www.swapshopracing.ca*. Owner André Brunet recommends using the stock Subaru replacement piston rings and has access to a large supply of internal engine parts at reasonable prices, many imported directly from Japan. André says the Subaru engine is designed like the engines used in aircraft, where you tear down, inspect and reassemble after a certain number of hours in the air. The Swap Shop ships rebuilt engines all over Canada. If you live in the Montreal area, and have a difficult problem to solve on a Subaru, this would be the place to go.

RATING: Above Average (New); Average (Used). The Impreza is Subaru's entry-level compact designed to compete with everything from the Chevrolet Cruze to the Volkswagen Golf, but with the benefit of standard all-wheel drive. It is advertised as Canada's lowest-priced all-wheel drive vehicle. It comes as a four-door sedan or five-door hatchback/wagon. Until 2011, the car was powered by Subaru's 2.5L flat-four engine that is shared with the Forester SUV and larger Legacy sedan. The sporty WRX features a 224 hp turbocharged version of the engine. As of 2012, the Impreza switched to a smaller 2L engine that puts out 148 dull horses. At the top of the line, the rally-inspired WRX STI features a powerful turbocharged engine (305 hp version of the 2.5L), lots of standard performance features, sport suspension, an aluminum hood with functional scoop, and higher quality interior trim and seats. The STI is a harder-edged version of the WRX and not worth the extra cash unless you're a weekend warrior with access to a track. *2013:* Subaru scores with the Crosstrek; it's an "off-road" lookalike version of the Impreza hatchback with a slightly raised suspension and trucky body decoration. The public loves it, and Subaru gets to charge a premium for some extra trim and larger wheels and tires. *2014:* The Crosstrek hybrid is introduced. The 2017 Impreza is all new, riding on the company's Global platform. Look for a slightly longer and lower sedan and hatchback with a nicely sculpted body – it actually looks handsome. **Road performance:** Subaru's all-wheel drive system is always sending torque to all the wheels, which provides quick reflexes on snow-covered and loose surfaces, at the expense of somewhat higher fuel consumption. *2008-2011:* The 4-speed automatic sometimes shifts harshly and uses more fuel on older models; it's reliable. There's some roll when cornering, but cornering is predictable. Fuel consumption with the 2.5L and automatic is in between a compact car and an all-wheel drive SUV. *2012-2016 Impreza:* The remake brought a softer riding car, with a smaller and more economical engine and a continuously variable CVT automatic transmission. The combo featured much improved fuel economy (7.5L/100 km is achievable in highway driving) at the expense of some additional engine noise. Road noise is also noticeable. *2015:* Advanced Eyesight collision avoidance system becomes available on the Premium and Limited models. In following years, it migrates down the range. *WRX 2009:* A 265 hp motor becomes available; it supersedes the 224 hp engine in 2010, and the handling is a bit sharper. **Strong points:** Superior and relatively trouble-free full-time all-wheel drive. *2012-2016 Impreza:* Roomy cabin with comfortable seats; lots of storage space with the hatchback; a nice control layout; and refreshingly good all-around visibility thanks to large windows and well placed mirrors. Attractive base price for the entry-level 2017 Impreza. *WRX:* Very quick with little turbo lag; solid feel, entertaining to drive; precise transmission, especially with the optional short-throw shifter; suspension surprisingly compliant over bumps; good steering feedback. Turbo whine and characteristic blatting sound from the flat four when you open up the throttle are music to the ears of *rallye* car fanatics. **Weak points:** The primary reason for *Lemon-Aid's* lowered rating on the Impreza and related models is the engines that consume oil and Subaru ducking its obligation to extend the warranty. Both the 2.5L and 2L engines are prone to high oil consumption and oil leaks; the 2L is worse to 2015. All models are fairly noisy. Highest retained value in the compact class makes a used Impreza or WRX expensive. *2008-2011 Impreza and 2008-2014 WRX:* Some cabin trim looks inexpensive. *WRX and STI:* Expensive to insure and high risks for theft. **Major redesign:** 2008, 2012 Impreza and 2017 Impreza. **Best alternatives:** If you don't need all-wheel drive, available compact hatchbacks include the Elantra GT, Mazda3, VW Golf and 2017 Honda Civic and Chevrolet Cruze. For a used car buyer looking for an all-wheel drive vehicle, the Toyota Matrix and Pontiac Vibe are more reliable, and the Suzuki SX4 is cheaper.

Prices and Specs

Prices: *2.0i:* $19,995, *2.0i Limited Tech:* $30,395; *WRX:* $29,995, *STI Sport Tech:* $45,395 **Freight:** $1,595
Powertrain (AWD): Engines: *2.0i:* 2.0L 4-cyl. (148 hp), *WRX:* 2.0L 4-cyl. Turbo (268 hp); *STI:* 2.5L 4-cyl. Turbo (305 hp); Transmissions: *2.0i:* 5-speed manual, CVT automatic; *WRX/STI:* 6-speed manual, CVT automatic. **Dimensions:** Passengers: 2/3; Length: 180 in.; Wheelbase: 104 in.; Weight: 2,910-3,384 lb.
Fuel economy: *2.0i:* 8.5L/100 km city, 6.4L/100 km highway; *STI:* 13.8L/100 km city, 10.2L/100 km highway. **Assembled in:** Japan.

RELIABILITY: Keep an eye on your dipstick! Offered until 2011 on the Impreza, the 2.5L can burn oil starting at 100,000 km and is notorious for head gasket failures. The 2012-2015 2L engine is even worse when it comes to burning oil. Reports show oil consumption starts by 20,000 km and that Subaru won't repair engines unless consumption is in the range of 1L/1,500 to 2,000 km, equivalent to 3 or 4 litres of oil between changes. Other reported problems include short-lived clutches, failed a/c compressor bearings, filmy windows in winter (burning coolant?). WRX models are less temperamental than the STI, which has experienced engine, exhaust, and fuel system complaints. *2008-2011 Impreza, 2008-2014 WRX:* Check the rear suspension struts (leaking, worn after 100,000 km), 2.5L engine (leaks at the head gaskets, valve covers, timing covers and oil pressure switch), power steering pump (leak at the pulley shaft), front differential (leak at the output seals), front and rear sway bar links (worn,

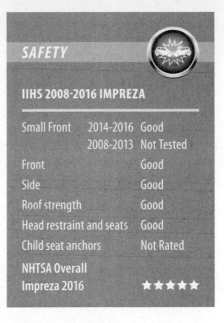

rattling), rear brakes (rusted, scored discs, have the calipers freed up and lubricated annually). *WRX:* Some manual and automatic transmission failures. *2012-2014 Impreza:* Some CVT automatic transmission complaints, covered under warranty.

"Boxed" by Subaru

Used 2.5L engines are in short supply and expensive; wreckers sell the engines within a couple of days of the donor car coming in. Subaru's "boxer" engine has two head gaskets that are prone to leaking; replacing them costs $1,200 or more per side. A light knocking due to "piston slap" when the engine is cold is generally a precursor to high oil consumption.

Subaru is cunning; the company interprets its original warranty generously if you are the original owner and is even more liberal if service was performed at a Subaru dealership. The APA has seen the Subaru powertrain warranty extended from the standard 5 years/100,000 km to over 6 years and nearly 150,000 km. Subaru will pay to replace head gaskets or to replace an engine block. Second owners are not treated as liberally out of warranty, and could find themselves being asked for service records Subaru knows they likely won't have. If all this sounds a lot like a secret warranty, you're right. Subaru should double its powertrain warranty with a notification to owners and offer refunds to customers who already paid for these expensive repairs. So far, the automaker's reputation in the marketplace doesn't appear to have suffered.

The APA recommends you purchase an extended warranty from Subaru, or lease a new Subaru. Just before the end of the powertrain warranty, have the dealer check the engine for head gasket leaks and other leaks at the front of the block.

INTERNAL BULLETINS, SECRET WARRANTIES: 2008-14—Replacement of faulty air intake duct that leaks turbo boost pressure, cuts power, and increases engine noise. 2012-13—Troubleshooting premature wear of rings and higher oil consumption, camshaft position sensor clearance could be out of specification, causing the Check Engine light to come on. Loose instrument panel vents. Highway speed, vibration, harshness, and noise diagnostic and correction tips.

FORESTER	NEW ★★★★
	USED ★★★

RATING: Above Average (New); Average (Used). The Forester is a tall wagon crossover that uses Subaru's ubiquitous 2.5L 4-cylinder engine or an optional turbocharged 4-cylinder. It is built on the Impreza platform. The 2011 Forester earned a significant mechanical update in the form of an updated 2.5L boxer engine with dual overhead camshafts (DOHC) in place of the single over head camshaft (SOHC) in each cylinder head. It still made 170 hp, but torque increased marginally to 174 lb-ft, and it was more fuel efficient and cleaner for emissions. Both engines perform nicely, despite being coupled to a dated 4-speed automatic prior to 2014. Subaru redesigned the Forester for 2014 with cleaner styling, a roomier and better-appointed interior, and better fuel economy. The XT received a 2.0L turbo 4-cylinder to replace the older 2.5L turbo. The 2017 models gain more sound insulation, better door seals and updated headlights and grille treatment. Fuel economy is once more supposed to have improved a little. The panoramic sunroof lowers the ceiling, cutting into cargo height a bit. **Road performance:** The standard Forester 2.5i is a nice all-rounder and reasonably equipped. The Forester was in the top tier of compact SUVs in APA comparison tests. Acceptable acceleration. The turbocharged XT model shares its robust engine with the WRX; fuel consumption increases and premium is required. Competent, agile and secure handling; the ride can get bouncy over broken pavement. **Strong points:** Effective full-time all-wheel drive and good ground clearance. Roomy cabin; comfortable seats; lots of storage space; convenient control layout; good all-around visibility; large windows and well placed mirrors. **Weak points:** Fuel consumption is a little heavy through 2013; expect about 12 L/100 km around town. Some dealer-only parts are expensive. Excessive oil consumption became a common complaint with the introduction of the 2.5L DOHC 4-cylinder engine in 2011 (*www.edmunds.com/subaru/forester/2015/suv/review/*):

> At around 4000 miles with my 2015 Forester, I started to notice excessive oil consumption. Checked with Subaru National, was given a case number, and was instructed to have the local dealer in Bedford, Ohio, do an oil consumption test. The service manager's statement, "One-third of a quart in 1200 miles is acceptable." If that answer sounds scripted, it was. Plus he talked down to me like I was a third grader. So that means that by the time your first scheduled synthetic oil change is due, you have blown through two quarts. That is not acceptable, that is frightening. There are lots of negative comments online about excessive oil consumption with these engines.

In addition, the CVT transmission can perform poorly:

> My 2015 with the change to CVT was bad, really bad. Bucking/surging/hesitating since day one and got worse. Dealer/mechanic saying that it needs to warm up is just wrong. It would never quit bucking, cold, hot or any other time.

Major redesign: 2009 and 2014. **Best alternatives:** Lots of choice in a compact all-wheel drive crossover. The likely alternatives are the Honda CR-V, Toyota RAV4, Mazda CX-5, and Nissan Rogue.

Prices and Specs

Prices: *2.5i:* $25,995, *2.0XT Limited:* $39,495 **Freight:** $1,675 **Powertrain (AWD):** Engines: 2.5L 4-cyl. (170 hp), 2.5L 4-cyl. turbo (224 hp), 2.0L 4-cyl. turbo (250 hp). Transmissions: 6-speed manual, CVT automatic. **Dimensions:** Passengers: 2/3; Length: 181 in.; Wheelbase: 104 in.; Weight: 3,295-3,651 lb. **Fuel economy:** *2.5i:* 9.2L/100 km city, 7.4L/100 km highway; *2.0XT:* 10.2L/100 km city, 8.6L/100 km highway. **Assembled in:** Japan.

ALERT! The back-up camera may be useless if you wear polarized sunglasses:

> The electronic screen on the 2015 Subaru Forester that includes the back-up display reflects a solid black bar down the middle if you are wearing polarized sunglasses... I checked at the dealer, and other 2015 Foresters have the same problem, but the Outback does not. Since I first noticed the problem I have driven a number of cars, including Toyotas and BMWs that do not have the problem. Subaru's suggested solution is that I don't wear polarized sunglasses. I wear corrective lenses, and it is virtually impossible to buy corrective sunglasses that aren't polarized.

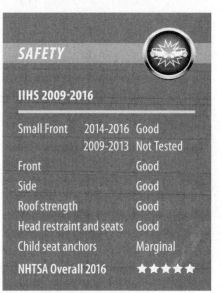

SAFETY		
IIHS 2009-2016		
Small Front	2014-2016	Good
	2009-2013	Not Tested
Front		Good
Side		Good
Roof strength		Good
Head restraint and seats		Good
Child seat anchors		Marginal
NHTSA Overall 2016		★★★★★

The passenger side airbag may be disabled for some obscure reasons:

> The Subaru occupant detection system in my 2014 Forester is defective. It does not detect my wife and the passenger airbag does not turn on. We have been told by Subaru that they have recently changed to an "electrostatic capacitance sensor" to replace the previous "weight sensor." My wife needs to sit on a seat cushion as the seats are too hard for her medical condition. Subaru told us the seat cushion will not allow the ODS to verify a person is sitting in the seat and will not turn on the passenger airbag. I also discovered that wet clothing (wet raincoat) will also defeat the sensor and the airbag will not be turned on. This is totally unacceptable... The only suggestion from Subaru was for my wife to sit in the back seat.

Owner-reported safety-related failures: Driver-side mirror and bracket detached; rearview mirror also falls off; and many reports of windshield cracks without any impact on recent Foresters and Imprezas:

> My 2015 Impreza windshield cracked when the defroster was turned on with temperature outside about 20F. We noticed a crack starting from the right bottom of the windshield (near the passenger side).

Cruise control malfunctions; front door corners can easily cut one's head when opened, due to their design. When accelerating, some model years lag, then the vehicle surges ahead. Head restraints push head forward at an uncomfortable angle, causing neck strain and backache. The moonroof system cavity allows debris and small animals to enter between the headliner and interior walls – the perfect place for fungi and mould to incubate.

RELIABILITY: As with the Impreza, the *Lemon-Aid* rating on the Forester dropped because of the recurring engine defects and Subaru's failure to extend the warranty. If you're buying used, check: Ball joints (wear), wheel bearings (wear). The two catalytic converters in the exhaust system can rust at their front flanges. The Swap Shop performs the repair for about $200 (see Subaru introduction, under A Reliable Supplier for Rebuilt 2.5L Subaru Engines). Slow moving power liftgate; heated seats are slow to warm; the Bluetooth screen can "freeze;" tiny back-up camera display washed out in sunlight. For additional reliability info consult the Impreza review.

INTERNAL BULLETINS, SECRET WARRANTIES: 2011-12— TCM computer reboot to cure harsh shifting. TSB #02-113-11R, published Jan. 26, 2011, addresses cold-start engine noise and suggests that the timing chain tensioner be changed. Excessive oil consumption; defective engine had to be replaced. White exhaust smoke may indicate leaking head gasket. Loose instrument panel vents. **2011-14—**TSB #02-141-13R outlines the design change to the rubber sealing cap oil pressure switch to prevent false low oil alerts. **2014—**TSB #02-152-14R, issued April 22, 2014, and revised June 12, 2014, announces the availability of free revised valve train components developed to reduce a tapping sound (sometimes described as "a sewing machine type" sound) which may be heard coming from the left-hand side of the engine when the engine is warm. The changes consist of: Design change to the valve rockers, Camshaft profile change, and 1.65mm longer intake and 2.45mm longer exhaust valve stem lengths. If a customer's concern over a tapping sound from the B2 cylinder head is confirmed, the dealer must replace the intake and exhaust camshafts, the four intake valves, four exhaust valves, and all eight rockers. Repair tips for an inoperative liftgate. Details on how to silence a rattling sound from the sunroof air deflector while driving with the roof panel closed. Some changes made to the oil level switch assembly designed to improve its accuracy. **2014-15—**Hard starts and extended cranking time can be corrected by re-calibrating the electronic control module (ECM). The rear door power window regulator/motor assembly gearing has been changed to prevent the mechanism from binding.

NEW ★★★★
USED ★★★

2015 Subaru Outback

RATING: Above Average (New); Average (Used). The Legacy sedan is the go-to choice in a mid-size, mid-price all-wheel drive sedan. The more practical Legacy wagon was discontinued at the end of 2009. The Outback is a Legacy on stilts, with larger wheels and tires and lower body cladding to bulk it up; it sells in much larger numbers. The Legacy and Outback are more fuel-efficient alternatives to a mid-size SUV. Subaru's "H6" flat-six boxer engine is optional at the top of the line; the cylinder arrangement is shared with Porsche. For 2010 both models were redesigned. A new CVT transmission saved gas, but contributed to more engine noise in the cabin. Interior space grew; the ride became softer and handling a bit less responsive. The H6 engine grew from 3L to 3.6L. *2013:* First year for Subaru's excellent EyeSight collision avoidance system; it migrated down to more models with every passing year. *2015:* Redesigned again, the cars are smoother, styling more mainstream. The infotainment system was upgraded and the base engine and CVT combo feels more like a conventional automatic. **Road performance:** The base 2.5L 4-cylinder is an acceptable, noisy performer. The 6-cylinder engine is quick and smooth but uses a lot of fuel. *The Outback wagon* adds higher ground clearance. **Strong points:** A refined and relatively reliable all-wheel drive system; predictable handling and a comfortable ride. A spacious interior, with lots of cargo room (innovative under-floor cargo storage area). Interior materials and fit and finish were upgraded for 2015. The Legacy depreciates more than other Subarus including the Outback, so your used car dollar will go further with it. **Weak points:** Defective 2.5L engines account for the lower rating as a used car buy. **Major redesign:** 2005, 2010 and 2015. **Best alternatives:** Honda CR-V, Hyundai Santa Fe, and Toyota Highlander and Highlander Hybrid.

ALERT! Owners say the head restraints force the driver's head into a painful and unsafe chin-to-chest position (worse for short drivers), a problem plaguing Subarus for several years. Check during test drive.

Owner-reported safety-related failures: Engine may default to very low idle, almost to the point of stalling out; cruise control and brake failures; steering shimmy and wobbles, and car sways from right to left (partially corrected by replacing the steering-column dampening spring and force-balancing the tires); excessive steering wheel, clutch, and brake vibration; airbag warning light comes on for no reason; and driver-side floor mats may "creep" toward the accelerator pedal. The location of the electronic brake button makes it easy to engage the brake inadvertently. *Outback:* Sudden, unintended downshifting or accelerating when using transmission paddles:

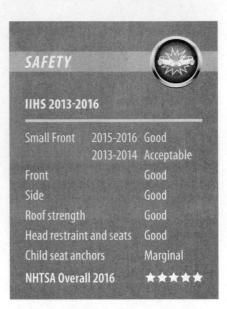

SAFETY

IIHS 2013-2016

Small Front	2015-2016	Good
	2013-2014	Acceptable
Front		Good
Side		Good
Roof strength		Good
Head restraint and seats		Good
Child seat anchors		Marginal
NHTSA Overall 2016		★★★★★

Situation: Travelling at 60 mph [97 km/h] up a steep hill in left passing lane. Cars following close, and cars in the right lane. For the first time (new car) I used the downshift paddle on the left side of the steering wheel to downshift to accelerate. I tapped it to downshift one gear. It instantly dropped to First gear. The engine rpms went to red line or above. The car decelerated dramatically, and I was tossed forward. I attempted to upshift using the right paddle but there was no response, and the car remained in First gear. The car behind nearly hit me. The only useful control that I had was the steering wheel (brakes or accelerator useless). Further, I assumed the brake lights were not lit. Due to the alertness of the driver behind and the drivers to my right as I slowed dramatically and got off the highway to the right shoulder, a serious accident was avoided.

• • •

Ever since purchasing the 2012 Outback we have had a serious issue when using the paddle shifters to slow down for a stop. When the tach slows to about 1100 rpm in First or Second gear the engine then accelerates to up to 2500 rpm, slowing down and then speeding up again, then repeating the cycle over, even if you apply the brakes. Sometimes it would just run at 2500 rpm until you braked to a stop.

Faulty cruise control/traction control:

Vehicle stopped cruise control and flashed Brakes and No Traction Control unexpectedly. Came close to a wreck shutting the vehicle down on the side of the road hitting various tire recaps and debris on the side of the road. Not told that this is a regular occurrence with this vehicle.

Passenger-side airbag may suddenly disable itself while vehicle is underway:

Drove the car for approximately 45 minutes, made a quick stop with car turned off, when restarting car, airbag warning light came on and also the passenger side airbag light said it was off even though there was an adult passenger on that side of the car. Light stayed on even after restarting car, readjusting seat belts, etc. Drove with warning light on for about an hour.

Excessive wander over the roadway:

When driving on the highway the vehicle exhibits very poor straight line stability. Vehicle wanders within the lane and requires excessive steering wheel correction to maintain straight direction. Vehicle has 500 miles [800 km] on it (350 driven by owner) but is now sitting in driveway for fear of personal safety if emergency manoeuvre is necessary on the highway.

RELIABILITY: Oil consumption is the most frequent complaint. See "Boxed" by Subaru, under Empreza review for more complete information. A lit engine emissions light could signal a defective oxygen sensor or PCV valve. Driveshaft center bearing can wear at high mileage. The replacement part from Subaru includes the entire shaft; check the aftermarket for a less expensive rebuilt drive-shaft. *2011-2012:* Frequent headlight failure and replacement. Spontaneous windshield/sunroof cracks appear for no reason:

When getting into the car in the afternoon, noticed a huge crack on the windshield starting between the wiper blades and going to the top of the windshield. There was no impact to have caused this. The car was parked in the open on a day where temperatures were mild. Looks like there are quite a few complaints in the Subaru forums complaining about the Subaru Legacy and Outback, which share the same platform.

Fuel filler door sticks; front seats need more padding; interior trim look and feel cheap; the flat six engine requires premium fuel; and the radio display "freezes" until vehicle is re-started. Subaru recalled the 2010-2014 Legacy and Outback because the windshield wiper motor can melt and catch on fire if obstructed by snow, ice or debris; free the wiper arms before turning on. If you're buying used, check: Ball joints (wear), wheel bearings (wear); rear coil springs on the wagon (occasionally broken); sway bar links (broken), rear brakes (rusted or grooved discs, have the calipers freed up and greased annually). The two catalytic converters in the exhaust system can rust at their front flanges. The Swap Shop performs the repair for about $200 (see Subaru introduction, under A Reliable Supplier for Rebuilt 2.5L Subaru Engines). Subarus are dealer-dependent for some parts, resulting in occasional delays.

INTERNAL BULLETINS, SECRET WARRANTIES: 2005-12—Replacement of the air intake duct that leaks turbo boost pressure, cuts power, and increases engine noise. 2005-14—Remedy for customer concerns of a "click," "pop," or "creak" sound heard coming from either the left or right side around the rear corners of the cowl/engine compartment/base of "A" pillar area. 2010-13—Water leaks from map light area. 2010-14—The Legacy and Outback may exhibit drivetrain vibration ("shimmy") and instability at highway speeds, linked to poor steering and suspension components. Technical service bulletin 05-48-10 outlines the fix, but it doesn't always resolve matters fully. 2013-14—Revised valve train parts to reduce a warm engine tapping sound from the left cylinder head. Engine chirp, squeak, or squeal (replace the existing V-belt (serpentine drive/accessory belt) with the upgraded version (Part No: #809221160). Sunroof doesn't open properly. 2015—Wind noise from the front door glass and rear door area. Whistling from the rear seat console air vents and side vents.

BRZ AND SCION FR-S/TOYOTA 86 ★★★★

RATING: Above average (2013-17). Subaru introduced the BRZ sport coupe in 2013 along with partner Toyota, which offered the Scion FR-S. As of 2017, the Scion brand has been dropped, and the car renamed Toyota 86. Unlike everything else in Subaru's range, the BRZ is a rear-drive coupe. It takes advantage of the Subaru's boxer engine that lies flat at the bottom of the engine bay; this lowers the centre of gravity to aid handling. The BRZ/FR-S is lightweight and small, with just enough room for two occupants up front, while the rear seats are relegated to carrying briefcases and groceries. The BRZ and Toyota 86 receive a mid-cycle refresh for 2017, with some powertrain, chassis and styling tweaks. Its 2.0L 4-cylinder engine gets new heads, cams and manifolds to yield 5 more horsepower than last year –

and only if you opt for the standard 6-speed manual gearbox (automatic-equipped cars remain at 200 hp). **Road performance:** With its low-slung engine positioned behind the front axle line sending power to the rear wheels, the BRZ is supremely balanced. This pays off handsomely in the handling. While not overtly powerful, the car is fun to drive and quick. Low-torque engine – you have to wind it up for max acceleration. The car sticks to the road. The minimalist interior hearkens back to the basic hot cars from the 1980s, like Toyota's Corolla GT-S and the original VW GTI. Among the small sporty vehicles, only the MINI Cooper S, a front-wheel drive car, and Mazda Miata have reflexes this sharp. The APA tested both the BRZ and its twin the FR-S and found them to be essentially the same car, save for a small difference in suspension tuning which you hardly notice in normal driving. **Strong points:** Balanced chassis; exceptional cornering response and turn-in; good steering; good fuel economy; comfortable and supportive front seats. Equipped with all the right features to make it a great track car. Reasonable price for the technology and exclusivity offered. The automatic transmission is a conventional 6-speed, not a CVT, which works better in this sporting application. **Weak points:** Tiny back seats, trunk opening and trunk size too small to be practical; hard to get in and out of due to its low profile; primitive audio controls. **Major redesign:** 2017s get a mid-cycle refresh. **Best alternatives:** Mazda MX-5 Miata and MINI Cooper S.

Prices and Specs

Price: *$27,995; Sport Tech:* $31,195 **Freight:** $1,650 **Powertrain (Rear-drive):** Engines: 2.0L 4-cyl. (200/205 hp); Transmissions: 6-speed manual, 6-speed automatic. **Dimensions:** Passengers: 2+2; Length: 167 in.; Wheelbase: 101 in.; Weight: 2,785 lb. **Fuel economy:** 11.1L/100 km city, 8.0L/100 km highway. **Assembled in:** Japan.

RELIABILITY: Insufficient data. Some first year launch issues with the fuel system and engine management. The 2013-2016 engine features both direct and conventional port fuel injection; this may help avoid the carbon buildup seen with direct injection engines. To date the cars appear to have avoided the oil consumption issues that are plaguing the Impreza 2L.

SAFETY

IIHS 2013-2016 BRZ & SCION FR-S

Small Front	2014-2016	Acceptable
	2013	Not Tested
Front		Good
Side		Good
Roof strength		Good
Head restraint and seats		Good
Child seat anchors		Poor
NHTSA Overall BRZ 2016		★★★★

After hanging tough for years with its stable of small cars and SUVs in a U.S. market obsessed with large pickups and SUVs, American Suzuki Motor Corporation filed for bankruptcy protection in November 2012, and announced it would discontinue making vehicles for the U.S. and focus on motorcycles, ATVs, and marine equipment instead. In the same statement, Suzuki reiterated its commitment to the Canadian market. Well, that lasted barely four months. In March 2013, Suzuki Canada Inc. declared it would discontinue its auto-building operations in Canada as part of the American bankruptcy proceedings and dealerships began to close, go independent, or look for other franchises.

Suzuki Motor Corp. remains a going concern in much of the world. Readers may be surprised to learn that Suzuki is a major player in the Far East and India, where its partnership with Maruti allowed it to dominate the Indian market with almost half of all vehicle sales in the world's most populous nation. Back here in Canada, three Suzuki models show up on the used car market with some regularity. Their prices dropped a lot soon after Suzuki pulled out, and have since stabilized. As owners of an "orphaned" brand, Suzuki owners don't have the benefit of a full-service dealer network, but the company committed to making replacement parts available through a limited number of its former dealers until 2023.

SX4 ★★★

RATING: Average (2007-2013). Canadians embraced the front-wheel drive SX4 five-door hatchback when it was launched here in 2007. Suzuki also produced an all-wheel drive hatchback version, which employed an electric solenoid-operated clutch pack to activate the rear wheels. A console switch allowed the driver to choose between locked four-wheel drive, computer-engaged all-wheel drive or front-wheel drive for fuel efficiency. The oddball styling provides an unusually tall greenhouse with lots of glass, including a pair of triangular sail windows that provide the illusion of riding in a minivan. Despite its small size, the SX4 is reasonably roomy inside with upright chair-like seating. A trunk was grafted on the end to add a four-door sedan in 2008. The engine is an all-aluminum, 143 hp 2.0-L DOHC 4-cylinder. Buyers could choose between a standard 5-speed manual transmission or a 4-speed automatic. For 2010, there was a small 7 hp power bump (to 150), and two new transmissions – a 6-speed manual, and a CVT to replace the conventional automatic. For 2012 all models received standard stability control and rear disc brakes. **Road performance:** The 2.0L engine is noisy and feels less powerful than its rating would suggest; acceleration is acceptable. Light and precise gearshift, with easy clutch and shift action. The rigid platform pays dividends in terms of accurate steering and a tolerable ride. The small turning circle is very handy during parking maneuvers. **Strong points:** Excellent visibility all around and tidy dimensions make this an ideal city car. The seating "hip-point" is at the right height for easy entry and exit, a boon for older drivers and passengers. Rear-seat room is acceptable, aided by a tall door opening. The seatbacks split and fold to allow flexible stowage capacity. **Weak points:** *NOISY.* Fuel consumption with the automatic and all-wheel drive is high for a small car, but lower than the contemporary Subaru Impreza. The small gas tank makes for a short cruising range. Cargo space is modest. **Major redesign:** 2007 hatchback, 2008 sedan introduced. **Best alternatives:** The obvious cross-shop is the similarly tall and odd Toyota Echo, or the Yaris. If you must have all-wheel drive, this is the cheapest way to get into a well-engineered reliable car.

Prices and Specs

Price: *FWD (2009):* $4,000; *AWD (2012):* $4,500; *FWD:* $9,000; *AWD:* $10,000 **Powertrain:** Engine: 2012: 2.0L 4-cyl. (150 hp); Transmissions: 6-speed manual, 4-speed automatic, CVT. **Dimensions:** Passengers: 2/3; Length: 162 in.; Wheelbase: 98.5 in.; Weight: 2,800 lb. **Fuel economy:** 10.1L/100 km city, 8.0L/100 km highway. **Assembled in:** Japan.

RELIABILITY: Assembled in Japan, the SX4 enjoyed very good build quality and has a reliable powertrain. The most commonly reported problem is a faulty front passenger seat occupancy sensor, which can falsely disarm the airbag. The sensor mat installed in the front passenger seat may fail due to repeated flexing resulting from sitting it. A U.S. recall covers 2007 to 2011 models, but owners complained that the Suzuki service network did not furnish enough parts to complete the recall. The accessory drive belt tensioner on the engine may weaken and cause the belt to become noisy; if not replaced, a failure of the belt will result in a loss of power steering. The Jatco-supplied CVT transmission used from 2010-2013 is not as durable as the previous 4-speed automatic. The air conditioning may stop working because the electromagnet compressor clutch has failed. Check for leaking struts that require replacement.

SAFETY	
IIHS 2007-2013	
Small Front	Not Rated
Front	Good
Side	Good
Roof strength	Not Rated
Head restraint and seats	Marginal
Child seat anchors	Not Rated
NHTSA Overall	★★★★

KIZASHI ★★

RATING: Below Average (2011-13). Sold in tiny numbers here for only three years, this compact four-door sedan offered nothing exceptional for its ambitious $30,000 original price tag. The Kizashi is a well-equipped family sedan with standard electronic stability control. All-wheel drive became standard in 2012. It doesn't share its platform with any other model. Reportedly, the suspension benefited from extensive development in Europe. Suzuki dealers could not understand what their manufacturer was smoking when they learned of the price tag and tried to order as few as possible; of all the Suzuki models this is the one that lost the most value after the pullout and a four-year-old car now sells for a third of what it cost when new. **Road performance:** The Kizashi uses the 180 hp 2.4L DOHC 4-cylinder from the Grand Vitara sport-utility, tied to a CVT transmission (a handful of Sport models with a 6-speed manual gearbox were imported). Hobbled by the power-sapping CVT, the Kizashi doesn't run like a sports sedan – unless you can find one with a stickshift, which transforms the car. Steering is the car's most athletic trait, although some drivers find it's heavy. Handling is better than average, especially with the Sport. Braking is excellent. The trunk has a useful pass-through. **Strong points:** The cabin is plush and well appointed – Suzuki pulled out all the stops to create a nice interior. The front seats are supportive and comfortable. **Weak points:** Sized in between a compact and an intermediate, but the back seat is smaller than many compacts. CVT automatic transmission. Middling fuel economy. Mediocre visibility. **Major redesign:** 2011. **Best alternatives:** For four-wheel-drive, the Subaru Impreza or a base Legacy, but they're also more expensive.

RELIABILITY: Incomplete data due to the small number sold; of all the Suzuki orphans this is the one with the most precarious parts availability. Made-in-Japan superior build quality, with a rigid, rattle-free body. The CVT transmission is its Achilles heel; a few needed their software reflashed and some transmissions were replaced outright. A major failure now could lead to the car being scrapped. If you can find a manual transmission car, it would be a much better choice. Secondary issues reported include a finicky pushbutton ignition and frozen windshield washer nozzles. Fragile paint that chips easily is an old Suzuki weakness.

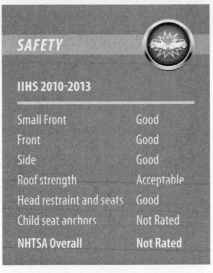

SAFETY	
IIHS 2010-2013	
Small Front	Good
Front	Good
Side	Good
Roof strength	Acceptable
Head restraint and seats	Good
Child seat anchors	Not Rated
NHTSA Overall	**Not Rated**

GRAND VITARA ★★★★

RATING: Above Average (2006-2013). The all-new Grand Vitara sport utility released for 2006 swapped its Japanese styling cues for a crease-and-fold design that incorporated Suzuki's trademark clamshell hood. It would wear the same crisp bodywork for eight model years. The Grand Vitara benefits from a boxed ladder-type frame underpinning its unibody structure (like a Range Rover) to doubly insure its integrity. The rear suspension is fully independent, and unlike car-based crossovers like the Honda CR-V, the Suzuki defaults to rear-wheel-drive, just like a real truck. The wheelbase and overall length grew enough to transform the Grand Vitara into a roomy compact SUV. Short overhangs and greater ground clearance made the Grand Vitara trailworthy. The interior leapfrogged ahead with improved materials and a contemporary design. The cargo door had the spare tire piggybacking on it, as was the fashion of the day. Mounting a spare that way precludes a conventional hatchback, because you'd have to lift the wheel and tire every time you opened the hatch, but it is actually preferred by shorter people. A 185 hp 2.7L DOHC V6 was the sole powerplant at launch, oriented longitudinally, not sideways. The manual and automatic transmissions both had five speeds. Premium models offered a serious full-time four-wheel-drive system with a locking centre differential. It had three selectable driving modes: "4-high" for on-road driving, "4-high locked" for slippery conditions and "4-low locked" for low-speed trail climbing. For 2009, Suzuki's truck was facelifted and two new engines arrived. A 166 hp 2.4L DOHC 4-cylinder was the base motor (using a 4-speed automatic), while the optional 3.2L V6 made 230 hp. Safety was enhanced with more airbags and standard traction control on all models. The V6 was dropped for 2011. **Road performance:** The 2.4L 4-cylinder is no powerhouse, but delivers similar acceleration to its 4-cylinder competitors. The V6 is the better choice; both versions provide smooth, usable power and a nice sound. Despite its four-wheel independent suspension, the Grand Vitara rides more like a truck than its competitors. Handling is predictable. Precise, nicely weighted steering. **Strong points:** The low cargo floor allows a lot of stuff to be stowed below the window line. The rear seat folds and then tumbles vertically against the front seat to maximum cargo space. Comfortable seats, with good legroom front and rear. The cabin is nicely assembled with big, clear instruments and logical controls. Visibility with the upright styling is far superior to most current SUVs. Available with a genuine 4x4 system that offers low gearing for real off-roading. And it can tow 3,000 lbs. **Weak points:** Handling is predictable, but clumsier than the better compact SUVs. The stiff ride is tiresome, and deteriorates noticeably as the suspension wears. Fuel economy is higher than average for the class, even with the 4-cylinder. **Major redesign:** 2006, 2009 update. **Best alternatives:** A Honda CR-V or Toyota RAV4, but both will cost thousands more. For similar or a little more money, a Hyundai Tucson, or Kia Rio. The Escape, Compass and Patriot compete on price but are all too unreliable to recommend.

RELIABILITY: The Grand Vitara sold well and parts availability in the aftermarket is very good. Durable engine, transmission and driveline and easy to service. First-owners of Grand Vitaras often bought them because they were cheap and tough, and many performed minimal maintenance. Have the driveline checked for oil leaks at the engine, transmission, transfer case and rear differential, as all can weep or leak slightly and only the level in the engine is likely to have been checked. Budget $300-$500 for new fluids, or more to cover the cost of any leak repairs. A common issue affecting several model years is blown headlamps, typically one or both bulbs every six months or so; replacement bulbs are inexpensive. Some reports of failed head gaskets on the 4-cylinder engine, which can lead to overheating and engine damage. Some failures of the air conditioner compressor; Suzuki recommends using it once a month to prevent its seals from drying out. The cabin ventilation fan can fail. Some owners report excessive tire wear and related alignment problems. Scratch-prone interior plastics and silver plating that rubs off high-wear areas like the shift knob are a Suzuki tradition. Like other Suzukis, the Grand Vitara is rust-prone. The APA recommends Krown Rust Control for an annual application available across Canada, or in Montreal, Barry's Rustproofing for a grease treatment (contact information is in the Part Four Introduction).

SAFETY	
IIHS 2009-2013	
Small Front	Not Rated
Front	Good
Side	Acceptable
Roof strength	Acceptable
Head restraint and seats	Marginal
Child seat anchors	Not Rated
NHTSA Overall	**Not Rated**

"Runaway" Bestsellers

When running properly, Toyotas hold up well over many years, are forgiving of owner neglect, and have reasonable servicing requirements.

I have recommended Toyota models since the early '70s, when they started gaining popularity in Canada. Their vehicles were reliable and cheap, and the company paid most warranty claims without forcing customers to file small claims court lawsuits.

All this came to an end more than a decade ago when bean-counters took over the company and adopted the mantra that profit and marketshare trump quality. That's why Tacomas are rust-cankered, and Tundras shake dentures loose. Speaking of rust, Toyota will be paying out about $3.4 billion U.S. to settle a class-action lawsuit as compensation for corroded Tacoma, Tundra, and Sequoia trucks.

In Canada, Toyota and its dealers used the Access Toyota program to keep retail prices artificially high. *Lemon-Aid* made a formal complaint to Ottawa, alleging Toyota price-fixing, and the next thing we knew, Toyota settled and agreed to give $2.3 million to a Canadian charity – without admitting guilt. Slick, eh? And prices for Toyotas remained "fixed" in some regions of Canada for some years afterward.

Fast-forward to Toyota's sudden-acceleration woes. As far as safety is concerned, Toyota's, "Oh what a feeling" jingle comes to mind – indeed, a "feeling" of betrayal. Although National Highway Traffic Saftey Administration (NHTSA)-logged complaints confirmed that Toyota reps stonewalled thousands of Toyota car and truck owners, these same Toyota executives, claims managers, and lawyers said they were unaware that the vehicles would suddenly accelerate out of control. Toyota's president cried as he testified before the U.S. Congress in 2010 when confronted with complaint records. Shortly thereafter, Toyota recalled almost its entire lineup to change floor carpets and throttles and paid almost $50 million U.S. in fines. In December 2012 another $1.6 billion was offered to Toyota owners in the States in a class-action settlement.

Toyota maintains that the problem isn't electronics. A brake override feature has been added on all models. The brake-to-idle failsafe system cuts engine power if both the accelerator and brake are pressed. European vehicles have had this safety device as a standard feature for years. Ultimately, the U.S. Department of Transportation (DOT) concluded that, other than in instances where accelerators were trapped by poorly fitted floor mats, the collisions were caused by drivers pressing the accelerator when they intended to apply their brakes, which DOT called "pedal misapplication" or, essentially, blamed on human error. The problem is that some motorists driving new Toyotas today with the override feature added, say their cars still suddenly accelerate without warning.

There are still complaints coming from owners of recalled models and service bulletins that point to a possible electronic failure in the throttle system apparently affecting recent models. To be fair, drivers of other makes of automobiles have reported experiencing unintended acceleration in their vehicles, as well.

Toyota's Quality Decline

Ten years ago *Lemon-Aid* warned readers that Toyota quality was declining. Reports of "runaway" cars were coming in through NHTSA owner-complaint Internet postings and brake failures were rampant. We immediately lowered our ratings on many Toyota models.

"Lag and Lurch"

Toyota has systematically rejected owner complaints over drivetrains that possibly affect its entire 1999-2014 lineup. A look at NHTSA's safety complaint database shows complaints alleging these vehicles have an electronic module glitch that causes a lag and lurch when accelerating, decelerating, or turning. Toyota knows that if it confirms the defect is electronic in nature, the company re-opens the sudden acceleration polemic and could be forced to replace electronic control modules on millions of vehicles – modules that cost far more than a floor mat anchor.

A perusal of *Lemon-Aid* readers' letters and e-mails, as well as NHTSA reports, shows that other recent-model Toyotas have been plagued by engineering mistakes. These include cars that pull to one side or require constant steering corrections; Corollas that wander all over the road; Prius hybrids that temporarily lose braking ability; and trucks with rear ends that bounce uncontrollably over the smoothest roadways. Other safety failures include engine and transmission malfunctions; fuel spewing out of cracked gas tanks; displays that can't be seen in daylight; and electrical system glitches that can transform a powered sliding door into a guillotine. The ever-popular 3.5L V6 used in many Toyota and Lexus models adopted a rubber hose to direct hot engine oil to the camshaft – an engineering bungle that predictably saw many engines lose their oil and grind themselves to smithereens in 2005 to 2008 models.

$2000 Dashboard Repairs

After a pummeling from owner complaints mounting class-action lawsuits, Toyota has extended the warranty on 3.5 million 2003-2011 cars with sticky, cracked, and melted dashboards. Warranty extensions allow owners to replace their dashboards free of charge at Toyota and Lexus dealerships. For owners who already paid out-of-pocket to replace their dashboards, Toyota will pay up to $1,500 per dashboard. The extended warranty only applies to dashboards that were damaged by heat and humidity. If the dealers find that the dashboards were damaged by other means, the extended warranty won't apply, unless an independent expert refutes Toyota's appraisal. Only Toyota and Lexus dealers are authorized to do the work.

RATING: Recommended (2006-2012), Above Average (2013-2016). The tiny Yaris hatchback is ancient mechanically speaking, but that's the source of its biggest strength: It doesn't break down and it is an ideal conveyance for people seeking basic transportation. Like the Echo that preceded it, the Yaris offered tall seating, easy entry and egress, good visibility and decent power for a subcompact. Its 1.5L DOHC 4-cylinder is an economical twin-cam engine equipped with variable valve timing, good for 106 hp. Canadians got three- and five-door hatchbacks. The Yaris sedan was offered from 2007 to 2012. The sedan is essentially as roomy as the Corolla and it has a large trunk. Except for a re-body in 2012, the Yaris has essentially remained the same throughout the years. The last visual change for the Yaris was a mid-cycle remake for 2015, which included mildly revised exterior styling, minor cabin updates, some structural enhancements and additional sound insulation. The big change for 2017 is Toyota's Safety Sense System C, with a pre-collision system and a lane departure alert. The exterior of the Yaris looks pert and quite European, appropriate as the Yaris sold in Canada is assembled in France. *2017 Yaris Sedan:* When Mazda elected not to launch its redesigned subcompact Mazda2 in North America, Toyota went ahead with a Toyota-branded version of the car, which it sells in Canada as the Yaris Sedan. Road performance: *2012-2017:* With only 106 hp connected to an old-school 4-speed automatic transmission, the Yaris is slower than competitors like the Hyundai Accent and its engine is spinning more quickly in top gear. The ancient 4-speed upshifts smoothly but can be reluctant to engage a lower gear when requested. The single windshield wiper creates significant wind noise when in its parked position. The ride which was quite supple on the 2006-2011 Yaris, is quite choppy, especially in the sporty-themed SE trim. The electric power steering is light and lacks road feel. Since its 2012 redesign, the Yaris features conventional gauges placed ahead of the driver, logical minor controls and cabin materials that are reasonably attractive at this price point. The front seats are small, but supportive enough, and except for legroom for really tall drivers, front occupants have enough space to be comfortable. Rear seat passengers enjoy good headroom and acceptable legroom for the class. Luggage space is fairly tall, but does not have a big footprint. **Strong points:** The best feature of the Yaris is its history of excellent durability and low running costs. Fuel economy is excellent. The car is easy to maneuver in tight spots. **Weak points:** As a new vehicle purchase, the Yaris is behind the times. Its raspy engine and ancient 4-speed automatic transmission are no longer competitive and its suspension is neither supple nor much fun in the twisties. The car gets buzzy beyond 100 km/h and becomes tiresome on long trips; the older Yaris sedan was softer and quieter and selling prices are now reasonable. **Major redesign:** 2006, 2012 hatchback, 2016 sedan. **Best alternatives:** The Hyundai Accent, Kia Rio and Honda Fit. A used Mazda2 hatchback is a good city commuter.

Prices and Specs

Price: *Hatchback CE manual:* $15,395, *SE automatic:* $19,430 **Freight:** $1,565 **Powertrain (FWD):** Engine: 1.5L 4-cyl. (106 hp); Transmissions: 5-speed man., 4-speed auto. **Dimensions:** Passengers: 2/3; Wheelbase: 98.8 in., 2,510 mm.; L: 155.5 in., 3,950 mm.; Weight: 2,335 lb., 1,050 kg. **Fuel economy:** *Automatic:* 7.8L/100 km city, 6.6L/100 km highway. **Assembled in:** Japan (sedan, hatchback), France (hatchback); Mexico (Mazda2-based Yaris sedan).

Owner-reported safety-related failures: One downside of the car's low weight and short overall length is its propensity to wander on the highway in high winds. More than a few drivers questioned the effectiveness of the electric steering system in such conditions.

RELIABILITY: Very few complaints for all years. Until 2012, the cars were assembled in Japan; production switched to France and recently to Mexico. The Yaris is tough and tolerates neglect. Some alternator failures on 2006-2011 sedans. Check the water pump to ensure it isn't leaking. 2007-2008 Yaris sedans with early ABS systems could experience water infiltration of their circuitry triggering an ABS warning light and an expensive repair involving replacement of a wiring harness. The 1.5L engine uses a durable timing chain, not a replaceable belt. A few owners had bad luck with the air conditioner when road debris punctured the condenser. Deep snow may pull the plastic engine fairing off the bottom of the car, and the paint appears

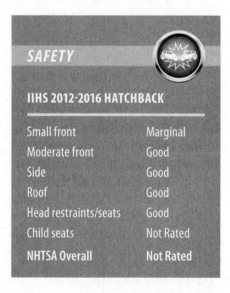

SAFETY	
IIHS 2012-2016 HATCHBACK	
Small front	Marginal
Moderate front	Good
Side	Good
Roof	Good
Head restraints/seats	Good
Child seats	Not Rated
NHTSA Overall	**Not Rated**

to chip easily. Corrosion resistance is good. The APA recommends aftermarket rustproofing to extend the life of the body because the rest of the car is so long-lived: Krown Rust control for an annual application, or in Montreal Barry's Rustproofing (contact information is in the Part Four Introduction).

INTERNAL BULLETINS, SECRET WARRANTIES: 2012-14—Remedies for vehicle pulling from one side to the other, requiring constant steering corrections. 2003-11—Eliminating a windshield ticking noise. 2006-11—Corroded front suspension lower control arm No. 2 bolts will be replaced for free up to 7 years/100,000 miles. An abnormal front-end noise when accelerating, turning, or braking is one symptom of this problem. 2006-12—Engine intermittently runs rough with engine misfires. Valve lifters and valve springs have been updated. Remedy for a front suspension clunk. 2007-08—Water on front and rear carpets. Noise, vibration with the blower motor on. Rattle from the upper instrument panel area. ABS light stays on (corrosion alert). 2007-09—Engine noise, vibration when vehicle accelerates. Automatic transmission shift cable rattles when car in Reverse. 2007-10—A/C blower motor noise and vibration. 2007-11—Front end clunk. 2007-14—A/C evaporator drain hose clogged by insect nests. 2011-12—What to do if the passenger-side airbag Off light comes on when the seat is occupied by an average-sized adult. 2012-13—Loose gindshield dam fix.

COROLLA		
	2000-2008	★★★★★
	2009-2010	★★★★
	2011-2017	★★★★★

RATING: Recommended (2000-2008 and 2011-2017); Above Average (2009-2011). The Corolla has long been Toyota's conservative standard-bearer in the compact sedan class, and like other cars in its class, is now big enough to fill the needs of intermediate sedan buyers. The redesigned 2014 Corolla was a fresh, modern design that grew marginally over its predecessor, which resulted in a genuinely roomy car for its segment. The '80s-themed dashboard is a bit of a throwback, but its compact design leaves more space for passengers and its displays and controls are easy to fathom. Underhood the same old 1.8L 4-cylinder drones away behind the firewall, tied to an ancient 4-speed automatic (a CVT is offered in higher trims). The Corolla is subject to a mid-cycle refresh for 2017. Changes include revised exterior styling, some cabin updates and the addition of the Toyota Safety Sense P with a pre-collision system with pedestrian detection, lane departure alert with steering assist, and dynamic cruise control – all offered as standard equipment. In addition, the ancient 4-speed automatic transmission option on the base CE trim level has finally been replaced by the CVT used in the rest of the lineup. **Road performance:** Though far from thrilling with the CVT, the Corolla gathers speed smoothly and is a relaxed cruiser. The ride is generally quite supple, and handling, while lacking any true sense of engagement, is tidy enough and will satisfy most buyers. Steering is accurate and nicely geared, but also numb and overly light. **Strong points:** Reliable with low running costs; used car prices are lower than for the Civic. Roomy cabin. **Weak points:** Uninvolving driving experience, improved a bit with the 2014 redesign. Prehistoric 4-speed slushbox assigned to base models (but it's reliable). **Major redesign:** 2003, 2009 and 2014. **Best alternatives:** Honda Civic, Hyundai Elantra and Mazda3.

Prices and Specs

Prices (2017): *CE manual:* $16,290, *SE-XSE CVT:* $25,210 **Freight:** $1,590 **Powertrain (FWD):** Engine: 1.8L 4-cyl. (132 hp and 140 hp-LE Eco); Transmissions: 6-speed man.; CVT auto. **Dimensions:** Passengers: 2/3; Wheelbase: 106.3 in., 2,700 mm.; L: 183.1; Weight: 2,855 in., 1,300 kg. **Fuel economy:** *1.8 CVT:* 8.3L/100 km city, 6.5/100 km highway. **Assembled in:** Cambridge, Ontario.

SAFETY

IIHS 2014-2016

Small front	Marginal
Moderate front	Good
Side	Good
Roof	Good
Head restraints/seats	Good
Child seats	Acceptable
NHTSA Overall 2016	★★★★★

Owner-reported safety-related failures: Many of the 2010's close calls involved faulty steering that caused the vehicle to veer back and forth, all over the road and sudden, unintended acceleration:

> While driving 50 mph [80 km/h] the vehicle suddenly accelerated. As the vehicle is accelerating, the contact is trying to slow the vehicle down by applying the brakes. At this time the brakes are malfunctioning and speed is increasing. The contact was unable to slow the vehicle down and crashed into another vehicle.

Airbags fail to deploy:

> The driver fell asleep at the wheel, awoke and tried to correct his lane position. Upon his attempt, the car could not be stabilized or controlled. This was a front end crash at a speed of approximately 50–55 mph going through a chain link fence, hitting hundreds of stacked lobster crates (like hitting a brick wall). The car was completely totalled, the driver had seat belt on. Not one airbag deployed. The driver side mirror smashed through the driver side window and a piece of wooden lobster crate with nails came through the front windshield and into the vehicle. This caused serious injury to the driver, severe facial and elbow lacerations, and major amounts of glass fragments in his body.

Other safety-related reports: Airbag warning light comes on for no reason; mysterious windshield cracks; and the rear defogger doesn't adequately clear the window.

RELIABILITY: The Ontario-built Corolla shines in terms of reliability, although there are a few known weaknesses, many due to Toyota cutting corners somewhat in the late 2000s. Check for an oil leak at the top of the engine timing cover; correction is free during the powertrain warranty. The 2009-2010 Corolla generated the most complaints, including a short-lived water pump (the replacement is reportedly better). A leaking water pump can potentially degrade the alternator, which may account for some of the reported alternator replacements. There are reports of oil consumption with the 1.8-L and 2.4-L engines, which may be related to fast-wearing piston rings. Toyota has rebuilt some engines after oil consumption tests, but not all engines are eligible. Check the oil level periodically between changes. The Corolla's electric power steering, part of the 2009 redesign, not only introduced some unwelcome wandering, but the has been known to quit altogether, with lots of complaints about steering issues in its first two years.

INTERNAL BULLETINS, SECRET WARRANTIES: All models/years—Special procedures for eliminating A/C odours and excessive wind noise. These problems are covered in TSBs #AC00297 and #BO00397, respectively. *All models:* 2002-14—Remedies for vehicle pulling from one side to the other, requiring constant steering corrections. 2009—According to TSBs #SB002411 and #SB009411, excess oil consumption in the 2.4L 4-cylinder engine was traced to the piston assembly. Toyota will replace the pistons and rings on a "goodwill" case-by-case basis. 2002-07—Repair tips for correcting a severe pull to one side when underway (TSB #ST005-01). 2004-10—Fixing front-seat squeaking. 2005-06—Grille mesh available to protect the AC condenser from road debris. 2009-10—Poor steering feel. Steering clunk, pop noise. A-pillar rattles. 2009-14—AC evaporator drain hose clogged by insect nests. 2012-13—Free fixes for a host of infotainment functionality failures. 2014-16—Free replacement of the rear wheelhouse plates that may be loose or leave a large gap where attached to the vehicle body.

MATRIX/PONTIAC VIBE ★★★★★

RATING: Recommended. Spun off the component set of the Toyota Corolla, the Toyota Matrix and Pontiac Vibe were launched for the 2003 model year. The first-generation vehicles were paragons of space efficiency, with good room for four adults and hatchback bodies that provide the versatility of a compact SUV without the weight and higher fuel consumption. Power came from the same 1.8L 4-cylinder that's in the Corolla. The XRS featured a high-power very high revving 1.8L tuned by Yahama rated at 165-170 hp. Second-generation models arrived for 2009. Pontiac's best car, the Vibe, was discontinued with the demise of the brand in 2010, while the Matrix lasted until the end of 2014. The 2009 models of both cars kept the mainstream 1.8L 4-cylinder but added a big 2.4L 4-cylinder option lifted from the Camry. The Matrix was more stylized but not necessarily better looking, while the Vibe appeared more conventional. Like the outside, the cabin of the Matrix, especially the dashboard, looks a bit wacky but works well. The

Vibe's different cabin finishes look less "out there." Though space and versatility are good, the cabins of the second-generation cars are not as roomy. All-wheel drive was offered on both generations, with the 2009 and later versions powered by the 2.4L engine. **Road performance:** *2009-2014:* The 1.8L engine coupled with the 4-speed automatic transmission delivers adequate performance and good fuel economy. The big-engined Corolla XRS and Vibe GT are quick, smooth and combine agility with a firmly resilient ride. Nicely weighted, precise steering. The manual transmission features a smooth clutch and a short-throw gear change. The 1.8L engine coupled with the 4-speed automatic transmission delivers adequate performance and good fuel economy. **Strong points:** Good use of space and hatchback versatility. Good blend of fuel economy and performance with the 1.8L 4-cylinder. Good supply on the used car market and prices have come down a bit. **Weak points:** *Second generation:* Small side windows and thick roof pillars impede outward visibility. Carpet quality akin to peach fuzz. Check for a cargo-area cover as it was not standard on all model years. **Major redesign:** 2003 and 2009. **Best alternatives:** As a tall hatchback, the main alternative to the Matrix/Vibe would be the Kia Soul or Hyundai Elantra Touring wagon.

Prices and Specs

Price (used): $14,000-16,000 (2014); $7,500-9,500 (2010). A Pontiac Vibe sells from $1,000 to $1,500 less than a Matrix of similar age and condition. **Freight:** N/A. **Powertrain (FWD/AWD):** Engines: 1.8L 4-cyl. (132 hp); 2.4L 4-cyl. (158 hp); Transmissions: 5-speed manual, 4- and 5-speed automatic. **Dimensions:** Passengers: 2/3; 102.3 in., 2,600 mm.; L: 171.6 in., 4,365 mm.; Weight; 2,844 lb., 1,290 kg. **Fuel economy:** *1.8 Automatic:* 8.3L/100 km city, 6.5L/100 km highway. **Assembled in:** Cambridge, Ontario (Matrix) and United States (Vibe).

RELIABILITY: The 2003-2008 generation is getting old now, but generated fewer complaints than the 2009-2010 cars. *2003-2014 with 1.8L engine:* Check the top of the timing chain cover (oil leak), the water pump (wet, possible coolant leak), a noisy accessory drive belt tensioner (replace), and rear differential on all-wheel drive models (small leak, check fluid level). A rattling noise on startup could signal a worn timing chain. *2.4L engine through 2009:* The engine warranty has been extended to 10 years/240,000 kilometres for excess oil consumption. Toyota considers oil consumption of 1L/ 2,000 km to be normal. If you've just purchased a used Matrix/Vibe with this engine,

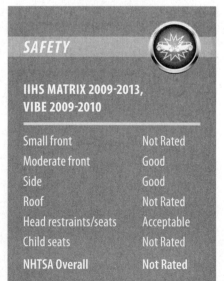

SAFETY

IIHS MATRIX 2009-2013, VIBE 2009-2010

Small front	Not Rated
Moderate front	Good
Side	Good
Roof	Not Rated
Head restraints/seats	Acceptable
Child seats	Not Rated
NHTSA Overall	**Not Rated**

be sure to monitor the oil consumption before your warranty is up. *2009-2014:* Some EGR failures reported. A steering creak could be caused by a faulty steering column; the replacement part costs up to $450. Some radio/infotainment failures, poorly sealed windshields, and chipped paint. Models wearing 18-inch wheels and tires have experienced a few blowouts and bent rims. *2009:* Water can infiltrate the ABS circuitry, triggering the ABS and stability control warnings; the repair can require rear wheel hub and/or wiring harness replacement, an expensive job. A Toyota service bulletin describes how to eliminate dash rattles.

INTERNAL BULLETINS, SECRET WARRANTIES: 2003—Loose or deformed front or rear glass door run. A/C doesn't sufficiently cool the vehicle. Headlights come on when turned off. 2003-06—Correction for rear-end whining, humming, or growling. *Vibe: 2003*—Transmission shifts too early when accelerating at full throttle and the engine is cold. Harsh shifting. Water leak from the A-pillar or headliner area. 2003-08—Silencing a hoot or whistle heard on light acceleration (replace the automatic transaxle cooler hoses).

PRIUS HATCHBACK ★★★★★

RATING: Recommended (2004-2017 5-door); Above Average (2012-2017 Prius V wagon); Above Average (2012-2017 Prius C subcompact hatchback). The original 5-door compact/intermediate Prius was introduced in 2004 and quickly became a cult car with the Green Crowd on the U.S. and Canadian west coasts. The car featured a complex drivetrain with a gas engine, an electric motor, batteries and a CVT transmission in a sleek body that became the template for many of the hybrids that followed in the next 10 years. The Prius was redesigned for 2010, retaining the essential features of the original with slightly better dynamics and a larger engine. It was redesigned again for 2016 with more "expressive" lines; depending on your point of view, the styling is either very distinctive or reminiscent of Mothra from the old cult horror films. For 2017, Toyota's Safety Sense system with pre-collision, lane departure alert and radar cruise control is standard.

A plug-in variant with a limited range on electric power returns sometime during the 2017 model year. Like its predecessor, the current Prius hatchback, offers good space for four within a narrow, tidy footprint that makes the car ideal for urban dwellers and those with challenging driveways or garages. The bigger Camry hybrid is quicker and more refined but also uses more fuel. The proven hybrid system of the Prius works well and is durable. In the mid 2000s, Vancouver cab companies bought rebuilt Prius insurance write offs for their taxi fleets and regularly broke 500,000 km with the original engine, transmission and batteries. (Many of these structurally compromised cabs were ordered off the road by BC's sleepy vehicle safety regulator just before the 2010 Winter Olympics.) **Road performance:** *2004-2015:* Lethargic acceleration; sloppy handling, lifeless steering. *2016-2017:* A revelation, compared to the previous two generations. Although not actually sporty, the steering is much sharper, the ride is more compliant and the car handles more crisply. Despite a small drop in advertised horsepower as of 2016, the Prius is a smoother, more relaxed performer, and the powertrain is not as noisy when pressed. **Strong points:** Ultra low fuel consumption and superior reliability. Great space utilization and a versatile interior. All generations easily accommodate four adults and luggage in a compact format. **Weak points:** A used Prius is expensive and hard to justify based solely on fuel savings. A good strategy to stretch you dollar is to look for an older car (six years plus) with low mileage and service records. *All years:* The transmission selector toggle is quite unconventional and Prius owners should show how it works before inviting someone else to drive the car. Dealer-only service for all but basic work. *2016-2017:* The high-tech display has become a visual cliché and needs to be rethought, as it lacks a compelling look and the ergonomics are a bit befuddled. Cabin materials should be more attractive for what is quite an expensive car. **Major redesign:** 2004, 2010, 2016. **Best alternatives:** The Honda Civic and Insight hybrids; the Civic isn't as economical and the Insight is more an engineer's experimental dream than a true family vehicle. The most common "green" decision was between a Prius and a Golf diesel, but since the discovery of VW's emissions cheating in 2015, there is only one correct answer.

Prices and Specs

Prices (2017 hatchback): *Prius Base:* $27,055, *Technology with Advanced Package:* $32,365 **Freight:** $1,690 **Powertrain (FWD):** Engine: 1.8L 4-cyl. (121 hp total); Transmission: CVT. **Dimensions:** Passengers: 2/3; Wheelbase: 106.3 in., 2,775 mm.; L: 178.7 in., 4,590 mm.; Weight: 3,065 lb., 1,390 kg. **Fuel economy:** 3.7L/100 km city, 4.0L/100 km highway. **Assembled in:** Japan.

ALERT! Head restraints still a recurring complaint:

The default setting is too far forward on my 2016 Prius, causing a forward head and neck posture, resulting in headaches, neck pain, etc., very uncomfortable to drive, and difficult to check blind spots. It also forces the driver's head very close to the airbag.

Owner-reported safety-related failures: Rear window spontaneously shatters when the trunk lid closes; the driver's head restraint could be used to interrogate terrorist prisoners; the low driver's seat and window distortions may impede visibility. Very few safety-related complaints registered from 2011-2016. *2010:* The car is extremely vulnerable to side winds, and light steering doesn't help much, causing the vehicle to wander all over the road and need constant steering corrections. *2012:* Cruise control doesn't disengage quickly enough:

> I have to press the brake harder than any prior vehicles I have owned to kill the cruise control and if I release the brake before the cruise control is released then the car lurches forward. Many other people have experienced this issue and have documented their experiences on the forum *priuschat.com*. They have even fixed the problem themselves by moving the cruise control disengagement closer to the top of the brake pedal.

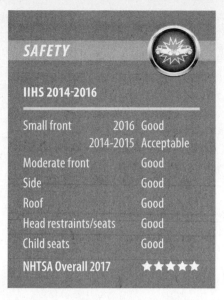

SAFETY

IIHS 2014-2016

Small front	2016	Good
	2014-2015	Acceptable
Moderate front		Good
Side		Good
Roof		Good
Head restraints/seats		Good
Child seats		Good
NHTSA Overall 2017		★★★★★

Transmission sometimes goes into Reverse when shifted into Drive, or goes into Drive when Reverse is selected (operator error predictable due to the design of the shifter); traction control engages when it shouldn't; and the headlights go on and off intermittently.

RELIABILITY: Fanatical assembly quality, low service and running costs. The Prius mostly avoided the decline in quality that hit other Toyota vehicles in the period between 2005-2010. The conventional disc brakes can seize. They don't get much use, because of the regenerative braking system charges the batteries when braking. Have the brake calipers deseized and lubricated annually to postpone expensive brake repairs. *2004-2009:* HID headlamps may shut off without warning, then turn on again. Usually one lamp will show symptoms, but if both lamps play dead on a rural highway the experience can be frightening. The centre multi-function display can go dark, caused by poorly soldered internal connections. The power inverter coolant pump may conk out, resulting in the Check Engine light illuminating. Other irritants include short-lived conventional batteries (every Prius has one) and faulty air conditioners and brake actuators – both rare but expensive fixes. *2010-2015:* Braking responds unpredictably to pedal pressure; Toyota recalled the model worldwide in 2010 to fix an antilock brake software glitch, and more recently to fix a brake pressure accumulator, and to reprogram software to correct a hybrid control unit glitch that could cause the car to revert to limp-home mode. Other irritants include faulty sound systems and backup cameras and conventional batteries that drain mysteriously. The plastic underside fairing and drag on the road.

INTERNAL BULLETINS, SECRET WARRANTIES: All years—It is surprising that with so complex a vehicle and several recall campaigns, most Prius service bulletins don't point to major deficiencies. **2000-08**—Multiple warning lights on; vehicle won't shift out of Park. Steering pulls to the right. **2002-14**—Remedies for vehicle pulling from one side to the other, requiring constant steering corrections. **2010**—Warped engine cover. **2010-14**—A/C evaporator drain hose clogged by insect nests. Cleaning tips to keep the HV battery cooling fan at peak efficiency. Troubleshooting rear windshield ticking. **2012-13**—Warm air comes out of the A/C vents. **2012-15**—Free fixes for a host of infotainment functionality failures.

CAMRY, HYBRID		
	2002-2006	★★★★★
	2007-2009	★★★
	2010-2017	★★★★★

RATING: Recommended (2002-2006 and 2010-2017); Average (2007-2009). The 2012 redesign offered good refinement, a supple ride and a nicely finished cabin; it was an improvement over the 2007-2011 Camry. Until 2009 most Camry's were powered by a sometimes troublesome 2.4L 4-cylinder making 158 hp; from 2010-2017 a better 2.5L 4-cylinder with 178 hp was standard. Unlike most competitors that migrated to turbo 4-cylinders, Toyota still offers a V6 engine upgrade that is both smoother and uses less fuel despite its larger size. In addition to conventional power, the Camry is also offered with a frugal and reliable hybrid powertrain. A conventional 6-speed automatic equips mainstream models, while the hybrid has a CVT. The 2015 update resulted in marginally sleeker exterior styling, an incrementally nicer cabin and crisper driving dynamics. For 2017, the premium XSE V6 receives a standard pre-collision system with radar cruise control and lane departure alert; in other respects the Camry is unchanged this year. **Road performance:** The 2015 and newer Camry offers sharper braking, a firmer ride and crisper handling that mimic the Honda Accord, even in the non-sporting LE and XLE trims. The steering is still light and numb. Try-before-you-buy the sportier SE and

XSE, as the ride is firm for traditional Camry customers. The 2.5L 4-cylinder is strong and smooth, except when pushed hard, when it takes on an appealing snarl. The V6 is refined and very fast. **Strong points:** Roomy, comfortable and quiet cabin. The dash is stocked with easily scanned gauges and easy-to-use controls. Seats are large and supportive, and the trunk is commodious. Very good blend of performance and fuel economy with the 2.5L four, and sparkling acceleration and surprisingly decent fuel economy with the V6. With a combined rating of 200 hp, the hybrid delivers good performance and exceptional fuel economy; after the fourth year, the premium to buy one is negligible compared to a gas Camry. **Weak points:** Reliability took a nose-dive in 2007-2009 as Toyota chased sales at the expense of quality. Uninvolving handling on 2007-2011 models. Visibility to the rear could be better. **Major redesign:** 2002, 2007, 2012, 2015 update. **Best alternatives:** The Honda Accord is the obvious cross shop. A Hyundai Sonata or Kia Optima will cost thousands less on the used car market. The Volkswagen Passat with the 2.5L 5-cylinder engine or base turbo and a full coverage VW warranty.

Prices and Specs

Prices (2017): *LE 2.4L:* $24,970, *Hybrid XLE:* $36,450 **Freight:** $1,690 **Powertrain (FWD):** Engines: 2.5L 4-cyl. Hybrid (200 hp), 2.5L 4-cyl. (178 hp), 3.5L V6 (268 hp); Transmissions: 6-speed auto.; CVT. **Dimensions:** Passengers: 2/3; Wheelbase: 109.3 in., 2,775 mm.; L: 190.9; Weight: 3,240 lb., 1, 467 kg. **Fuel economy:** *2.5L:* 9.8L/100 km city, 7.1L/100 km highway; *Hybrid:* 6.2L/100 km city, 5.6L/100 km highway. **Assembled in:** U.S.A.

ALERT! Warranty to cover excessive oil consumption extended to 10 years/240,000 km on the troublesome 2.4L engine in 2007-2009 models. Keep your fingers crossed as Toyota considers oil consumption of 1L/2,000 km is normal, and may ask for oil change records a second owner doesn't have.

Owner-reported safety-related failures: Airbags fail to deploy; when accelerating from a stop, the vehicle hesitates, sometimes to a count of three, before suddenly accelerating. When decelerating, the vehicle speeds up, as if the cruise control were engaged. The close placement of the brake and accelerator pedals contributes to driver error. The centre console below the gear shift becomes extremely hot; Hybrid's low-beam headlamps are inadequate on the highway; excessively bright LED tail/brake lights irritate drivers in trailing vehicles; and

SAFETY

IIHS 2015-2016

Small front	Good
Moderate front	Good
Side	Good
Roof	Good
Head restraints/seats	Good
Child seats	Acceptable
NHTSA Overall 2017	★★★★

wheels may lock up. Reports of the front windshield cracking from the driver-side upper left corner and gradually extending toward the middle of the windshield. Glass sunroof shatters, front windshield distortion looks like little bubbles are embedded in the glass; rear window distortion when viewed through the rearview mirror during night driving; the passenger-side windows may fall out. Trunk lid "beans" people's heads when the weak struts fail. Rodents in the underhood area or ductwork

RELIABILITY: *2002-2006:* Check the steering column before changing the rack if you hear a knocking sound. Water pump (wet, coolant). *2007-2011:* Sway bar links (broken, rattling over bumps), rear suspension knock over bumps (blown bushings), rear struts (leaking, worn), wheel bearings (noisy, worn), 2.4L engine (oil consumption, leak at the rear of the block). For 2007, the most common complaint involves a lag in the automatic transmission's ability to respond to changes in speed. Owners report the vehicle hesitating then lurching ahead, making merging with traffic difficult. The remedy involves three stages: A computer reflash (update), a solenoid replacement and, if required, transmission replacement. *2007-early 2010 V6:* A defective external rubber oil supply line to the camshaft mounted on the side of the block can rupture and ruin the cylinder heads or entire engine; check to make this important product improvement has been performed. If it hasn't, pay the dealer to do it, as Toyota's warranty extension ended in 2013. *2012-2014:* The air conditioner may leak water (condensate) into the cabin and onto the carpet, resulting in a moldy smell. Report failures of the electric power steering to Transport Canada (1-800-333-0510). Stressed out sunroof glass.

INTERNAL BULLETINS, SECRET WARRANTIES: 2002-14—Remedies for vehicle pulling from one side to the other, requiring constant steering corrections. 2006-09—*2006-08 RAV4, 2007-08 Solara, 2007-09 Camry, 2007-11 Camry Hybrid, 2009 Corolla, and 2009 Matrix.* The 2.4L 4-cylinder engine may be an "oil-burner." In TSBs #SB002411 and #SB009411, Toyota says the problem was traced to the piston assembly. The automaker will replace the pistons and rings on a "goodwill" case-by-case basis. No shift from Park; multiple warning lights come on. 2007—Engine oil leaks from the timing cover. Rough idle, stalling; shift flare. 2007-08—No crank; engine starts and dies. Excessive steering-wheel vibrations, flutter, and noise. Instrument panel rattle. Frame creaking noise. Rear suspension squeaking, rubbing. Engine oil leak from camshaft housing. Engine ticking noises. Torque converter shudder. Moonroof knocking when underway. Troubleshooting brake pulsation/vibration. Rattle from trunk area. 2007-09—The 2.4L 4-cylinder engine burns oil rapidly. 2007-11—Sunroof leaks at headliner and floor areas. 2007-14—AC evaporator drain hose clogged by insect nests. 2009—Silencing engine ticking and floor pan creaking. Inoperative moonroof. 2007-10—Braking vibration, pulsation. A rattle or buzz coming from the driver's side dash may require an updated vacuum check valve. Tips on correcting a roof knocking sound. Intermittent noxious AC odours. 2007-11—Water leaks from sunroof onto headliner and into footwell area. 2008-09—TCM update for shift improvements. 2008-10—Ignition coils may need replacing if the MIL alert is illuminated. *Hybrid:* 2007-09—No shift from Park; multiple warning lights come on. Water leaks onto headliner and footwell area. Inoperative moonroof. 2007-10—Ways to fix a knocking sound from the roof area. 2007-11—The 2.4L 4-cylinder engine burns oil rapidly. Front strut insulator noise. 2011-12—Passenger-side airbag OFF light will come on even though the seat is unoccupied. Uneven rear brake wear. Insufficient alternator charging may be corrected with an updated pulley assembly. Remedy for a front/rear suspension noise that occurs when passing over bumps in the road. A front door trim panel rattle. Underbody rattling. Troubleshooting a windshield back glass ticking noise. 2012-14—Toyota has extended its warranty up to 8 years/150,000 miles (it's an American decision) to cover repairs to correct transmission torque converter shudder. This "goodwill" warranty applies no matter if the Camry was bought new or used. Trunk lid won't stay up on an incline. Condensation drips from the headliner. Transaxle high-pitch whine when cruising. 2012-14—Free upgrades for a host of infotainment functionality failures. 2012-16—Free fix for vehicles that exhibit a knocking popping ticking or snapping noise from the moon roof area while driving. 2015—Reduced air flow through the cabin air filter due to snow intrusion through the cowl. A free cowl louver sub-assembly with integrated mesh is available.

AVALON ★★★★

RATING: Above Average. Along with the Nissan Maxima, the Avalon resides in a market limbo-land where non-prestige branded luxury cars, regardless of their inherent merits, fail to sell. The stylish, roomy Avalon released for the 2013 model year did suffer from a number of fit and finish issues. Loose headliners, distorted windshield view, or reflective interior trim that distracts drivers are complaints received regarding the current Avalon. Based on the 2012 Camry, 2017 should be the last year for the current Avalon. **Road performance:** A smooth and responsive powertrain that provides quick acceleration combined with good fuel economy; steady handling and a ride that is on the firm side of resilient. The steering is still light and too detached but better than in years past. The dashboard houses crisp gauges and intuitive controls and occupants repose on large, supportive seats with copious legroom. **Strong points:** Built on the same platform and wheelbase as the more prestigious ES350, the Avalon is a comparative bargain. One of the best-looking Toyotas in years. Iconoclasts will love it for its reverse snob appeal and exclusivity. **Weak points:** Except for a bit more rear seat legroom and the handsome exterior, is the Avalon really worth more than a top-spec Camry V6? Assembly quality seems to be an issue. **Major redesign:** 2005 and 2013. **Best alternatives:** Toyota Camry XLE V6, Honda Accord V6, Nissan Maxima, and Buick LaCrosse.

Prices and Specs

Prices (2016): *Touring:* $38,990, *Limited:* $44,170 **Freight:** $1,690 **Powertrain (FWD):** Engine: 3.5L V6 (268 hp), Transmissions: 6-speed auto. **Dimensions:** Passengers: 2/3; Wheelbase: 111 in., 2,820 mm.; L: 195.3 in., 4,960 mm.; Weight: 3,548 lb., 1,610 kg. **Fuel economy:** 11.4L/100 km city, 7.6L/100 km highway. **Assembled in:** Kentucky, U.S.A.

ALERT! Avalon dashboard trim reflects sunlight directly into driver's eyes. Tan-coloured dashboards are especially reflective. During mid-day sun, blinding beams of sunlight may also bounce off several areas of the mirrored-chrome-coloured plastic trim that surrounds the dashboard and wraps around the instrument cluster. Sunlight is reflected off chrome trim beneath the tachometer and speedometer … off trim on both sides of the steering wheel, and other points across the trim depending on time of day and direction of car. Because the trim is bevelled, instead of a vertical surface, it focuses the sunlight directly back into the driver's eyes.

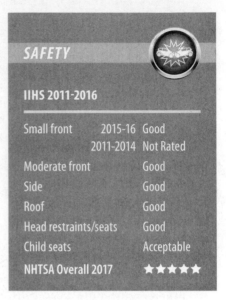

SAFETY

IIHS 2011-2016

Small front	2015-16	Good
	2011-2014	Not Rated
Moderate front		Good
Side		Good
Roof		Good
Head restraints/seats		Good
Child seats		Acceptable
NHTSA Overall 2017		★★★★★

Owner-reported safety-related failures: Sudden unintended acceleration; rear-corner blind spots and excessive rear glare and distortion. Other reported driving hazards: "Lag and lurch" when accelerating; when cruise control is engaged, applying the brake slows the car, but as soon as the foot is taken off the brake, the car surges back to its former speed; vehicle rolls backward when parked on an incline; "chin-to-chest" head restraints; a defective telescopic steering-wheel lever may cause the steering wheel to collapse towards the dash when the vehicle is underway; steering column is unusually loose; high-intensity discharge headlights only partially illuminate the highway; and electrical shorts that may suddenly turn off dash lights.

RELIABILITY: *2005-2008:* The most serious complaint involves a poorly designed rubber hose that routes hot high-pressure oil outside the V6 engine block. The rubber deteriorates over time and can rupture unexpectedly, causing the engine to go dry and self-destruct. Check to see if this repair was done when purchasing the vehicle (affects 2005-2008 models mostly). *2005-2012:* Jerky transmissions (requiring a reflash), bad ignition coils, faulty steering columns, leaky moonroofs, cracked dashboards, short-lived HID headlamps, broken radios and chipping paint. *2013-2017:* Deteriorating cabin trim is the concern with newer models; the front seatback covers can fall off and the ceiling headliner can sag badly – that's unusual for Toyota. Other reported issues in small numbers include droopy trunk lids, recalled sub-woofers, sunroofs that shatter spontaneously, engine and rear windshield/window ticking; problems with the trunk opener; and sunshade switches that are located too close together.

INTERNAL BULLETINS, SECRET WARRANTIES: 2005-09—Front power seat grinding, groaning. 2005-11—Sunroof leaks at headliner and floor areas. 2005-12—Telescopic steering column adjustment lever detent clip replacement is at no charge for 10 years under a "goodwill warranty" (Warranty Enhancement Program #ZTY). 2005-14—Front strut insulator noise. 2007-14—A/C evaporator drain hose clogged by insect nests. 2008-10—High-beam headlight failures. 2008-11—Underbody rattling noises. 2011-12—Torque converter shudder at low acceleration. Insufficient alternator charging may require an updated pulley assembly. 2012-14—Free fixes for a host of infotainment functionality failures. 2013-14—Free replacement of the driver and passenger front seatback board until July 31, 2017 (Limited Service Campaign #E0J). The driver's seat bottom outer bolster may have a ridge/bulge in it, or the seat is uncomfortable. Fuel door may be difficult to open. 2013-16—Free fix for vehicles that exhibit a knocking, popping, ticking, or snapping noise from the moon roof area while driving.

SIENNA ★★★★★

RATING: Recommended. The Sienna is the chief competitor to the Honda Odyssey and in many years it was more reliable. The all-new 2004 model was larger and featured a 3.3L V6 that used a replaceable timing belt; it was retired when Toyota switched to the chain-driven 3.5L V6 for 2007 (with a 36 hp increase). Stability control arrived in 2008. The current Sienna debuted for 2011 and received a mid-cycle refresh for 2015; a backup camera and Bluetooth became standard. The 2017 updates include direct injection, resulting in an extra 30 hp for the 3.5L V6, and a new 8-speed automatic transmission that replaces the old 6-speed. The Sienna is the only minivan currently available with all-wheel drive. Toyota dealers report that the Sienna will be in short supply in Canada this year, which could mean delivery delays and high transaction prices. **Road performance:** The Sienna's 2015 update included an attractive new dash, nicer cabin fittings and better sound insulation, rectifying the van's deficits when it debuted for 2011. The powertrain updates for 2017 improve both acceleration and refinement. The Sienna is now a very competent all-rounder that is approaching the ride-handling balance of the Honda Odyssey which has been traditionally, if one can say it, the "sportiest" of the large family vans. **Strong points:** *All years:* Clear gauges, logical controls, comfortable seats and generous space for passengers and cargo. *2015-2017:* Punchy powertrain and a good ride-handling compromise. Lower prices than the Odyssey on the used vehicle market, though much more expensive than the Grand Caravan. **Weak points:** Little to complain about. The redesigned 2011 models were attractive, but the cabin was de-contented in an obvious show of cost cutting. Offered from 2011-2014, the 4-cylinder was an unsuccessful experiment; its 2.7L engine barely saved any fuel compared to the V6 and Toyota wisely dropped it. **Major redesign:** 2004, 2007 update, 2011. **Best alternatives:** The Honda Odyssey is the closest alternative. The redesigned Kia Sedona is worth looking at. A used Dodge Grand Caravan or Chrysler Town and Country will cost thousands less; no Toyota buyer would cross shop a new one.

Prices and Specs

Prices (2017): *Base V6:* $33,420, *XLE Limited AWD:* $51,445 **Freight:** $1,760 **Powertrain (FWD/AWD):** Engine: 3.5L V6 (296 hp); Transmission: 8-speed auto. **Dimensions:** Passengers: 2/3/2; 2/3/3; Wheelbase: 119.3 in., 3,030 mm.; L: 200.2 in., 5,086 mm.; Weight (2017 FWD): 4,430 lb., 2,010. **Fuel economy:** 12.5L/100 km city, 8.9L/100 km highway. **Assembled in:** U.S.A.

ALERT! Run-flat tires on all-wheel drive models are fast-wearing and expensive. Consider Michelin or Pirelli, instead of the original equipment Bridgestone or Dunlop run-flats. Some owners report that the brake and accelerator pedals are too close together; see if this is noticeable during the test drive.

Owner-reported safety-related failures: Be wary of the power-sliding door and power-assisted rear liftgate, especially if you have children. Parents, especially those who do the bulk of the carpooling, love the hands-free convenience but it comes at a price. The doors pose risks to other occupants, while the liftgate can injure someone standing under it.

My 17-month-old's head got jammed between the right rear wheel and the right rear door panel while the electric door slid open. Even though my wife pulled on the door handle the door kept sliding open. My baby's head was crushed between the tire and door panel. This is a very unsafe design as my wife tried to stop the door from sliding back and the door kept moving.

. . .

My 2-year-old daughter got her leg caught in the back part of the sliding door of a 2011 Toyota Sienna. She was inside the car. The door was opened. Her leg fell into the space while the door was opening. The door opened as far as it could and constricted her leg. Her leg was so constricted we could not reposition her body to open the door. ... She was trapped (screaming) for 20-25 minutes. Her leg was cold and turning blue before it was freed. ... I'm very concerned about the design of the door. I've looked at other mini vans (even the same make and model but different year) and they don't have the gap in the back part of the door like the 2011 Toyota Sienna.

. . .

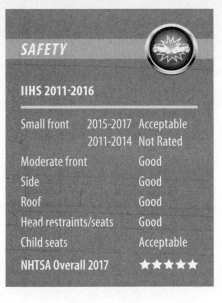

SAFETY

IIHS 2011-2016

Small front	2015-2017	Acceptable
	2011-2014	Not Rated
Moderate front		Good
Side		Good
Roof		Good
Head restraints/seats		Good
Child seats		Acceptable
NHTSA Overall 2017		★★★★★

Couple of months after I got the car, there were several incidents [in which] me and family members were hit on our heads and shoulders by the self-closing liftgate [and we] didn't know what the cause was. After researching this problem, Toyota had recalled Sienna in the past about this same problem for older models for weak liftgate struts.

Other owner reports: The slightest touch of the gear shifter causes a shift into Neutral or Reverse; multiple warning lights come on, and the vehicle cannot shift; front windshield distorts the view; rear window may spontaneously explode:

The rear window on my 2013 Sienna hatchback door blew out. The vehicle had been parked in my garage overnight – the next morning it was shattered. I contacted the dealer to find out if this was a common problem – I was told no. However, upon performing a Google search, I found hundreds of instances of people complaining of the same issue. It was also interesting to learn that rear windows were/are on national backorder from Toyota.

Excessive rearview mirror vibration; front passenger seatback tilts forward when braking and second-row seats may be wobbly. Three more things to remember, particularly on the 2013 models: If the battery "dies" you will have to climb over the console to extract kids from the backseat; the A/C is known for emitting a foul, moldy smell.

RELIABILITY: The most reliable minivan over the years. 2004-2010 Complaints about a slow-shifting automatic and electronic throttle response; both require reprogramming by the dealer and should have been resolved long ago. 2007-2010 V6

engine external oil tube (see the Camry evaluation). 2004-2006 models were prone to leaky radiators and gas tanks (both recall items). The power sliding doors can malfunction; their cables are ridiculously thin and susceptible to corrosion. Weak tailgate struts and some interior rattles. *2004-2010:* The coolant line to the rear heater is subject to corrosion and its replacement is expensive. If the underbody is not too corroded consider aftermarket oil or grease-based rustproofing. The APA recommends Krown Rust Control or in Montreal, Barry's Rustproofing (contact information is in the Part Four Introduction). *2011-17:* The most common complaint has to do with the power sliding doors (again) whose thin cables can snap; the repair is expensive. The 2011-2016 models were recently recalled to correct a problem with an open fuse that could see a door open while the van was in motion with the door not locked. The power-assisted rear hatch is also known to fail. Best advice: Avoid buying any used van with power doors or purchase a comprehensive Toyota used vehicle warranty. The cable assembly that controls the power sunroof can fail; the repair can involve replacing the entire sunroof assembly for an astronomical $3,600; most owners pass on the repair and leave the roof closed. Other reported mechanical weaknesses include fast-wearing tires – both the conventional ones and the run-flats that come with all-wheel drive – seats that squeak and a few interior rattles. Some reports of the electrically assisted power steering system may fail spontaneously, leaving drivers to strong-arm the vehicle to the side of the road (report the incident to Transport Canada at 1-800-333-0510). Until 2010, a clunking noise when turning may be traced to the intermediate steering shaft. *All-wheel drive:* Check the left-side transmission output shaft for an oil leak as well as the rear differential. Rotating tires to maintain even wear at all four corners is important to reduce stress on the driveline.

INTERNAL BULLETINS, SECRET WARRANTIES: All years—Sliding-door hazards, malfunctions, and noise are a veritable plague affecting all model years and generating a ton of service bulletins. Owner feedback confirms that front brake pads and discs are often replaced under Toyota's "goodwill" policy if they wear out before 2 years/ 40,000 km (in spite of Toyota's pretension that brakes aren't a warrantable item) and the customer is adamant that the brakes aren't "reasonably" durable. Rusting at the base of the two front doors will usually be repaired at no cost, often with a courtesy car included. **2002-14**—Remedies for vehicle pulling from one side to the other, requiring constant steering corrections. **2003-09**—Upper, lower windshield ticking noise. **2004-05**—Remedy for hard starts in cold weather. Transmission lag, gear hunting. Premature brake pad wear. Fuel-injector ticking. Inoperative A/C light flashing. A/C blower or compressor noise; seized compressor. **2004-10**—Front seat squeaking. Sliding doors don't operate smoothly (change the lock assembly). Sliding-door rattle. Brake rattle, buzz from driver's side of the dash. Underbody spare tire carrier was recalled for corrosion; dealers are installing an improved carrier at no cost. **2006-09**—No shift from Park. **2011-12**—Engine ticking; more ticking from the windshield/back glass. Vehicle may exhibit insufficient charging performance from the alternator. An updated pulley assembly is available to address this condition. Transfer-case fluid leaks. Water puddles in the van's rear storage area near the back door. 2011-13—If the A/C doesn't work properly, an A/C line retainer (piping clamp) may have become unlatched and caused a refrigerant leak. This is a simple and cheap repair; try it first. 2011-14—Some Siennas may have a front brake vibration/pulsation that can be felt while lightly applying the brake pedal. New front brake pads and a new field fix repair procedure have been developed to improve this condition, says TSB # T-SB-0045-14, issued July 8, 2014. A/C evaporator drain hose may be clogged by insect nests.

RAV4 ★★★★★

RATING: Recommended. Like the better compact SUVs, the RAV4 combines comfort and utility with a nice blend of performance and fuel economy. *2006-2012:* The optional 3.5L V6 with 269 hp transforms the RAV4 into cruise missile. In 2009 the base 4-cylinder engine grew from 2.4L to 2.5L and picked up 13 hp. Active head restraints appeared. An optional third-row seat suitable for children may offer just enough additional versatility for carpooling or family outings with grandparents. The current RAV4 was introduced for the 2013 model year and received a mid-cycle update for 2016. The V6 and 3-row seating were dropped. The conventional RAV is still powered by a 2.5L 4-cylinder engine sending power to the front, or all wheels, now via a 6-speed automatic transmission. The RAV4 Hybrid uses the powertrain from the Camry. For 2017, the principal change is the addition of the Toyota Safety Sense system as standard equipment, including a pre-collision system with pedestrian detection, lane departure alert with steering assist and dynamic cruise control. **Road performance:** Good acceleration and relaxed cruising from the 2.5L 4-cylinder that powers mainstream RAV4s. The conventional 6-speed automatic transmission is well matched to the engine. Some owners would appreciate a bit more power when passing on two-lane roads but the RAV4 is quick enough for most owners. Good steering and nice handling. **Strong points:** *2006-2017:* Comfortable seats, front and rear, and plenty of space for passengers and cargo. Good balance of fuel economy and performance. The 2006-2012 V6 was top rated in APA comparison tests; the 4-cylinder was ranked fairly close behind, with other leaders in the class. *2013-2017:* Superior handling dynamics. Very economical hybrid. **Weak points:** Some people find the interior design too overtly a truck-wannabe, especially the tacky dashboard on the 2006-2012 generation. Pre-2013 models have a side-hinged rear door that carries the spare tire, but it is hinged on the wrong side to aid loading at the curb, and the cargo lamp is mounted on the swinging door and casts no light into the vehicle. Fairly high theft risk. **Major redesign:** 2006 and 2013. **Best alternatives:** Honda CR-V, Mazda CX-5, or the somewhat smaller 2016-2017 Hyundai Tucson. If you're buying new, a Subaru Forester with an extended warranty on the powertrain.

Owner-reported safety-related failures: Fire erupted in the engine compartment; steering angle sensor malfunction causes the vehicle to stall out; a "thumping" rear suspension noise; cracking front windshields; the defroster/air circulation system is weak; and wide rear roof pillars obstruct visibility.

RELIABILITY: Best in class for most years, equal to or better than the Honda CR-V and Suzuki Grand Vitara. *2006-2012:* A knocking or popping noise in the steering column when turning, traced to either the intermediate steering shaft or the steering rack. In either case, replacement is required, which is expensive. A lit engine service light and EVAP code can indicate a leak in the evaporative emissions system that is common to other Toyota models. Both the 2007-2009 2.4L 4-cylinder and 2006-2009 3.5L V6 share the same defects with other contemporary Toyota models (check the review for the Camry). Other potential issues include short-lived water pumps, suspension struts (check for leaks after 100,000 km), erratic transmissions, prematurely worn mufflers, faulty stereos and chipped paint. *2010:* Some failures of the limited slip rear differential ($1,100 for the replacement part). *2013-2017:* The optional navigation screen is difficult to see in bright sunlight. Some hesitating automatic transmissions and drivetrain vibrations. Air conditioner may produce a musty smell. Lubricate the hinges on the swinging rear door.

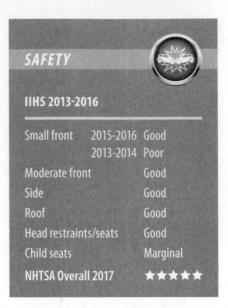

SAFETY		
IIHS 2013-2016		
Small front	2015-2016	Good
	2013-2014	Poor
Moderate front		Good
Side		Good
Roof		Good
Head restraints/seats		Good
Child seats		Marginal
NHTSA Overall 2017		★★★★★

INTERNAL BULLETINS, SECRET WARRANTIES: 2002-06—Correction for vehicles that pull to the right when accelerating. 2003-11—Windshield ticking noise considered a factory-related problem (TSB-0142-08). 2004-10—Front-seat squeaking. 2006-08—The 2.4L 4-cylinder engine may be an "oil-burner" covered by a Toyota "goodwill warranty" (see Camry section). Engine compartment squeaks. Steering clunk, pop, knock. 2006-09—Engine ticking noise. Multiple warning lamps lit; no shift from Park. Inoperative moonroof. 2006-10—No-crank, no-start requires the installation of a revised Neutral switch assembly. Rough idle. **2006-12**—A rear-end clunking sound may signal that one or both rear stabilizer links are damaged. A growling noise from the rear differential is likely caused by the contamination of a bearing. **2006-14**—A/C evaporator drain hose may be clogged by insect nests. **2012-13**—Free fixes for a host of infotainment functionality failures. **2013**—One or both power back door actuator units may separate from the ball mounts on the hatch or the body. Additionally, wiring on the actuator may be damaged causing the power back door to become inoperative. **2015**—Correction for an intermittent HVAC buzzing noise. Key fob reduced remote range.

VENZA   *2009-2016* ★★★

RATING: Above Average (2009-2016). Essentially a Camry hatchback on stilts, the five-door Venza was introduced as a 2009 model and discontinued in Canada at the end of the 2016 model year. Front-wheel or all-wheel drive can be linked to either a 2.7L 4-cylinder or a 3.5L V6. The Venza uses the Camry's platform to good effect; the wheelbase remaines comfortably long for room to stretch, while ground clearance is a generous 20.5 cm. The extra height makes entry and egress easy, especially for seniors. Since it didn't offer third-row seating the Venza accepts only five; the seats were praised for being broad, supportive and comfortable. The rear seat reclines. **Road performance:** The Venza's big 4-cylinder is reasonably quick and smooth, and is the choice of most Venza buyers. The V6 is powerful and not much harder on gas; however it's not especially quiet or smooth sounding. Noise from a variety of sources is higher than expected from a car in this segment. The 6-speed automatic transmission upshifts smoothly, but downshifts reluctantly. With a flinty ride over short, sharp bumps (courtesy of 19 and 20 inch wheels) and a lack of composure when roads get twisty, the Venza's suspension delivers the worst of both worlds. Prices vary widely depending on the engine and trim level. To stretch your dollar, choose front-wheel drive and buy four winter tires – that's safer than all-wheel drive with worn all season tires. **Strong points:** Roomy interior and comfortable seats. Big, clear instruments. Controls for the heating and audio system look odd at first but are a snap to use once you are used to them. The vast centre console can hold a massive amount of stuff, all accessed via a number of cleverly conceived lids. Seamless all-wheel drive system works well. **Weak points:** Subpar cabin materials and poor assembly on the early models are letdowns. Shallow cargo area. Big wheels and tires hurt the ride and are expensive to replace. Quite noisy for a large Toyota. **Major redesign:** 2009. **Best alternatives:** A Honda Accord Crosstour is the closest vehicle to the Venza in concept and execution.

RELIABILITY: The Venza was introduced at the end of Toyota's market-share-at-all-cost binge. The first two model years showed it, with quality control issues affecting the steering, suspension, interior trim and assembly, and they are rated lower. Toyota and its dealers worked on getting the bugs out and many owners had their vehicles corrected under warranty. Reliability issues over the years have included some juddering transmissions (there have been a few outright replacements), faulty wheel speed sensors, poor navigation system displays and interior rattles. The internal cable of the sunroof can fail, requiring a complete assembly to repair it for an astronomical

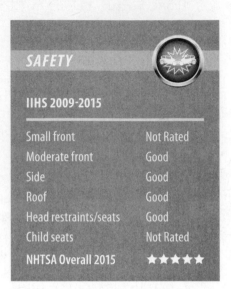

SAFETY	
IIHS 2009-2015	
Small front	Not Rated
Moderate front	Good
Side	Good
Roof	Good
Head restraints/seats	Good
Child seats	Not Rated
NHTSA Overall 2015	★★★★★

$3,600. Check the sway bar links (noisy, broken), wheel bearings (noisy, worn), rear differential on all-wheel drive models (a leak at the pinion seal), and suspension struts (leaking, defective top plates). A leaking rear crank seal is no small matter on all-wheel drive models, because the repair takes 20 hours. In addition, a few faulty steering columns have been replaced, and the paint chips easily.

INTERNAL BULLETINS, SECRET WARRANTIES: 2009-13—Some Venzas equipped with the 2GR-FE V6 may not start in sub-freezing temperatures (approximately -4°F [-20°C] and lower). An Engine Room Junction Block Assembly is available to address this condition. Some vehicles equipped with the 1AR-FE engine may exhibit one or more of the following conditions: An inoperative A/C, or rising engine temperature when stopped. Some vehicles may exhibit a condition where the seat heater is inoperative. Cold start engine knock/rattle. 2009-14—Remedies for vehicle pulling from one side to the other, requiring constant steering corrections. A/C evaporator drain hose clogged by insect nests. 2011-12—Vehicle may exhibit insufficient charging performance from the alternator. An updated pulley assembly is available to address this condition. 2013-14—Entune infotainment and navigation issues and concerns.

good buy

HIGHLANDER, HIGHLANDER HYBRID ★★★★★

RATING: Recommended. The previous generation, also based on the front-wheel drive Camry platform, debuted for 2008. With its optional third-row bench, the Highlander could seat up to seven. Included was a trick middle-row perch that could be folded up and tucked under the front centre console to create two captain's chairs in back. Toyota's ubiquitous 3.5L DOHC V6, good for 270 hp, worked through a conventional 5-speed automatic transmission. A 4-cylinder model returned to the lineup for 2009; it used a 187 hp, 2.7L engine coupled with a 6-speed automatic transmission, and was available in front-wheel drive only. The current Highlander was a hit from the moment it debuted for 2014 and its popularity never waned, meaning that delivery delays and high transaction prices are the norm. The Highlander receives a mid-cycle remake for 2017. Updates include revised exterior styling, a few cabin trim tweaks, direct injection and automatic stop-start for the 3.5L and a new 8-speed automatic transmission for non-hybrid models. Standard for 2017 is the Toyota Safety Sense system that features pre-collision braking with forward collision warning, automatic emergency braking, pedestrian detection and dynamic radar cruise control. **Road performance:** The Highlander's smooth, punchy V6 sends power to a slick shifting automatic transmission that gets its job done without calling attention to itself. Though too light for some, the Highlander's steering is precise and ride and handling are very well sorted and will suit the tastes of most buyers. Clear gauges and, despite a mild excess of buttons, the climate and audio controls are fairly straightforward. Interior materials are attractive and a step up from the pre-2014 model. First and middle row passengers enjoy supportive seats and have abundant legroom. The third-row seats, like the steerage rows in most SUVs, require agility to access but can actually accept smaller adults. Cargo space is ample with the third-row seat folded down but minimal if the seatback is up. The Hybrid is quick and fuel-efficient and can propel itself on electric power alone. The rear wheels of the hybrid's all-wheel system are driven by electric motors. **Strong points:** Quick, quiet, roomy, comfortable and nicely finished. The optional V6 makes the Highlander one of the quicker SUVs in the segment. The Highlander Hybrid works really well, but it makes no economic sense with gas at $1/litre; it's a good choice for those who want to look green. **Weak points:** High prices on the used vehicle market, even for previous generation models. Insufficient production contributes to delivery delays and high transaction prices for new Highlanders. High theft risk. **Major redesign:** 2008, 2014. **Best alternatives:** From Detroit, try the Buick Enclave, Chevrolet Traverse and GMC Acadia trio, as well as the Ford Flex and Explorer. The Honda Pilot is the most direct competitor, but like the Highlander, it can experience delivery delays and inflated transaction prices. Though not quite as good for third-row passenger space, the Hyundai Santa Fe XL and Mazda CX-9 are worth looking at.

Prices and Specs

Prices (2016): *LE V6:* $33,555, *Hybrid Limited:* $55,160 **Freight:** $1,760 **Powertrain (FWD/AWD):** Engines: 3.5L V6 (285 hp estimated), 3.5L Hybrid (280 hp); Transmissions: 8-speed auto., CVT. **Dimensions:** Passengers: 2/2/3, 2/3/2, Hybrid: 2/3; Wheelbase: 109.8 in., 2,790 mm.; L: 191.1 in., 4,855 mm.; Weight: 4,398 lb., 1,995 kg. **Fuel economy:** *3.5L:* 13.0L/100 km city, 9.8L/100 km highway. **Assembled in:** U.S.A. Starting with the 2010 models, production shifted from Japan to Toyota's Indiana plant.

ALERT! Check the front seat and head restraint on 2014-2017 models. Some front seat occupants find the design is uncomfortable enough to be a deal breaker.

Owner-reported safety-related failures: NHTSA's safety-defect log sheet shows very few complaints registered against the Highlander. Lag and lurch acceleration, airbag failed to deploy; transmission will not hold vehicle parked on an incline; sudden brake failure; brake and steering both went out as driver was making a turn; engine replaced after overheating (due to road debris damaging the radiator); engine loses power in turns; and windshield distortion.

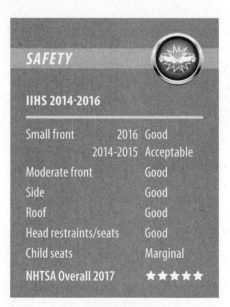

SAFETY

IIHS 2014-2016

Small front	2016	Good
	2014-2015	Acceptable
Moderate front		Good
Side		Good
Roof		Good
Head restraints/seats		Good
Child seats		Marginal
NHTSA Overall 2017		★★★★★

RELIABILITY: *2008-2013:* Reliability issues have included concerns about some transmission shudders (there have been a few outright replacements), malfunctioning audio systems, and failed water pumps and batteries. A few owners report paying to have a noisy steering intermediate shaft replaced. The sun visors may sag and the fix is not inexpensive. *2014-2017:* Non-functioning infotainment systems (including Bluetooth), recalcitrant power liftgates and hesitating transmissions found in small numbers of the latest generation of the Highlander. The Highlander uses Toyota's popular 3.5L V6, which has a problem with the 2GR-FE (V6) engines manufactured from 2005 to May 2008. The rear bank VVT-I oil line uses a rubber hose to deliver motor oil to the camshaft. Due to heat and fatigue, the hose can rupture over time, spraying oil on the passenger-side wheel, the brakes, on the serpentine belt, seemingly everywhere, and could lead to an inability to steer or brake, and even cause a fire in the engine bay. Six litres of oil rapidly drained out of the engine can also result in a complete engine seizure. A telltale sign is a big oil slick under the vehicle when parked. The problem was first reported by owners of the Avalon sedan, and then Highlander, RAV4, Sienna and drivers of various Lexus V6 models. Toyota began installing a new all-metal line on the 3.5L V6 engine beginning in May 2008. Check with a Toyota dealer to see if the upgrade modification was performed.

INTERNAL BULLETINS, SECRET WARRANTIES: 2002-14—Remedies for vehicle pulling from one side to the other, requiring constant steering corrections. 2008-13—Vehicles equipped with the 5-speed automatic transaxle may exhibit a whine noise from the final drive gear assembly. This noise is noticeable above 50 kph. A new automatic transaxle assembly may be needed. A clunk, pop, or knock-type noise when turning the steering wheel can be silenced by replacing the intermediate shaft. 2008-14—A/C evaporator drain hose may be clogged by insect nests. 2011-12—Insufficient alternator charging may require an updated pulley assembly. 2011-13—If the A/C doesn't work properly, an A/C line retainer (piping clamp) may have become unlatched and caused a refrigerant leak. This is a simple and cheap repair; try it first. 2012-13—Difficulty in folding down or stowing the third-row seat assembly may be due to binding between the seat frame and the banana bracket guide in the seat assembly. 2013—Free fixes for a host of infotainment functionality failures. 2014—An abnormal noise or squeak from the rear suspension is likely caused by a faulty rear trailing arm bushing. Indeed a warrantable item. 2014-15—Repair for an inoperative power back door and a torn sunroof seal. 2015—Key fob reduced remote range.

4RUNNER ★★★★★

RATING: Recommended. The 4Runner is one of the few genuine body-on-frame sport utilities left on the market, evidenced by its tall step-in height and the fact your pant leg will brush the running boards clean every time. With its old school four-wheel drive apparatus and best-in-class ground clearance, the 4Runner feels unapologetically brash, invincible. Like the Tacoma pickup and recently discontinued FJ Cruiser, the 4Runner employs a fully boxed frame. Off-road equipment, includes a locking centre differential and 2-speed transfer case, a "crawl control" low-speed cruise control, and anti-roll bars that disconnect for greater wheel travel.

"Limited" models use a sophisticated full-time, all-wheel drive system. The low-mounted seating of previous 4Runners was corrected somewhat in the 2010 redesign and the sightlines are good all around. There's ample space for five occupants; an optional third-row bench adds two spots for smaller passengers. Cargo loading in back is aided by a slide-out tray that can hold up to 200 kg. Every 2010 and newer 4Runner is powered by a 4.0L V6 making 270 hp (10 more than the old 4.7L V8) tied to a standard 5-speed automatic transmission. The only choice is what type of 4x4 system to get: Old-school or full-time all-wheel drive. The 4Runner got a styling update for 2014 and audio/infotainment upgrades since then. **Road performance:** The 4Runner's V6 provides good power and has enough low-end torque to pull with authority. By comparison, the lamented V8 model, last sold in 2009, generated 306 lb-ft of torque, versus the V6's 278 lb-ft. Despite being built on a truck chassis, there is very little of the bouncy, over-sprung ride you expect from a body-on-frame vehicle capable of serious off-roading. Body roll is considerable, of course, given the truck's off-road mission, so it doesn't compare well with crossover-type SUVs like the Honda Pilot or Toyota's own Highlander. Likewise, the steering feels disconnected and uncommunicative on the pavement – but it's ideal for rocky forest trails. **Strong points:** Goat-like off-road capability; decent on-road demeanour; capable V6 engine. There's ample space for five with good cargo capacity, and there's even an available third-row bench, though it's cramped. Great build quality. Phenomenal resale value (good for new vehicle buyers). **Weak points:** Some owners still regret the loss of the previous V8 and its copious torque (which makes the V8 model a coveted used buy). The V6 feels sleepy by comparison, and sometimes displays an annoying lag off the line seen in other Toyotas. High fuel consumption. Extra height means it won't fit in some underground parking areas. Closing the doors sounds surprisingly tinny for what is an expensive vehicle. Very high theft risk. Phenomenal resale value (bad for used vehicle buyers). **Major redesign:** 2003 and 2010. **Best alternatives:** Most of the remaining body-on-frame SUVs are big trucks, such as the Chevrolet Tahoe, Suburban and Ford Expedition. The only other vehicle with a comparable off-road pedigree is the Jeep Wrangler but its build quality and refinement are nowhere near those of a 4Runner. For used truck buyers, the obvious choice is the Toyota FJ Cruiser that uses a lot of the same component set; it's expensive but considerably less so than the 4Runner. A late-model Nissan Xterra also provides body-on-frame construction and some off-road capability.

Prices and Specs

Prices (2016): *Base V6:* $44,540, *Limited:* $51,240 **Freight:** $1,760 **Powertrain (4x4/AWD):** Engine: 4.0L V6 (270 hp); Transmission: 5-speed auto. **Dimensions:** Passengers: 2/3/2; Wheelbase: 109.8 in., 2,790 mm.; L: 190 in., 4,824 mm.; Weight: 4,400 lb., 1,995 kg. **Fuel economy:** *4.0L:* 14.2L/100 km city, 11.1L/100 km highway. **Assembled in:** Japan.

RELIABILITY: Assembled in Japan at Toyota's Tahara plant and at Toyota's Hino truck division, the 4Runner enjoys a sterling reputation for reliability. Still, there are a few complaints including some leaking shocks, worn wheel bearings, bad batteries and door lock actuators, as well as weak liftgate struts. A few owners got their transmission serviced to address the annoying hesitation that seems to dog some Toyota models. Brake performance has also been characterized as inconsistent, requiring varying levels of foot pressure. Some driver's seats required new lumbar supports and servo motors. Older models can experience intermittent problems with the stability control cycling on and off, the ventilation fan motor can fail, and the optional sunroof can have rattles.

SAFETY

IIHS 2014-2016

Small front	Marginal
Moderate front	Good
Side	Good
Roof	Good
Head restraints/seats	Good
Child seats	Marginal
NHTSA Overall 2017	★ ★ ★ ★

SEQUOIA ★ ★ ★ ★

RATING: Above Average. The Sequoia was the first model from a Japanese automaker to wade into the full-sized SUV segment in North America, aimed squarely at the Ford Expedition and the Chevrolet Tahoe. Like its domestic competition, the Sequoia has a station wagon body built on the stout frame of a pickup truck (the Tundra). A multi-link rear suspension with coil springs is different from the Tundra's leaf spring, but like the pickup, the Sequoia retains a live axle. The 2008 redesign saw the arrival of independent rear suspension with double wishbones and coil springs. The new suspension yielded an enhanced ride quality, a tighter turning radius and made room for fold-flat third-row seats. The Sequoia was available with a bounty of posh accoutrements in a spacious cabin; most models offer seating for eight; the Platinum trim featured seats seven. Carried over from the old truck was the 271 hp 4.7L V8; a larger 381 hp 5.7-L DOHC V8 was optional. The smaller engine came coupled to a 5-speed automatic, while a 6-speed automatic was mated to the V8. For 2010 the 4.7L V8 was replaced by a 310 hp 4.6L V8, which was then dropped in 2013, leaving just the big iForce 5.7-L. Like other very large SUVs the Sequoia won't fit in some indoor garages. **Road Performance:** Equipped with the energetic 5.7L V8, 0 to 100 km/h came up in under 7 seconds – a very impressive performance for an SUV that tips the scales at a Goliath-like 2,722 kg. Owners say the truck is maneuverable for its size in the city, with a tighter turning radius than many minivans. The ride and handling are accomplished for a behemoth. **Strong points:** Commodious interior with flexible eight-passenger seating, a good ride, predictable handling for its size, brisk acceleration and big towing capacity with the 5.7L V8. Exceptional reliability. **Weak points:** Gas guzzler, partly because this truck has not been redesigned in almost a decade. Audio controls are hard to reach from the driver's seat. Theft target. Expensive new and used. **Major redesign:** 2001 and 2008. **Best alternatives:** The Detroit Three offer several body-on-frame models between them, including the GMC Yukon and Ford Expedition, which are very refined and offer better fuel economy than the aging Sequoia, though likely not the same reliability. If you don't require the towing capacity, a crossover SUV like the Honda Pilot or Toyota's own Highlander may work better.

Prices and Specs

Prices (2017): *4WD:* $56,525; *4WD Platinum:* $71,395 **Freight:** $1,760 **Powertrain (Four-wheel drive):** Engine: 5.7 L V8 (381 hp); Transmission: 6-speed auto. **Dimensions:** Passengers: 2/3/3 or 2/2/3; Wheelbase: 122 in., 3,099 mm; L: 205 in., 5,209 mm; Weight: 6,000 lb., 2,722 kg. **Fuel economy:** *5.7L:* 18.7L/100 km city, 13.8L/100 km highway. **Assembled in:** U.S.A.

SAFETY: Not crash tested by the IIHS.

RELIABILITY: *2008-2017:* The Indiana-built Sequoia has presented few mechanical failings, a big reason why buyers will pay a premium over some good domestic products. Teething problems with the 2007 Tundra pickup, which included wonky driveshafts, oil leaks, short-lived tires and flimsy trim, had largely been addressed when the redesigned Sequoia arrived a year later. Drivers who used their SUV extensively for towing noticed that the plastic rear bumper cover melted near the exhaust pipe. An exhaust tip extension may alleviate the problem. Other reported issues included failed water pumps, warped brake rotors and cracked exhaust manifolds in small numbers. Toyota recalled 2008 and 2010 Sequoias that required the installation of a small shim to relieve unwanted friction and restore fluidity to the accelerator pedal. The VSC (vehicle stability control) lamp may light continuously, indicating an issue with the system, which can lead to expensive fixes. If the frame is not already too rust damaged, the APA strongly recommends aftermarket rustproofing, with either Krown Rust Control (annual oil-based) or in Montreal, Barry's Rustproofing (grease). (Contact information is in the Part Four Introduction.)

TACOMA

NEW ★★★★★
USED ★★★★

good buy

RATING: Recommended (New); Above Average (Used). The 2005 redesign was warmly welcomed at the time; the Tacoma had become a mid-sized pickup for the first time, and North Americans embraced the more accommodating cabin and cargo boxes. A 236 hp 4.0L DOHC V6 provided the go-power; there was also a 2.7L 4-cylinder on the base two-door pickup. The same chassis underpinning the Toyota 4Runner, featured a thick box-section front member, seven cross-members and reinforced steel C-channels to boost frame stiffness. Too bad Toyota didn't do more to protect all that metal from rusting – it will be paying out about $3.4 billion U.S. to settle a class-action lawsuit as compensation for rapidly decaying Tacoma, Tundra, and Sequoia trucks. The Tacoma was redesigned for 2016 with only minor trim and equipment changes for 2017. The 2016-2017 models use a 278 hp version of the 3.5L V6 working through a 6-speed automatic transmission; a 4-cylinder is still the base engine. Rear-wheel drive is standard, with a traditional 4x4 system available, tied to the automatic or a manual gearbox. Styling for the current truck is not that far removed from that of its predecessor, which is a good strategy as owners are fanatical about the previous generations of the Tacoma. Toyota added more high strength steel and re-engineered the suspension, rear differential and rear axle to improve the ride and handling without compromising its off-road prowess. The cabin incorporates the infotainment options expected of a contemporary pickup. **Road performance:** Hooked up to the 6-speed automatic, the potent 3.5L V6 delivers quick acceleration and flexible power. On road, the Tacoma's steering is accurate but slow, light and a bit numb, and the ride is quite firm. However, in challenging terrain, the Tacoma transforms from a slightly too rough and ready day-to-day driver into a super-capable supple leopard, with impressive stability and bump absorption. The cabin has easy-to-read gauges and logical controls. The Tacoma's seats are comfortable and legroom is good up front and, on the Double Cab (crew cab) models, good access to the back seat and acceptable rear legroom for adults. **Strong points:** Lusty V6 and prodigious tough terrain capability. Limited but good selection of cabin and box configurations. Towing capacity is significant at 2,950 kg or 6,500 lbs with the V6. **Weak points:** All years are very expensive used; there are buyers for trucks at any age and in any condition. *2005-2015:* Low seats with flat cushions. Lots of roll in corners – owners don't care. Cabin design is a bit jagged, blocky and constructed from drab materials – owners don't care. High theft risk. Structural corrosion. **Major redesign:** 2005 and 2016. **Best alternatives:** The new Canyon-Colorado twins from General Motors, and if you have the taste for a used vehicle, something fossilized with a smaller footprint, like the ancient Ford Ranger, or a Nissan Frontier.

Prices and Specs

Prices (2017): *Access Cab 4x2 Auto:* $29,560, *4x4 V6 Double Cab Limited:* $45,635 **Freight:** $1,760 **Powertrain (Rear-drive/AWD):** Engines: 2.7L 4-cyl. (159 hp), 3.5L V6 (278 hp); Transmissions: 5-speed man., 6-speed man., 6-speed auto. **Dimensions:** Passengers: 2/2 or 2/3; Wheelbase: *Access Cab and Double Cab short box:* 127.4 in., 3,235 mm., *Double Cab:* 140.6 in., 3,571 mm., L: *Access Cab and Double Cab short box:* 212.3 in., 5,392 mm., *Double Cab:* 225.5 in., 5,727 mm.; Weight: *4WD Limited Double Cab:* 4,355 lb., 1,975 kg. **Fuel economy:** *3.5L 4x4:* 13.2L/100 km city, 11.6L/100 km highway. **Assembled in:** Mexico and U.S.A.

ALERT! Payload capacity is overly optimistic:

My 2012 Toyota Tacoma TRD Off Road does not meet its payload capacity. It has a limit of 1240 lbs and routinely bottoms out with 300-500 lbs in the bed of the truck. Toyota knows about the issue on its 2005-11s [and] has issued TSBs on the leaf springs but refuses to solve the issue on its 2012 trucks.

Front windshield may distort night visibility:

At night, the top one-third of the windshield causes double vision of lights. This occurs for all headlights, taillights, signal lights, and streetlights. This doesn't occur lower in the windshield, but it's unavoidable for taller drivers (I'm over 6' tall). This affects the entire width of the windshield.

Owner-reported safety-related failures: Less than average number of incidents registered for all model years. But the same safety hazards reappear year after year. Airbags fail to deploy; sudden, unintended acceleration accompanied by loss of braking ability; truck surges forward when braking; brakes come on by themselves when turning or slowly release, allowing truck to "drift" into car ahead; there is no brake light warning to others when brakes are applied; and ABS braking is unpredictable. The plastic piece found within the rear seat head restraints may exacerbate head injuries in a collision. Clutch pedal sticks in cold weather; spare tire fell off the vehicle in traffic; and false low-pressure tire alerts. The 2005-2015 Tacoma generated the following complaint for excessive driveline vibration:

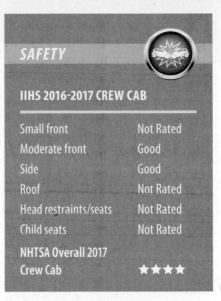

SAFETY

IIHS 2016-2017 CREW CAB

Small front	Not Rated
Moderate front	Good
Side	Good
Roof	Not Rated
Head restraints/seats	Not Rated
Child seats	Not Rated

NHTSA Overall 2017
Crew Cab ★★★★

> There was severe vibration inside the cab of our 2014 Tacoma and it felt like the driveshaft was going to fall out. The dealer has changed the suspension and motor mounts; tires have been balanced, re-balanced and replaced; the driveshaft was trued and balanced; and the driveshaft was replaced, no change. We are told that the vibration is normal and a characteristic of the Tacoma.

Windshield seal lifts in high winds and allows air into the cab:

> I heard wind noise coming into the vehicle. I stopped at the next rest area and checked the vehicle out and found that the windshield seal had lifted and was causing wind noise and flexing of the windshield. This could have been catastrophic had the windshield blown completely out.

Rodent marauders continue to snack on wiring, hoses, and plastic components, running up huge repair bills:

> Electronic stability control turns off when check engine light turns on. Vehicle stability is compromised. Almost rolled the truck over. Dealer technician reports that rodents ate the hose connecting fuel injector air pump to valve which triggers the ECU to fault and cascades failure to stability control. Technician reports that Toyota is using edible soy-based plastics for engine hoses and wiring harness and rodents are causing extensive damage in Toyota vehicles. Toyota does not cover related repairs under manufacturer's warranty. Was quoted $1000 to replace one hose.

RELIABILITY: *2005-2015:* A tough vehicle that tolerates severe usage and casual maintenance, it has consistently ranked at the top of pickup truck reliability. The Tacoma appeared to make it through 2005-2010 without experiencing the quality control issues that bedeviled other Toyota models. A few reported transmission problems; more often it was the manual gearbox that was faulty (short-lived clutches, bad synchros). The original tailgate could bend under heavy loads; Toyota made an improved, reinforced tailgate available. Faulty front wheel bearings, noisy gearboxes (transmission pops out of gear); noisy rear brakes; A/C malfunctions; noisy fuel pump; suspension bottoms out at 300-500 lbs; instrument panel is poorly lit; loose front passenger seat. Rusty frame components are the bane of Tacoma owners' existence. Toyota had to recall the older, pre-2005 trucks to apply rust-proofing and make repairs to those frames. A program is expected for 2005-2010 trucks; repairs can take the vehicle out of service for weeks. *2016-2017:* Owner reports of rough/harsh downshifts with the automatic transmission, especially when cold. The Tacoma may lurch into gear at low speeds or while parking. Toyota dealers can apply and now the 2005-2010 models are the subject of a U.S. class-action settlement. TSB that updates the ECM firmware for better shifting. Even the manual gearbox has displayed some hard shifting characteristics. Drivers have also noted some drivetrain vibration. Excessive wind noise may be attributed to poor windshield and window seals. Acoustic windshield is said to be susceptible to cracking easily.

INTERNAL BULLETINS, SECRET WARRANTIES: 2002-14—Troubleshooting tips for a vehicle that continually pulls to one side. 2004-14—Some Tacoma, FJ Cruiser, and 4Runner vehicles may exhibit a front differential cyclical grinding or groaning noise. Replace the needle bearing on the left side of the front differential. 2005-13—A rear differential whine at 50-60 mph may be heard by some owners of Tacoma pickups. In TSB #005713 issued on April 26, 2013, Toyota says replacing the differential is the cure. TSB #0016-13 says some 4x4 Tacomas equipped with an automatic transmission may exhibit a clunk/thunk noise from the rear of the vehicle or a "bump-from-behind" sensation just before a stop or when accelerating from a stop. An upgraded rear propeller shaft (driveshaft) may reduce this condition. 2006-14—Driveline vibration at 24-40 km/h. 2011-12—A bouncy rear suspension ride with a heavy load can be corrected by installing upgraded rear spring assemblies. 2012-13—A wind whistle from the front of the vehicle may be coming from the radiator grille where it meets the hood. An upgraded radiator grille seal will silence the noise. 2016—Remedy for a 2-3 upshift flare.

TUNDRA ★★★★

RATING: Above Average. The full-size Tundra pickup offers a roomy interior and better than average off-road ability and reliability, but the truck lags behind more modern rivals in terms of ride quality, refinement and interior design and materials – even after its thorough refresh for 2014. The APA ranked the Tundra fourth in comparison tests with the three domestic trucks. Tundra's larger V8 is responsive and powerful, with plenty of low-end torque for trailering. It was redesigned all big and blustery for 2007, finally groomed to take on the competition from Ford, Dodge, GM and the Nissan Titan. The Tundra offered three cab styles – standard two-door, Double Cab and CrewMax (both with four doors), along with three wheelbases and three cargo bed lengths. Canadians could choose from two capable V8s: A DOHC 4.7L, good for 271 hp, and an all-aluminum 5.7 L V8 making 381 hp. The smaller engine was replaced in 2010 with a 310 hp 4.6L V8. The 2007-2008 models are the subject of a recent U.S. class-action settlement that will see trucks inspected, the frames repaired and rustproofed to correct defective factory corrosion resistance. **Road Performance:** Tested with Toyota's robust 5.7L V8, the Tundra moves out with authority. The abundant power is accompanied by oppressive exhaust noise, which could be fun if it was a switchable "sport" mode, but the constant drone becomes tiresome. Ride is not the Tundra's best attribute as it's pretty bouncy; owners talk about "bed bounce" and excessive vibrations throughout the vehicle. Steering and handling are quite competent. **Strong points:** Strong 5.7L V8; spacious, comfortable cabin on Crew Cab models. The Tundra's gauges are easy enough to scan and controls are straightforward. Simple, popular configurations make it easy to order. **Weak points:** Rough ride, excessive exhaust noise and the cabin appointments feel a little cheaper than some rivals. Heavy fuel user, even for its segment. Entune system is cumbersome to set up. Owners in the know report the cargo payload ratings are overrated. Not an ideal commercial vehicle choice as few Toyota dealers are prepared with the available parts and extended repair hours to keep downtime to a minimum. **Major redesign:** 2007 and 2014. **Best alternatives:** GM's Silverado/Sierra twins, the Ford F-150 and Ram 1500 are all good new or used alternatives. A used F-150 from 2011-2013 with the EcoBoost engine is probably best avoided.

Prices and Specs

Prices (2017): *Regular Cab 4x2 Auto:* $30,425, *4x4 V6 Crewmax 1794:* $58,540 **Freight:** $1,760
Powertrain (Rear-drive/AWD): Engines: 4.6 L V8 (310 hp) 5.7 L V8 (381 hp); Transmission: 6-speed auto.
Dimensions: Passengers: 2/3; Wheelbase: 145/7 in., 3,700 mm. (except long box) 164.6 in., 4,180 mm.
L: 228.9 in., 5,815 mm. (except for long box) 247.8 in., 6,295 mm. Weight (4WD 5.7 L CrewMax): 5,677 lb.,
2,575 kg. **Fuel economy:** *4.6L:* 16.8L/100 km city, 12.6L/100 km highway; *5.7L:* 18.1L/100 km city, 13.9L/
100 km highway. **Assembled in:** U.S.A.

RELIABILITY: In return for the Tundra's steep price premium, buyers thought they were getting Toyota's legendary quality for their money, but early adopters discovered that the 2007 production run at the Indiana and Texas assembly plants was rife with teething problems. Yet, despite the hiccups, the Tundra is recommended by *Consumer Reports* and is the only full-size truck to have an above average reliability rating from them. Some owners ended up replacing transmissions, differentials and driveshafts early on. Toyota ended up recalling the driveshaft, and there was a recognized problem with the torque converter on vehicles equipped with the 5.7L V8. The tailgate often bent under the strain of ATVs being loaded or a couple of hefty guys having lunch; Toyota had to reinforce it. Other issues included leaky drivetrain seals, errant engine codes, faulty radios, flimsy bodywork and paint, and some rattles. After the initial production bugs were corrected, the Tundra performed well, but there were nagging complaints about a lag in the automatic transmission and brakes that required inconsistent pedal force to stop the heavy truck. The Tundra seems to go through tires (of various brands) rapidly. Some seat frames cracked and required replacement. Aftermaket rustproofing with an oil or grease based product is strongly recommended; a settlement was recently announced to cover 2007-2008 pickups trucks with structural corrosion.

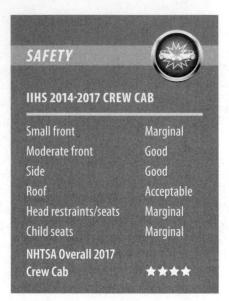

SAFETY

IIHS 2014-2017 CREW CAB

Small front	Marginal
Moderate front	Good
Side	Good
Roof	Acceptable
Head restraints/seats	Marginal
Child seats	Marginal

NHTSA Overall 2017
Crew Cab ★★★★

EUROPEAN VEHICLES

Luxury Lemons

European vehicles are a driver's delight and a frugal consumer's nightmare. They're noted for having a high level of performance and made of beautiful materials, combined with a complement of leading edge safety and convenience features. They're usually fun to drive, well appointed, and attractively styled. On the other hand, you can forget the myth about European luxury vehicles holding their value – most don't. They're also more expensive, less reliable, and can be a pain in the neck to service.

It's hard to believe now, but for a couple of decades the best-selling luxury import in Canada was Volvo. The company's stodgy cars, with styling that was current for a decade or more, and pricing that was lower than Mercedes-Benz appealed to Canada's conservative luxury car buyers of the day. All that began to change after the year 2000. Volvo made some missteps that cost it its dominance in the market, and Canada's auto guru, Dennis Desrosiers, finally found a receptive audience for his luxury market analysis. Desrosiers appears to have been the original person to appreciate the extent to which Canada's luxury class buyers are not just American Mini-Me's. Compacts were a natural for Canada, whereas Americans preferred mid-size cars. All-wheel drive was an asset in Canada, whereas Americans often preferred rear-wheel drive. The automakers began to realise that if they could get an advertised monthly lease payment into the $500 range, many more Canadians could be coaxed out of their medium-price vehicles into something more "special." Eventually Mercedes-Benz and BMW followed Audi's example and adopted all-wheel drive almost across the board. Rear-wheel drive was relegated to limited high performance models or base versions of the Mercedes C-class and BMW 3-series cars, primarily to advertise a low entry-level price. When Canada became one of the few G8 countries to survive the real estate correction of 2007-2008 relatively unscathed, the European carmakers who were desperate to keep their factories running, really turned their sites toward our market. Dennis Desrosiers of Derosiers Automotive Consultants imparted to us that the share of luxury vehicles, as a percentage of the total market, has now doubled from its historic 6% and is predicted to rise even more going forward. Canadian preferences are somewhere between those of Americans and Europeans. We buy smaller vehicles than Americans on average, but fewer diesels and more SUVs than the Europeans.

Servicing problems and costs can be attenuated by purchasing a model that's been sold in relatively large quantities for years and has parts that are available from independent suppliers. If you buy a European make, be sure you know where it can be serviced by independent mechanics in case the dealership's service becomes "lemony." Independent BMW, Mercedes, Volkswagen, and Volvo service seems to be fairly well distributed in larger centres, while Jaguar, Saab, and Smart repairers are very limited.

So what's wrong with European cars? First, they can't compare to Asian competitors in terms of affordability and durability. Why get a quality-challenged VW when you can have less trouble with a Mazda3 Sport? Second, when times get tough, the less established European automakers get out of town or go belly up. Remember Lada, Dacia, Peugeot, Renault, Skoda, Yugo, GM's Saab and Ford's Merkur line? Finally, European vehicles require frequent, expensive maintenance as they become older, and European automakers are currently adding complicated, failure-prone electronics that drive up servicing costs even more.

The following European car ratings include some of the most popular offerings from the four major German automakers: Audi, BMW, Mercedes and Volkswagen. Low-volume models are not reviewed in *Lemon-Aid*. Leasing a new European vehicle can make sense. After all, almost any luxury product is to some extent a discretionary purchase, with value and economy taking a back seat. The higher long-term ownership cost of leasing brings with it the convenience of a full coverage warranty in the first three or four years, and the ability to drive the latest thing on the market. If you're purchasing a new European vehicle and plan to keep it past the end of the warranty, the Automobile Protection Association (APA) recommends purchasing an extended warranty from the carmaker with full coverage. If you're buying used, you'll find that the higher prices at franchised dealerships for three-to-four-year-old lease returns compared to independent dealers are offset to some extent by the lower mileages of vehicles on new car dealer lots, subsidized interest-rate loans from their manufacturers, and much better extra-cost full-coverage warranties.

AUDI

"Only a masochist owns an Audi outside of its warranty period. VW too, for that matter."
— Wall Street Journal *reader comment (March 13, 2015)*

From a quality and safety perspective, both Audi and the other European luxury makes have reputations they don't deserve. Audis aren't that bad; BMWs and Mercedes aren't that good; while Volkswagen is stuck somewhere in the middle, floating in a sea of prevarication and misrepresentation. Audi is part of the Volkswagen Group, so it shares some platforms and technology with VW. Saddled with a reputation for making poor quality cars that would suddenly accelerate out of control in the early '80s, Audi fought back for two decades and staged a spectacular comeback with well-built, moderately priced, front-wheel drive and all-wheel drive ("quattro ") sedans and wagons that delivered "Performance" with a capital "P."

Audi was an early adopter of aluminum to lighten its platforms, a material that's found in all of its products to some degree. Through an expanded lineup of sedans, coupes, and cabriolets during the last decade, Audi became known for making sure-footed, all-wheel drive luxury cars loaded with high-tech bells and whistles – and they look drop-dead gorgeous. However Audi's quality control, servicing, and warranty support have been uneven.

The fact that Audi powertrains are covered under warranty for only 4 years/ 80,000 km is far from reassuring, since engines and transmissions have traditionally been Audi's weakest components, and almost all of the non-luxury automakers offer longer powertrain warranties. In some cases, Audi extends its warranty to cover complaints collectively or more often offers coverage on a case-by-case basis through 'goodwill' settlements not widely known to Canadian owners. If you're in the market for a used vehicle, Audi dealers offer a well-priced 2 year/40,000 km used car warranty and low-cost financing that may tip the balance in their favour.

A3		2006-2010	★ ★
		2011-2016	★ ★ ★
		2017	★ ★ ★ ★

RATING: Below Average (2006-2010); Average (2011-2016); Above Average (2017). The 2006-2013 A3 hatchback defined the compact luxury segment when it came out. Based on the Volkswagen Golf, the A3 is Audi's entry-level, compact. Offered as a practical 4-door hatchback in Canada, it had more rear legroom and a larger cargo area than the contemporary A4 sedan when it came out in 2006. Although Audi shared the platform with VW, it asked Audi prices and provided Audi features. Sparkling performance with the base 4-cylinder turbo; the 6-speed automatic was ahead of its time, and available quattro all-wheel drive gave the car all weather capability that made it hit with the ski set. Interior finish defined compact luxury in Canada at that time, with available leather and wood trim. An even stronger 3.2L V6 arrived for 2007; it was very smooth but unnecessary, and affected chassis balance. For 2010 the V6 was dropped, and a 2L turbodiesel joined the lineup. A panoramic sunroof became standard in 2012. After a full eight years on the market, production of the 2006-generation car ended in 2013. There was no 2014 model. When the A3 was reintroduced for 2015, the hatchback body was replaced by a sedan in North America. Still sharing a Golf platform, the new A3 is a well-appointed, nicely powered vehicle that is smaller and costs less than Audi's A4 compact; it may be more reliable, and is just as much fun to drive. Power came from turbocharged 4-cylinder gas and diesel engines, until diesel sales were halted in September 2015 following the discovery of emissions cheating software. The 2016 A3 e-tron is Audi's first plug-in hybrid. The e-tron is an A3 hatchback with a 1.4L turbo 4-cylinder and an 102 hp electric motor working in tandem, with an all-electric range of only 26 km. VW-Audi bet the farm on diesel tech and the e-tron is best viewed as a remedial class assignment, as the company plays catch-up with this new technology. **Road performance:** *2006-2013:* The A3 is a sophisticated performer, thanks to its powerful and smooth-running engines and transmissions. Handling is responsive, steering is accurate, and the ride is nicely controlled. *2015-2017:* No longer alone in its segment, the A3 is a nicer can than its chief rival, the Mercedes-Benz CLA. The A3 platform is much newer and totally unrelated to that of the Audi Q3 SUV. **Strong points:** *2006-2013:* Luxury finish and attractive design in a small package. Versatile hatchback body is a favourite with the sporty outdoors set and young urban families. *All years:* The A3 is loaded with safety, performance, and convenience features; plus, it provides a dynamic driving experience. **Weak points:** Premium fuel required, and insurance premiums are higher than average. High retained value means a used A3 is no bargain. Second owners hoping to cash in on Audi cachet sometimes get a hangover from the repair bills. *2015-2017:* Navigation feature is confusing. Small back seat. If you want a hatchback, you'll have to switch to the Q3. **Major redesign:** 2006 and 2015. **Best alternatives:** Acura ILX or TSX, Mercedes CLA, Volvo C30 or S/V40, VW Golf or GTI. If rear wheel drive is not a problem for you, take a look at the Lexus IS200t.

Prices (2017): *A3:* $32,800; *S3 Cabriolet:* $51,300 **Freight:** $2,095 **Powertrain (FWD/AWD):** Engines: e-tron 1.4L 4-cyl. Turbo (202 hp), 2L 4-cyl. Turbo (186 hp, 220 hp, 292 hp), Transmissions: 6-speed auto., 7-speed auto. **Dimensions:** Passengers: 2/3; Length: 175 in.; Wheelbase: 104 in.; Weight: 3,175 lb. **Fuel economy:** *2.0T:* 9.7L/100 km city, 7.5L/100 km highway; *1.4 e-tron Hybrid:* 7.2L/100 km city, 6.6L/100 km highway. **Assembled in:** Germany and Hungary.

ALERT! During the test drive check out the headlight intensity:

> As others have previously mentioned, the low beams/regular headlights on the A3 are set too low and so much of the road ahead remains black.

Sunroof explodes from the inside out. Before paying for a replacement or making an insurance claim, ask Audi to pay for this relatively frequent occurence.

Owner-reported safety-related failures: Brake master cylinder failure leading to brake loss. False low tire pressure warnings, TPMS must be reset regularly by the dealer. Very low-profile tires (aspect ratio less than 50 with some sport packages) require care to avoid blowouts and other issues:

SAFETY	
IIHS 2008-2013	
Small Front	Good
Front	Good
Side	Good
Roof strength	Good
Head restraint and seats	Good
Child seat anchors	Good
NHTSA Overall	No data

> Since purchasing my Audi A3 on 2/8/2015 I have had four flat tires. My tires are OEM and are Contiprocontact 225/40 18 92H. Online it seems that there are many complaints for Continental tires having sidewall issues (bubbling) with no or minimal road hazard and at low speeds. A dealership service employee said they have been overwhelmed with tire issues, mostly in newly sold Audis.

Many reports that the A3 stalls out in traffic or hesitates when accelerating. Owners also report a sudden loss of diesel power.

> Purchased a used 2013 Audi A3 TDI... Driving onto I80 west when I heard/felt car hiccup, lost power. Coasted to the stop sign, tried multiple times but car would not start. Dealer said that the fuel pump (HPFP) had come apart spewing metal shards into the system and that the entire system had to be replaced. Internet research shows documented failures in VW TDI (same engine) HPFP in 2010, 2011 and 2012. Is this system safe?

Many incidents where the transmission engages and then disengages when accelerating from a stop or when parking:

While pulling out into an intersection the DSG transmission briefly went into Neutral and I saw the tachometer needle shoot up and heard the engine whine. I was in manual mode at the time. I downshifted and let off the gas and it re-engaged. The following day ... the same thing happened again. This time I was also in manual mode and was again pulling out into traffic from an almost complete stop. I have since learned that this is an ongoing and known issue with VW/Audi DSG transmissions.

RELIABILITY: The recommended oil change interval is too long for most Canadian driving conditions; don't exceed 6 months or 8,000 km and use the correct grade of synthetic oil. A sudden increase in oil consumption can signal a defective crankcase ventilation valve (PCV); have it checked or replaced and the PCV system reprogrammed if possible before agreeing to more extensive repairs. A lit engine service light, hesitation or an unstable idle may indicate a carbon buildup in the valvetrain; this is a consequence of direct fuel injection not cleaning the valves the way conventional port fuel injection does. The repair, which takes several hours, can sometimes be done without removing the cylinder head by soaking the top in an approved solvent or blasting it with walnut shells and then vacuuming out the deposits. A misfire code, especially on 2006-2008 models likely means one or more defective coil packs. Audi introduced a variety of fixes over the years and dropped the price of replacement coil packs. It may be worth checking with a dealer, as there is a small possibility the car could still be covered by a recall or special policy on the parts. A lit engine service light could also indicate fuel "reflux" from the gas tank into the evaporative emissions system; this repair is covered by a free recall repair to install a stronger backflow valve on 2006-2010 models. The TDI turbodiesel is a poor used car investment and many owners have learned the hard way that fuel savings are eaten up by post-warranty repairs. The high-pressure fuel pump can "explode" and circulate metal particles through the vehicle's fuel system, destroying the engine. The complex 6-speed manumatic transmission can bang into gear when coming to a stop or beginning to move, causing uncontrollable lurches. Check your owner's manual for the recommended service interval; it requires expensive VW-Audi fluid and costs a few hundred dollars. Although it's less common on high-spec models and in later years, the manual transmission causes less trouble. Check the air conditioner compressor (operation, refrigerant leaks), turbo (leaks, bearing), water pump (leak), rear brakes (clean rust off the rear brake pads and free the system up annually to postpone expensive service), power steering system (a noisy pump means the fluid is probably low, check for a leaking hose), steering rack (leak at the output seals) and rear differential on all-wheel drive models (leak). Water pumps fail frequently. Models equipped with sunroofs use sunshade clips that can break. If you own the original 2006-2013 A3, you may want to know that it would be familiar to VW specialist shops that have by now picked up a lot of experience working on the contemporary Golf; look for one of these shops.

INTERNAL BULLETINS, SECRET WARRANTIES: 2005-10—Headlights go on and off. 2005-11—Noisy sunroofs. Inoperative windshield wipers. 2005-13—Audi says in TSB #40 12 28 that "it's normal to hear creaking and squeaking noises coming from the front axle when driving at low temperatures on rough roads. The sound comes from the rubber and metal mounting of the front track control arms. ... Track control arm bushings that are completely cracked through should be replaced." 2006-09—No acceleration when shifted into gear. Inoperative low beams. Xenon headlights flicker and fail. 2006-10—Cluster lights dim, flicker. Electrical malfunctions in door. 2006-15—A loud cracking or rubbing noise coming from the steering or suspension is likely caused by the shock absorber stop contacting the suspension strut's plastic cap. Check out this possibility before spending lots of dough replacing parts needlessly. 2008-11—Warranty extended on fuel injectors and the intake manifolds up to 10 years/120,000 miles on 2.0L engines. 2008-13—Rattling and/or jarring noises heard from the engine compartment/exhaust system between 1800 and 2900 rpm are likely caused by the wastegate flap and rods vibrating at the start of the boost air control. A spring clip (06J145220A) fitted on the wastegate adjustment should eliminate the noise. 2008-15—If the radio turns On and Off and the doors lock and unlock while driving, the S-contact lubricant needs to be changed. 2009—Stiff steering. 2009-10—Airbag light stays on. Hard start; timing chain noise. Automatic transmission control module update. Inoperative headlight washer system. 2010—TDI catastrophic fuel-pump failure; sudden engine shutdown; metal shavings found in the fuel system (an $8,000 repair awaits). Automatic transmission suddenly downshifts to M1, inviting a rear-ender. 2010-11—A faulty thermostat may cause the engine to overheat. 2010-12—Engine exhaust flap will be replaced free of charge up to 10 years/120,000 miles (when it fails the MIL light will come on). 2010-13—Diesel engine won't start, rough running, or excess moisture found in intake piping. 2011-12—Tiptronic DSG transmission malfunctions can be corrected via a software upgrade. Parking Assist System false warnings. Bose Radio erratic sound volume. Cannot pair Bluetooth phone to vehicle. Poor cell phone voice recognition. No-start due to discharged battery. Electrical malfunctions after window tint. Excessive engine noise. Front window binds or is noisy during operation. Inaccurate "distance to empty" display. Noises from the sunroof area. Disc brake squeal. Can't eject navigation DVD. Rattling, humming noise from speakers. Radio turns on/off, locks self-activate. Inoperative remote key. Dash cluster lighting appears to flicker. Fuel system malfunction warning. Moisture accumulation in exterior lights. Cold weather intercooler kit. 2014-16—Reasons why the Adaptive Cruise control may not work. 2015—AC may not cool sufficiently; noisy compressor. If the AC doesn't cool sufficiently or the compressor is noisy, a faulty N280 valve may be the culprit. 2015-16—There may be small crack lines in the top area of the headlight lens. Tips for improving the functionality of the infotainment system. Troubleshooting headliner/sunroof squeaks and rattles. 2015-17—The cap on the control knob for the dash panel backlight dimming switch may be missing or damaged. Background static noises (crackling) heard when music is streamed to the MMI using the Bluetooth audio player (A2DP).

A4/S4/A5/S5	2006-2010 ★★
	2011-2016 ★★★
	2017 (NEW) ★★★★

RATING: Below Average (2006-2010), Average (2011-2016); Above Average (2017 (New)). *A4:* The A4 is consistently Audi's best-selling car. Four-cylinder all-wheel drive models are the most sought after. A continuously variable transmission with a chequered reputation equips front-wheel drive models. The second-generation A4 that arrived for 2002 received a major mid-cycle update for 2006, with all new exterior panels, new engines and transmissions and revisions to the suspension. A major facelift took place for 2006 with Audi's new keystone grille and more flamboyant exterior lines. The 4-cylinder engine grew from 1.8L to 2L, and the V6 increased in size from 3L to 3.2L. Both engines gained direct injection. Interior materials outclassed all the other luxury compacts. Styling was timeless, and quattro all-wheel drive in the majority of cars provided a level of winter convenience that many contemporary BMWs and Mercedes didn't have. The third-generation A4 arrived for 2009. The cabin grew wider, and rear seat legroom increased, making the A4 one of the roomiest cars in the compact luxury class. More powerful engines improved performance. The 2009 A4 was noisier than the car it replaced, interior trim a bit cheaper, and Audi saved money here and there on the body (compare the trunk finish in the two generations and it's immediately obvious). Steering on cars equipped with the Audi Drive Select feature felt a bit odd. *A5:* Appearing in 2007, the A5 is a coupe version of the A4. The gorgeous styling made it an immediate hit. Unlike some other sport coupes from the German and Japanese automakers, the A5 offered standard all-wheel drive and a usable back seat. It provided medium-high performance that was usable every day and quickly became popular. The base engine is the 4-cylinder turbo from the sedan; it's the one with the best chassis balance. The performance S5 offered a supercharged V6 and V8; the V8 sounds like it's in training for NASCAR. The supply of coupes is more limited than for the equivalent sedan on the used car market and prices are higher. The A5 was redesigned for 2017; critics note the lines are not as handsome. The 2017 S5 uses a supercharged V6. **Road performance:** Balanced performance with the 2L that also boasts reasonably good fuel economy. The manual gearbox, Tiptronic automatic transmission, and the CVT perform well. Comfortable ride; superior handling, though not quite as responsive as the BMW 3 Series. Consider a 2013-2014 A4, with some of the factory warranty left, and depreciation to your advantage. **Strong points:** *Pre-2009:* Best-in-class interior finish. Good availability with convenient all-wheel drive. Practical wagon body style; the All-Road and Avant wagons perform more nicely than most well-equipped sport-utility vehicles. **Weak points:** Infotainment features aren't user-friendly on models with the Audi

MMI interface, and voice controls and climate adjustments are overly compli-cated. Expensive upkeep. *Coupe:* Poor visibility to the rear. **Major redesign:** 2002, 2006 update, 2009 and 2017. **Best alternatives:** A4 alternatives are the Acura TLX, BMW 3 Series/2 Series, Mercedes-Benz C-class, Infiniti G37/Q50 and Lexus IS series. If you like the S4 or S5 tire burners, also consider the BMW M3 or perhaps the G37 Coupe.

Prices and Specs

Prices (2017): *A4 Komfort:* $38,500; *S5 Cabriolet:* $73,650 **Freight:** $2,095 **Powertrain (FWD/AWD):** Engines: 2.0L 4-cyl. Turbo (190-252 hp), 3.0L SC V6 (333 hp); Transmissions: 6-speed man., 8-speed auto., 7-speed auto., CVT. **Dimensions:** Passengers: 2/3; Length: 186 in.; Wheelbase: 111in.; Weight: 3,665 lb. **Fuel economy:** *2.0T:* 8.6L/100 km city, 6.4L/100 km highway. **Assembled in:** Germany.

ALERT! Electric power-steering system has been fingered for road wander. Check the steering during your road test.

> After 3500 miles the vehicle developed a "notchy" sensation in the steering feel that varied in intensity and would occur at random times. This notchy sensation would occur at any speed above 20 mph, as if switched on. When symptoms would occur there would be a heavy, notchy feeling on either side of straight steer that would take a lot of force to overcome and then once feeling like the wheel is over the notch, it would over-correct making it difficult to maintain a lane... The notchiness is also felt throughout all wheel travel, not just on center... This makes stay-ing on a given path difficult... At random times steering was so heavy that it felt like there was no power steering in manoeuvres. Turning the car off and on or turning the wheel lock to lock alleviates the symptoms. This is the first year Audi has introduced electromechanical steering into their cars in the United States. Many other 2013 Audi (varying models) owners have had the same issue.

SAFETY

IIHS 2009-2017 A4 SEDAN

Small Front	2017	Good
	2009-2016	Poor
Front		Good
Side		Good
Roof strength		Good
Head restraint and seats		Good
Child seat anchors		Good
NHTSA Overall 2016		★★★★★

Owner-reported safety-related failures: NHTSA logs show few safety-related com-plaints. Reports of continued acceleration while braking; acceleration lag and engine surge; vehicle lunging every time the Tiptronic transmission is downshifted; stalling caused by faulty fuel injectors; CVT allows the vehicle to roll down an incline when stopped. The following problems are reported on models prior to 2009: Airbag fails to deploy; excessive steering shake due to a faulty lower control arm; fuel system (fuel injectors, principally), and powertrain component failures; defective brakes; and chronic electrical shorts.

RELIABILITY: The A4 has enjoyed healthy sales over a long stretch with relatively few model changes, which helps with repairs. Sustained digging will usually find you the parts and an independent mechanic who has experience servicing the car. Items to monitor: Dirty oil (check for brown deposits on the dipstick and oil filler) could be indicative of a sludge buildup, turbo (oil leak, bearing), power steering pump and steering rack (leaks, if the pump is noisy the fluid ran low at some point), rear differential (oil leak). *2002-2008:* The front suspension ball joints are expensive to replace and available only as part of an assembly that includes the suspension arms. *1999-2004 models with the 1.8L turbo:* The warranty on the engine was increased to 8 years/unlimited kilometres for engine failure due to internal sludge (warranty now expired). Stick with the factory-recommended timing belt replacement; replace the water pump at the same time as it is accessible, saving hours of labour if it fails between belt changes. Check: 1.8L turbo and 3L engines (valve cover leaks and hard to diagnose oil consumption problems). A lit "Check Engine" warning could signal one of the following defects: oxygen sensors, intake airflow sensor, or one or more ignition coils. Check that all the power windows and locks are operating. *2L turbo and 3.2L V6 with direct injection:* Because gasoline with detergent additives no longer flows past the valves into the combustion chamber, the intake can become dirty and cause an unstable idle and hesitation. Cleaning the valves costs from $500 to $600. The first ignition coil to fail on non-V8 cars will be replaced after the warranty is over (policy now expired). Excellent factory rust protection. Front-wheel drive A4s use an unreliable CVT automatic transmission that failed in sizable numbers during the warranty period; the fluid should be changed every 60,000 km, ideally at a dealership using the recommended VWAudi fluid. If the transmission has been acting up, the dealer may be able to install a programming update to calm it down. *2009-2016:* For an engine that has earned a spot on Ward's Ten Best Engines list, the 2.0T 4-cylinder can be troublesome. Owners describe oil consumption deteriorating to as much as one litre burned every three or four tankfuls. Some engines were rebuilt with new pistons, rings and seals under warranty or replaced. Other issues reported on 2009 and newer models include faulty suspension control arms and power-steering hoses, bad fuel pumps, a few leaking water pumps and sunroofs, and assorted electrical snafus. The secondary radiator is easily damaged from road debris; and the wipers may stop working when the vehicle comes to a stop. Cabriolet tops are known to leak or malfunction. The optional 19-inch alloy wheels resist impacts poorly and can bend; ride comfort and impact protection are better with smaller rims and higher profile tires. Repair frequency improved significantly since 2011, although the trend may be partly attributable to the cars being more recent.

INTERNAL BULLETINS, SECRET WARRANTIES: 2002-06—Audi agreed to refund repair and other expenses to drivers who bought or leased 2002-06 Audi A4s and A6s with factory-installed CVTs (program long-since expired). Faulty glove compartment door. Noisy power steering. 2003-04—Service campaign to replace the engine wire harness. 2005-06—Remote won't lock/unlock doors. 2005-07—Xenon headlights flicker and fail. 2005-08—Remedy for a vehicle that pulls to one side. Dash clicking noises. Headlights vibrate. 2006-07—Inoperative low beams. 2006-08—Front, rear brake squealing. Brakes moan when accelerating or turning. 2007—Multiple electrical failures. 2009-11—Sunroof noises, concerns. 2011-15—Harsh shifting. 2012-15—Rattling noises can be heard coming from underneath the vehicle, most likely caused by contact between the exhaust heat shield and the body of the vehicle. Apply a section of PVC sealer to the area. *A4, A5, Q5, and A6:* 2009-13—A coolant leak may signal the need for a new water pump, says TSB #191336 issued on April 15, 2013. Replacing the pump, hose, and seal ring ought to stop the dripping. *A4, A5, and Q5:* 2009-14—Stiff steering on turns can be fixed by installing an upgraded intermediate steering shaft under warranty, says TSB: #48-14-61. Improper operation of the AC fresh air blower could be caused by a faulty printed circuit board in the blower control module, or the carbon brushes are losing contact with the fresh air blower's motor commutator. Install an improved fresh air blower or blower module. 2013—Troubleshooting tips to smooth out harsh First to Second upshifts or braking downshifts. Intermittent cruise control malfunctions. Water accumulation in xenon headlights may cause serious electrical short-circuits elsewhere. A constantly lit ABS alert could mean the wiring harness is damaged. *A4, A5, A6, Q5, and TT:* 2009-14—If the engine judders when accelerating or runs erratically, a faulty air mass meter is the likely culprit. 2013-14—The wastegate linkage may be disconnected, and the car loses power. 2013-15—GPS gives inaccurate readings. 2014—Clunking or rattling noises coming from the rear suspension area when driving over bumps is likely caused by an improperly seated rear bump stop. *A4, A5, A6, A8, Q5 Q7, and TT:* 2010-14—Correction for coolant loss from the coolant valve. Symptoms: Engine warning light on, "Limp Home" mode active, and insufficient cabin heating. Water ingress into the connector housing of the brake pad wear indicator can lead to the oxidation of the pins. This oxidation can increase contact resistance in the connector, which can generate a false brake pad wear warning. 2011-14—Ice can form on the locking surface of the touch sensor (inside the door handle), preventing proper locking operation. *A4, A6:* 2005—Fuel gauge reads empty with a full tank. 2005-06—Rough-running cold engine. Inoperative sunroof. 2005-09—Long warm-engine crank time. 2005-11—Sunroof noises. Brakes moan when accelerating or turning. 2006-11—Front, rear brake squealing. 2007—AC doesn't cool. Loose, broken control knobs. 2008-09—Erratic operating radio and door locks. *A4, A5, A6:* Automatic transmission will not engage, or shifts only after key cycle. 2009-15—Illegal emissions software on diesel-equipped models may need to be replaced before vehicle can be registered. Replacement is free. 2013—Coolant leak at water pump and hose area. *A4, A6, S6:* 2002-05—Vehicles equipped with the Multitronic automatic transmission buck when accelerating. 2002-08—Noisy power steering. Inoperative daytime running lights. 2005—Cold engine stumble; warm engine stall. 2005-08—Eliminating brake moan on low-speed turns. Front window reverses direction when closing. Inoperative sunroof switch. Inoperative One Touch window feature. 2005-09—Long warm-engine crank time. 2005-10—Headlights go on and off. 2007-08—Paint spots or stains on upper surfaces. 2009—Hard start; timing chain noise. 2009-10—Airbag light stays on. 2009-13—A coolant leak in some models may mean a new water pump is in order. In TSB #191336, issued on April 15, 2013, Audi said owners of 2009-13 A4, A5, Q5 and A6 models might notice leaks from the hose connecting the water pump to the heater core. Replacing the pump, hose and seal ring under this "goodwill warranty" ought to correct the problem. Water pooling in xenon headlamp assemblies is covered in TSB #941314 issued on April 5, 2013. Audi said the headlight adjustment screw or the bonding channel between the housing and the lens might let water enter. The problem affects some 2013 A4, S4, A5, S5 and RS5 models. Replacing the headlamp assembly will prevent further leakage. 2011-15—Harsh shift concerns. 2012-14—Coolant loss from coolant valve, engine warning light on, "Limp Home" mode active, cabin heating is insufficient. 2013-14—Waste linkage disconnected resulting in reduced engine power. On the camshaft adjustment valve, the filter element can loosen, also causing a loss of power. 2014-16—A defective fuel level sensor may cause erratic fuel level readings. Clunking or rattling noises are heard from rear suspension area when vehicle is driven over bumps. Look for an improperly seated rear bump stop.

ELECTRICAL—HARNESS DAMAGE FROM ANIMAL BITES

BULLETIN NO.: 2021169/2   DATE: JULY 1, 2010

Audi

MODEL(S)	YEAR	VIN RANGE	VEHICLE-SPECIFIC EQUIPMENT
All Audi	2007–2010 2012–2015	All	
R8	2011	All	
A3	2011	All	
A4, S4	2011	All	
A4 Cabriolet	2011	All	Not Applicable
A5, S5	2011	All	
A5 Cabriolet	2011	All	
A6	2011	All	
Q5	2011	All	
Audi Q7	2011	All	

CONDITION: The customer may report:
- Engine warning light illuminated in IP cluster
- Reduced driving performance
- Engine does not start

- Coolant warning light illuminated
- ABS warning light illuminated
- Parking system warning illuminated in IP cluster
- Cable or rubber hose damages in the engine compartment.

TECHNICAL BACKGROUND: Animal damage primarily occurs on easily accessible, exposed cables and on thin cables. To avoid future animal bites, advise the customer to clean the engine compartment. Electrical deterrents and cable protection have proven effective, but 100% protection cannot be guaranteed.

WARRANTY: This damage is due to outside influence and is not covered by any Audi warranty.

RECOMMENDED ANIMAL PROTECTION MEASURES: Electric deterrents. Similar to electric fences, these deterrents ensure effective and sustainable protection. Animals are driven away by harmless electric shocks.

Audis, Hondas, and Toyotas represent a "Moveable Feast" to mice, rats, squirrels, etc. Rodent bites can cause up to $18,000 in wire/hose damage, make the car unsafe, and scare the dickens out of some drivers if "Mickey" decides to ride shotgun. Lawyers say Audi is 100% responsible for not building barriers to animal entry as other automakers have done. "Honey, what just scurried under your seat?"

A6/S6	
	2005-2011 ★★
	2012-2016 ★★★
	2017 (NEW/LEASE) ★★★★

RATING: Below Average (2005-2011); Average (2012-2016); Above Average (2017 (New or Lease)). Audi has never been a major player in the mid-size luxury sedan market in North America. For every A6 sold in 2010, Mercedes sold seven E-Series models and BMW sold five 5 Series sedans. This means you can haggle to your heart's delight because Audi dealers will do what it takes to capture buyers from their competitors in this slow-selling segment for them. The A6 is a comfortable, spacious mid-size luxury vehicle that comes as a sedan or wagon. Its redesign for 2012 included an extensive diet of aluminum, which yielded a bigger car that weighed less, and paid off in terms of performance and efficiency. Inside, the new cabin treatments certainly won over fans; the appealing dash layout, excellent materials and exceptional fit and finish contributed to a stylish environment. The base sedan uses the familiar 252 hp 2.0L turbocharged 4-cylinder engine or an optional 333 hp 3.0L supercharged V6 (a supercharger provides forced induction by way of an accessory belt driven by the engine; a turbocharger harnesses exhaust gas flow). Both engines are mated to a CVT or an 8-speed automatic transmission with manual-shift capability; Audi's quattro all-wheel drive is also available. After a one-year hiatus, the high-performance Audi S6 returned for 2013 powered by a new twin-turbocharged 4.0 L V8, which put out 420 hp and 406 lb-ft of torque through a dual-clutch, 7-speed automated transmission. All-wheel drive was standard. The A7 is a low-slung four-door "coupe" variant of the A6. **Road performance:**

The 2016-2017 models have a bit more horsepower. The potent V6 engine produces incredible acceleration times with acceptable gas mileage. Base A6 2.0L models are cheaper and more fuel-efficient than many competitors, but offer less power than other cars in the segment. Handling and braking are responsive. The Servotronic steering is improved, but it is still both over-boosted and uncommunicative in "Comfort" mode and ponderous and numb in its "Dynamic" setting. **Strong points:** Sumptuous interior finish. Comfortable seating; interior includes a competent navigation system and an analog/digital instrument panel that is pleasing to the eyes; plenty of passenger and cargo room (it beats out both BMW and Mercedes in this area); easy front and rear access; and very good build quality. Dropping the failure-prone DSG automatic transmission in favour of an 8-speed automatic on the A6 was smart. Quiet. The A6's reputation for expensive repairs and poor reliability contribute to used car prices that are lower than its major competitors. **Weak points:** Some controls on models with the MMI interface can take getting used to. Servicing can be a challenge. Limited resale market. **Major redesign:** 2005 and 2012. **Best alternatives:** The BMW 5 Series and Mercedes E-Class are the obvious alternatives. Other vehicles worth a look are the Hyundai Genesis and Lexus GS.

Prices and Specs

Prices (2017): *A6:* $58,600, *S6:* $90,850 **Freight:** $2,095 **Powertrain (AWD):** Engines: 2.0L 4-cyl. (252 hp), 3.0L V6 (333 hp); Transmissions: 7-speed S tronic, 8-speed auto. **Dimensions:** Passengers: 2/3; Length: 194 in.; Wheelbase: 115 in.; Weight: 3,803 lb. **Fuel economy:** *2.0T:* 10.9L/100 km city, 7.5L/100 km highway. **Assembled in:** Germany.

ALERT! The multi-tasking joystick control for all the entertainment, navigation, and climate-control functions can be confusing. The rear parking assist feature may suddenly shut down (see below).

Owner-reported safety-related failures: Very few safety-related complaints have been recorded over the past two model years, except for the new electric steering, which owners say can cause the car to weave from side to side with no driver input. Other reports: Power brake failure, and the brake and accelerator pedals are mounted too close together. Brake Guard, an advanced safety feature, is jumpy and can suddenly apply the brakes unnecessarily when it senses an object ahead.

SAFETY

IIHS 2012-2016 AUDI A6 SEDAN

Small Front	2016	Good
	2012-2015	Not tested
Front		Good
Side		Good
Roof strength		Good
Head restraint and seats		Good
Child seat anchors		Good

NHTSA Overall Audi A6 2016 ★★★★★

RELIABILITY: Limited sales of the A6 in Canada mean that reports are incomplete. Expect the usual Audi electrical issues, drained batteries, errant oil leaks. Among the other reported items, faulty thermostats that lead to overheated engines, short-lived water pumps, failed air conditioners, wonky sensors and servo motors, and faulty ignition coils. The optional oversized 20-inch alloy wheels are easily damaged by potholes and their replacement is expensive; buyers might be wise to stay away from extremely low-profile tire and wheel sizes. Purchase of a full-coverage extended warranty is strongly recommended with a used A6.

INTERNAL BULLETINS, SECRET WARRANTIES (See also Internal Bulletins section of A4/S4 models): *A6, S4, S5 Cabriolet, Q5:* 2011—TSB #131106 says that some models with 3.0L or 3.2L V6 engines may experience problems with the accessory drive belt or its guide due to a guide that is out of line, causing damage to the belt. Audi will do a free inspection of vehicles it suspects of having the problem and replace the guide and the belt for free as needed. 2011-12—Countermeasure to prevent electrical harness damage caused by animal snacking. 2011-15—Troubleshooting headlight failures. Harsh shift concerns. 2012-13—Coolant loss from coolant valve, engine warning light on, "Limp Home" mode active, cabin heating is insufficient. 2012-15—False taillight bulb warning in the instrument cluster caused by a failure-prone taillight transistor. Tips to fix an inoperative lane assist system. Inoperative hands-free trunk release. Inoperative overhead view camera. 2013-14—The circlip connecting the turbo wastegate actuator rod and the wastegate flap lever can fall off and the car loses power. 2013-15—GPS gives inaccurate readings. 2014-16—False fuel level readings. 2015—The rear parking brake assist may be inoperative, or the warning won't turn off (A7, included).

TT

1999-2007	★★
2008-2016	★★★
2017	★★★★

RATING: Below Average (1999-2007), Average (2008-2016), Above Average (2017). The TT sport coupe provides a delightful combination of creative styling, agility and comfort. The third-generation TT is drawn more angular and muscular, with less of the Bauhaus influence that inspired the original TT. The TT debuted in the spring of 1999 as a sporty front-wheel drive hatchback with 2+2 seating, and extraordinary styling that managed to be both a look backwards and forwards. The interior with its rounded forms, splashes of satin finish metal, and beautiful stitched leather sent many other automakers back to the drawing board. The TT is built on a platform shared with the Golf and Jetta, and the majority of TTs use the 1.8L and 2L turbo 4-cylinders from contemporary VWs. The TT RS, the series' most robust model, is powered by a 360 hp 2.5L 5-cylinder turbocharged engine hooked to a revised 6-speed manual transmission (there is no automatic). **Road performance:** The TT and TTS both come exclusively with the less reliable dual-clutch manumatic 6-speed transmission ("S tronic"). Owners like the handling, and the TT is best seen as a sporty all-rounder that is primarily about style. Most versions are not as handling-focused as other sporty small cars like the VW's GTI, or MINI Cooper S. **Strong points:** Beautifully styled, TTs are well-appointed and provide a tastefully designed interior; comfortable, supportive seats; and sufficient passenger space up front, and good cargo space when the rear seatbacks are folded. All-wheel drive quattro is a plus but not really necessary (it's standard now). Used bargains abound, especially the first-generation cars. Familiar to competent independent repair shops that service Volkswagens. **Weak points:** A useless back seat; tough rear-seat access; awkward navigation system interface; and lots of engine and road noise. The hatch is heavy to raise, and a rear windshield wiper would be nice. Think twice about getting a moonroof-equipped model if you're a tall driver. **Major redesign:** 2008 and 2016. **Best alternatives:** For Canada, no sporty car offers this combination of unique elegance, handling and all-wheel drive. The VW GTI shares the same component set as a front-wheel drive TT in a more practical body, but hasn't got the style. The 2 Series BMW is a possible cross shop. Among the small community of stylyish retro-inspired coupes the Chrysler Crossfire, a two-seater, or Hyundai Veloster turbo might be worth a look. Rear-drive sports coupes like the Hyundai Genesis are a compromise for all-weather use.

Prices and Specs

Prices (2017): *2.0 quattro Coupe:* $52,400; *TTS:* $62,700 **Freight:** $2,095 **Powertrain (AWD):** Engines: 2.0L 4-cyl. (220 hp), 2.0L 4-cyl. Turbo (292 hp), Transmissions: 6-speed man. auto. **Dimensions:** Passengers: 2+2; Length: 165 in.; Wheelbase: 98.6 in.; Weight: 3,164 lb. **Fuel economy:** *2.0T:* 10.1L/100 km city, 7.8L/100 km highway. **Assembled in:** Hungary.

SAFETY: The Audi TT has not been crash tested by the IIHS or NHTSA, likely due to its small sales volume.

ALERT! The TT's timeless styling doesn't betray the car's true vintage and three- to five-year depreciation takes the sting out of the car's original premium price.

Owner-reported safety-related failures: Brake and accelerator pedals are too close together. Outside door handles may present problems opening the car door. Poor rear and side visibility.

RELIABILITY: The early models (2000-2007) were plagued by numerous glitches, partly stemming from the problematic 1.8L turbo gasoline engine, reputed for its short-lived MAF sensors, coils, timing belts and turbo, as well as leaks and oil consumption. Audi's electrical problems are legendary and the TT is no better: Entire instrument panels have been replaced, as well as fuel tank sending units, window motors, lights and numerous sensors. One owner reported spending $7,000 on repairs after the warranty ended. Reliability concerns on the 2008 and newer TT have been fewer in number, but the traditional Audi/Volkswagen failings haven't disappeared entirely. The automated-manual transmission can be a little troublesome, sometimes resulting in the control module being replaced. Other weaknesses include faulty ignition switches and taillamp clusters, oil consumption, lousy radios/Bluetooth, squeaky brakes and some bent alloy wheel rims. Older roadster owners reported broken "flap" motors that power the top.

INTERNAL BULLETINS, SECRET WARRANTIES: 2000-10—Low power, won't move after stopping. Inoperative keyless entry. Excessive oil consumption. 2002-11—Front, rear brake squealing troubleshooting tips. 2006-09—No acceleration when shifted into gear. 2007-10—Multiple electrical malfunctions. Headlights go on and off. Inoperative headlight washer system. 2007-11—Interior buzzing vibrating noises. 2007-15—Convertible top adjustments. 2007-16—The rear spoiler extends slowly or operates erratically. An error light for the rear spoiler may be illuminated. Corrosion is the likely culprit. 2008-11—Front suspension cracking, rubbing noise. 2008-15—Inoperative DVD/CD EJECT button. Loud cracking or rubbing noise when steering. 2009—Hard start; timing chain noise. Stiff steering. 2009-11—Steering squeak when turning. 2009-13—Under an extended warranty, Audi will remove excess 3.0L/3.2L engine carbon buildup in the cylinder head secondary air ports, free of charge, up to 10 years/120,000 miles. 2010-14—Tips on silencing centre console noises. 2011-12—Countermeasure to prevent electrical harness damage caused by animal snacking. Rattling, jarring engine noise. Door can be opened from the inside only. No-starts due to dead battery. Window tint causes electrical malfunctions. Inaccurate Distance to Empty display. False warnings from the parking-assist system. Radio turns on/off, locks self-activate. DSG transmission software update. Fuel-system malfunction alert. Dash cluster lighting flickers. Moisture accumulation in exterior lights. 2012-13—When the car is underway, squeaks or rattles can be heard coming from the A-pillar area (near the corner of the windshield). This occurs because the openings in the reinforcement panel of the A-pillar structure are slightly off-center from the carrier plate. 2012-14—Squeaks and rattles from the A-pillar area. 2013-14—The turbo wastegate actuator rod and the wastegate flap lever can fall off and the car loses power. 2013-15—When the battery is fully charged, the energy generated by the alternator is sometimes too great for the power system to absorb. This may cause the lights to flicker. This is normal, says Audi. 2014-15—The rear spoiler's movement may be restricted due to corrosion in the spoiler drive unit. Poor AM radio reception. Ambient noise affects the quality of Bluetooth calls.

Q3 ★★★★

RATING: Above Average (2015-2017). Building on the strength of crossover sales, Audi discontinued the A3 hatchback and replaced it with the Q3 compact SUV for 2015 in North America. The Q3 had been on sale in Europe for four years; by the time it arrived to Canada, the smaller crossover segment was getting crowded with models from Buick, BMW and Mercedes-Benz. The Q3 is based on a previous generation of the Volkswagen Tiguan and Golf platform, and reprises the attractive design of its bigger siblings, the Q5 and Q7, to help close the deal. **Road performance:** Acceptable, linear power from the 200 hp 2.0L turbocharged 4-cylinder VW engine; it's mated to a front-wheel drive or an all-wheel drive drivetrain. The 6-speed automatic performs agreeably. Nicely weighted and precise steering; handling feels more Tiguan than GTI. Well appointed cabin. Rear seat space is acceptable but not class leading. **Strong points:** A nice all-rounder that was preferred to the Mercedes GLA in APA comparison testing. Few first year complaints. **Weak points:** The Q3 gets pricey once you add some features, crossing into Q5 territory on price or payments. All-wheel drive adds about $2,500 which you'll recover upon resale. **Major redesign:** 2015. **Best alternatives:** Lots of good choices in this burgeoning segment, including BMW X1, Infiniti QX30, Lexus NX200t, Mercedes-Benz GLA250 and Buick Encore.

Prices and Specs

Prices: $34,600, *Tecknik:* $44,200 **Freight:** $2,095 **Powertrain (FWD/AWD):** Engines: 2.0L 4-cyl. (200 hp). Transmissions: 6-speed automatic. **Dimensions:** Passengers: 2/3; Length: 173 in.; Wheelbase: 102.5 in.; Weight: 3,494 lb. **Fuel economy:** *2.0T:* 11.9L/100 km city, 8.4 L/100 km highway. **Assembled in:** Spain.

RELIABILITY: Few reported issues to date with this relatively new model. The familiar 2.0L turbocharged 4-cylinder (TFSI) engine has a tendency to consume oil. Audi tolerates a significant amount of oil consumption as "acceptable." Keep your service records. The direct fuel injection system design requires a cleaning of the upper valve area every two or three years prevent excess carbon buildup. Audi sells a scheduled maintenance program at a reasonable price around $750. It's recommended, as is a full-coverage warranty from the manufacturer if you're buying a used model.

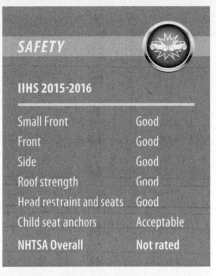

SAFETY	
IIHS 2015-2016	
Small Front	Good
Front	Good
Side	Good
Roof strength	Good
Head restraint and seats	Good
Child seat anchors	Acceptable
NHTSA Overall	**Not rated**

Q5		2009-2016 ★★★
		2017 ★★★

Not-yet-released second-generation 2018 Q5.

RATING: Average (2009-2016) Above Average (2017). The mid-size Q5 debuted in 2009 as a stylish five-passenger luxury crossover compact full of high-tech gadgetry, including an adaptive suspension that allows for firm, sporty handling, if so desired. It's been described as having a luxury-car interior, the handling of a sports sedan, and the ground clearance of a crossover SUV. Standard power comes from the familiar 2.0L turbo 4-cylinder; a smooth or a potent 3.2L V6 with 270 hp.

Audi has had a history of factory-related engine and transmission glitches, but original owners are apparently satisfied with Audi's servicing on the Q5. **Road performance:** The Q5 is an adroit driving machine. Braking and lateral grip are very good, and the ride quality is firm but never harsh. The quattro all-wheel drive system is always at the ready to compensate for any overly enthusiastic driver inputs. **Strong points:** The Q5 borrows heavily from the A4 sedan, as the dashboard and instruments are nearly identical. It has the nicest interior finish in its segment. Backseat occupants get a split-folding bench that slides forward or backward to increase legroom, along with a reclining backrest. Driving dynamics. More plentiful at prices that overlap the All Road station wagon, this is a good alternative. **Weak points:** Cargo capacity does not approach the segment leaders. Audi's MMI controller interface, while improved, is still a little counter-intuitive. Steering judged somewhat artificial in terms of feel and feedback. **Major redesign:** Second-generation Q5 will be released for the 2018 model year. **Best alternatives:** BMW X3, Lexus RX 350, Volvo XC60, Acura RDX.

Prices and Specs

Prices (2017): $43,800, *Technik:* $50,700; *SQ5:* $58,500, *Dynamic:* $64,900 **Freight:** $2,095 **Powertrain (AWD):** Engines: 2.0L 4-cyl. (220 hp); 3.0L V6 (272 hp); 3.0L V6 (354 hp SQ5); Transmissions: 8-speed automatic. **Dimensions:** Passengers: 2/3; Length: 183 in.; Wheelbase: 110.5 in.; Weight: 4,079 lb. **Fuel economy:** *2.0T:* 12.0L/100 km city, 8.6 L/100 km highway; *3.0L V6:* 13.2L/100 km city, 9.2 L/100 km highway. **Assembled in:** Germany.

ALERT! The optional front sunroof glass panel on 2012 model-year Q5s is susceptible to shattering, sometimes in extremely cold temperatures, and sometimes in moderate temperatures. Because falling glass could injure drivers and passengers, Audi has issued a recall.

RELIABILITY: The 2012-2015s generated fewer complaints; insufficient data on the V6. Audi tolerates oil consumption of 1L/2,000 kilometres. Oil consumption is indicative of a faulty engine and a condition that should be repaired. When pressed, Audi has sometimes pays to replace defective piston rings. Other concerns include water and fuel pump failures, broken air conditioners, jerky transmissions, faulty LED lighting, bad radios and assorted warning lamps. Audi service bulletins reveal drivetrain concerns, including defective 2.0L engine head gaskets,

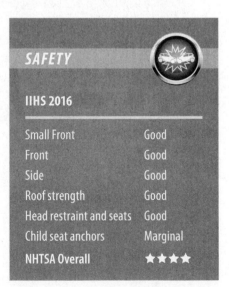

SAFETY	
IIHS 2016	
Small Front	Good
Front	Good
Side	Good
Roof strength	Good
Head restraint and seats	Good
Child seat anchors	Marginal
NHTSA Overall	★★★★

fuel injectors; intake solenoids on 2011-2012 models (covered by a secret warranty); and harsh shifting with 2011-2012s. There's a campaign to improve the intermediate steering shaft on 2008-2014 Q5 and A5 models; a turbocharger warranty extension on U.S. market vehicles to 7 years/70,000 miles; another warranty extension for 10 years/120,000 miles covering the intake manifold, fuel injectors, and other emissions components; servicing for clogged parking aid control units; free carbon buildup removal from the engine cylinder head secondary air ports on 2009-2012 models; and Bosch ignition coil failures.

Q7 ★★ *2017* **NOT RATED**

RATING: Below Average. Pre-2016, Audi's big, luxury SUV shares its platform with the first-generation Volkswagen Touareg and Porsche Cayenne. The Audi version is a complicated five- or seven-passenger machine that offers limited seating in the third row and modest storage space, but looks good compared to the more cumbersome and even more complicated big Mercedes GL-Class SUV. The previous-generation Q7 offers both gasoline and diesel powertrains hooked to an 8-speed automatic transmission. Popular with owners for its performance and long cruising range, the 225 hp 3.0 L turbodiesel V6 making an incredible 406 lb-ft of torque is no longer available, a victim of VW's "Dieselgate." There was no 2016 model year. A second-generation Q7 has arrived for 2017, having shed 120 kg and gained some headroom and legroom. A turbocharged 4-cylinder engine is offered on base models, a first for the Q7. It's not recommended during its first year on the market. **Road performance:** Drivers rave about the Q7's un-SUV-like driving dynamics; braking and lateral grip are good. Handling feels relatively nimble for such a heavy vehicle and the ride is nice despite the low-profile rubber. **Strong points:** The interior furnishings are posh, to say the least. Tech features are top-drawer. Quiet on the highway with comfortable seats. **Weak points:** Earlier versions of the MMI controller interface are not user friendly. The third row of seats is best considered kids only. **Major redesign:** 2007, 2017. **Best alternatives:** Mercedes-Benz GL/GLS-class, Volvo XC90, Infiniti QX60, Acura MDX, BMW X5.

Prices and Specs

Prices (2017): *Komfort:* $61,900; *Technik:* $73,500 **Freight:** $2,095 **Powertrain (2017 AWD):** Engines: 2.0L 4 Turbo (252 hp), 3.0L V6 Supercharged (333 hp); Transmissions: 8-speed automatic. **Dimensions:** Passengers: 2/3/2; Length: 200 in.; Wheelbase: 118 in.; Weight: 4,938 lb. **Fuel economy:** *3.0L V6 S:* 12.6 L/100 km city, 9.4 L/100 km highway. **Assembled in:** Slovakia.

RELIABILITY: Owners report short-lived brakes and tires, a function of the Q7's well-disguised corpulence. Don't try to get through winter on the strength of the quattro all-wheel drive system alone; the Q7 will become a handful in the snow when the all-season tires are in their second or third winter. Purchase of dedicated winter tires in a narrower size if possible, is strongly recommended. On older Q7s, sunroof leaks can wreak havoc with the electronics – entire instrument panels have gone dark – and the multi-panel skyroof may jam on occasion, too. Watch for a weak or broken air conditioner, oil leaks, faulty high-pressure fuel pump, and a recalcitrant transmission.

SAFETY

IIHS 2017

Small Front	Good
Front	Good
Side	Good
Roof strength	Good
Head restraint and seats	Good
Child seat anchors	Good
NHTSA Overall	**Not rated**

Owners have noted Audi's Advanced Key feature allows driver to lock the vehicle with the key inside (how advanced is that?). The all-new 2017 Q7 has generated a few complaints; the head-up display can produce glare; the runflat tires ride roughly and cost a lot to replace. An extended warranty from Audi is strongly recommended if you purchase a used Q7 and stick with a low mileage vehicle with comprehensive warranty coverage.

BMW: Bring My Wallet

Following the post-Brexit turmoil in the European Union, BMW wants to hold the line on prices for its 2017 models in order to maintain its considerable market share in North America. To this end, the automaker will be offering more discounts, favourable financing and other incentives this year to fend off Volkswagen and Audi's "fire sale" pricing, in addition to Mercedes-Benz's stepped up competition. Last year, European automakers largely held a lid on prices in Canada, despite our devalued loonie. They can be expected to do more of the same this year.

Canadian buyers haven't balked at BMW's high prices yet, inasmuch as lease deals, ultra-low interest rates and lower fuel prices have stretched their purchasing power by thousands of dollars. Shoppers are also beguiled by BMW's reputation (undeserved) for offering well-built and reliable vehicles. Unfortunately, there's barely a whisper to warn you of the plethora of bizarre and frustrating factory-related faults hiding in these beautifully styled, gadget-infused machines. Owner surveys show, and internal service bulletins confirm, BMW vehicles are afflicted with fuel, electrical system and powertrain deficiencies that can be expensive to troubleshoot and repair.

I love this online post from one disillusioned BMW owner:

> I figure the car smells like a wallet to remind you of how much money you will need to continue to put into it.

Read on about "out-gassing" fumes that permeate the BMW cabins and form a sticky, image-distorting film on windshields; or windshield/sunroofs that suddenly shatter with a sound like a gunshot; or deadly door locks that suddenly open while underway, throw the dog out through the rear hatch, or hold children hostage unless the window is broken to get them out. Worst of all, these door lock failures span a period of 22 years and involve locks on all doors and the rear hatch.

2014 X5 passenger-side door lock failed while car was underway.

Doors opened (on multiple occasions) by themselves, while my 2014 X5 was in motion. The vehicle has soft close automatic doors; yet driver's door as well as rear passenger doors opened while driving. The dealer claimed to have repaired it (based on BMW service bulletin), yet it occurred again within a few days. Eventually BMW North America bought the vehicle back.

2014 X5 door lock failure trapped toddler in summer heat.

On three separate occasions the electric door locks have locked the car with the key fob inside. On the first occasion, a 2 y/o child had just been strapped into his car seat, a purse, with the key inside the purse, was placed on the floor behind the driver's seat, the rear door was closed and all locks were activated. This occurred in the heat of summer and required another driver with a spare fob to quickly drive to the site of the parked car and avoid having to break a window. This was a very scary moment! Same thing happened (no child in car); all doors locked when a briefcase containing both key fobs was placed on back seat and rear door was closed. A call to BMW's hot line resulted in the doors being unlocked via the airways. The same incident occurred this week with only one key fob in the car.

BMW electronic and fuel delivery components head the list of parts most likely to cause owners grief. Three authoritative websites that list BMW problems and fixes are *carcomplaints.com*, *ALLDATA.com*, and *safercar.gov*. Here are just a few incidents from BMW's "dark side" found at *safercar.gov*.

2011 X5 35i: Quit stalling, pay up!

Started the car and the engine light came on with "Engine Malfunction – Reduced Power" and drove a few hundred yards and then the car completely died… Because there was no power, the car could not be put into Neutral to be put on a flatbed. The X5 had to be put on a crane and lifted onto a flatbed tow truck. (Engine replaced.)

2007 X5: "Raindrops keep falling on my head."

This is my second complaint of problems caused by water intrusion of my 2007 BMW X5. First complaint was the passenger-side floorboard carpet getting wet. Now, I have a problem with electrical components getting wet. My satellite radio receiver was destroyed by moisture.

Owners also mention poor transmission performance with gear hunting and abrupt engaging, believed to be caused by a faulty Mechatronic unit; premature fuel and water pump failures leading to stalling, no starts, and engine overheating; exhaust fumes that invade the cabin; faulty TPM tire sensors; no power assist for the brakes; and high maintenance costs with dire consequence if not performed (simultaneous engine shutdown, and loss of brakes and steering). Going in for warranty work? Parts delivery may take weeks in some instances.

Car needed a muffler, which took 10 days for BMW service Port Chester to get it from Germany. Then they decided it needed another muffler part, which was backordered 2 months! In all it would be 2.5 months to fix a muffler! They couldn't care less about the inconvenience to me.

When shopping new, keep in mind that base models are reasonably well equipped, and just a few options can blow your budget. The upscale, gizmo-laden, better-finished high-end models aren't worth their premium price when compared with less expensive and more reliable Japanese and South Korean competitors.

2013 BMW 1 Series

RATING: Average (2008-2016); Above Average (2017). *2008-2013:* Used-car shoppers can look to the previous-generation 128i and 135i models in either a two-door coupe or convertible with a power-folding soft top. These mini-Bimmers are a joy to drive – but reliability was uneven. A niche product in Canada, the 1 Series coupe bowed out in 2013, BMW's entry-level 2 Series coupe is a few inches wider and longer, providing useful gains in cabin and trunk space, along with the required luxury and technology upgrades. The 2 Series convertible debuted in 2015. The styling is more successful, without the stubby look of the old 1 Series. Otherwise, the mission statement is the same: To bring the BMW "Ultimate Driving Machine" experience to a younger sport coupe demographic. BMW's smallest offering is priced only a few thousand dollars less than the immensely popular 3 Series sedan. **Road performance:** *2 Series:* Good acceleration from the base 230i coupe, which employs a strong, turbocharged 4-cylinder engine that gives equal measures of performance and fuel economy. The high-performance option is the M240i with its 335 hp turbocharged 6-cylinder. Light and precise gear shifting with easy clutch and shift action; predictable handling on dry surfaces. The suspension and steering are tuned to deliver a rewarding drive. Strong braking – a BMW tradition – produces short stopping distances. The older 1 Series models perform similarly well. The best bet among them is the 128i with its classic inline 6-cylinder engine sans turbocharger. **Strong points:** The 2 Series, and the previous 1 Series, cars are classic BMWs in their most unadulterated form. Small and lighter (though not truly "light"), these cars are ideal for people who love to drive on a winding road early on a Sunday morning. Buyers of all 1 Series cars and the M235i get the venerated inline 6-cylinder engine, which is immensely smooth by virtue of its architecture. The 2 Series is available with xDrive all-wheel drive, which has broadened its appeal, compared to the rear-wheel drive only 1 Series. **Weak points:** Expensive for an entry-level car when new; the popular 3 Series lineup starts at only a few thousand dollars more, and you get four handy doors and more space inside. The 1 and 2 coupes have snug back seats, though there are certainly less hospitable sports cars around. **Major redesign:** 2008 introduction, 2014. **Best alternatives:** Acura TSX, Audi A3, Mercedes C-Class coupe, Lexus IS.

Prices and Specs

Prices (2017): *230i:* $36,700; *M235i xDrive:* $49,450; *M2:* $61,900 **Freight:** $2,145 **Powertrain (Rear-drive/AWD):** Engines: 2.0L 4-cyl. turbo (248 hp), 3.0L inline-6 turbo (335 hp), 3.0L inline-6 turbo (365 hp. M2); Transmissions: 6-speed man., 7-speed dual clutch auto (M2), 8-speed auto. **Dimensions:** Passengers: 2/2; Length: 175 in.; Wheelbase: 106 in.; Weight: 3,295 lb. **Fuel economy:** *2.0T:* 9.8 L/100 km city, 6.8L/100 km highway. **Assembled in:** Germany.

RELIABILITY: *1 Series:* The powertrain, fuel, and electrical systems are trouble spots. Fuel pump failures, covered by a 10-year secret warranty. Failure-prone and expensive components include the high-pressure fuel pump, electrical and infotainment systems, and some body trim and accessories. Rattles and excessive vibration are common in older models. Other grievances noted in the 1 Series include malfunctioning taillamps, window regulators and air conditioners, poor radios and speakers, high oil consumption with the turbo engine in the 135i, and interior creaks and rattles. Beware of run-flat tires; owners have long complained about their short service life, noise and ride harshness, and high replacement cost. Interior materials (leather, steering wheel) can show wear quickly. *2 Series:* Insufficient data. The mechanical components set are largely shared with the new 3 Series so it should be similar.

SAFETY

IIHS 2016 BMW 2 SERIES COUPE

Small Front	Good
Front	Good
Side	Good
Roof strength	Good
Head restraint and seats	Good
Child seat anchors	Good
NHTSA Overall 2 Series	Not rated

RATING: Above Average (2006-2011); Average (2012-2016); Above Average (2017). With BMW's constant mechanical and electronic upgrades, styling changes, and increased exterior and interior dimensions, the 2006 and later 3 Series came to resemble the more expensive 5 Series, with super-smooth powertrain performance and enhanced cabin space. Still, competitors deliver more interior room and standard features for less money. The 2010 335d was powered by a 3.0 L turbocharged inline-six "clean" diesel rated at 265 hp and 425 lb-ft of torque, tied to an automatic transmission. Fans cried out in 2012 when BMW introduced the new-generation 3 sedan with a turbocharged 4-cylinder engine in place of BMW's trademark inline 6-cylinder engine. The change was made to meet ever-higher fuel economy goals. Note that after 2013, the 3 Series coupe became the all-new 4 Series coupe, a sleeker, updated version of the former two-door. There's also an available 3 Series convertible and wagon. **Road performance:** *2006-2011:* Very good acceleration; the 6-cylinder engines and the transmissions are the essence of harmonious cooperation, even when coupled to an automatic transmission – there's not much difference between the manual and the automatic from a performance perspective. The 3 Series is one of the only sedans left whose value doesn't take a beating in the used car market when it's equipped with a stickshift. *2012-2017:* The turbo 4-cylinder engines introduced in 2012 are similarly athletic but coarser, and the base 3 Series lost some of its exclusivity. Hotfoots will probably prefer to pass on the entry-level 184 hp version. The optional Sport suspension does enhance handling and steering, but it also produces an overly harsh, jiggly ride on rough pavement. Wider tires compromise traction in snow. **Strong points:** *2006-2011:* Light and precise gear shifting with easy clutch and shift action; competent and predictable handling on dry surfaces; no-surprise suspension and steering make for crisp high-speed and emergency handling; a somewhat harsh ride; great steering feedback, and smooth, efficient braking that produces short stopping distances. *2012-2017:* Larger back seat. BMW retuned the power steering, with new front struts and upgraded rear dampers, to improve handling in the 2016s and 2017s back to pre-2012 levels. **Weak points:** *2006-2011:* Confusing navigation system controls; iDrive electronics interface is not very intuitive. Overpriced on the used car market. *2016-2017:* Reliance on turbochargers to energize its drivetrains has meant high maintenance and repair costs. **Major redesign:** 2006 and 2012. **Best alternatives:** Smart BMW buyers will stick with the simple, large volume, entry-level models; pre-2012 gets you a non-turbo inline six that was the soul of the brand. If it fits the bill, a car with rear-wheel drive, or no sunroof will save you thousands. Used Bimmers with naturally aspirated engines like the 328i are your best bet for sustained reliability and cheaper, independent servicing. Plus you get the smoothness of the classic inline 6-cylinder. Other cars worth considering are the Infiniti G35/37, the Lexus IS series and Acura TSX or TL (used).

SAFETY

IIHS 2012-2016 SEDAN

Small Front	Marginal
Front	Good
Side	Good
Roof strength	Good
Head restraint and seats	Good
Child seat anchors	Marginal
NHTSA Overall 2016	★★★★★

ALERT! Loss of power on the highway may be due to the high-pressure fuel pump failing, especially on older turbocharged models, with some 335i owners having reported replacing the pump three or four times. More than a few have had the engine replaced. The high-pressure fuel pump is covered by an extended warranty to 10 years/120,000 mi. (193,000 km), according to bulletin #SI B13 03 09, announced in BMW's November 2010 dealer letter (see: *www.scribd.com/doc/153404704/BMW-N54-HPFP-Warranty-Extension-TSB#scribd*).

Owner-reported safety-related failures: Powertrain defaults into 'limp mode' and loses power, airbag failed to deploy, brake failures, premature tire wear and tire failures; Bridgestone Tire tread separation. *320i:* Tires leak air, possibly through faulty TPMS feature; sunroof explodes without cause. *325i:* Excessive hesitation on acceleration:

> When the driver demands a sudden increase in acceleration, the car hesitates anywhere from 1.5 to 3 seconds. This is a dangerous condition when someone is making a left turn in traffic, or getting onto a highway, or passing on a 2-lane country road, etc. Other cars traveling at 60 mph [96.5 km/h] are moving at 88 ft./sec. [27 m/s]. The amount of leeway this car needs is much too excessive.

328: Some of the failures reported during the past few years: Airbags fail to deploy; underhood fire ignited while car was parked; premature tire failure (bubbles); sudden acceleration; engine slow surge while idling at a stoplight; when accelerating, engine cuts out and then surges forward (suspected failure of the throttle assembly); car loses all engine and electrical power (blamed on a faulty electronic module); severe engine vibrations after a cold start as Check Engine light comes on; poor rain-handling; First gear and Reverse are positioned too close together, as are the brake and gas pedals; sunroof spontaneously shattered:

Front windshield covered with sparkling chips; seat rails that project a bit into the foot area could catch the driver's feet; and the front passenger head restraint won't go down far enough. *330i:* Side airbag deployed when vehicle hit a pothole; vehicle overheats in low gears; and vehicle slips out of Second gear when accelerating. *335i:* Delay in throttle engagement when slowing to a roll and then accelerating; frequent false brake safety alerts; sunroof suddenly exploded; tires lose air due to defective tire rims; faulty fuel injectors; and engine stalling and loss of power, which was fixed by replacing the fuel pump – now exhaust is booming, fuel economy has dropped, and there's considerable "turbo lag" when accelerating. Overheating engines may be caused by a failed water pump. *335d:* After a short downpour, engine started sputtering. Dealer and BMW said there was water in the fuel and held the car owner responsible for the full cost of the repairs.

RELIABILITY: High-pressure fuel pumps, electrical and infotainment systems, and some body trim and accessories are the most failure-prone components. Rattles and excessive vibration are also common with older models. Engine overheating is a serious problem experienced by owners of the pre-2012 cars. While many drivers are pleased with how their 3 Series drives, an unsettling number of reliability complaints should raise the alarm for used BMW shoppers in the market for lease returns:

Rear bearings replaced at 8,000 kms, trunk latch broken, rear suspension unbolted itself out of the frame, right rear brake caliper replaced, added 1 litre oil every month, power window switch defect, interior panels shook loose, wiper motor burned out… reads one owner's litany of problems with a '07 model.

The run-flat tires topped the list of complaints, with many owners grumbling about their replacement cost, as well as their short service life and harsh ride. Drivers also saw numerous warning lamps lighting up to indicate airbag issues, engine problems and more. Faulty sensors are often the culprits. Entire engines have been trashed after throwing a rod. Disconcertingly, some owners discovered their engines burn considerable quantities of oil between changes. A few have had their engines replaced. Other common maladies include overheated engines, faulty power seats and windows, leaky sunroofs, transmission woes, short-lived batteries and annoying rattles. *2012 and newer:* Leaky valve cover gaskets and noisy steering columns are a couple of the early annoyances. Owners also report troubling vibration in the steering wheel at highway speeds. Watch for ignition coil failures. Some turbocharger failures. BMW parts are expensive post-warranty. *All years:* A lit Check Engine light or unstable idle may indicate it's time to clean the upper valve area; the service takes a few hours and is typically done with the cylinder head still on the car to save on labour. It's a consequence of using direct fuel injection instead of conventional port fuel injection in which atomized gasoline cleans this area of the cylinder head during normal vehicle operation.

 INTERNAL BULLETINS, SECRET WARRANTIES: All models: Many of the service bulletins listed here apply to other cars in the BMW lineup, due to common engines and drivetrain componentry. If you are not sure there is an overlap that includes your car, ask a BMW dealer. If that doesn't work, go to *www.safercar.gov* and look up the service bulletins applicable to your car. As a last resort, pay $26.95 (U.S.) to ALLDATA (*www.alldatadiy.com/buy/index.html*) to get an overnight digital copy of every bulletin applicable to your vehicle. *3 Series:* 2007-10—High-pressure fuel pump failure. An 8-year/82,000 miles warranty extension covers the free correction of turbocharger wastegate rattles (see: *www.scribd.com/doc/151944416/BMW-N54-Turbo-Wastegate-Rattle-TSB-Extended-Warranty*). 2008—Instrument cluster displays go blank. Intermittent engine valve lash adjuster noise. 2008-09—Water leaks into footwell area. 2009—Airbag warning light stays on. No start, or reduced engine power. No start, or false fuel reading. Poor AC performance. Rattling noise from the radio area. No Reverse or Forward gear. An oil leak at the right-hand side of the 6-cylinder engine crankcase may require that the crankcase be replaced. Excessive engine vibration. Front suspension creaking and groaning. Silencing brake squeak and squeal. Steering column noises. 2013—During operation with high temperature fluctuations, the different materials used in the ignition coil construction can deteriorate over time, leading to a failure. For vehicles with the N51, N52, and N52K engines, which have been in service for over 24 months or 10,000 miles, during the first service visit due to an ignition coil failure, replace all Bosch ignition coils with the replacement Bosch coils. 2015—Engine misfires due to ignition coil failure. The power-assisted steering fails with a warning lamp in the instrument cluster or a check control message (CCM) in the Central Information Display. In some cases, the Dynamic Stability Control warning lamp in the instrument cluster may also be illuminated. A CCM for "luggage compartment open" may come on, even though the lid is closed. Additionally, the convertible top cannot be opened. Both problems may be caused by a luggage compartment micro-switch that isn't activated. Don't take diesel power claims as gospel; the system is much more complicated to service and repair than earlier versions, plus independent researchers say BMW diesels aren't as "clean" nor as fuel-efficient as advertised.

RATING: Average (2005-2016); Above Average (2017). The 5 Series sedan and wagon is BMW's "business athlete" that has long brought premium levels of luxury and comfort, but with a dollop of performance to satisfy serious drivers. The sedan was redesigned for 2011 with familiar styling (the wagon was retired), but chock-full of the latest technology. Despite the extensive use of aluminum to keep the weight down, the new car was substantially larger and unavoidably heftier. Careful engineering ensured the car maintained ideal 50/50 weight distribution over the front and rear axles. Starting in 2012, however, the base model 528i got a direct-injected 4-cylinder turbocharged engine, replacing the vaunted inline six. It made 240 hp, the same as the normally aspirated 3.0 L 6-cylinder, as well as 255 pound-feet of torque, an increase of 30 lb-ft, which made itself felt. The redesign brought a new 8-speed automatic transmission for better fuel economy. A manual transmission remained on the equipment sheet, reinforcing the notion that BMWs are built for drivers, but it has become increasingly rare. The diesel-fueled 535d sedan was added in 2014. All late models incorporate BMW's xDrive all-wheel drive system standard. An "all-new" 5 Series sedan has arrived for 2017, resembling an enlarged 3 Series sedan. An aluminum trunk, hood and doors take some weight out of the vehicle. There are just two engines at launch: A turbocharged 2.0L 4-cylinder making 248 hp, and a turbocharged 3.0 L inline 6-cylinder making 335 hp. The new car offers a cornucopia of electronic driving aids, but at a steep price BMW commands. **Road performance:** Good acceleration from any of the engines, including the 4-cylinder and the diesel. Impressive fuel economy in most forms, despite the car's size and mission. The high-quality interior offers a plethora of high-tech features; it's also supremely comfortable and quiet. The ride is composed and refined in the European tradition. **Strong points:** The silky smooth engines and transmissions work seamlessly together, especially its trademark inline 6-cylinder. BMW's notorious iDrive telematics interface works better than it used to, with some intuitive features in the newest examples.

Cabin materials are top-drawer. The xDrive all-wheel drive is now *de rigueur* in this class. More rapid depreciation than the 3 Series makes the 5 Series a better used buy. **Weak points:** The 5's steering is less communicative than it used to be, making the handling less responsive. While the cabin is roomy, the trunk is smaller than the class average. The automatic stop-start ignition system, which shuts off the engine at red lights to save fuel, is intrusive and annoying to some drivers. BMW pricing is always ambitious when new. **Major redesign:** 2008, 2011 and 2017. **Best alternatives:** Lots of choices if you have the cash or credit rating: Audi A6, Mercedes-Benz E-Class, Cadillac CTS, Lexus GS 350, Infiniti M-Series, Genesis G80, and Acura TLX or TL (used).

Prices and Specs

Prices (2016): *528i xDrive Sedan:* $60,500; 550i xDrive Sedan: $82,500 **Freight:** $2,145 **Powertrain (2016) (AWD):** Engines: 2.0L 4-cyl. turbo (241 hp), 3.0L inline-6 turbo (300 hp), 3.0L inline-6 Diesel (255 hp); 4.4L V8 turbo (445 hp). Transmissions: 6-speed man., 8-speed auto. **Dimensions:** Passengers: 2/3; Length: 193 in.; Wheelbase: 117 in.; Weight: 3,814 lb. **Fuel economy:** *2.0T:* 10.5L/100 km city, 6.9L/100 km highway; *3.0T:* 11.9L/100 km city, 8.1L/100 km highway; *3.0 Diesel:* 9.2L/100 km city, 6.3L/100 km highway; *4.4T V8:* 14.4L/100 km city, 9.6L/100 km highway. **Assembled in:** Germany.

ALERT! Some 2007-2012 BMW models have faulty fuel pumps with wiring that may be "insufficiently crimped," which can increase electrical resistance and melt the surrounding plastic. As a result, gasoline may leak during refueling or while the car is running. The fuel pump itself may fail, leading to stalls or the engine failing to start. The 2007-2011 X5, 2008-2011 X6, 2011-2012 5 Series sedans and Gran Turismo models, and 2012 6-Series models are affected. The telltale sign is a gasoline odour inside the cabin, as well as starting problems.

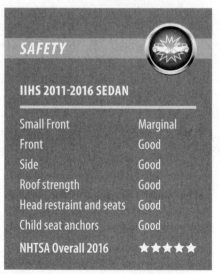

SAFETY	
IIHS 2011-2016 SEDAN	
Small Front	Marginal
Front	Good
Side	Good
Roof strength	Good
Head restraint and seats	Good
Child seat anchors	Good
NHTSA Overall 2016	★★★★★

RELIABILITY: Purchase with a full-coverage extended warranty, or lease a new vehicle. *Ward's AutoWorld* anoints the industry's top-rated powerplants annually with its 10 Best Engines awards – recommendations that shoppers should take with a big grain of rock salt. Editors rate engines based on power, torque, technology, observed fuel economy, and vibration and harshness characteristics, but what's missing from the criteria list is reliability. Case in point is BMW's multiple 10 Best winner, the N54 twin-turbo 3.0 L 6-cylinder, which some BMW owners have come to loathe for its spontaneous fuel pump and injector failures. BMW has a campaign to replace the high-pressure fuel pump feeding the twin-turbo 535i, but some vehicles are on their third pump already. Fuel injectors also fail. Engine overheating may be the result of a faulty water pump. Other common complaints include drained batteries, jerky transmissions, oil leaks, faulty taillamps and numerous electronic glitches. The 2.0 L turbocharged engine released in 2012 has seen numerous failures related to the turbocharger, powertrain, oil filter housing and coolant system. The gas-saving stop/start system introduces an annoying shudder, and the car may hesitate during acceleration from a stoplight.

INTERNAL BULLETINS, SECRET WARRANTIES: All years: Water inside of headlight. Erratic performance of the navigation system. 2008-13—A rattling or clattering noise may be heard from the driver's or passenger footwell area while driving. This likely caused by excessive tolerance between the footwell air duct and the securing hooks. 2013—Transmission intermittently goes into Park or Neutral. Loss of performance and turbocharger noise may mean the oil supply is restricted, causing oil starvation and resulting in the seizing of the turbocharger assembly. 2013-15—Clicking noises are heard from the front axle area while maneuvering at low speeds (e.g., parking lot maneuvers). Confirm the noise is coming from the front wheel bearing area and remove the front wheel bearing. Use repair kit P/N 83 19 2 298 825 to clean up the mating surfaces of the wheel bearing and the swivel bearing (steering knuckle). Troubleshooting side-view camera malfunctions. 2014-15—Fixing adaptive headlights that malfunction in cold weather. Tips on correcting speaker cover rattles. *525i:* 2009—Reduced engine power. Automatic transmission jumps out of Drive or Reverse into Neutral (requires a software adjustment). Troubleshooting front seat noise. Front brake squeak or squeal upon light brake application. An oil leak at the right-hand side of the V6 engine crankcase may require that the crankcase be replaced. Intermittent engine valve lash adjuster noise. Exhaust system vibration or drone at idle. Poor AC performance. Steering column noises. *530i:* 2005-07—Front brake squeak or squeal upon light brake application. Sunroof wind noise and water leaks. 535i: 2008-14—The turbocharged 3.0L V6 is notorious for faulty high-pressure fuel pump; in addition, some turbo assemblies have been replaced after failure.

X1

| | 2012-2016 ★★★ |
| | 2017 ★★★★ |

RATING: Average (2012-2016); Above Average (2017). BMW's entry-level sport-utility came to Canada in 2012 (U.S. in 2013), but it was already a couple of years old upon arrival. Critics described it being more of a 3 Series wagon than a sport utility in its own right. It was a cramped conveyance for families. The redesigned, entry-level 2016-2017 X1 offers increased interior space and interior upgrades. The 2016 redesign was based on the more efficient front-wheel drive platform of the enlarged, new-generation MINI Countryman, rather than the previous 3 Series rear-wheel drive car. The switchover allowed engineers to create a more accommodating cabin. All-wheel drive system is standard, which makes the X1 a useful all-weather vehicle, but remember, winter tires are required just the same. **Road performance:** The 228 hp 2.0 L turbocharged 4-cylinder engine coupled to the 8-speed automatic transmission and xDrive deliver power seamlessly to all four tires as needed. Acceleration is brisk. Not quick enough? Consider that the pre-2016 models offered the turbocharged 3.0 L inline 6-cylinder with 300 horses on tap as an optional feature on a limited number of vehicles. Add to that crisp handling, precise direct steering, and the original X1 can be quite the nimble compact speedwagon. **Strong points:** *2012-2015:* An exception to the rule for small BMWs, the X1 depreciates fairly quickly, making it a more affordable used BMW option. The new-generation 2016 model has more headroom and legroom than the outgoing version and is 66 pounds lighter. Cargo capacity leaps to the head of the class with the redesign. **Weak points:** *2012-2015:* Very noisy. Mediocre cabin finish. Premium fuel required and the observed fuel consumption in APA testing was much higher than the Energuide rating. The fuel-saving start-stop system feels abrupt at times. **Major redesign:** 2010 and 2016. **Best alternatives:** Audi Q3, Mercedes-Benz GLA250, Lexus NX 200t, Acura RDX.

Prices and Specs

Prices (2017): *xDrive 28i:* $39,500 **Freight:** $2,145 **Powertrain (AWD):** Engines: 2.0L 4-cyl. turbo (228 hp) Transmission: 8-speed automatic. **Dimensions:** Passengers: 2/3; Length: 175 in.; Wheelbase: 105 in.; Weight: 3,660 lb. **Fuel economy:** *2.0T:* 10.4L/100 km city, 7.4L/100 km highway. **Assembled in:** Germany.

Owner-reported safety-related failures: *X1:* Sudden unintended acceleration; recalled Takata airbags not available; airbag failed to deploy. Windshield and interior "off-gassing" can create a film on the windshield. Spontaneous shattering of the panoramic sunroof is not uncommon.

RELIABILITY: For Internal Bulletins information, check the X3 review.

SAFETY	
IIHS 2011-2016	
Small Front (Marginal 2011-2015)	Good
Front	Good
Side	Good
Roof strength	Good
Head restraint and seats	Good
Child seat anchors (Not rated 2011-2015)	Acceptable
NHTSA Overall 2016	Not rated

2017 BMW X4

RATING: Average (2005-2016); Above Average (2017). The original X3 "sport activity vehicle" won fans for its agility, engaging steering, strong braking and energetic powertrains. It simply didn't drive like most plodding SUVs. The X3 was redesigned for 2011, gaining sharper styling, a new turbocharged engine, an 8-speed automatic transmission, and an updated interior design with the latest iDrive electronics interface. The revised strut front and new multilink rear suspension improved the ride quality, while speed-sensitive electric power steering became standard issue. Overall the second generation X3 uses considerably less fuel, but traded some of the sharp reflexes of the original for a softer experience. Designers upgraded the interior with better plastics and more luxury finishes. All X3s featured the third-generation xDrive all-wheel drive system; an electronically actuated multi-plate clutch seamlessly varied torque between the axles beyond the normal 40/60 front-rear torque split. Second-generation X3 production shifted from the Canadian-run Magna Steyr facility in Austria to South Carolina, where it shares a factory with the X5 and X6. The oddball X4, new in 2015, shares the same X3 platform, but sits 1.5 inches lower and wider, with a sloping coupe-like roofline; it's a sort of mutation between a sports car and an SUV that manages not to combine the better features of both. **Road performance:** Smooth and flexible 6-cylinder on first-generation models and higher trim level of the second-generation X3. Crisp handling; precise, predictable steering. Recent changes provide a more forgiving suspension; a softer, less choppy ride; but steering is less communicative. The original X3 rides more stiffly. Braking is strong. **Strong points:** The X3 is a great driving machine, thanks to the engineers' insistence that its weight be distributed almost evenly between the front and rear axles. The X3 has abundant cargo space, good cabin access and a quiet, nicely appointed interior with a well-integrated information screen up front. The second-row seats have good leg and elbow room, and rear seating is relatively comfortable. **Weak points:** Many owners are unhappy with BMW's reliance on run-flat tires to solve its storage issue (no spare tire means more cargo space). Run-flats are notoriously hard-riding, don't last long and are expensive to replace, especially in the sizes that BMW specifies. Don't spill drinks on the iDrive controller on the console! Unhappy drivers have had to pay big bucks to replace the controller, which is hyper-sensitive to liquids. **Major redesign:** 2004 and 2011. **Best alternatives:** Audi Q5, Mercedes-Benz GLC-Class or GLK-Class (used), Lexus RX 350, Acura RDX, Volvo XC60.

Prices and Specs

Prices (2017): *X3 xDrive 28i:* $45,950; *xDrive 35i:* $51,250; *X4 xDrive 28i:* $48,700; *xDrive M40i:* $60,700 **Freight:** $2,145 **Powertrain (AWD):** Engines: 2.0L 4-cyl. turbo (241 hp); 2.0L 4-cyl. turbodiesel (184 hp), 3.0 inline-6 turbo (300 hp X3/355 hp X4); Transmission: 8-speed automatic. **Dimensions:** Passengers: 2/3; Length (X3): 183 in.; Wheelbase: 110.5 in.; Weight: 4,112 lb. **Fuel economy:** *2.0T:* 11.1L/100 km city, 8.5L/ 100 km highway; *3.0T:* 12.7L/100 km city, 9.1L/100 km highway. **Assembled in:** Austria and South Carolina.

SAFETY

IIHS 2011-2016 BMW X3

Small Front	Not rated
Front	Good
Side	Good
Roof strength	Good
Head restraint and seats	Good
Child seat anchors (Not rated 2011-2015)	Marginal
NHTSA Overall BMW X3	★★★★★

Owner-reported safety-related failures: Poor rearward visibility. *X3:* Fewer than usual safety-related failures reported to the government. Some examples include sudden unintended acceleration, brake failures, airbags fail to deploy, flimsy seatbelt latches and electronic steering that suddenly shuts off while the car is being driven. Acceleration lag is also a problem for the X3:

> The car didn't move for about a second or two when I tried to make a left turn in an intersection and then again when I was on the highway changing lanes. There were cars heading towards me but the initial distance was quite comfortable and safe. With the hesitation of the X3, I was actually in a panic and stepped really hard on the gas pedal to avoid a potential collision. I have seen countless Internet threads of people complaining about the same thing with the X3 model.

Car accelerates when the brakes applied; sudden stalling on the highway; vehicle will roll backwards even if in Park. Reports of total shutdown of the electrical system.

The windshield wipers don't work, the headlights operate sporadically, the power door locks and power windows do not operate, the A/C doesn't work, the horn honks periodically, the tailgate won't open to facilitate replacement of fuses. The fuel gauge is inoperative and the cruise control doesn't work. Run-flat tires are noted for their short tread life; steering failures; car veers to the right with sudden stops; protruding exhaust pipe can burn your leg when unloading cargo through the rear hatch.

RELIABILITY: There was an epidemic of seat heaters in early X3 models that exhibited propensity to burn a hole in the upholstery. Small numbers of automatic transmissions intermittently reverted to fail-safe mode due to multiplexing problem, requiring reprogramming. The 6-speed unit in 2007 models may be more troublesome. Other gripes centre upon the entertainment and navigation units whose displays may fade or may require reloading. Some drivers have reported sudden failure of the electric steering system, forcing the pilot to steer manually, greatly compromising path control. Entire steering racks have been replaced, along with the electric motor, under a recall. Faulty electronic sensors continue to be a BMW weakness, which can cause poor A/C cooling capacity, rear hatch and window failures, truculent locking systems, wonky windshield wipers and instrument panels. The battery can drain quickly if the vehicle is not driven regularly (a BMW affliction). Beware of high-pressure fuel pump failures in the xDrive35i turbo engine. The turbo 2.0 L 4-cylinder in newer models has proven to be troublesome, with failed turbos topping the list. See comment on cleaning vehicles with direct fuel injection at the end of the 3 Series review. *Diesel engine:* The emissions system goes into "limp mode" in very cold weather on 2010-2012 models, triggering an engine service light. After a few trips to the dealer for a reset, many owners just live with it.

X1, X3/X4

INTERNAL BULLETINS, SECRET WARRANTIES: 2011-14—BMW says headlight failures can often be traced to a defective LED main light module. *X1:* 2012-14—The Service Engine Soon lamp (MIL) may light up; the engine may run poorly or no longer start; and various faults may be stored in the DME memory. This could be caused by water damage and corrosion to the DME pins and harness connectors because the harness connectors aren't properly sealed. 2013—The vehicle judders or surges repeatedly while accelerating in hot ambient temperatures between 3,000 rpm and 5,000 rpm. The EPDW (electropneumatic pressure convertor) for the turbocharger wastegate valve is probably binding internally. 2015-16—There may be a transmission fluid leak around the oil cooler lines. *X3:* 2011-13—Incorrect fuel gauge readings. 2013—Intermittently noisy cooling fan. Water leaks into the cargo area. In most cases, the customer is not aware of any water in the lower compartments of the cargo area, but complains of an electrical malfunction or failure, as a result of water intrusion. Water leaks from A/C centre console into the left and right footwell. Condensation is leaking from the HVAC housing water drain connection (not fitted correctly). Various electrical system failures leading to no-starts. Repeated juddering or surging on acceleration. Intermittent loss of power. The EPDW for the turbocharger wastegate valve may bind. Vehicle drifts to the right when traveling straight ahead. Possible Causes: Tires or improper tolerance in the coil springs of the front axle.

X5/X6

2000-2006	★
2014-2016	★★
2017 (NEW)	★★★★

bad buy

2017 BMW X6

RATING: Not Recommended (2000-2006); Average (2005-2013); Above Average (2017). BMW's first incursion into the sport-utility category began in 2000 with the well-received X5, which was assembled in BMW's first American plant in South Carolina. It was redesigned in 2007 and again in 2014, though casual observers likely wouldn't notice. The 2007 model was cast considerably bigger and, despite the fact that it weighed almost as much as a Chevy Tahoe, it still drove like a Bimmer, thanks to its new control-arm suspension up front. However, the ride can be a little stiff and choppy, in part due to its massive tires. The similar X6, billed as BMW's "sports activity coupe," was unveiled in 2009. It uses a turbocharged 3.0 L 6-cylinder engine or a powerful optional 4.4 L V8. Like the X4, its claim to fame is its radically sloping "fastback" roof, which reduces cargo capacity. Originally it had only two bucket seats in back, but later versions offered the option of a regular rear bench seat with room for three. A new plug-in hybrid version introduced for 2016, the X5 xDrive40e boasts a combined output of 308 hp, a 0-60 run in 6.5 seconds, and better fuel economy (55 mpge) through all-electric mobility with zero tailpipe emissions and a 13-mile electric driving range. Consider it a toe-in-the-water move toward electrification, as the European carmakers come to realize the sunset on diesel may not be that far off. **Road performance:** Engines deliver plenty of power, and there's a 265 hp turbodiesel option, too. Smooth, responsive power delivery; secure handling; and good steering feedback. *X6:* Capable handling, the all-wheel drive system can vary the torque from side to side to minimize understeer. **Strong points:** BMW managed to imbue its corpulent SUV with sedan-like handling and performance. Comfortable first- and second-row seating in a high-quality cabin. Suspension improvements have smoothed out the ride. The uniquely styled X6 has the benefit of retaining its value better than most luxury SUVs. **Weak points:** Despite its girth, the X5 seats five, though there is a provision for optional jump seats for two more (small) riders in back. With the exception of the turbodiesel and hybrid models, the X5 is a gas hog (the fat-tired X6 is even worse). Once punctured, run-flat tires must be replaced rather than patched, at more than $500 apiece. That's par for the course: Everything on the X5 is dear to fix post-warranty. **Major redesign:** *X5:* 2007 and 2014; *X6:* 2009 and 2015. **Best alternatives:** Consider the Lexus RX Series, Acura MDX, or GM's Acadia, Enclave, or Traverse. If the reports of poor quality don't faze you, get an almost identical and much cheaper 2012 X5 or X6 with a full-coverage warranty. But keep cash on hand for the inevitable repair bills.

Prices and Specs

Prices: *X5 xDrive35i:* $67,000; *xDrive50i:* $89,400 **Freight:** $2,145 **Powertrain (AWD):** Engines: 3.0L inline-6 turbo (300 hp), 3.0L inline-6 Diesel (255 hp); 4.4L V8 turbo (445 hp); Transmission: 8-speed auto. **Dimensions:** Passengers: 2/3/2; Length: 193 in.; Wheelbase: 116 in.; Weight: 5,265 lb. **Fuel economy:** *3.0T:* 13.0L/100 km city, 9.8L/100 km highway; *3.0T Diesel:* 10.3L/100 km city, 8L/100 km highway; *4.4T:* 15.7L/100 km city, 11.3L/100 km highway. **Assembled in:** South Carolina.

Owner-reported safety-related failures: At times, most of the X5's electronics can suddenly fail while the vehicle is underway, though the engine keeps running because the shut-off button doesn't work. Underbody splash shield falls off ($400 U.S.). Inoperative taillights. Airbags fail to deploy. Engine surges and stalls:

> I leased my 2012 BMW X5 35I in May 2011. I was driving on the interstate with 2 toddlers at around 65 mph [105 km/h], when the car suddenly lost power and the message displayed "Engine Malfunction, Reduced Power." I pulled over on the shoulder, and tried to re-start the car, but it wouldn't start. The next

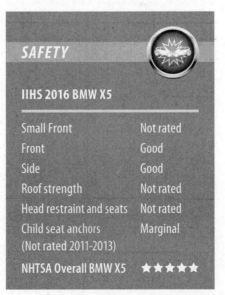

SAFETY

IIHS 2016 BMW X5

Small Front	Not rated
Front	Good
Side	Good
Roof strength	Not rated
Head restraint and seats	Not rated
Child seat anchors (Not rated 2011-2013)	Marginal
NHTSA Overall BMW X5	★★★★★

Then there are the overheated engines reported when the short-lived water pump fails. Also troubling are broken automatic transmissions and transfer cases, inexplicable stalling, and water leaks that can wreak havoc with the electronics.

RELIABILITY: Purchase of a full-coverage warranty is strongly recommended with this expensive X5 and X6, or leasing a new vehicle for no longer than the basic warranty. The most common complaint made by X5 owners involves the electric auxiliary water pump, which can spontaneously fail, letting the engine overheat and leaving the driver stranded. BMW's VANOS valve system is notorious for failing, too (see Internal Bulletins). Other typical mechanical faults reported by X5 and X6 owners include short-lived alternators, batteries, idler pulleys, air conditioners and rear wheel bearings, along with leaking sunroofs and myriad electrical faults including faulty gas gauges. The electronic parking brake can lock and leave the driver stranded (there is a manual override tow-truck drivers don't know about). The turbo 6-cylinder gas engine has a notorious high-pressure fuel pump that fails regularly. The turbodiesel engine can be troublesome and expensive to repair, wiping out any fuel savings. The diesel emissions system goes into "limp mode" in very cold weather on 2010-2012 models, triggering an engine service light. After a few trips to the dealer for a reset, many owners just live with it. More recent models have exhibited issues with the door latches refusing to close, or releasing the doors while the vehicle is in motion.

INTERNAL BULLETINS, SECRET WARRANTIES: 2010-15—Front driveshaft/universal joint may wear out prematurely, says BMW bulletin. 2010-12—BMW has recalled 2010-12 models with the N55 inline 6-cylinder gasoline engines equipped with VANOS and Valvetronic technologies to replace the bolts holding the VANOS housing. There are owner reports of complete engine failure when the engine bolts shear and drop into the timing chain causing metal shavings to contaminate the engine oil. 2011-15—Incorrect fuel gauge readings. Fuel injectors commonly fail early. Electronic parking brake can fail. Watch for leaking coolant reservoirs. 2013—Intermittent loss of power. Idle may fluctuate or cut off. Lag and lurch acceleration continues; various faults concerning the automatic tailgate that flies open on the highway and BMW's admission that its door locks malfunction on most models. 2013-14—Driving with a cold engine knocking could damage the engine. 2014—Cold temperatures may reduce brake booster vacuum. Door opens while driving. Rear shocks rattling. Poor chrome material adhesion. 2014-15—Troubleshooting defective door locks. Tire pressure monitor failure.

MERCEDES-BENZ

More Profits, Less Quality

Mercedes-Benz, as well as the other German luxury brands, have been doing phenomenally well in Canada since the 2008 financial crisis, seemingly operating inside a bubble detached from the general economy. The enduring allure of the Mercedes three-pointed star has spurred the company to offer surprisingly rich lease incentives to build volume and keep customers coming. The brand is also reaching downmarket to capture younger buyers by selling its front-wheel drive entry-level cars in Canada. Mercedes-Benz increased its sales at a time of general economic malaise, despite having a product line that included some vehicles with appalling reliability. With the recent redesign of the C-Class and E-Class models, Mercedes-Benz has fully re-engaged the luxury market it all but abandoned in the period from 1996 to 2005. Currently, Mercedes-Benz is once again a company that is building luxury cars whose design, finish, and performance can be considered benchmarks for their respective classes.

Daimler AG, Mercedes' governing company, is registering record-breaking profits. Shoppers in Mercedes' segment want luxury, but they also value prestige. Automobile alchemists capable of creating fancy and *desirable* cars will be the winners in 2017. Mercedes is doing just that and it is paying off handsomely.

The company has pulled off this turnaround by increasing sales of smaller and less expensive cars in Canada and the United States, while selling fewer – but larger and more expensive – models in Europe and Asia. This means we'll see more compacts, crossovers, and a proliferation of turbocharged engines that have mostly been offered offshore. Gasoline hybrid and electric vehicles may eventually start to squeeze out the popular Mercedes diesel.

As oil prices hover around $45 U.S. a barrel, luxury car sales in North America are shifting to more expensive European vehicles that appeal even to Millennial buyers (age 18-34) because of favourable leasing deals. According to data supplied by Polk, leasing accounts for 29% of all new car purchases by Millennials in 2015 – a couple of points higher than leasing by the general population. Why the attraction? Simple. Leasing gets more car for less money up front; younger buyers are used to carrying a heavy debt load (school or mortgage debt); and in the age of 3-year cell phone contracts, they want a different vehicle every few years.

More Models, Less Quality

Contrary to popular perceptions, Mercedes hasn't been very consistent at making reliable or top-quality cars and SUVs over the past 15 years. Industry insiders say quality control went downhill after M-B extended its product lineup in 1996. Since then, the company has settled multimillion-dollar lawsuits for engine failures and other major defects.

In a recent U.S. class action, owners say about 1.6 million cars built from 2006 to 2015 were sold with defective wheels. Court documents show approximately 30% of the 50 wheels the plaintiffs' expert tested, including ones that didn't appear to be abused in any way, had visible cracks. The expert determined the cracks were "clearly induced by cyclic deformation" during normal use of the cars. (*Vincent Luppino v. Mercedes-Benz USA LLC, et al.*, Case No. 2:09-cv-05582, in the U.S. District Court for the District of New Jersey.)

In addition to faulty components, a number of M-B's models have been lemony as well. The 2001-2007 C-Class sedan and 1998-2005 M-Class sport utility were trouble-prone; and the Smart car is still considered a "cute" marginal player outclassed by more refined, reliable Japanese and South Korean mini-compacts. Although Mercedes' quality is improving, especially with the E-Class, some models continue to do much worse than others. For example, recent model years of the C-Class, M-Class, and GLK-Class still have reliability shortcomings, including engine, driveline, and electrical faults – similar defects are also evident in Audi, BMW, and VW models.

Higher-end models like the CLK, GL-Class, and M-Class SUV have a history of quality failures that can lighten your wallet and make your life miserable. Don't assume a high price tag ensures high quality: The most expensive models, like the $100,000+ S-Class sedan, can also be very troublesome over time. Along with the upper-class cachet, buyers going in for servicing sometimes end up feeling like they're wearing a sign on their back, reading, "Kick me – and take my wallet, too."

Mercedes' first SUVs were a disaster and are still a work in progress. From the very beginning, the U.S.-built 1998 M-Class proved to be abysmally bad. You couldn't have made a worse vehicle, judging by the unending stream of desperate-sounding service bulletins sent from head office to dealers after the vehicle's official launch. Two bulletins stand out in my mind. One was an authorization for dry-cleaning payouts to dealers whose customers' clothing had been stained by the dye from the burgundy-coloured leather seats. The other was a lengthy scientific explanation as to why it was "normal" for occupants to be "tasered" by static electricity when entering or exiting their vehicles

The S-Class (S for *Sonderklasse*: German for "special class") is a series of flagship vehicles built by Mercedes-Benz since 1972. Sadly, owners say these super-luxury cars aren't as "special" as Mercedes says or the general public thinks. Costing over a hundred thousand dollars each, they can't begin to approach the reliability of something like a Honda Civic. The following two NHTSA sample complaints show why:

Collision Avoidance System crashes

Salesman reached across driver and set cruise at 40 mph and encouraged driver to test the collision prevention system – traffic ahead was stopped at light – salesman continued to tell driver to not apply brakes – driver did not apply brakes – collision avoidance system failed – seat belt tensioners failed – air bags did not deploy when S550 collided with rear of stopped vehicle (an E-class) at approx 40 mph. Back seat passenger (driver's wife) was hospitalized with a cracked sternum.

Sunroof an "Improvised Explosive Device" (IED).

The 2015 S-class 550 was underway on the freeway when the sunroof exploded and broke off in chunks hitting driver repeatedly until approximately 80% of the glass collapsed. Glass shards cut driver. MBworld shows similar incidents reported on other Mercedes-Benz vehicles. Mercedes-Benz would not cover under warranty or admit defect. See sample of postings: *http://mbworld.org/forums/e-class-w212/405329-2011-e350-exploding-sunroof. html; http://mbworld.org/forums/c-class-w204/544374-exploding-shattered-sunroof-tristar-mercedes-st-louis-mo.html; http://mbworld.org/forums/c-class-w203/346317-c230-sunroof-exploded.html; http://mbworld.org/forums/c-class-w203/525268-sunroof-blew-out-exploded. html; http://mbworld.org/forums/gl-class-x166/550965-panoramic-roof-blew-up.html.*

Used-model Pricing

Luxury vehicles tend to depreciate a little more quickly than most, partly because they are priced high and have that much further to fall in terms of their value. The news that a vehicle is unreliable occasionally filters down to the used car market and can impact prices negatively. Buying an M-B Star-certified used model will cost an extra $3,000 to $4,000 compared to purchasing at an independent dealer or non-Mercedes franchised dealer, but the stronger warranty will cover known expensive repairs and comes with the assurance of dealer parts and service with the latest upgrades. Franchised luxury car dealers also offer low-cost financing on some of their inventory that offsets part of the higher purchase price.

With uneven reliability and more off-lease Mercedes vehicles coming back onto the market, residual values have fallen dramatically from what they used to be. And counter to tradition, Mercedes' diesel models don't hold their value as well anymore either. Adding to the diesel's uncertain future, German investigators suspect its emissions software may not perform as well on the road as in the lab.

So, what should a smart buyer do?

Consider a Japanese or South Korean alternative (Hyundai's Genesis is making waves). If you are really attracted to the brand, lease a new Mercedes and return it at the end of the term, or protect yourself from your new purchase with a full coverage warranty, ideally for as long as you'll own your car. Sign up for a prepaid Mercedes maintenance plan too, if it's available.

If a used European luxury model is on your list, look for a vehicle with some warranty left, or buy it with a full coverage used car warranty that pays out up to the value of the car. Luxury carmaker component costs can be astronomical.

> *Defective Gears Cost Big Money*
>
> Mercedes-Benz V6 and V8 gasoline engines sold in model years 2004 to 2008 (and to a lesser extent up to 2010) experience balance shaft and idler gear failures, as well as timing chain problems. The defects are typically seen in the C-Class, E350, M-Class and other models. Defective gears on the balancer shafts and defective idler gears can wear

out prematurely, causing the vehicle to malfunction, the Check Engine light to illuminate, and the vehicle to misfire or stop driving. Another warning sign is engine clatter at idle — uncommon to gasoline engines. Engines with the worn balance shaft sprocket were Mercedes-Benz "350" models that were equipped with the V6 (M272) engine.

Timing chain failures can cause catastrophic engine damage when the pistons strike the valves and cause head damage. Mercedes-Benz "450" models have the V8 (M273) engine that exhibited problems with a worn guide idler gear. Replacement parts are improved. Repairs are very expensive, in the range of $4,500 to $7,000 depending on the extent of the damage. A class-action settlement in the U.S. and one in Quebec reimbursed some repair costs, but the deadline for making a claim is over.

B-CLASS	*2006-2011*	★
	WITH MANUAL TRANSMISSION	★★
B250	*2013-2017*	★★★

2017 Mercedes-Benz B250

RATING: *B200:* Not Recommended (2006-2011); Below Average (manual transmission). *B250:* Average (2013-2017). The B-Class is a compact five-door hatchback that was introduced in March 2005 in Europe and six months later in Canada. It's one of the few automobiles that Canadians get to enjoy while Americans don't (they can buy an all-electric B model now). The B200 was the only front-wheel drive Mercedes sold in North America (an all-wheel drive 4Matic model was introduced in 2015). The B's two-box configuration makes the most of its tidy footprint by building up instead of out. You step up to get in, much like a minivan.

The extra-long wheelbase places the wheels far in the corners, improving the ride and minimizing cabin intrusion. The redesigned 2013-2017 B250 is actually roomier for passengers and cargo than the CLA and GLA, and doesn't suffer from their poor visibility. Unlike the B200, a mechanical breakdown in the U.S. can be easily rectified as it uses the same components as the contemporary CLA and GLA, but in the event of collision damage, body parts may be hard to obtain. The B-Class benefits from a full suite of safety gear and robust construction. **Road performance:** The cabin is fronted by an oversized dashboard displaying clear gauges. The seats are comfortable with good room front and rear and the interior is finished in attractive materials. The B200 turbo performs well, but the 134 hp normally aspirated model feels a bit lazy and its CVT is poorly calibrated. That said, the car is roomy and comfortable, soft riding, and pleasant to drive with a polished demeanour. *2013-2017:* The B250 is more refined and a big step up with additional performance, safety and convenience features. Only one engine, a 208 hp 2.0L gasoline turbo 4-cylinder is offered in Canada. Power reaches the front wheels via a 7-speed dual clutch automated manual transmission with Economy, Sport, and Manual modes. The engine is acceptably smooth. While the 7-speed automatic shifts smoothly, it can be reluctant to downshift. Ride and handling are nicely sorted. **Strong points:** Easy occupant ingress and egress with a perfect seat height and extra headroom to accommodate occupants with mobility concerns; comfortable rear seat with good legroom for three adults. Good cargo space with a large opening hatch, and low load height. Back seat folds flat to provide a practical cargo hold. Safe vehicle based on European-market crash testing. **Weak points:** Premium fuel required, the only compact people mover to specify it. The 2006-2011 B-Class was not ready for prime time in North America and had multiple problems, including rust, engine and CVT transmission failures. The B200 is to be avoided unless it is a gift or you can afford to send it to a wrecker after the first major component failure. The optional panoramic sunroof presented defects, including water leaks and improperly closing panels. Long-term durability of the B-250 is uncertain; lease it for no longer than the warranty period or purchase an extended warranty. Expensive to replace run-flat tires are fitted to all B-250s. **Major redesign:** *2006:* B200 introduced. *2013:* Redesigned B-250. **Best alternatives:** Space-efficient micro-vans like the Kia Rondo and Mazda5 are worth a look, but don't have the brand cachet.

Prices and Specs

Prices: *B250 FWD:* $31,850, *B250 4Matic AWD:* $34,150 **Freight:** $2,075 **Powertrain (FWD/AWD):** Engines: 2.0L 4-cyl. Turbo (208 hp); Transmissions: 7-speed dual clutch automatic. **Dimensions:** Passengers: 2/3; Length: 173 in.; Wheelbase: 106 in.; Weight: 3,230 lb. **Fuel economy:** *2.0T FWD:* 9.7L/100 km city, 6.6L/100 km highway; *2.0T AWD:* 10.2L/100 km city, 7.6L/100 km highway. **Assembled in:** Germany and Hungary.

SAFETY: IIHS and NHTSA crash testing have not been conducted in the U.S. However, the B250 scored 15.78 out of 16 in the Euro NCAP offset crash test. The passenger compartment held its shape well; there was a slight risk of serious leg injury for the passenger. All other injury values were good. The vehicle scored 16 out of 16 in the side impact crash test and a further two points in the pole test. Conclusion: The B250 is an exceptionally safe compact vehicle.

ALERT! The paddle shifters take getting used to and may discourage spirited driving. Check out the left side-view mirror's blind spot.

Owner-reported safety-related failures: The B250's 7-speed automatic transmission can't make up its mind as to which gear it should choose; it randomly shifts up and down and lingers in one gear when it should be in another. Cold starts exacerbate the problem. M-B's Eco Start/Stop is a fuel-saver that shuts off and re-starts the engine when stopped and accelerating; performance is anything but smooth. Consider de-activating it with the dash-mounted switch.

RELIABILITY: *B200:* Predicted reliability is a disaster waiting to happen. The B200 is afflicted with CVT transmission, turbo (20 hours of labour to replace when it fails), and engine timing chain failures ($400), as well as premature rust complaints. The CVT fails just out of warranty; first owners are covered at least partially until 6 yrs/150,000 km under a Mercedes secret warranty. Transmission repair parts are sold as an expensive complete assembly and a rebuild will set you back $5,500-$6,000 at Mercedes. If you're in the Montreal or Quebec city areas, the APA has located shops that will perform the big repair jobs for about 40% less than dealer prices. Try to obtain information on the service history of the vehicle you are looking at; the B200 has an expensive scheduled service at 96,000 km ($800 at a dealer) and many first owners who plan to sell will put it off. On the turbo, replacing the spark plugs requires removing the intake manifold, a big job. The consequence: Some owners don't bother. According to *Benzworld.org* the root cause of corrosion is the steel itself; some batches were improperly zinc-coated, which allows rust to develop early. Check the area around the front strut towers for structural corrosion. If damage is not too advanced the APA recommends Krown Rust Control for an annual rustproofing application, or in the Montreal area, Barry's Rustproofing for a one-time grease application (contact information is in the Part Four Introduction). The optional panoramic sunroof is made up of multiple glass panels. Owners report water leaks and improperly closing panels. The best bet is the very rare non-turbo B200 sold with a manual transmission between 2006 and 2008. Other concerns include short-lived batteries and noisy steering. *B250:* Insufficient data to date.

INTERNAL BULLETINS, SECRET WARRANTIES: All Years—Owners report premature rusting of the rear hatch and door seams, especially the early 2006-08 models. M-B paid to repair the damage on a case-by-case basis under a secret warranty offered to original owners. Look for bubbling paint and rust on the bottom edges of the doors where the metal is folded over.

C-CLASS	2005-2008	★★
	2009-2016	★★★
	2017	★★★★

RATING: Below Average (2005-2008); Average (2009-2016); Above Average (2017). The 2008-2014 C-Class had more sporting intentions to compete with the best-selling BMW 3 Series cars. For 2012, a 1.8L turbo 4-cylinder replaced the V6 on the base rear-wheel drive C250 and the interior was retouched. The redesigned 2015 C-Class marked the return of the model to the front rank of luxury cars. The 2015-2017 C-Class emerged during one of the "elegant" periods of Mercedes exterior design, and the cabin is roomy, chic and assembled from top-notch materials. The appearance of Mercedes' budget CLA allowed the C-Class to shift upmarket and the money spent on the current car clearly shows. A station wagon was announced for 2016 but never launched. A restyled C-Class coupe emerged for the 2017 model year. **Road performance:** *2008-2014:* Smooth V6 performance coupled to a 7-speed automatic that shifts very well. *2015-2017:* The bulk of C-Class vehicles sold in Canada are C300s, powered by a 241 hp 2.0L turbo 4-cylinder hooked up to a 7-speed automatic transmission. The engine delivers good performance and acceptable refinement. The turbocharged V6 model, sold as the C450, is fast but really overkill for this car. Very good ride-handling compromise. Strong brakes. Noise isolation has returned to the high levels expected of a Mercedes. The coupe shares the same engine/transmission combinations as the sedans. **Strong points:** *2008-2014:* The previous C-Class was valued for its styling, suave road manners, quiet interior and big trunk. The back seat was small and some controls like the factory navigation system were cumbersome. *2015-2017:* Elegant, luxuriously finished with room for four adults to be comfortable. As of 2016, Mercedes' 4Matic all-wheel drive became standard equipment even on the base model. **Weak points:** With the new models, you pay the Mercedes premium to get a four-banger under the hood. Some confusing controls, including cruise control, the shift selector and turn signals. Durability is a question mark, so if you want one of these cars, it's best to lease it for no longer than the warranty period or pay extra for additional warranty coverage. **Major redesign:** 2008 and 2015. **Best alternatives:** The Audi A4 and BMW 3 Series are the obvious cross shops. If you are buying for the long term, the Lexus IS or ES or Infiniti Q50 are worth a look.

Prices and Specs

Prices: *C300 4matic AWD:* $44,000; *AMG C63 S 4Matic AWD:* $84,100 **Freight:** $2,075 **Powertrain (AWD):** Engines: 2.0L 4-cyl. Turbo (241 hp), 3.0L V6 Turbo (362 hp), 4.0L V8 Turbo (469 hp); Transmissions: 7-speed automatic. **Dimensions:** Passengers: 2/3; Length: 184.5 in.; Wheelbase: 112 in.; Weight: 3,583 lb. **Fuel economy:** *2.0T AWD:* 10.1L/100 km city, 7.8L/100 km highway; *3.0T AWD:* 11.5L/100 km city, 8.3L/100 km highway. **Assembled in:** Germany and the U.SA.

IIHS 2015-2016 SEDAN

Small Front	Good
Front	Good
Side	Good
Roof strength	Good
Head restraint and seats	Good
Child seat anchors	Good
NHTSA Overall Sedan 2017	★★★★★

Owner-reported safety-related failures: Airbags fail to deploy. *C250:* Turn-signal control light is barely visible in daylight, and steering-column-mounted levers (cruise control, for instance) are hard to see behind the steering wheel. *C300:* Driver's door popped open and interior lights suddenly came on, says this owner of a 2015 C300:

> It was very frightening, and caught me by surprise. Luckily at the time there were no other cars near me. I was told by dealer they couldn't duplicate the door opening. However, looking at forums on the internet, this exact issue has been reported by others in the US and Australia at least. Some were the driver's door, others were the passenger's door. One reported it happening a second time after the dealer inspected the vehicle.

Vehicle fails to accelerate on the highway:

> The accelerator pedal was depressed but my 2015 C300 would not accelerate. The stability control, collision preventive assistance, and cruise control shut down. Warning indicators illuminated. The failure recurred three times. The radar sensor was replaced, but the failure recurred.

Electric power steering failures reported:

> My 2015 C300's steering malfunction light came on and the steering wheel lost power assist and locked up.

RELIABILITY: Needlessly complex systems in various areas of the car lead to various failures as the cars age. The 2004-2008 C280 and C350 V6 engine in the previous-generation have a history of balancer shaft failures that cost a fortune to fix (see Defective Gears Cost Big Money, under Mercedes-Benz introduction). If a used C-Class with an engine that has the suspected defect does not come with proof that the balancer shaft gears have been replaced, the car may not be worth considering. Even Mercedes dealers are reluctant to take these engines in trade and will make low-ball offers of $3,000-$5,000 for pristine cars. A rattling noise in the drive system when accelerating could signal a defective bearing in the 4-Matic drive system. At the time of writing, Mercedes sells only the complete transfer case assembly at $12,000. Contact the APA for the name of a shop in the Montreal area that can replace just the bearing. Ignition switch failures reported; replacing the defective part and reprogramming the keys will cost $500-$700. *2008-2014:*

Common complaints include a faulty electronic steering lock and faulty wiring harness that shorts out the tail lamps (a potential fire hazard). Some tail lamps have actually caught on fire and melted. Why does electricity confound the European automakers? Also reported are troublesome moonroof mechanisms, erratic-shifting automatics (addressed with a software update) and leaking 4Matic transfer cases. The blower motor is known to fail and the air conditioner can leak on occasion, requiring a recharge. Batteries can drain down when the car is parked for a few days; blame the car's overly complex systems, which draw power 24 hours a day. Engine and transmission mounts may wear quickly. Failing high-pressure fuel pump can result in occasional poor fuel delivery, rough acceleration and Check Engine light. Rattling V6 upon start-up may indicate metal fatigue in wrist pins; requires removing engine and replacing all six pistons/rods as per TSB. There is a TSB for a timing chain secondary pulley that also can cause a rattle on start-up. It calls for an anti-drain valve to be installed in each oil supply orifice serving the pulley. Leaking seals in transmission and differential. Wheel bearings can wear prematurely.

INTERNAL BULLETINS, SECRET WARRANTIES: **All C-Class (2009-13), CLK-Class (2009-10), E-Class (2009-13) models:** Correction for steering knock. **All C-Class and E-Class models: 2011-13**—Bulletin advises dealers to replace noisy automatic transmissions under warranty. **2013**—Oil loss near the rear crankcase-transmission bell housing. Corrosion spreads under wheel hub sealing ring. Dirt and water are washed in front of the sealing ring of the wheel hub via the rpm sensor bore in the steering knuckle or through corresponding gaps between the anchor plate and steering knuckle. Corrosion forms on the contact surface of the sealing ring and spreads under the sealing lips. As a result, moisture can penetrate the wheel bearing and cause corrosion. Moisture in area of A-pillar trim/headliner at front left or right. Replace water drain grommet. Casting porosity in crankcase or leaks in oil filter housing (seal might be damaged at the oil filter housing plate). The steering boot heat shield with aluminum ring may be loose and could scrape on the steering shaft. **2005**—Engine oil leaks from the oil-level sensor. Harsh shifts with the automatic transmission. Transmission fluid leaks at the electrical connector. Inoperative central locking system and A/C heater blower motor. Steering assembly leaks fluid. Sliding roof water leaks, rattling. Moisture in the turn signal lights and mirrors. Tail lights won't turn off; trunk light won't turn on. A Service Campaign calls for the modification of the lower door seal. **2007**—Rough shifting. Automatic transmission shift chatter. Steering rack leaks. Inoperative A/C blower motor. Remedy for brake squealing. Front-end/dash noise. Front axle knocking when parking. Torsion bar front-end creaking. Inoperative turn signals. Rear seatback rattle. Loose head restraint. Horn may not work due to premature corrosion of the assembly. *C350:* **2009**—Oil leaks at the rear of the engine may be fixed by changing the camshaft cover plugs. Hard 1-2 shifts. Harsh engagement when shifting from Park to Drive. Delayed Reverse engagement. What to do if the automatic transmission goes into "limp home" mode? Front axle noise when maneuvering. Front axle dull, thumping noise when going over bumps. Front-end suspension or steering grinding noise. Front seat backrest noise. Interior lights flickering. Four-way lumbar support fails. Internal steering gear leakage. A/C is inoperative or supplies insufficient cooling. *C250: 2011-12*—Oil leakage at the seam between the automatic transmission and the transfer case housing. Suspension noise from front axle suspension struts on vehicles equipped with a 1.8L engine. Automatic transmission hard Second-Third upshift or slipping, no Third gear. *C300, C350, C63 AMG, and CL550: 2013*—Vehicle doesn't perform automatic engine stop. Repair tips for engine cylinder head cover leaks. Consumer electrical shut-off intermittently active. Automatic transmission switches default to "limp home" mode for no reason. Automatic transmission hard Second-Third upshifts, slipping, or no Third gear. Oil leaks at the seam between the automatic transmission and the transfer case housing. Front suspension noise. Correcting various Parking Assist malfunctions. *C220, C250, C300: 2013-15*—Sluggish steering; instrument cluster display power steering warning message is activated. *2014-15*—Vehicle shuts down at 8 kph due to software mis-match. Engine clattering, knocking, and rattling noises in cold weather. *2015-16*—Leakage from turbocharger oil feed line.

E-CLASS		
2006-2007	★★	
2008-2011	★★★	
2012-2017	★★★★	

The pre-2017 E-Class looks a bit odd but marked a return of the E-Class series to the luxury market it abandoned in the mid 1990s.

RATING: Below Average (2006-2007); Average (2008-2011); Above Average (2012-2017); New (2017 C300 sedan). Groomed as the essential doctor's car and direct competitor to BMW's 5 Series sedans, the E-Class is all-new for 2017, its first remake since 2010. As Mercedes is apt to do, the car is on a slow roll-out with the E300 4Matic sedan introduced first with the turbo V6 E400 and E43 AMG following. A station wagon and coupe versions of the newest E-Class have been introduced elsewhere and will make it to Canada eventually. A diesel engine has traditionally been offered in this model but no announcements have been made for 2017. AMG E 43 4MATIC. A station wagon and two-door versions will surely follow, as will diesel. **Road performance:** The pre-2017 E-Class is offered with a multitude of engines, and performance ranges from lively to very fast. Most used E-Class models in Canada are equipped with the 4Matic all-wheel drive system. The E-Class is distinguished by its refinement and solidity, smooth ride and predictable handling. **Strong points:** Elegant, well-appointed interior with acceptable space for this type of car. The redesigned 2010 models also offered a remarkably buttoned-down and comfortable ride, thanks to the rigid chassis and communicative steering. Broad product line with coupe, convertible and wagon versions, but they're not always easy to locate. **Weak points:** Like other Mercedes-Benz branded cars, the E-Class is best experienced as a new car leased for no longer than the warranty period. Needless complexity – attributed to "overengineering" – leads to various issues as the cars age. Cruise control and turn signals are poorly placed. Mercedes' COMAND interface is fussy and can get tiresome. **Major redesign:** 2010, 2014 update and 2017. **Best alternatives:** The Audi A6 and BMW 5 Series are the usual alternatives. If you are buying for the long term, the Lexus GS, Genesis G80 or Infiniti Q70 are good alternatives. A discounted 2014 E-Class represents a good buy after steep depreciation with a full coverage warranty from Mercedes or transfer of the extended warranty purchased by the original owner.

Prices and Specs

Prices: *E300 4Matic AWD:* $61,200 **Freight:** $2,695 **Powertrain (AWD):** Engines: 2.0L 4-cyl. Turbo (241 hp); Transmissions: 9-speed automatic. **Dimensions:** Passengers: 2/3; Length: 194 in.; Wheelbase: 116 in.; Weight: 3,891 lb. **Fuel economy:** *2.0T AWD:* 10.8L/100 km city, 8.1L/100 km highway. **Assembled in:** Germany.

Owner-reported safety-related failures: Few owner safety complaints: Airbags failed to deploy in a 2.016 E350; sudden, unintended acceleration; stall-out in traffic; cruise control won't cancel; steering stiffened and car crashed; windshield wipers are too slow for moderate speeds in the rain.

RELIABILITY: Check the review for the C-Class, as many engine/driveline issues are common to both cars. A battery that dies frequently could be due to a fault in the Keyless Entry System staying on instead of going to sleep. Auxiliary battery can also die prematurely. Outer transfer case bearing

SAFETY

IIHS 2016 SEDAN

Small Front	Good
Front	Good
Side	Good
Roof strength	Good
Head restraint and seats	Good
Child seat anchors	Good
NHTSA Overall 2016	★★★★

can become noisy at speed. There is a service program for all 4Matic Mercedes relating to this issue. Dealers have ordered and replaced entire transmissions (see Defective Gears Cost Big Money, under Mercedes-Benz introduction). Engine mounts can wear out prematurely, permitting vibration to enter the cabin. Artico "pleather" (vinyl) can crack and tear, especially on driver's seat. Broken seat heaters. Door handles can malfunction and break. Bluetec turbodiesel models use an AdBlue urea fluid heating element that commonly fails; replaced under warranty, but it's expensive afterward ($1,500-$2,000) and will fail again if the car is parked outdoors in very cold weather for extensive periods. Oil cooler seal fails; oil cooler gasket and housing all replaced. Heater blower motor often conks out. The air suspension system is notorious for failing over time; exorbitantly expensive to replace. Sunroof may not seal properly, allowing air leakage.

INTERNAL BULLETINS, SECRET WARRANTIES: 2006-07—Rough transmission shifts. Upshift/downshift chatter or shudder. Front axle creaking, grinding, knocking noise when parking, and other front-end noises. Rivet replacement to prevent water leakage. 2011-12—Automatic transmission switches to "limp home" mode. Hard Second-Third upshifts, slipping, or no Third gear. Oil leakage at the seam between the automatic transmission and the transfer case housing. Also, the vehicle doesn't perform automatic engine stop. The front suspension may be noisy. Repair tips for Parking Assist malfunctions. 2011-13—No crank/no start. 2012-14—Rear brake squeaking, scraping, or rattling may require replacing the brake shoes, stator, and expansion lock. 2014—An engine crank assembly knocking might be attributed to a defective connecting rod in the piston. Remedy for harsh shifts when going from Park to Drive. The automatic transmission may default to limp-home mode while driving (gearshifts no longer possible) and/or one or more fault codes will be stored. A knocking/creaking noise from the front axle may occur when manoeuvring with steering almost at full lock. This noise is caused by the inner stop plug in the hydro-mount colliding with the outer sleeve. Noise from the front seat backrests can occur when there's contact between the upper rivets inside the backrest cover and the backrest frame. Slight pressure on the center console can cause the rear blower fan wheel to scrape on the housing. Check the rear blower to see whether the cable set is badly installed or trapped. Replacing the blower is not necessary. 2014-15—Even after a software update of the Keyless-Go control unit, the vehicle cannot be opened either via Keyless-Go or via the radio remote control. The failure is caused by a software error in the Keyless-Go control unit. Mercedes says it is developing new software (TSB #L180.61-P-061174). Water can enter into the control unit tray under the driver/front passenger seat and damage the control units installed there. Problems with the on-board power supply voltage may also occur. It's possible the condensation hose (right/left) on the AC housing may either be dislocated, pinched/crushed (water collects in AC housing) or leaking, resulting in water entering the interior. 2015—A clunking noise from the front axle on rough roads can be traced to a damaged piston threaded section within the suspension damper. The piston may be bolted incorrectly. Enhancement of transmission shift quality following owner complaints. **2015**—PCM and TCM electronic modules need to be updated under warranty.

GLK-CLASS/GLC-CLASS

2010-2011	★★
2012-2016	★★★
2017 (LEASE)	★★★★

RATING: Below Average (2010-2011); Average (2012-2016); Above Average (2017 (Lease)). After watching its competitors churn out a slew of compact luxury sport-utilities, Mercedes joined the fray with a *Geländewagen Luxus Kompaktklasse* of its own for 2010. The GLK was priced aggressively, because the premium SUV segment has proven to be an effective way to attract new customers; Mercedes estimated that 70% of GLK buyers would be new to the brand. Not coincidentally, the three-pointed star on the grille was big enough to be seen from space. The all-new GLK rode on the C-Class sedan chassis, utilizing the same strut-type front suspension with lower control arms, and a multilink configuration at the rear. Inside, Artico premium vinyl upholstery was standard fare, but most riders mistook it for leather. While the seats up front provided ample first-class space, the rear bench was second class. Initially, there was but one powertrain: An all-aluminum 3.5L DOHC V6, good for 268 hp, working through a 7-speed automatic transmission. The standard all-wheel drive's torque split was fixed at 55/45% front to rear, although to aid traction the ABS brakes could individually retard any wheel that was spinning needlessly. The GLK was redesigned for 2016, and was renamed GLC under Mercedes's new nomenclature. It shares 70% of its parts with the C-Class sedan, including the same 2.0L turbocharged 4-cylinder engine. There will be a four-door "coupe" variation of the GLC released sometime in 2017 with a sleeker roof profile that's less practically shaped than the upright GLC wagon. **Road performance:** Despite the C-Class's underpinnings, the GLK was less sporting; its steering felt a little disconnected and the brake pedal was "wooden;" the overall driving experience was popular with owners. The optional 20-inch wheels and tires are excessive, and expensive to replace. In terms of fuel consumption, the V6 drinks deeply in the city. The all-new GLC for 2016 smoothed a lot of the GLK's rough edges. The GLK's modest cabin space and elevated wind noise were duly attended to. **Strong points:** *GLK:* Rigid made-from-a-solid-ingot feel, supremely controlled ride and handling, tailored cabin, high-tech gear aids driver. *GLC:* Pampering interior; cleaner exterior design; excellent balance of performance and comfort; enormous amount of safety equipment; generous, family-friendly backseat; fuel-efficient turbocharged engine. **Weak points:** The COMAND controller interface can be confusing to use, though the 2016 version is better. Inflexible navigation system. Expensive upkeep after the warranty expires. **Major redesign:** 2010 and 2016. **Best alternatives:** Lots of choice in this segment, the Audi Q5 and BMW X3 are direct competitors. For the long term, the

Acura RDX and Infiniti QX50 are good alternatives. The Volvo XC60 is a family-oriented option.

Prices and Specs

Prices: *GLC300 4Matic AWD:* $45,150; *GLC45:* $59,900 **Freight:** $2,075 **Powertrain (AWD):** Engines: 2.0L 4-cyl. Turbo (241 hp); 3.0L V6 Turbo (362 hp); Transmissions: 9-speed automatic. **Dimensions:** Passengers: 2/3; Length: 183 in.; Wheelbase: 113 in.; Weight: 4,002 lb. **Fuel economy:** *2.0T AWD:* 11.1L/100 km city, 8.5L/100 km highway. **Assembled in:** Germany.

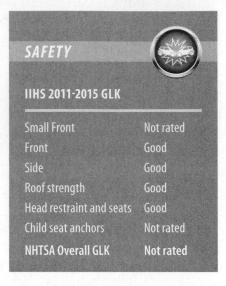

SAFETY

IIHS 2011-2015 GLK	
Small Front	Not rated
Front	Good
Side	Good
Roof strength	Good
Head restraint and seats	Good
Child seat anchors	Not rated
NHTSA Overall GLK	**Not rated**

RELIABILITY: The usual niggling Mercedes bugaboos include problematic electrics that operate the power seats, and especially the optional power rear hatch. Some owners reported faulty windshield washer pumps and, oddly, leaking washer tanks. Other repair items include failed wheel bearings, faulty thermostats, broken door lock actuators, truculent navigation systems and A/C controls. Spontaneously shattered sunroofs experienced in the GLK, as in many other models and makes. Dealers are accustomed to directing owners to make an insurance claim. In the absence of an impact, a cracked or shattered sunroof is a manufacturing defect. Driveline vibration may be traced to worn engine and transmission mounts. Power rear liftgate may malfunction; motor often needs replacing. Timing chain can wear out prematurely, as can wheel bearings. Weatherstripping can detach from door bottoms. Faulty fuel injectors on Bluetec turbodiesel engine, as well as short-lived DEF (urea) tank heater that's expensive to replace.

M-CLASS/GLE-CLASS

2005-2008	★
2009-2016	★★
2017 (LEASE)	★★★★

RATING: Not Recommended (2005-2008); Below Average (2009-2016); Above Average (2017 (Lease)). Mercedes-Benz updated its well-known M-Class mid-size luxury sport-utility in 2016 with revised styling, more sophisticated technology and the latest COMAND interface, then dubbed it the GLE-Class as part of its new nomenclature regime. Much of the discussion here will be about the pre-2016 M-Class, which was Mercedes' first foray into U.S. assembly when it opened a plant in Alabama. The first ML320 models leaving the factory were disastrously bad in terms of fit and finish and reliability issues, including ill-fitting doors, a cacophony of squeaks and rattles, failed power windows, electrical gremlins, fragile interior trim pieces, faulty batteries and leaky fuel lines. DaimlerChrysler reportedly spent $600 million U.S. on plant improvements before the second-generation M-Class was released for 2006. By switching to a unibody platform, the 2006 M-Class gained more interior room and rigidity while trimming about 40 kg. There were two engines initially: A 268 hp 3.5L V6 (replacing the original 232 hp 3.7L) in the ML350, while the ML500 used a 302 hp 5.0L V8. A 7-speed automatic was the sole transmission. Additional engine choices were added in subsequent years, including the popular Bluetec 210 hp 3.0L turbodiesel V6 in 2009. The M-Class was again redesigned for 2012, featuring a more luxurious cabin, more potent engines and all-new, but familiar, sheetmetal. The switch to the CLE-Class naming system for 2016 brought new front and rear fascias, and a revised cabin, but the same M-Class running gear. **Road performance:** Given its tall stance, the ML350 leans a little when pressed, but the ride is reasonably compliant without being floaty; a Dynamic Handling package does a good job of quelling body motions, at the expense of additional complexity. The all-electric steering assist is overly light and doesn't provide the sort of subtle feedback German vehicles are regarded for. Otherwise, the ride is composed and supremely quiet, indicative of the class. **Strong points:** Sumptuous luxury, with handsomely stitched leather, more "soft" design cues and up-to-date switchgear quality and functionality. New are a few interior styling options, such as quilted leather upholstery and matte-finish wood accents. Available V8 power makes the M competitive with SUVs from BMW and others. The ML350 Bluetec turbodiesel works the other end of the spectrum, with a focus on fuel economy. Robust construction and numerous systems make the vehicle supremely safe. **Weak points:** The M-Class has a long history of expensive reliability issues, everything from failed engines and transmissions, to a cornucopia of electrical issues that can sideline this beast. The turbodiesel option, while more efficient, has not been a model of reliability, and repair costs can erase any fuel savings. **Major redesign:** 2006, 2012 and 2016. **Best alternatives:** Direct competitors include the BMW X5 Series, Audi A7 and Range Rover Sport. The Porsche Cayenne is a performance-oriented alternative. The Volvo XC90 is another alternative. The Acura MDX and Lexus RX 350 are much more reliable used buys.

Prices and Specs

Prices: *GLE400 4Matic AWD:* $63,800; *GLE550 4Matic AWD:* $81,500 **Freight:** $2,075 **Powertrain (AWD):** Engines: 3.0L V6 Turbo (329-362 hp); 4.7L V8 Turbo (449 hp); Transmissions: 9-speed automatic. **Dimensions:** Passengers: 2/3; Length: 190 in.; Wheelbase: 115 in.; Weight: 4,927 lb. **Fuel economy:** *3.0T AWD:* 13.3L/100 km city, 10.1L/100 km highway; *4.7T AWD:* 15.3L/100 km city, 11.3L/100 km highway. **Assembled in:** Alabama.

RELIABILITY: *2006-2011:* Avoid the inaugural 2006 model. The V6 is a risky buy until 2008 (see Defective Gears Cost Big Money, under Mercedes-Benz introduction). The automatic transmission may develop a rough shifting condition and eventually fail outright. Harsh downshifts from Second to First when braking may require a software upgrade, a revised valve body, or both. It's important to follow Mercedes' maintenance regimen. The camshaft adjuster solenoid can reportedly fail, or balance shaft components may wear, resulting in a lit Check Engine Light and drivability issues. Repairs are expensive. The engine may also develop a stalling or no-start condition due to a bad crankshaft position sensor. Other malfunctions include oil leaks from the camshaft caps, failed air conditioners, drained batteries, sundry fluid leaks, overheated driver's seat, bad seatbelt retractors and short-lived tires. Bluetec turbodiesel engines are notorious for failing DEF tank heater, which can cost more than $2,000 to replace (recent model years as well). Check out this rant by a 2009 Mercedes ML-320 Bluetec owner on *Edmunds.com* listing his itemized repairs over a 7-year period (all figures in U.S. funds):

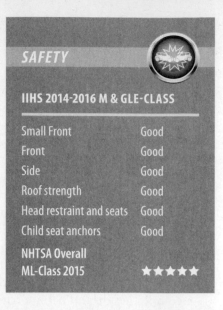

SAFETY

IIHS 2014-2016 M & GLE-CLASS

Small Front	Good
Front	Good
Side	Good
Roof strength	Good
Head restraint and seats	Good
Child seat anchors	Good
NHTSA Overall ML-Class 2015	★★★★★

01. Factory recall: Tail lamps, rear lights, power lift gate module replaced (cost not known) at 5,176 miles

02. Warranty work: Noise from front end; replace right front wheel bearing at 27,670 miles

03. Warranty work: Replace left strut assembly front and replace buttons on steering wheel at 32,477 miles

04. Warranty work: Removed and lubricated shift paddles on steering wheel to fix squeaky noise at 32,620 miles

05. Warranty work: Replaced defective NOX sensor at 35,866 miles

06. Warranty work: Left rear door lock assembly replaced at 42,541 miles

07. Repair NOT covered by warranty: replaced auxiliary heater in AdBlue tank diagnosed at 49,671 although it is part of the emissions control system but NOT covered by MB emissions control warranty (read the small print); paid out of some slush fund after my vociferous complaints to MBofUSA; cost estimate almost $2,200; fixed problem at 50,843 miles

08. Repair: Front passenger door lock assembly (same broken part as above, different door) $833.99 after 15% dealer courtesy discount at 53,277 miles

09. Repair: Noise from engine department – loose NOX sensor – tightened – no charge at 56,633 miles

10. Repair: Replace 2nd NOX sensor and EGR temperature sensor and air cleaner turbo seal at 60,028 miles; this NOX sensor lasted 24,162 miles; cost of repair $1,350.92

11. Repair Turbocharger intake shut-off motor, seals, gaskets, pipes (almost left me stranded) at 66,241 miles; cost $1,675.89

12. Repair: Bad Glow Plug Control Module at 68,9921 miles; cost $503.64

13. Repair: Oil leak in front engine area. Turbo Pipe O-Ring Seal and seal on oil breather assembly black o-ring seal; oil squirted on V-belt; replaced free of charge by dealer as it was possibly related to repair #11 not performed 100%; dealer otherwise very good and VERY HONEST. Same mileage as Repair #12 done at same time.

14. Replace 3 engine mounts/support struts. They were leaking fluids; at 73,696 miles; $1,774.38

15. Replace temperature sensor upstream of turbo at 73,696 miles (as in #14); cost $737.98

Estimated cost of warranty repairs $5,000+; repairs paid by owner $6,876.80; additional regular maintenance cost incl. tire replacement $8,391.98. Total estimated cost for all repairs, including warranty work and regular maintenance ~ $20,268.78.

2012-2017: COMAND interface system can stop working, also back-up camera, radio, navigation and many more related issues, including Bluetooth malfunctions. Exterior mirrors may not fold and power liftgate stops in the middle of opening. Frequent and expensive brake service. Experiencing latency in some functions: Lagging garage remote, starting procedure, etc. When in standard mode the engine can almost stall before lurching forward before the turbos kick in during quick highway merges. Unresolved drivetrain vibration. Plenty of oil leaks from engine seals and from transfer case. Engine can stall at speed or go into slow "limp-home mode" without warning, endangering drivers and passengers. Some fuel pumps and crankshaft position sensors have been replaced, and some engines have been replaced outright. Loud noise from engine during cold start-up may be traced to the right and left timing chain tensioners, which may need to be replaced. Electric power steering system can become inoperative without warning while driving, leaving driver to strong-arm the steering wheels to stop safely. A software update is usually installed to address steering problems. Optional air-suspension system is failure-prone and should be avoided. Power sunroof may not auto-close to proper position. Short-lived ignition coils. Suspension bushings can wear quickly. Transmission failure is not uncommon. Short-lived NOx sensors and wheel bearings.

MINI

The original Austin Mini was such a groundbreaking automobile in 1959 that many modern automobiles owe something to it: Unibody construction, front-wheel drive, transverse engine orientation, and four-wheel independent suspension, among other features. Creator Sir Alec Issigonis didn't invent all this, but he successfully married it all in one fantastically compact package (legend has it he designed the car around four chairs arranged in two rows) and sold it for an equally minuscule price. Mr. Bean's Mini was sold in various markets until 2000, although 1967 marked the last year it was exported to America. Canadian sales petered out in 1979.

BMW bought the ailing Rover Group in 1994 and, having failed to stem its heavy losses, dismantled the British automaker in 2000, selling Land Rover to Ford. BMW retained the rights to the Mini nameplate and took charge of the plans for an all-new MINI Cooper. Arriving for 2002, the new MINI was considerably larger than the 10-foot-long original, a requirement of contemporary crash and occupant comfort standards, but reproduced many of its styling cues. Rather than confine itself to a lone "entry-level" model, BMW created a whole hipster brand it could use as a stepping stone into BMW showrooms.

This eye-catching classic British-cum-German car is a very competent performer, but high maintenance bills make this cutie costly. MINI has traditionally dwelled in the basement of J.D. Power's dependability studies, often rated as the nameplate with the most reported mechanical problems. Early adopters of the car suffered through random stalling, fast-wearing clutches, defective automatic and manual transmissions, faulty air conditioners, electrical glitches, broken latches and rattles galore. Newer MINIs are better, but the brand has yet to match the reliability of an Asian brand, not that it seems to matter, because MINI sales are healthy, thanks to clever marketing, impossibly cute styling and a fun driving experience.

Vintage Mini

MINI COOPER

2007-2016	★★
2017 (LEASE)	★★★★

WITH CVT AUTOMATIC

2002-2008	★

WITH 1.6 TURBO

2007-2012	★

bad buy

bad buy

EUROPEAN VEHICLES · PART FOUR

RATING: Below Average (2007-2016); Above Average (2017 (Lease)). Timeless styling with an attractive interior and nimble handling. The back seat in the two-door is uncomfortably cramped. There's a history of costly, premature mechanical and fit and finish deficiencies in older models. Although the base MINI has an average reliability rating, the Cooper S has been much less reliable. The third-generation MINI, introduced for 2014, rode on a new front-wheel drive platform engineered by BMW for a number of future models. The result is an enlarged MINI that's awkwardly stretched over the longer wheelbase. While it is less well proportioned than previous models, the redesign provided a bigger interior with upgraded materials, two new turbocharged engines, a much-improved automatic transmission and a bevy of high-tech features. The new platform also allowed for the creation of a four-door MINI in 2015, which was sorely lacking in the lineup (the Countryman was a lot more expensive). The revised 2016 Clubman is the longer station-wagon version of the four-door Cooper hatchback with an extended cargo area; the split rear doors (rather than top-hinged hatch) hinder visibility. **Road performance:** Mediocre acceleration with the base engine; stiff-riding, especially with optional larger wheels, but the chassis pays dividends in terms of remarkably agile handling that conjures up sensations of go-karting. Light and precise gear shifting with easy clutch and shift action. A conventional 6-speed automatic transmission is available (early MINIs used a CVT automatic, which should be avoided). The base MINI Cooper hatchback comes with a 134 hp turbocharged 1.5L

3-cylinder engine; the Cooper S hatchback packs a turbocharged 2.0L 4-cylinder engine that produces 189 hp. **Strong points:** The MINI Cooper is great fun to drive, and the funky styling inside delights passengers. It's also easy to maneuver on city streets and in parking lots, and is very good on gas. Strong acceleration with the Cooper S. The four-door model has a usable back seat with acceptable access. IIHS top safety pick in terms of crash survivability. Lots of paint colours and customization options, including a Union Jack motif for the roof. Four-seater convertible model is also available. The Clubman wagon offers optional "ALL4" all-wheel drive. **Weak points:** MINIs demand premium fuel. The audio and climate controls are unnecessarily complicated. The stiff, choppy ride can become tiresome. Blame the rigid run-flat tires, which are disliked by owners for their harshness, short service life and expensive replacement. MINIs require dealer servicing, or the services of a specialized independent repair shop. Some parts can take weeks to come from Europe. **Major redesign:** 2002 introduction, 2007 and 2014. **Best alternatives:** Normally, we would suggest buying a cheaper 3-year-old model with some original warranty left, but used MINIs are too often synonymous with "money pit." Instead, consider a Mazda3 Sport, Volkswagen Golf GTI, Hyundai Veloster, Mazda MX-5 Miata or Fiat 500/500L.

Prices and Specs

Prices: *Cooper:* $21,990; *John Cooper Works convertible:* $40,240 **Freight:** $2,045 **Powertrain (FWD):** Engines: 1.5L 3-cyl. turbo (134 hp), 2.0L 4-cyl. turbo (189 hp), 2.0L 4-cyl. turbo (228 hp); Transmissions: 6-speed man., 6-speed auto. **Dimensions:** Passengers: 2/2 or 2/3; Length: 151 in.; Wheelbase: 98 in.; Weight: 2,605 lb. **Fuel economy:** *1.5T:* 8.7L/100 km city, 6.6L/100 km highway; *2.0T:* 9.2L/100 km city, 7.0L/100 km highway. **Assembled in:** England.

RELIABILITY: Purchase of a full-coverage extended warranty recommended unless you're leasing a new car. With a new MINI inquire about the prepaid maintenance plan. *2002-2006:* BMW's first-generation MINI is a lemon. Problems include prematurely worn clutches, failed CVT transmissions (very expensive), faulty air conditioners, electrical glitches, power steering failures (often traceable to an inoperative tiny plastic cooling fan that allows the power steering system to overheat), broken latches and interior trim pieces, and rattles galore. One owner identified the following common repair items:

SAFETY	
IIHS 2016	
Small Front	Good
Front	Good
Side	Good
Roof strength	Good
Head restraint and seats	Good
Child seat anchors	Marginal
NHTSA Overall	★★★★

If you keep it after the warranty expires, be ready to pay $1,000 and up for each repair, and there will be numerous repairs, for example, the water pump (replaced 2x), thermostat housing, oil pan seal (replaced 2x), moonroof repairs, rear door latch (replaced 2x), cylinders misfiring, oil leaks, axle seal replacement, etc.

2007-2017: The BMW-Peugeot engine is notorious for its failing timing chain and tensioners. A telltale "death rattle" underhood and oil leaks are often the first signs of pending engine seizure. A U.S. class-action lawsuit singles out 2007-2010 models. Excessive carbon build-up in the turbo engine can introduce start-up and drivability issues. Long list of other ailments includes leaky water pumps, turbo failures, short-lived fuel pumps and oxygen sensors, oil consumption, truculent power windows, broken turbochargers and exhaust manifolds, dead batteries, electrical glitches, weak air conditioners, power-steering woes and cold-weather starting issues. Manual transmission aficionados should know that the clutch can wear out in as little as 20,000 to 30,000 kilometres and the synchros will not stand up to the turbo engine in the Cooper S.

MINI COUNTRYMAN

WITH 1.6 TURBO ★★ ★

2017 NOT RATED

bad buy

RATING: Below Average (2011-2016). Imagine a MINI that can actually seat four people in comfort and carry all their luggage. Enter the chubby Cooper Countryman crossover with four adult-sized doors, a taller stance and optional all-wheel drive for 2011. It uses an enlarged platform (not related to the front-wheel drive BMW platform introduced more recently) that made room for the "ALL4" all-wheel drive system. An electro-hydraulic differential, working off the transmission's final drive, varies power distribution from front to rear. Inside, the MINI's cartoonish instruments and switches adorn a decidedly more upright cabin with bolstered chairs raised 7 cm higher off the floor. Two bucket seats grace the rear seating area, with a three-across bench available as a no-cost option. The Paceman is the two-door coupe variant of the Countryman with a sloped roof and standard ALL4 all-wheel drive. There's a new-generation Countryman coming in early 2017 that will use BMW's front-wheel drive/all-wheel drive platform and current generation of turbocharged engines found in the MINI Cooper. **Road performance:** Somnolent acceleration with the normally aspirated 1.6-L DOHC 4-cylinder that produced 121 hp in older models. The Countryman S used a turbocharged version of the same 1.6-L, churning out much more useful 181 hp. The steering is quick and accurate, braking is superb and the optional ALL4 system is supremely balanced. The ride quality ranges from decent to rough, depending on the size of wheels and tires. Avoid the sport-tuned suspension. **Strong points:** The Countryman manages to retain much of the sharp reflexes of the smaller MINI. Strong acceleration with the S turbo engine and also with the John Cooper Works edition, which extracts

208 hp from just 1.6 litres of displacement. Designers created a roomy back seat in a MINI for the first time. An IIHS top safety pick in terms of crash survivability. Comes in myriad colours with lots of options for customizing. **Weak points:** Slow acceleration with base engine in older models; the ride is quite stiff – avoid the sport-tuned suspension; less cargo capacity than most competitors. Like other MINIs, a new Countryman gets expensive if you indulge in the extensive options catalogue. Turbo engines require premium fuel, and real-world economy is not that great. **Major redesign:** 2011 introduced and 2017. **Best alternatives:** Subcompact all-wheel drive crossovers are all the rage these days, and we're seeing lots of choice in this burgeoning segment, including Mazda CX-3, Honda HR-V, Subaru Crosstrek, Chevrolet Trax, Buick Encore, Nissan Juke, Fiat 500X, and the VW GTI 5-door.

Prices and Specs

Prices: *Countryman Cooper S ALL4:* $29,950; *John Cooper Works ALL4:* $38,500 **Freight:** $2,045
Powertrain (AWD): Engines: 1.6L 4-cyl. turbo (181 hp), 1.6L 4-cyl. turbo (208 hp); Transmissions: 6-speed man., 6-speed auto. **Dimensions:** Passengers: 2/2 or 2/3; Length: 162 in.; Wheelbase: 102 in.; Weight: 2,954 lb. **Fuel economy:** *1.6T:* 10.1L/100 km city, 7.7L/100 km highway. **Assembled in:** Austria.

RELIABILITY: Purchase of a full-coverage extended warranty recommended unless you're leasing a new car. With a new MINI inquire about the prepaid maintenance plan. *2011-2016:* Assembled by Canada's Magna Steyr in Graz, Austria, the Countryman has exhibited plenty of mechanical lapses, especially short-lived clutches that burn up quickly, owners reported. Also noteworthy are high-pressure fuel pump failures that can leave motorists stranded. Owners reported ongoing issues with the thermostat housing and frustrating oil leaks around a sending unit. The timing chain can slacken and cause drivability issues; owners are accustomed to seeing the Check Engine Lamp frequently lit. Other issues include temperamental door locks, broken power window actuators, overheated radios, leaky sunroofs, unusually short-lived spark plugs and ignition coils, and other electrical gremlins.

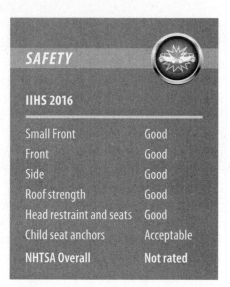

SAFETY

IIHS 2016

Small Front	Good
Front	Good
Side	Good
Roof strength	Good
Head restraint and seats	Good
Child seat anchors	Acceptable
NHTSA Overall	**Not rated**

"Smoke and Mirrors"

> *Diesel*
>
> Volkswagen is a crooked company. It concocted an onboard "defeat device" to sup-press diesel-engine emissions during mandatory emissions tests, a deception that will likely cost the automaker $30 billion by the time all the fallout settles. The auto-maker will be cutting back its workforce in Germany in order to help pay fines, settle-ments and judgments. In the meantime, affected Canadian diesel owners should consider VW's buyback, compensation and corrective repairs proposal as a possible prelude to unloading their cars.

What to Do

- You can't buy a new VW diesel; don't buy a used one, either.
- If selling one, make sure you tell the buyer the car has to be "fixed" – and watch their hasty retreat.
- Sit tight and have the car fixed only after you know what will be done.
- Ask how engine performance and fuel mileage will be affected.
- Ask what the long-term effects will be on the powertrain.
- Consider a lawsuit against dealer and VW for loss of use, misrepresentation, inconvenience, and loss of value, or sign up for one of the class actions.

Does VW Have a Future?

Yes, but not in its present form. VW is sorely lacking a mid-sized SUV as one example. Consequently, the company is using cheap leasing offers to keep produc-tion humming and buy Volkswagen time to improve its product mix over the next three years as leasing contracts expire and owners return to the dealership. Leasing accounts for as much as 45% of the company's transactions – double the rate of other mainstream makes.

Still, in spite of the discounts, cheap leases and high-tech drivetrains, Volk-swagen's North American sedans and SUVs are not dazzlers. They embody bland styling and offer only basic safety and infotainment technology – a niche already dominated by the conservatively designed, bestselling Honda Accord and Toyota Camry.

VW's 2017 lineup beyond the popular Jetta includes the mid-size Passat, small Golf hatchback, and the sportier GTI and Beetle. Its sport utility vehicles, the aging Tiguan and upscale Touareg, have been laggards in a market hungry for crossovers and SUVs. However, the next-generation Tiguan is coming next year and the all-new Atlas mid-size SUV, based on the enlarged Passat platform, will begin selling in the summer of 2017. The only thing that's fresh right now is the Golf Alltrack, an outdoorsy station wagon with VW's 4Motion all-wheel drive that channels the Subaru Outback.

VW's e-Golf

Volkswagen launched its first all-electric car, the $33,450 e-Golf, two years ago in the U.S. and is scheduled to bring it to Canada in mid-2017. With Canadian tax credits and the obligatory $2,000 freight charge, the car should retail for similar money here. Virtually indistinguishable from a regular Golf hatchback, the e-Golf is a city car with a range of about 130 kilometres that will already be out of date when it hits the market. VW has indicated its future is in electric cars and not diesels, and the e-Golf is playing catch-up.

Be Wary of Volkswagen DSG Transmissions

Quality has been the company's Achilles' heel, from the first Beetle's no-heat heaters that chaperoned your mom and dad on their first date, to gear-hopping, dual-clutch DSG automated transmissions afflicting Volkswagen's 2007-2013 models:

> I own a 2009 Jetta TDI with a DSG transmission. I feel like I am going to get hit when I start from a stop. The transmission jumps and hesitates. It has been to the dealer without being fixed. It is terrifying to drive a car that may or may not accelerate, which also jumps in and out of gear!

We can all agree that Volkswagens are practical drivers' cars that offer excellent handling and great fuel economy without sacrificing interior comfort. But overall reliability goes downhill after the fifth year of ownership and servicing is often more competent and cheaper at independent repair shops, which have grown increasingly popular as owners flee more expensive VW dealerships.

With rare candour Volkswagen now admits that car buyers see its products as failure-prone, and the automaker has vowed yet again to change that perception by building a more reliable, durable product and providing timely, no-return servicing. Taking a page out of Toyota's sudden, unintended acceleration/brake failure Congressional testimony in February 2010, Volkswagen says it is now paying more attention, sooner, to problems reported by fleet customers and dealers in order to find and fix problems before they become widespread among individual customers.

VW's quality control efforts seem to be working – more on some models than others. A check of the National Highway Traffic Safety Administration (NHTSA) owner complaints log at *safercar.gov* does show safety-related incidents have dropped during the last five years, probably as a result of the recall of the DSG transmission and subsequent "goodwill" warranty extensions to address DSG claims. In spite of all these efforts, automatic powertrain-related problems are still the number-one failure reported to NHTSA's safety complaint website.

Seven years ago *Lemon-Aid* exposed the DSG problem and rated Audi and VW new and used models equipped with DSG transmissions as lemons (Not Recommended), and we called for a warranty extension and recall. Since then, VW and Audi have recalled the transmission several times and extended the warranty to 10 years/100,000 miles on 2007-2010 models.

Incidentally, after *Lemon-Aid's* intervention, Australian VW/Audi car owners, irate that VW stonewalled their DSG complaints, sought the help of local media. The *Sydney Morning Herald* and *The Age* championed their case, leading to Volkswagen pulling its advertising from both publications. Shortly thereafter, VW recalled the affected VW, Audi and Skoda models.

GOLF/RABBIT ★★★
2017 (NEW) ★★★
DIESEL ★

bad buy

RATING: Average (2006-2016); Average (2017 (New)); *Golf TDI:* Not Recommended (2009-2015 turbodiesels and all models using the DSG transmission). Although they use similar components, the Golf hatchbacks are more reliable than the Jetta sedans, because of the Jetta's greater use of the failure-prone DSG drivetrain. Golf's nemesis has been primarily turbocharger failures and defective high-pressure fuel pumps that disintegrate and spew metal particles throughout the fuel delivery system, killing the engine. All gasoline- and diesel-powered models equipped with the DSG automatic transmission are risky buys. The Golf was nostalgically marketed as the Rabbit between 2007 and 2009, a half-baked notion that conjured up memories of roadside emergency calls, dead batteries and maddening electrical faults. Fortunately, it came with what was arguably VW's most reliable powertrain engine: A 2.5L DOHC 5-cylinder that worked well with the automatic transmission North Americans favour. The hatchback was redesigned for 2010 and got its Golf badge reinstated. The new car looked similar to the Rabbit, but the interior was all new and rendered in upscale materials that would not look out of place in an Audi. The durable 2.5L 5-cylinder returned, as did the popular TDI turbodiesel. The Golf was redesigned again for 2015, receiving an all-new unibody structure and a more efficient 1.8L turbo gasoline engine in place of the aging 2.5. New for 2017 is the Golf Alltrack, a jacked-up, all-wheel drive compact wagon that takes a page out of Subaru's playbook. **Road performance:** Golfs are superior all-around performers. The DSG's shifts are soft in full-auto mode, but subject to a lag when most needed, such as on turns, or merging into traffic. The sporty GTI, with its turbocharged 200 hp 2.0L 4-cylinder engine, delivers high-performance thrills without much of a fuel penalty. **Strong points:** "Practical and fun to drive" pretty well sums up why the Golf is popular. It offers a flexible, accommodating interior, plenty of power and responsive handling. Like most European makes, these VWs are drivers' cars with lots of road feedback; a comfortable ride; plenty of headroom, legroom and cargo space; a standard tilt/telescope steering column; a low load floor and good fuel economy. Owners point to its bank vault construction as a point of distinction in the econobox class. **Weak points:** With 2015-2017 models, watch for jerky and shuddering automatic transmissions, excessive shaking at highway speeds and a malfunctioning Bluetooth infotainment system that "freezes." The Golf is relatively pricey and is missing some common features found in other economy cars. Other weaknesses: Engine noise; folding rear seats don't lie flat; and restricted rear visibility. **Major redesign:** 2007, 2010 and 2015. **Best alternatives:** Other handy hatchbacks worth considering are the Honda Fit and new Civic Hatchback, Mazda3 Sport, Hyundai Elantra GT and Veloster, Kia Forte and Subaru Impreza.

Prices and Specs

Prices (2017): *Golf:* $19,195; *Golf GTI:* $29,495; *Golf Alltrack:* $35,295; *Golf R:* $40,695 **Freight:** $1,625
Powertrain (FWD/AWD): Engines: 1.8L Turbo 4-cyl. (170 hp), 2.0L Turbo 4-cyl. (210-292 hp); Transmissions: 5-speed man., 6-speed man., 6-speed auto., 4 Motion AWD Dimensions: **Passengers:** 2/3; Length: 167.5 in.; Wheelbase: 103.8 in.; Weight: 2,900 lb. **Fuel economy:** *1.8T:* 9.3L/100 km city, 6.5L/100 km highway; *2.0T:* 9.5L/100 km city, 7.2L/100 km highway. **Assembled in:** Mexico and Germany.

RELIABILITY: Purchase of a full-coverage extended warranty from VW recommended. German-sourced Golfs may have an inaccurate speedometer, which can be out by as much as +/- 7%. Sensors and wiring harnesses have been replaced in an attempt to address drivability issues. Powertrains on the DSG-equipped 2011 through 2013s are showing failures similar to the recalled 2007-2010 models. Reported trouble areas include failed fuel injectors and timing chain tensioners, broken turbochargers and clogged diesel particulate filters. *GTI:* Watch for short-lived clutches, faulty intake manifolds, frequent water pump failures and a Check Engine lamp that pops up every other month due to sensor failures. *TDI Turbodiesel:* Emissions scandal aside, maintenance costs increase after the fifth year of ownership; it takes six years for fuel savings to equal the car's higher purchase cost; and depreciation accelerates as you approach the end of the 4-year warranty. Expensive high pressure fuel pump failures. See Jetta, under Reliability, for information on direct fuel injection maintenance issues.

For Reliability and Internal Bulletin information check the Jetta review.

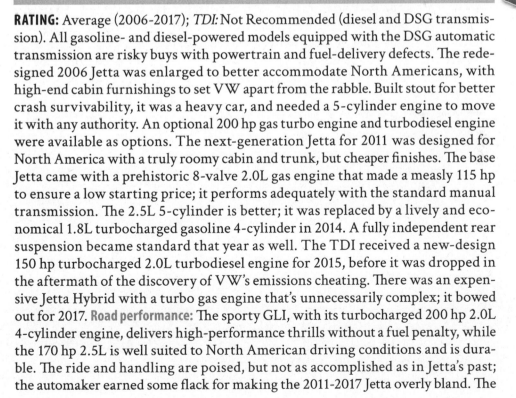

SAFETY

IIHS 2011-2016 GOLF

Small Front	Good
2011-2014	Not Rated
Front	Good
Side	Good
Roof strength	Good
Head restraint and seats	Good
Child seat anchors	Acceptable
2011-2015	Not Rated
NHTSA Overall Golf 2017	★★★★★

JETTA ★★★

DIESEL AND DSG AUTOMATIC ★

bad buy

RATING: Average (2006-2017); *TDI:* Not Recommended (diesel and DSG transmission). All gasoline- and diesel-powered models equipped with the DSG automatic transmission are risky buys with powertrain and fuel-delivery defects. The redesigned 2006 Jetta was enlarged to better accommodate North Americans, with high-end cabin furnishings to set VW apart from the rabble. Built stout for better crash survivability, it was a heavy car, and needed a 5-cylinder engine to move it with any authority. An optional 200 hp gas turbo engine and turbodiesel engine were available as options. The next-generation Jetta for 2011 was designed for North America with a truly roomy cabin and trunk, but cheaper finishes. The base Jetta came with a prehistoric 8-valve 2.0L gas engine that made a measly 115 hp to ensure a low starting price; it performs adequately with the standard manual transmission. The 2.5L 5-cylinder is better; it was replaced by a lively and economical 1.8L turbocharged gasoline 4-cylinder in 2014. A fully independent rear suspension became standard that year as well. The TDI received a new-design 150 hp turbocharged 2.0L turbodiesel engine for 2015, before it was dropped in the aftermath of the discovery of VW's emissions cheating. There was an expensive Jetta Hybrid with a turbo gas engine that's unnecessarily complex; it bowed out for 2017. **Road performance:** The sporty GLI, with its turbocharged 200 hp 2.0L 4-cylinder engine, delivers high-performance thrills without a fuel penalty, while the 170 hp 2.5L is well suited to North American driving conditions and is durable. The ride and handling are poised, but not as accomplished as in Jetta's past; the automaker earned some flack for making the 2011-2017 Jetta overly bland. The

115 hp weakling base engine sold until 2015 is reliable. **Strong points:** Jettas offer an accommodating interior, plenty of power with the higher-end models, and agile handling and good braking. Doors close with a solid "thunk." Like most European makes, these VWs are drivers' cars with a refined ride and good fuel economy from an array of engines. **Weak points:** Interior finish was cheapened with the 2011 redesign. With 2016-2017 models, watch for jerky and shuddering automatic transmissions. Owners have seen plenty of warning lamps lit up on the dashboard – never a welcome sign. The imitation leather seating surfaces can be uncomfortable in hot weather. The Fender-branded audio system rattles (covered by a special service campaign). **Major redesign:** 2005 and 2011. **Best alternatives:** Other cars worth considering are the Honda Civic and Accord, Hyundai Elantra, Kia Forte, Mazda3, Mazda6, and Toyota Corolla and Camry.

Prices and Specs

Prices (2017): $16,395, *GLI:* $34,995 **Freight:** $1,625 **Powertrain (FWD):** Engines: 1.4L Turbo 4-cyl. (150 hp), 1.8L Turbo 4-cyl. (170 hp), 2.0L Turbo 4-cyl. (210 hp); Transmissions: 5-speed man., 6-speed man., 6-speed auto. **Dimensions:** Passengers: 2/3; Length: 182.2 in.; Wheelbase: 104.4 in.; Weight: 3,090 lb. **Fuel economy:** *1.4T:* 8.5L/100 km city, 6.2L/100 km highway; *1.8T:* 9.4L/100 km city, 6.8L/100 km highway; *2.0T:* 9.8L/100 km city, 7.4L/100 km highway. **Assembled in:** Mexico.

ALERT! VW has not perfected the power sunroof (ditto the old manually operated sunroof) as owners report water and air leaks, and unexpected and spontaneous shattering:

> I was traveling on an interstate highway in my 2015 VW Golf and my sunroof exploded without warning. Temperatures outside were in the mid 90s [F], time of day was 6:00 pm, I had air conditioning running and sunroof and interior shade totally closed. After the explosion, the sunroof was bowed from the inside out (convex curve) and the safety glass was shattered in web-like pieces. I was missing glass from the middle of the roof about the size of an oblong watermelon.

Owner-reported safety-related failures: Many of the NHTSA-posted complaints on 2013 and earlier models involve DSG transmission and high-pressure fuel pump failures:

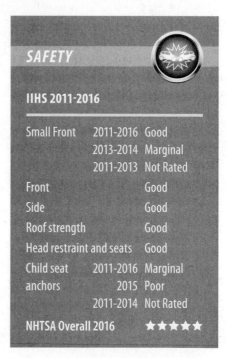

SAFETY

IIHS 2011-2016

Small Front	2011-2016	Good
	2013-2014	Marginal
	2011-2013	Not Rated
Front		Good
Side		Good
Roof strength		Good
Head restraint and seats		Good
Child seat	2011-2016	Marginal
anchors	2015	Poor
	2011-2014	Not Rated
NHTSA Overall 2016		★★★★★

2013 DSG Transmission Issues: When making a left hand turn across traffic, I coasted up to the light when it was my turn, then I pressed the accelerator and the car had no power. It crossed through the intersection at approximately 1 to 2 mph. It took 5 to 10 seconds for the power to return. This has happened at quite a few intersections. Also it happened when I was accelerating then had to release the accelerator due to a vehicle slowing in front of me, I re-engaged the accelerator and there was no power for 5 to 10 seconds.

Another owner report:

I was notified by the dealer that the fuel pump (commonly referred to as HPFP) basically imploded and sent metal throughout the entire fuel system, which now needs to be replaced. … This is a design failure and/or oversight on the part of both Volkswagen and Bosch, the HPFP manufacturer. I am a veteran member of the TDI Club VW Diesel online community, and there is extensive information and documentation there of these repeated failures.

Let's make it a troika:

Without warning, the engine shut down while driving down a busy road. Check Engine and Glow Plug warning light came on. Was just able to coast to the shoulder of the road. Car would turn over, but engine would not start. Car towed to dealer. Was told there was a catastrophic failure of the high-pressure fuel pump, and metal shards were found throughout the fuel system. VW replaced the entire fuel supply system (including fuel tank) and fuel injection system.

Owners warn that engine repairs after a fuel pump failure can easily total $7,500. The German-sourced components are exorbitantly expensive. VW has redesigned the fuel pump three times to improve its service life, yet even some late-model TDIs continue to exhibit pump failures. Also be wary of premature brake wear, and electrical and electronic failures. The cruise control can disengage suddenly, unintentionally braking the car. *GTI:* DSG transmission won't shift into gear, and sometimes the engine suddenly surges or stalls, accompanied by total brake failure:

During rush hour traffic, I had to slow down a little in order to allow the car next to me to pass so I could change lanes without hitting the car in front of me. My 2013 GTI seemed to shift into Neutral and did not respond when I hit the accelerator. The accelerator pedal actually sank to the floor with no response. After a few seconds, the transmission did shift into gear and took off too fast. In the meantime, I was almost rear-ended. This happens almost every day that I drive in heavy traffic. I can't control it so I have to make sure there is not a car within a mile behind me when I change lanes because the car frequently almost stalls.

RELIABILITY: Owners of previous-generation Jettas (pre-2011) complain about the Jetta 2.0T's tendency to consume plenty of motor oil between oil changes. Those who have pushed the issue with their dealer have had their piston rings replaced under warranty. 2006-2011 cars with Direct Injection gas engines can trigger an engine service light due to excessive carbon buildup in the intake manifold and around the valvetrain because the area is not cleaned by atomized incoming fuel like a conventional port fuel injection system; a cleaning, with walnut shells and with the head still on the engine, will take a few hours to restore engine performance. If you don't perform this cleaning the head may have to come off for a thorough cleaning or the vehicle could end up with a ruined engine. The Jetta is hard on its brakes, with expensive brake pad-and-rotor replacement coming early, and sometimes at the rear wheels before the front; have the rust cleaned off the rear brakes and all four brake calipers lubricated annually, or more often as needed, and you will prolong brake life into the normal range or better. Other complaints centre on the Jetta's troublesome electrical system, errant sensors, bad transmissions and turbos, poor paint and lousy radios. By comparison, drivers of the Jetta 2.5 have been relatively happy with the 5-cylinder engine, though it isn't fuel-thrifty, which is why it was dropped. Diesel owners grumble that the fuel savings are eaten up by the TDI's expensive service regimen. The newer turbodiesel engine presented owners with numerous headaches, including imploding fuel pumps, failed fuel injectors, broken turbochargers, intercooler icing and clogged particulate filters. *2011-17:* TDIs have been plagued by high-pressure fuel pump failures that see the pump grinding itself to smithereens and contaminating the fuel system. Engine restoration runs in the thousands of dollars. Other TDI faults include failed fuel injectors, bad fuel pressure sensors, broken turbochargers, intercooler icing and clogged particulate filters. Engine coils may fail prematurely in gasoline models, sometimes cutting out on the highway at speed and stalling the vehicle. High oil consumption continues to be an issue with the 2.0T turbo gasoline engine; owners have reported adding a litre as often as every 1,000 km. Other reported weaknesses in the Jetta include short-lived air conditioners, lousy radios, broken horns and power-lock actuators, wonky electrical components, sagging door seals and trunk lids that open on their own. Some owners continue to complain about the automatic Jetta's poor shifting quality. The DSG transmission requires an expensive service, best done using the actual VW-approved fluid, and possibly at a VW dealership to obtain the latest software upgrade. *Carcomplaints.com* gave the 2011 Jetta its "Beware of the Clunker" seal of disapproval.

INTERNAL BULLETINS, SECRET WARRANTIES: 1995-2013—Squeak and rattle kit available. **1999-2013**—Abnormal vibration when braking caused by excess corrosion or an out-of-round rotor; tackling unpleasant odours coming from the A/C vents; reducing exterior light moisture accumulation, removing headlight lens blemishes; and servicing the cooling fan if it runs with the ignition turned off. **2004-11**—DSG transmission lag and lurch troubleshooting. **2008-11**—VW has extended the Emissions Control Systems Warranty for the intake manifold under specific conditions to 10 years or 120,000 miles. **2008-13**—Remedy for a hard-starting, noisy, and rough-running engine. **2008-14**—A faulty high-pressure fuel pump may be the cause for no starts or a rough-running engine. Pump can "grenade" and send metallic debris throughout the fuel system, killing the engine. VW has advised owners of an extended 10-year/120,000-mile warranty on the pump for certain model years. **2011-12**—Free engine repairs and injector replacements:

SUBJECT: Warranty Extension for Intake Manifold & Fuel Injectors. Certain 2011-12 Model Year Volkswagen Vehicles with 2.0 TFSI Engine.

"We are informing you of our decision to extend your Emissions Control Systems Warranty for the intake manifold and fuel injectors under specific conditions to 10 years and 120,000 miles, whichever occurs first, from the vehicle's original in-service date." – Volkswagen of America.

VEHICLE MODEL AND YEAR(S):

2011-2012 BEETLE	2211 R3
2011-2012 CC	2011-2012 RABBIT
2011-2012 EOS	2011-2012 ROUTAN
2011-2012 GOLF	2011-2012 TIGUAN
2011-2012 GTI	2011-2012 TOUAREG
2011-2012 JETTA	2011-2012 TOUAREG HYBRID
2011-2012 PASSAT	

2011-14—A seam sealer skip or hole in the area around hood hinge or behind front fender will allow water to leak into the front passenger compartment. **2011-15**—Front outside door handles may stick due to cold outside temperatures. **2012-13**—Correcting an MIL warning light that comes on for no reason. **2013**—Engine intermittently shuts off immediately after starting. UV radiation can cause fading of the burred walnut veneer wood finish trim parts. Various door function control failures. Steering honking/squeaking noises. **2013-14**—Rough idling and poor engine timing may be corrected cheaply by first reprogramming the engine control module (ECM). **2014-2015**—Sticking camshaft adjuster control valve as the Malfunction Indicator Lamp (MIL) comes on. **2015**—Sticking A/C doesn't cool; compressor is noisy. Front seat creaking noise. Rear washer leaks; install upgraded part. Paint concerns on front or rear bumper. *Rabbit, GTI, R32:* **2010**—Noise from the B-pillar area. Front door gap causes some wind noise. Can't open liftgate after locking. **2010-11**—Poor front seat heater performance. **2011-12**—How to prevent electrical harness damage caused by animal snacking. If the heater doesn't blow hot enough, reboot the system with upgraded software. *TDI Turbodiesel:* What to do about engine hesitation; harsh shifting in low gear and cold weather no-starts. **2009-11**—Moisture from the air intake may condense in the intercooler and freeze solid.

RATING: Average; Not Recommended (diesel and DSG automatic). Volkswagen traced the classic Beetle profile and refashioned it with modern materials and technology as both a hatchback and soft-top convertible. The New Beetle sold well around the world when it was introduced in 1998, then VW promptly forgot about it and sales declined over the next 13 years. It was modestly refreshed for 2006 and got a 150 hp 2.5L 5-cylinder gas engine standard, later upgraded to 170 hp. To appeal to a broader audience (read: males), the second-generation 2012 Beetle was reshaped to give it a more muscular, hunkered-down profile. It was cast 18 cm longer and 8 cm wider, with a lower roof, longer hood and crisper sheetmetal – it looked like an original 1998 New Beetle had been left in a Panini press a little too long. It was underpinned by the contemporary front-wheel drive Jetta platform, complete with its strut front suspension and simple twist-beam rear suspension (the Beetle Turbo got the GTI's sophisticated multilink setup instead). Although no longer boasting top-hat-friendly front seats – thanks to the squashed roof – the Beetle's interior still offered plenty of space up front, less so in back. It's configured as a three-door hatchback with seating for four people, not five. The convertible version with a power-folding softtop arrived for 2013. New models use VW's 1.8L turbo 4-cylinder gas engine, good for 170 hp. **Road performance:** Early base models were powered by an underwhelming, 115 hp 4-cylinder engine (or optional 1.8L turbocharged gas or 1.9L turbodiesel), replaced in 2006 by a 2.5L 5-cylinder engine that offered all the power of a 4-cylinder combined with the economy of a 6-cylinder. The 200 hp 2.0T turbo gas variant was better, bundled with a sport-tuned suspension and other performance enhancements. Engine and automatic transmission hesitate when accelerating. The suspension provides a more comfortable ride than the usual Germanic fare, and the electric steering is accurate and communicative. The TDI turbodiesel is no longer sold until VW's fraudulent emissions system has been addressed. **Strong points:** Owners can't get enough of the Beetle's retro looks, funky interior, tidy size and refined drive. There's very little out there that looks anything like a Beetle. Handles like any other front-wheel drive Jetta or Golf, which is to say, competently. Pricing is surprisingly reasonable for a German icon. **Weak points:** The DSG dual-clutch automatic transmission's past failure rate doesn't bode well for long-term reliability. The car is easily buffeted by crosswinds; large head restraints and large front roof pillars obstruct front visibility; rear visibility is limited; there's insufficient rear legroom and headroom, and you won't find much trunk space due to the car's bug profile. New models haven't change much, except for a new infotainment system that allows for Android Auto and Apple CarPlay connectivity, as well as a new value-packed 1.8T S model. Watch for special editions, a cheap way to attract showroom traffic for an aging model. The Beetle's competitors are better handling and provide higher fuel economy (legally!) and more cargo space for a lower price. **Major redesign:** 2012. **Best alternatives:** Nothing else is a Beetle, but if you like the idea of driving a conversation starter, consider the MINI Cooper, Fiat 500, Nissan Juke, Hyundai Veloster, Kia Soul, or the Scion xB as a solid used buy.

Prices and Specs

Prices (2017): *Trendline 1.8T:* $19,990, *Comfortline Convertible:* $30,550 **Freight:** $1,625 **Powertrain (FWD):** Engines: 1.8L 4-cyl. Turbo (170 hp); Transmissions: 5-speed man., 6-speed auto. **Dimensions:** Passengers: 2/2; Length: 168 in.; Wheelbase: 100 in.; Weight: 3,012 lb. **Fuel economy:** *1.8T:* 9.6L/100 km city, 7.0L/100 km highway. **Assembled in:** Mexico.

ALERT! Beetle TDI owners can petition VW to buy back their car and include compensation for inconvenience and embarrassment.

RELIABILITY: *2012-2016:* By far the biggest reported issue with the Beetle is malfunctioning power windows. Owners complain online about the windows having a minds of their own, stopping halfway up and then lowering to where you see about an inch of the glass. Dealers were baffled by all the complaints, and offered some sage advice: "Don't use them." At least one service manager scolded his customer in this manner, while another recommended carrying plastic sheeting in case of rain. VW eventually did supply improved window actuators, but the problem may persist in used models. Some early builds exhibited peeling paint

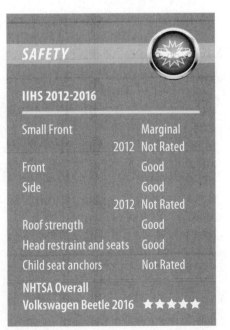

SAFETY

IIHS 2012-2016

Small Front	Marginal
2012	Not Rated
Front	Good
Side	Good
2012	Not Rated
Roof strength	Good
Head restraint and seats	Good
Child seat anchors	Not Rated
NHTSA Overall	
Volkswagen Beetle 2016	★★★★★

on the front bumper, and owners noted the Beetle's design invited lots of chipped paint on the hood and cracks in the upright windshield. Other mechanical ailments included faulty door locks, disintegrating seat foam, high-pressure fuel pump failures (turbo engines), underperforming air conditioners and intermittent stalling. *2004-2010:* Owners have noted persistent electrical issues, especially concerning the power windows, trunk release, door locks and short-lived headlamps. The convertible's power top may become inoperable, while the manual top may see the cords snap. Some have had their roof liners fall down, making driving difficult. Nagging mechanical issues include faulty ignition coils, broken air conditioners, truculent transmissions, overheating engines, leaking fuel lines and stalling. Owners have to put up with a fair bit to drive an icon. The Jetta and Golf share the Beetle's running gear; check their reviews for a list of additional trouble areas.

PASSAT/CC ★★★
2017 (NEW) ★★★★

RATING: Average; Above Average (2017 (New)). The Passat is an attractive mid-sized car built for the North American market. In its plans for world domination, Volkswagen collected $727 million (CDN) in local, state and federal incentives to build an assembly plant in Chattanooga, Tennessee, for its all-new 2012 Passat. Unlike the previous B6-generation Passat (2006-2010) that offered a wagon, the U.S. version was available only as a four-door sedan and it was super-sized to appeal to North Americans along with Costco-like pricing, which cut $8,000 off the sticker. The front-wheel drive car, partially based on the PQ46 platform used by the European Passat, grew 10 centimetres in length with a stretched wheelbase to yield class-leading legroom and a comfortable, roomy interior. The long wheelbase gives it an unshakable presence and provides good all-around performance for highway and city driving. *CC:* This "four-door coupe" makes use of the more expensive European-market Passat platform sourced in Germany, which explains why the sticker price is so much higher than the entry price of the Tennessee-made model. The CC provides a sharper road experience that delights driving enthusiasts, and the "coupe" styling looks attractive enough to belong on an Audi or Mercedes. It employs some of the same VW powertrains, but adds an optional V6 engine also available in the Passat. **Road performance:** Impressive acceleration with the turbocharged engine hooked to the smooth-performing manual gearbox. Pre-2012 models also offered sophisticated 4Motion full-time all-wheel drive. Refined road manners; better-than-average emergency handling; quick and predictable steering; handling outclasses most of the competition's and the suspension is both firm and comfortable. However, the engine/automatic transmission hesitates when accelerating. **Strong points:** Well-appointed and every bit as comfy as a Buick, and then some. Finally competitive with the Accord/Camry juggernauts. Quiet running; plenty of passenger and cargo room; impressive interior fit and finish;

and an exceptional long-distance runner. **Weak points:** Passats remain a favourite among thieves – whether for stealing radios, wheels, VW badges, or entire cars. (No, the delayed tranny shifts, fire-prone fuel system, and sticking outside door handles are not anti-theft measures – hmm, that's a thought.) Interior finish on the American Passat is no longer class leading. The 5-cylinder engine drones. **Major redesign:** 2006 and 2012. The 2016 models received a mid-cycle facelift that includes new headlights and taillights, wheels, and a reworked infotainment system, instrument panel and upgraded interior. **Best alternatives:** Other choices include the BMW 3 Series, Honda Accord, and Toyota Camry. The most reliable used Passat is one with the 2.5L 5-cylinder engine, without the DSG transmission.

Prices and Specs

Prices (2017): *Trendline 1.8T:* $23,295, *Highline 3.6L:* $35,745, *CC Wolfsburg Edition:* $41,990 **Freight:** $1,760 **Powertrain (FWD):** Engines: 1.8L 4-cyl. Turbo (170 hp), 2.0L 4-cyl. Turbo (200 hp), 3.6L V6 (280 hp); Transmissions: 5-speed man., 6-speed auto., 6-speed manumatic. **Dimensions:** Passengers: 2/3; Length: 192 in.; Wheelbase: 110 in.; Weight: 3,263 lb. **Fuel economy:** *1.8T:* 9.4L/100 km city, 6.4L/100 km highway; *3.6 V6:* 11.9L/100 km city, 8.5L/100 km highway. **Assembled in:** Germany and Tennessee.

ALERT! Function is sacrificed to style with rear corner blind spots and head restraints that impede rear visibility. Speaking of which, it's not the car for drivers or passengers who are tortured by the poorly designed head restraints:

> Recently I drove several new cars (the latest being the 2012 Passat) and found one common complaint: The headrests on these cars are tilted forward way too much with no adjustments available. My understanding is that NHTSA requires vehicles' headrests to be higher and close to the head to reduce whiplash injuries. How do you improve safety if it's impossible to find a comfortable driving position? The new headrest regulation forces the driver to slouch forward (and looking down) while driving, causing fatigue to set in quickly.

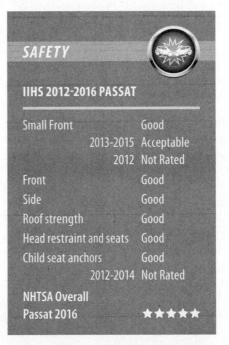

SAFETY

IIHS 2012-2016 PASSAT

Small Front		Good
	2013–2015	Acceptable
	2012	Not Rated
Front		Good
Side		Good
Roof strength		Good
Head restraint and seats		Good
Child seat anchors		Good
	2012–2014	Not Rated
NHTSA Overall		
Passat 2016		★★★★★

The fault isn't with government regulation, however, it's with VW's design engineers who picked the cheapest, most uncomfortable restraints possible – ones that would give Freddy Krueger nightmares. Ford had a similar inhumane design until buyer protests forced the company to phase in versatile and comfortable head restraints later that year. In your test drive, check out the car's ability to accommodate parallel parking on a hill, after first making sure there are no cars parked nearby that you might hit:

> We have a problem controlling the car while using Reverse on a hill. It appears that VW has tied the accelerator and braking function together in a way that the driver may lose control of the vehicle while in Reverse. If the brake is pressed, the accelerator is disengaged thus allowing the engine [to] fall to an idle and not develop any thrust. If the driver is using both feet to control the vehicle, left foot on the brake, right foot on the accelerator while depressing the brake, the engine develops no power even if the accelerator is depressed fully. By releasing the brake while the accelerator is depressed fully, the vehicle will lurch at full throttle in Reverse in an out of control condition until the driver realizes what is happening and removes the foot from the accelerator.

Owner-reported safety-related failures: Owner safety-related complaints are down significantly; however, the failures reported relative to the steering, brakes and powertrain are troublesome. Sudden unintended acceleration; vehicle pulls or drifts to the right or shuts off when slowing down; the electronic stability control engages erratically; exploding sunroofs; steering wheel controls and horn don't work; and a problematic navigation system:

> My wife is afraid to drive it because of concerns with the aforementioned radio navigation system. When putting the vehicle in Reverse and waiting from 3-7 seconds the rearview camera shows a picture. When placed in drive it stays on the screen for around 8-9 seconds. Multiple touches to get a channel change, again a distraction to the driver. Now the navigation system in this unit also is a pain. When my wife would use the navigation system the map would freeze up on the original streets

Some of the transmission failures are eerily similar to complaints heard from owners 8 years ago:

> My 2014 Passat will not stop smoothly and gives whip lashes after pumping the brakes pedal twice to ensure the car stops. The DSG system fails to engage smoothly while in automatic but runs smoothly while in "sport" mode. We have almost rear ended several cars while driving in automatic due to the jerky DSG gear shifting and poor response time in the braking systems while in stop and go traffic conditions.

> . . .

> Harsh downshift with my 2016 Passat associated with a very audible clunk or bang in the drivetrain or transmission since new. Occurs when utilizing the auto-shift (aka tiptronic(tm)) shift to downshift when decelerating to a stop. Bang occurs at low rpm (<700) and low speed (<10mph) and only when shifting 2nd gear to 1st gear.

RELIABILITY: Deficiencies dating back to the 2006 model year include failure of the powertrain, fuel, and electrical systems, and various fit and finish flaws. Power windows freeze shut in cold weather and driver-side door locks freeze shut on more recent models:

> Whenever outside temperature reaches -20 degrees Fahrenheit the driver side lock freezes making it impossible to open this door. The only means of entry and egress is through the passenger side door. In the event of a crash, submerging in water, fire, or other type incident, there is significant risk. I have found countless websites and forums that address this same concern with driver side door lock freezing on Volkswagen products.

On more recent models, there have been complaints concerning turbocharger and fuel pump failures that cause highway stall-outs or reduced power (see Internal Bulletins, below). Many complaints about older Passats involve the TDI model, whose engine has been plagued by short-lived turbochargers, self-destructing fuel pumps, failed fuel injectors, bad fuel pressure sensors and inoperative particulate butterfly valves – the usual refrains. Other problems include melted headlamp assemblies, clogged heater cores, faulty steering-column clock springs, and slow-acting reverse cameras and navigation systems. The DSG transmission requires expensive fluid changes at $500 each; it is best to have the service performed with VW fluid at a VW dealer to receive the latest software upgrades. A new wrinkle involves broken AdBlue fluid heating elements that reportedly cost $1,000 to replace post-warranty. In addition, the TDI uses a timing belt that requires changing. Owners of newer TDIs have often come to the realization that everything they gained in fuel savings has been completely erased by repair bills. *CC:* When coming to a stop, the car still inches forward; factory-installed GPS tells the driver to turn just moments before the turn must be made; the navigation system goes blank; and the horn doesn't sound immediately. See Jetta, under Reliability, for information on direct fuel injection maintenance issues.

INTERNAL BULLETINS, SECRET WARRANTIES: 1997-2009—Class action settlement to pay for and mitigate water damage to components and interiors of numerous models, and reimburse expenses caused by leaking sunroofs. 2004-11—DSG delay on acceleration. 2006-07—Airbag light constantly lit. 2006-10—Inoperative front-seat back recliner. 2008-11—Silencing a front suspension knocking. 2008-13—Remedy for a hard-starting, noisy, and rough-running engine. 2008-14—A faulty high-pressure fuel pump may be responsible for hard starts or a rough-running engine. 2011-12—Free engine repair and injector replacements up to 10 years/120,000 miles (see Warranty Extension under Jetta Internal Bulletins). A transmission whistle or whine at highway speeds requires the installation of an updated shifter cable bracket. A harsh engagement from Park to Drive or Reverse may signal the need for a software update. 2011-13—Possible oil leak from the oil filter housing. Troubleshooting tips to correct brake vibration/pulsation when brakes are applied. 2011-15—Front outside door handles may stick in cold weather. 2012-13—Troubleshooting tips for a malfunctioning navigation system. 2012-14—Engine may not operate properly due to a broken turbocharger fan or seized shaft. Models equipped with a 2.0L TDI diesel engine may experience exhaust failure after initial startup. Cold temperatures could compromise the exhaust turbocharger's performance. **2012-15**—Water/snow may enter the fresh air port of the blower housing contaminating the blower. The blower motor bearings may fail and create a high-pitched noise. Excess water/snow may also enter the water box through the drain port located in the wheel housing. VW countermeasures: A new passenger-side wheel liner in production (CW20/2014) and a new blower air intake cover and water deflector in production (CW28/2014). **2013-14**—Rough idling and poor engine timing may be corrected cheaply by first reprogramming the engine control module (ECM). Sunroof/sun shade won't open. Noise from the right-side door panel when driving. **2015**—Sticking camshaft adjuster control valve; steering upgrade will assist in keeping the vehicle straight on the road.

TIGUAN ★★★

RATING: Average (All years). Bred to steal sales from the Ford Escape, Honda CR-V and Toyota RAV4, the Tiguan compact crossover was spun off from the front-wheel drive Golf and Passat platforms in 2009, with all-wheel drive running gear for 4MOTION models (the base model is front-wheel drive only). The Tiguan is reasonably roomy inside, thanks to tall, chair-like seating that provides ample legroom front and rear, but cabin space was never perceived to be segment leading in North America, and roomier and cheaper SUVs like the Honda CR-V and pre-2013 Ford Escape continue to win the sales race. The split-folding rear bench slides fore and aft to optimize the space requirements of occupants and their cargo. VW dispatched just one engine to North America: The turbocharged and direct-injected 2.0L 4-cylinder gasoline engine, good for 200 hp. Buyers could choose between a 6-speed manual and automatic transmission, the latter gracing 4MOTION models exclusively. The Haldex all-wheel drive system uses a multi-plate centre clutch controlled by a computer that monitors the ABS wheel-speed sensors' information for signs of slippage. VW is finally readying a new Tiguan for 2018. Looking a lot like Audi's Q3, it will actually grow in size to accommodate an optional third row jump seat. Production will move to Mexico to give the Tiguan a more competitive (lower) starting price. **Road performance:** The Tiguan has been called a "GTI on stilts," an apt description with the latter's suspension geometry making the transition to a crossover. Acceleration is among class-leaders, thanks to the 2.0T turbocharged gasoline engine from the GTI. The steering is ideally weighted and accurate, making it easy to place. Brake feel and performance are very good. It earned demerits, however, for the automatic transmission's occasional jerky gear changes. **Strong points:** Teutonic engineering and design; tidy dimensions make it easy to drive and park. Good visibility all around. There's not a line or crease out of place, and the cabin appointments earned raves from buyers. Disciplined road manners reward drivers who like to drive. **Weak points:** Other compact crossover SUVs provide more for the money. Owners characterize the entertainment/navigation interface as confusing and unfriendly. Fuel economy is not great – driving a turbo engine efficiently requires a very light foot – and the Tiguan demands premium grade. **Major redesign:** 2009 and 2018. **Best alternatives:** Lots of choice in this crowded segment, including Honda CR-V, Toyota RAV4, Mazda CX-5, Nissan Rogue, Ford Escape, Subaru Forester.

Prices and Specs

Prices (2017): *Trendline:* $25,990, *Highline:* $37,198 **Freight:** $1,625 **Powertrain (FWD/AWD):** Engine: 2.0L 4-cyl. Turbo (200 hp); Transmissions: 6-speed manumatic. **Dimensions:** Passengers: 2/3; Length: 175 in.; Wheelbase: 102.5 in.; Weight: 3,393 lb. **Fuel economy:** *2.0T:* 11.7L/100 km city, 9.5L/100 km highway. **Assembled in:** Germany.

ALERT! The 2.0T turbo gasoline engine uses a timing chain in newer applications like the Tiguan and CC sedan. Volkswagen and Audi 2.0T (TSI) engines from 2008 to 2015 have issues relating to the lower timing chain tensioner. An early version of this tensioner may fail, losing its hydraulic tension. When that happens, it can cause the intake or exhaust valves to contact the piston while the engine is running, bending the valves. The cylinder head would have to be removed and the valves replaced, which is typically a $2,000 to $4,000 repair bill, depending on the damage done. There is a TSI Tensioner Update Kit available to owners of older Tiguans and other VWs that use this engine.

SAFETY	
IIHS 2009-16	
Small Front	Marginal
Front	Good
Side	Good
Roof strength	Good
Head restraint and seats	Good
Child seat anchors	Acceptable
2009-15	Not Rated
NHTSA Overall 2016	★★★★

RELIABILITY: One of the more aggravating mechanical issues is a broken plastic intake manifold, which can present drivability issues in the 2.0T gas engine in early Tiguans. Failed ignition coils are a very common problem with this engine. Short-lived fuel injectors and fuel pumps are also commonplace – the warning sign is usually stalling at speed – as are faulty sensors and other electrical bugaboos. The remote keyless entry transmitter may quit working due to a synchronization issue. Squeaking brakes are a common gripe, which some dealers claim is resolved with thorough cleaning, best done annually or more often to postpone expensive rear brake service. The 2.0T engine can be troublesome: The high-pressure fuel pump can fail spectacularly. See Jetta, under Reliability, for information on direct fuel injection maintenance issues.

Volvo

Volvo's Canadian sales are up by over 25%, the result of all-new models finally gracing showrooms. But the automaker isn't a volume seller in Canada, and its North American sales have been a volatile roller-coaster ride. Now owned by Geely, a Chinese truck manufacturer that has limited experience in automobile manufacturing and marketing, Volvo may find itself cut off at the knees if it takes another wrong turn in the future. If the automaker again makes poor product decisions, there may be demands for new management and increased insistence from its board to market Volvos as high-end, chauffeur-driven, luxury cars – which is not what the brand is known for in North America and Europe. This is too bad considering that the twice-married Swedish automaker is finally recovering from a "reality show" experience, with Sweden, the U.S. (former Ford ownership) and China each presenting conflicting visions of Volvo's target clientele.

In the recent past, *Lemon-Aid* rated the Volvo lineup "Not Recommended" for the same reasons that the uncertainties surrounding pre-bankrupt Saab earned that company a low rating. Jeremy Cato, one of Canada's better auto writers, once had his own misgivings about the company's future. Despite Volvo's emphasis on research and new products, he concluded that Canada might not be much of a player in Volvo's future global growth plans.

Lemon-Aid considers Volvo's new vehicle lineup a good candidate for leasing, mainly because there are so many storms on the horizon that could compromise quality/reliability, servicing and resale value. A low-volume automaker like Volvo would once again be unable to meet the requirements of its small, loyal customer base. Shoppers don't want to buy a car with a residual value that flows faster downhill than the Yangtze River. And most traditional Volvo customers who longed for that safe, solid and understated liberal college professor's car that was always more functional than fashionable have migrated into Subaru wagons and other SUVs. This isn't your uncle Olaf's Volvo any longer.

On the plus side, Volvo's designs and collision avoidance have improved considerably over the past couple of years. As for passenger crash safety, the S60, S80, V60, XC60 and XC90 have all been recognized as Top Safety Picks by the Insurance Institute for Highway Safety (IIHS). This ranking is not surprising, since Volvo built its reputation upon the active and passive safety features its vehicles provide. Here's a look at the present offerings from Volvo in Canada.

S60/V60/XC60	USED ★★
	NEW (LEASE) ★★★★

RATING: Average (2004-2017). Unveiled for 2001, the four-door-only S60 replaced the S70, which itself was a rebadged 850, Volvo's first front-wheel drive model in North America. The S60's stiff platform was the same one underpinning the S80, but with an 8-cm shorter wheelbase that becomes apparent when you compare

their rear-seat legroom. Shoehorned between the strut towers was an inline 5-cylinder engine in three strengths: A naturally aspirated 2.4L rated at 168 hp; a light-pressure turbocharged version making 197 hp in the 2.4T; and a full-blown 2.3L intercooled turbo that cranked out 247 hp in the performance-oriented T5. Engineers added a Haldex all-wheel drive option for 2002. It was sold for nine model years without any wholesale changes beyond minor updates. *2011-2017:* The second-generation S60 was a big departure from the old car, stylistically and otherwise. Extraordinarily supportive seating up front embraced all who sat down. The folding rear bench remained a little cramped, and the trunk was markedly small for its class – the result of the car's four-door coupe profile. Following the Volvo nomenclature, the S60 is the sedan and the V60 is the wagon version. There were three engine choices: A 250 hp, 2.5L inline 5-cylinder turbo driving the front wheels; a sideways-mounted 300 hp 3.0L turbo inline 6-cylinder in the all-wheel drive T6; while the T6 R-Design got a boost to 325 hp with added athletic gear. The S60 and V60 adopted new, powerful turbo 2.0L 4-cylinder front-wheel drive powertrains for 2015, including a base engine that made 240 hp. The 4-cylinders migrated to the all-wheel drive models in 2016. That one engine, in its various strengths, powers the entire Volvo lineup in 2017. *XC60:* This is a compact cross-over SUV with seating for five; essentially, a jacked-up V60 wagon with a chunkier look that plays well in the suburbs. The panoramic sunroof is a popular option. **Road performance:** Owners relish the mid-size S60/V60 for its spirited turbo engines and refined ride and comportment. The inline 5- and 6-cylinder engines are inherently smoother than the new 2.0L 4-cylinder. The stronger-rated 4-cylinder (302 hp) uses a larger turbocharger, but to combat lag, Volvo incorporated a supercharger, too – which draws power from the engine rather than the exhaust stream – to provide immediate boost, then hands the baton over to the turbo-charger above 3500 rpm. It's a very complex system that could be difficult to diagnose and repair. Bear in mind the transverse-mounted bigger motors were a tight fit and contributed to the car's unusually wide turning circle. **Strong points:** This stylish Swede delights with its superb seating and Scandinavian cool interiors. It boasts excellent safety ratings in the Volvo tradition, with advanced collision avoidance. The new 4-cylinder engine is both a good performer and quite fuel efficient, thanks in part to the standard 8-speed automatic transmission. **Weak points:** Rear-seat legroom and trunk space are both smaller than the class average. The unrefined 4-cylinder engine sounds raspy (especially at higher rpms) and there's some clatter at idle. Front-wheel drive models have some torque steer in spirited cornering. Expensive parts, and uncertain reliability. Low resale value makes these models a better lease proposition or a used car purchase, ideally with a full coverage Volvo warranty. **Major redesign:** 2001 and 2011. **Best alternatives:** Acura TLX, Audi A4, BMW 3 Series, Infiniti Q50 and Lexus IS series. Subaru Outback is a good alternative to the V60 and XC60, especially as a used buy.

RELIABILITY: A common lament concerns the car's entertainment and navigation system, Sensus. Owners have had their systems reset and even replaced. Other electrical and sensor failures have also been reported. The automatic transmission can exhibit harsh shifting. A computer reflash is a common remedy, but it doesn't always work. A small number of transmissions have been replaced outright. Other complaints include groaning air conditioning compressors, faulty fuel pumps, a few leaky sunroofs, peeling chrome trim and some annoying rattles. Long-term durability of the Haldex all-wheel drive components is a potential question mark, given some failed differentials reported at high mileage. Many consumers do not like the absence of a spare tire in the trunk. Monitor the dipstick for oil consumption, especially in the T6 engine. Worn piston rings are the likely culprit. An intermittent door ajar warning or water leaking into the cargo area may point to a defective hinge on the rear tailgate; the repair is expensive because Volvo sells it only with the complete hatch door.

SAFETY

IIHS 2011-2016 S60 SEDAN

Small Front	Good
Front	Good
Side	Good
Roof strength	Good
Head restraint and seats	Good
Child seat anchors	Acceptable
2011-2014	Not Rated
NHTSA Overall 2017 S60	★★★★★

S90/V90   NOT RATED

RATING: Unrated; all-new models for 2017. Volvo's range-topping luxury car, the S90 replaced the S80 as the flagship in the lineup for 2017. It is a large "executive class" sedan that acts as the brand's ambassador in a pretty formidable segment. Like the XC90, it makes use of Volvo's new Scalable Product Architecture platform, which meets collision-testing standards throughout the world. The wagon variant is the V90, and there's a Cross Country version of the wagon that provides additional ground clearance to telegraph a more rugged all-terrain capability. Like other raised wagons, it's more of an all-weather vehicle. All versions use the new, powerful 2.0L 4-cylinder in one strength at the moment: A complex turbocharged

and supercharged powerhouse that makes 316 hp out of two litres of displacement. The standard all-wheel drive system puts down all that power without annoying torque steer.

XC90	USED ★★
	NEW (LEASE) ★★★

RATING: Volvo's first sport-utility, the 2003 XC90 was a five-door wagon on stilts, offering unusually generous ground clearance for a car-based SUV. Building on its safety reputation, Volvo reinforced the XC90's safety cage with boron steel, a resilient alloy that's especially resistant to crushing forces. Despite being roomy inside, when optional third-row seating was ordered, the second-row chairs were mounted closer to the front, compromising legroom. Early models used a 5- or 6-cylinder turbocharged engine, which felt just adequate for the XC90's portly weight. An optional 311 hp V8 engine, supplied by Yamaha of Japan, was more athletic. Remarkably, the first-generation XC90 remained in production for 13 model years, with the requisite cosmetic tweaks and equipment upgrades. Later versions of the first-gen XC90 offered only a 240 hp 3.2L inline 6-cylinder engine. *2016-17:* The second-gen XC90 (finally!) was the first to use the automaker's Scalable Product Architecture that will eventually underpin all of its models. This big, blocky wagon, with seating for up to seven in three rows, uses the same 4-cylinder turbo engine that Volvo has assigned to all of its models in 2017. In this application, it makes 316 hp, working through an 8-speed automatic transmission supplied by Aisin, Toyota's transmission supplier. Standard all-wheel drive is supplied by Europe's Haldex. **Road performance:** Volvo elected to endow the big-boned XC90 with its tiny "Drive-E" engine: A direct-injected 2.0L DOHC turbocharged 4-cylinder that forms the basic powerplant for every model Volvo sells in 2017. The fortified version (316 hp) it specified for the XC90 uses a larger turbocharger *and* a supercharger. The supercharger draws power from the engine rather than the exhaust stream to provide immediate boost, then lets the turbocharger take over at above 3500 rpm. Despite the enormous complexity and lots of plumbing around the engine, the wee motor actually works as advertised, hauling the big XC90 to 60 mph in about 6.5 seconds. The ride quality is composed and serene, but nothing that suggests sporty. The XC90 is built for comfort and not speed. **Strong points:** Authentic Scandinavian design with requisite cool interior design, seating and appointments. Tall road presence means good sightlines for the most part. The 4-cylinder engine feels strong and is reasonably fuel efficient. There's a "Twin Engine" hybrid model that boasts 400 hp and some electric-drive capacity. Brake performance is good for such a large vehicle, and safety features are above reproach. **Weak points:** Driver infotainment interface is confusing, and sometimes it doesn't even work. Clunky transmission exhibits odd lurches from a standstill and sometimes at parking-lot speeds. The unrefined 4-cylinder turbo engine does not make expensive sounds befitting the class and the price tag. More importantly, will that tiny, over-stressed four-banger prove durable over the long run? **Major redesign:** 2003 and 2016. **Best alternatives:** Acura MDX is a strong and reliable alternative; Audi Q7 and BMW X5 are two sporting contenders that command high prices.

Prices and Specs

Price: *XC90 T5 AWD:* $55,650; *XC90 T8 AWD:* $77,650 **Freight:** $2,015 **Powertrain (AWD):** Engine: 2.0L turbo 4-cyl. (250 hp), 2.0L turbo+supercharged 4-cyl. (316 hp), 2.0L turbo+supercharged+electric 4-cyl. (400 hp); Transmissions: 8-speed automatic. **Dimensions:** Passengers: 2/3 or 2/3/2; Length: 195 in.; Wheelbase: 117.5 in.; Weight: 4,733 lb. **Fuel economy:** 11.5L/100 km city, 9.5L/100 km highway. **Assembled in:** Sweden and China.

RELIABILITY: *2003-2014:* The previous XC90 exhibited a number of expensive problems, most notably bad transmissions that frequently failed in the T6 model dating back to 2003. It's best to avoid the early T6, which came with the 2.9L 6-cylinder. Owners most commonly reported fast-wearing brakes and tires that scarcely lasted 40,000 km. There's no shortage of other headaches: Short-lived wheel bearings, suspension components, half-shafts, fuel pumps, batteries, air conditioners, bad turbos and wonky electrical faults. Purchase with a full-coverage warranty recommended with a repair limit equal to the value of the car or higher. *2016-2017:* The second-generation model arrived for 2016 based on Volvo's new Scalable

SAFETY	
IIHS 2011-2016	
Small Front	Good
Front	Good
Side	Good
Roof strength	Good
Head restraint and seats	Good
Child seat anchors	Acceptable
2011-2015	Not Rated
NHTSA Overall 2017	★★★★★

Product Architecture platform; It's longer, lower and wider. Unfortunately, the new XC90 was Not Ready for Prime Time, as owners have had to contend with myriad electronic glitches, from non-operative instrument and GPS displays, to slipping transmissions to faulty door locks and air conditioners, and other electrical malfunctions. Most disconcertingly, the accident prevention automated braking reportedly may activate at random, which could lead to a collision (this may be irony). Best is wait. The cars is now in its third year. Naturally, the automotive press couldn't wait to heap praise on it.

MODEL INDEX

Acura CSX 361
Acura ILX 361
Acura MDX 366
Acura RDX 364
Acura TL 362
Acura TLX 363
Audi A3 565
Audi A4 570
Audi A5 570
Audi A6 575
Audi Q3 580
Audi Q5 581
Audi Q7 583
Audi S4 570
Audi S5 570
Audi S6 575
Audi TT 577
BMW 1 Series 587
BMW 2 Series 587
BMW 3 Series 589
BMW 5 Series 593
BMW X1 595
BMW X3 597
BMW X4 597
BMW X5 600
BMW X6 600
Buick Allure 325
Buick Enclave 346
Buick Encore 342
Buick Lacrosse 327
Buick Verano 329
Cadillac ATS 330
Cadillac CTS 331
Cadillac Escalade 349
Cadillac SRX 348
Chevrolet Camaro 334
Chevrolet Colorado 353
Chevrolet Corvette 337
Chevrolet Cruze 324

Chevrolet Equinox 344
Chevrolet Impala 325
Chevrolet Malibu 322
Chevrolet Malibu
   Hybrid 322
Chevrolet Silverado 355
Chevrolet Sonic 312
Chevrolet Spark 310
Chevrolet Spark EV 310
Chevrolet Suburban 349
Chevrolet Tahoe 349
Chevrolet Traverse 346
Chevrolet Trax 343
Chevrolet Volt 320
Chrysler 200 218
Chrysler 300 225
Chrysler Aspen 233
Chrysler Aspen
   Hybrid 233
Chrysler Pacifica 233
Chrysler Sebring 218
Chrysler Town &
   Country 230
Dodge & Ram 1500 236
Dodge & Ram 2500 236
Dodge & Ram 3500 236
Dodge Avenger 218
Dodge Caravan 230
Dodge Challenger 221
Dodge Charger 223
Dodge Dart 216
Dodge Durango 233
Dodge Durango
   Hybrid 233
Dodge Grand
   Caravan 230
Dodge Journey 227
Dodge Magnum 223
Fiat 500 214

Ford Edge 285
Ford Escape 281
Ford Explorer 293
Ford F-150 Pickup 296
Ford Fiesta 264
Ford Five Hundred 275
Ford Flex 290
Ford Focus 267
Ford Fusion 271
Ford Mustang 277
Ford Taurus 275
GMC 1500 355
GMC 2500 355
GMC Acadia 346
GMC Canyon 353
GMC Sierra 355
GMC Terrain 344
GMC Yukon 349
Honda Accord 382
Honda Accord,
   Hybrid 382
Honda Civic, Hybrid 373
Honda Crosstour,
   Hybrid 382
Honda CR-V 379
Honda Fit 370
Honda HR-V 378
Honda Odyssey 387
Honda Pilot 390
Honda Ridgeline 393
Hyundai Accent 398
Hyundai Elantra 400
Hyundai Elantra GT 400
Hyundai Genesis
   Coupe 408
Hyundai Genesis
   Sedan 406
Hyundai Santa Fe 412

647

Hyundai Santa Fe Sport *412*
Hyundai Santa Fe XL *412*
Hyundai Sonata, Hybrid *403*
Hyundai Tucson *409*
Infiniti EX35 *421*
Infiniti EX37 *421*
Infiniti G25 *416*
Infiniti G35 *416*
Infiniti G37 *416*
Infiniti JX35 *422*
Infiniti Q50 *419*
Infiniti QX50 *421*
Infiniti QX60 *422*
Jeep Cherokee *248*
Jeep Compass *242*
Jeep Grand Cherokee *255*
Jeep Liberty *247*
Jeep Patriot *242*
Jeep Renegade *244*
Jeep Wrangler *251*
Kia Forte *429*
Kia Forte Koupe *429*
Kia Forte5 *429*
Kia Optima *431*
Kia Optima Hybrid *433*
Kia RIO *424*
Kia RIO5 *424*
Kia Rondo *434*
Kia Sorento *438*
Kia Soul *426*
Kia Sportage *436*
Lexus 300H *443*
Lexus 330 *443*
Lexus 350 *443*
Lexus 350 *447*
Lexus 400H *447*
Lexus 450H *447*
Lexus ES 300 *443*
Lexus IS *445*
Lexus RX 330 *447*
Lincoln MKX *287*
Lincoln MKZ *271*
Mazda CX-5 *462*

Mazda CX-7 *464*
Mazda CX-9 *466*
Mazda MX-5 Miata *460*
Mazda3 *451*
Mazda5 *455*
Mazda6 *457*
Mercedes- Benz B250 *606*
Mercedes- Benz B-Class *606*
Mercedes- Benz C-Class *609*
Mercedes- Benz E-Class *612*
Mercedes- Benz GLC-Class *614*
Mercedes- Benz GLE-Class *616*
Mercedes- Benz GLK-Class *614*
Mercedes- Benz M-Class *616*
MINI Cooper *621*
MINI Countryman *623*
Mitsubishi Lancer *470*
Mitsubishi Mirage *469*
Mitsubishi Outlander *472*
Nissan 350Z *495*
Nissan 370Z *495*
Nissan Altima *487*
Nissan Cube *482*
Nissan Frontier *502*
Nissan Juke *484*
Nissan Leaf *485*
Nissan Maxima *492*
Nissan Micra *476*
Nissan Murano *500*
Nissan Pathfinder *506*
Nissan Rogue *497*
Nissan Sentra *480*
Nissan Titan *505*
Nissan Versa *477*
Nissan Versa Note *477*
Nissan Xterra *508*
Pontiac Torrent *344*
Saturn Outlook *346*

Scion FR-S *520*
Subaru BRZ *520*
Subaru Forester *514*
Subaru Impreza *511*
Subaru Legacy *517*
Subaru Outback *517*
Subaru WRX *511*
Subaru WRX STI *511*
Suzuki Grand Vitara *525*
Suzuki Kizashi *524*
Suzuki SX4 *522*
Toyota 4Runner *553*
Toyota 86 *520*
Toyota Avalon *541*
Toyota Camry, Hybrid *538*
Toyota Corolla *531*
Toyota Highlander *551*
Toyota Highlander Hybrid *551*
Toyota Matrix *533*
Toyota Pontiac Vibe *533*
Toyota Prius Hatchback *535*
Toyota RAV4 *547*
Toyota Sequoia *555*
Toyota Sienna *543*
Toyota Tacoma *557*
Toyota Tundra *561*
Toyota Venza *549*
Toyota Yaris *529*
Volkswagen Beetle *634*
Volkswagen CC *636*
Volkswagen Golf *627*
Volkswagen Jetta *629*
Volkswagen Passat *636*
Volkswagen Rabbit *627*
Volkswagen Routan *230*
Volkswagen Tiguan *640*
Volvo S60 *642*
Volvo S90 *644*
Volvo V60 *642*
Volvo V90 *644*
Volvo XC60 *642*
Volvo XC90 *645*